Michael Landy,
Saleem Siddiqui,
Jeff Swisher, et al.

JBuilder Developer's Guide

SAMS

201 West 103rd Street, Indianapolis, Indiana 46290

JBuilder Developer's Guide

International Standard Book Number: 0-672-32427-X

Library of Congress Catalog Card Number: 2002104738

Printed in the United States of America

First Printing: December 2002

05 04 03 02 4 3 2 1

Trademarks

Warning and Disclaimer

Associate Publisher
Michael Stephens

Acquisitions Editor
Carol Ackerman

Development Editor
Songlin Qiu

Managing Editor
Charlotte Clapp

Project Editor
George E. Nedeff

Copy Editor
Geneil Breeze

Indexer
Erika Millen

Proofreader
Katie Robinson

Technical Editors
David Sampson
Todd Story

Team Coordinator
Lynne Williams

Multimedia Developer
Dan Scherf

Interior Designer
Gary Adair

Cover Designer
Alan Clements

Page Layout
Michelle Mitchell

Contents at a Glance

Table of Contents

Part III JBuilder for Java Client Applications

About the Lead Authors

Michael Landy is Director of Business Applications and is part of a senior strategic team that sets direction for Dunn Solutions Group. He has been instrumental in the promotion of Java as an effective business solution for Dunn Solutions Group clients. As a result, Java-based solutions have become a focal point of the company's delivery mechanisms.

Michael has a master's degree in electrical engineering from the University of Missouri at Columbia. Michael and his wife have been transplanted to suburban Chicago from their native St. Louis. Michael, his wife, and their children have remained true to their roots and cheer on the St. Louis Cardinals, Rams, and Blues. Michael can be contacted at `mike@landy.net`.

Saleem Siddiqui takes pleasure in dealing with all things Java at Dunn Solutions Group. His key contribution at Dunn has been to provide consulting services and business application development for government and Fortune 500 clients. Saleem is a technical architect and trainer at Dunn and is a Sun Certified Developer and Borland Certified Instructor in JBuilder.

Saleem has a master's degree in computer science from Loyola University, Chicago. He welcomes e-mail at `siddiqui_saleem@hotmail.com` and has even been observed responding to most of it.

Jeff Swisher is thoroughly versed in Java development. He has worked as a programmer, trainer, architect, and instructional designer for Dunn Solutions Group for more than nine years. Jeff is also a Sun Certified Developer and Borland Certified Instructor in JBuilder.

Jeff attended Taylor University in Upland, Indiana. He lives with his wife and two children in Northwest Indiana. He can be reached at `theswishers@attbi.com`.

Contributing Authors

Erik Nickelson is a technical architect of business applications for Dunn Solutions Group, as an architect and developer in Java, among other languages. He has helped both government and Fortune 500 clients develop software solutions in the Chicago and Raleigh metro areas. Erik majored in Chemistry/Computer Science at Houghton College in Houghton, New York. He divides his time between Chicago and Raleigh and welcomes e-mail at `erik@pfoa.com`.

Todd Story is Enterprise Architect for Distributed Systems for Aelera Corporation, a marketing IT consultancy with a long-standing reputation for completing engagements with unparalleled speed and success. For 2 years, he has overseen all Java projects and is technical lead on Aelera's most complex initiatives. During half of his 10-year software development career, Story has focused specifically on distributed software applications. He initially developed his JBuilder Web services expertise at Borland and adds to this knowledge daily as he applies it to his work at Aelera. Story holds a B.S. in Computer Science with a concentration in Information Systems from the University of Tennessee at Chattanooga. He currently lives in the Atlanta area.

Dedication

Dedicated to my lovely wife Rosa and our children. —Michael

Dedicated to my parents and the memory of Yusuf. —Saleem

Dedicated to my wife, for her patience, and to my children for typing on the computer when I went to get some soda and responding "I help daddy." Thanks! —Jeff

Acknowledgments

Writing a book requires an author to spend time alone. Anyone related to an author will tell you at whose expense this solitude is purchased! Of all the challenges that writers face, perhaps few are as unpleasant as the thought of neglecting loved ones for the sake of writing. We want to thank our families for their patience and understanding during the seemingly endless weekends and evenings spent at our computers. Without this cherished support, this book would not have materialized.

We also want to thank the wonderful staff at Sams for their help and guidance throughout the complex process of writing the manuscript. Geneil Breeze, George Nedeff, Songlin Qiu, David Sampson, and others at Sams did a wonderful job of guiding us newbie authors in the proper direction and getting our idiosyncrasies squared away. Special thanks go to Carol Ackerman for her consistent support and gentle nudging when deadlines loomed. Carol: We'll miss your reminders!

And finally, we want to express our gratitude to the people at Borland for helping us out with licensing and product issues, and for their generosity in repeatedly providing us with the latest releases of JBuilder.

We Want to Hear from You!

As the reader of this book, *you* are our most important critic and commentator. We value your opinion and want to know what we're doing right, what we could do better, what areas you'd like to see us publish in, and any other words of wisdom you're willing to pass our way.

As an associate publisher for Sams Publishing, I welcome your comments. You can email or write me directly to let me know what you did or didn't like about this book—as well as what we can do to make our books better.

Please note that I cannot help you with technical problems related to the *topic* of this book. We do have a User Services group, however, where I will forward specific technical questions related to the book.

When you write, please be sure to include this book's title and author as well as your name, email address, and phone number. I will carefully review your comments and share them with the author and editors who worked on the book.

Email: feedback@samspublishing.com

Mail: Michael Stephens
Associate Publisher
Sams Publishing
201 West 103rd Street
Indianapolis, IN 46290 USA

For more information about this book or another Sams Publishing title, visit our Web site at www.samspublishing.com. Type the ISBN (excluding hyphens) or the title of a book in the Search field to find the page you're looking for.

Introduction

Welcome to *JBuilder Developer's Guide*. This book teaches you how JBuilder can help you develop better Java code. This book focuses more on leveraging the built-in features, wizards, and tools provided by the JBuilder development tool rather than focusing on how to code Java. Plenty of books talk about Java coding techniques and specific Java related topics. This book shows you how to decrease your development time by leveraging the features of JBuilder on advance topics such as unit testing, refactoring, Java Server Pages, Enterprise JavaBeans, CORBA, and database access.

Who Should Read This Book

JBuilder Developer's Guide is written for experienced programmers at the intermediate level or above. It leverages JBuilder's capability to build quality Java code in a fraction of the time.

You will need to have a working knowledge of the Java 2 platform and will need to be running JBuilder 6, 7, or 8 Enterprise edition with the Borland Enterprise Server installed. Although most of the examples in this book will work on JBuilder 6, 7, and 8 standard editions, some of the more advanced topics and features, such as Java Server Pages, Enterprise JavaBeans, and CORBA, will work only on JBuilder Enterprise versions. In addition, some of the menu options and features will only be available in the JBuilder 7 and later versions.

Most of the source code presented in this book has been executed on the Windows version of JBuilder 7 and JBuilder 8, but it should also work on other platforms.

Conventions Used in This Book

This book uses several common conventions to make it easier to read and understand the material. Look for these special conventions throughout the book to enhance your learning experience.

Source Code

Source code listings appear in almost every chapter. We have made an effort to keep superfluous source code listings to a minimum, trying to show only the source code that pertains directly to the topic at hand. For example, we don't show the main application source code for every sample project we create because it would be identical for every project and would make it difficult to find the real meat of the chapter topic.

All the source code for all the chapters is on the companion CD-ROM.

Source code is always shown in a `monospaced font`. Source code can appear in two locations: either mixed in with other text or in separate code listings. For example, if we are referring to the `jbInit()` method in text, it appears as source code in text.

Short code fragments used to illustrate specific topics are simply listed inline with the text.

Longer source code listings appear in numbered listings. These numbered listings are referenced in the text with a callout, such as "see Listing *xx.nn*" where *xx* is the chapter number, and *nn* is the listing number within the chapter. Here is an example of a listing:

LISTING 5.1 Sample Unit Test (handCodedUnitTest.java)

```
package jbbook.ch05;

import junit.framework.*;

public class handCodedUnitTest extends TestCase {

  public handCodedUnitTest(String name) {
    super(name);
  }
```

Listing 5.1 is in Chapter 5 and is the first code listing in that chapter.

Code Continuation Character

Many JBuilder program listings appear in this book. Because of space limitations, some source code lines must be wrapped (continued on the next line). In actual use, you would enter this code as one extended line without a line break. To indicate such lines, a special code continuation character (➥) is used. When you see this character at the beginning of a line, it means that line should be added to the previous line.

Shortcuts and Typefaces

In this book, shortcut key combinations are joined with plus signs. For example, Ctrl+V means hold down the Ctrl key while pressing the V key.

This book also has typeface enhancements to indicate special text, as shown in the following table:

Typeface	Description
Italic	Indicates new terms.
`Computer Type`	Indicates text the user types and onscreen messages, commands, and code.
`Computer Italic Type`	Indicates placeholders in code and commands.

"Design Guidelines" Section

The "Design Guidelines" sections represent a modern classical design using elegant solutions to common problems in software design. These sections describe patterns and guidelines for managing object creation, coordinating control flow between objects, and surfacing business logic and user interface design. These sections provide numerous examples of using practical applications to improve the reusability and flexibility of your code and design.

"In Practice" Section

To reinforce the knowledge presented in that chapter, most chapters end with an "In Practice" section, which is a hands-on lab exercise using JBuilder to create a portion of an ongoing project. The project is common throughout all chapters to provide consistency while practicing new techniques and skills.

"Reflections" Section

To encourage you to think about what you have just read, a "Reflections" section appears at the end of each chapter. This section gives you food for thought about the topic you just read in the form of rhetorical questions, ideas, and bits of advice.

Contacting the Authors

If you want to contact a specific author, some of the authors' email addresses are shown on the "About the Authors" page. Please feel free to contact us.

PART I

Starting Out—A First Look at JBuilder

IN THIS PART

1 Viva Java

IN THIS CHAPTER

- From Oak to J2EE—A Brief History of Java
- Borland JBuilder, a First Look
- What Is Next?

Why Java? Java was described in the original 1991 white paper as a "simple, object-oriented, network-savvy, interpreted, robust, secure, architecture-neutral, portable, high-performance, multithreaded, dynamic language."

It has also been described, somewhat facetiously, as having the elegant simplicity of C++ and the blazing speed of Smalltalk!

In essence, Java is a language, a standard, and a platform. This, perhaps, makes a fair comparison with other languages difficult because many architectural decisions in Java reflect concerns that are totally absent in other languages.

Figure 1.1 shows an architectural view of the Java platform.

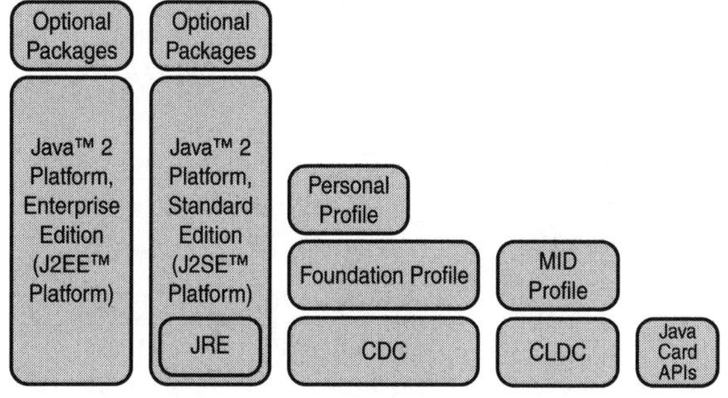

FIGURE 1.1 An architectural view of the Java platform.

It is clear from Figure 1.1 that Java the platform exists in three distinct flavors: J2EE (Java 2 Enterprise Edition), J2SE (Java 2 Standard Edition), and J2ME (Java 2 Micro Edition).

As far as the Java language goes, it has a syntax and grammar like any other computer (or human) language. This specification is available as a book or online at `http://java.sun.com/docs/books/jls/second_edition/html/j.title.doc.html`. This language specification is comparable to the ANSI specifications of the C and C++ languages.

Java the standard, which has its roots in the "architecture-neutral, portable" features stipulated by its designers, is largely embodied in the erstwhile "100% Pure Java program" (`http://java.sun.com/products/archive/100percent/4.1.1/index.html`) and the currently active Java Community Process (`http://www.jcp.org/aboutJava/communityprocess/java_community_process.html`). This collective means of standardizing ensures smooth progression and nonfragmentation of the standards—something C and C++ programmers have to contend with even today.

The popularity of Java can thus be attributed to its simplicity, wide availability (on multiple platforms and operating systems), and relative robustness.

From Oak to J2EE—A Brief History of Java

Figure 1.2 shows a brief timeline of the history of Java.

Java was born in the early 1990s as Oak, an interpreter written by James Gosling in the C language. From these humble beginnings came the language and the platform that were to become the dominant driving force for the enterprise applications of today.

In the early part of the 1990s, the growth of this new language coincided with the growing popularity of the Internet and the release of the first Web browser, the NCSA Mosaic version 1.0 from the National Center for Supercomputing Applications at the University of Illinois. This confluence was responsible, at least in part, for determining the initial direction the language would take. The first substantial application written in Oak was a browser later named HotJava. The impetus generated by HotJava was used to write the Java compiler—in Java.

At this juncture, Sun (which had been funding this development since 1994) decided that Java was ready for prime time. Sun demonstrated both HotJava and the new language at SunWorld on May 23, 1995. You could say that Java debuted on that date.

By the end of 1995, many companies large and small had announced plans to license Java. The new language was object oriented and provided simplicity, portability, and memory management among other things.

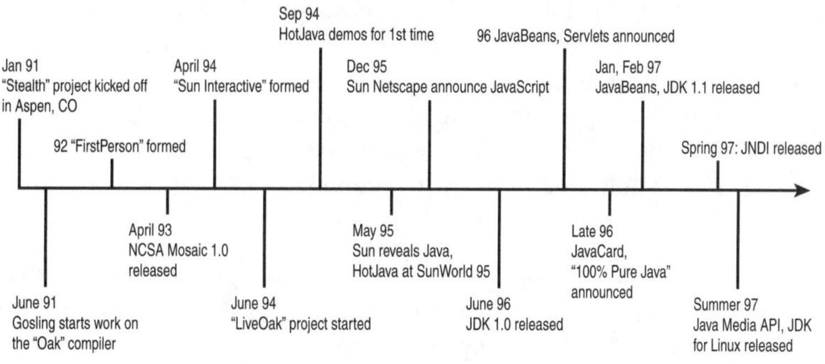

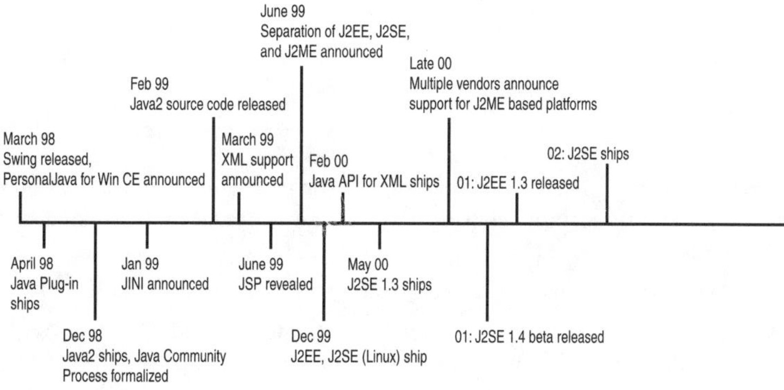

FIGURE 1.2 A brief timeline of the evolution of the Java language.

Soon it became obvious that the new language was capable of much more than client-side, browser-based applets. The language was object oriented, and there was nothing to prevent its use on traditionally server-side "serious" programming. Thus work began on the JavaBeans framework and the Servlet API in 1996. That same year, the Java Language Specification was formalized and published. This led to the 100% Pure Java initiative—an objective and measurable metric by which the interoperability and compatibility of Java applications could be judged. This gave immense credibility to the nascent language.

The year 1997 was nothing short of a banner year for Java. The JavaBeans Development Kit—JDK 1.1, Java Web Server, and Java Servlet Developers Kit were released. New APIs and technologies such as the Java Naming and Directory Interface, Java Media and Communication, and Smart Card were released. Work commenced on the Enterprise JavaBeans API. All this was received by the early adopters with glee. Subscriptions to the Java Developer Connection program topped 100,000.

In the following years, Java made a firm place for itself in all tiers of the enterprise with technologies such as Java Server Pages, servlets, Jini, Java XML support, and others. The applicability became so wide that in mid 1999, Sun announced the logical separation of the platform into three editions: Java 2 Standard Edition, Enterprise Edition, and Micro Edition (affectionately called J2SE, J2EE, and J2ME, respectively). The J2SE licensing terms were made flexible (licensing for binaries was made essentially free).

The new millennium has brought new successes for Java. Release of version 1.4 of J2SE extended the capabilities of the standard edition. Next generation virtual machines such as the KVM offer more efficient just-in-time compilation and better performance. Whichever aspect of modern technology you look at, you are bound to find yourself face to face with Java—from PDAs and cell phones to mainframes and everything in between.

THE JVM AND KVM

The JVM, or Java Virtual Machine, is a specification that describes an abstract computation machine on which applications can be developed. The machine is virtual in the sense that it has a significant software component (the Java runtime). Specific implementations of the JVM are available from Sun, Borland (as part of JBuilder), and many other vendors.

The complete JVM specifications are located at `http://java.sun.com/docs/books/vmspec/`.

The KVM is a lightweight virtual machine written in C and is intended for handheld and micro devices (mobile phones, palm-top devices, and so on). KVM stands for K Virtual Machine, where K signifies the small memories of micro devices, usually on the order of a few kilobytes.

Borland JBuilder, a First Look

In the words of Blake Stone, JBuilder's architect, "from day one the goal of the JBuilder team was to push the limits of Java." This goal was realized in large part by writing substantial portions of JBuilder in Java.

Thus, the very existence of JBuilder has been a Java success story. This is also a reason that JBuilder has won a number of awards for simply being a decent Java product, let alone other awards for being the best IDE for developing Java programs.

From the release of version 1.0 in 1997, JBuilder has gone from a Java/Delphi product to one that is 100% Pure Java. This is neither a mere philosophical improvement nor a sheer marketing move; it affects the way JBuilder itself may be enhanced and improved as an IDE.

Figure 1.3 shows the architectural view of JBuilder.

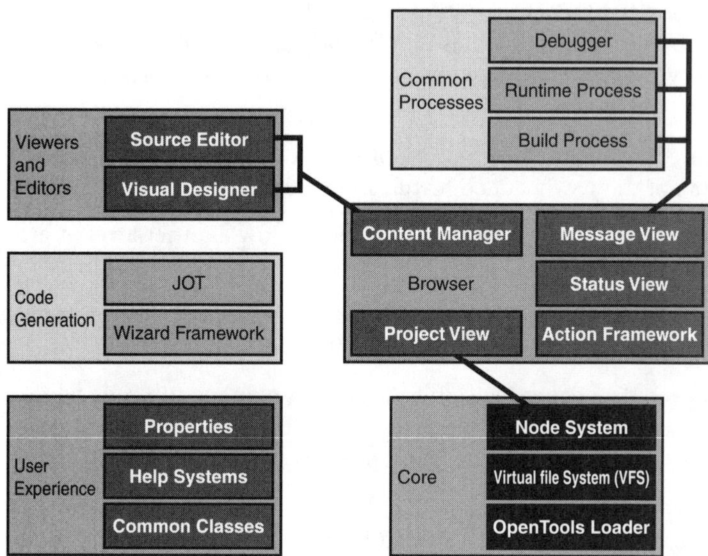

FIGURE 1.3 The architectural view of JBuilder, courtesy of Borland, Inc.

As you can see, the entire design of JBuilder consists of collaborating and cohesive subcomponents. Each of these subcomponents is written in Java and hence is extensible in the same manner that any other Java API is extensible and reusable.

This fact allows you to customize the look, feel, and behavior of JBuilder to achieve interesting and useful results. In fact, an amazing array of JBuilder Open Tools are available as shareware and freeware on the Internet. The easiest way to find them is to start at `http://info.borland.com/jbuilder/resources/jbopentools.html` and follow the many resources present on that Web page.

JBuilder has grown from a useful editor of Java source to an all-in-one development tool for all manner of class design, code generation, testing, deployment, and debugging involving Java, XML, and HTML among other languages. It can be used to build applications targeted for different platforms with varying computing power. In other words, Java code can be built, tested, debugged, and deployed for J2ME, J2SE, and J2EE platforms.

What Is Next?

As these lines are being written, exciting changes are underway both in the Java community at large and at Borland. J2SE version 1.4 has been released, so has

JBuilder version 8. JBuilder now integrates with the latest versions of the software from many other vendors, such as BEA Weblogic, Rational (Rose and ClearCase), Microsoft (PVCS, Windows Explorer), Apache Group (Web server, Tomcat, Ant, Struts), IBM (WebSphere), and others.

To appreciate the enhanced versatility of the recent versions of JBuilder, an enumeration of some of the newly added features may help:

- Project groups (new in version 8)—These allow another level of grouping related projects.
- Support for Struts (version 8)—This effective Web-application framework has gained popularity and is now part of JBuilder.
- Enhanced debugging (version 8)—You can now modify code while debugging as well as debug native code according to the specifications of JSR 45 (see `http://www.jcp.org/aboutJava/communityprocess/review/jsr045/`).
- Support for the latest version of third-party software—Products such as Ant 1.5, Weblogic Server 7.0, Xalan 2.2, and Xerces 2.02 are now supported.
- Multiple runtime configurations (version 7)—Many configurations can be specified and then used either to run or to debug the project.
- Enhanced refactoring support (version 7)—Features such as extract method, change method parameter, and introduce variable allow you to constantly allow refactoring nudges while aggressively developing code. Rapid application development is no longer synonymous with rapid application degeneration!

In the remainder of this book, we will build a course registration application using JBuilder that illustrates the use of the preceding features and many others.

We chose a full-blown application that is developed iteratively throughout the book because that is closer to what most developers do for a living. We consider this approach to be better than developing several toy applications, unrelated to each other, largely useless, and cobbled together simply to illustrate the menu options and wizards in JBuilder. We hope you'll enjoy the continuity this offers. Despite this continuity, each chapter is self-contained (including the corresponding files on the companion CD-ROM) and can be referenced individually.

Summary

The Java language and the JBuilder product have come a long way in the last several years. Maturity of the Java platform is both a cause and an effect of its wide acceptance by the commercial and academic programming community.

As a comprehensive Integrated Development Environment, JBuilder is a clear favorite (if not an outright leader) among software practitioners who want to develop applications in Java.

With this, let's begin our exploration of JBuilder!

2

Exploring JBuilder

IN THIS CHAPTER

- The JBuilder Integrated Development Environment
- The Main Menu
- The Toolbar

The topics in this chapter are

- The JBuilder IDE
- The Main menu, especially the Project Properties, IDE Options, and Editor Options dialog boxes
- The Welcome and Hello World projects

If you are not familiar with the JBuilder IDE, this chapter should be useful to you. If you have used JBuilder (or other Borland tools) before, you can skim this chapter.

The JBuilder Integrated Development Environment

If you have used any Integrated Development Environment for writing code, JBuilder's IDE should be intuitively familiar to you. (Of course, you might belong to the "real programmers use vi" club—in which case, we respect your point of view but don't share it!) What might be new to you is

- JBuilder is a "two-way" tool.
- It does not pollute your source code with any proprietary, cryptic-looking tags.

A "two-way" tool enables you to build your application either by writing code or by modifying the application entities visually with "point and click" programming. You can switch between these two modes as often as you want. The tool keeps a single, consistent, and unified codebase with which you interact using these two modes. For JBuilder, this unified codebase is simply the set of Java source files that are part of your project (see "The Skinny on JBuilder Projects" sidebar later in this chapter).

JBuilder's primary window, which is divided into multiple panes, is called the *AppBrowser* (see Figure 2.1).

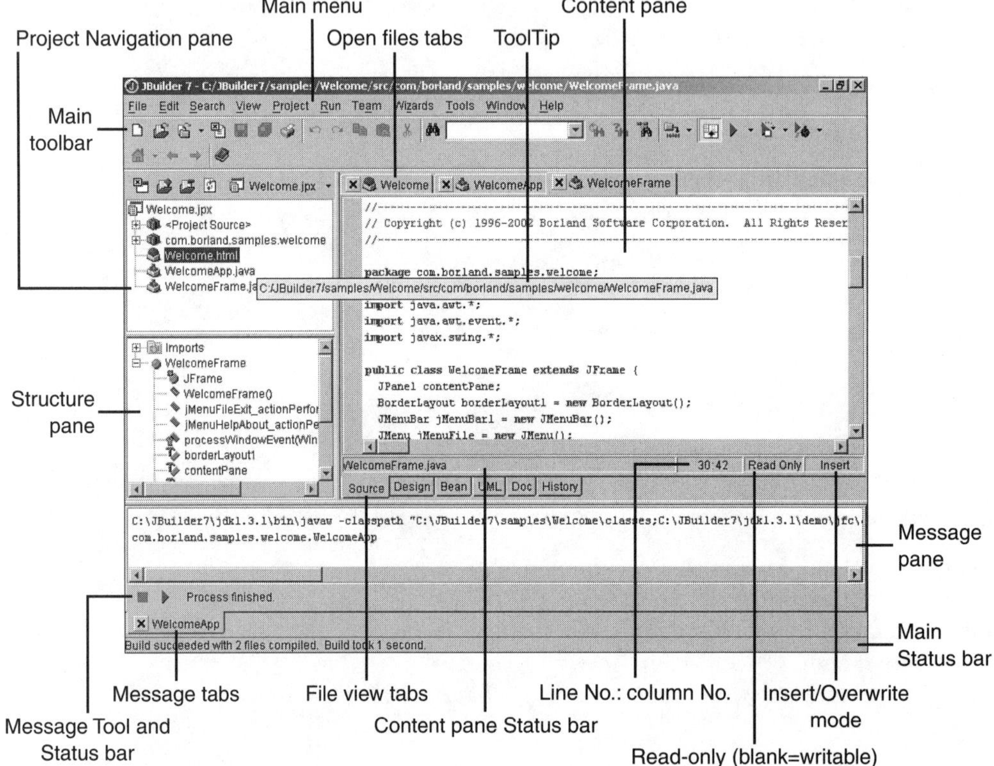

FIGURE 2.1 JBuilder's AppBrowser presents a detailed yet uncluttered view of your project.

The AppBrowser enables you to interact with and control your project from a single location. JBuilder does not have any "floating" toolbars or windows on top of the AppBrowser. JBuilder's AppBrowser is compact—yet sophisticated.

There might be many files open simultaneously in the AppBrowser; however, only one file is viewable at a time. This is the current file. (You can open another AppBrowser window—see the "Window Menu" section later in this chapter.)

The Main Menu

At the top of the AppBrowser is JBuilder's main menu bar. It contains the following 11 menus:

- File
- Edit
- Search
- View
- Project
- Run
- Team
- Wizards
- Tools
- Window
- Help

Some of the menu items in these menus are standard or self-explanatory. The following sections describe the more interesting or uncommon menu items.

File Menu

The File, New menu item opens the Object Gallery. The *Object Gallery* is where you can select which one out of a variety of objects you want to create. You probably recognize some of them (Class, Interface, and so on) already.

The File, New Project menu item creates a new JBuilder project. We will talk about the place of projects in JBuilder later in this chapter.

The File, Compare Files menu item is a useful and quick way to compare the differences between two text files. Figure 2.2 shows how the differences in two files appear in the Diff View tab of the Compare Files dialog box.

The File, Revert menu item reverts to a previously saved version of the current file.

Edit, Search, and View Menus

The Edit menu contains the usual edit commands (Cut, Copy, Paste, Select All, and so on). The Edit, Undo and Edit, *Redo* menu items in JBuilder support multiple levels of undoing/redoing actions—not just the last action.

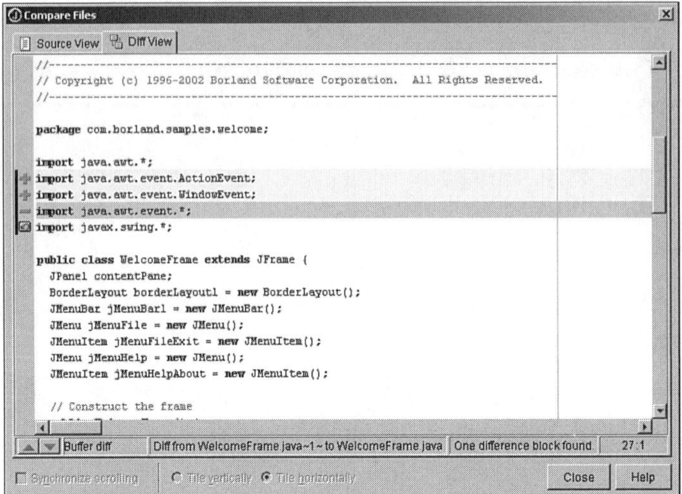

FIGURE 2.2 The Diff View tab of the Compare Files dialog box provides visual cues for added, deleted, and changed lines of text.

The Edit, Format Menu Option

Seven options in the Edit menu deal with refactoring your code. These are

- Edit, Optimize Imports—Optimizes the `import` statements for the current Java source file
- Edit, Rename—Renames the currently selected class, field, or method
- Edit, Move—Moves the currently selected class to a new package
- Edit, Change Parameters—Modifies (adds, removes, renames, repositions) the parameters of the currently selected method
- Edit, Extract Method—Pulls the selected lines of code into a method and puts a call to that method in place of the selected lines
- Edit, Introduce Variable—Pulls the selected expression into a variable and replaces the selection with the variable name
- Edit, Surround With Try/Catch—Puts a `try` clause around the selected lines, followed by a `catch` construct

Import Optimization is explained in the next section on the Project menu. The other options are discussed in Chapter 7, "Refactoring."

Three options in the Edit menu provide code assistance by providing lists from which you can select an item and hence minimize typing code. These menu items are MemberInsight, ParameterInsight, and ClassInsight.

The Edit, MemberInsight shows the methods and data members for the visible context. For example, say that you have the following line of code in your source file:

```
System.out.println("Hello World!");
```

If you put the cursor after the period following `out` and select the Edit, MemberInsight menu option, you get the Member Insight dialog box shown in Figure 2.3.

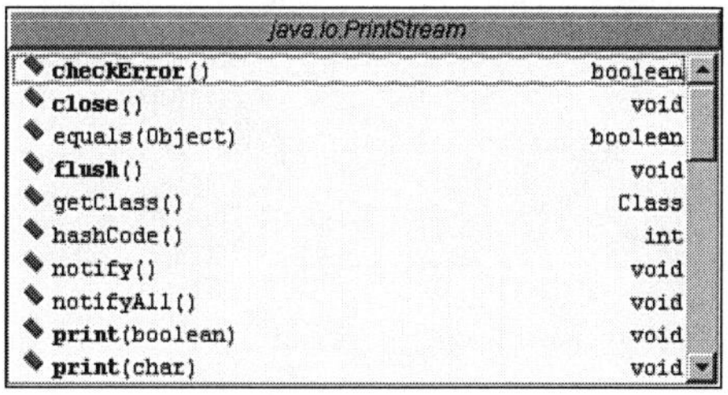

FIGURE 2.3 The Member Insight dialog box for a variable of type `java.io.PrintStream`.

Because the type of `System.out` is `java.io.PrintStream`, the Member Insight dialog box shows the data members and methods for the `PrintStream` class.

Similar to Edit, MemberInsight, the Edit, ParameterInsight menu item opens a dialog box that shows all the parameter choices for the current method. You must place the cursor within the parentheses of the method call for Parameter Insight to work. Parameter Insight comes in handy when you can't recall the different parameter lists for overloaded methods.

The Edit, ClassInsight menu item launches a dialog box that shows all the classes that are close matches to the currently selected class name. To see how this can be useful, imagine that you want to use the `Timer` class in your code, but you can't remember which package the `Timer` class is in. Worse, you have an uneasy feeling that there might be multiple `Timer` classes in different packages, and you'll end up using the wrong one. This will soothe you: Type **`Timer`** where you want to declare the variable, and select the Edit, ClassInsight menu item. You get the Class Insight dialog box shown in Figure 2.4.

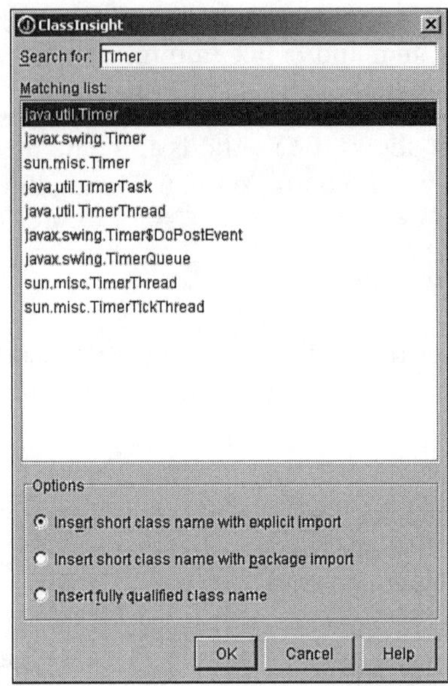

FIGURE 2.4 The Class Insight dialog box for all classes that match `Timer`.

The Search, Find in Path menu item works like the Windows Find or the Unix `grep` command. It searches all files (of a certain type) for a given text. The results are shown in the Message pane at the bottom of the AppBrowser.

The Search, Incremental Search menu item gives you a little yellow text box. As you type characters into the text box, the current file is searched and the first location of the text you have typed is highlighted.

Figure 2.5 shows a search for the text "packf" in a file.

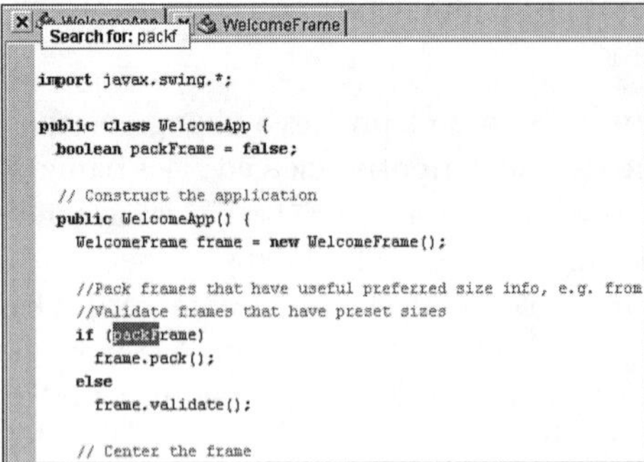

FIGURE 2.5 The incremental search feature looks for the next matching text pattern in the current file.

The Search, Browse Classes menu item enables you to browse classes. If the source (.java) file for the class is available, it is shown in the Content pane within the AppBrowser. Otherwise, the bytecode (.class) file is decompiled (using the javap decompiler) and shown in the Content pane. In this case, the method implementations are not shown—just the method signatures.

The View menu enables you to show or hide the various panes and toolbars in the AppBrowser to your liking.

The View, Toolbars submenu enables you to select which toolbars to show. Because all the standard toolbars can be comfortably displayed even on an 800×600 display, you'll probably not need to hide individual toolbars.

The View, Toggle Curtain menu item is a nice way to hide or show both the Project and Content panes—the curtain on the left side of the AppBrowser. This is useful—especially if you use the three-key shortcut of Ctrl+Alt+Z to expand or contract the Content pane quickly.

Project Menu

The Project menu contains useful menu items related to managing the current project.

THE SKINNY ON JBUILDER PROJECTS

JBuilder uses the notion of a "project" to group together all the text files (Java, JSP, HTML, IDL, XML, and others including Java autogenerated files); binary files (image and audio files, Jar, Zip archives, and so on); and properties (such as the location of various files, the version of the JDK, and so on) you work on as a unit. You need to organize your work in a project to take advantage of JBuilder's features.

The overhead of a JBuilder project is little more than a few text files that contain references to all the other resources (files, processes, servers, and so on) and properties. The primary project file is the one that has the extension .jpx or .jpr. There might be other project-related text files (such as .library files).

It is important to realize that creating a project requires absolutely no changes to the files that are part of the project. In other words: The project knows about and depends on the resources it contains; the resources neither know about nor depend on the project files in any way. This means that creating a JBuilder project is a "noninvasive procedure"—it does not affect the files you choose to include in the project in any way. This has important ramifications:

- You can make a JBuilder project to include files that have already been created.
- You can safely modify any file (say, a Java source file) that is part of a JBuilder project without using JBuilder. However, if you delete, move, or rename files, you'll obviously have to update the JBuilder project separately; otherwise, your project will become stale.

- JBuilder projects have no deployment footprint. That is, the deployed application has no overhead just because JBuilder was used to develop it.

Most of the time, you interact with a project not by editing the project files in an editor, but by modifying the project properties.

The first group of menu items under the Project menu contains options to compile and clean up the project. Menu items can be added to and removed from this group, as discussed in the "Build Tab" section later in this chapter.

Project, Make Project and Project, Rebuild Project both compile the current project. The difference is that "making" a project compiles only the source files (and the files they import) that have changed since the last time the project was compiled. "Rebuilding" a project always compiles all the source files (including imported files) in the project.

THE "DEPENDENCY" FILE

JBuilder keeps track of the dependencies between files in special binary files in the output path of the project. These binary files—although JBuilder specific—are not indispensable because

- They do not have to be part of the deployment modules.
- Even during development, you can delete these files and your project will still compile. JBuilder will simply compile all the Java source files. However, if you have many source files in your project, this will take a long time.

In JBuilder versions 6 and 7, the dependency files have a .dep2 extension. In earlier versions of JBuilder, they had a .dependency extension.

Similar to a project, the current file can also be "made" or "built" using the Project, Make and Project, Rebuild menu items, respectively. Making a file compiles it (and imported source files) only if there have been changes; rebuilding a file always compiles it (and imported source files).

Both Project, Properties and Project, Default Project Properties menu items open a dialog box detailing the project properties. The difference is that the former menu item deals with the current project's properties, whereas the latter sets the default values for all projects (which can be overridden per project). Understanding the various options in the Project Properties dialog box is crucial to properly managing your projects.

The Project Properties dialog box, shown in Figure 2.6, has nine tabs.

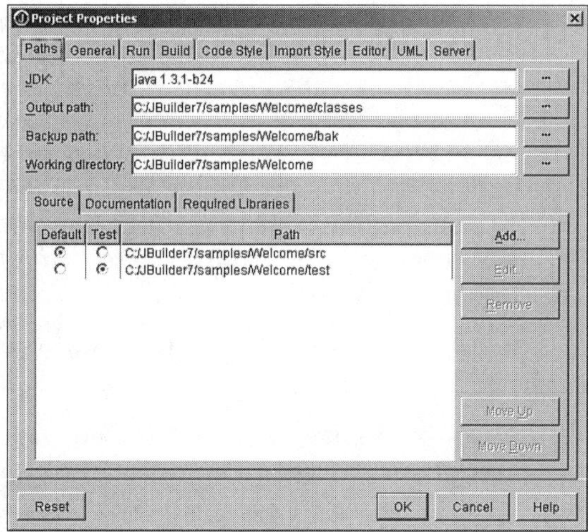

FIGURE 2.6 The Project Properties dialog box presents a myriad of properties related to your JBuilder project.

Let's look at the various Project Properties options closely.

Paths Tab

In this tab, you specify the paths to various resources and directories. The options on this tab are as follows:

- JDK—Points to the Java Development Kit used for this project. This is a powerful means to build projects targeted for older or specialized JDKs. You can use the JDK that comes with JBuilder or another JDK for your project. You can set up multiple JDKs, but a project can logically use only one at a time.
- Output Path—This points to a directory where the compiled (.class) files of your project would go. In almost all cases, this should be different from any of your source paths. (Otherwise, your class files will start mingling with your source files. Yuck!)
- Backup Path—Keeps local backups (in addition to any source control system you use—which we cover in Chapter 30, "Team Development with JBuilder"). This path points to a directory where backups are kept.
- Working Directory—This is the project's working directory, which contains all the working files (the project files). In practice, it is almost always a good idea to make this directory the immediate parent of the source directory or directories. This keeps a project's "bookkeeping" files close to the actual Java source files.

- Source Tab—This is where you specify the directories where JBuilder looks for Java source files. There are two distinct and separate types of paths: Default and Test. Although you can add as many paths as you want you can choose exactly one default and one test path each at one time. The *default path* is where you store your "work-in-progress" source files. The *test path* is where you store a relatively more stable release of source files for unit testing purposes. Although you can choose the same path to be both the default and test path, it's more appropriate to choose distinct paths and thereby separate your test environment from your working environment.
- Documentation Tab—This is where you specify the directories containing Javadoc documentation for your project.
- Required Libraries Tab—If you have done any Java programming, you have probably experienced classpath woes at one time or another. This is where you get "Class Not Found" errors during compilation and/or `java.lang.NoClassDefFoundError` errors during execution. All this because of the darn classpath!

NOTE

The *classpath* is the collection of directories and archive files where the Java executables (`javac`—the compiler and `java`, `javaw`, `jre`, or `jrew`—the runtime environments) look to find files. In JBuilder, you specify the classpath by including libraries in the Required Libraries tab within the Paths tab of the Project Properties.

To add an existing library to the current project, click on the Add button on the Required Libraries tab. This opens the Select One Or More Libraries dialog box.

You can select from the libraries in this dialog box. If you want to add a brand new library that is not in this list, click on the New button to open the New Library Wizard.

To add a new library throughout the New Library Wizard, all you need to provide is a unique and human-readable name for the library and specify the locations (directories or archive files) that are included in the library.

General Tab

The General tab includes the important Enable `assert` Keyword check box. Enabling this check box causes JBuilder to follow the JDK 1.4 standards for the `assert` keyword.

THE `assert` KEYWORD

Assertions have long been included in the core language definitions of other programming languages. In Java, the behavior of the `assert` keyword is new—first defined in version 1.4 of the J2SE (Java 2 Standard Edition). To allow smooth transition from a universe where `assert` is a legal Java identifier (you can name a variable or method `assert` in JDK 1.3) to one where `assert` is a reserved Java keyword, you are allowed to make your intentions clear by saying "I am going to use assert in the special way specified by J2SE 1.4," or "I'm going to use assert as just another string identifier." If you use the command-line compiler (`javac`), you specify this by using the `-enableassertions` or `-disableassertions` options, respectively. In JBuilder, you specify this choice by checking or unchecking the Enable `assert` keyword check box. You will get warnings if you keep this check box unchecked and still use `assert` as an ordinary identifier—a polite reminder to you to rename your identifiers because assertions are now a part of the core Java language.

Turning on the Enable Source Package Discovery and Compilation check box causes JBuilder to discover and show packages in the Project pane. The discovered packages are included in the compilation (Make or Build scenarios) as well.

The last check box on this pane is the one labeled Include References From Project Library Class Files. Turning this on affects the way UML diagrams and the Find References menu item on the context menu work. If this check box is checked, references to your class from library files are included in UML diagrams and through the Find References menu. We recommend that you keep it unchecked—because you are often interested in the references from your source files only, not from library files (for which you might not have the source, anyway).

Run Tab

The Run tab allows you to specify the run and debug configurations for applets, applications, server components (including JSPs, servlets and EJBs), and test environments.

You can set up multiple configurations using the buttons on the Run tab. You can create a configuration (New button), clone it (Copy button), modify it (Edit button), or delete it (Remove button). The New, Copy, and Edit buttons launch the Runtime Properties dialog box, shown in Figure 2.7.

The Runtime Properties dialog box has a tab each for Run and Debug options. Let's take a look at each in turn.

The Run Options tab (within the Run tab) contains Application, Applet, Server, and Test tabs. Let's look at the Applet and Application tabs—saving the other tabs for later chapters.

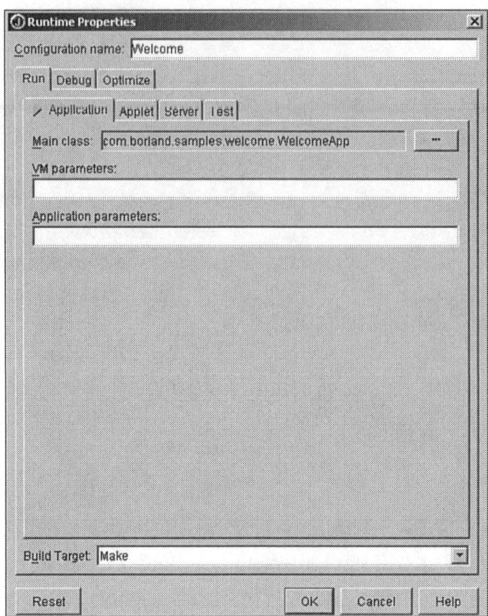

FIGURE 2.7 The Runtime Properties dialog box enables you to specify details for a run configuration.

The Application tab lets you select the Main class (class with `public static void main(String[] args)` method) and any parameters you want to pass to the Main class or to the Java runtime. You can also select whether you want to compile before you run and/or debug. These choices—Compile Before Running and Compile Before Debugging—appear on all the tabs under the Run tab.

The Applet tab enables you to select which applet you want to run. You can specify either the applet class (subclass of `java.applet.Applet`) or an HTML file as the starting point. If you specify an applet class, you can additionally specify the applet parameters and the screen size the applet should be granted. (An HTML file internally describes these parameters as tags within the `<applet>` tag.)

The Debug Options tab enables you to control how JBuilder works in Debug mode.

If you Enable Smart Step, you can control whether JBuilder should "step inside" constructors, static initializers, and synthetic methods. It's usually a good idea to keep the defaults (skip static initializers and synthetic methods). Turning on Warn If Break in Class with Tracing Disabled lets JBuilder warn you when you (inadvertently, perhaps) put a breakpoint in classes for which you have disabled tracing. You should therefore keep this check box selected.

STATIC INITIALIZERS AND SYNTHETIC METHODS

A *static initializer* is executable Java code in a class enclosed within "`static {`" and "`}`". It is executed once when the class is loaded by a classloader.

A *synthetic member* (method or variable) is one that is generated by the Java compiler and is not specified in the source code. Such members can be generated by the compiler as implementation mechanisms. For example, a compiler can generate a synthetic member variable to keep a reference to the current object (that's the reference provided by the `this` keyword).

Remote debugging allows you to debug an application running on a different computer. We'll discuss this in detail in Chapter 6, "Debugging."

Build Tab

The Build tab has seven tabs: Java, IDL, JSP, Resource, Ant, SQLj, and Menu Items. Let's look at the Java, Resource, Ant, SQLj, and Menu Items tabs in more detail. The IDL and JSP tabs will be discussed later (IDL is discussed in Chapter 25, "CORBA," and JSPs in Chapter 17, "Java Server Pages").

The important (and what might appear at first to be misplaced) option on the Java tab is the Debug Options list box. This list box is here (and not in the Debug tab) because you have to select how much information is put into the compiled files for the debugger to be useful. We recommend that you keep the highest level (Source, Line, and Variable Information) all the way to integration testing and even deployment if possible. Only settle for a lower level if performance becomes a real issue, and you're convinced that removing debug information will improve performance measurably.

The Make Stable Packages option tells JBuilder to mark a package (and all its subpackages) as "stable" after that package is compiled for the first time. The package will not be subsequently compiled unless its contents (that is, classes within that package) change. Leave this option off (unchecked) during development. This indicates that packages should not be marked stable when they successfully compile—a natural choice when packages and their contents are constantly changing.

The Check Stable Packages option allows you to tell JBuilder to check packages marked stable to see whether their contents have changed (and to recompile if necessary). If you turn off this check box (unchecked), stable packages are not checked. Leave this option on (checked) during development—except for packages containing classes for which you do not have the source, or packages that you faithfully trust.

The Obfuscate option tells JBuilder to mangle the names of private members (both methods and variables), so that they become cryptic. This protects you from reverse engineering to a greater extent. It's clear that from a security perspective, a cryptic name such as `$_1` is better than `strPassword`.

The Resource tab within the Build tab lists all the file types that JBuilder copies from the source directories to the output directory when the project is compiled. By default, you need compiled class files, image files, audio files, and any other resources to be copied to the output directory. However, not all file types need to be copied (for instance, Java source files). The Resource tab lets you control which file types should be copied over and which should not. You can change this option for all projects (by editing Default Project Properties) or for the current project (by editing the Project Properties). In addition, you may choose to include or exclude individual files from being copied to the output directory by right-clicking on the file in the Project pane and selecting Properties. This is shown in Figure 2.8.

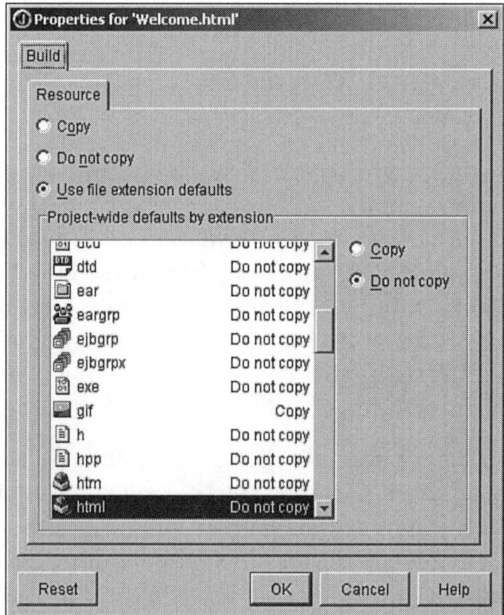

FIGURE 2.8 The Properties dialog box for an individual file allows you to include, exclude, or follow the default behavior regarding copying that file.

The Ant tab relates to Ant—not the hard-working insect but the open-source, Java-based build tool available freely from the Apache Software Foundation. Ant allows you to build a project by executing build tasks and build targets. You can find more details at Ant's home page, `http://jakarta.apache.org/ant/index.html`.

The build tasks that are part of an Ant build may require the inclusion of custom libraries. This is where the Ant tab comes in. On this tab, you can include libraries containing Java class files for specific Ant tasks that your project needs.

The SQLj tab lets you select a database vendor–specific SQLj translator. SQLj is a standard that defines how to call Structured Query Language statements from Java to access relational databases. SQLj is discussed in Chapter 15, "Database Connectivity."

The Menu Items tab allows you to add menu items to the first group within the Project tab. By default, the first two menu items in the Project menu are Make Project and Rebuild Project. You can add or remove other menu items to this group to provide easy access to your Project-specific tasks, such as generating Javadoc files or cleaning up the project directory.

Code Style Tab

The Code Style tab enables you to select curly-brace location and event-handling style. We'll discuss this in Chapter 3, "Employing the JBuilder Designers."

The Visibility of Instance Variables combo box enables you to select the visibility of variables generated through the JBuilder wizards. We recommend that you set this to "private" in accordance with good object-orientation principles (see the design guideline section on Encapsulation in Chapter 4, "Modeling").

Import Style Tab

The Import Style tab enables you to specify how JBuilder should put import statements in your code when you use the Optimize Imports menu item from the Content pane context menu. The options you select on this tab affect the behavior of the Edit, Optimize Imports menu item.

If you select Always Import Classes, JBuilder always imports classes one by one, rather than using the "*" wildcard—even if this means importing all the classes in the package. If you turn off this option, you can specify the threshold level beyond which JBuilder should use the "*" wildcard in the Package Import Threshold text field. If you put "3" in this text field, you're telling JBuilder to use the "*" prefix to import all classes from a package if you use three (or more) classes from that package.

You can also specify the order in which package import statements occur in your source files by arranging the packages in the same order in the Package Prefix Order.

Editor Tab

The Editor tab lets you specify what character combination to use for end-of-line characters. If you (or other members in your team) use JBuilder on different platforms, you might want to choose Platform Native; otherwise, the default Preserve Current Line Endings Within Files is sufficient.

UML Tab

The UML tab allows you to exclude certain packages and/or classes from appearing in UML diagrams. You might choose to do so to minimize clutter from your UML diagrams.

The Diagram References from Generated Source check box enables you to include autogenerated files (for example, Java files generated from compiling IDL files) in your UML diagrams. Again, you can minimize clutter in your UML diagrams by keeping this check box off.

Server Tab

The Server tab allows you to select which application server and which Web server JBuilder should use for various services. You may select one server for all the services (such as Borland Enterprise Server) or different servers for individual services (such as Tomcat for JSP/Servlet, Weblogic Application Server for EJBs, and Borland Enterprise Server for all other services). We will discuss these topics in detail in later chapters (in Parts IV and V of this book).

Tools Menu

The Tools menu contains commands to manage the JBuilder IDE, code editor, and libraries among other tools. The first two menu items (IDE Options and Editor Options) are discussed later in this section. Let's look at the other menu items in this menu first.

The Tools, Configure Libraries menu item enables you to add or modify and remove libraries. Libraries can exist at the Project, User, or JBuilder levels.

The Tools, Configure JDKs menu item enables you to manage the JDKs known to JBuilder. As mentioned before, you can configure multiple JDKs in JBuilder and choose any one for a project.

The Tools, Configure Palette menu item enables you to add or remove JavaBeans from the Component Palette. We'll look at the palette again in Chapter 10, "AWT," and Chapter 11, "Swing."

The Tools, Enterprise Setup menu item is for managing CORBA and application servers and configuring the database drivers known to JBuilder.

The Tools, Bean Insight menu item opens the BeanInsight dialog box. This dialog box presents a quick and easy way to examine a JavaBean.

TIP

You can use the BeanInsight dialog box to examine any Java class—JavaBean or not. BeanInsight, however, is most useful when examining true JavaBeans.

The Tools, Package Migration menu item opens the Package Migration Tool dialog box, through which you can define and execute various package migration strategies.

JBuilder comes complete with a database—JDataStore—and the Tools, JDataStore Server and Tools, JDataStore Browser menu items let you start or stop the server and browse through your deployed schemas, respectively. We'll look at these menu items again when we look at databases in Chapter 15.

Now let's look at the first two menu items in the Tools menu—IDE Options and Editor Options.

IDE Options

The Tools, IDE Options menu item opens the IDE Options dialog box, shown in Figure 2.9.

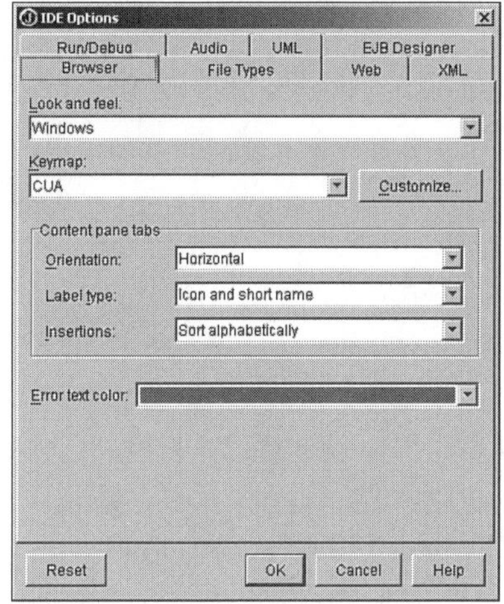

FIGURE 2.9 The IDE Options dialog box lets you modify various properties of the JBuilder IDE.

Let's take a look at the various tabs of the IDE Options dialog box:

- Browser—Enables you to change the "look and feel" of your IDE, set key mappings, and determine the location of tabs and colors. Feel free to change these options to suit your mood and style!

- File Types—Enables you to manage the file extensions that JBuilder associates with the recognized file types. You can add a file extension if you want to use JBuilder to open or edit it. Remember that you can edit only textual files in JBuilder (you can, however, open a wider variety of files, such as image and audio files).
- Web—Enables you to select whether JBuilder should copy the URL of a Web application to the Clipboard when it is run (so that you can then paste it to an external Web browser). Another option is whether JBuilder should use its internal Web browser ("internal process"), an external Web browser ("separate process"), or both.
- XML—Gives you options for displaying and transforming XML files. (XML is discussed in Chapter 20, "XML.")
- Run/Debug—Lets you control the update intervals for run and debug environments. Running frequent updates might degrade the overall responsiveness, so the default values (100 to 150 ms) should be acceptable in most cases.
- Audio—Lets you select whether JBuilder should play sounds to provide you feedback when key operations finish (normally or with errors).
- UML—Lets you select some adornment levels for the UML diagrams generated by JBuilder. You can also specify colors for the various UML elements.
- EJB—Is similar to the UML tab in that you can customize the color and font details for the EJB designer.

Editor Options

The Tools, Editor Options menu item opens the Editor Options dialog box, shown in Figure 2.10.

The following is a brief description of the tabs on this dialog box:

- Editor—On this tab, you can select the key mapping, as well as set the tab and indent options. The Backup Level determines how many local backup files JBuilder will create before the files start to "rollover."
- Display—Here you can set the font, which is used in the code editor within the Content pane. You can also choose to display a right margin, which is useful to ensure that your lines don't get wrapped awkwardly when you print your text files.
- Color—You might very well feel like a kid in a candy store playing with all the color options that the Color tab gives you! Often, the defaults suffice, but for people with visual impairments such as color blindness, the options on this tab are sure to provide workable color schemes.

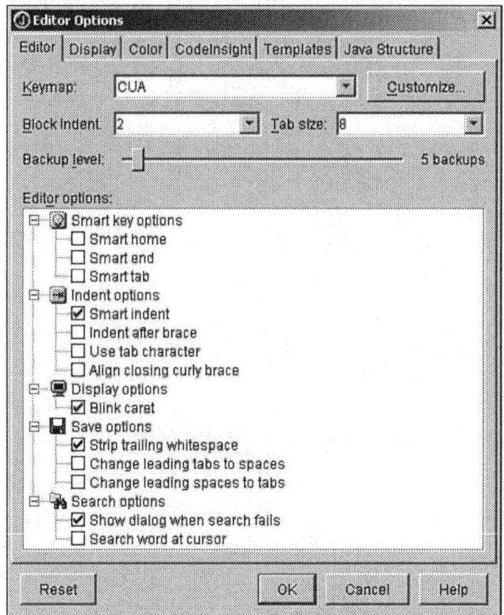

FIGURE 2.10 The Editor Options dialog box enables you to modify various features of the code editor.

- CodeInsight—The options on this tab enable you to set the delay after which JBuilder automatically pops up dialog boxes to show you members (methods and variables) and parameters to a method. This is a helpful feature to avoid making typing errors while coding.

TIP

You can make the CodeInsight windows pop up on command, even if you have turned off these options in the CodeInsight tab.

Press Ctrl+Spacebar after the dot (.) following a variable name to pop up the MemberInsight dialog box.

Press Ctrl+Shift+Spacebar within the parentheses of a method to pop up the ParameterInsight dialog box.

- Templates—Templates are another great way to reduce typing (and hence typing errors) while coding. Each code template has a name and an associated code snippet. You can type the name of the code snippet anywhere in your source code and press Ctrl+J, and the code snippet associated with the template name will be added to your current file at the cursor location. The cursor is placed at the appropriate location, so that you can immediately start typing the remaining code.

TIP

It might take you a while to memorize some of the template names, but when you do, using the templates is always quicker than typing code.

What's more, you can even add your own templates. This works great if you have a recurring code snippet. You can make a template out of it, and then use the magic of Ctrl+J to do the trick!

- Java Structure—On this tab, you can specify how JBuilder should arrange the elements in the Structure pane when the source code of a Java file is being viewed in the Content pane. You can control how often JBuilder parses your source file (necessary to provide you all the code assistance features) by using the Parse Delay slider. For large files, you might want to set this to a large value so that the JBuilder IDE remains crisp and responsive.

The Other Menus

In this section, we'll briefly look at the other menus: Run, Team, Wizards, Window, and Help.

Run Menu

The Run menu has commands to run or debug the current project, run or debug the current file (if it can be run), and other debug-related commands to control how the debugger steps through code.

The Run, Configurations menu item enables you to add and modify more than one run configuration. A single run configuration specifies which application, applet, JSP, servlet, EJB, or test application to run, and any parameters specific to the run setting.

All the run configurations you specify appear in the drop-down next to the Run button in the toolbar (discussed in "The Toolbar" section later in this chapter).

Team Menu

The Team menu includes commands to select which Version Control System (VCS) you want to use and commands to check files into or out of the VCS.

Wizards Menu

The Wizards menu includes wizards for implementing interfaces, overriding methods and resource strings, creating Javadocs, archiving, using data modules, generating EJB code, and using CORBA interfaces.

Window Menu

The Window menu lets you select any one of the open files within the AppBrowser. You can open up another AppBrowser—or more. This is much better than actually launching multiple instances of the JBuilder application.

Help Menu

The Help menu lets you access all the help features of JBuilder. We will have more to say about accessing help in JBuilder in the "In Practice" section later in this chapter.

The Toolbar

The JBuilder toolbar provides quick "at your fingertips" access to the most commonly needed services. All but one of the toolbar buttons have corresponding menu items, and most of them have shortcut key combinations as well.

The only toolbar button to which there is no menu bar equivalent is the drop-down button next to the Run and Debug buttons, shown in Figure 2.11. These drop-downs enable you to choose which configuration to run.

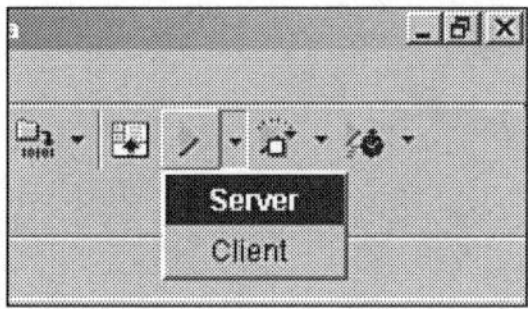

FIGURE 2.11 The Run and Debug configuration buttons are available on the toolbar as drop-down lists.

Specifying multiple run configurations is useful in many situations. You might need multiple configurations for the following and other reasons:

- You have a project that contains a server application and a client application. You'll need two run configurations to run the two separate "main" classes—one each for the server and the client. (The Chess sample that comes with JBuilder exhibits this situation.)
- You may want to run the same "main" class with different command line and/or VM parameters. You can create a separate run configuration for each parameter set.

In Practice

Now that you know your way around the JBuilder IDE, let's put our skills to the test by first looking at the Welcome project, and then creating our very own Hello World project using JBuilder.

The Welcome Project

When you start JBuilder for the first time, the Welcome project opens automatically for you. Figure 2.12 shows what the project file (an HTML file) for the Welcome project looks like.

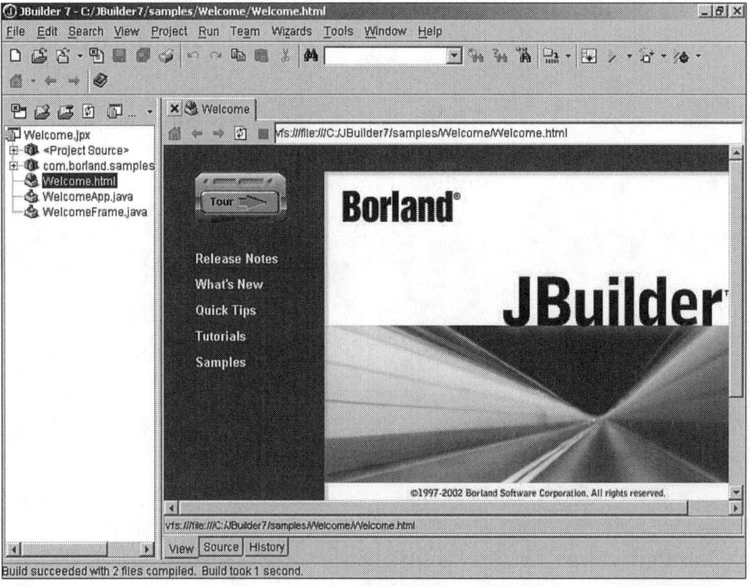

FIGURE 2.12 The Welcome project's HTML file provides links to useful resources.

> **TIP**
>
> You can open the Welcome project at any time by selecting the Help, Welcome Project (sample) menu item.

The Welcome project is a good place to start (even after you've used JBuilder for a while) because the HTML project file provides excellent links to samples, tutorials, and a virtual gold mine of useful information. For now, we will focus on actually running the application within the Welcome project:

1. Open the Welcome project, if it's not already open.
2. Run the application by clicking on the Run button on the toolbar. You should get a bland-looking frame with File and Help menus.
3. The File, Exit menu item works. You can use it to close the frame.

The Hello World Project

If you feel underwhelmed by the nominal nature of the Welcome application, wait a little longer. Next, we'll build our own simple project and see how easy it is.

Creating a New Project

1. Select the File, New Project menu item to open the Project Wizard.

TIP

The File, New Project and File, New Class menu options provide convenient shortcuts to the same options in the Object Gallery.

2. On the first screen of the Project Wizard, enter **`HelloWorld`** as the name of the project, **`jpx`** for the type, and **`C:/Projects/HelloWorld`** as the directory (where the project files are located). Leave the template set to (Default project). Check Generate Project Notes.
3. Click Next.
4. You don't need to make any changes on the second screen of the wizard. Observe how all the paths are set up. Notice how JBuilder by default recommends separate directories for the output (.../HelloWorld/classes); backup (.../HelloWorld/bak); the working directory (.../HelloWorld) where all the project files are stored; the default source (.../HelloWorld/src); the test source (.../HelloWorld/test); and the documentation (.../HelloWorld/doc).
5. Click Next.
6. On the third screen, enter some values for the Javadoc fields (title, description, and @author).

TIP

Javadoc treats fields that start with the @ sign in a special manner. These fields are included in the HTML documentation generated through the Javadoc Wizard. We'll demonstrate this in Chapter 8, "Documenting in JBuilder."

7. Click Finish.
8. At this point, you have a brand new project, which has one HTML file. Your AppBrowser should look as shown in Figure 2.13.

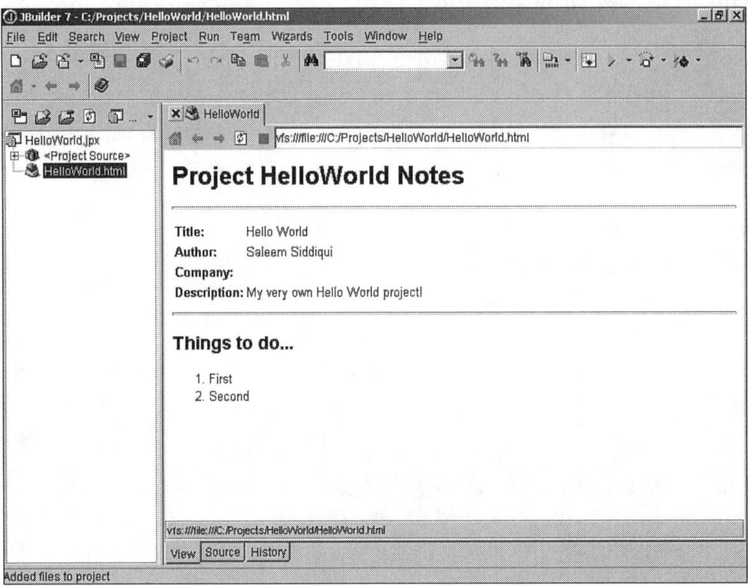

FIGURE 2.13 The newly created Hello World project contains only the HTML project file.

9. With the Project notes (HTML) file open in the AppBrowser, switch to Source file view tab at the bottom of the Content pane. We will now put some comments and "notes-to-self"—a common usage of the project file.
10. Notice that the Structure pane changes to show you the HTML structure of the file. Locate the word "First" in the Structure pane and click on it.
11. Change the "First" and "Second" items in the HTML text to the next steps that we're really going to do: "Create Hello World application" and "Compile and run Hello World application".
12. Switch back to the View file view tab at the bottom of the Content pane. You should now see the changes you made in your project notes file.
13. Save your project (File, Save All).

Creating a New Application

Now that we have a project, let's continue with creating an application within this project.

1. Select File, New to open the Object Gallery. Select Application from the New tab and click OK. This opens the Application Wizard.
2. On the first screen of the Application Wizard, select `helloworld` as the package, and enter **`HelloApp`** as the name of the application. Check the Generate Header Comments check box.
3. Click Next.

> **PACKAGE NAMES IN JAVA**
>
> You might have noticed that the package name suggested by JBuilder is the same as the project name—except that is all lowercase. Why is that? The Java naming standards recommend that all package names should be comprised of lowercase letters (and possibly digits) only. Uppercase letters in package names are frowned upon. JBuilder subtly suggests this naming scheme and converts all uppercase letters to lowercase. You could choose to ignore this naming scheme. We recommend that you avoid doing so. It's no fun to needlessly swim against the tide!

4. On the second screen of the wizard, enter the name (**`FrmHello`**) and title (**`Hello World!`**) of the main Frame class that will be created. Select all the other options (generate menu bar, toolbar, status bar, and About dialog box, and then center frame onscreen).
5. Click Finish.

That's it! We have created our first project and application, without so much as writing a single line of code.

Running the Hello World Application

Run the application by clicking the Run button on the toolbar. The application opens a frame shown in Figure 2.14.

Voila! We have an application—admittedly trivial—but nevertheless with a toolbar, a menu bar, and a status bar. The Help, About menu item works (pops up the dialog box), and so does the File, Exit menu item. All in all, it's a nice starting point for you if you want to develop a Java client.

FIGURE 2.14 The simple Hello World application in action.

Browsing Through the Java Files and Accessing Help

We've already looked at the Help menu in detail. Now we want to explore what other ways exist in JBuilder to summon the help genie.

Context-Sensitive Help with F1 You would expect F1 to bring you the customary help window—and indeed it does. The F1 help in JBuilder is context sensitive, which adds to its great value. Let's access this context-sensitive help in the Hello World project. Follow these steps:

1. With the Hello World project still open, select the FrmHello file in the AppBrowser.
2. Make sure that the Source view is selected in the Content pane.
3. Click on the JFrame node in the Structure pane.
4. Press F1. You should get the context sensitive help for the `javax.swing.JFrame` class in a new window, as shown in Figure 2.15.

"Definition" Help with the Context Menu If all you need is to look up a class or method definition, then you can do it by following these steps:

1. Make sure that you're looking at the FrmHello file with the Source tab selected in the AppBrowser.
2. Place the blinking cursor in the word `JMenuBar` near the top of the class definition.
3. Right-click to open the context menu.

4. Select the Find Definition menu item. This opens the source file for the class `javax.swing.JMenuBar` in your AppBrowser.
5. Click the Doc file view tab at the bottom of the Content pane. You're now looking at the documentation of the `JMenuBar` class in place.

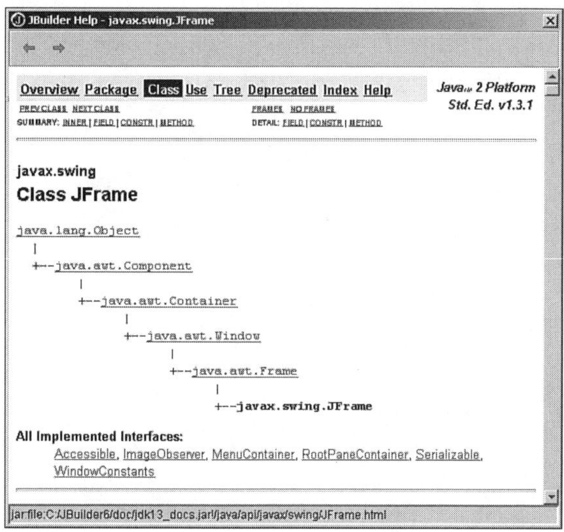

FIGURE 2.15 The context-sensitive F1 help in JBuilder pops up windows similar to this one showing the `JFrame` class.

Summary

In this chapter, we looked at the JBuilder IDE. One of the keys to using any IDE effectively is to learn the commonly used options, their purpose, and their shortcuts. In JBuilder, the Project Properties, the Object Gallery, and the menu items in the File menu are often the most commonly used options. With JBuilder, it is also comforting to know that there are no smoke and mirrors. The source code is pure Java, the documentation is pure HTML, and even the project file is human-readable. (All jpx files are XML; all jpr files are text.) If you are curious about what a jpx file looks like, feel free to open up one in your favorite text editor. Just make a copy of it beforehand in case you accidentally delete portions of it! In it, you will find references to all the files included in the project and environment settings related to your project.

Like any other tool, it may take you a while to get acquainted with the various menus and options in JBuilder. Take time to get familiar with the environment. Run the samples. See how they work.

In Chapter 3, we will develop a more substantial application with a user interface.

Reflections

- How many files did JBuilder create for the Hello World project and application? How many Java files?
- At first blush, does the code generated by the wizards seem difficult to you, easy, or trivial?
- How long do you estimate it would take you to build the HelloWorld application without using any Java IDE? Using an IDE other than JBuilder?

3 Employing the JBuilder Designers

IN THIS CHAPTER

- Screen Designer
- Writing Event Handlers
- Menu Designer

JBuilder provides many different designers and wizards to allow you to be more productive in the development of your application. In this chapter, we will look at these designers and wizards to build our application efficiently and effectively. You will learn how to use these designers to produce a simple user interface, hook up events, and build navigation. As we explore these designers, you will experience the single biggest reason to use JBuilder and its available designers—productivity! We will investigate the following objectives:

- Using the Screen Designer
- Implementing event handling
- Building a menu with the Menu Designer

Screen Designer

The JBuilder Screen Designer uses an amazing feature called a *two-way* designer. This allows user interfaces to be constructed either with code or by using the Screen Designer, interchangeably. This gives you the flexibility to use whatever technique works best. Often, you will find that you might switch back and forth between both, depending on what needs to be accomplished. For example, it might be easier to make changes to the code to change properties based on variables. Whereas in other instances, the designer would better meet the need to change the graphical layout of the user interface. We'll now look at the Screen Designer and see where to start.

Activating a Designer

Activating any designer, in this case the Screen Designer, is rather simple, although the response to the activation of the designer is more dramatic. This result includes parsing the user interface, building the interrelationship between all the components, and finally checking for syntactical errors. To access any of the design tools, you must open a source file (java, XML, jsp, and so on) in the Content pane and then click on its Design tab to load the appropriate designer. The designer in which the JBuilder initiates is the designer that was last used if multiple designers are appropriate for that situation. For example, if the Screen Designer, shown in Figure 3.1, was last used on a frame, the Designer pane defaults to the Screen Designer.

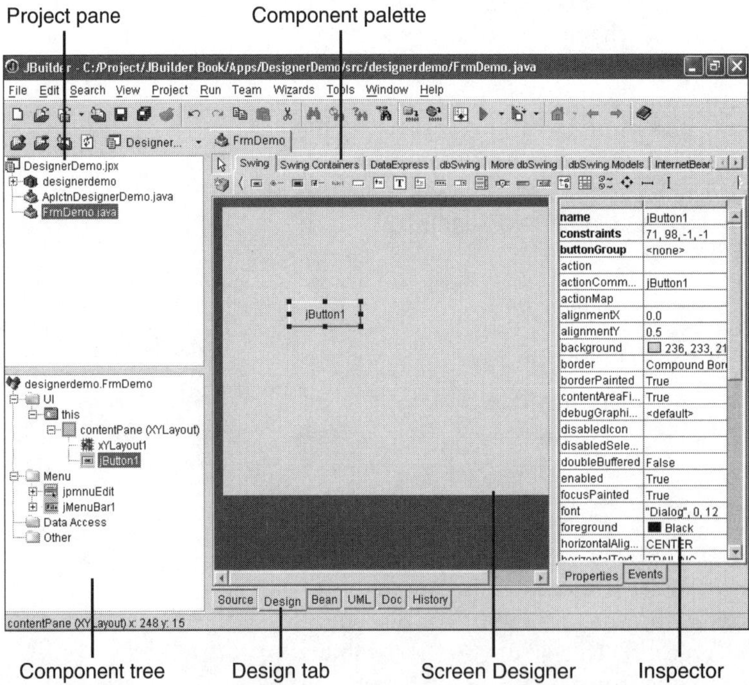

FIGURE 3.1 JBuilder in Design view.

JBuilder provides tools for visually designing and programming Java classes, giving you the ability to produce new complex user interfaces. Like an artist having many different tools at his disposal, the visual design tools offer many options. The designer contains four main compartments: the Component tree, an Inspector, one of three different designers, and finally a Component palette. These three designers include a Menu Designer, Screen Designer, and Database Component Designer. The

Database Component Designer will be addressed in Chapter 15, "Database Connectivity."

NOTE

If you have an error in the `jbInit()` method of the class, you will not be able to enter the Screen Designer. This is not limited to just the Screen Designer, but also affects the Menu Designer and Database Component Designer. You may receive a variety of errors if the designer cannot parse the `jbInit()` method. For example, a missing semicolon on any line of code would produce `com.borland.jbuilder.cmt.CmtParseException: Class '' not found`, but all errors will be displayed under the Design tab of the Compiler window.

Component Tree

Let's drill down and look specifically at what the component tree offers. It is one of the most useful and often overlooked portions of the JBuilder IDE. The component tree replaces the source code Structure pane when the Design tab becomes activated. Its display contains a structured/organized view of all the components owned/contained within the frame. Its purpose is simple: to display the interrelationships between all components and containers for a given frame. The Component tree is divided into folders to allow for better organization of components within a user interface. For example, Figure 3.2 shows how the Component tree of the Screen Designer is divided into these folders.

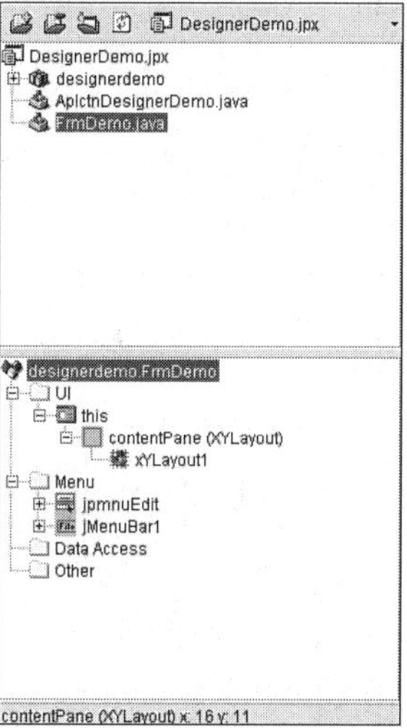

FIGURE 3.2 The Component tree is used to navigate either between designers or components within a designer.

The Component tree offers a number of productive features, such as

- Add and manage non-UI components from the Component palette into your class by dragging and dropping them on the Component tree.
- Move the mouse over a component to identify the base class name.
- Select a visual or non-UI component to modify its properties and associated events in the Inspector.
- Open a visual or non-UI component's associated designer (for example, the Menu Designer or Database Component Designer).
- Rename a component.
- Cut, copy, and paste components in your UI design.
- Reorganize the relationship of components to containers.

The tree is organized into a number of different folders to allow for easy traversal through the frame design. These folders enable you to have an organized view of all components contained within this module. The following is a list of each of the folders and its containership rules:

- UI components—This folder contains all the user interface components of a frame. More specifically, it demonstrates visually the relationship between containers and components.
- Menu components—All menu components and containers appear under this folder. This includes pop-up menus in addition to fixed menus.
- Data Access components—All nonvisual data model components appear in this location.
- Other—Any JavaBean that is not defined in one of the three preceding categories (for example, Socket component).

Component Palette

The Component palette will be the most used section of JBuilder's Screen Designer. The palette divides all the building blocks, components, and other JavaBeans, of an application into a number of different categories and offers the ability to add many of your own. These building blocks are organized into different categories depending on the requirements and capabilities of the component. Each component ultimately represents a program element as a user-interface object, a database, or a system facility (see Figure 3.3). Each component, therefore, represents a true implementation of object-oriented behavior with properties, methods, and events.

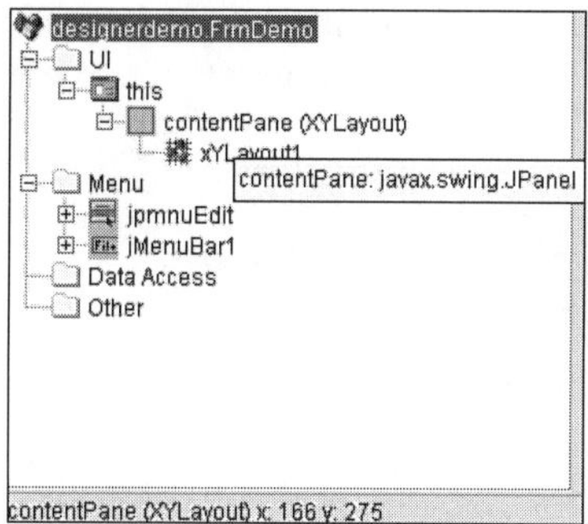

FIGURE 3.3 ToolTip text represents the component under design. The hierarchies represent the containership of each component in the tree. Each component is grouped into similar types of components in the tree (UI, Menu, Data Access, and Other).

Component Palette Organization The organization of the Component palette is actually simple. Each component is grouped into an interrelated set. The following is a list of many of these sets:

- Swing—This grouping contains all the components of swing that are not a container.
- Swing Container—This set contains all the container swing level components.
- DataExpress—The DataExpress tab contains all the Borland DataExpress JavaBeans.
- db*—Any of the tabs that start with db contain swing or AWT components that have been extended to support a data model.
- XML, CORBA, JClass, and many more—These will be discussed in subsequent chapters.

Managing the Component Palette One of the great features of JBuilder is its capability to be customized and extended. One extension enables you to add new components to the Component palette. For example, you might want to include your own custom controls or add new components from third-party vendors. To do this, choose Tools, Configure Palette from the menu. This allows you to configure your palette properties either by reorganizing the existing components or adding new components under the Add Components tab. Figure 3.4 demonstrates the folder's visual. From this Palette Properties page, you have access to the following:

- Add/reorganize component groups—To add a component group, select any existing component group and choose the Add button. You can also reorganize the order of the components within a group.
- Add a new component—Choose the Add Components tab of the Palette Properties page. You can use this tool to add JavaBean components from a third-party class library or JavaBean-compliant object you have created.
- Add a component image—Each component may have an associated image to aid in its functional clarity.

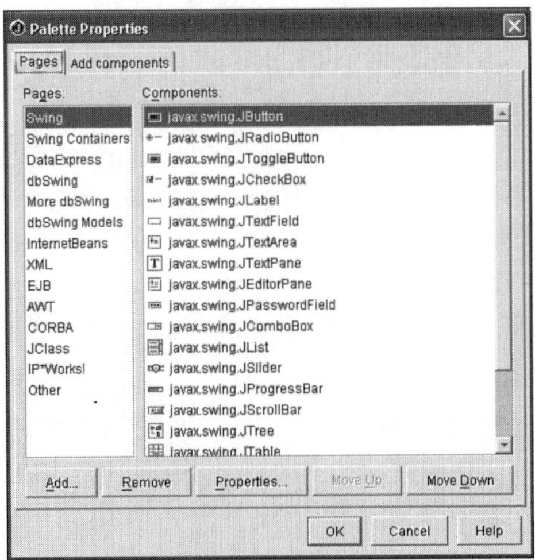

FIGURE 3.4 The Configure palette enables you to customize any component group or component in addition to inserting new components.

Inspector

The Inspector displays to the right of the design window. Its purpose is to display and manipulate the properties of a given component at design time. As changes are made in the Inspector, source code is immediately written to implement the change. As in the Screen Designer, the Menu Designer is also a two-way tool. In Figure 3.5 for example, the code written to configure the menu is also shown in the Menu Designer.

The associated properties available to the Inspector for any given component are implemented in the `BeanInfo` class. This class defines for the Inspector what name and attribute types each property must be. In any case, JBuilder's Inspector reads the appropriate properties when the component is selected, in addition to making an appropriate custom editor available or using the default editors. In Listing 3.1, notice that when we changed the text for `jButton1` in the Inspector, it created the code that is in **bold**.

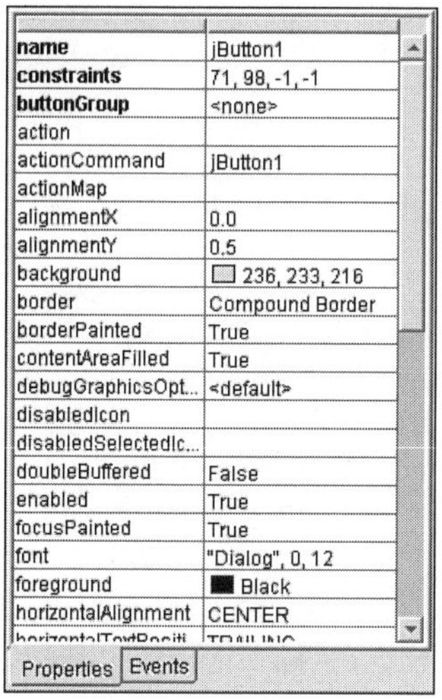

name	jButton1
constraints	71, 98, -1, -1
buttonGroup	<none>
action	
actionCommand	jButton1
actionMap	
alignmentX	0.0
alignmentY	0.5
background	236, 233, 216
border	Compound Border
borderPainted	True
contentAreaFilled	True
debugGraphicsOpt...	<default>
disabledIcon	
disabledSelectedIc...	
doubleBuffered	False
enabled	True
focusPainted	True
font	"Dialog", 0, 12
foreground	Black
horizontalAlignment	CENTER

Properties | Events

FIGURE 3.5 The Inspector is used to change any design-time property and the designer interprets it to code.

NOTE

In Listing 3.1, notice that as you build your user interface, no custom tags are included in your source code; that is the magnificence and simplicity of JBuilder and its patented two-way tool technology.

LISTING 3.1 The Results of Changing the Property Text for `jButton`

```
private void jbInit() throws Exception  {
    //setIconImage(Toolkit.getDefaultToolkit().createImage(
➥ FrmDemo.class.getResource("[Your Icon]")));
    contentPane = (JPanel) this.getContentPane();
    contentPane.setLayout(xYLayout1);
    this.setSize(new Dimension(400, 300));
    this.setTitle("Designer Demo");
    //Code to setup the menu
    contentPane.addMouseListener(new FrmDemo_contentPane_mouseAdapter(this));
    jButton1.setText("Exit");
    contentPane.add(jButton1, new XYConstraints(82, 63, -1, -1));
}
```

NOTE

Properties not exposed in the `BeanInfo` class remain hidden. This means that they will not be displayed in the Inspector property list. The designer does not know about them unless a property manipulated for a given attribute was manipulated within the `jbInit()` method. In this case, the property will then appear in the Inspector, but only the default editors will be enabled for that attribute.

Writing Event Handlers

Event code is executed upon a given associated action. This is programming based on the event-driven programming model. In other words, code is executed as a reaction to a given event or events. This code is written within an event-handling stub to allow for better organization of code. JBuilder then manages the relationship or the attachment of these code snippets or business logic to the corresponding component's event.

Using the Events tab of the Inspector, you can easily attach a new or modify an existing event handler. To attach event-handling code to a component event, you need to do the following:

1. Choose the appropriate component by selecting it on the user interface or in the Component tree.
2. Choose the Event page of the Inspector.
3. Find the appropriate event you want to add a handler to and double-click on it.

NOTE

After completing the first three steps, you will be positioned in the implementation section of the code to enter the event business logic.

4. Write your business logic to implement the desired effect.

Just like in the Screen Designer, JBuilder does not add any special tags; it simply inserts standard Java code into your source file. In Listing 3.2, you will see the code generated by JBuilder.

LISTING 3.2 The Code Generated to Respond to an `actionPerformed` Event

```
jButton1.addActionListener(new java.awt.event.ActionListener() {
  public void actionPerformed(ActionEvent e) {
    jButton1_actionPerformed(e);
```

LISTING 3.2 Continued

```
      }
    });
...
  void jButton1_actionPerformed(ActionEvent e) {

  }
```

How an Event Is Processed

Many things have to be aligned properly for an event to be processed. When you first look at an event handler in Java, it can be overwhelming. Objects have to be created and assigned to the proper handler. The beauty of its design and implementation is that it works and gives you lots of flexibility for future design. To create an event handler for a given action, see Figure 3.6 and follow the five steps:

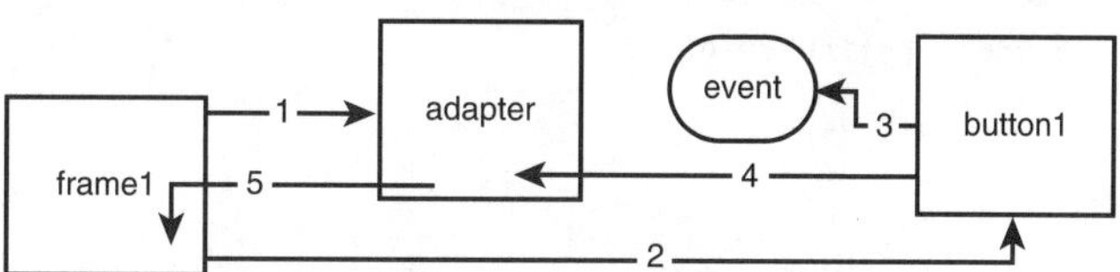

FIGURE 3.6 The interrelationships for event processing. Each number on the diagram represents a snippet of code included in the five steps.

The process for creating an event handler, although it does not contain much code, is actually not as easy as it looks. The process to create these lines of code by hand is defined in the following five steps:

1. Create an Adapter object. More specifically in this instance, we are creating an Adapter object of the ActionListener type.

   ```
   jButton1.addActionListener(new java.awt.event.ActionListener() {
     public void actionPerformed(ActionEvent e) {
       jButton1_actionPerformed(e);
     }
   });
   ```

2. Register the adapter with the component.

   ```
   jButton1.addActionListener(new java.awt.event.ActionListener() {
     public void actionPerformed(ActionEvent e) {
   ```

```
      jButton1_actionPerformed(e);
    }
  });
```

3. Create an Event object.

4. Send the Event to the Adapter.

```
jButton1.addActionListener(new java.awt.event.ActionListener() {
  public void actionPerformed(ActionEvent e) {
    jButton1_actionPerformed(e);
  }
});
```

5. Send the Event to the original object.

```
jButton1.addActionListener(new java.awt.event.ActionListener() {
  public void actionPerformed(ActionEvent e) {
    jButton1_actionPerformed(e);
  }
});
```

Just like in the rest of JBuilder, events can also be added by means of a shortcut. It is as simple as double-clicking on the component in the Screen Designer, and the default action is attached. For example, the default action for a jButton, defined within its BeanInfo class, is actionPerformed. To this point, we have ignored that there is more than one method for implementing an adapter. You have at your disposal two different adapter types: anonymous and standard.

Using Anonymous Adapters

Anonymous adapters use a special convention in Java that is seldom used in other places. That is Java's capability to define an inner class. An inner class is defined within or inside another class. Because an adapter is defined inside the frame and is owned by the frame, it has full access to all the methods and properties of that class. Listing 3.3 shows an example of an anonymous adapter. Contrast that with Listing 3.4, which is a standard adapter implementation.

LISTING 3.3 An Example of an Anonymous Adapter Implementation

```
jButton1.addActionListener(new java.awt.event.ActionListener() {
  public void actionPerformed(ActionEvent e) {
    jButton1_actionPerformed(e);
  }
});
```

Using Standard Adapters

Standard adapters are only standard in that they allow for an adapter to be defined externally from a class before Java allowed inner classes. Using anonymous adapters is actually more of the norm in user interface construction today. Listing 3.4 demonstrates this in an implementation of `actionPerformed`.

LISTING 3.4 An Example of a Standard Adapter Implementation

```
    jButton1.addActionListener(new FrmDemo_jButton1_actionAdapter(this));
…
class FrmDemo_jButton1_actionAdapter implements
➥ java.awt.event.ActionListener {
  FrmDemo adaptee;

  FrmDemo_jButton1_actionAdapter(FrmDemo adaptee) {
    this.adaptee = adaptee;
  }
  public void actionPerformed(ActionEvent e) {
    adaptee.jButton1_actionPerformed(e);
  }
}
```

Changing Adapter Settings

Changing the adapter style is easy in most cases, although the anonymous adapter is normally used in JDK 1.1.3 and greater development. To change the object adapter type, you must use the Project Properties dialog box. Figure 3.7 shows the Code Style tab of the Project Properties page.

Following these steps enables you to change your adapter style generated by JBuilder:

1. Select Project, Project Properties.
2. Select the Code Style tab.
3. Make an adapter choice (Standard—External Class, Anonymous—Internal Class).
4. Decide whether to Match Existing Code—use the same adapter as the others defined within this frame/class.

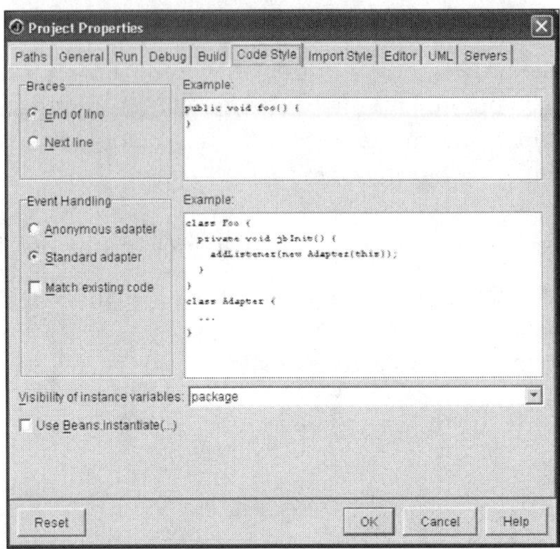

FIGURE 3.7 The Project Properties page/Code Style tab affects event processing code construction by JBuilder.

Menu Designer

The Screen Designer is used to show all graphical aspects of your screen, but it does not show a menu assigned to a given frame. They are available only in the Component tree on the bottom left, but not shown graphically. If the Component tree is not enough to visually interpret the menu, you can also see the menu graphically by activating the Menu Designer. There are two methods by which you can activate the designer. Double-clicking on the Component tree menu item starts the Menu Designer in addition to right-clicking on and selecting Activate Designer. The Menu Designer toolbar becomes available. To ultimately use the Menu Designer, you must first drop the component for a menu onto the desired frame. The following menu types are available within the JBuilder environment:

- From the Swing Containers palette: `JMenuBar` `JPopUpMenu`
- From the AWT palette: `MenuBar` `PopUpMenu`

Drop a menu component anywhere onto on the frame or drop it onto the Component tree. Menu components are always placed under the Menu folder of the Component tree regardless of where it is dropped.

Menu Designer Buttons

When the Menu Designer is instantiated by JBuilder, many tools become available, which were not seen in the Screen Designer, to build your menu. For a description of all the Menu Designer tools, see Table 3.1.

TABLE 3.1 Action Buttons for the Menu Designer

Button	Action
Insert Item	Adds a new menu item before the selected one.
Insert Separator	Adds a separator between items to divide them into logical groupings.
Insert Nested Menu	Adds a submenu or nested menu to the selected menu item.
Delete Item	Deletes the selected menu item.
Enable/Disable Toggle	Enables or disables the selected item. (This is the initial state unless changed programmatically.)
Checkable/Uncheckable	Makes the selected item have an initial state of checked or unchecked.
Toggle	Toggles the menu item between being a `JMenuItem` or a `JradioButtonMenuItem`.

Building a Menu with the Menu Designer

Now we'll build a simple menu and see the results that JBuilder gives us. Just like in the Screen Designer, JBuilder is a two-way tool in the Menu Designer also. As a menu is constructed graphically, JBuilder is developing the physical source code.

NOTE

A menu is visible only while either in the Menu Designer or during application execution. You will not see a menu while in the Screen Designer.

When you build a menu, JBuilder implements the menu in the `jbInit()` method of your frame class. This also includes any design-time properties for the menu, such as disable/enable and accelerators. For example, let's build a menu that has two headings File and Help. Under File, we will place a menu item to exit us from the system. Under Help, we'll create Help Topics and About menu choices. Place a keyboard accelerator for the exit to be Ctrl+X. The following code demonstrates the successful implementation of a menu constructed by JBuilder. We'll go step-by-step through the process of building the menu. To help in this construction, the following steps are required to build this menu:

1. Select the Screen Designer—yes, the Screen Designer. This enables you to drop a container to hold your menu.

2. Drop a `JMenuBar` anywhere on your frame. This component is located under the Swing Containers tab.

3. Right-click on the `jMenuBar1` object created under the Menu folder of the Component tree and choose Activate Designer.
4. In the blank of the first menu item, type **`File`**. The Menu Designer automatically adds a blank menu item to append to a menu list.
5. In the Inspector, change the properties as desired.
6. Repeat until all the menu items are completed.

Now that the menu is complete, Listing 3.5 shows the code that JBuilder constructed while we were building the menu. We did not write any code; the Menu Designer did it all.

LISTING 3.5 The Results of Building a Menu with the Menu Designer

```
...
  private void jbInit() throws Exception  {
    //setIconImage(Toolkit.getDefaultToolkit().createImage(
➥ FrmDemo.class.getResource("[Your Icon]")));
    contentPane = (JPanel) this.getContentPane();
    contentPane.setLayout(xYLayout1);
    this.setSize(new Dimension(400, 300));
    this.setTitle("Designer Demo");
    //Code to setup the menu
    jmnFile.setText("File");
    jmnitmExit.setText("E&xit");
    jmnitmExit.setAccelerator(javax.swing.KeyStroke.getKeyStroke(88,
➥ java.awt.event.KeyEvent.CTRL_MASK, false));
    jmnitmExit.addActionListener(new FrmDemo_jmnitmExit_actionAdapter(this));
    jmnHelp.setText("Help");
    jmnitmHelpTopics.setText("Help Topics");
    jmnitmAbout.setEnabled(false);
    jmnitmAbout.setText("About");
    jMenuBar1.add(jmnFile);
    jMenuBar1.add(jmnHelp);
    jmnFile.add(jmnitmExit);
    jmnHelp.add(jmnitmHelpTopics);
    jmnHelp.addSeparator();
    jmnHelp.add(jmnitmAbout);
  }
...
```

Implementing a Menu Action

When a menu is defined, it may—but nothing requires it—have an event handler just like the event handlers identified earlier with GUI components. To create an event handler and implement an action for a menu item, execute the following steps:

1. Activate the Menu Designer.
2. Select the menu item to create an event handler.
3. Click on the Events tab of the Inspector pane.
4. Double-click on the appropriate event.
5. Add implementation code for desired business logic. For example, add `System.exit(0)` for the Exit menu item of your menu.
6. Finally, associate the newly created menu with the panel. This is accomplished by setting the `JPanel` property for `JMenu` to the menu name.

Notice after the event has been produced that the code generated follows the same rules as anonymous and standard adapters for the events in components. For example, every application needs the capability to exit. The following example implements the `System.exit(0)` to shut down the application. Listing 3.6 shows what the generated code looks like.

LISTING 3.6 Implementing an Event Within a Menu Item

```
  private void jbInit() throws Exception  {
    …
    jmnitmExit.setText("Exit");
    jmnitmExit.setAccelerator(javax.swing.KeyStroke.getKeyStroke(88,
➥ java.awt.event.KeyEvent.CTRL_MASK, false));
    jmnitmExit.addActionListener(new FrmDemo_jmnitmExit_actionAdapter(this));
…
  }
…
  void jmnitmExit_actionPerformed(ActionEvent e) {
    System.exit(0);
  }

}

class FrmDemo_jmnitmExit_actionAdapter implements
➥ java.awt.event.ActionListener {
  FrmDemo adaptee;
```

LISTING 3.6 Continued

```
  FrmDemo_jmnitmExit_actionAdapter(FrmDemo adaptee) {
    this.adaptee = adaptee;
  }
  public void actionPerformed(ActionEvent e) {
    adaptee.jmnitmExit_actionPerformed(e);
  }
}
```

Creating a Pop-Up Menu

A *pop-up menu* is simply a menu that is not attached to any menu bar but floats when activated. The activation sequence for a pop-up menu is typically implemented using the secondary mouse button. A pop-up menu is useful for context-sensitive actions that need to be accomplished based on a certain selection or range. A good example is cut, copy, and paste. You can create a pop-up menu by doing the following:

1. In the UI Designer, click on a `PopupMenu` component from the AWT page of the Component palette or a `JPopupMenu` component from the Swing Containers page and drop it onto the Component tree.
2. Name the component `jpmnuEdit`.
3. Activate the Menu Designer for the dropped objects.

   Add Cut, Copy, and Paste menu items as you did with `JMenu`.
4. Select any component on the UI and activate the Screen Designer.
5. Select the component you want to activate the pop-up menu with.
6. Select the event to activate the pop-up menu. The event normally tasked with this event is mouse click.
7. Add this code to the event chosen to activate the pop-up menu.
8. Review what has been generated by the designer by switching to the Source tab. Listing 3.7 demonstrates what the generated code should look like.

LISTING 3.7 Generation of a Pop-Up Menu Using the Menu Designer

```
void contentPane_mouseClicked(MouseEvent e) {
  contentPane.add(jpmnuEdit);
  if (e.getModifiers() == Event.META_MASK)  {
   // Make the jPopupMenu visible relative to the
```

LISTING 3.7 Continued

```
➥ current mouse position in the container.
      jpmnuEdit.show(contentPane, e.getX(), e.getY());
    }
  }
```

9. Add event handlers to the pop-up menu to support the required functionality.

In Practice

We are going to put the principles we just investigated into practice in addition to the guide design and application development process. Often as a project is moving it becomes difficult to elicit good and correct requirements from end users. You are asking them to visualize something that has not been created yet. More likely than not, you are forced to create any number of the following:

- Storyboards—The process for which screen layout and flow are designed without focus on any of the underlying details of the form.
- Screen mock-ups—The process for which a requirements gather may use something like Microsoft's Visio or similar tool to mock up a screen.
- Screen prototype—The process for which a developer analyzes and designs a nonfunctional but viable user interface for an application. This adds the clarity and accuracy of the collected requirements.

You might ask why these are important. Designing your application before you start developing is extremely important. Often, designing a screen aids in the solicitation of requirements. For the ChalkTalk application, we are going to create screen prototypes. The ChalkTalk application allows us to schedule and register students and facilities for a set of courses. Because we are creating prototypes to elicit requirements, we will build a more detailed design in Chapter 4, "Modeling." When we build this application, we want to make sure that we use an appropriate prototyping process. The rules we are going to use are simple:

- The application will be discarded after the requirements collection is completed.
- Naming standards and other programming techniques are simply ignored to focus on one item: the correct implementation of the user interface to aid in the elicitation of requirements.

Creating the Application Framework

First, we need to create the shell of the user interface to gain consensus among the users of the ChalkTalk application.

1. Choose File, New Project and fill in the following information. Use the name ChalkTalk for the project.
2. Click Finish.
3. Choose File, New and select the Application tab.
4. Change the class name using a name standard, such as Hungarian Notation, which would change the name of the class to `aplctnChalkTalk`.
5. Change the frame name to `frmMain` and the title to ChalkTalk Administrator.
6. Start laying out the frame using ideas of how you think the application should look.
7. Compile and run your application.

Summary

JBuilder provides tools that enable you to visually design user interfaces without having to visualize what the interface will look like from code. The visual design tools, such as the Screen Designer, are two-way tools. When you write code, it is interpreted visually; when you design visually, it generates code.

Reflections

- Should I hand code or use the designer?
- What happens if I change the code? Can I go back to the designer?
- Can I mix hand coding with the use of designers?

PART II

JBuilder for Application Design, Modeling, and Testing

IN THIS PART

4 Modeling

IN THIS CHAPTER

In all but the most trivial software systems, the practice of modeling—deciding what to build and how to build it—both precedes and is concurrent with the actual writing of code. Modeling is an integral part of the design and analysis of any major system, and software systems are no exception.

Modeling requires a language all its own—a language that is precisely expressive (unlike natural languages) yet at the same time abstract (unlike programming languages à la Java). Various such modeling languages exist. The vocabulary of many of them consists of graphical, rather than textual, symbols. Graphical symbols, in general, are more expressive than textual symbols. One graphical symbol expresses much more information than can be described by one word or even one sentence. In fact, it could even be argued that graphical languages are more natural to humans than the so-called "natural" languages—after all, humans created hieroglyphs before they created any alphabet. If you have ever doodled on a napkin or a whiteboard to express the design of some software module to your colleagues (or to yourself), you would probably agree that it is easier to explain concepts by drawing pictures than by writing words.

Many graphical modeling languages are available, but the Unified Modeling Language (UML) is the most widely accepted of them all. This chapter looks at UML and how to use the relevant JBuilder features.

A "Warp 6" Overview of UML

The Object Management Group (OMG) defines UML as a language that "helps you specify, visualize, and document models of software systems, including their structure and design" (see `http://www.omg.org/gettingstarted/what_is_uml.htm`).

UML has been around for more than five years now; version 1.1 of UML was adopted by the OMG in late 1997. It was born out of the "unification" of various object modeling languages that grew in the 1980s and early 90s. Even though it encompasses the ideals of other languages—such as Booch, OOSE, OMT, and others—it does so with a reasonably small set of symbols and diagrams. UML provides extensibility through stereotyping some of these symbols, so that the overall vocabulary remains manageable.

In this section, we will discuss the various elements of UML. Then we will look at those elements—class and package diagrams—supported by JBuilder.

Elements of UML

UML's basic elements are *entities*—which may be physical or software—and their *relationships*. The relationships, too, can be physical (for example, a node representing a server can contain four other nodes, each representing a processor), or logical (for example, a class can subclass or "specialize" another class).

Entities and relationships are shown in UML in the form of various diagrams. A *diagram* in UML is a collection of entities and relationships drawn observing UML's syntactical and semantical rules. The various kinds of diagrams in UML are

- Class diagram—Shows a static view of classes and their relationships.
- Object diagram—Shows a dynamic (runtime) view of objects and their relationships to each other.
- Sequence diagram—Shows the time sequence of an operation as ordered steps representing suboperations and the objects that initiate (or are influenced by) those suboperations.
- Collaboration diagram—Conveys the same information as a corresponding sequence diagram but uses notation that clearly exposes the structural relationships among the collaborating objects (rather than the time sequence of suboperations).
- Use case diagram—Shows various "use cases" and the "actors" that initiate and/or are affected by each use case. (An *actor* is an entity external to the system that interacts with the system. A *use case* is a sequence of steps that yield a result valuable to an actor.)

- Deployment diagram—Shows the deployment view with hardware nodes (computers, processors, routers, and so on) and software components (deployable units such as dynamic link libraries or shared objects) and their relationships.

Class Diagrams in UML

In UML, the most common diagram used to show static (as opposed to runtime) entities and relationships is the class diagram. You could argue that it is also the most important static diagram.

A class diagram can contain the following elements:

- Class—In UML (as in object-oriented languages), a *class* is a named set of attributes and operations. The symbol for a class is a rectangle with usually three compartments showing the name, attributes, and operations of the class, respectively. The UML notation allows a class to have additional compartments at the bottom (for example to show responsibilities or properties of the class).

  A UML class maps (that is, corresponds) to a Java class.

- Interface—An interface is similar to a class except it cannot have any attributes, only operations. An interface is symbolized by a rectangle, too. However, the name of the interface is shown in italicized font. (For foreign language character sets that do not permit italics, a different font may be used to achieve the same effect.)

  A UML interface maps to a Java interface.

- Package—A package can appear not just on class diagrams but on other types of static UML diagrams as well, such as deployment or use case diagrams. A package in UML is simply an organizational unit that can contain other static elements. In class diagrams, packages are used to show the organizational hierarchy of UML classes and interfaces.

  A UML package (containing classes or other packages) maps to a Java package.

- Dependency relationship—A dependency relationship means that the dependent entity (for example, a class) may be affected by a change in the specifications of the entity on which it's dependent. Dependencies are shown by a dashed arrow with the tail of the arrow resting on the dependent object.

  A UML dependency relationship maps to a Java dependency (meaning that the dependent class uses a public attribute or method of the class or interface on which it is dependent).

- Generalization relationship—A generalization is a relationship where one entity (a class or interface) represents a more generic (or less specific) type of another entity (another class or interface). In UML, "generalization" spelled backward is "specialization!" This means that "class 'Baked Food' generalizes 'Doughnut'" and "class 'Doughnut' specializes 'Baked Food'" are semantically equivalent statements. Generalizations are represented by a line with a triangular, filled arrow head that rests on the more generic class. If the line is solid, it represents that the generalization is either from a class to another class or from an interface to another interface. A dashed line means that the generalization is from an interface to a class. (An interface cannot specialize a class because specialization cannot be used to make things more abstract, and interfaces are more abstract than classes.)

  A UML specialization relationship maps to a Java `extends` or `implements` relationship.

- Association relationship—An association is the most general of all relationship types. It means that the two connected entities are associated with each other. An association is shown by a solid line between the two related entities. The exact meaning of the association is almost always clarified either by placing a name for the association (such as "provide treatment") in the middle of the line or by placing two roles near the two entities (such as "patient" and "doctor"). An association can have *navigability*, which indicates whether the association can be traversed both ways or only one way. Navigability is shown by means of arrowheads. An association can be unidirectional (one arrow head indicating the direction of traversal) or bidirectional (two arrow heads or omission of arrow heads altogether).

  A UML association relationship translates to a Java association (meaning that the class at the tail of the association has a member variable referencing the class or interface at the head of the association).

Figure 4.1 illustrates most of these elements.

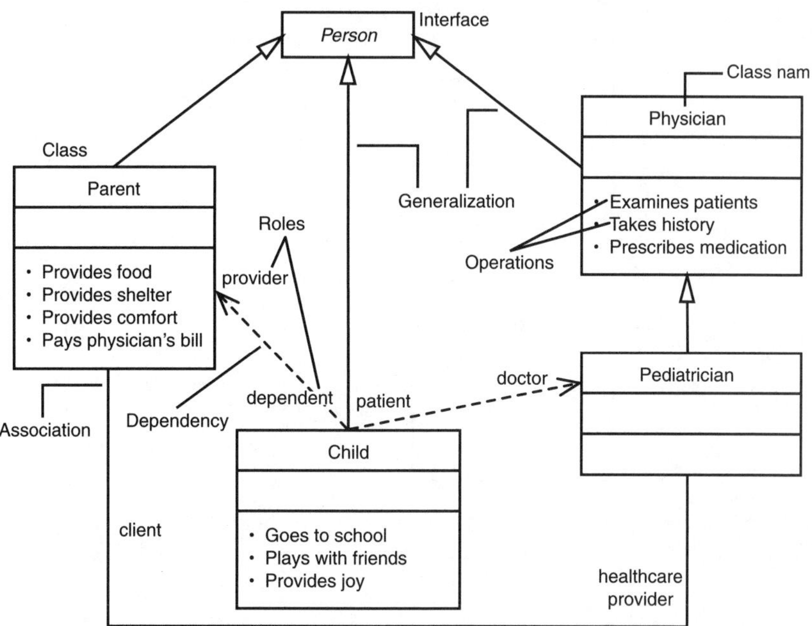

FIGURE 4.1 The admittedly oversimplistic scenario of parent, child, and pediatrician captures many UML elements.

Showing Packages in Class Diagrams

The one UML element that is conspicuous by its absence from Figure 4.1 is the package. The omission was purely to minimize clutter on the diagram—packages can be legitimately depicted on UML class diagrams (and often are). Furthermore, it's possible to have a static diagram where only packages (and their dependencies) are shown. Such a diagram, which is called a *package diagram* in JBuilder, provides useful information about the high-level distribution of a system's (or subsystem's) architecture, without revealing unnecessary details about the classes within those packages.

The only relationship possible between two packages is one of dependency, which identifies which packages are susceptible to changes to another package. One goal of design is to minimize circular dependencies among packages.

If we were to implement a hypothetical Java-based health-care software system based on the entities shown in Figure 4.1, we might get something similar to Figure 4.2.

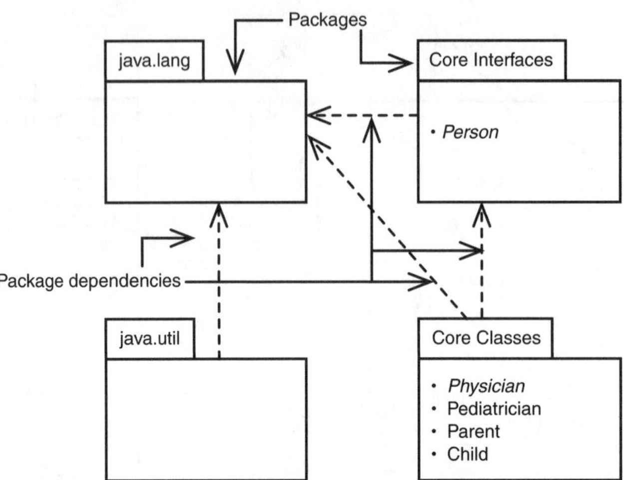

FIGURE 4.2 Package diagrams provide key information about package dependencies while maintaining a high level of abstraction.

JBuilder and UML

JBuilder is not a full-fledged UML modeling tool. It provides useful UML features that assist you in visualizing and changing (or refactoring) your code. It does not provide features such as drawing dynamic diagrams (activity, sequence, and collaboration) or many other features for which commercial UML tools are available.

JBuilder supports class and package diagrams of the type described in the previous section. Let's take a look at the features JBuilder provides to work with these diagrams.

Class Diagrams in JBuilder

When a Java file is opened in the AppBrowser, the UML tab at the bottom of the content panel becomes visible. Clicking on this tab allows you to switch to the UML diagram for that class, as shown in Figure 4.3.

It's that simple! The only thing you need to ensure is that the source file is free from compilation errors (in Source view, just glance at the structure pane to see whether an "Errors" folder is at the top). This is another benefit of JBuilder being a two-way tool—the UML diagram is generated simply by parsing the source code.

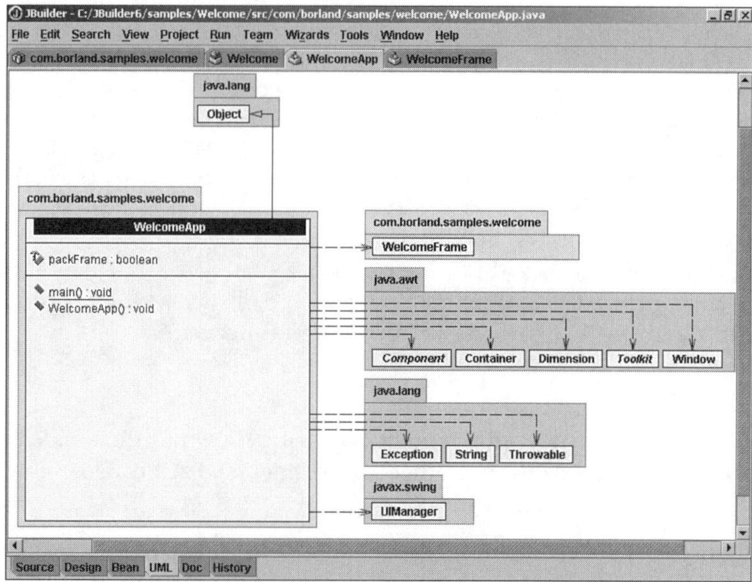

FIGURE 4.3 UML class diagram for the `WelcomeApp` class from the Welcome project. The "curtain" and toolbars have been hidden for clarity.

CAUTION

If the source code contains errors, the UML diagram cannot be generated.

If you know your UML, the diagram should be fairly clear to you. The current class occupies the central position, with all its attributes and operations visible by default. In addition, JBuilder provides another compartment at the bottom where properties are shown.

PROPERTIES OF A CLASS

A *property* is a named attribute of a class that can be read and/or modified through the use of IDE tools, as well as programmatically. Additionally, properties can be *bound* (that is, changes to them may be observed by other classes) and "vetoable" (changes to them may be rejected).

Some programming languages (and products) require different syntactic requirements to distinguish between the properties and simple member variables of a class. In Java, the distinction is more subtle in the sense that it does not require any "special" keywords. The language and tools, like JBuilder, use introspection and secondary classes to gather details about properties (and events) of a class.

> In the simplest case, a property in Java is a private member variable that has either an accessor (`get`) or a mutator (`set`) method or both. The accessor for a property `propX` must be named `getPropX` (or optionally `isPropX` for Boolean properties), and the mutator must be named `setPropX`. Note the capitalization of the first letter after `get` or `set` in the method names. If these simple rules are followed, then properties in Java are no different from other member variables. (Additional rules apply in case of array-properties and so on.) If these rules are not followed, or if additional control is desired over how properties are exposed, the class author needs to specify these details in a `BeanInfo` class.
>
> In JBuilder, you view and modify properties through the property inspector in the Design view. You define your own properties using the Property editor in the Properties tab, which is visible after the Bean tab at the bottom of the AppBrowser is selected.

Apart from the current class, all the other classes are shown in their elided form (only their names are shown—not other compartments). Each class is shown inside its package using the package element.

All—and only those—dependencies, associations, and generalization relationships are shown that involve the current class. To keep the diagram manageable, JBuilder uses the following conventions:

- Generalizations in which this class (or interface) is the "child" are shown at the top of the UML diagram. Generalizations in which this class (or interface) is the "parent" are shown at the bottom.
- Association relationships are on the left side of the diagram. They are ordered in a specific way from top to bottom. Associations that allow navigation to this class from another class are at the top left. Associations that are navigable both ways are in the middle. Those in which the navigability is to another class from the current one are at the bottom left. (Simply put: Incoming arrows top, two-way arrows middle, outgoing arrows bottom.)
- Dependencies are on the right side of the diagram and are ordered similarly to associations.
- Relationships not involving the current class are not shown.

In the UML view, you can do simple things such as save the diagram as an image (through the context-sensitive pop-up menu) or print it (through the File, Print menu item on the main menu). However, other goodies allow you to navigate through documentation and code, and change (refactor) your code in a consistent manner as well. We'll look at these options in more detail in later chapters, but first let's look at the other type of UML diagram that JBuilder supports.

Package Diagrams in JBuilder

In addition to class diagrams, you can also view package diagrams that represent a "zoomed-out" view of the dependencies for one package. Viewing a package diagram is also simple. In the UML view for a class, simply double-click on the package name (or select Go to Diagram through the context-sensitive pop-up menu). This opens up the UML view of the selected project as a new tab in the AppBrowser, as shown in Figure 4.4.

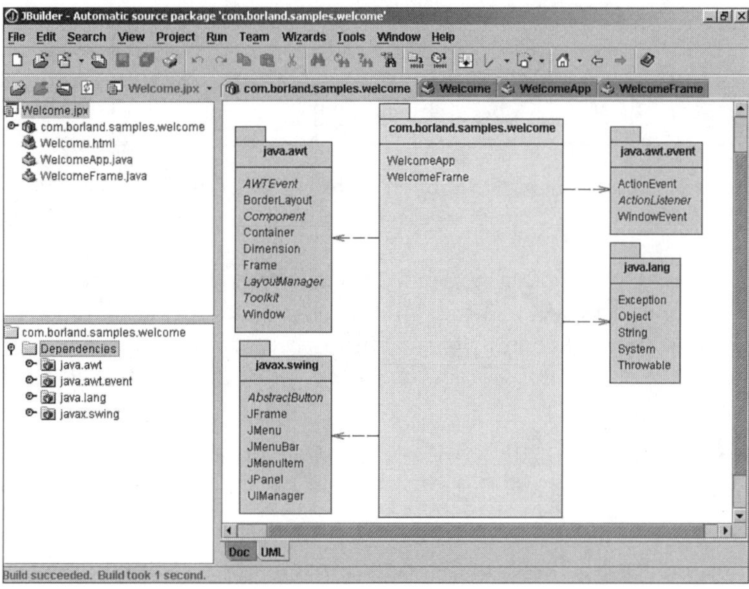

FIGURE 4.4 Package diagram for the `com.borland.samples.welcome` package from the Welcome project.

On the package diagram, dependencies involving only the current package are shown.

From the package diagram, you can rename the package, browse its documentation, or save the diagram.

Design Guidelines—Modeling

The purpose of UML is to aid modeling. Modeling a software system, like any other creative activity, requires discipline and awareness of certain guidelines. Even when a guideline is not followed, it is important (in fact, more important) to be cognizant of the guideline so that the decision to break the rule is taken consciously and deliberately—not in ignorance.

In this section, we will examine some common design guidelines that are useful during modeling.

"Avoid Circular Dependencies"

Circular dependencies, such as those shown in Figure 4.5, are often an error and represent unclear partitioning of responsibilities.

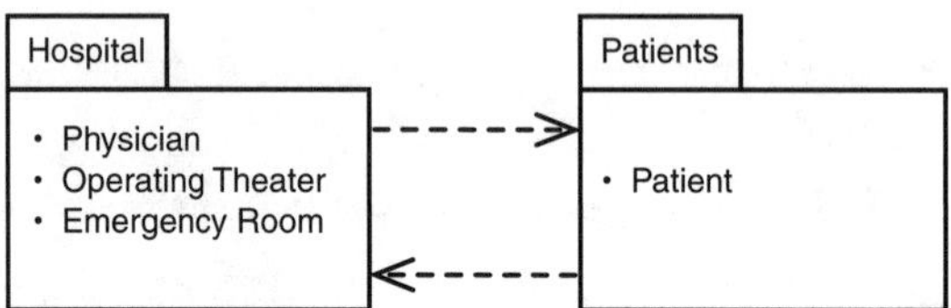

FIGURE 4.5 Circular dependencies often represent an unclear understanding of responsibilities.

Circular dependencies should be avoided because they prohibit you from changing any of the entities (packages, classes, interfaces—whatever is involved in the circular dependency) without changing at least one other entity. In effect, you cannot think about any of the entities in isolation because none of them is truly independent.

For example, in Figure 4.5, the two packages Hospital and Patients are mutually dependent, making it difficult to modify or even conceptualize either one without thinking about the other.

The solution to circular dependencies is straightforward. Partition one (or more) of the entities (packages, classes, and so on) so that a "core" entity is discovered that is not dependent on any other entity. Two or more entities may then depend on this core entity. This will break the cycle. You will be able to conceptualize and design this core entity without getting bogged down with the other parts of your UML diagram.

Figure 4.6 shows one such partitioning for the health-care system.

You can arrive at the design shown in Figure 4.6 by realizing that the Hospital package can be split into two packages: Hospital Staff and Hospital Resources. The latter is a core package in the sense that it is possible to think about (and design) classes representing Emergency Room and Operating Theater without directly thinking about the other classes (physicians, nurses, and patients) that use these resources. This partitioning breaks the cycle.

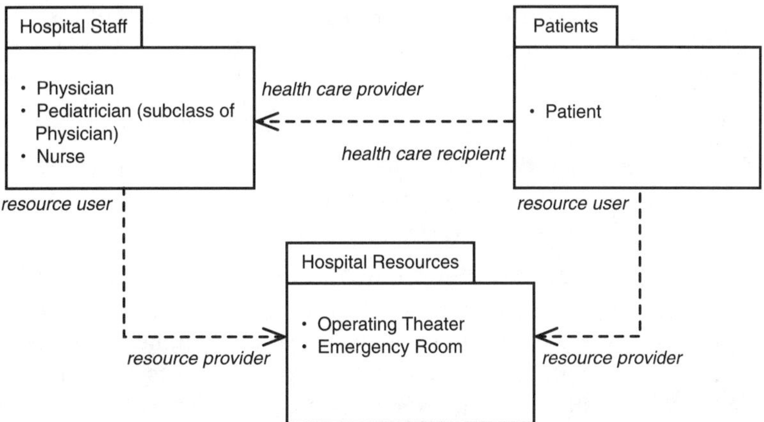

FIGURE 4.6 One possible solution to break the previous circular dependency is to introduce a new "core" package.

"Do One Thing—Do It Well"

Design your operations (methods), classes, and packages to do just one thing—and do it completely and self-sufficiently. Another way to say this is that your entities should be "single-minded." The easiest way to test whether your entities lack this single-mindedness is to say the name of the entity aloud and see whether it makes sense. If you decided to put a Java method in your design called `admitPatientAndCollectHistory`, it's almost certain that such a method will exhibit poor design. It tries to do multiple, unrelated things in one place. (Of course, this assumes that you name your entities appropriately to begin with—another good design principle!)

Two criteria often used to measure this quality of "doing one thing" are cohesion and coupling. *Cohesion* is a measure of the interrelationship of the code in an entity (class or method). *Coupling* refers to the dependency of one entity on another. High cohesion is good. High coupling is bad.

Cohesion can be maximized by breaking up (refactoring) those entities that do more than one thing. The previously mentioned method may be split into two separate methods—`admitPatient` and `collectPatientHistory`—to increase cohesion.

"Encapsulation: Show Operations and Hide Data"

The intent of this design principle is to reduce the coupling between entities (classes and methods) by minimizing what they can "see" of each other. If you make only your operations (methods in Java) public and keep the data (variables) they operate on private, other classes will interact with your class only through your operations, not by directly modifying your data in unexpected or undesirable ways.

"Think at the Appropriate Level of Abstraction"

It is said that perfection in design is achieved not when there is nothing more to add, but when there is nothing more to take away. The simplest way to achieve this is to learn to think in terms of abstractions.

In a model for a health-care system, you will eventually need to model many different types of patients. Some are outpatients; others are admitted to a ward. There are patients in the ER, in the OT, and in their beds. Patients can be differentiated based on their method of payment, the seriousness of their ailments, and a host of other criteria. Is all this significant at first when you are simply identifying the different components of the system? Certainly not! If you cannot stop yourself from thinking about the details when you should be thinking about abstractions, you are bound to make mistakes when it comes time to really consider the details.

Abstraction is not the same as imprecision. It is possible to specify a design at an abstract level yet be precise in what is actually expressed. If you have ever looked at the blueprint of a house with all the outside measurements, you know what we mean. The blueprint gives no details about the interior dimensions of the house, or what the paint scheme should be, or whether the windows are double-paned. Those are details at a lower level of abstraction. Yet the blueprint clearly lists all the outside measurements to the nearest inch—in another word, precisely.

Thinking abstractly is somewhat of an art, but there is no reason that it cannot be learned. Many books dedicated to software modeling teach abstraction through various recursive design techniques. In a nutshell, if you employ the other design principles (such as those discussed earlier in this section), you will be able to think at the appropriate level of abstraction and not get bogged down by unnecessary details.

In Practice

In this section, we will model our ChalkTalk application. This application will be used in subsequent chapters as well. For now, we will focus on the high-level design of packages and classes based on the requirements given in the following sidebar.

THE CHALKTALK APPLICATION—REQUIREMENTS

ChalkTalk is a simple course-scheduling application that may be used in a college or other institution that offers classes to students. We will refer to the institution simply as the School.

The high-level requirements of this application are

- It will allow students to register for courses, unregister from courses, make payments for courses, and monitor the courses offered by the School.
- It will allow the School administrator(s) to add, remove, and modify course instances (an actual scheduled offering of a course) and to assign a room and an instructor to the course instance. Administrators may monitor any aspect of the system.
- It will allow the instructors to add themselves as certified teachers of a course. Instructors may monitor courses and the course instances for which they have been selected as the instructor.

This is admittedly a simple list of requirements. The purpose is to illustrate a nontrivial system, yet keep the requirements and analysis simple and manageable.

The first task is to identify which services will lie in the client tier and which in the server tier. Figure 4.7 shows one such partitioning. The reasons for partitioning this way are best discussed in a book on architecture and design.

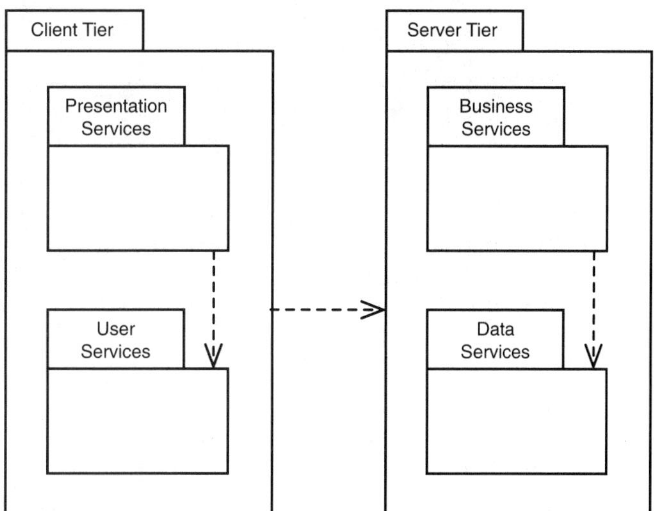

FIGURE 4.7 The high-level design of the ChalkTalk application.

Note that the partitioning in Figure 4.7 does not mean that this system will be designed as what's commonly known as a client/server system. In other words, do not think that the "client" necessarily means a Windows desktop PC and the "server" means a database server. They do not! The model shown in Figure 4.7 is at a high enough level of abstraction that the exact deployment details (How many server-nodes are there? Do the user-services have to reside on a smart desktop?) are hidden. Yet the design is precise in that it identifies the tiers of services that must be offered.

In the following sections we will model the server and the client tiers, respectively.

Modeling the Server

The server consists of two packages: Data Services and Business Services. We'll look at these individually.

Data Services Package

The Data Services package consists of persistent entities that are part of the ChalkTalk system. These entities are really UML classes. Again, without going into the steps of analysis, we'll simply present the classes that have been identified by analyzing the requirements. These are shown in the UML diagram in Figure 4.8.

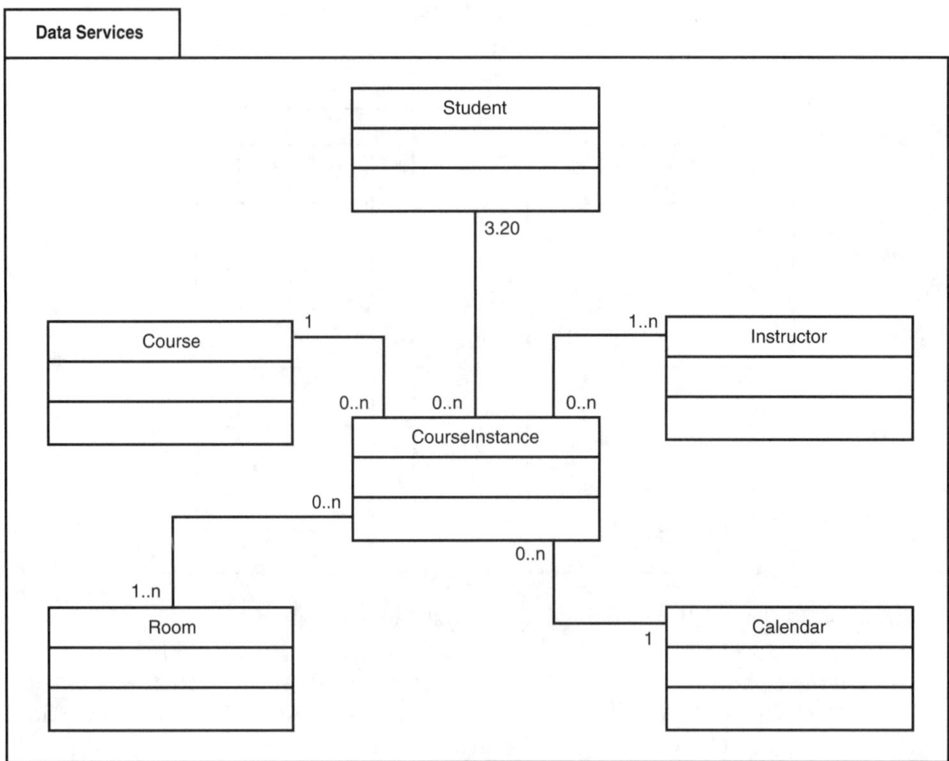

FIGURE 4.8 The classes in the Data Services tier represent the persistent entities of the ChalkTalk application.

You may notice that all the relationships in Figure 4.8 have been specified as associations. This is normal. As discussed previously, associations are the most generic form of relationship. Often, you start by simply associating two classes, and later change that relationship to one of dependency (or even generalization).

Also notice that we have captured some business rules about association between classes in the multiplicity numbers (such as "each `CourseInstance` must have between 3 and 20 students, inclusive").

A brief description of the objects follows:

- `Course`—The `Course` class represents all the courses offered by the School at one time or another. A `Course` may not be in offering now or may even have been cancelled (for example, "Introduction to JBuilder 2.0" would probably be cancelled because of obsolescence).
- `CourseInstance`—A particular instance of a `Course` being offered. A `CourseInstance` is a course when it is actually taught in the School. One `Course` may have multiple (or zero) `CourseInstances` at any given time. A `CourseInstance` must have between 3 and 20 `Students` (both limits inclusive).
- `Student`—Any person who registers to take a `CourseInstance`.
- `Instructor`—A person who can teach a `Course`. An `Instructor` is authorized to teach `Courses` for which she is qualified. An Instructor may be selected to teach zero or more `CourseInstances`.
- `Room`—A `Room` is where a `CourseInstance` is scheduled to be held or taught. The `Room` class represents a fixed resource that cannot be created or destroyed for the purpose of the ChalkTalk application.
- `Calendar`—A `Calendar` represents a set of dates and times on which a particular `CourseInstance` is offered. A `Calendar` class can represent all the possible scheduling scenarios for a `CourseInstance` (recurring or one-off time slots).

Business Services Package

The Business Services package describes the operations that can be performed on the classes that are part of the Data Services package. At this level of analysis, all these operations are in only one class called `BusinessOperations`.

Table 4.1 lists all the operations that can be performed on the different Data Services classes. Each column represents a Data Services class, and each row corresponds to an operation. The letters "A," "S," and "I" indicate that the operations will be performed by Administrators, Students, and Instructors. (This information is not needed at this level of abstraction, but will be needed when we design the client tiers.)

TABLE 4.1 The Operations (Methods) of the `BusinessOperations` Class in the Business Services Package

	Course	Student	Instructor	CourseInstance	Room	Calendar
Add	No	Yes (S)	No	Yes (A)	No	No
Remove	No	Yes (S)	No	Yes (A)	No	No
Modify	Yes (A)	Yes (S)	Yes (I)	Yes (A)	No	No

Figure 4.9 shows the UML diagram for the Business Services tier.

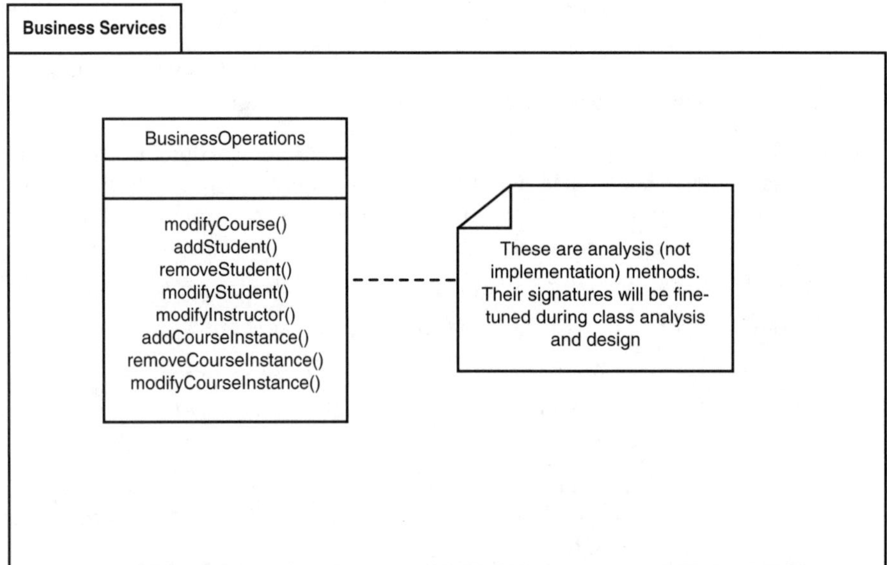

FIGURE 4.9 The Business Services tier contains the operations that can be performed on the Data Services classes.

Modeling the Client

Because we have (purposefully) not defined the full functionality extent of the client, we will design only the common operations at this stage. This is consistent with iterative design, where you visit each class as a designer multiple times—specifying the operations in increasing detail in each iteration.

Another consideration specific to the Presentation Services tier is that the design of that tier depends on its exact nature (for example, Web-based versus Java application versus Java applet). For now, we will design only the User Services tier.

Figure 4.10 shows the design of the User Services tier.

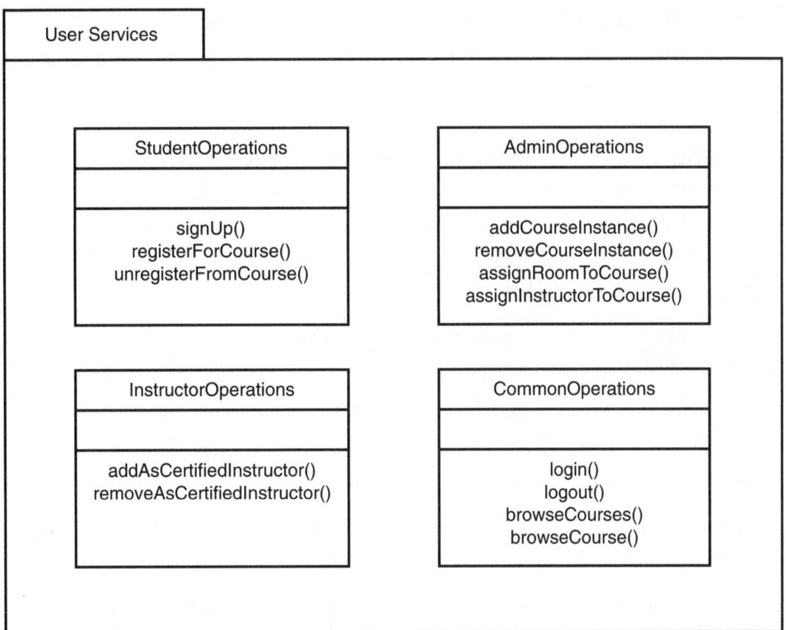

FIGURE 4.10 The User Services tier contains the operations visible to the users (through appropriate mechanisms in the Presentation Services tier).

The user operations are, logically, dependent on the different types of users of the system. Thus there are four main packages—one for each type of user (student, administrator, or instructor) and one for the common operations. It is important to recognize that (just as in the Business Services tier) the signatures of these operations will change as analysis and design gets more detailed.

The design of the user operations uses the information from the requirements and also from Table 4.1 described earlier.

Summary

UML has been crowned as the modeling language of choice because of its adoption by the OMG and its rich modeling features.

Modeling is often a neglected activity simply because it is widely assumed to be a distraction to the "real" task of building the software. Although this is bad habit, it is justified on the basis of two excuses, which are largely true:

- Models have a tendency to drift from the actual design because the tools used to model are different from the tools used to build the software.

- Keeping the model in harmony with the design requires substantial effort, usually at the expense of other important activities (such as building and testing the application).

JBuilder nullifies these excuses by offering a unified view of the model and the implementation. Thus the model stays with the implementation (no drift), and the ease of switching between the UML diagram and the code makes the job of manually updating the model unnecessary. All that is needed is a constant validation of the model to ensure that no design principles are being violated.

In this chapter, we designed the high-level packages of the ChalkTalk application. In subsequent chapters, we will evolve this design into an actual application.

Reflections

- How much time do you and your team typically spend in design?
- How much of this design is expressed formally in UML (or some other modeling language)?
- Do you spend time keeping your UML (or other modeling) diagrams in sync with the actual code as your projects move along? If so, how much effort do you spend in this endeavor?
- Can you think of two uses of the UML functionality in JBuilder for which you currently have no alternative (or have a tedious, manual alternative)?

5 Unit Testing

IN THIS CHAPTER

- JBuilder Test Options
- JUnit Testing Framework
- JBuilder Test Runner, Test Cases, and Test Suites
- Comparison, JDBC, and JNDI Fixtures

JBuilder transforms unit testing from a boring chore often skipped to a quick and workable reality. Some independent studies have shown that unit testing can reduce the time and cost of delivering a system by 80 percent! Unit testing describes the process by which a developer tests the methods of an object with a variety of inputs to ensure that the method works as expected.

JBuilder's Enterprise edition includes a unit testing framework based on the open standard JUnit. JBuilder integrates the JUnit framework by using wizards to create test cases and test suites. JBuilder extends the standard `JUnit.TextUI` and `JUnit.SwingUI` classes into the `JBTestRunner` class. In addition, JBuilder includes testing fixtures that provide utility functions for common testing requirements.

This chapter covers the use of the JUnit framework and how JBuilder facilitates good programming practices. To get more in-depth information on JUnit, visit `www.junit.org`.

Learning how to use the integrated unit testing framework will increase the robustness of your code and the ability to regression test your code after modifications. This chapter teaches you the fundamentals of the unit testing framework in the JBuilder environment. The fundamentals include

- Review of JBuilder test options
- JUnit testing framework
- JBuilder Test Runner, test cases, and test suites
- JDBC, JNDI, and comparison test fixtures

JBuilder Test Options

JBuilder has integrated the capability to perform unit testing into the IDE. JBuilder provides unit test options and the JBuilder Test Runner application.

Unit test options can be controlled through the Project, Project Properties menu or the Default Project Properties menu. In Figure 5.1, the Project Properties dialog box is displayed with the Run tab selected.

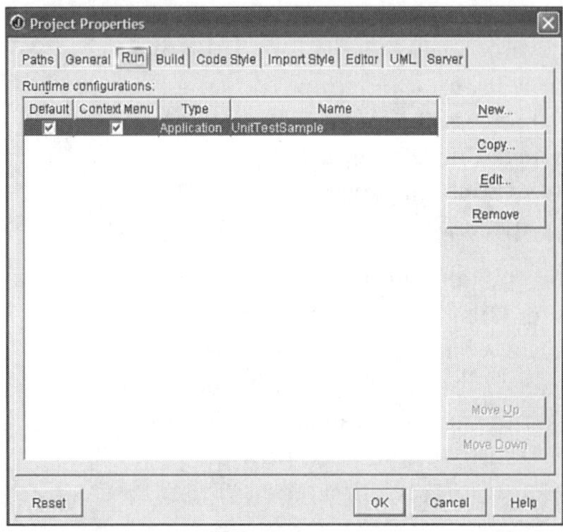

FIGURE 5.1 The Runtime options in the Project Properties dialog box.

The Run tab on the Project Properties dialog box allows you to set up multiple runtime configurations. A runtime configuration allows you to specify the Java Virtual Machine parameters, how debugging will be set up, how applets will be executed, and many other runtime settings.

If you create multiple runtime configurations, you will have to choose which configuration you want the application to run under by default. The default check box on the Run tab determines which configuration is automatically selected. The Context Menu check box determines which configurations will show up in the pop-up context menu when selecting a Java class to run.

When a runtime configuration is created or edited, the Runtime Properties dialog box is displayed. The Runtime Properties dialog box has many configuration options for applications, applets, tests, and server-based applications. For unit testing, we will look at the test configuration settings. Figure 5.2 shows the Test tab and the different options available for performing unit testing. These are the Main Class, VM Parameters, and Test Runner.

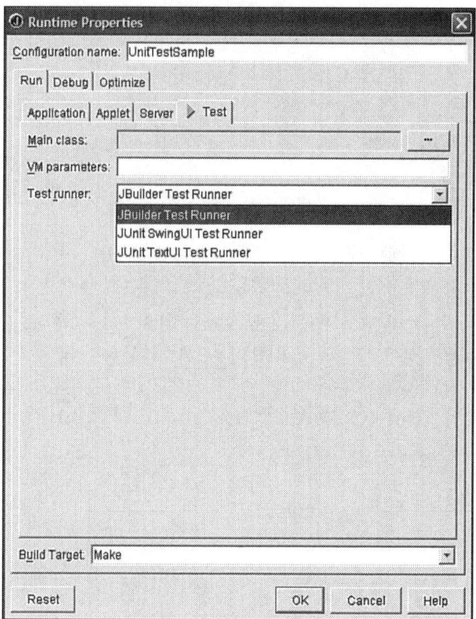

FIGURE 5.2 The Test options in the Runtime Properties dialog box.

The Main Class box contains the name of the class containing a test case or test suite that is instantiated in the Java Virtual Machine. Therefore, this class must have a main method. Typically, this field will be left blank, and the IDE will automatically run unit tests based on the class chosen in the Project pane.

The VM Parameters field allows you to set additional Virtual Machine settings for the unit test. If you need to modify the parameters of the Java Virtual Machine, enter the parameters into this field. Typical Java Virtual Machine parameters include stack size, memory allocation, and garbage collection handling.

The Test Runner field displays all the unit test applications that will execute the unit tests. The test runner applications listed are

- JUnit TextUI Test Runner provides the standard JUnit text output.
- JUnit SwingUI Test Runner provides the standard JUnit graphic and text output.
- JBuilder Test Runner provides enhancements over the JUnit default test runners.

The JBuilder Test Runner appears in Figure 5.3. The JBuilder test runner provides a hierarchical view of all unit tests and the success or failure of those tests.

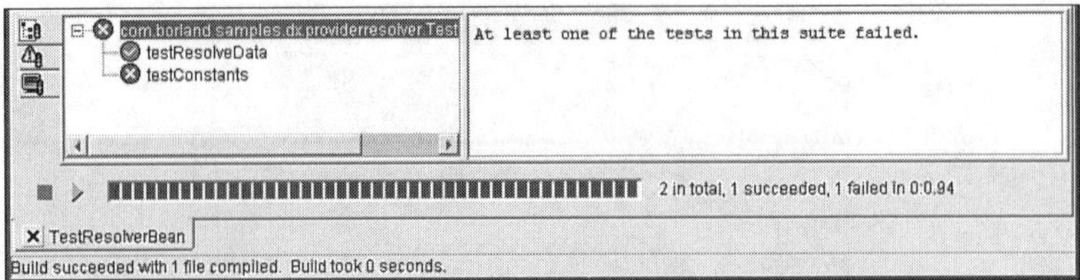

FIGURE 5.3 JBuilder Test Runner view with success and failure icons.

The JBuilder Test Runner view is comprised of a status bar, command bar, and three tabbed views. The status bar has a count of the tests, successes, and failures. The command bar enables you to execute the unit tests or stop the unit tests. The three tab views represent the unit test hierarchy, unit test failures, and unit test output. Table 5.1 explains the different tab views.

TABLE 5.1 JBuilder Test Runner Views

View	Description
	In the test hierarchy view, a red circle with an "X" in the middle displays for each unit test failure, and a green circle with a check mark appears for successful unit tests.
	In the test failure view, all the tests that failed are listed. Clicking on a test results in the line with the test method called to be highlighted.
	In the test output view, all the output from the tests are displayed.

NOTE

There is a huge difference between running your application and unit testing your application. Unit testing your application executes methods and functionality you decided should be tested. Test cases are executed and analyzed. When you run your application, the test cases are not executed, and the application performs as it would for your end user.

JUnit Testing Framework

JUnit is an open source testing framework developed by Erich Gamma and Kent Beck. The JUnit framework uses Java's reflection capabilities to run unit tests created in your classes.

The JUnit framework provides you with the ability to create test cases and group those test cases into a test suite. The test suite can then be executed as many times as required.

JBuilder enhances the JUnit framework by providing wizards to build skeleton unit test code, create test suites, and provide utility functions for comparing JDBC and JNDI results.

The JUnit package `junit.framework` contains the classes `TestCase` and `TestSuite`. These classes are used in the creation of unit tests and are recognized by JBuilder as unit test classes.

The following sections show the key elements of the JUnit framework. A complete JBuilder exercise that uses the JUnit framework can be found in the "In Practice" section at the end of the chapter.

Creating a Test with JUnit

Creating a test case with the JUnit framework requires the following:

- Extend the testing class from `junit.framework.TestCase`.
- All test methods return void, take no parameters, and begin with the word `test`.

The first requirement is that the testing class extends from the `junit.framework.TestCase` class. Listing 5.1 contains the beginning of a sample unit test class.

LISTING 5.1 Sample Unit Test (`handCodedUnitTest.java`)

```
package jbbook.ch05;

import junit.framework.*;

public class handCodedUnitTest extends TestCase {

  public handCodedUnitTest(String name) {
    super(name);
  }
```

The next requirement is that all the test methods begin with `test`. The `JUnit` framework will use reflection to run all the methods beginning with `test`. In Listing 5.2, the method `testFunctionalClass()` is the test method. It uses the `assertEquals` method to compare the driver's age with 16 and the full name with "Mike."

LISTING 5.2 Sample Unit Test (continued) (`handCodedUnitTest.java`)

```
  public void testFunctionalClass()  {
    FunctionalClass fc = new FunctionalClass();
    assertEquals("Drivers Age Test", 16, fc.getDriversAge());
    assertEquals("FullName Test", "Mike", fc.getFullName("Mike","Landy"));
  }
} // end of code example
```

The `FunctionalClass` code is in Listing 5.3.

LISTING 5.3 Functional Class Code (`FunctionalClass.java`)

```
package jbbook.ch05;

public class FunctionalClass {
  public FunctionalClass() {
  }
  public String getFullName( String sFirst, String sLast) {
    return sFirst + " " + sLast;
    }
  public int getDriversAge() {
    return 16;
    }
} // end of code example
```

The sample code in Listing 5.2 and Listing 5.3 shows that the `getFullName()` method returns a value different than `assertEquals` is expecting. The mismatch in values causes the test to indicate a failure. The method `getDriversAge` always returns 16, and `assertEquals` is expecting 16. No failure will be indicated on the `getDriversAge` test.

When creating many unit tests, you might want to log information or store data in a file or database. Instead of every test method opening a connection to a file or database, you can globalize these settings. JUnit provides this globalization by exposing two protected methods. These methods are `protected void setUp()` and `protected void tearDown()`. These methods are executed prior to the execution of a test and at the end of a test.

Running a Test with JUnit

The JUnit framework classes `junit.framework.TestSuite` and `junit.textui.TestRunner` provide an easy way to execute a unit test on a series of test cases. The

TestSuite class creates a group of tests based on a class name or a passed-in method. The JUnit framework makes it easy for you by pulling the "test" methods out of your class and putting them into a test suite.

The next step in running the unit test is to instantiate the junit.textui.TestRunner class to run the test suite. Listing 5.4 shows how to execute the test created in Listings 5.1, 5.2, and 5.3.

LISTING 5.4 Running the Test Suite (handCodedTestSuite.java)

```
package jbbook.ch05;

import junit.framework.*;

public class handCodedTestSuite extends TestCase {
  public handCodedTestSuite(String name) {
    super(name);
  }
  public static void main(String[] args) {
  TestSuite ts = new TestSuite(handCodedUnitTest.class);
  junit.textui.TestRunner.run(ts);
  }
}
```

When the handCodedTestSuite.java class is executed, it executes the test and returns a success or failure on each test executed. The TestSuite class ts in Listing 5.4 looks through the class passed in and pulls out all methods that fit the test case signature. In our case, it pulls the method testFunctionalClass from the handCodedUnitTest class. Sample output from running Listing 5.4 can be seen in Listing 5.5.

LISTING 5.5 Output from the handCodedTestSuite.java

```
C:\JBuilder6\jdk1.3.1\bin\javaw -classpath $CLASSPATH
➥ jbbook.ch05.handCodedTestSuite
.F
Time: 0
There was 1 failure:
1) testFunctionalClass(jbbook.ch05.handCodedUnitTest)junit.framework.
➥ AssertionFailedError: FullName Test expected:
➥ <Mike> but was:<Mike Landy>
    at jbbook.ch05.handCodedUnitTest.testFunctionalClass
➥ (handCodedUnitTest.java:23)
```

LISTING 5.5 Continued

```
    at jbbook.ch05.handCodedTestSuite.main(handCodedTestSuite.java:22)

FAILURES!!!
Tests run: 1,  Failures: 1,  Errors: 0
```

From the output in Listing 5.5, you will notice that one failure occurred on the `FullName Test`. The output shows the expected value `<Mike>` and the actual value `<Mike Landy>` from the test method.

JBuilder provides wizards to help create the code in Listing 5.1 and Listing 5.2. JBuilder has additional utilities and IDE enhancements that eliminate the code shown in Listing 5.4.

JBuilder Test Runner, Test Cases, and Test Suites

The JBuilder IDE has integrated many of the manual tasks needed to take advantage of the JUnit testing framework. JBuilder enables you to add test cases, test suites, and test fixtures.

This section looks at how JBuilder makes it easier to do unit testing by integrating the JUnit testing framework.

The Object Gallery that is shown when you add a new file to a project contains many tabs. The Test tab contains the various testing options provided by JBuilder. Figure 5.4 depicts the Object Gallery's Test tab.

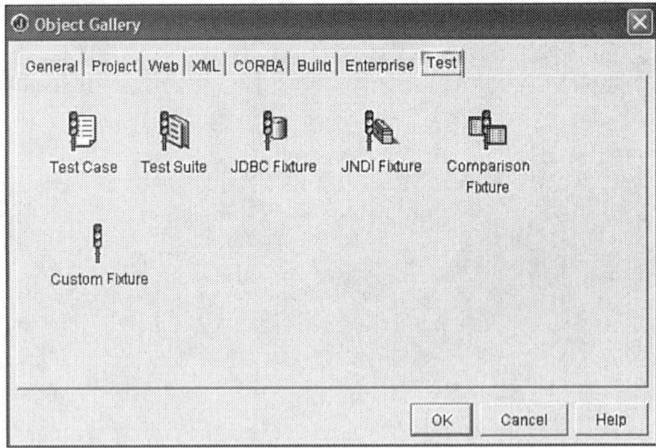

FIGURE 5.4 JBuilder's Test tab in the Object Gallery.

Table 5.2 describes the testing objects contained in JBuilder.

TABLE 5.2 JBuilder's Test Tab in the Object Gallery

File Type	Description
Test Case	The test case object adds a skeleton file for creating a JUnit `TestCase` object. The JBuilder Test Case Wizard is invoked and asks for the parameters of the test case.
Test Suite	The test suite object adds a skeleton file for creating a JUnit `TestSuite` object.
JDBC Fixture	The JDBC Fixture is a set of utility functions to help in the unit testing of resultsets from JDBC.
JNDI Fixture	The JNDI Fixture is a set of utility functions to help in the unit testing of Java Naming services.
Comparison Fixture	The Comparison Fixture is a set of utility functions to help compare previous results with current results. The comparison fixture is used to create regression testing scenarios based on dynamic data elements.
Custom Fixture	The Custom Fixture is a user-defined set of utility functions to help a particular project(s) with repetitive testing functions.

Creating a Test Case Using JBuilder

After you choose to add a test case to your project, JBuilder invokes the Test Case Wizard. JBuilder provides a Test Case Wizard that scans your project for classes and methods. Figure 5.5 illustrates the Test Case Wizard in action.

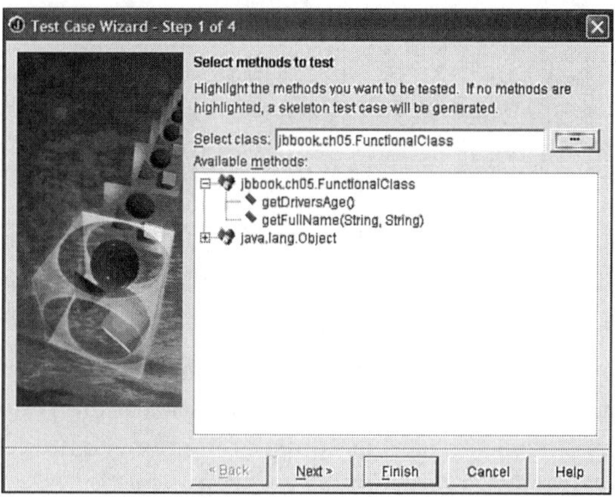

FIGURE 5.5 JBuilder Test Case Wizard (1 of 4).

The first step the wizard requires is to name the class or group of methods that you want to generate a test case skeleton file. If no methods are selected, JBuilder generates a skeleton file with no methods. If methods are selected, JBuilder generates test stubs for all the methods and adds Javadoc `ToDo` comments. The `ToDo` comments identify where in the code you need to make changes.

Figure 5.6 represents the next step in the Test Case Wizard. You are asked to name the test case class and the base class the test case is to extend. In our case, this is the JUnit framework class `TestCase`.

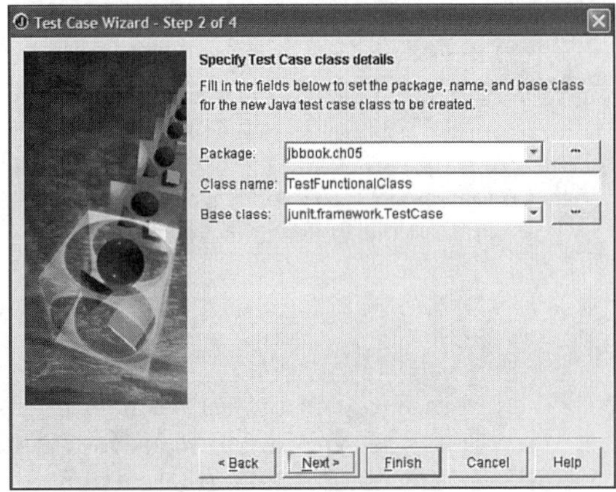

FIGURE 5.6 JBuilder Test Case Wizard (2 of 4).

The third step in the wizard asks you about test fixtures. Test fixtures are utility functions used to help simplify the creation of unit tests. Test fixtures are covered in the next section, "Comparison, JDBC, and JNDI Fixtures." Figure 5.7 gives you the ability to add test fixtures to the skeleton code.

The final step in using the Test Case Wizard is to define the test configuration. If you plan on making the runtime test configuration different than the design-time configuration, select the check box for creating a runtime configuration.

A runtime configuration can be accessed under the Run, Configurations menu option. A runtime configuration can be set up to use different debugging defaults, unit test runners, and Java Virtual Machine parameters. Figure 5.8 gives you the ability to make runtime configuration decisions for the test case you are creating.

After running through all the wizard screens, JBuilder generates a new class file for your project that provides the skeleton code for testing. If you open that file, you will notice that `ToDo` items are shown in the Structure pane for all methods you selected to test.

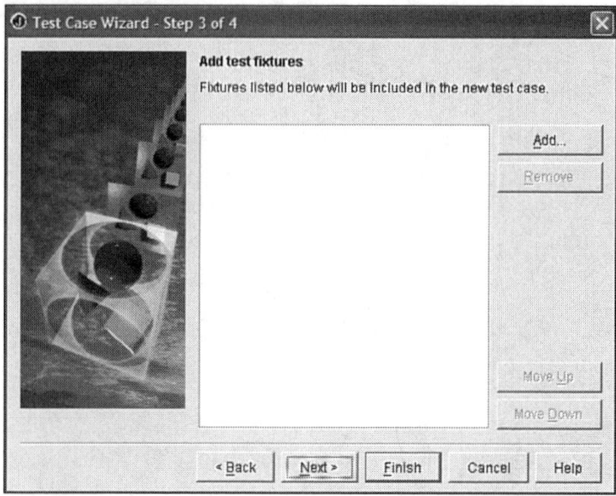

FIGURE 5.7 JBuilder Test Case Wizard (3 of 4).

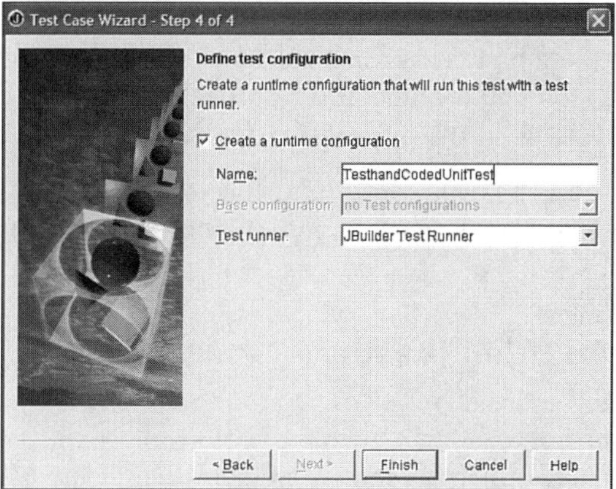

FIGURE 5.8 JBuilder Test Case Wizard (4 of 4).

Most of the time, you will have to add `assertEqual` commands to your test cases and pass in appropriate parameters to the method calls. Listing 5.6 shows part of the generated code created by the Test Case Wizard. Notice the `@todo` line in the generated code and the generated instantiation of your class, parameters, and return variable type.

LISTING 5.6 Code Added After `ToDo` Placements

```
public void testGetDriversAge() {
  FunctionalClass functionalclass = new FunctionalClass();
  int intRet = functionalclass.getDriversAge();
```

LISTING 5.6 Continued

```
  /** @todo:  Insert test code here.  Use assertEquals(), for example. */
  }
  public void testGetFullName() {
    FunctionalClass functionalclass = new FunctionalClass();
    String sFirst1=  "STRING0";
    String sLast2=  "STRING0";
    String stringRet = functionalclass.getFullName(sFirst1, sLast2);
  /** @todo:  Insert test code here.  Use assertEquals(), for example. */
  }
```

The following lines of code replaces the `@todo` lines. This line provides the conditions of the unit test and when to throw an assertion:

```
assertEquals("Drivers Age Test", 16, intRet);
assertEquals("Full Name Test", "Mike", stringRet );
```

JBuilder has done the job of generating skeleton code for creating a unit test on existing methods. After you create a unit test for the methods, you can run the test directly by right-clicking on the new unit test class and selecting Run Test.

On large projects, you will need to run multiple test cases on a wide variety of classes and record the results. JUnit's `TestSuite` class automates the running of multiple test cases for many classes.

Creating a Suite Using JBuilder

JBuilder's Test Suite Wizard enables you to select the classes to be included in a test suite. To create a test suite, add a new file to your project and select the Test Suite object from the Object Gallery as shown previously in Figure 5.4.

After the Test Suite object is selected, JBuilder begins the Test Suite Wizard. Figure 5.9 is the first screen in the wizard, and it asks for the classes to be included in the test suite. Any classes in the project that extend the `TestCase` object are automatically selected for inclusion.

Figure 5.9 enables you to add `TestCase` classes or do a recursive inclusion of many `TestCase` classes. `TestCase` classes can also be removed from the list.

Figure 5.10 shows the next wizard screen. Figure 5.10 allows you to specify the package name, class name, and the base class that is extended for the Test Suite class you are creating.

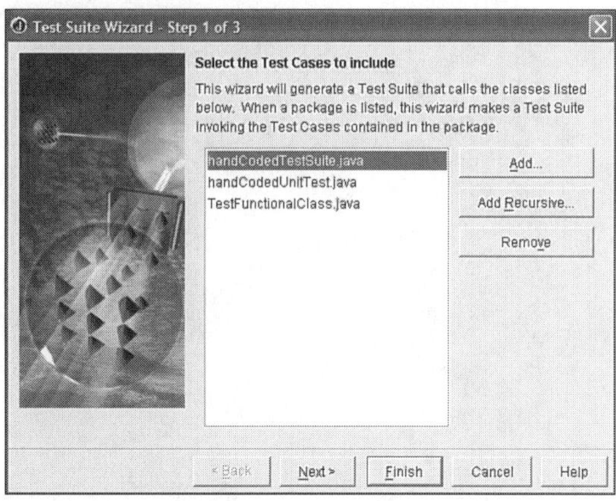

FIGURE 5.9 JBuilder Test Suite Wizard (1 of 3).

FIGURE 5.10 JBuilder Test Suite Wizard (2 of 3).

Finally, the last wizard screen (see Figure 5.11) enables the setup of additional runtime configuration options. The runtime configuration options shown previously in Figure 5.2 consist of VM parameter settings, debugging options, and other parameters. Figure 5.11 lets you select the test runner to run the test suite.

Based on the information selected in the Test Suite Wizard, a new class file is added to the project that contains the generated test suite code. Listing 5.7 shows the typical code generated by JBuilder's Test Suite Wizard.

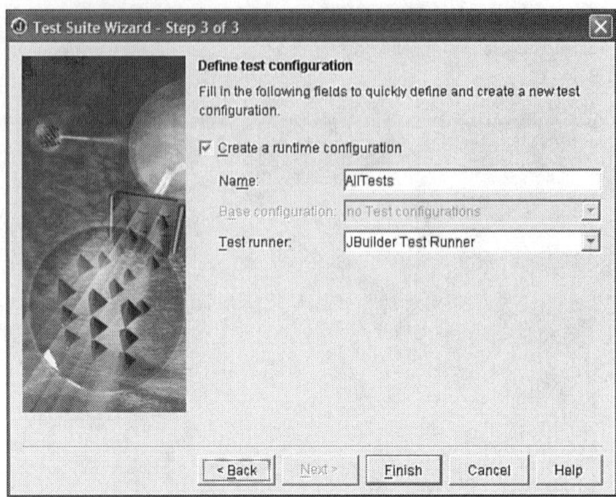

FIGURE 5.11 JBuilder Test Suite Wizard (3 of 3).

LISTING 5.7 Generated Test Suite Code

```
package jbbook.ch05;

import junit.framework.*;

public class AllTests extends TestCase {

  public AllTests(String s) {
    super(s);
  }

  public static Test suite() {
    TestSuite suite = new TestSuite();
    suite.addTestSuite(jbbook.ch05.handCodedUnitTest.class);
    suite.addTestSuite(jbbook.ch05.TestFunctionalClass.class);
    return suite;
  }
}
```

The code generated by JBuilder calls all the methods beginning with the name `test` in the two classes added to the `TestSuite` object. The Test Runner class executes the test suite and records the results.

Comparison, JDBC, and JNDI Fixtures

Testing fixtures are utility classes that extend the functionality provided by the JUnit testing framework. JBuilder has defined three sets of testing fixtures and provides you the ability to create your own fixtures.

The Object Gallery in Figure 5.4 and Table 5.2 describe the available fixtures. In this section, we will look at the comparison, JDBC, and JNDI fixtures.

Comparison Fixture

The comparison fixture provides a utility class to your project that allows the creation and comparison of test data. The comparison fixture makes it easy to record the data results in your unit tests. Those results are saved to a file as a baseline for your unit tests. Subsequent tests result in comparisons to the baseline results. A failure in a comparison issues an assertion failure.

The comparison fixture extends the `com.borland.jbuilder.unittest.TestRecorder` class, which extends the `java.io.Writer` class. This allows the comparison fixture to be used wherever a `Writer` class is allowed.

To add a comparison fixture to your project, select the File, New menu item and select the Comparison Fixture from the Test tab in the Object Gallery. Figure 5.12 enables you to set the Java package, class name, data file location, echo, and verbose output options.

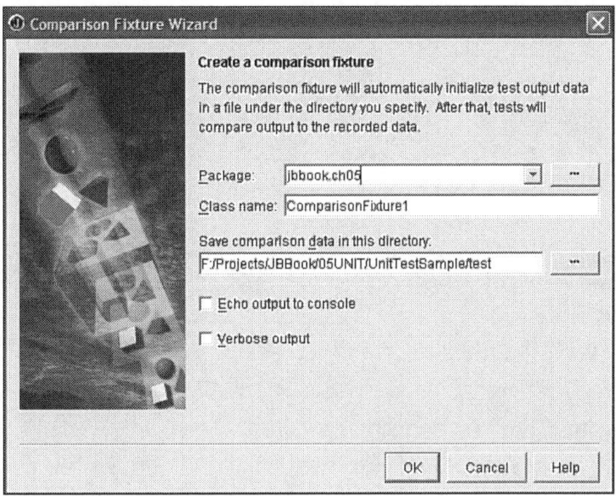

FIGURE 5.12 JBuilder Comparison Fixture Wizard.

The data file location specifies the location of the comparison data file. The name of the data file is the same as the class that instantiates the comparison fixture class with no file extension.

The echo and verbose options will send all the output from the `TestRecorder` to `System.out`.

Listing 5.8 shows the class generated by the Comparison Fixture Wizard.

LISTING 5.8 Generated Comparison Fixture Code

```
package jbbook.ch05;

import com.borland.jbuilder.unittest.TestRecorder;

public class CompareUnitTest extends TestRecorder {

  public CompareUnitTest(Object obj) {
    super();
    super.setMode(UPDATE);
    super.setVerbose(true);
    super.setEcho(true);
    String fileName = super.constructFilename("C:/UnitTestSample/test", obj);
    super.setOutputFile(fileName);
  }
  public void setUp() {
  }
  public void tearDown() {
  }
}
```

In Listing 5.8, the `setMode(UPDATE)` method controls the behavior of the `TestRecorder` class. Table 5.3 contains the valid constants for the `setMode` method and the behavior of `TestRecorder` class.

TABLE 5.3 `TestRecorder`'s `setMode` Constants and Behavior

`setMode` **Values**	**Description**
`OFF`	Turns off the test record and does not record or compare.
`RECORD`	Creates a new file or overwrites an existing file with data. The data written becomes the new baseline for comparisons.
`COMPARE`	Uses an existing data file to perform a compare with the runtime data and the existing data.
`UPDATE`	If the data file does not exist, the `TestRecorder` class acts in `RECORD` mode. If the data file does exist, the `TestRecorder` class acts in `COMPARE` mode.

The next step in using the comparison fixture is to use the `recordObject` method of the comparison class. The `recordObject` either records or compares an object based on the `setMode` constant. Listing 5.9 shows an example of creating the comparison fixture and then recording information.

LISTING 5.9 Using the Comparison Fixture Code

```
CompareUnitTest compareunittest = new CompareUnitTest(this);
compareunittest.recordObject(unittest.getName());
```

The code in Listing 5.9 creates a comparison fixture and records the information passed to the `recordObject` method. A file is created in a test directory off the project's root directory. The file will be named the same as the class that is creating the comparison fixture, but without an extension.

The file is a binary file that can be opened but should not be modified. The `recordObject` method will behave differently depending on the existence of the file. If the comparison file does not exist, it is created and the `recordObject` method writes data to the comparison file. If the comparison file already exists, the `recordObject` method compares the data in the file with the object being passed in the method.

The comparison fixture provides you the ability to set up a baseline of data and compare against that baseline multiple times.

JDBC Fixture

The JDBC fixture is a utility class that provides methods for manipulating JDBC connections and resultsets, and running SQL scripts. The benefit of a utility class that connects to the database can be seen when used in conjunction with the comparison class. Database resultsets that are generated can be written to a file as a baseline. The database data is initially written to a file and then compared to during subsequent tests. Mismatches in the resultsets will result in a unit test failure.

JBuilder provides a wizard to generate the JDBC fixture class based on your selections. Figure 5.13 asks for the package, class name, and the base class name for the JDBC fixture.

After the basic information is filled in Figure 5.13, the JDBC Fixture Wizard asks for the JDBC database information. Figure 5.14 asks for the JDBC Driver, URL, User Name, Extended Properties, and Password. The wizard also gives you the ability to save your connection and to test the connection to make sure that it is valid prior to generating the JDBC fixture code.

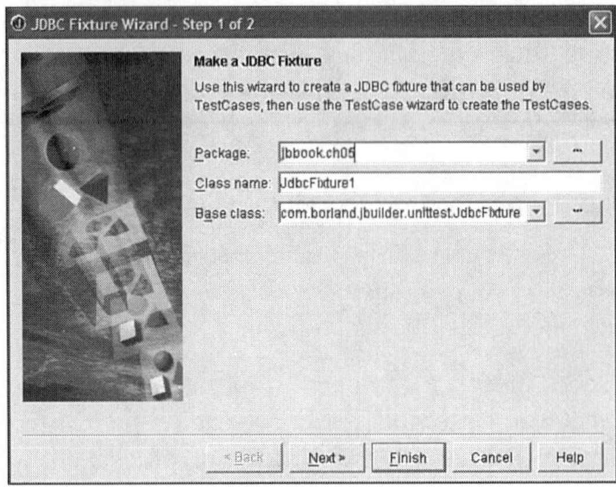

FIGURE 5.13 JBuilder JDBC Fixture Wizard (1 of 2).

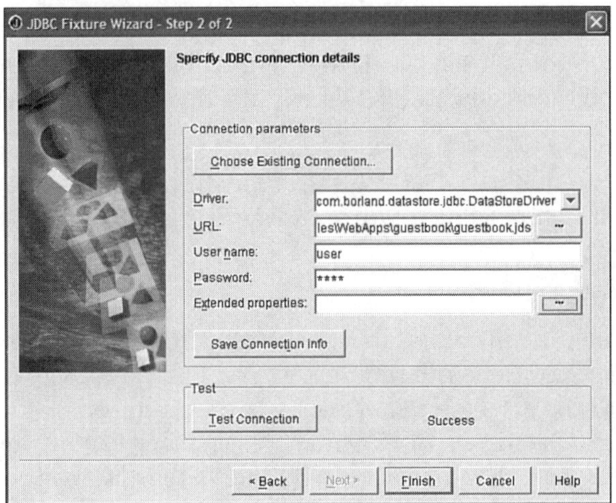

FIGURE 5.14 JBuilder JDBC Fixture Wizard (2 of 2).

Listing 5.10 shows the code generated for the JDBC fixture.

LISTING 5.10 JDBC Fixture Generated Code

```
package fixture;

import java.sql.*;
import java.io.*;
import com.borland.jbuilder.unittest.JdbcFixture;
```

LISTING 5.10 Continued

```
public class JdbcFixture1 extends com.borland.jbuilder.unittest.JdbcFixture {

  public JdbcFixture1(Object obj) {
    super();
    super.setUrl("jdbc:borland:dslocal:C:/JB6/samples/WebApps/guestbook.jds");
    super.setDriver("com.borland.datastore.jdbc.DataStoreDriver");
    super.setUsername("user");
    super.setPassword("user");
  }
  public void setUp() {
    super.setUp();
  }
  public void tearDown() {
    super.tearDown();
  }
}
```

The code in Listing 5.10 extends JBuilder's `JdbcFixture` class and generates a skeleton class that connects to the database.

The typical usage of the JDBC fixture class follows these steps:

1. Get a connection to the database.
2. Execute a SQL script or statement.
3. Get the resultset from the script or statement.
4. Dump the resultset to a comparison object.
5. Close the database connection.

The JDBC fixture class contains the following utility methods to help the typical usage scenario. The methods for each of the steps are

1. Get a connection to the database.

   The `getConnection()` method gets a connection to the database that was described in the JDBC Fixture Wizard.

2. Execute a SQL script or statement.

   The `runSqlBuffer()` or `runSqlFile()` methods execute a SQL statement in a `StringBuffer` or in a file. Typically, this sets up the database with sample data or temporary tables.

3. Get the resultset from the script or statement.

   With the connection established in step 1, a `Statement` object and a `ResultSet` object can be created based on a SQL query.

4. Dump the resultset to a comparison object.

   The `dumpResultSet()` method takes a `java.sql.ResultSet` object and writes out the results to a `java.io.Writer` object. This is where the comparison fixture class can be used to write the resultset to a file.

5. Close the database connection.

   Finally the connection in step 1 can be closed using the `close` method.

TIP

The `dumpResultSet()` method is an important feature of the JDBC fixture class. You do not have to write a function to iterate through the resultset and write it out to a file. Allowing the test case to take a resultset and write the resultset out to a file through a single method call makes it easy to implement. The comparison fixture can be used to compare the existing resultset with the runtime resultset to determine whether they are equal.

JNDI Fixture

The JNDI fixture is the most basic of the fixtures and extends from the `java.lang.Object`. By filling in the default settings for the JNDI server, the test cases you create can gain immediate access to the naming context server.

The `getContext()` method of the JNDI fixture is the primary method of the JNDI fixture class. The `getContext()` method returns the context of the current Java naming server. This is similar to the JDBC `getConnection()` method. After access to the naming context server is obtained, you can create unit tests on the naming server.

In Practice

The following unit testing tutorial helps you gain experience using JBuilder's unit testing features. To learn more about the JUnit testing framework, visit `www.junit.org`.

The application's goal is to unit test a class named `FunctionalClass`.

The exercise shows you how to set up a test case and a comparison test fixture.

Step 1: Opening the Unit Testing Sample Project

In this step, you open the sample project and the source code file that contains errors.

To open the example project, follow these steps:

1. Select File, Open Project from the JBuilder menu.
2. Locate the `jbbook/ch05/UnitTestSample.jpx` and click on OK.
3. The project opens in the Project pane. The project is composed of five Java files:
   - `FunctionalClass.java`—The file containing the class methods to be unit tested.
   - `handCodedUnitTest.java`—The file containing the hand-generated unit testing code.
   - `handCodedTestSuite.java`—The file containing the hand-generated test suite code.
   - `FrameUnitTest.java`, `UnitTestSample.java`—The standard JBuilder-generated files; these can be ignored in our tutorial.
4. Double-click on the `FunctionalClass.java`. The Content pane displays the file.
5. Notice the functions `getFullName` and `getDriversAge`. `getFullName` returns a concatenation of the first and last names passed to it. `getDriversAge` always returns 16.

Figure 5.15 shows the `UnitTestSample` project with the `FunctionalClass.java` code.

Step 2: Adding a Unit Test Case to the Project

In this step, you add a test case to the project and write the code to test the class.

To add the test case file to the project, follow these steps:

1. Select File, New from the JBuilder menu.
2. From the Object Gallery, select the Test tab.
3. Select the Test Case icon and click OK.
4. A dialog box appears with the name Test Case Wizard—Step 1 of 4. Highlight the methods `getDriversAge()` and `getFullName(String,String)` in the dialog box as shown in Figure 5.16.

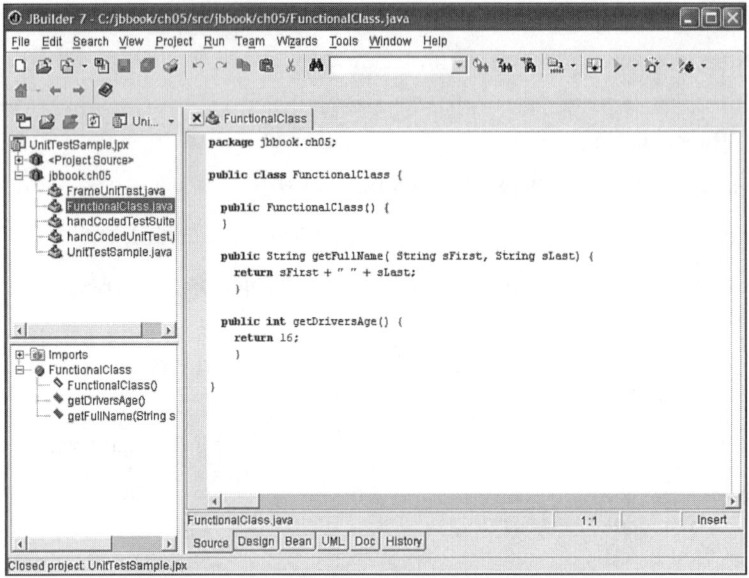

FIGURE 5.15 Unit test sample—getting started.

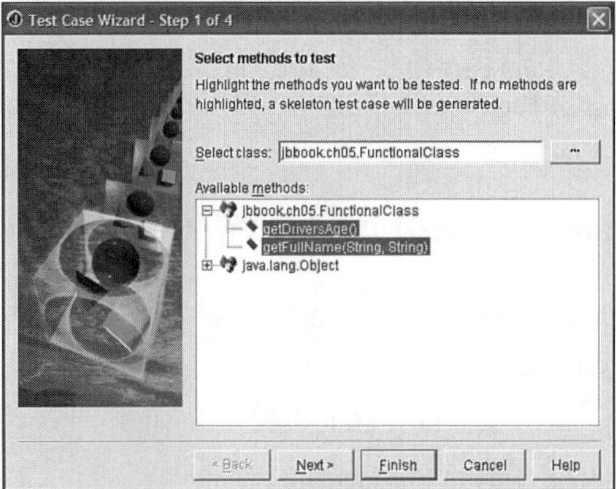

FIGURE 5.16 Unit test sample—Test Case Wizard.

5. Click on the Finish button to accept the defaults of the Test Case Wizard.
6. The class `TestFunctionalClass` is added to your project. Double-click the file so that it appears in the Content pane.

7. The Structure pane should have the To Do folder available. Expand the folder and select the first `todo` item: `todo:: Insert test code here...`. The code in the Content pane should scroll to the `todo` line in the method `testGetDriversAge()`.

8. Replace the `todo` line with the following line:

```
assertEquals("Drivers age test:", 16, intRet);
```

9. Select the remaining `todo` item in the Structure pane. The code in the Content pane should scroll to the `todo` line in the method `testGetFullName()`.

10. Replace the `todo` line with the following line:

```
assertEquals("Full Name Test:", "Mike Landy", stringRet);
```

11. Right-click on the class `TestFunctionalClass` in the Project pane and select the `Run Test using "TestFunctionalClass"` menu item.

Figure 5.17 shows the `UnitTestSample` project with the `TestFunctionalClass.java` code after it has been tested. Notice how the `testGetDriversAge` method succeeded and the `testGetFullName` method failed. By selecting the failed test, the Content pane scrolls to the assertion that caused the failure.

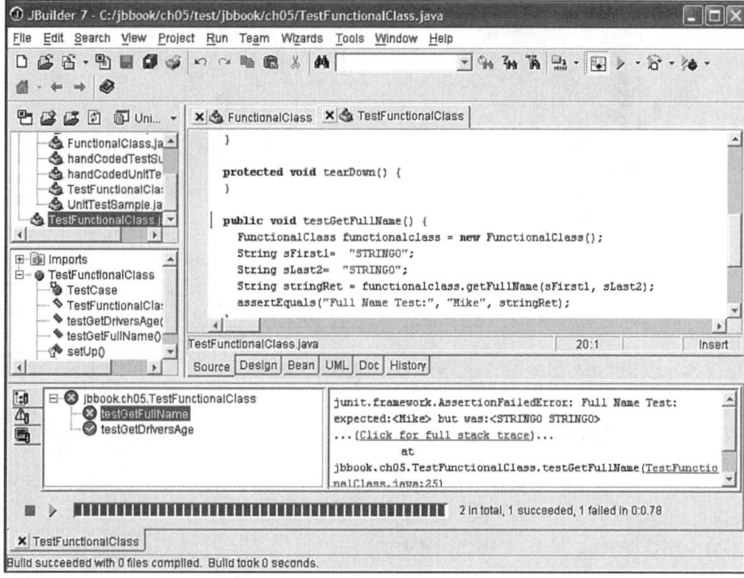

FIGURE 5.17 Unit test sample—test case code after running the test.

TIP

How would you fix the code to make both unit tests succeed?

Answer: Modify the expected value to be `"Mike Landy"`. Modify the variables `sFirst1` to be `"Mike"` and the variable `sLast2` to be `"Landy"`.

Step 3: Adding a Comparison Fixture to the Project

In this step, you add a comparison fixture to the project and write the code to compare the results.

To add the comparison fixture file to the project, follow these steps:

1. Select File, New from the JBuilder menu.
2. From the Object Gallery, select the Test tab.
3. Select the Comparison Fixture icon and click OK.
4. A Comparison Fixture Wizard dialog box appears. Modify the class name in Figure 5.18 to `ComparisonFunctionalClass`.

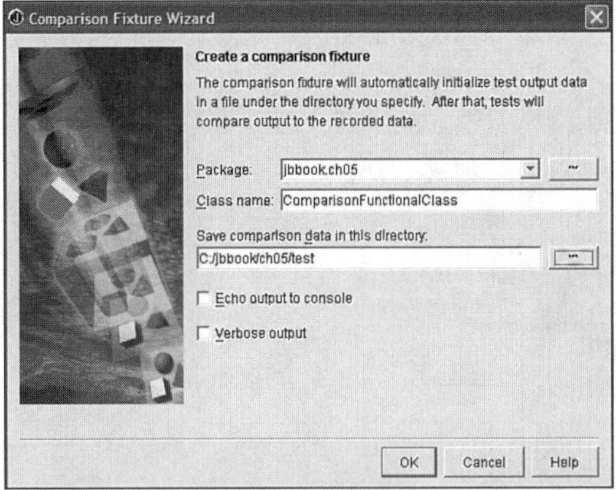

FIGURE 5.18 Unit test sample—Comparison Fixture Wizard dialog box.

5. Click on OK. The class `ComparisonFunctionalClass` is added to your project under the `fixture` package folder.
6. Double-click on the `TestFunctionalClass.java` file in the Project pane. The file should be loaded in the Content pane.

7. Replace the following line in the `testGetFullName()` method:

```
assertEquals("Full Name Test:", "Mike", stringRet);
```

with the following lines:

```
ComparisonFunctionalClass cfc = new ComparisonFunctionalClass(this);
cfc.recordObject(stringRet);
```

8. Right-click on the class `TestFunctionalClass` in the Project pane and select the Run Test using "TestFunctionalClass" menu item.

Figure 5.19 shows the `UnitTestSample` project with the `TestFunctionalClass.java` code after it has been tested. Notice that both methods have now succeeded.

The comparison fixture did not find an existing data file and therefore created one. The file can be found under the test directory in the root directory of the project. In our example, that would be the jbbook/ch05/test/jbbook/ch05 directory and have a filename of `TestFunctionalClass`. The file will record the object passed in the `recordObject` method the first time it is run. Subsequent running of the test will compare the results in the file with the results in the `recordObject` method. If the value of that object changes, the comparison will fail.

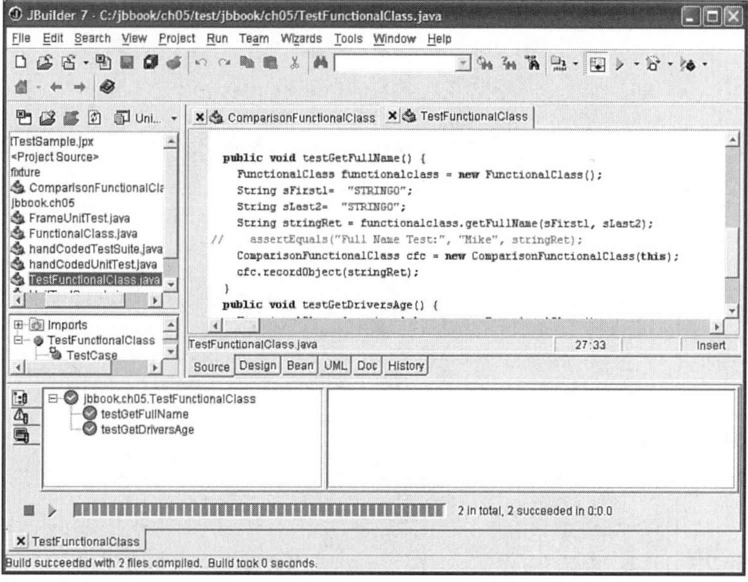

FIGURE 5.19 Unit test sample—comparison fixture code.

TIP

How would you fix the code to make the unit test on the `getFullName` method fail?

Answer: Modify the variables `sFirst1` or `sLast2` to contain different values. The test will fail because the comparison file exists. The comparison file contains the expected value, and the expected value was changed by modifying the contents of the `sFirst1` or `sLast2` variables.

When a test fails, the `java.lang.NoSuchFieldError` exception is thrown. The error message will reveal the source code line where the comparison failed.

What is the name of the file created to hold the comparison values?

Answer: The filename created to hold the comparison data values is `TestFunctionalClass`, and it can be found in the test subdirectory in the project folder.

How do you clear the comparison values stored in the data file?

Answer: There are two ways to clear the comparison values stored in the data file. The easiest is to delete the file `TestFunctionalClass`. Be careful not to delete the .java file! The other method is to open up the `ComparisonFunctionalClass.java` file and modify the `setMode(UPDATE)` to `setMode(RECORD)`. The `RECORD` mode will overwrite the existing file and record new values to the file.

Summary

The JBuilder IDE makes it easier to implement unit testing using the open JUnit testing framework. JBuilder's fixture utility classes provide quick methods to connect to a database or naming service, making unit testing setup easier.

Best practices state that you should unit test every method in your class. In reality, the time to unit test every method may result in unreasonable delays and wasted effort. Our recommendation is to create unit tests only for complex methods and/or nonprivate methods. Complex methods are ones that manipulate the database or make several method calls into your other classes. By unit testing the most complex portions of your code, you can greatly reduce the cost of maintaining that code.

Finally, most studies show that 60 to 80 percent of time and costs can be saved by implementing testing early in the development of your code. With the built-in unit testing facilities of JBuilder, you have no excuse for not building unit tests.

Reflections

- How often do you unit test your code?
- What is your biggest complaint about unit tests and does JBuilder's IDE address them?
- Before you build elaborate test suites to unit test your application, you may consider automated testing tools. Automated testing tools can provide reporting and load analysis, which the JUnit framework does not provide.

6 Debugging

IN THIS CHAPTER

- Integrated Debugger
- Fundamental Debugging
- More Debugging Options

JBuilder's integrated debugging facility provides a wealth of information for finding compile-time, runtime, and logic errors. The JBuilder integrated debugger provides you the ability to stop a program, step through the code, view and modify variables, execute expressions, log expressions, and provide remote debugging facilities. JBuilder can debug Java applications, applets, JSP/Servlets, and Enterprise Java Beans.

Learning how to use the integrated debugger is essential to minimizing the time spent in finding and correcting errors. Chapter 26, "Debugging Your Enterprise Application," takes you through the more advanced debugging features. In this chapter, you will learn the fundamentals of debugging in the JBuilder environment. The fundamentals include

- Setting up, running, and controlling the debugging environment
- Viewing and modifying variables during runtime
- Setting conditional breakpoints
- Learning the advanced features of JBuilder's debugger

Integrated Debugger

JBuilder's IDE provides a rich interface for controlling all sorts of debugging information. When running under the debug Virtual Machine (VM), the IDE displays debug controls, debug views, debug status, and a debug session.

Figure 6.1 shows the major features of the JBuilder IDE while in Debug mode. To enter Debug mode, click on Run, Debug Project from the menu.

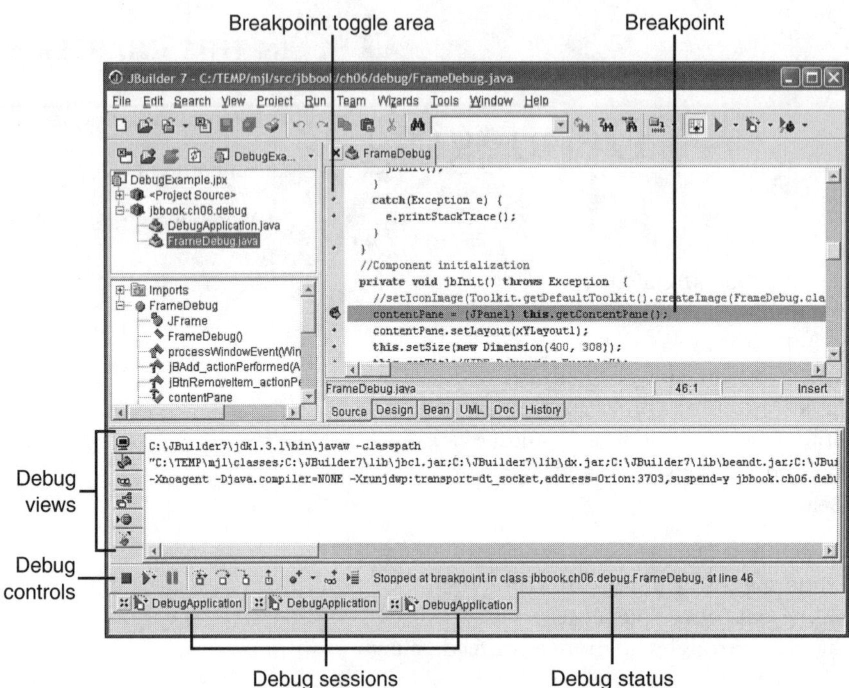

FIGURE 6.1 The JBuilder IDE in Debug mode.

Debug Controls

JBuilder provides many ways to continue execution of your application after it is paused. All the continuation commands are available from the Run menu. A subset of the available continuation commands is available in the Debug Control section shown in Figure 6.1.

Table 6.1 defines the code continuation features of JBuilder's debugger.

TABLE 6.1 Debug Controls

Control	Description
Reset	Reset stops the current instance of your application. Modifications to code while debugging require you to reset the application before they take effect. `[shortcut Ctrl-F2]`
Resume	Resume continues the execution of your application.
Pause	Pause stops the executing application and loads the relevant source file with the pause location.

TABLE 6.1 Continued

Control	Description
Toggle Smart Step	JBuilder includes Smart Step technology, which allows you to define what classes should not be stepped into during a debugging session. This is useful when stepping through code that includes calls to third-party libraries or core Java libraries.
Step Over	The Step Over command executes the current command and moves to the following statement. This command will not trace into called functions. `[shortcut F8]`
Step Into	The Step Into command attempts to follow the code line-by-line into every function call. `[shortcut F7]`
Step Out	You will undoubtedly find yourself stepping into code that you did not want to step into. For example, the method `getStudent()` calls the method `getStudentSchedule()`, and the method `getStudentSchedule()` calls the method `getDBConnection()`. You step into the method `getDBConnection()` by accident. The Step Out command provides a way to resume execution but stop on the next line of code in the calling method `getStudentSchedule()`. In this case, if you accidentally stepped into method `getDBConnection()`, the Step Out command would execute the remaining method `getDBConnection()` and then stop on the next line in the method `getStudentSchedule()`.
Run to Cursor	The Run to Cursor command works in conjunction with the Content pane. The application continues execution until it reaches the line where the cursor is located. When it reaches the line with the cursor, the application is paused. `[shortcut F4]`
Run to End of Method	The Run to End of Method command completes execution of a method but stops on the return to the calling method. Run to End of Method is useful when you want to execute a method but review all the variables, objects, and expressions prior to returning to the calling function.
Set Breakpoints	This command allows you to add a breakpoint to the code. See the section "Setting Breakpoints" later in this chapter for more information.
Set Watches	This command allows you to set up a watch variable. See the section "Watching Variables" later in the chapter.
Show Current Frame	This command locates the class and line of code at which the current application is paused.

Typically, the standard debugging steps include putting one or more breakpoints in your code, starting the debugger, stepping into your code, and watching variables. Using these basic guidelines, you will be much better off than putting `System.out.println` throughout your code.

When you enter Debug mode, the system creates several views to help you manage the information from all aspects of the runtime environment. These are called *debug views*.

Debug Views

Six debug views show various pieces of information on the executing program. The views are described in Table 6.2.

TABLE 6.2 Debug Views

View	Description
Console Output, Input, and Errors	All program output and errors are displayed in this tabbed view. It is useful for debugging output, program output, and the execution commands used to compile and run your project.
Threads, Call Stack, and Data	When you pause your program, this tabbed view shows all the threads in your project, the call stack based on the project's current location, and the relevant data values. Unexpected errors can be tracked through all levels of code back to the line that started the problem.
Data Watches	The Watch view is used to set up custom views of data and expressions. The Watch view is updated after each line of code is executed. In addition, you can modify the value of variables while the program is in Debug mode thereby affecting the outcome of the code.
Loaded Classes and Static Data	This view shows the current set of classes loaded by the VM and the static data associated with those classes.
Data and Code Breakpoints	All program breakpoints show up in this window. Breakpoints can be enabled, disabled, and modified from this tabbed view.
Classes with Tracing Disabled	When debugging a project, you can tell the debug ger not to single-step through certain classes. By not single-stepping through core Java or other vendor libraries, you can focus your debugging on the code written for the project.

Builder has the capability to have multiple debugging panes open at once and displayed in a floating window.

Each of these debug views has context-sensitive pop-up menus. Some options are available only on a selected value in the debug view. Tables 6.3 and 6.4 list the pop-up menus for the Watch view and the Data and Code Breakpoint view.

TABLE 6.3 Watch Context Pop-up Menu

Menu Option	Description
Create Field Watch	Creates a duplicate of the selected watch expression
Create Object Watch	Creates a duplicate of the selected watch object
Create Field Breakpoint	Creates a breakpoint whenever the variable or expression is accessed
Change Value	Allows you to change the current value of a variable or expression
Change Watch Expression	Changes the current expression for the selected watch expression
Change Watch Description	Allows you to change the description associated with the selected watch expression
Remove Watch	Removes the watch expression from the debug view
Show Hex Value	Shows the value of a watch expression in hex
Show Decimal Value	Shows the value of a watch expression in decimal

TABLE 6.4 Breakpoint Context Pop-up Menu

Menu Option	Description
Enable Breakpoint	Enables a breakpoint so that it can perform whatever actions have been set.
Remove Breakpoint	Removes a breakpoint from the application.
Breakpoint Properties	Displays the Breakpoint Properties dialog box. For more information see Figure 6.6.
Break on Read	For field level breakpoints, pauses the application every time the code reads the field.
Break on Write	For field level breakpoints, pauses the application every time the code writes to the field.

Finally, the debug views provide a wealth of information to diagnose problems in your application. Learning which views to use and their options can help you locate your errors quickly.

Debug Session and Status

A project running under Debug mode gets its own tab for every process being debugged. The tab is associated with one debug session and contains all the debug view information for that program.

You can have multiple copies of the same program being debugged at the same time, or, more practically, you can debug a client program and server program at the same time from the same IDE instance.

Because multiple programs can be debugged at the same time, it is possible that each program can be stopped at different places or not stopped at all. The Debug Status line displays for each Debug Session tab to notify the developer of the current status of the program.

Fundamental Debugging

Debugging is a common process that a developer undertakes for two main reasons. The first reason is "Why the heck doesn't this compile?". The second reason is "That's not how it is supposed to work!"

Before the maturity of the Java Debugging API, many developers had to determine why the program was not running as coded and what it was doing when executing the code. Developers had to read cryptic error messages from the Java compiler and resort to `System.out.println` to determine where their application was breaking. Some brave developers worked with the `jdb` as their debugger, but most found it too cumbersome.

The JBuilder IDE enables you to debug much more efficiently by

- Supporting real-time error checking
- Locating compile-time errors
- Setting breakpoints in code during runtime
- Watching and modifying variables during runtime
- Setting conditional breakpoints
- Logging debug information during runtime

Real-Time Error Checking

The JBuilder IDE automatically parses a source code file when it is opened. If errors are found, they can be seen in the Structure pane menu View, Structure. The JBuilder IDE is constantly checking for errors in the open source code file as you type.

Figure 6.2 displays the Structure pane with an Errors folder. Expanding the Errors folder reveals that a semicolon was expected at line 47. By clicking on that error, the system highlights the line containing the error.

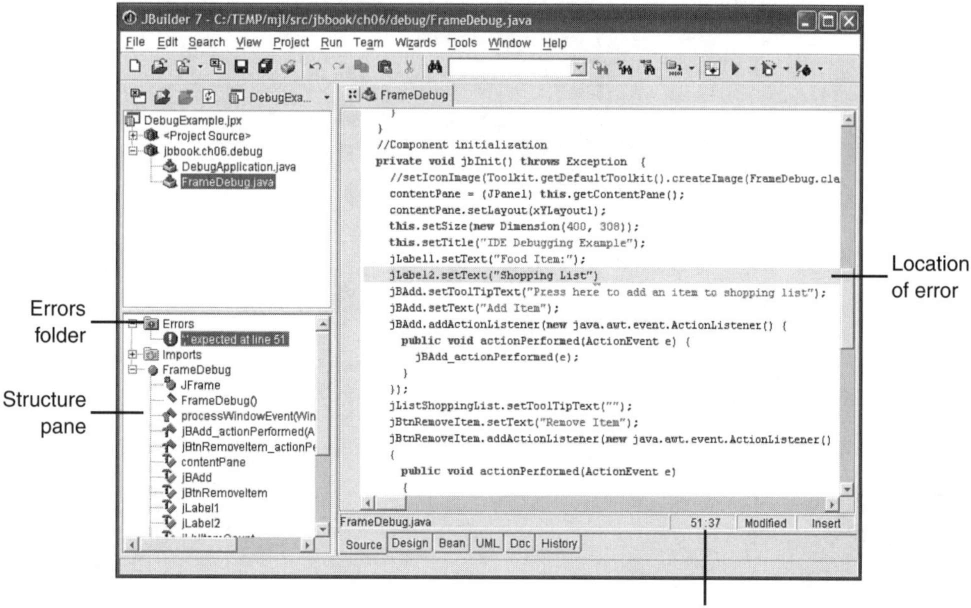

FIGURE 6.2 Real-time error checking in the JBuilder IDE.

JBuilder's integrations of real-time error checking make it easier to spot errors before an attempt to compile code.

Compiler Errors

Compile-time errors occur when an attempt is made to compile a project or a single source code file. If you attempt to compile a project that contains errors, JBuilder lists those errors in a *compiler status window*. Figure 6.3 displays the compiler window that identifies all the compile-time errors that exist in the application.

There are many different ways to compile a project. Under the Project menu, you can use the options to Make or Rebuild the project or just the currently selected source code file. In addition, any attempt to run or debug the project forces a compile of all project modules.

Setting Breakpoints

Breakpoints give you the ability to mark a line of code as the place the application should stop while maintaining the current state of the runtime environment. The ability to stop an executing Java application and single-step from one line of code to the next is a huge advantage when tracking down problems.

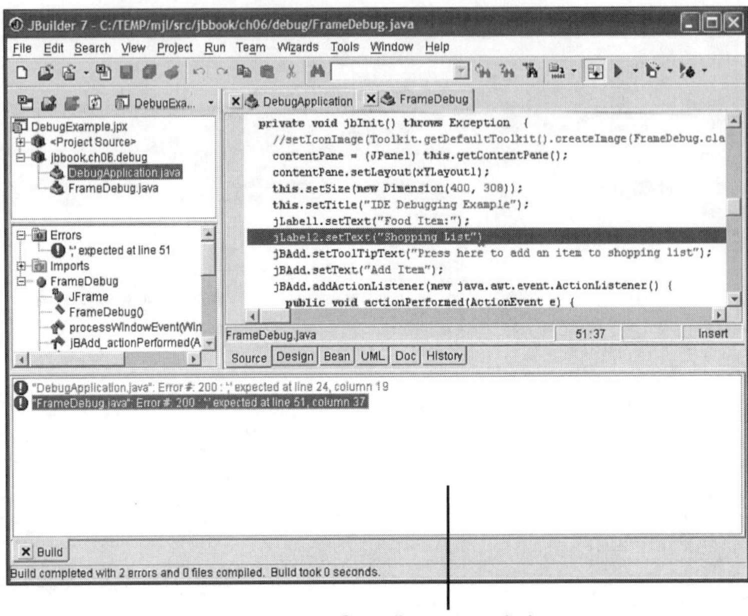

FIGURE 6.3 Compile-time errors in two Java source files.

Even today, the most common solution to finding out why an application is behaving in a certain manner is to use the ever-popular `System.out.println` all over your code. Breakpoints allow the JBuilder developer to graphically select a line of code to pause execution of the application.

Breakpoints are recognized only when running a project in Debug mode. Breakpoints may be set and removed as well as enabled and disabled.

A breakpoint that is removed from the project loses all its settings. A breakpoint that is disabled maintains its settings but is ignored by the project running in Debug mode.

Setting breakpoints can be accomplished by selecting a line of code and pressing F5 or clicking in the left gray margin (gutter) on a line with code. A breakpoint can be identified by the red dot at the beginning of the line of code. The line of code is also highlighted in red. The red highlighted line indicates that the application will be paused when the line is about to be executed.

An application running under Debug mode is slower than the same application not running under Debug mode. Figure 6.4 gives a rough idea of what an application does when running under Debug mode.

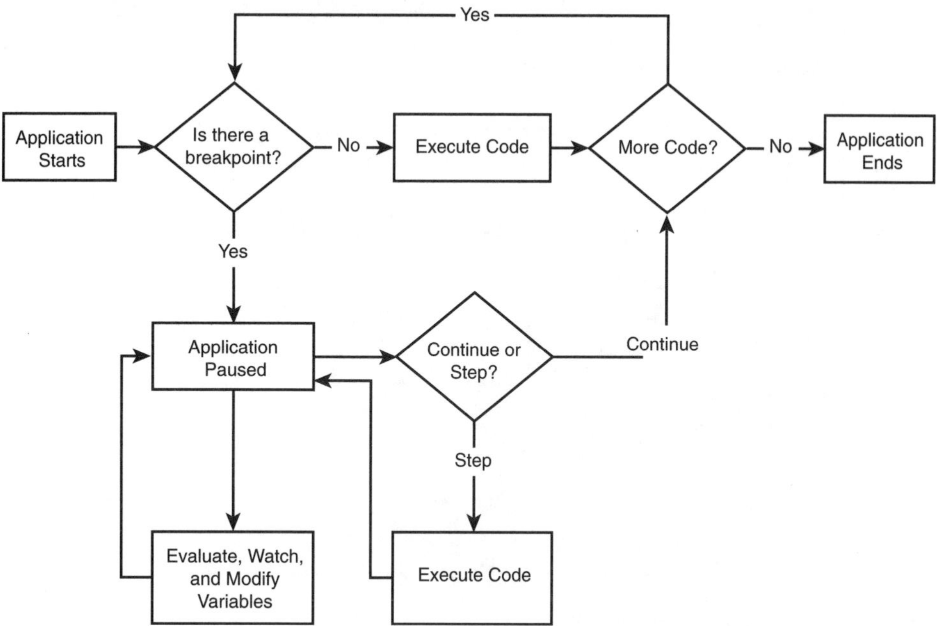

FIGURE 6.4 Application running under Debug mode.

When an application is paused, you may choose from many different actions. These include watching variables, changing the value of variables, and evaluating expressions.

Watching Variables

When an application is paused, all the in-scope variables can be accessed and reviewed. The floating ToolTip and the watch variable are two methods used in inspecting the contents of objects, variables, and expressions.

The floating ToolTip method requires the mouse cursor to hover over a variable causing a ToolTip window to appear and show the contents of the variable. The ToolTip window disappears when the mouse is moved off the variable.

When you need to see the contents of many variables, a watch variable is more practical. A watch variable appears in the Watch view window. The contents of a watch variable may be a primitive variable, an object, or an expression. To set a watch variable, select Run, Add Watch from the menu.

In Figure 6.5, the `String s` and the `int a` have been defined and are in scope. The integer `b` has not been set and is therefore not in scope. The Watch view knows how to handle in-scope and out-of-scope variables. The Watch view also contains an expression watch that multiplies `a` by `10`.

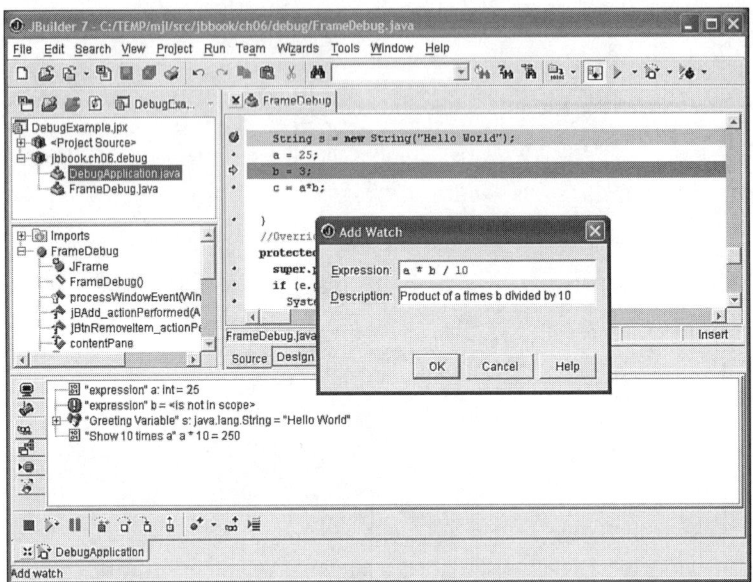

FIGURE 6.5 Watching the variables.

TIP

If you right-click on the watch variable, you have the ability to create a field breakpoint. The Create Field Breakpoint menu option allows you to set a breakpoint on whenever that variable is accessed. From the Debug view of breakpoints, you can set properties on a field watch so that the application pauses if the variable is accessed for reading and/or writing.

Finally, Figure 6.5 shows an Add Watch dialog box with an expression that will be evaluated in the Watch view. Every time you step through the lines of code, the watch window updates the value of all expressions affected.

Evaluate and Modify On-the-Fly

JBuilder's IDE can evaluate expressions and change values while the application is paused. Expressions can operate on any in-scope variables, methods, or objects. Variables can be modified directly or manipulated by evaluating an expression.

To evaluate or modify an expression, select Run, Evaluate/Modify from the menu.

More Debugging Options

JBuilder offers additional features to help debug an application. These additional features are used only a fraction of the time, but represent huge time savings when debugging code. The additional features are

- Conditional breakpoints
- Breakpoint logging
- Exception breakpoints
- Class breakpoints
- Method breakpoints
- Class tracing

Breakpoint Options

Conditional breakpoints become active if conditions are true. Breakpoints by default will stop execution of an application and put the application on pause. Breakpoints can also be used to log messages without stopping the application. In Figure 6.6, the breakpoint becomes active based on the condition `c>70`.

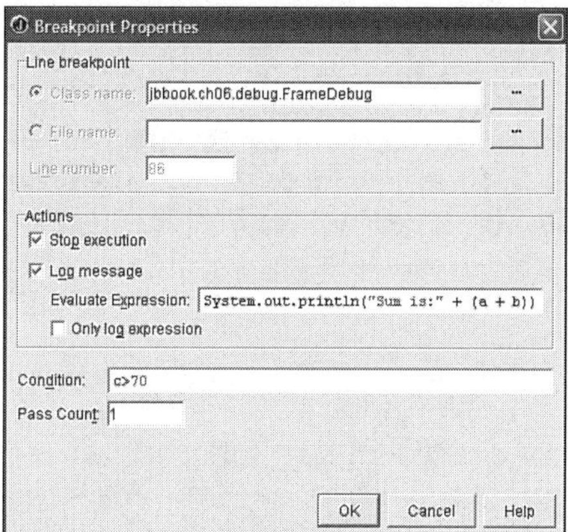

FIGURE 6.6 Conditional breakpoint properties.

In Figure 6.6, when the application encounters the breakpoint and the condition `c>70` is true, it evaluates the expression. The application stops and logs the expression to the Console view. The application remains stopped until you resume or reset the application.

The Breakpoint Properties dialog box has additional options: Pass Count and Log Message.

The Pass Count condition determines the number of times the line with the breakpoint must be executed prior to enabling the breakpoint. This is useful in situations where you know an error occurs after many execution iterations, and you don't want to waste time stepping through all the iterations.

The Log Message action sends an expression to Console view. In Figure 6.6, the Console view is shown with the output from the Log Message expression `System.out.println("Sum is:" + (a + b))`.

Exception Breakpoints

Exception breakpoints are identical to line breakpoints except that an exception breakpoint is tied to a particular exception class. Exception breakpoints can be set on exceptions that are caught and uncaught. The application stops the program execution when the exception is about to be thrown. Exception breakpoints have the same logging and condition options as the line breakpoints. To set an exception breakpoint, select Run, Add Breakpoint, Add Exception Breakpoint from the menu.

Class Breakpoints

Class breakpoints stop execution anytime a method of a class is called. Class breakpoints have the same logging and condition options as the line breakpoints. To set a class breakpoint, select Run, Add Breakpoint, Add Class Breakpoint from the menu.

Method Breakpoints

Method breakpoints stop execution when the specified method of a class is called. Anytime that method is called by any piece of code, the breakpoint activates causing execution to stop. Method breakpoints have the same logging and condition options as the line breakpoints. To set a method breakpoint, select Run, Add Breakpoint, Add Method Breakpoint from the menu.

Class Tracing

Java includes the core classes and interfaces often used in every application. You may set a breakpoint in your code and step through it. While stepping through the code, the code may call a method that is part of the standard Java core libraries. You do not want to step into the core library code because you know that it has already been debugged.

To prevent this from happening, JBuilder includes the capability to mark a class or package as tracing disabled. When you attempt to step into one of the classes in the list of tracing disabled, the debugger steps over these classes and continues to the next traceable class.

For JBuilder to acknowledge the list of tracing disabled classes and packages, the Smart Step option must be enabled. The Smart Step option is located on the Debugging tab in the Project Properties dialog box.

To view the list of classes and packages with tracing disabled, select Run, View Classes with Tracing Disabled from the menu. The dialog box shown in Figure 6.7 displays the current set of classes and packages with tracking disabled. To add an entry into this list, right-click on the window and select Add Class or Package.

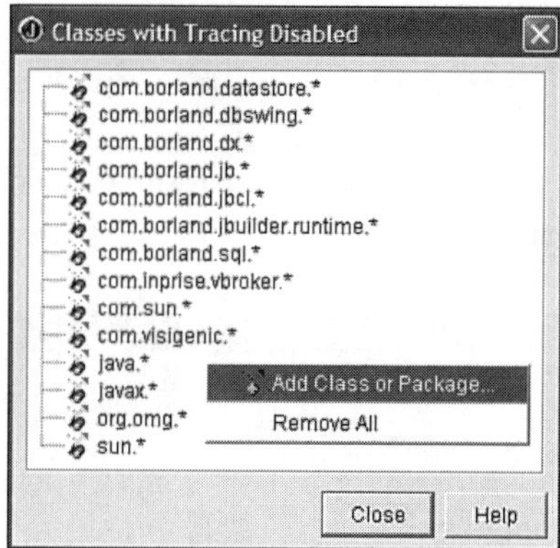

FIGURE 6.7 List of tracing disabled classes and packages.

The list in Figure 6.7 shows that all the core libraries and JBuilder libraries have tracing disabled. The Smart Step feature prevents the developer from accidentally stepping into code libraries that have already been debugged.

In Practice

The following debug tutorial helps you gain experience using JBuilder's debugger. We cannot stress enough how important it is to learn the features of the debugger. Debugging is really about making the coding environment find the error for you.

The application we have written takes user input of food items and adds them to a `JList` list box. Although this seems simple enough, it is filled with syntax and runtime errors.

We will take you through debugging compile-time errors, runtime errors, and logic errors.

Step 1: Opening the Debugging Example Project

In this step, you open the example project and the source code file that contains errors.

To open the example project

1. Select File, Open Project from the JBuilder menu.
2. Locate the `jbbook/ch06/DebugExample.jpx` and click on OK.
3. The project opens in the Project pane. The two files in the project are
   - `DebugApplication.java`—The file containing the `main()` method
   - `FrameDebug.java`—The file containing the primary code of the application
4. Double-click on the `FrameDebug.java`. The Content pane displays the file.

Figure 6.8 shows the `DebugExample` project with the `FrameDebug.java` code. Notice the Errors folder in the lower-left pane, the Structure pane.

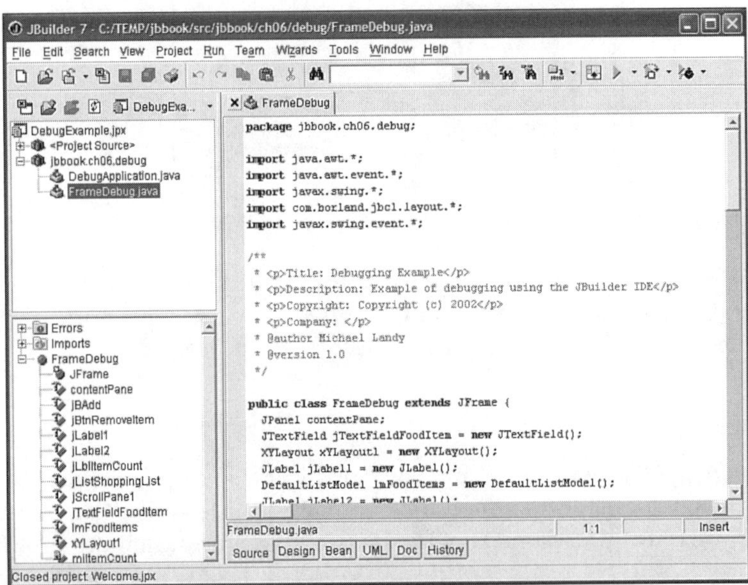

FIGURE 6.8 Debug example—getting started.

Step 2: Fixing the Syntax Errors

In this step, you open the Errors folder in the Structure pane and resolve the syntax errors:

NOTE

The following exercise refers to specific lines of code in the `FrameDebug.java` file. If you modify the code outside this example, the following steps will report different line numbers than the ones specified. The same errors will appear but on different lines.

1. With the `FrameDebug.java` code in the Content pane, expand the Errors folder in the Structure view. You see the statement `';' expected at line 31.`
2. Click on the statement, and the Content pane should automatically scroll to line 31. Line 31 reads

   ```
   private int miItemCount
   ```

3. Add a ";" to the end of the line so that it now reads

   ```
   private int miItemCount;
   ```

4. The Errors folder should now display the next syntax error. It should read `Illegal start of expression at line 88.`
5. Click on the error, and the Content pane should automatically scroll to line 88. Line 88 should read

   ```
   if (!jTextFieldFoodItem.getText().trim() <> "" )
   ```

6. Line 88 is incorrect because strings are not compared for equality using logical operators. In addition, the operator for not equal to is `!=` rather than <>. This line should read

   ```
   if (!jTextFieldFoodItem.getText().trim().equals("") )
   ```

7. After this line is corrected, the Errors folder displays one more error in the Structure pane. Ignore this error for now; we will fix it in "Step 3: Fixing the Compile-Time Errors."
8. Select File, Save `FrameDebug.java` from the menu.

The Figure 6.9 shows the `DebugExample` project with some additional errors. Having the errors appear in the Structure pane is a nice feature, but to open all the source code files in a project and check for errors can be tedious. An easier way to find errors is to try and compile the application. "Step 3: Fixing the Compile-Time Errors" deals with compile-time errors.

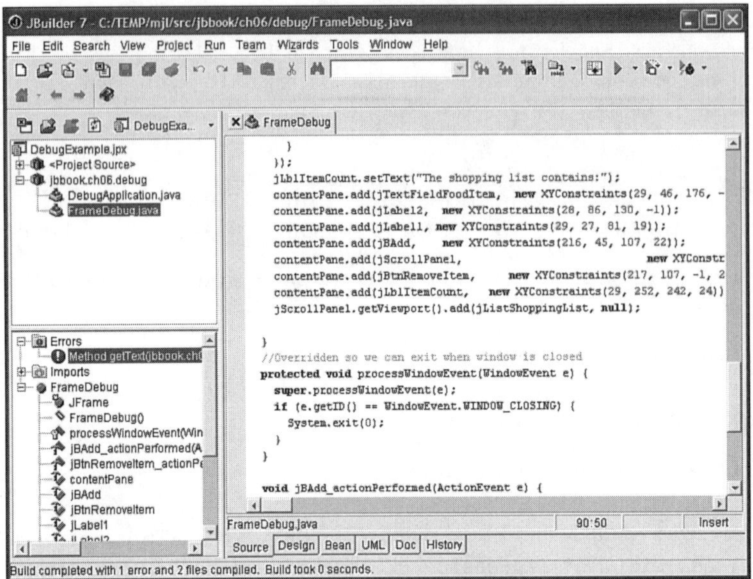

FIGURE 6.9 Debug example—removing syntax errors.

Step 3: Fixing the Compile-Time Errors

In this step, you fix the compile-time error and run the application:

1. Select Run, Run Project from the menu.
2. A compiler window appears on the bottom of the screen with the compile-time error

```
"FrameDebug.java": Error #: 300 : method
getText(jbbook.ch06.debug.FrameDebug) not found in class
javax.swing.JTextField at line 90, column 50.
```

3. The compile-time error refers to the method `getText` with an argument of `this`. The `getText` method does not take an argument, and `this` should be removed. The final line should read

```
lmFoodItems.addElement( jTextFieldFoodItem.getText().trim() );
```

4. Select Run, Run Project from the menu. The application appears. Figure 6.10 shows the application running.

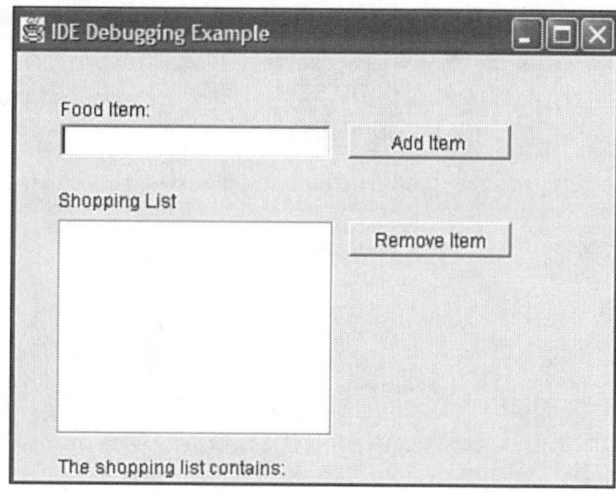

FIGURE 6.10 Debug example—application is now running.

Step 4: Fixing the Runtime Errors, Setting Breakpoints, Evaluating Variables, and Modifying Variables

In this step, you fix the runtime error and run the application:

1. Select Run, Run Project from the menu.

2. Click on Remove Item. In the Console view, you find that an exception has been thrown. Figure 6.11 shows the Console view and the exception that was thrown. If you scroll to the beginning of the exception in your debug windows, it tells you the cause of the exception. Find the line

   ```
   java.lang.ArrayIndexOutOfBoundsException: Array index out of range: -1.
   ```

3. Stop the application by closing the window or clicking the Reset button on the debug control toolbar.

4. The exception in the Console view shows a trace of all method calls that led to the exception. Figure 6.11 shows that the exception was raised in the `Vector.java` file. The `Vector.java` file was called by the `DefaultListModel.java` file. It would be rare to find an error in these files because they are standard Java class files.

   Searching the exception trace to find code that is part of the project is the primary goal in determining the cause of the exception. The `DefaultListModel.java` file was called by our code `FrameDebug.java:100`. The 100 indicates the line number of the method in FrameDebug that called `DefaultListModel.java`, which in turn called `Vector.java`.

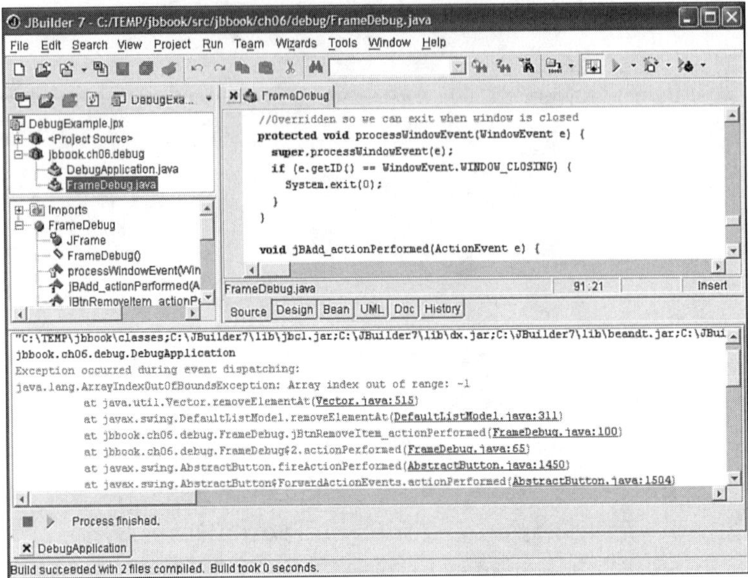

FIGURE 6.11 Debug example—exception in the application.

Look through the `FrameDebug.java` source code and find the following code at line 98 through 101:

```
void jBtnRemoveItem_actionPerformed(ActionEvent e)
{
  lmFoodItems.removeElementAt(jListShoppingList.getSelectedIndex());
}
```

5. Right-click on line 100 and select Toggle Breakpoint from the pop-up menu. The line now appears highlighted in red. Figure 6.12 indicates the location of the breakpoint.
6. Select Run, Debug Project from the menu.
7. Click on Remove Item. The application is now paused.
8. Highlight the code `jListShoppingList.getSelectedIndex()`. Right-click to bring up the pop-up menu. Select Add Watch from the pop-up menu. The Add Watch dialog box is displayed. Verify that the expression is `jListShoppingList.getSelectedIndex()`. Click OK.
9. Select the Data Watches debug view. The view should have the expression `jListShoppingList.getSelectedIndex()=-1`. Figure 6.13 shows the Watch debug view and the current value of the selected item in the list box.

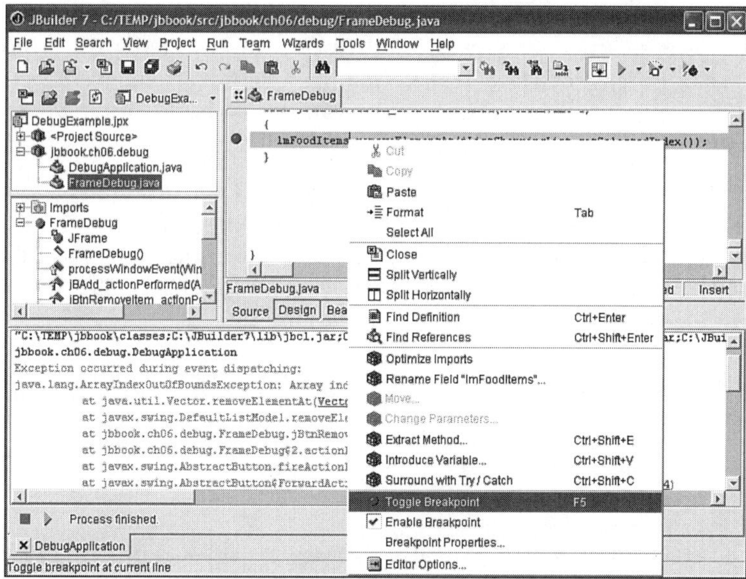

FIGURE 6.12 Debug example—setting a breakpoint.

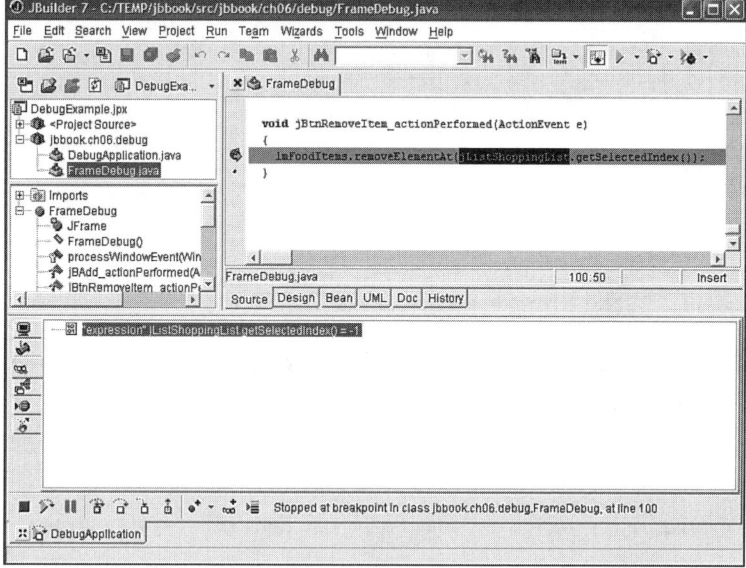

FIGURE 6.13 Debug example—watching the variables.

10. From this, you understand that an item cannot be removed from the list if one was never selected. If an item is not selected, the selected index returns a -1. You can fix this code later by determining whether a value has been selected before trying to remove the element from the list box. Click the Resume button or select Run, Resume Program from the menu.

11. While the program is still running, let's watch the variables in action during an add item request. To do this, find the function `jBAdd_actionPerformed` in the Structure pane or in the Content pane on line 87. Select line 88 and press F5, the shortcut for toggling a breakpoint. Line 88 appears highlighted in red. Figure 6.14 shows the highlighted breakpoint line.

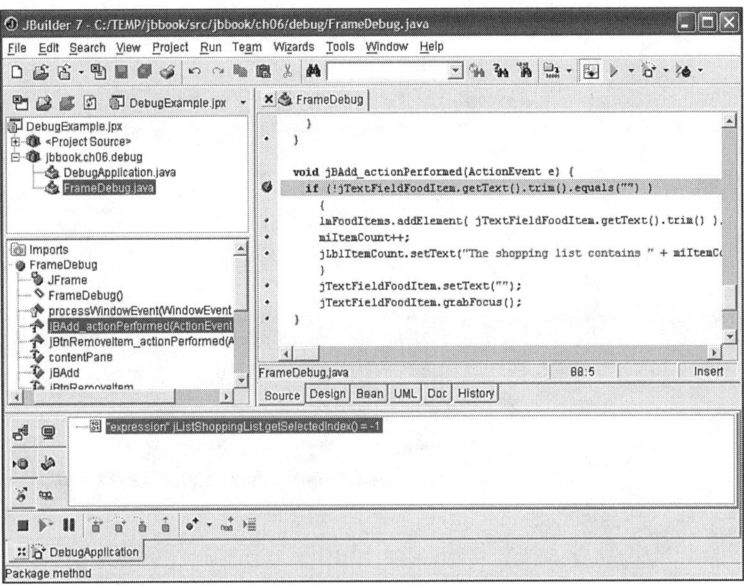

FIGURE 6.14 Debug example—setting a new breakpoint in the application.

12. Type in the food item "Carrots" and click Add Item. The application pauses on line 88.

13. Press F7 three times. F7 is the shortcut for the Step Into command. The line that should be highlighted is

```
jLblItemCount.setText("The shopping list contains " + miItemCount +
➥"items");
```

Figure 6.15 shows the highlighted line indicating the breakpoint, and the arrow highlighted line indicating the current line to be executed.

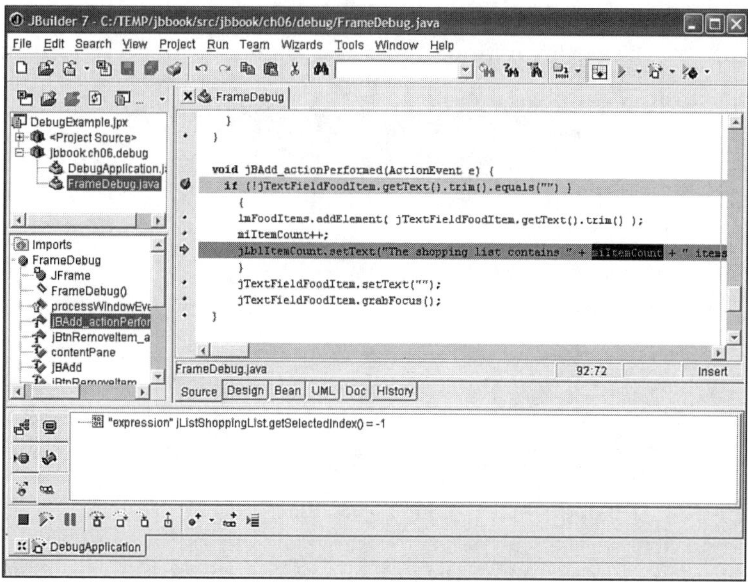

FIGURE 6.15 Debug example—single-step through the method.

14. Because this is the first item being added to the list, the `miItemCount` should have a value of one. To verify this, right-click on the line to bring up the pop-up menu. Select Evaluate/Modify from the pop-up menu.

15. In the Evaluate/Modify dialog box, type in `miItemCount` and click the Evaluate button. The value of `miItemCount` returns a 1. Figure 6.16 shows the current value of `miItemCount`.

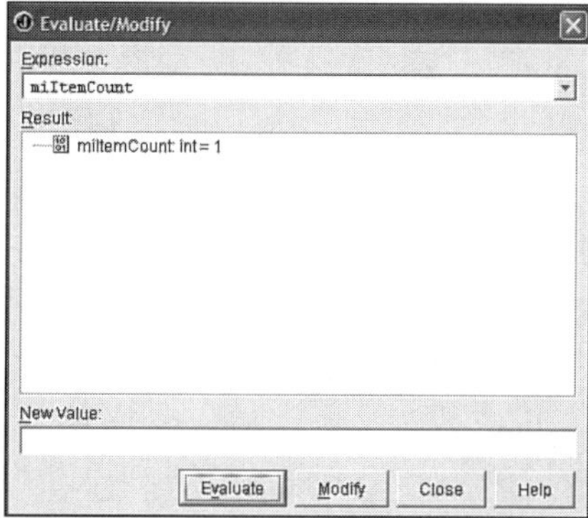

FIGURE 6.16 Debug example—evaluate and modify a variable.

16. In the New Value box on the Evaluate/Modify dialog box, type in the value 5 and click the Modify button. Figure 6.17 shows the modified variable.

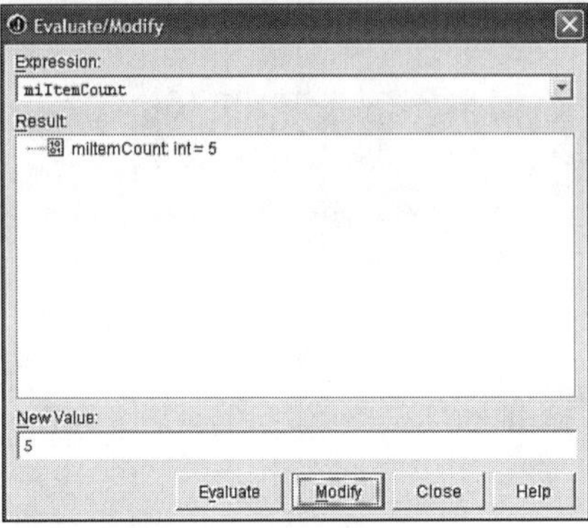

FIGURE 6.17 Debug example—modify a variable.

17. Click the Close button on the Evaluate/Modify dialog box. The dialog box closes. Click Resume on the debug controls or press F9 to resume the application execution. F9 is a shortcut for resume execution. The application shown in Figure 6.18 now displays "The shopping list contains 5 items."

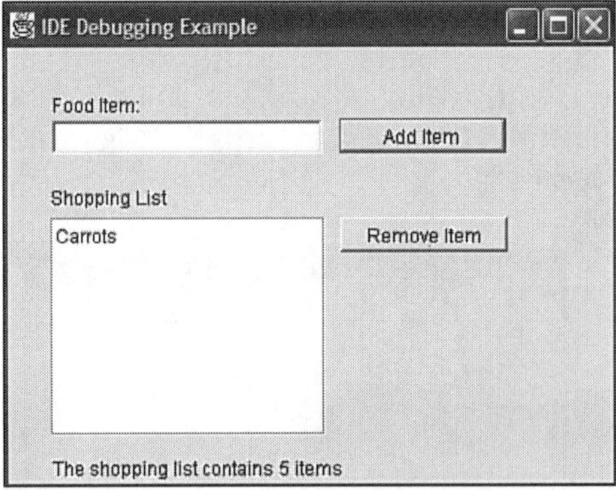

FIGURE 6.18 Debug example—application running with modified values.

Summary

The debugger provided by JBuilder's IDE is easier to use and far more powerful than putting `System.out.println` code throughout your application. The tight integration of the debugger with JBuilder's IDE allows the developer to work completely in one tool.

JBuilder's capability to stop an application and allow you to view and modify variables and fields brings a new level of power to your debugging. Learning how and when to apply the many debugging features takes practice and experience.

This chapter only touched the tip of the iceberg of JBuilder debugger's capabilities. In Chapter 26, you will see the debugger being used to debug applications running on other machines.

Reflections

- Of all the debugger features covered in this chapter, which one appears to make the most compelling argument to use the debugger and why?
- Did you happen to choose "run program" rather than "debug program" during the "In Practice" section? If so, what was the result?

7 Refactoring

IN THIS CHAPTER

- What Is Refactoring?
- Move Refactor
- Rename Refactor
- Changing Parameters
- Extract Method
- Introduce Variable
- Optimize Imports
- Surround with Try/Catch

Refactoring is the process of improving the infrastructure of your code while not changing the perceived behavior of your application. The refactoring process is a controlled method of improving the design of your code after it has been written. By following the process to refactor existing code, you will increase the maintainability and improve the design architecture of your application while minimizing the introduction of bugs.

JBuilder's IDE provides the many refactoring features. This chapter will teach you how to refactor existing code using the JBuilder environment. The refactoring concepts we will cover are

- What is refactoring?
- Move refactoring
- Rename refactoring
- Change parameters
- Extract method
- Introduce variable
- Optimize Imports
- Surround with Try/Catch

What Is Refactoring?

The saying "hindsight is 20/20" refers to the clarity one has about a situation after the situation has passed. A similar thing can be said after an application has been coded. The code design an application should have been built with becomes much clearer after the application has been coded.

In its strictest sense, refactoring is a controlled process of modifying and improving existing code while not changing the external behavior of the application. Refactoring is done in a way that minimizes the introduction of new bugs while changing the design of the code. Hindsight in this case provides clarity on what classes and methods are necessary, where code bottlenecks appear, and how the maintainability and scalability of the application can be improved.

AUTHOR'S EXPERIENCE

Many times I have ripped out the code of an application and redesigned it because of performance or understanding. I would ask myself what the developer of the code was trying to achieve and clean up the method. Most of the time, I focus on making the code simpler to understand by breaking up large routines into smaller, more logical ones.

I'll readily admit that at first, redesigning my own or someone else's code didn't make me think "why." I just did things certain ways because they made sense. Later I heard about refactoring. It turns out that many smart developers sat down and figured out that there are methods to improving the design of existing code. These methods define processes for renaming variables, extracting methods, breaking apart complex classes, and many others.

JBuilder now supports refactoring capabilities in its IDE. Given the OpenTools API in JBuilder, I expect more complex refactoring capabilities to be added to the IDE. JBuilder supports five refactoring processes and two IDE coding enhancements. The refactor methods are move, rename, change parameter, extract method, and introduce variable. The coding enhancements are Optimize Imports and Surround with Try/Catch.

Move Refactor

When working on a project, time and effort must be spent on organizing the code into certain packages using a standard naming convention. If the package organization changes or the package name changes, a developer has to go through all the classes and change the imports and class creation code. Depending on the number of classes and where the class is created, it is a tedious and manual effort. The move refactor method automatically moves a class from one package to another package.

NOTE

The move refactor does not work if the package you are moving the class to already contains a class with the same name.

To move a class from one package to another, the project must be compiled and up-to-date. After the project is up-to-date, the class must be selected either in the Code view or the UML view.

To move the class, you must first select the class in your code and bring up the context-sensitive pop-up menu. Figure 7.1 shows the Code view of the class you want to move and the context-sensitive menu.

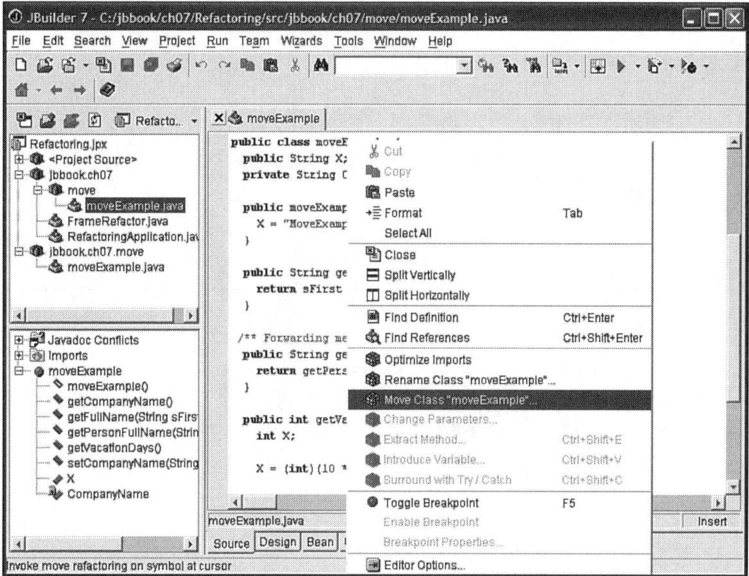

FIGURE 7.1 Moving a class in the Code view.

When you select the Move Class *classname* option from the pop-up menu, a Move Class dialog box appears. Figure 7.2 shows the Move Class dialog box options.

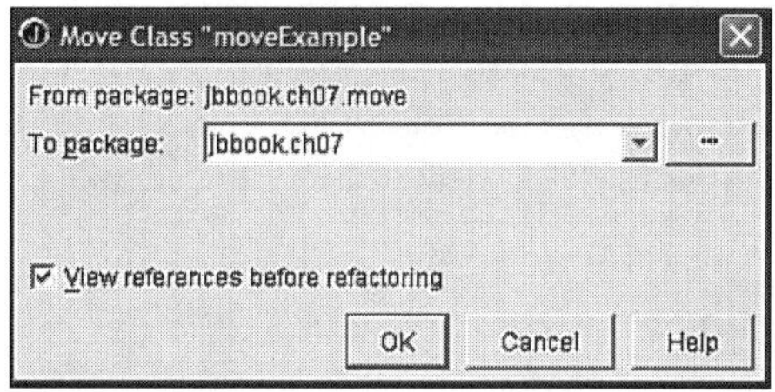

FIGURE 7.2 The Move Class dialog box.

The Move Class dialog box allows you to enter the new package name for the class and to view references before refactoring. If you cannot remember the package name, you can click on the button after the To Package field to get a list of packages.

The View References Before Refactoring check box displays a list of changes that will be made to each of the source code files to support the move refactoring. In the move refactoring, the `import` statement may be added or changed to reflect the new location of your class. Refactoring is more than a simple textual search and replace.

The Refactoring tab view in Figure 7.3 shows the list of changes that will be made to the source code files.

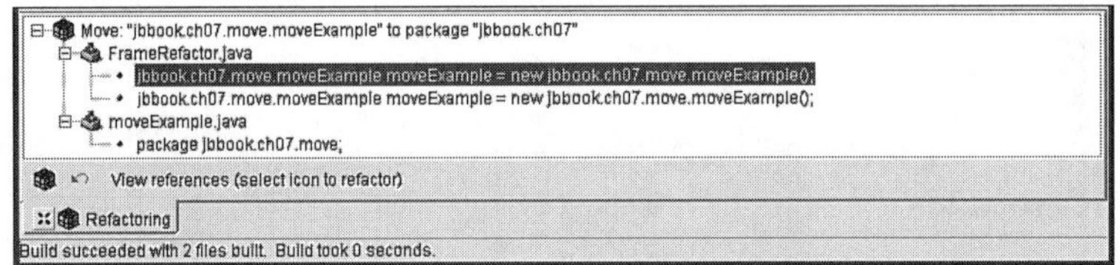

FIGURE 7.3 Refactoring tab view.

The Refactoring view has a command bar to apply the refactoring changes as well as undo the refactoring changes. By clicking on a line in the Refactoring view, the IDE highlights that line in the Code view. This is a convenient way of reviewing the changes prior to the changes being made.

NOTE

If you do not check the View References Before Refactoring check box, the class will be moved automatically. The list of changes and the Undo Refactoring buttons will still be available.

If you check the View References Before Refactoring check box, the class will not be moved automatically, and you will need to click the Refactor button on the command bar.

Another way to move a class from one package to another is through the class's UML tab. The project must be compiled and up-to-date for the UML for the class to be displayed. When it is displayed, you may select the class name and pull up the context-sensitive menu. Figure 7.4 shows the project UML and the context-sensitive menu.

The Move menu item displays the Move Class dialog box shown earlier in Figure 7.2. The remainder of the moving process is the same as described previously.

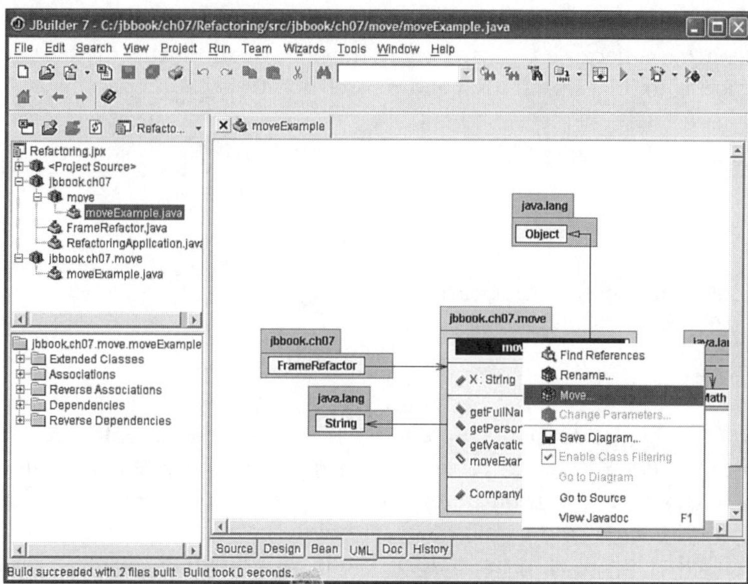

FIGURE 7.4 UML view of the class.

NOTE

After moving a class from the UML view, JBuilder displays a warning message stating that the "Diagram may not be correct because project class files are out of date." This warning tells you that your class needs to be compiled again for the UML view to reflect the changes you have made. If you recompile the class, the UML view will be updated and reflect the new package you assigned your class.

Moving a class from the UML screen provides more visual context information about the class versus the Code view.

Rename Refactor

The rename refactor method allows you to rename a package, class, method, field, variable, and property in your project. The rename refactor method is a sophisticated search and replace mechanism. The renaming has to be done based on what is being renamed, its scope, and its visibility.

For example, suppose that you are reviewing the code in Listing 7.1 and notice that the variable to represent an employee's age is called `X`. `X` does not clearly represent its purpose or follow the coding standards. You intend to change the variable from `X` to `nAgeOfEmployee`. Because `X` is used many times throughout this method, your first inclination is to do a search for `X` and replace it with `nAgeOfEmployee`.

LISTING 7.1 Refactoring a Variable—Concept Code 1

```
...
int X;
...
X = Employee.calcEmployeeAge( dateOfBirth);
System.out.print( "Employee Age" + X);
...
```

Being the intelligent developer, you notice that a search and replace routine may introduce bugs that were not present in the application before the modification. In other words, you do not want to replace every instance of the uppercase letter `X`, but you want to rename your variable `X` according to Java's scoping rules. In Listing 7.2, you notice that `X` is used in multiple methods with different meanings. A search and replace would have to be done intelligently so that you do not accidentally rename a variable being used for a different purpose.

LISTING 7.2 Refactoring a Variable—Concept Code 2

```
getEmployeeAge()
{
...
int X;
...
X = Employee.calcEmployeeAge( dateOfBirth);
System.out.print( "Employee Age" + X);
...
}

setEmployeeName( String X )
{
...
X = Employee.getFullName();
System.out.print( "Employee's Name is" + X);
...
}
...
```

JBuilder's rename refactor capability intelligently searches your code and makes the desired changes. For JBuilder to perform a rename refactor, the source code must be compiled and up-to-date.

JBuilder allows you to rename the following:

- Package
- Class
- Interface
- Method
- Field
- Local variable
- Property

Renaming a Package

JBuilder enables you to rename a package and all the subpackages in a project. When a package is renamed, all code references and import statements are modified to work with the new package name. If a package with the new name already exists, it will not rename the package. In this situation, use the move refactor method to move the classes into the package.

You can rename a package in the Source tab or the UML tab. Figure 7.5 shows the Source tab with the context-sensitive menu open on the `package` statement.

The context-sensitive menu knows that your cursor is on the `package` code line and enables the package Rename Package *packagename* menu option. When you choose Rename Package *packagename* from the pop-up menu, you are presented with the Rename Package dialog box as shown in Figure 7.6.

The Rename Package dialog box enables you to give the new name of the package and gives you the ability to view references before refactoring. The View References Before Refactoring check box opens a Refactoring view of all the references that will be renamed. Figure 7.7 displays the references for the rename procedure prior to the renaming process. The command bar on Figure 7.7 enables you to apply the renaming process or roll back the renaming process.

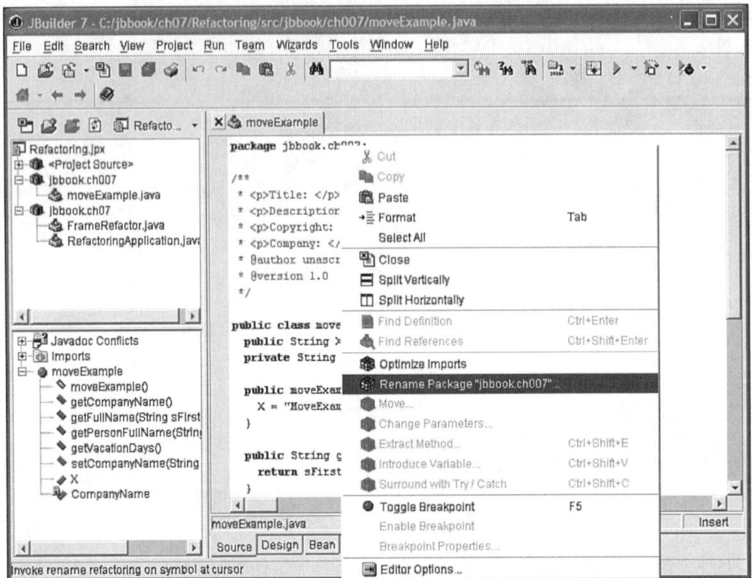

FIGURE 7.5 Context-sensitive menu with Rename highlighted.

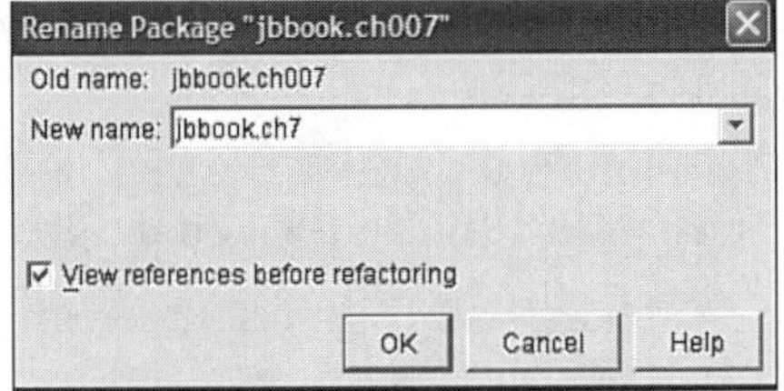

FIGURE 7.6 The Rename Package dialog box.

The Refactoring references view shows all the places in the project that will be modified due to the renaming package process. Clicking on the reference highlights the code that will be modified. In Figure 7.7, the package name will be modified from `jbbook.ch007` to `jbbook.ch7`.

Another way to rename a package is through the UML tab on the Code view window. For the UML tab to display, the project must be compiled and up-to-date. Figure 7.8 shows the UML view of the code shown in Figure 7.7.

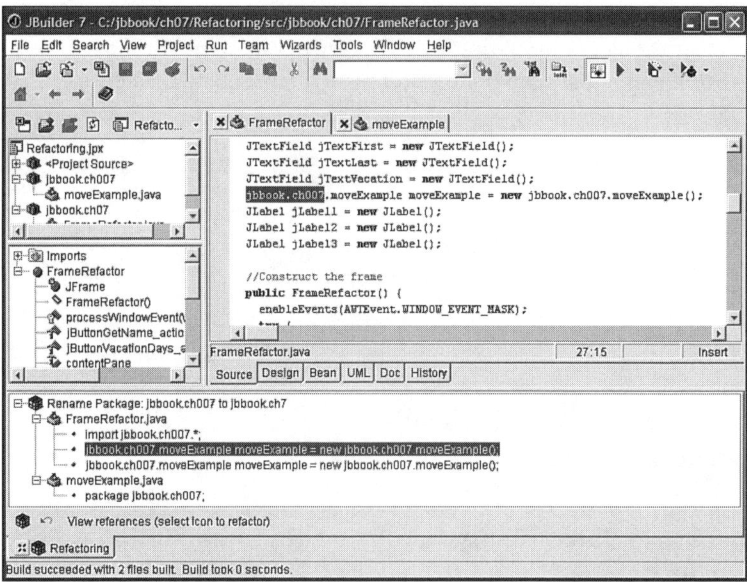

FIGURE 7.7 Refactoring references view.

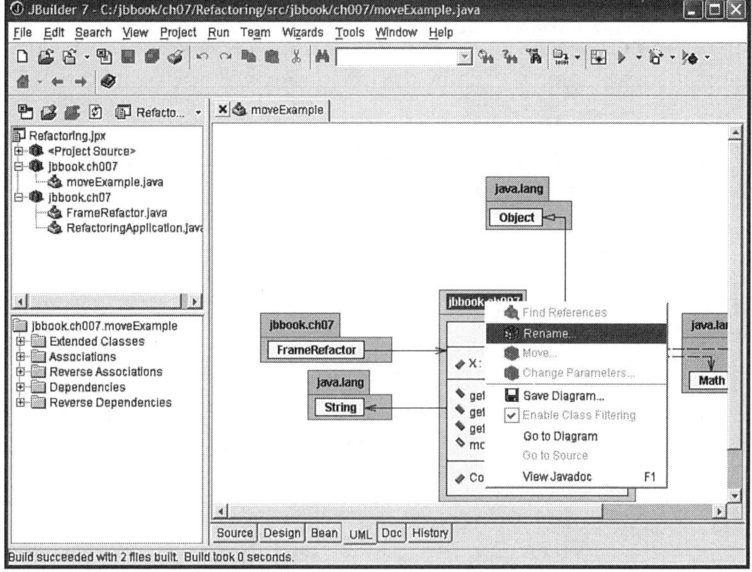

FIGURE 7.8 UML Refactoring view.

By selecting the package name and pulling up the context-sensitive pop-up menu, you can select the Rename menu option. After the Rename menu option has been selected, the Rename Package dialog box shown previously in Figure 7.6 appears.

NOTE

After renaming a class from the UML view, JBuilder displays a warning message stating that the "Diagram may not be correct because project class files are out of date." This warning tells you that your class needs to be compiled again for the UML view to reflect the changes you have made. If you recompile the class, the UML view will be updated and reflect the renamed package you assigned your class.

Renaming a Class or Interface

A class or interface can be renamed in a project.

If the class to be renamed is the public class or interface, a new file with the new name is created for that class. If a class already exists with the new name, the rename class or interface will not be created, and the rename refactor will fail.

If the class is an inner class, the class will be renamed as long as no other inner class exists with that name.

To rename a class or interface, select the class in the Code view to open the context-sensitive pop-up menu. Select the Rename Class *classname* option from the menu. Figure 7.9 shows the selected class in the Code view and the context-sensitive pop-up menu.

After the Rename Class *classname* menu option is selected, the Rename Class dialog box shown in Figure 7.10 appears.

NOTE

The title caption of the dialog box that displays for each rename or move operation displays the scope of the change.

The rest of the renaming process is identical to what is shown in Figure 7.7. You are shown the references to all the code that will be modified to support the renaming of the class.

The renaming of a class can also be done in the UML view of the class. From the context-sensitive pop-up menu in Figure 7.8, select the Rename menu option. The Rename menu option opens the Rename Class dialog box shown in Figure 7.10.

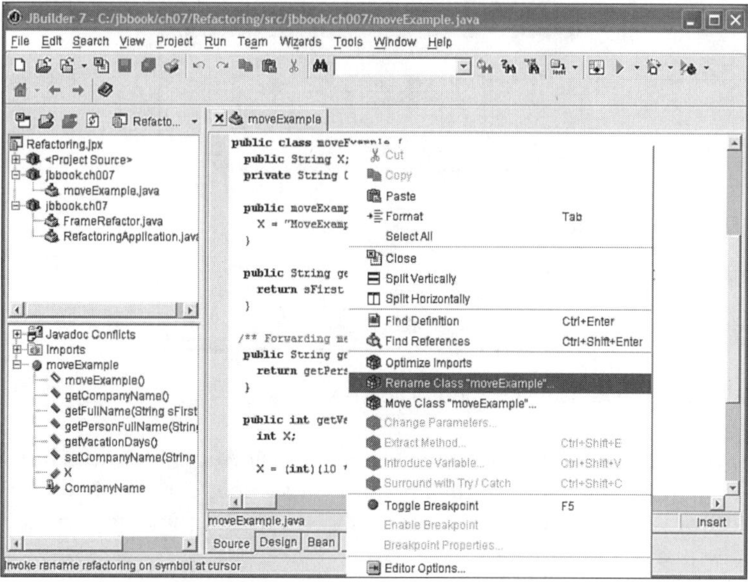

FIGURE 7.9 Rename Class menu.

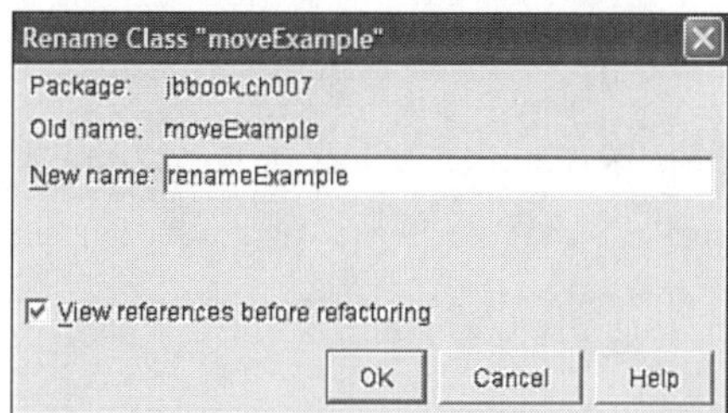

FIGURE 7.10 The Rename Class dialog box.

Renaming a Method

Renaming a method follows the same process as renaming a package or class except that a method is the chosen target for renaming. By selecting the method in the Code view or the UML view, the Rename Method dialog box in Figure 7.11 appears.

The Rename Method dialog box differs from the other rename dialog boxes by adding two options. These two options control the renaming of the method through the project's hierarchy. These additional options are necessary because renaming methods directly affects polymorphism if the methods are overridden.

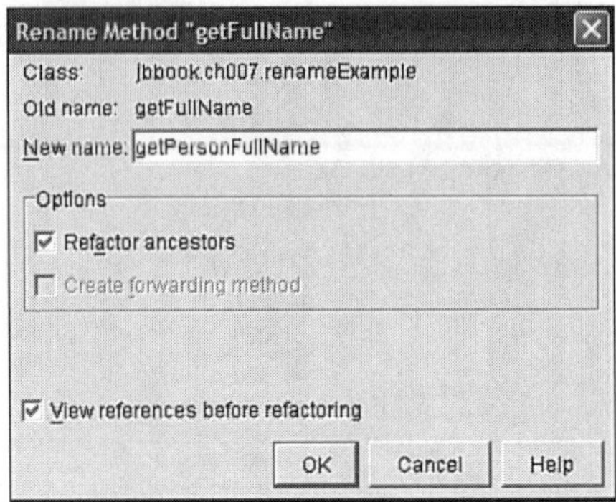

FIGURE 7.11 The Rename Method dialog box.

The first option is Refactor Ancestors. If the Refactor Ancestors check box is selected, JBuilder attempts to rename all the ancestor classes that contain this method. If this option is not selected, JBuilder renames only this method for the current class and all the descendants of this class.

The second option is Create Forwarding Method. The Create Forwarding Method check box renames your method in the class but creates a new method with the old name that forwards the request to the new method. Listing 7.3 shows the code after the Create Forwarding Method option is selected.

LISTING 7.3 Renamed Method and New Forwarding Method

```
 public String getPersonFullName( String sFirst, String sLast) {
   return sFirst + " " + sLast;
 }

/** Forwarding method*/
 public String getFullName(String sFirst, String sLast)  {
   return getPersonFullName(sFirst, sLast);
 }
```

In Listing 7.3, the original method name was `getFullName`. This method was renamed to `getPersonFullName`, and a forwarding method was created.

The Refactor Ancestors option refactors the method name in the entire hierarchy in the current class and all superclasses. The forwarding method allows the public interface to remain the same for applications that are using the class and are not aware of the renamed method. In conjunction with the Java feature of deprecation these two options can be used to elegantly change the architecture of Java code.

Renaming a Field or a Local Variable

Renaming a field or a local variable is almost identical to renaming a package or a class. Renaming a field or a local variable will rename that field or variable based on its scope.

For example, a public field will be changed in other places in the project that reference the field.

To rename a field or a variable, select the field or variable in the source file or the UML view to open the context-sensitive pop-up menu. Select the Rename menu option to begin the renaming process. The title caption of the rename box will be Rename Field or Rename Variable.

The process of renaming a field or variable is identical to the preceding class renaming example. The user has the same options and rollback capabilities.

Renaming a Property

Unlike the other renaming methods discussed previously, renaming a property can be done only from the UML view. In the UML view, a property is represented in the fourth box of a UML class drawing. In Figure 7.12, the property `sCompName` is made up of a private variable, getter method, and setter method. The property name is renamed to `CompanyName`.

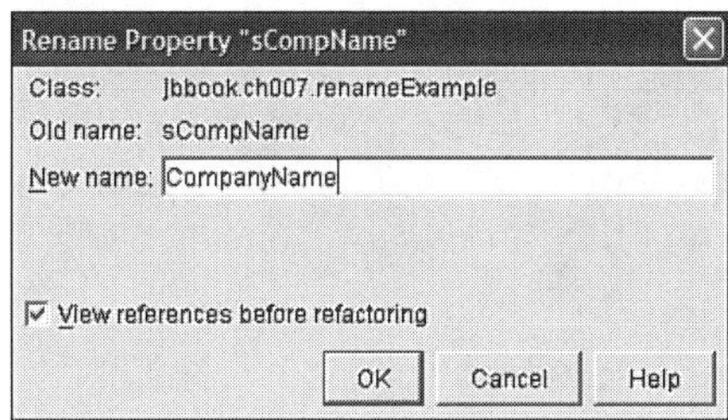

FIGURE 7.12 Rename Property is available only from the UML diagram.

The renaming of a property renames the private variable name, getter, and setter methods for that property. In addition, any other source files in the project that access that property are renamed as well.

Changing Parameters

JBuilder allows you to change a method signature by reordering existing parameters or adding new parameters. By pulling up the context-sensitive pop-up menu on a method, you can select the menu item Change Parameters for *methodname*. Figure 7.13 displays the Change Parameter for Method *methodname* dialog box.

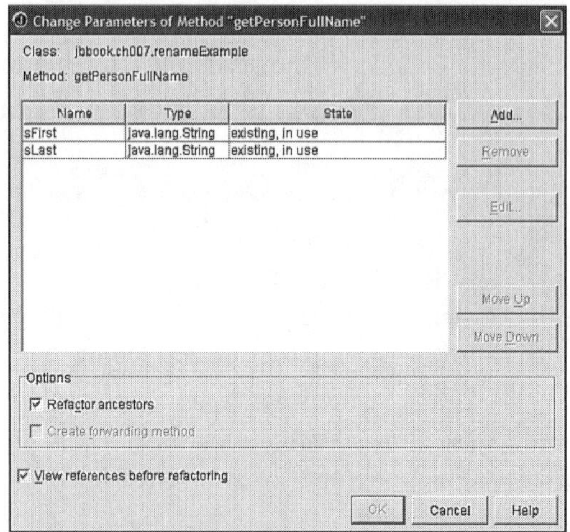

FIGURE 7.13 Change Parameters of Method methodname.

Figure 7.13 displays the method and any existing parameters. Existing parameters can be reordered using the Move Up and Move Down buttons. Existing parameters cannot be removed.

Three options perform identical operations as the Rename Method dialog box. The first option is to Refactor Ancestors. This allows the changing of parameters to propagate up and down through the class hierarchy. The second option maintains the original function interface while adding the new method signature. The original method calls the new method signature. The third option is to View references before refactoring. Selecting this option shows you the code that will be changed by changing the method's parameters.

To add a new parameter to the method, select the Add button. Figure 7.14 displays the Add New Parameter dialog box.

FIGURE 7.14 The Add New Parameter dialog box.

The Add New Parameter dialog box allows you to add a new parameter to the method. The Type field defines the parameter's data type. The Name field lets you assign a name to the parameter. The Default Value field assigns a default value to the new parameter. The default value will be added to the method calls in your project.

Extract Method

When reviewing code, you may encounter a situation where a defined method is extremely long and performing many actions. JBuilder lets you select portions of the code and extract them into a separate method. JBuilder determines parameters, local variables, and the return type.

JBuilder also determines whether the selected lines of code can be refactored. For example, if more than one variable is written to or read after the selected code, the method cannot be refactored automatically.

Figure 7.15 selected some code for the extract method. Notice how the selected code fills in the Statements field in the Extract Method dialog box.

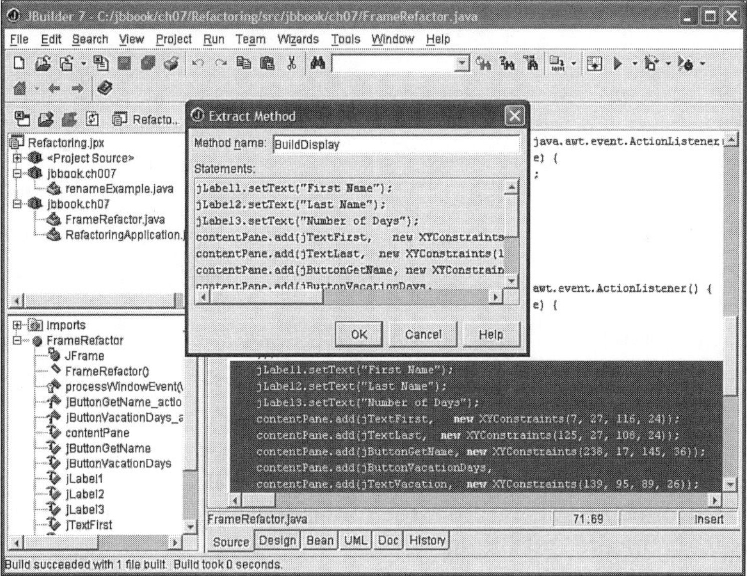

FIGURE 7.15 The Extract method.

Figure 7.15 resulted in a new method being added to the code named *BuildDisplay*. The new method contains the highlighted code, and the highlighted code is replaced with the method call.

Introduce Variable

To increase readability and sometimes to increase performance, introducing temporary variables into a method is necessary. For example, consider the code in Listing 7.4.

LISTING 7.4 Calculate Vacation Days

```
public int getVacationDays( ) {
 int X;

 X = (int)(10 * java.lang.Math.random());

 if (X + 2 < 5 )
 {
   return X + 2;
 }
 if (X + 2 > 5 )
 {
   return X + 2 - (X + 2) / 7;
 }

 if (X + 2 == 5)
 {
   return 5;
 }
   return X;
 }
```

In Listing 7.4, notice the number of times that `X + 2` is used. Every time that expression is evaluated, a calculation takes place. Calculations are typically one of the more CPU-intensive operations.

By using Introduce Variable, a temporary variable can be created to replace the expression `X + 2`. To display the Introduce Variable dialog box, select the expression and choose Introduce Variable from the context-sensitive pop-up menu. Figure 7.16 displays the Introduce Variable dialog box.

Figure 7.16 allows you to name the introduced variable. The Type field displays the data type for the expression contained in the Expression field. The option Include all read expressions substitutes the introduced variable name for all occurrences of the expression within the defined scope. Listing 7.5 shows the code after introducing a temporary variable for the expression.

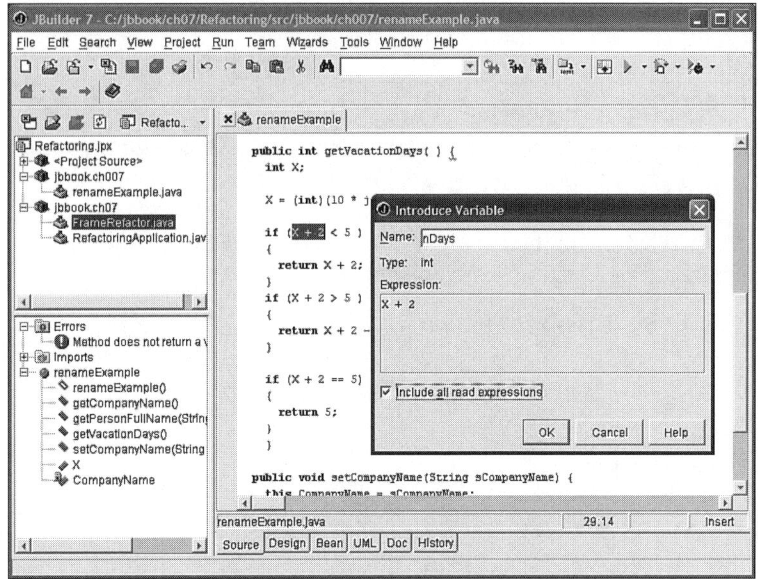

FIGURE 7.16 Introduce Variable.

LISTING 7.5 Calculate Vacation Days (after Introduce Variable)

```
public int getVacationDays( ) {
  int X;

  X = (int)(10 * java.lang.Math.random());

  int nDays = X + 2;
  if (nDays < 5 )
  {
    return nDays;
  }
  if (nDays > 5 )
  {
    return nDays - (nDays) / 7;
  }
  if (nDays == 5)
  {
    return 5;
  }
    return X;
  }
```

The variable `nDays` has replaced all the `X + 2` expressions.

Optimize Imports

Optimize Imports is a coding enhancement that makes managing your code easier. When creating an application, you add and remove classes from your code resulting in a list of used and unused `import` statements at the top of your class. The Optimize Imports capability of JBuilder removes unused imports from your class and rewrites the import sections based on customizable settings.

Listing 7.6 shows a class with imports.

LISTING 7.6 Imports in FrameRefactor.java

```
import java.awt.*;
import java.awt.event.*;
import javax.swing.*;
import com.borland.jbcl.layout.*;
import jbbook.ch07.move.*;
import jbbook.ch007.*;
```

From the context-sensitive pop-up menu, select Optimize Imports. JBuilder evaluates your class and optimizes the import section based on the required imports. Listing 7.7 shows the same import section after Optimize Imports has been selected.

LISTING 7.7 Optimize Imports on FrameRefactor.java

```
import com.borland.jbcl.layout.*;
import java.awt.*;
import java.awt.event.*;
import javax.swing.*;
```

Because the application was no longer using classes from the jbbook.ch07.move.* and jbbook.ch007.*, they were removed. The import section was rewritten, and some of the `import` statements were moved around.

The order of the `import` statements and the class qualification statements can be controlled through the Project, Project Properties menu. Figure 7.17 displays the Import Style tab of the Project Properties dialog box.

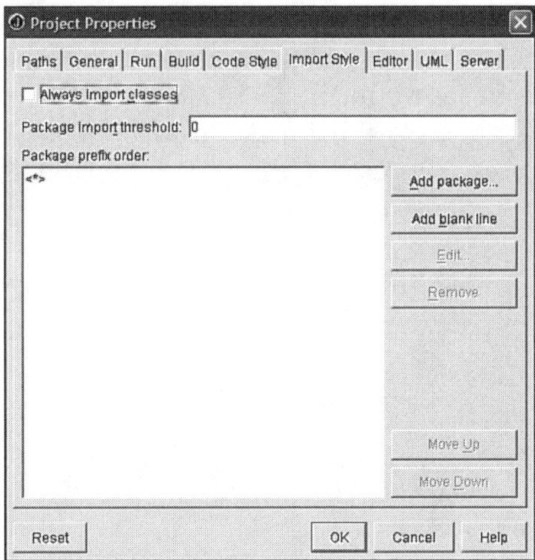

FIGURE 7.17 The Import Style tab.

The package prefix order in Figure 7.17 allows you to specify the ordering of the `import` statements when the Optimize Imports command is executed. Packages and blank lines can be added to the package prefix order to customize the generation of the import section.

The option Always import classes controls whether individual classes are imported. With this option selected, the import section shown in Listing 7.7 would be rewritten during Optimize Imports. The rewritten import section is shown in Listing 7.8.

LISTING 7.8 Always Import Classes Option on FrameRefactor.java

```
import com.borland.jbcl.layout.XYConstraints;
import com.borland.jbcl.layout.XYLayout;
import java.awt.AWTEvent;
import java.awt.Dimension;
import java.awt.event.ActionEvent;
import java.awt.event.WindowEvent;
import javax.swing.JButton;
import javax.swing.JFrame;
import javax.swing.JLabel;
import javax.swing.JOptionPane;
import javax.swing.JPanel;
import javax.swing.JTextField;
```

The individual classes used in the class are explicitly named in the import section rather than a wildcard. When the option Always import classes is not selected, the package import threshold shown in Figure 7.17 is used. The package import threshold refers to the number of classes that must be added to an import section before the `import` statement uses a wildcard. Listing 7.9 is the import section with the threshold set to four.

LISTING 7.9 Package Import Threshold on FrameRefactor.java

```
import com.borland.jbcl.layout.XYConstraints;
import com.borland.jbcl.layout.XYLayout;
import java.awt.AWTEvent;
import java.awt.Dimension;
import java.awt.event.ActionEvent;
import java.awt.event.WindowEvent;
import javax.swing.*;
```

The threshold setting removes the multiple `javax.swing` classes and replaces them with a wildcard. Had there been one more `java.awt` class added to the import section, the Optimize Imports would have replaced the classes with a wildcard.

Surround with Try/Catch

Surround with Try/Catch is another coding enhancement provided by JBuilder. Surround with Try/Catch is accessible from the context-sensitive pop-up menu during code editing.

JBuilder detects all exceptions for a highlighted set of lines. After detecting the possible exceptions, JBuilder places `try` and `catch` statements around the highlighted lines.

Listing 7.10 displays sample code that makes a call to the database. Most database calls return a `SQLException` if there are any problems.

LISTING 7.10 Sample Database Code

```
      stmtCommand.executeUpdate("insert into JDBCSample values('Michael', 45)");
      stmtCommand.executeUpdate("insert into JDBCSample values('Jeff', 22)");
      stmtCommand.executeUpdate("insert into JDBCSample values('Saleem', 36)");
```

Listing 7.11 displays the same code shown in Listing 7.10 after applying the Surround with Try/Catch. JBuilder examines the lines of code and determines that a `SQLException` can occur. The code is surrounded with a `try` and `catch`.

LISTING 7.11 Sample Database Code After Surround with Try/Catch

```
try {
  stmtCommand.executeUpdate("insert into JDBCSample values('Michael', 45)");
  stmtCommand.executeUpdate("insert into JDBCSample values('Jeff', 22)");
  stmtCommand.executeUpdate("insert into JDBCSample values('Saleem', 36)");
}
catch (SQLException ex) {
}
```

In Practice

The following lab focuses on the refactoring capabilities of JBuilder. The exercise moves a class to a new package, renames a class, and renames a variable. After each refactoring, you run the application to verify that the application has not been broken.

Step 1: Opening the Example Project and Reviewing the Code

To open the example project,

1. Select File, Open Project from the JBuilder menu.
2. Locate the jbbook/ch07/refactoring/Refactoring.jpx file and click OK.
3. The project opens in the Project pane. The project consists of three files in two packages. The project files are
    - moveExample.java—The file containing the `moveExample` class that is called by the main frame window. This file belongs to the package `jbbook.ch007`.
    - FrameRefactor.java—The file containing the main window frame and calls the `moveExample` class. This file belongs to the package `jbbook.ch07`.
    - RefactoringApplication.java—The file that sets up the application and creates the `FrameRefactor` window. This file belongs to the package `jbbook.ch07`.
4. Double-click on the moveExample.java file. The Content pane displays the file. Review the contents of this file.
5. Run the project. Type in a first name and a last name. Click the Get Full Name button. A message box with the full name appears. Click the Get Vacations Days button, and a number appears in the text box to the left of the button. The number is random.

Step 2: Moving the Class `moveExample`

To move the class `moveExample` from the `jbbook.ch007` package to the `jbbook.ch07` package, do the following:

1. Make sure that the application has been stopped and the moveExample.java file is displayed in the Content pane. Right-click on the RefactoringApplication tab at the bottom of the screen and select the Remove All Tabs option.
2. Place the cursor on the line

   ```
   public class moveExample
   ```

3. Click the right mouse button to display the context-sensitive pop-up menu. Select the Move option from the menu.
4. The Move Class dialog box as shown previously in Figure 7.2 appears. Change the To Package name from `jbbook.ch007` to `jbbook.ch07`. Make sure that the View References Before Refactoring check box is selected. Click OK when ready.
5. In the Refactoring view, expand the changes that will be made to the moveExample.java and FrameRefactor.java files. Review the changes. When ready, click the Refactor icon on the command bar.
6. If successful, the Project pane should now show only one package, `jbbook.ch07`. The package `jbbook.ch007` is no longer available.
7. Run the application and confirm that it still works.
8. Right-click on the RefactoringApplication tab at the bottom of the screen and select the Remove All Tabs option.

Step 3: Renaming the Class `moveExample`

Rename the class `moveExample` to `renameExample` and then undo it as follows:

1. Make sure that the application has been stopped and the moveExample.java file appears in the Content pane.
2. Select the UML tab at the bottom of the Code view screen.
3. Click on the `moveExample` class name in the UML diagram.
4. Click the right mouse button to display the context-sensitive pop-up menu. Select the Rename option from the menu.
5. The Rename Class dialog box should be displayed. This box is similar to Figure 7.10. Set the New Name value to `renameExample`.

6. Make sure that the View References Before Refactoring check box is *not* selected. Click OK when ready. The code will automatically be refactored.
7. JBuilder should have displayed a warning message that the "Diagram may not be correct because the project class files are out of date." Click OK.
8. Click on the Source tab at the bottom of the Content pane. Check that the class has been modified to `renameExample`.
9. Run the application and make sure that it works.
10. Select the Refactoring tab at the bottom of the page. Click on the Undo button. The application will undo the rename operation, and the class will be named `moveExample` again.
11. Run the application and make sure that it works.
12. Right-click on the RefactoringApplication tab at the bottom of the screen and select the Remove All Tabs option.

Step 4: Renaming a Variable

Rename a variable to give it context meaning:

1. Make sure that the application has been stopped and the moveExample.java file is displayed in the Content pane.
2. Locate the method `getVacationDays`.
3. Place the cursor right before the `X` on the line

    ```
    int X;
    ```

4. Click the right mouse button to display the context-sensitive pop-up menu. Select the Rename option from the menu.
5. The Rename Variable dialog box appears. Make sure that the title of the dialog box says Rename Variable X. If it does not say this, go back to step 2 and start again.
6. Change the name of the variable `X` to `nVacationDays` by typing `nVacationDays` into the New Name field.
7. Make sure that the View References Before Refactoring check box is *not* selected. Click OK when ready. The code will automatically be refactored.

8. Verify that the code for the method `getVacationDays` has been modified to the following code:

```
public int getVacationDays( ) {
  int nVacationDays;

  nVacationDays = (int)(10 * java.lang.Math.random());

  return nVacationDays;
  }
```

9. Run the application and make sure that it works.

Summary

Refactoring code is an old idea that has been getting a new look. JBuilder's IDE is only getting better at supporting code refactoring. If you are ambitious, you can extend JBuilder's IDE to support other refactoring methods.

This chapter showed you simple code and the rename and move refactor methods. Refactoring makes much more sense in large projects with hundreds of classes. Think of the time savings of having an automatic way to rename a method or class that increases the developers' understanding of the code!

Reflections

- When would creating a forwarding method during a rename refactoring be appropriate?
- Say that you were authoring a Java interface `javax.servlet.http.HttpServletResponse`. You name two of the methods in that interface `encodeUrl` and `encodeRedirectUrl`. Later, you realize that better names for the methods would be `encodeURL` and `encodeRedirectURL`, respectively (with the acronym spelled in uppercase letters). How would you use JBuilder's refactoring options, together with the deprecation feature of Java, to make this change?

8 Documenting in JBuilder

IN THIS CHAPTER

- Adding Comments
- Javadoc Tags
- Javadoc Provides More than Documentation
- Documentation Doesn't Match Code
- Automatic Javadoc Templates
- Using the JavaDoc Wizard
- Design Guidelines

The Java SDK comes with a tool that allows technical documentation and source code to be combined into one. As a developer completes coding, coding usually takes the highest priority; hence the technical documentation tends to remain incomplete. Often, the documentation is done after the fact, when the greatest benefit for its use has passed. The utility to accomplish integrated documentation is called `Javadoc`. This utility generates HTML documentation based on the comments defined within the source. Note the phrase "within the source"—the comments are not in a separate file. JBuilder supports many different capabilities to keep you productive even in the creation and management of documentation.

This chapter covers the following list of the capabilities provided by `Javadoc` within the JBuilder environment:

- Comment template that enables you to add many common commenting elements
- Template for adding `@todo` tags
- Management of `Javadoc` comment conflicts
- Document viewer to generate `Javadoc` on-the-fly documentation
- `Javadoc` generation documentation archiving with the Archive Builder

Adding Comments

You can add many different types of `Javadoc` comments to your application source. The application source can contain documentation at many different levels: class and interface as well as methods, constructors, and attributes. When these special comments are merged with the source code, the Javadoc utility follows a few simple rules to dynamically build the documentation. The identifying mark of a Javadoc comment is /** at the start of the comment and */ at the end. Listing 8.1 is an example of Javadoc commenting tags within a source file, and Figure 8.1 displays the documentation generated.

LISTING 8.1 Java Code Including Javadoc

```
package designerdemo;

/**
 * <p>Title: Demo Designer</p>
 * <p>Description: JBuilder Developers Guide</p>
 * <p>Copyright: Copyright (c) 2002</p>
 * <p>Company: Dunn Solutions Group</p>
 * @author unascribed
 * @version 1.0
 */

public class Employee {

  public Employee() {
  }
  /**
  Raise the salary of an employee a given percentage.
  @param percentRaise  This is the percentage for which
➥ the raise will be applied (e.g. 25%)
  @return The total amount of the employees new raise
  */
  public double raise(double percentRaise)
  {
    Return (0.0);
  }
}
```

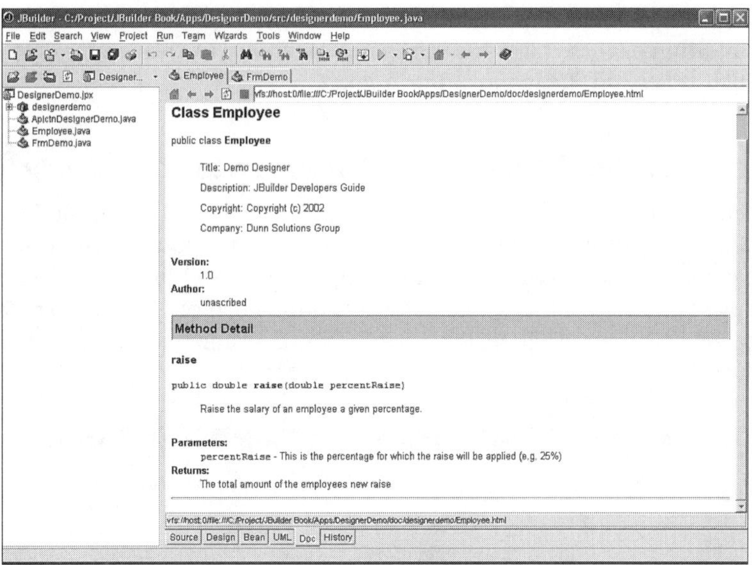

FIGURE 8.1 When you click on the Doc tab, JBuilder produces documentation using the `Javadoc` on-the-fly parser.

Javadoc Tags

`Javadoc` contains many tags to customize the expansion and control of the generation of your documentation. JBuilder generates some of these tags automatically such as `@author` or `@version`. Table 8.1 presents a list of many frequently used tags (for a complete list see `http://java.sun.com` for your specific version of the JDK).

TABLE 8.1 Javadoc Tags Available within Java Source

Tag	Description
`@author` *`name`*	Identifies the primary author for a class
`[@docroot]`	Identifies the generated document's root directory for the generated documentation
`@version` *`version`*	Captures the current version of the source code
`@param` *`param description`*	Generates the parameter list for a method
`@return` *`param`*	Generates information about the return variables
`@depreciated` *`text`*	Indicates that this API call is depreciated
`@exception` *`class`*	Documents the exceptions thrown
`@throws` *`class`*	Documents the exceptions thrown
`@see reference`	Identifies cross references

We will look later at the implementation and usage of these tags within the JBuilder IDE. In addition to these tags, you also have the ability to create your own custom tags, which is beyond the scope of this book.

Javadoc Provides More than Documentation

One often overlooked JBuilder Javadoc tag is the @todo tag. In fact, JBuilder has some additional features that give the @todo tag an extra punch. When the @todo tags are placed inside a Javadoc comment, they appear in JBuilder's Structure pane under a new folder. The To Do folder appears only when one or more @todo tags are present within that source file. Figure 8.2 shows an example of the @todo tag in a JBuilder project.

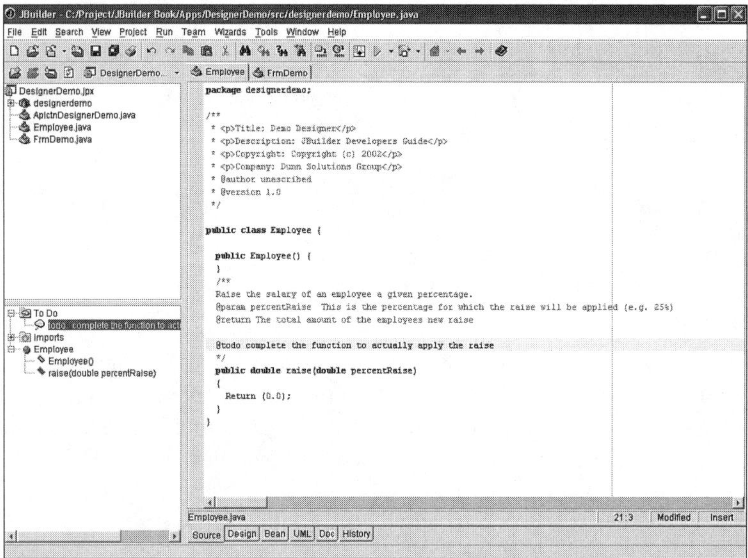

FIGURE 8.2 When you click on the @todo tag, it automatically highlights the to-do task.

To add the @todo tag, add this to your code:

1. Type **todo** in the position where you want the tag.
2. Press Ctrl+J. The @todo tag then expands in your code to the following:

```
/** @todo */
```

Documentation Doesn't Match Code

How often have you looked at technical documentation only to find that it does not come close to matching the real thing? Wouldn't it be nice if when the documentation did not match the code, you received an error or at least an indication of the inconsistency? That is what JBuilder offers to developers. As JBuilder parses the Javadoc tags, it searches for mismatches between the source definition and the Javadoc definition. For example, if you only document one parameter, but two parameters are defined for the method signature, you will receive an error. Let's take a look at an example in Figure 8.3.

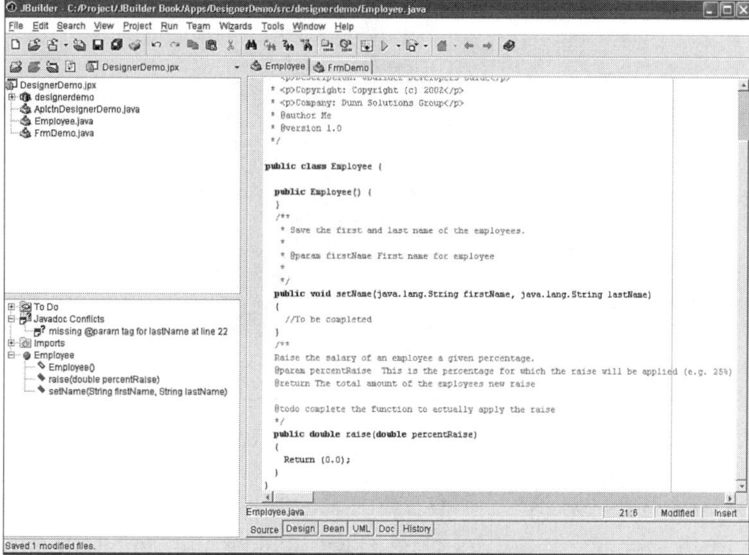

FIGURE 8.3 The Structure pane identifies the Javadoc conflict and even describes the problem.

These Javadoc mismatches can be resolved one conflict at a time. As the mismatches are corrected, they are removed from the conflicts list.

Automatic Javadoc Templates

JBuilder gives you a number of templates (such as class, function, or member) for documenting with Javadoc tags. The ingenious part is that you do not have to remember many different commands. You use the same command, and the result changes within the contextual location of the comment. The command is simple; just type /** and press Enter. JBuilder automatically creates the appropriate Javadoc comment for the given context. Table 8.2 presents a list of the behavior of the expansion based on its context.

TABLE 8.2 Demonstrate the Expansion of /** Based on the Given Context

Context	Sample Result
Before a class or interface definition	/** * * <p>Title: Demo Designer</p> * <p>Description: Jbuilder Developers Guide</p> * <p>Copyright: Copyright (c) 2002</p> * <p>Company: SAMS Publishing/p> * @author unascribed * @version 1.0 */
Before a method	/** * * @param percentRaise * @return * @throws Exception */
Before an attribute	/** * */

Using the JavaDoc Wizard

Besides the on-the-fly parsing of Javadoc tags, JBuilder also contains a wizard to generate a documentation node within your project. This node contains all the information required to create the Javadoc-generated files. The properties defined for the Javadoc node include items such as the following:

- Format of the output
- Name of the documentation node
- Output directory
- Javadoc build trigger
- Scope of the documentation
- Tags to process

This wizard differs from the on-the-fly parsing in a number of different ways. The most noticeable, though, is the completeness of the documentation generated. It generates documentation not only for an individual class, but also for all the classes and their interrelationships as well. In addition to the documentation being more complete, index pages and a table of contents are also generated by the wizard. After the initial node in the project is created, you can change its properties by entering into the node properties.

The `Javadoc` Wizard is divided into four main steps. These steps ultimately construct a node in your project with the given parameters specified. The first step, shown in Figure 8.4, is to identify the output format of the `Javadoc`-generated files.

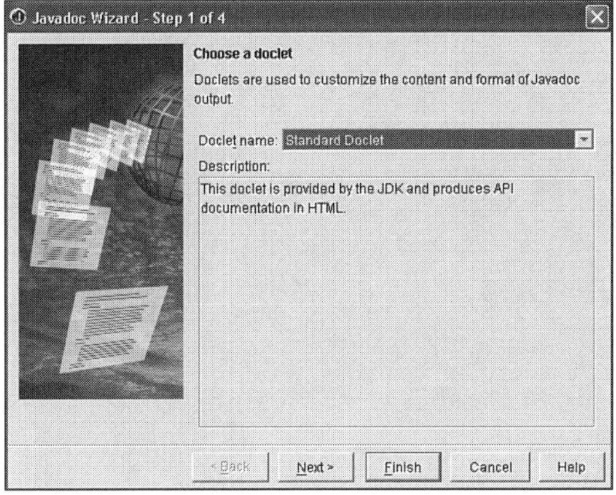

FIGURE 8.4 Step 1: Identify the doclet format you want.

JBuilder supports two primary doclet formats, although you may construct your own `Javadoc` parser and support your own format. One is the JDK 1.1 format; the second is the JDK 1.3 format. The two doclets use completely different directory and naming structures. JBuilder determines at design time which one to display. The following list, in order of priority of format to display, represents the different documentation formats supported by JBuilder:

- JDK 1.3—generated documentation (standard doclet)
- JDK 1.1—generated documentation
- On-the-fly documentation

NOTE

The doclet choice you make corresponds to command-line options that JBuilder passes to the `Javadoc` utility. This way, JBuilder gives a more intuitive interface to the `Javadoc` parser.

The following steps are the options provided by the JavaDoc Wizard as shown in Figure 8.5:

1. Enter the name of the node you want to add to the project. Typically, you should change the name to be more descriptive.
2. Supply an output directory where the documentation will be generated. The output directory will be set to the default properties in the Project Properties dialog box (select Project, Project Properties).

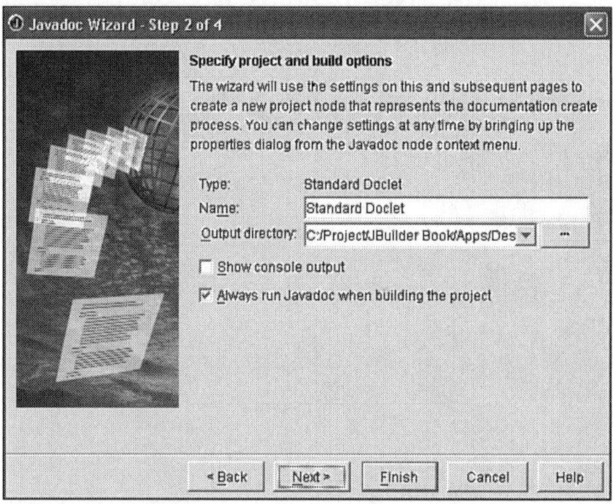

FIGURE 8.5 Step 2: Specify the project and build options.

NOTE

Typically you should store the documentation in a different directory from the source code.

3. Show Console Output displays the runtime parsing of the `Javadoc` standard output. This is the same as specifying the `-verbose` flag on the command line.
4. Always Run `Javadoc` When Building the Project creates new generated documentation every time the project is rebuilt. If this check box is unselected, you must manually remake the `JavaDoc` generated documentation.

The package and visibility level lets you proactively decide which portions of a project are going to be parsed by `Javadoc` (see Figure 8.6). In most situations, the entire project is selected; but in some instances, you may want to have separate documentation for the different logical tiers of your project. For example, you may want to have server persistence documented separately from business rules and utilities. Two different package visibilities are available:

- Entire Project—This option is on by default and tells `Javadoc` to document the entire project.
- Package Level—Using the Add and Remove buttons you can specify which packages you want to include.

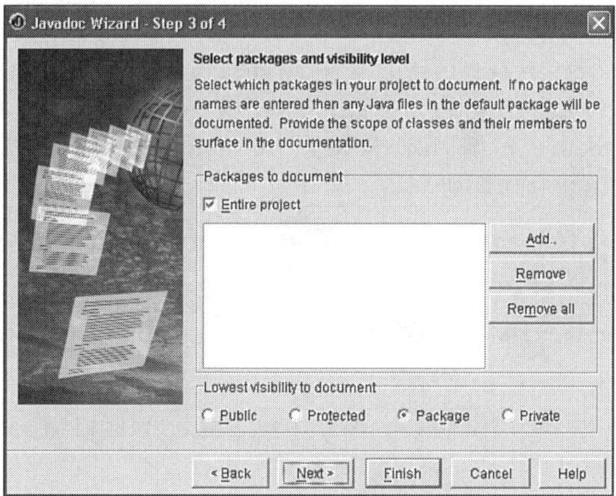

FIGURE 8.6 Step 3: Select packages and visibility level.

The visibility level instructs `Javadoc` to include the methods and attributes in the generated documentation. The following is the list of rules:

- Public—Includes only the public classes in the documentation. This is the same as using the `-public` switch on the `Javadoc` command line.
- Protected—Includes only the public and protected classes in the documentation. This is the same as adding `-protected` to the `Javadoc` command line.
- Package—Includes only the public, protected, and package classes in the documentation. This is the same as adding `-package` to the `Javadoc` command line. This option is the default and typically is the option selected.
- Private—Includes all classes in the documentation. This is the same as adding `-private` to the `Javadoc` command line.

The following, demonstrated in Figure 8.7, is a list of options available to change the results of the generated documentation:

- Generate hierarchy tree—The tree is a list of all packages, classes, and interfaces in the generated documentation. This tree is stored in `overview-tree.html` in the root of the documentation path.

- Generate navigation bar—A navigation bar includes links to the next and previous packages and classes. This bar is used for easy navigation.
- Generate index—An index will be created containing each method, field, package, class, and interface. This index is similar to the index in the back of this book. The index is stored in `index-all.html`, again in the root documentation path.
- `@use`—If this option is selected, a separate Use page is generated for each package and one for each class and interface. For packages, the file will be called `package-use.html`; for classes, the name will be `class-use/classname.html`.
- `@author`, `@version`, `@deprecated`—These options will either generate or ignore these tags.
- Generate `@deprecated list`—If selected, a list of all the deprecated items will be produced.
- Additional options—These commands are directly added to the `javadoc` command line.

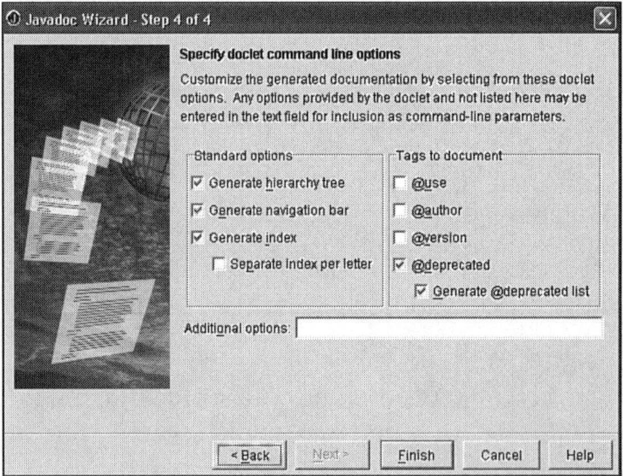

FIGURE 8.7 Step 4: Specify doclet command-line options.

JBuilder uses the `Javadoc` utility to generate all the requested documentation using the parameters specified in the documentation node. All the `Javadoc`-generated files are produced in HTML format. Table 8.3 gives a summary of the generated files.

TABLE 8.3 All Files Generated by Javadoc

Filename	Description
classname.html	Each class or interface in your project.
package-summary.html	A file for each package in your project.
overview-summary.html	A file containing the entire set of packages.
overview-tree.html	The class hierarchy for all the packages.
package-tree.html	Class hierarchy for each individual package.
package-use.html	A file for every package, class, and interface. The `@use` option indicates the creation or suppression of this file.
deprecated-list.html	This file contains all the deprecated names. Similar to the previous option, if `@deprecated` is not specified, the creation of this file will be suppressed.
index-*.htm	This file contains every class, interface, and field.
help-doc.html	This file describes the navigation of the documentation files.
index.html	Creates the frame page for the documentation.

Let's take a look at a sample source code using a number of different `Javadoc` features. The example is supplied with a JBuilder installation, shown in Listing 8.2. As you look through the source code, notice all the different `Javadoc` tags.

LISTING 8.2 Example of Integrated Javadoc Documentation

```
/**
 * Copyright (c) 1997-2002 Borland Software Corporation. All Rights Reserved.
 *
 * This SOURCE CODE FILE, which has been provided by Borland as part
 * of a Borland product for use ONLY by licensed users of the product,
 * includes CONFIDENTIAL and PROPRIETARY information of Borland.
 *
 * USE OF THIS SOFTWARE IS GOVERNED BY THE TERMS AND CONDITIONS
 * OF THE LICENSE STATEMENT AND LIMITED WARRANTY FURNISHED WITH
 * THE PRODUCT.
 *
 * IN PARTICULAR, YOU WILL INDEMNIFY AND HOLD BORLAND, ITS RELATED
 * COMPANIES AND ITS SUPPLIERS, HARMLESS FROM AND AGAINST ANY CLAIMS
 * OR LIABILITIES ARISING OUT OF THE USE, REPRODUCTION, OR DISTRIBUTION
 * OF YOUR PROGRAMS, INCLUDING ANY CLAIMS OR LIABILITIES ARISING OUT OF
 * OR RESULTING FROM THE USE, MODIFICATION, OR DISTRIBUTION OF PROGRAMS
 * OR FILES CREATED FROM, BASED ON, AND/OR DERIVED FROM THIS SOURCE
 * CODE FILE.
 */
```

LISTING 8.2 Continued

```
package com.borland.samples.micro.stopwatch;

import javax.microedition.lcdui.*;

/**
 * <p>This file creates a Main Menu for our StopWatch MIDlet by extending
 * javax.microedition.lcdui.List.  There will be two choices in our menu:</p>
 * <ul>
 *   <li>Run StopWatch: Will load the main StopWatchDisplay screen.</li>
 *   <li>Options: Will load the Options screen to allow user to select time
 *     display format.</li>
 * </ul>
 */
public class MainMenu extends List implements CommandListener {

  // --- Class Constants ----------------------------------------------------//
  // These are our menu choices that will be in our List.
  private static final String[] MENU_CHOICES = new String[2];
  static {
    MENU_CHOICES[0] = "Run StopWatch";
    MENU_CHOICES[1] = "Options";
  };

  // --- Class Variables ----------------------------------------------------//
  // (none)

  // --- Instance Variables -------------------------------------------------//
  // StopWatch screen.  (the screen that displays the actual stopwatch time).
  private StopWatchDisplay stopWatchDisplay = new StopWatchDisplay(this);

  // Options screen to allow user to set preferences.
  private Options optionsScreen = new Options(this);


  // --- Constructors -------------------------------------------------------//
  /**
   * <p>Construct the displayable.</p>
   */
  public MainMenu() {
    // Create a new List containing our defined menu choices.  We will title
    // our list "StopWatch Menu".
    super("StopWatch Menu",  // List title.
```

LISTING 8.2 Continued

```
        List.IMPLICIT,        // List type.
        MENU_CHOICES,         // Our defined array of menu choices.
        null);                // Images.  (we're not including any images).

    try {
      // Initialize the visual elements of this list.
      jbInit();
    }
    catch(Exception e) {
      e.printStackTrace();
    }
  }

  // --- Class Methods ------------------------------------------------------//
  /**
   * <p>Component initialization.</p>
   */
  private void jbInit() throws Exception {

    // Set up this Displayable to listen to command events.
    setCommandListener(this);

    // Add the Exit command for quitting the MIDlet.
    addCommand(new Command("Exit", Command.EXIT, 1));
  }

  /**
   * <p>Handle command events.</p>
   * @param command      a Command object identifying the command
   * @param displayable  the Displayable on which this event has occurred
   */
  public void commandAction(Command command, Displayable displayable) {
    // First, get the type of command that was just received.
    int commandType = command.getCommandType();

    // Now perform an action based on the type of command received.
    if (commandType == Command.EXIT) {
      // We just received the EXIT command (user just pressed EXIT), so quit
      // the MIDlet.
      StopWatch.quitApp();
    }
```

LISTING 8.2 Continued

```
    else {
      // User must have selected one of the menu items.  Find out what is
      // selected and display the appropriate screen.
      String selectedItem = getString(getSelectedIndex());

      if (selectedItem.equals(MENU_CHOICES[0])) {
        // Show the StopWatch screen.
        Display.getDisplay(StopWatch.instance).setCurrent(stopWatchDisplay);
      }
      else if (selectedItem.equals(MENU_CHOICES[1])) {
        // Show the Options screen.
        Display.getDisplay(StopWatch.instance).setCurrent(optionsScreen);
      }
    }
  }

  /**
   * <p>Retrieves the selected display format from the options screen.</p>
   * @return time display format
   */
  public int getDisplayFormat() {
    return optionsScreen.getDisplayFormat();
  }

  /**
   * <p>Sets the selected display format in the options screen.</p>
   * @param format  time display format
   */
  public void setDisplayFormat(int format) {
    optionsScreen.setDisplayFormat(format);
  }

  /**
   * <p>Releases references.  Used when quitting the MIDlet to make sure that
   * all variable references are null.</p>
   */
  void destroy() {
    optionsScreen = null;
    stopWatchDisplay.destroy();
    stopWatchDisplay = null;
  }
}
```

Design Guidelines

Defining design guidelines for documentation is like trying to explain to someone else what art is. The important focus of documentation is to remember that you are communicating the purpose, describing the input/output behavior, and explaining the complexities for a given module. These guidelines are meant to assist you in producing high-quality and descriptive documentation for your modules.

Documentation Usage Focused

It is important to understand the usage of the documentation you are creating so that you can address the appropriate needs of the user. Documentation usage in Java with `Javadoc` is divided into two main categories. Because of these different usages, you should develop or write the documentation comments in a variety of different ways. First we will explore the usage of API specification, and then we will model the design guidelines as a programming guide.

API Specification Usage

API specification focuses only on the public interface of the implementation. It is not as concerned about the inner workings but focuses more on the assumptions and reactions. The de facto standard for style guidelines for generated `Javadoc` is Sun's *How to Write Doc Comments for the* `Javadoc`™ *Tool*. The following is a subset of the style rules for API specification standards:

- The Java Platform API Specification is defined by the documentation comments in the source code and any documents marked as specifications reachable from those comments.

NOTE

Notice that the specification does not need to be entirely contained in doc comments. In particular, lengthy specifications are sometimes best formatted in a separate file and linked to from a doc comment.

- The Java Platform API Specification is a contract between callers and implementations.

  The specification describes all aspects of the behavior of each method on which a caller can rely. It does not describe implementation details, such as whether the method is native or synchronized. The specification should describe (textually) the thread-safety guarantees provided by a given object. In the absence of explicit indication to the contrary, all objects are assumed to be *thread safe*. (It is permissible for multiple threads to access them concurrently.) It is recognized that current specifications don't always live up to this ideal.

- Unless otherwise noted, the Java API Specification assertions need to be implementation independent.
- Exceptions must be set apart and prominently marked.
- The Java API Specification should contain assertions sufficient to enable Software Quality Assurance (SQA) to write complete Java Compatibility Kit (JCK) tests.

  This means that the Javadoc comments must satisfy the needs of the conformance testing by SQA. The comments should not document bugs or how an implementation that is currently out of spec happens to work.

Programming Guide Usage

Traditionally, programming guide usage is influenced by the commenting standards of your organization. The focus of this documentation is to provide the future developer with the necessary tools, documentation, and source code to give the developer insight into maintaining, or correcting his source code.

Style Guide

The following list contains useful tips and conventions for writing descriptions in doc comments:

- Use the <code> HTML style for all keywords and names. The keywords to offset with this tag include Java keywords, packages, classes, methods, interfaces, attributes, arguments, and code examples:

```
/**
* This will include methods from the <code>java.lang</code>
*/
```

- Use hyperlinks or in-links sparingly. API link tags call attention to themselves with different color and font attributes. It may make your comments difficult to follow. Some simple guidelines to follow would include linking only the first occurrence of a method and only including APIs that are not well known.
- When referring to the general form of an overloaded method or constructor, omit the parentheses. This ensures that the signature is generic. If you want to refer to a specific signature, only then specify the signature. Consider the following two examples:

The `add` method enables you to insert items. (Preferred.)

The `add()` method enables you to insert items. (Avoid this use if the generic message is desired.)

- It is acceptable to use phrases rather than complete sentences. The best use for phrases is the documentation of `@param` tags.
- When referring to methods or variables, avoid the use of second person; instead, use third person. This makes the documentation more declarative. Consider the following two examples:

  Gets the database cursor. (Preferred.)

  Get the database cursor. (Avoid this usage.)

- All method descriptions should begin with a verb phrase. In other words, the method must perform some operation, and this is normally represented with a verb phrase. Consider the following two examples:

  Gets the preferred date format. (Preferred.)

  This method gets the preferred date format. (Avoid.)

- Refer to the object created by a class with "this" rather than "the." For example, the documentation for the `getToolkit` method would be

  Gets the toolkit for this component. (Preferred.)

  Gets the toolkit for the component. (Avoid.)

- Make sure that more description of the API is given beyond just repeating the method/attribute name. If you cannot provide relevant information to the user, provide nothing. The comment should provide extra insight into the API usage and results.

  Avoid just repeating the obvious:

```
/**
     * Sets the tool tip text.
     *
     * @param text  The text of the tool tip.
     */
    public void setToolTipText(String text) {
```

A preferred solution completely defines the use of the method:

```
/**
     * Registers the text to display in a tool tip.   The text
     * displays when the cursor lingers over the component.
     *
     * @param text  The string to display.  If the text is null,
     *              the tool tip is turned off for this component.
     */
    public void setToolTipText(String text) {
```

- Be careful when using the term "field," which has two different meanings. A *static field* is another name for a class variable, and a *text field* is a field that holds text.
- Avoid the use of abbreviations. For example, use "also known as" rather than "aka," and use "to be more specific" rather than "i.e."

Summary

Javadoc commenting is a feature-rich and productive way of embedding your documentation and implementation together. This embedding of documentation in code guarantees that the documentation matches the implementation developed. Using JBuilder to help generate the tags is easy and does not take much effort, but the reward of being diligent will save you weeks of documentation after the fact.

In addition to the benefit of helping other developers, documenting your code will also benefit you. Documentation can help return you to the reference point or reasons for why something is done. Time will cause you to forget corrections you have made or the reasons behind them. Documentation will put you back into the context of the code quickly.

Reflections

- What is the importance of placing documentation with code?
- Why should I create different documentation for different audiences?

9 Deployment

IN THIS CHAPTER

- Java Archive Files
- Manifest File
- Java Archive Tool
- JBuilder's Archive Builder
- Design Guidelines

Deploying a Java program is an essential process that does not take long, but is required for every Java program you will ever develop. The deploying of a Java program is nothing more than the bundling of all the resources required for program execution. In this chapter, we will perform the deployment process two different ways: manually, using Sun's `jar` tool, and using JBuilder's Archive Wizard.

NOTE

Only JBuilder's Professional and Enterprise editions include the Archive Wizard, but it is simple to use the `jar` tool that comes with the JDK.

We will cover a number of different issues associated with the deployment of a Java program. We will address the following objectives:

- Java archive files—what they are and how they are used
- Contents and format of a Java Archive Manifest
- Using the JDK `jar` tool to build a Java archive
- Employing the JBuilder Archive Wizard

Java Archive Files

The Java archive file, or JAR file, is the central piece of any deployment. Whether it is a small Java applet or a large enterprise application, you cannot get away from the JAR file. The main purpose of these JAR files is to allow a convenient way to bundle and distribute your application, applet, or JavaBean.

A JAR file is a simple format that many developers already use day in and day out. Actually, a JAR is just a ZIP file with two differences: It has a different extension, and it includes a manifest. Just like a shipping manifest informs the receiver of the contents of a package, the manifest of a JAR informs the user of its contents. The JAR file may bundle many class files, various resource files, property files, or documentation. If you choose to use this JAR format for deployment, you get not one but two types. The first type is just an uncompressed file containing all the resources for an application, and the second type is, you guessed it, a compressed JAR file also containing all the resources.

A JAR file also implements many advanced features; these features are implemented by adding tags to JBuilder's Archive node. Sun has developed documentation to show how the `jar` utility works and the implementation of these advanced features. For more information about all the features in the `jar` utility, see `http://java.sun.com/j2se/1.3/docs/guide/jar/jarGuide.html`.

CAUTION

JDK versions prior to Java 1.1 did not allow the use of JAR files. The deployment units in these versions were plain ZIP files.

Manifest File

As mentioned earlier, the manifest for a JAR is simple information about the classes bundled within a JAR. This manifest must be named `manifest.mf` and is required to be located in the meta-inf/ directory within the JAR.

When using the JBuilder Archive Builder, a default manifest file is generated. The following example of a manifest, Listing 9.1, is for a simple project.

LISTING 9.1 The Required Portion of a Manifest File

```
Manifest-Version: 1.0
```

The manifest version tells the user of the JAR what version of the manifest specification was utilized. Notice, that a manifest does not require any resources to be defined, although this makes the JAR not very useful. For a more practical example, Listing 9.2 is a subset of the JAR file manifest for the `java.math` package.

LISTING 9.2 A Portion of the `java.math` Package Manifest

```
Manifest-Version: 1.0

Name: java/math/BigDecimal.class
SHA1-Digest: SDFSeasf23DFuoD83=
MD5-Digest: z7asf34AB7dJHD89=

Name: java/math/BigInteger.class
SHA1-Digest: SDFSeasf23DFuoD83=
MD5-Digest: z7asf34AB7dJHD89=
```

If an application is bundled within a JAR, the manifest file has to indicate this. The manifest file contains an entry indicating which class contains the main entry point—that is, a class containing a method with the signature `public static void main(String[] args)`. For example, we have a class called `AplctnDemo`:

```
Main-Class: AplctnDemo
```

Java Archive Tool

Sun provides, with the JDK, a tool to create and modify JAR files. The command-line utility is the Java Archive tool (`jar` tool) provided in most versions of the JDK. The `jar` command line has many different parameters to build and modify JAR files. The basic format is as follows:

```
jar cf jar-file input-file(s)
```

After a JAR file is created using the `jar` tool, it is easy to use the contents of the JAR—for example, `CLASSPATH=demoapp/demojar.jar`, or add it to the `-classpath` setting of the `java` command line:

```
Java -classpath demoApp/demojar.jar demoApp.AplctnDemo
```

Table 9.1 shows a list of all the available options for creating a JAR file.

TABLE 9.1 Available Options for the `jar` Utility

Switch	Description
`v`	This switch produces verbose output to `stdout` during the production of the JAR.
`0` (zero)	Specifies that the JAR is not to be compressed.
`M`	Default manifest should not be produced.
`m`	Specifies that the manifest should be created from an existing manifest: `jar cmf existing-manifest-file jar-file input-files`.
`-C`	Change directories during execution of the command.

NOTE

When using version 1.1, the JAR file format supports only ASCII filenames, but version 1.2 supports UTF-8 names. UTF-8 stands for Universal Transformation Format, 8-bit encoding form. It is a transmission format for Unicode that is suitable for use with many network protocols and Unix file systems.

Viewing an Archive

Because an archive file is binary, you cannot list its contents in the way you can list the files in a directory. It is important to have the ability to view the contents of a given archive. The basic format to view the contents of an archive is

```
jar tf jar-file
```

The arguments for viewing an archive are simple. The `t` indicates that you are to view the table of contents of the JAR file. The `f` option informs the utility that the JAR file is passed on the command line. If you omit the `f` option, the `jar` utility will expect a JAR file through `stdin`. Let's look at an example that demonstrates the usage of the `jar` utility:

```
jar tf HelloWorld.jar
```

The results would be displayed to the `stdout`:

```
META-INF/MANIFEST.MF
AplctnHelloWorld.class
fHelloWorld.class
img/world.gif
```

Notice that the archive includes images for our application. The output also shows that the JAR file contains a manifest file, `META-INF/MANIFEST.MF`, which is automatically produced if it is not supplied during the creation of the archive.

Updating an Archive

In addition to creating a JAR file, the `jar` utility contains the functionality to update a JAR file. In addition to adding new resources to the archive, it also modifies the existing manifest within the JAR. The basic command format for updating a JAR is

```
jar uf jar-file input-file(s)
```

The `u` option directs the utility to execute an update of the specified JAR. The `f` indicates to the utility which JAR file to perform the operation on. The `input-file` contains a space-delimited list of all the resources to add to the JAR.

Suppose that you want to add a new image to your JAR. Say that this image is hand.gif in the images directory. You accomplish this task with the following command:

```
jar uf HelloWorld.jar images/hand.gif
```

Extracting an Archive

When extracting files from an archive, the `jar` tool simply makes a copy of the contents of the JAR and writes them to the current directory. The basic format for extracting the contents of a JAR is as follows:

```
jar xf jar-file
```

The `x` option directs the utility to extract the contents of the archive, whereas the `f` option indicates which JAR file to extract from.

> **CAUTION**
>
> Be cautious when extracting the files. The utility overwrites any files that already exist, without any warning!

Suppose that you want to extract from HelloWorld.jar the file named `fHelloWorld.class`. To do so, you must execute the following command:

```
jar xf HelloWorld.jar fHelloWorld.class
```

This command places a copy of fHelloWorld.class into the current directory, and the original JAR remains unchanged.

JBuilder's Archive Builder

JBuilder offers an Archive Builder to make the process of building a JAR easier. This process searches through your project and identifies the requirements for the JAR. The following are the basic steps for deployment of an application:

1. Create your application with JBuilder.
2. Create a JAR file using the JBuilder Archive Builder.
3. Specify an install process.
4. Deliver the JAR file and necessary third-party libraries.

Although a JAR file can be created using the JDK `jar` tool, the Archive Builder is employed to speed up the process. As we look at the Archive Builder, you will notice that it greatly simplifies the process for future deployment. A feature of the Archive Builder that speeds up this process is searching for the required resources for the JAR. The default behavior of the builder is to include/bundle all the required resources. This includes images, sounds, property files, source, and classes.

NOTE

Before executing the Archive Builder, you must save and compile your application. The class files are required for the Archive Builder to execute correctly.

To start the Archive Builder process, choose Wizard, Archive Builder. After selecting the Archive Builder, the first of six steps is initiated. Figure 9.1 shows the first step of the process using the Archive Builder.

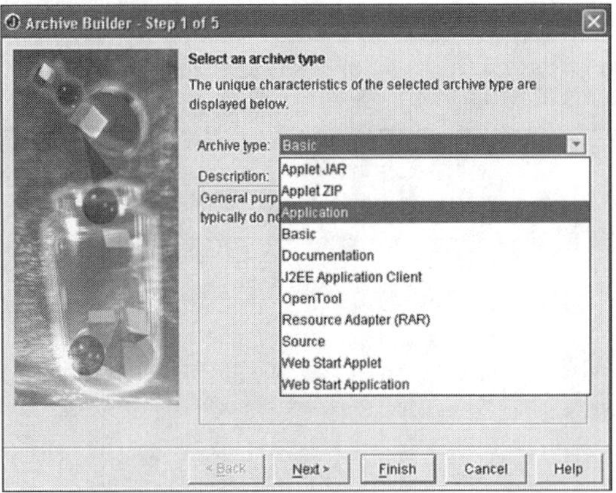

FIGURE 9.1 The first step is to select an archive type.

When selecting the archive type, you have many different options. Table 9.2 describes the usage of these archive types.

TABLE 9.2 Archive Types Available Within JBuilder

Archive Type	Description
Applet JAR	A compressed file designed to deliver an applet to a browser. The compression of the JAR file gives a quick download to the browser. The JAR format for an applet is available only in JDK 1.1 and greater. For earlier JDK versions, you must use an Applet ZIP. This archive type is normally compressed, and that is the selected default.

TABLE 9.2 Continued

Archive Type	Description
Applet ZIP	Similar in style to an Applet JAR with one noticeable difference—the extension is ZIP. This is required for browsers that support only JDK 1.0.2 or earlier. This archive type is normally compressed, and that is the selected default.
Application	Typically used to bundle not only the libraries but also the main class for an application. This file format is typically uncompressed to give better performance in loading classes. In addition, you will see the `Main-Class: class-name` in the manifest file.
Basic	An uncompressed file similar to an application JAR except that it does not carry any main class information in the manifest. Just like an application, JAR is uncompressed for increased performance; the same holds true for a basic JAR.
Documentation	Contains all the applicable documentation. This archive by default is uncompressed to decrease load time.
J2EE Application Client	Contains all the applicable deployment descriptors that describe all the external resources required.
OpenTool	Specific to JBuilder, this JAR is used to deploy new OpenTools within the JBuilder IDE, which extend the features of JBuilder. The manifest for OpenTool specifies how it interfaces with the IDE.
Resource Adapter(RAR)	Contains connector class implementations.
Source	Contains all the source and resource files for a given project. Default source archives are normally uncompressed.
Web Start Applet	Used to bundle the resources for a Web Start Applet. The default for this archive type is compressed.
Web Start Application	Similar to a Web Start Applet except that an application runs externally from a browser.

NOTE

The number of steps required to create your archive changes based on the selected archive type. For example, a documentation archive requires only two steps. In contrast, an application archive requires six steps.

The next step is to identify the name and location of the archive. You can also select the compression requirements for an archive. Figure 9.2 examines the options for naming and storage location of the archives.

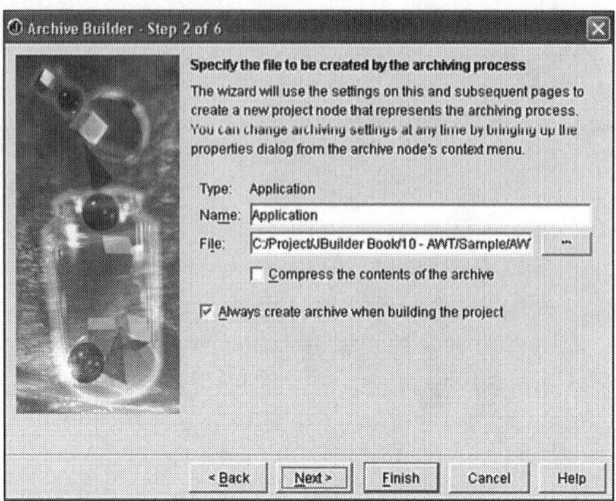

FIGURE 9.2 The second step in creating an archive is specifying its location and compression.

The name of the archive will be the name of the node created within the active project. The archive name's main purpose is to differentiate this archive from another archive within the same project. In other words, make sure the name of the archive node is descriptive. The archive's filename and location are also specified within this step. This will be the file created when you build the archive node. By default, the archive is saved in the default project directory. It also creates both ZIP and JAR files depending on the archive type selected.

The compression of the archive can be selected by choosing the Compress the Contents of the Archive check box. Most archives are created uncompressed to benefit load-time performance, although you can override the default by checking this box. An uncompressed archive is smaller than the total size of the individual files. If the archive you are creating is an applet, the default for the compression will be turned on.

In this next step, you specify exactly the scope of the archive. In other words, identify the classes that will be included within this archive. Figure 9.3 demonstrates this step.

Typically, all the required classes and known resources are included. This option scans through the project and includes only the resources specified. Known resources are specifically identified using the Add Classes or Add Files buttons. Choosing the Include Required Classes and All Resources button selects all classes used by one or more classes.

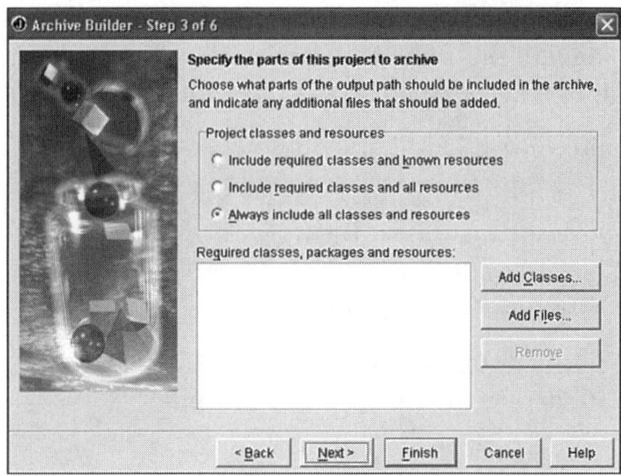

FIGURE 9.3 The third step is to specify the scope of the archive.

This step lets you define with whatever granularity you want to build your archive. You can identify specific classes and files. It takes an understanding of the application to determine what method will produce the most efficient results.

The next step is to determine the dependency of other libraries. These libraries can be either third-party libraries or libraries provided within the JBuilder environment. Figure 9.4 demonstrates the selection dependencies.

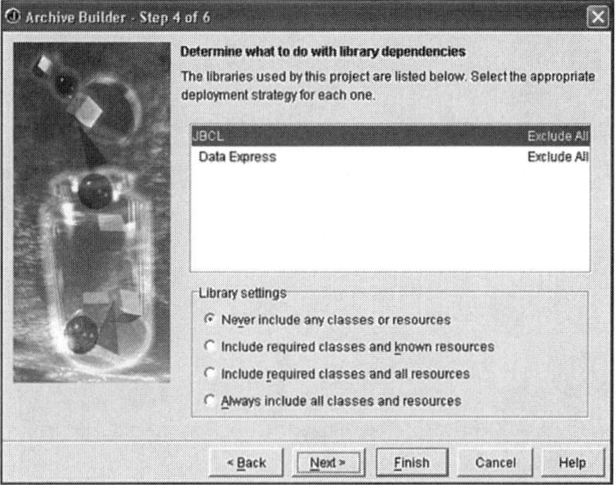

FIGURE 9.4 The fourth step is to identify the dependencies with third-party libraries.

There are many different deployment strategies for third-party libraries, and the Archive Builder needs to support them. The four main archive-building options are as follows:

- Never include any classes or resources—This option does not include anything other than the implementation classes and resources as part of the project. This is the default option for all archives except for an applet.
- Include required classes and known resources—The Archive Builder determines which classes and resources are required for a necessary deployment.
- Include required classes and all resources—With this option selected, the Archive Builder determines which classes are required and includes them. It also gathers resources for the project based on their usage.
- Always include all classes and resources—This option includes all classes and resources, whether or not there is a dependency.

In the next step, the Archive Builder asks you to either select or generate a manifest. This manifest is the packing slip for the archive to be built. The default option is to create a manifest as demonstrated in Figure 9.5.

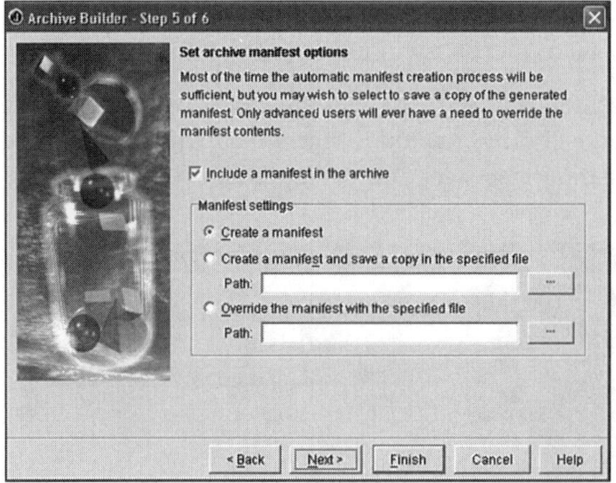

FIGURE 9.5 Select whether to create a new manifest or use an existing one.

NOTE

The majority of the time, you will automatically create a manifest, but you do have the ability to design and include your own.

Create a Manifest is the default option for all the archives except for an OpenTool archive. This option creates a manifest based on the information specified in the Archive Builder. The manifest created will be stored in a file called `manifest.mf` in the meta-inf/ subdirectory. Specifying the manifest file within the field titled Create a manifest and saving a copy in the specified file will save a copy of the manifest to the indicated location. The most advanced option is to override the manifest. It allows you to specify options that are not capable without intervention in the generated manifest. A typical use of this option is to utilize the OpenTool archive.

The last step is available only if you are building an application archive. This step allows the builder to specify the `Main-Class:` entry in the manifest for a runnable archive (see Figure 9.6).

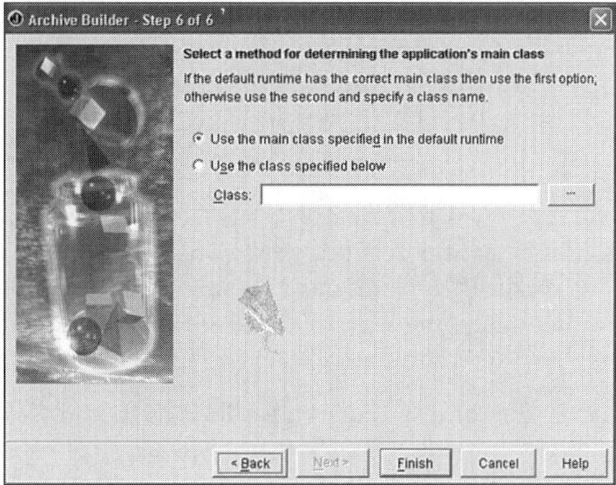

FIGURE 9.6 The last step is to specify the runnable class interface (Application Archive).

A successful archive node has been created. Remember that the archive has not yet been created, only the information required to build the archive. The archive will be generated later, when Build is selected. This node contains all the options and preferences required to build the archive, passing this information to the `jar` tool.

After the project node has been created, you will not have an archive until you either specifically build the archive or rebuild the project. Two options are available to build your archive file: the menu selections Project, Make Project or Project, Rebuild Project.

Quick Deployment

Quick deployment is designed to help you deploy a given type of solution without having to complete the process yourself. Although deployment is simple, many Java developers have never deployed a full system, or if they have, they have usually done it only a few times. These steps guide you in deploying your system correctly for the first time.

Application Deployment

Deploying an application requires only a few steps. The step that differentiates application deployment from the others is the `Main-Class: class-name` in the manifest file. The following are the typical steps used to build an archive for the deployment of an application and the archive's deployment:

1. Make sure that all resources are included in the project.
2. Produce a clean build of all required resources.
3. Create a JAR using the Archive Builder.
4. Copy the JAR file to the target computer.
5. Set the `CLASSPATH` or command line `-classpath` before you execute your application.

Applet Deployment

Applets run within a browser and depend largely on the JDK support within the specific browser. This makes the creating and deploying of the applet the most complex of all the other deployment types. The following steps guide you in producing an applet archive and deploying the applet:

1. Make sure that all files and resources are added to the project.
2. Compile all the classes for the applet.
3. Create a JAR or a ZIP archive. If you are deploying to JDK 1.0.2 or earlier, you must deploy with a ZIP archive.
4. Add to the HTML page the `ARCHIVE` attribute with the name of the JAR file inside the `<applet>` tags. If you have multiple JAR files, list them separated by commas: `ARCHIVE="archive1.jar, archive2.jar, archive3.jar"`.
5. Add the `CODEBASE` attribute to indicate where classes are located. The location of the class files is specified in their relationship to the HTML file. If the classes are in the same directory as the HTML file, the `CODEBASE` attribute becomes optional.
6. Copy the file to the desired location with the HTML file.
7. Test the applet by accessing the HTML file.

JavaBean Deployment

The final type of deployment we will discuss is JavaBeans. JavaBean deployment is required for any JavaBean development. Often, you will use other JavaBeans that have been deployed for you to use within the JBuilder IDE. The following steps show you how to deploy a simple JavaBean:

1. Verify all classes and resources in your project. If you are missing any, make sure that they are added.
2. Compile the JavaBean project.
3. Use JBuilder's JavaDoc Wizard to create the appropriate documentation for your JavaBean.
4. Build an archive using the Archive Builder.
5. Copy your archive to the targeted deployment location.

Design Guidelines

Design guidelines help ensure that you are successful in the deployment of your module or system. These guidelines help you deploy correctly the first time. Because deployment is typically the last task in a project's life cycle, it is also sometimes the most neglected. The following guidelines are important to consider when starting this process:

- Emulate/test your deployment.

  Java has been described by Sun as "Write once run anywhere." In reality, it is more like "Write once test everywhere." Java works well in similar Java Virtual Machine (JVM) versions, but it is important to have an idea of all the different versions of the JDK being deployed to. It is important to test your deployment on all the platforms desired for deployment. Different versions of the JDK along with different platforms have dissimilar abnormalities in operation. In other words, test your deployment on every platform and OS that you target.

- Redistribution of JBuilder classes.

  You may include portions of JBuilder redistributed JAR files. These files include JavaBeans and other portions included within the JBuilder environment. These JAR files are located in the <jbuilder install dir>/redist/ directory. The archive redistribution files are located under the <jbuilder install dir>/<jdk>/lib/ directory.

  If you use the JBuilder Archive Builder to build your archive, it automatically detects any redistribution archives that need to be included. The detected archives will be saved with the archive node when it is created.

NOTE

The terms of using and deploying JBuilder redistribution files are located in the license.txt file within your JBuilder installation. Make sure that you comply with these terms when deploying these archives.

Package Sealing

Sealing a package within a JAR indicates that all classes within that package must be within that JAR file. The reasons for package sealing are ensuring version consistency and guaranteeing security. To seal a package, you need to add some instructions to the manifest. To seal a package, follow these simple steps:

1. Open the manifest file.
2. Add the name of the package you want to seal and indicate the requirement to seal the package. An example for sealing the package `SAMS/util/` is

   ```
   Name: SAMS/util/
   Sealed: true
   ```

3. Rebuild the archive node.

In Practice

After creating an application in JBuilder, you are now ready to deploy your project. JBuilder uses an archive node within your project to maintain the settings and deployment properties. We will take a look at the steps required to deploy an existing application. These steps will be similar regardless of the application. To demonstrate the use of the Archive Builder, we will create an archive node within the JBuilder Welcome Project and deploy it.

1. Either open an existing project or choose Help, Welcome Project from the menu.
2. Now it is time to create an archive node. Either select Wizards, Archive Builder, or select File, New Build tab, Archive Builder from the menu.
3. Choose the archive type of Basic. Normally, when an application is being deployed, the basic archive type is chosen.
4. Name the archive node. Typically, the archive node is a descriptive name. Name the archive Welcome Archive.
5. Specify the parts of this project to include within the archive. If a library is required for your deployed application, it will be listed here.

6. Determine what to do with library dependencies. For this project, no libraries dependencies are required.
7. Set the archive manifest options. Create a default manifest for this project. This is normally the base course of action for your first attempt at creating this archive.
8. Select Finish. Your archive node is now complete.
9. Right-click on the newly created archive node. Select Build.
10. Copy or move your archive to the target deployment location. Remember that the target location must also have the Java Runtime Environment (JRE) installed.
11. Execute your application. Use the `java` runtime to launch your `jar`:

```
java welcome.jar
```

Summary

Deploying an application requires an archive file to be created first. This archive is made up of class files, resources, and other files required by the application. Next, the archive must be copied to the target computer. Finally, the runtime environment must be properly set. Remember that archives may contain just source files. Archives may also be created to contain resources for internationalization or documentation only.

Reflections

- What is the best archive type to use for the deployment of your system?
- How many JAR files should you create for your application?
- What is the best way to maintain your JAR files?

PART III

JBuilder for Java Client Applications

IN THIS PART

10

AWT

IN THIS CHAPTER

- AWT Basics
- Applications Versus Applets
- Working with AWT Containers
- Working with AWT Components

The Java language contains a toolkit to assist in the construction of user interfaces. This toolkit, called the Abstract Windows Toolkit (AWT), is powerful enough to create functional user interfaces. User interfaces are not easy to build by hand, but using both the AWT and the Screen Designer helps make the process easier. Using the Screen Design a developer can design a user interface, using AWT, graphically. For more information about the Screen Designer, see Chapter 3, "Employing the JBuilder Designers."

As we look at the details of building a user interface, we will cover the following basics of building a user interface with AWT:

- AWT basics
- Developing an application or applet
- Working with AWT containers and components

AWT Basics

All user interfaces created using AWT have one thing in common: They all have the same superclass, `java.awt.Component`. The second important superclass to understand is `java.awt.Container`. `Containers` contain `Components`, the building blocks of a user interface. A `Container` can also contain other `Containers` because it also is a `Component`.

Each component in AWT uses native platform code to draw itself to the screen. In other words, it is a surface for the system level API for drawing a screen. If an AWT button is running under Windows, the button is a Windows button. If the button running on an Apple Macintosh, it is a Macintosh button, and likewise for other hardware and software platforms.

As we look at AWT basics, we need to first discuss the difference between applets and applications. After we discuss whether we need an application or an applet, we will discuss how user interface components interact with the system and the user.

Applications Versus Applets

First let's define an applet and an application, and then we will address the advantages and disadvantages of each. JavaSoft defines an *applet* as "a component that typically executes within a Web browser, but can execute in a variety of other applications or devices that support the applet programming model." On the other hand, an *application* is defined as "a first-tier client program that executes in its own Java Virtual Machine." If you look strictly at the definitions, an applet runs within a device or context of another container, and an application runs within its own context directly communicating with a Java Virtual Machine (JVM). The more robust the Java environment becomes with the enhancement of JVM features (such as trusted applets and the Java plug-in), the more the lines blur. For example, applets can do almost anything that applications can. Typically, the division is this: An applet runs in a Web browser, and the bytecode is downloaded at runtime. An application, however, is run like a standard application on a desktop using its own JVM to execute and maintain the environment.

Many browsers by default do not support *Swing*, a set of JavaBeans for building a user interface; they include AWT capabilities. When applets are being constructed, they typically use AWT components. Although Swing can be used within an applet, it requires downloading the Swing libraries, if the browser does not already contain them. This increases the time it takes the applet to load. To address this issue, some newer browsers include the Swing libraries as a default installation.

Basic GUI Logic

Creating a GUI application or applet using AWT takes four simple steps:

1. Start with a `Container` to hold any `Component`(s).
2. Compose your GUI by adding components to `Container` objects.
3. Place event handlers to react to user interactions.
4. Display the user interface. This is automatic for applets and requires a few lines of code for an application.

What the system actually does with this GUI is more complicated. When the AWT GUI is created, the interpreter starts a new thread to watch for user interaction with the GUI. The new thread that is created waits until a user presses any key, clicks or moves a mouse, or responds to any other event. When an event is created, the thread calls the appropriate event handler.

NOTE

It is important to note that the event handler code is executed within the thread that watches the GUI.

The JVM exits when all nondaemon threads in it finish running (that is, return from their `run()` method either normally or exceptionally). Because both the event dispatching thread and the main thread are nondaemon threads, exiting one but not the other causes the JVM to stay alive. A *daemon thread* is a thread that is running continuously for the purpose of handling periodic service requests.

A Simple Example

To demonstrate the use of AWT, we will look at a simple example, an `Applet`. The `Applet` class contains a default container, in which you can place components easily. For example, Listing 10.1 is a simple example.

LISTING 10.1 A Simple AWT Example

```
package awt_sample_10;

import java.awt.*;
import java.awt.event.*;
import java.applet.*;
import com.borland.jbcl.layout.*;

//Step 1 - Create a container to hold components.
public class ApltAWT extends Applet {
  boolean isStandalone = false;
  Button btnHelloWorld = new Button();
  TextField txtfldMessage = new TextField();
  //Get a parameter value
  public String getParameter(String key, String def) {
    return isStandalone ? System.getProperty(key, def) :
      (getParameter(key) != null ? getParameter(key) : def);
  }
```

LISTING 10.1 Continued

```
//Construct the applet
public ApltAWT() {
}
//Initialize the applet
public void init() {
  try {
    jbInit();
  }
  catch(Exception e) {
    e.printStackTrace();
  }
  /* Step 4 - Wait for a response. This happens
     after the init() is finished. */
}
//Component initialization
private void jbInit() throws Exception {
  //Step 2 - Add Components to the container
  this.add(btnHelloWorld, null);
  this.add(txtfldMessage, null);
  btnHelloWorld.setLabel("Hello");

  //Step 3 - Add Event Handler for Objects
  btnHelloWorld.addActionListener(new java.awt.event.ActionListener() {
    public void actionPerformed(ActionEvent e) {
      btnHelloWorld_actionPerformed(e);
    }
  });
  txtfldMessage.setText("I haven\'t said anything");

}
//Get Applet information
public String getAppletInfo() {
  return "Applet Information";
}
//Get parameter info
public String[][] getParameterInfo() {
  return null;
```

LISTING 10.1 Continued

```
  }

  void btnHelloWorld_actionPerformed(ActionEvent e) {
    txtfldMessage.setText("Hello World!!!");
  }
}
```

Working with AWT Containers

A container is one of the most important class supertypes in AWT. This supertype class is used to provide containership for all components managed by it. The most common containers are frames, panels, and dialog boxes. Containers are also components, so as with other components, you interact with them by getting and setting their properties, calling their methods, and responding to their events. In addition to containers managing GUI components, they can also manage non-GUI components, including menus, for example. Table 10.1 lists many of the Java containers derived from the `Container` class.

TABLE 10.1 AWT `Container` Subclasses

Class	Description
`Applet`	An extension of `Panel`. The class is used to render an applet within a browser.
`Dialog`	An extension of `Window` that can have both model and nonmodel properties.
`FileDialog`	An extension of `Dialog` that allows selections of a file.
`Frame`	An extension of `Window`, `Frame` is the container for an application. A `Frame` may have a menu, whereas an `Applet` may not.
`Panel`	An extension of `Container`, `Panel` is a simple container.
`Window`	An extension of `Container`, `Windows` have no menu or border. `Window` is rarely extended directly; it is the superclass of `Frame` and `Dialog`.

Spatially, components must fit completely within the container's boundaries. The nesting of components (including containers) into containers creates a tree of elements, starting with the container at the root of the tree and expanding to the leaves, which are components such as buttons. All components that reside within the container are child nodes of the tree. Figure 10.1 shows a simple graphical user interface, and Figure 10.2 shows the components' interrelationships.

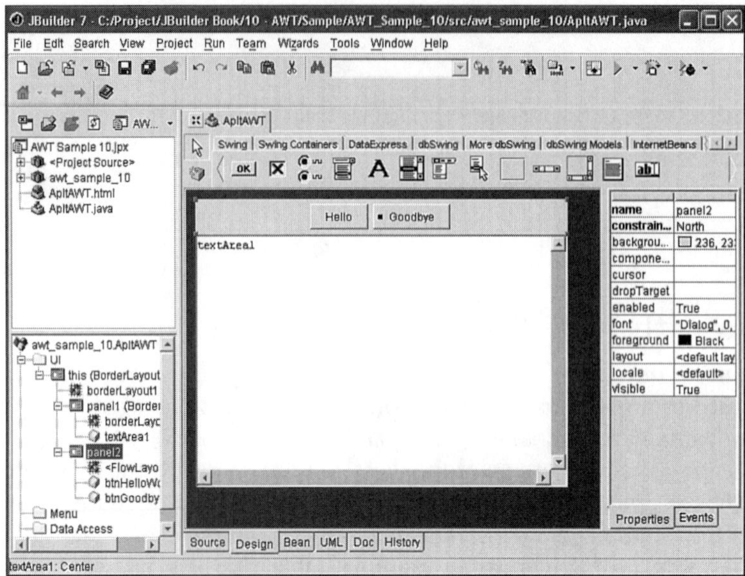

FIGURE 10.1 A simple graphical user interface using AWT.

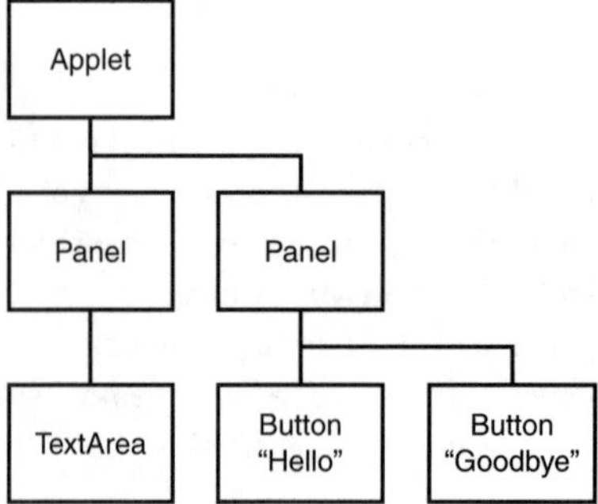

FIGURE 10.2 User interface interrelationships based on Figure 10.1.

Creating a Container

Before you can create a user interface, you must create a container. When building an application, you must first create an instance of class `Window` or class `Frame`. When building an applet, the browser or applet viewer provides a frame within which the applet appears.

Listing 10.2 demonstrates the creation of a simple empty frame. A frame is not visible until the method `show()` is invoked. To create an empty frame, choose File,

New from the menu, and on the General tab select Frame. This launches the Frame Wizard and creates a new blank frame within your project.

LISTING 10.2 Creating an Empty Frame Without JBuilder's Designers

```
package awt2;

import java.awt.*;

public class frmMain extends Frame {

  public frmMain() {
  }
  public static void main(String[] args) {
    frmMain frmMain = new frmMain();
    frmMain.show();
  }
}
```

Listing 10.3 adds to Listing 10.2. The method `add()` of the container allows the frame to manage the `Panel`. The results of Listing 10.2 and Listing 10.3 look exactly the same from the end user's perspective. Listing 10.2 was created by hand, and Listing 10.3 was created using the JBuilder IDE.

LISTING 10.3 Creating an Empty Frame with JBuilder's Designers

```
package awt2;

import java.awt.*;

public class frmMain extends Frame {
  Panel pnlMain = new Panel();

  public frmMain() {
    try {
      jbInit();
    }
    catch(Exception e) {
      e.printStackTrace();
    }
  }
  public static void main(String[] args) {
    frmMain frmMain = new frmMain();
```

LISTING 10.3 Continued

```
    frmMain.show();
  }
  private void jbInit() throws Exception {
    this.add(pnlMain, BorderLayout.CENTER);
  }
}
```

Common Container Methods

All different `Container` types have common functionality because they are all derived from `Container`. In addition to common functionality implemented in methods, they also include a number of predefined event handling routines. A list of common container methods appears in Table 10.2.

TABLE 10.2 `Container` Subclasses, Standard Methods

Method	Behavior
`add(Component)`	Adds the specified component to the end of this container
`add(Component,ObjectConstraints)`	Adds the specified component to this container with defined layout constraints
`Remove(Component)`	Removes the specified component from this container
`getComponents()`	Returns a list of all the components placed on the given container
`setLayout(LayoutManger)`	Sets the layout manager for this container
`getLayout()`	Gets the layout manager for this container

Working with AWT Components

If a container is simply the holder and organizer of components, components supply the real work of the user interface. Do not get this confused with layout managers, whose responsibility is to lay out graphically the components contained within a container. Some common AWT components include `Buttons`, `TextArea`, `TextField`, and so on.

AWT components, defined within JBuilder's Screen Designer, exhibit true object-oriented programming behaviors:

- *Encapsulation* describes the binding of data and behavior into one unit.
- *Inheritance* is behavior and data passed on from a parent or more accurately from a superclass.
- *Polymorphism* means classes operating interchangeably with other objects derived from a common superclass.

Each component, therefore, encapsulates many elements of a program, such as a window or dialog box, a field in a database, or a system timer. AWT components must ultimately extend either `java.awt.Component` or any other class that derives it, such as `java.awt.Panel` or `java.awt.Canvas`. Other JavaBean components do not have this requirement.

We will examine some of the frequently used AWT components. In the JBuilder IDE, the AWT components are available within the Component palette on the AWT tab. Figure 10.3 shows the JBuilder AWT components available on the palette.

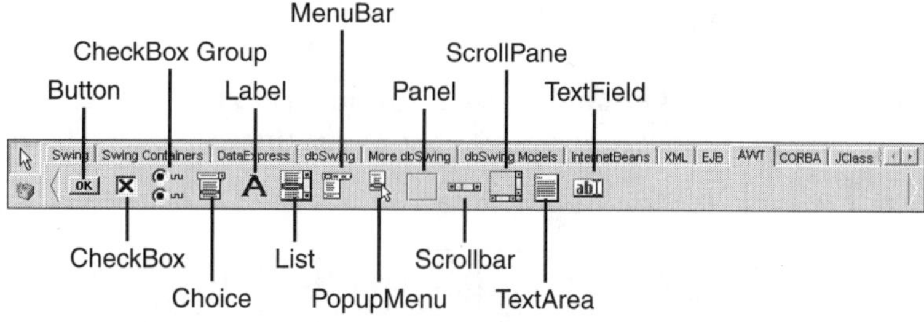

FIGURE 10.3 AWT Component palette in JBuilder's designer.

Finally, because every AWT component uses a peer, objects are instances of peer classes. These peer classes are written using native code rather than Java, the results of which make it difficult to override their defined system behavior. Table 10.3 lists the available components in AWT.

TABLE 10.3 AWT Components in JBuilder's Component Palette

Component	Description
`Button`	A component that you click to take an action
`Checkbox`	A component that displays a check mark when selected
`CheckboxGroup`	A group for grouping check box components into a set of mutually exclusive choices (sometimes called radio buttons)
`Choice`	A drop-down list from which a user can make a selection
`Label`	A component that displays text on the given frame
`List`	A component that displays multiple items within a scrolling window
`Scrollbar`	The control used to scroll information provided within a `ScrollPane`
`TextArea`	An area in which multiple lines of text can be displayed and edited
`TextField`	A small area designed to display and edit a single line of text and many more (`Menu`, `PopupMenu`, `Canvas`, and so on)

It is important not only to understand each individual component, but also to understand how the components interact with each other. We will look at these different components and sample usage of them in the following sections.

NOTE

We can only cover a portion of the components within AWT.

Button

```
java.lang.Object
  |
  +--java.awt.Component
        |
        +--java.awt.Button
```

The `java.awt.Button` class creates a labeled button. Typically, clicking on a button causes some action to happen. Figure 10.4 shows the three states of a button labeled "Hello."

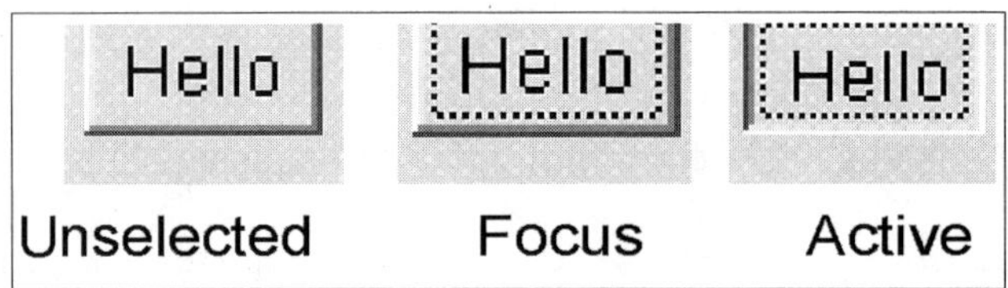

FIGURE 10.4 AWT button states in the Windows operating system.

As you look at the buttons, the first one appears normal, unselected and nonactivated. The second view shows the focus applied to the button. Notice the dashed border around the button indicating that it currently has focus. This differs from operating system to operating system. For example, in Solaris, the button will have a dark border around it. The last view shows a button when the user either presses Enter on the focused button or selects the button with the mouse.

When you click on a button with the mouse, it is associated with an instance of `ActionEvent`, which is then sent out when the mouse is both pressed and released over the button. If you want to have more detailed events, such as a button pressed but not released, you can use a `processMouseEvent`, or you can register for mouse events by calling `addMouseListener`. Listing 10.4 demonstrates the implementation of `java.awt.Button`.

LISTING 10.4 Create and Process Events for `java.awt.Button`

```
package awt_sample_10;

import java.awt.*;
import java.awt.event.*;
```

LISTING 10.4 Continued

```
import java.applet.*;

public class ApltAWT extends Applet {
  boolean isStandalone = false;
  Button btnSayHello = new Button();
  TextField txtfldLabel = new TextField();
  //Get a parameter value
  public String getParameter(String key, String def) {
    return isStandalone ? System.getProperty(key, def) :
      (getParameter(key) != null ? getParameter(key) : def);
  }

  //Construct the applet
  public ApltAWT() {
  }
  //Initialize the applet
  public void init() {
    try {
      jbInit();
    }
    catch(Exception e) {
      e.printStackTrace();
    }
  }
  //Component initialization
  private void jbInit() throws Exception {
    //Set the properties for the button
    btnSayHello.setLabel("Hello");
    //Add a listener to process then event
    btnSayHello.addActionListener(new java.awt.event.ActionListener() {
      public void actionPerformed(ActionEvent e) {
        btnSayHello_actionPerformed(e);
      }
    });
    //Set default for the label
    txtfldLabel.setText("Haven\'t Said Anything Yet!");
    //Add objects to container
    this.add(btnSayHello, null);
    this.add(txtfldLabel, null);
```

LISTING 10.4 Continued

```
  }
  //Get Applet information
  public String getAppletInfo() {
    return "Applet Information";
  }
  //Get parameter info
  public String[][] getParameterInfo() {
    return null;
  }

  //Perform the action for the associated event
  void btnSayHello_actionPerformed(ActionEvent e) {
    txtfldLabel.setText("Hello World");
  }

}
```

Canvas

```
java.lang.Object
  |
  +--java.awt.Component
        |
        +--java.awt.Canvas
```

`Canvas` is a component that represents a region where you can draw elements such as circles, squares, and text strings. The name comes from a painter's canvas. The `Canvas` class is typically used to define your own custom objects. For example, use subclass `Canvas` to override the `paint()` method to define your own components. Listing 10.5 creates a new custom object using the AWT `Canvas`.

LISTING 10.5 Subclassing `Canvas` to Create a Graphic Object

```
package awt_sample_10;

import java.awt.Canvas;
import java.awt.Graphics;

class DrawingRegion extends Canvas {
  public DrawingRegion(){
    setSize(100,100);
```

LISTING 10.5 Continued

```
  }

  public void paint(Graphics g){
    g.draw3DRect(0,0,99,99,true);
    g.drawString("Hello World",20,20);
  }
}
```

The preceding class creates an AWT `Canvas` that can be used to create your own components. Although the preceding component implements only a simple rectangle and a text string within the rectangle, you have the ability to create an object of any complexity. Listing 10.6 implements this newly created class within a test applet.

LISTING 10.6 Creating a User Interface Using the Newly Created Class

```
package awt_sample_10;

import java.awt.*;
import java.awt.event.*;
import java.applet.*;

public class ApltCanvas extends Applet {
  boolean isStandalone = false;
  DrawingRegion drRegion = new DrawingRegion();
  //Get a parameter value
  public String getParameter(String key, String def) {
    return isStandalone ? System.getProperty(key, def) :
      (getParameter(key) != null ? getParameter(key) : def);
  }

  //Construct the applet
  public ApltCanvas() {
  }
  //Initialize the applet
  public void init() {
    try {
      jbInit();
    }
    catch(Exception e) {
      e.printStackTrace();
```

LISTING 10.6 Continued

```
    }
  }
  //Component initialization
  private void jbInit() throws Exception {
    this.add(drRegion, null);
  }
  //Get Applet information
  public String getAppletInfo() {
    return "Applet Information";
  }
  //Get parameter info
  public String[][] getParameterInfo() {
    return null;
  }
}
```

Checkbox

```
java.lang.Object
  |
  +--java.awt.Component
        |
        +--java.awt.Checkbox
```

A `Checkbox` component is made up of a caption and a box that indicates its state. The state of the `Checkbox` is either true (box is checked) or false (box is blank). When the check box is selected, the state of the check box is then toggled. The default check box state is false. Listing 10.7 shows how to define and use a check box.

LISTING 10.7 Demonstrating the Usage of a `java.awt.Checkbox`

```
package awt_sample_10;

import java.awt.*;
import java.awt.event.*;
import java.applet.*;

public class ApltAWT extends Applet {
  boolean isStandalone = false;
  Checkbox cbFirst = new Checkbox();
  //Get a parameter value
  public String getParameter(String key, String def) {
```

LISTING 10.7 Continued

```
    return isStandalone ? System.getProperty(key, def) :
      (getParameter(key) != null ? getParameter(key) : def);
  }

  //Construct the applet
  public ApltAWT() {
  }
  //Initialize the applet
  public void init() {
    try {
      jbInit();
    }
    catch(Exception e) {
      e.printStackTrace();
    }
  }
  //Component initialization
  private void jbInit() throws Exception {
    cbFirst.setLabel("Test");
    this.add(cbFirst, null);

  }
  //Get Applet information
  public String getAppletInfo() {
    return "Applet Information";
  }
  //Get parameter info
  public String[][] getParameterInfo() {
    return null;
  }
}
```

CheckboxGroup

```
java.lang.Object
  |
  +--java.awt.CheckboxGroup
```

A `CheckboxGroup` combines multiple `Checkbox` objects together to create a state relationship between them. Only one `Checkbox` at a time within a `CheckboxGroup` can have a true state. In the Windows environment, we typically refer to a `Checkbox` with this behavior as a radio button. In addition to the behavior change, there is also a presentation change, from a check box to a selected or open circle. Building a group of check boxes takes only one extra line of code and a new parameter for the check box constructor, or you can set the `CheckboxGroup` property, as shown in Listing 10.8.

LISTING 10.8 Building a `CheckboxGroup`

```
...
  private void jbInit() throws Exception {
    cbFirst.setCheckboxGroup(checkboxGroup1);
    cbFirst.setLabel("Test");
    checkbox1.setCheckboxGroup(checkboxGroup1);
    checkbox1.setLabel("Test 2");
    this.add(cbFirst, null);
    this.add(checkbox1, null);
  }
...
```

Choice

```
java.lang.Object
  |
  +--java.awt.Component
        |
        +--java.awt.Choice
```

A Windows programmer will typically think of a drop-down combo box when using a `Choice`. The `Choice` object displays a defined list of items when it is dropped down. A `Choice` object is typically used to display a small set of choices—three to seven different items. Listing 10.9 demonstrates the usage of a `Choice` class.

LISTING 10.9 Using the `Choice` Class

```
...
  //Component initialization
  private void jbInit() throws Exception {
    this.add(cTest, null);
    //Add Elements to Choice
    cTest.add("First Choice");
    cTest.add("Second Choice");
    cTest.add("Last Choice");
  }
...
```

`Label`

```
java.lang.Object
  |
  +--java.awt.Component
        |
        +--java.awt.Label
```

A `Label` displays a portion of text on the screen. A `Label` is restricted to one line of text with a length of the current display. Usually a label is used to display textual information, such as the description for a `TextField`. To see a label implemented, look at Listing 10.10.

LISTING 10.10 Implementing a `Label` Class

```
…
  //Component initialization
  private void jbInit() throws Exception {
    lblName.setText("Name:");
    this.add(lblName, null);
  }
…
```

`List`

```
java.lang.Object
  |
  +--java.awt.Component
        |
        +--java.awt.List
```

A `List` is a scrolling list box that allows you to select one or more items. The default for the `multipleMode` property is false, indicating single selection only. Although the `List` constructor supports the setting of the `multipleMode` property, JBuilder uses the method `setMultipleMode` mutator. For an example of using the `List` class, see Listing 10.11.

LISTING 10.11 Using the `List` Class

```
import java.applet.*;
import java.awt.*;

public class ApltAWT extends Applet {
```

LISTING 10.11 Continued

```
  boolean isStandalone = false;
  List lstChoice = new List();
  //Get a parameter value
  public String getParameter(String key, String def) {
    return isStandalone ? System.getProperty(key, def) :
      (getParameter(key) != null ? getParameter(key) : def);
  }

  //Construct the applet
  public ApltAWT() {
  }
  //Initialize the applet
  public void init() {
    try {
      jbInit();
    }
    catch(Exception e) {
      e.printStackTrace();
    }
  }
  //Component initialization
  private void jbInit() throws Exception {
    lstChoice.setMultipleMode(true);
    this.add(lstChoice, null);
    lstChoice.add("First Choice");
    lstChoice.add("Second Choice");
    lstChoice.add("Last Choice");
  }
  //Get Applet information
  public String getAppletInfo() {
    return "Applet Information";
  }
  //Get parameter info
  public String[][] getParameterInfo() {
    return null;
  }

}
```

JBuilder supports the building of a `List` box through the mutators, set methods, to assign different properties. This component does not support the setting of the visible rows using a mutator. You must change the constructor for the class.

```
List lstChoice = new List();
```

becomes

```
List lstChoice = new List(2);
```

Notice the only change made was specifying the number of elements to create within the list.

Scrollbar

```
java.lang.Object
  |
  +--java.awt.Component
        |
        +--java.awt.Scrollbar
```

A `Scrollbar` is a "slider" component with characteristics defined by integer ranges defined during construction. As with other components, JBuilder supports only the default constructor. To implement the minimum and maximum, use `setMinimum()` and `setMaximum()`. The same component is used to display both horizontal and vertical sliders. Listing 10.12 demonstrates using the `Scrollbar`.

LISTING 10.12 Sample Implementation of a `Scrollbar`

```
...
  //Component initialization
  private void jbInit() throws Exception {
    scrollbar1.setMaximum(200);
    scrollbar1.setMinimum(100);
    scrollbar1.setOrientation(0);
    this.add(scrollbar1, null);
  }
...
```

TextField

```
java.lang.Object
  |
  +--java.awt.Component
        |
        +--java.awt.TextComponent
              |
              +--java.awt.TextField
```

A TextField is a scrollable text display object with one row of text. In most cases, this will be the most frequently used component. Listing 10.13 shows the TextField in use.

LISTING 10.13 Sample Implementation of a TextField

```
...
  //Component initialization
  private void jbInit() throws Exception {
    textField1.setComponentOrientation(null);
    textField1.setText("Test");
    this.add(textField1, null);
  }
...
```

One common behavioral operation when using a TextField is the ability to set a component as read-only. Use `setEditable(false)`. For a password, you set the echo character to be something other than the typed character. This is done by calling `setEchoChar('?')`.

TextArea

```
java.lang.Object
  |
  +--java.awt.Component
        |
        +--java.awt.TextComponent
              |
              +--java.awt.TextArea
```

A TextArea is similar to a TextField, except that a TextArea supports multiple lines of text. One important item to remember that will be different from platform to platform is the newline indicator; `'\n'` or `'\n\r'` or `'\r'` ends each row. To elevate this issue, Java includes a method to indicate the representation of a new line—`System.getProperty("line.separator")`. Listing 10.14 implements a TextArea.

LISTING 10.14 Sample Implementation of a TextArea

```
...
  //Component initialization
  private void jbInit() throws Exception {
    textArea1.setText("This is a really long text display component");
    this.add(textArea1, null);
  }
...
```

Common Component Methods

As with containers, each component has some similar available behaviors. These methods are used to either affect the behavior of or access information about the component. Some of the most frequently used methods are listed in Table 10.4.

TABLE 10.4 `Component` Common Methods

Method	Description
`getSize()`	Returns the current size of the component
`getLocation()`	Gets the current location of the component
`getLocationOnScreen()`	Retrieves the component location relative to the upper-left corner of the user interface
`setEnabled(Boolean)`	Toggles the state of the component
`setVisible(Boolean)`	Toggles the visibility of the component
`setBackground(Color)`	Changes the background and foreground color of a component
`setFont(Font)`	Changes the font of the text within a component

Separate User Interface Logic

Separation of the user interface from the business logic is an important concept to implement in your application. AWT 1.1 and the associated listener were designed to facilitate this function.

In Practice

In this section, we will create a user interface applet for registration for a specified course. This will allow remote users to register for the class themselves. When creating an applet, remember that you must also create an HTML page to service the applet. The applet will then be launched from the Web browser by displaying the generated HTML page. Figure 10.5 shows the applet we will create.

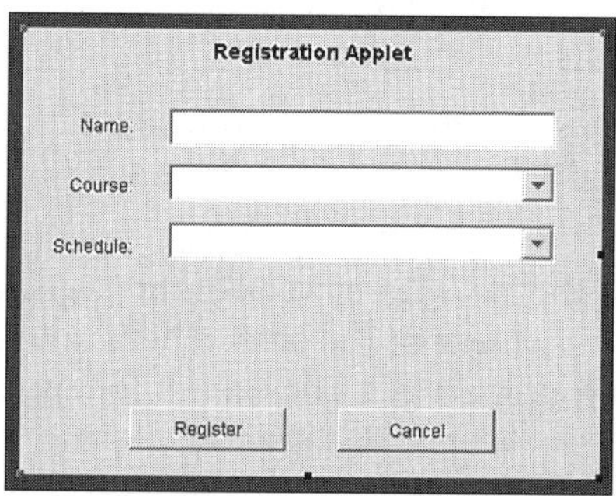

FIGURE 10.5 The Course Registration applet in its final form.

Creating an Applet with the Applet Wizard

Let's start with creating a new project using the Project Wizard. After that has been completed, we will use the Applet Wizard to build an empty applet and will also build the HTML file to run it in as well.

1. Select File, New Project. The Project Wizard steps you through the naming and directory structure for your project.
2. Using File, New, create a new applet.
3. Specify the following defaults for the project:
    - Name: Registration
    - Title: Registration Applet
    - Description: Register for a class
4. Choose File, New. The New dialog box appears.
5. Select the Web tab and the Applet Wizard.
6. Specify the following defaults for your applet:
    - Classname: ApltRegistration
    - Remaining properties should be left with default settings.
7. On the Navigation pane, select `ApltRegistration.java` and select the Design tab.
8. Under the Component palette, select the AWT tab. Add a `java.awt.Label` onto your design frame. JBuilder names the first one `label1`.
9. Change the following properties on your Properties tab:
    - Name: lblTitle
    - Text: Registration Applet
    - Font: "Dialog",1,14 (bold, 14 pt)
10. Choose Run, Run Project. This actually runs the HTML page, which in turn contains the applet.

We have now completed the basic framework of the Registration applet. Notice that you cannot control the placement of the label. The location of the label is determined by the selected layout manager. The default for applets is `FlowLayout`. You will learn more about layout managers in Chapter 11, "Swing."

Building the Interface

Now it is time to really build the user interface. We will need to add text fields, labels, and various other components to create the user interface. We will also add buttons to submit or cancel the course registration. To simplify the layout of the user interface, we are going to use the XYLayout manager.

Now we will start to add the required components to complete the user interface. The user types the important information and saves the registration.

1. Change the layout of the frame to XYLayout. This makes it easier to create the user interface without the obstruction of the layout manager at this point. You will only see the layout manager property for the existing panel if you select the node titled `this` in the Component Structure window.
2. Add the new `java.awt.Label` objects to display Name, Course, and Schedule.
3. Add the `java.awt.TextField` object to accept the input of the student's name.
4. Place two `java.awt.Choice` components on the frame. The first is to contain the course title, and the second is to show the schedule for the selected course.
5. Add two `java.awt.Buttons` to support the submission of the registration and canceling it.
6. Add a sample list of courses to the course `Choice` object. Within the method `jbInit()`, at the end, use the `add(string)` method to create a default list. To prevent you from losing focus with implementing JDBC, we will not connect to a database for course information at this time. Listing 10.15 shows the portion of code you need to implement at the end of the `jbInit()`.
7. Run and test your applet.

LISTING 10.15 Default Course and Schedule Information Loaded into the Instantiated `Choice` Objects

```
/* Add Default Classes - This will change when we read
 the information from the database. */
cCourse.add("Introduction to JBuilder");
cCourse.add("Introduction to Java");
cCourse.add("Advanced J2EE");
cCourse.add("JSP and Servlets");
//Schedule
cSchedule.add("5/5-5/8 - Chicago");
cSchedule.add("7/20-7/25 - San Diego");
cSchedule.add("9/10-9/13 - New York");
```

Accepting Input

We built the user interface, but nothing happens when we click on any of the buttons. Now that the basic components are put together, it is time to start making them work. We will write code to handle both cancelation and registration.

1. Double-click on the Cancel button within the Design window.
2. Within the method generated, place the following code:

```
System.exit(0);
```

3. Double-click on the Register button.
4. Type the following code within the method to save the information:

```
String sName = textField1.getText();
String sCourse = cCourse.getSelectedItem();
String sSchedule = cSchedule.getSelectedItem();
//We will later save this information to the database
System.exit(0);
```

5. We want the schedule to load based on the course selected. We must use the event `itemStateChanged` that will be processed whenever the user selects a new course. Using the Event tab of the Property Editor, choose the event and double-click on it.
6. Add the following code to load the schedule. We will load the information from the database later.

```
/** @todo Read information from database */
cSchedule.add("5/5-5/8 - Chicago");
cSchedule.add("7/20-7/25 - San Diego");
cSchedule.add("9/10-9/13 - New York");
```

7. Run and test your applet.

Summary

Although AWT (Abstract Windows Toolkit) is used rarely to create new applications, millions of lines of code in production today still use AWT. AWT is a powerful windowing environment that uses the operating system to manage and paint all components, thus depending on the OS for look and feel. Ideally, the AWT enables any Java application to appear the same whether it runs in a Windows, Macintosh, or Unix environment.

The AWT is both powerful and flexible. With proper guidance, the creation of a GUI using the AWT is not only possible but relatively straightforward.

Reflections

- Should I still be using AWT?
- How does AWT affect my system performance?
- Should I make the application look the same regardless of the platform?

11 Swing

IN THIS CHAPTER

It's not a dance; it's a GUI toolkit that is part of Java 2 Standard Edition (J2SE). Swing provides a pure Java alternative to the AWT. Swing is just one of the features of Java Foundation Classes (JFCs). JFC subsumes and extends AWT to provide the following additional features:

- Swing (`javax.swing` and subpackages)
- Accessibility, also known as assistive technologies (`javax.accessibility` package)
- Java2D (`java.awt.geom` and new classes and methods in `java.awt` package)
- Drag-and-drop (`java.awt.dnd` package)
- Clipboard (`java.awt.datatransfer` package)
- Printing (`java.awt.print` package)

In this chapter, we will look at Swing components, as well as the data transfer features that are part of JFC. We will put what we learn to good use by designing the user interface for our ChalkTalk application.

Why Use Swing Instead of AWT?

Swing offers many advantages over AWT. First, Swing components are pure Java. They do not depend on any platform-specific code. This not only makes them more portable from one VM implementation to another, it also allows for their look and feel to be changed. Whereas AWT components inherit the look and feel of the native platform, Swing components can be made to look like Windows, CDE Motif, or any other look and feel for which appropriate classes are present.

Second, Swing components follow the MVC pattern more closely than their AWT counterparts. MVC—Model View Controller—is discussed in detail in the next section. Some Swing components such as `JTable` and `JList` have model classes (`TableModel` and `ListModel`, respectively). Others support MVC through `Document` and other interfaces derived from it.

Third, Swing components provide a richer set of events and properties. For example, you can have a `JButton` with an image, but not a `Button`. `JComponent` allows `VetoableChangeListeners`, but `Component` does not.

Another difference that is historically important is that AWT initially supported the older, component-containment based event model. It is also called the JDK 1.0 event model because it was superseded by the observer/observable based event model in versions 1.1 and later of the Java SDK. The component-based event model relied on passing an AWT event (such as a mouse click or key press) to the component hierarchy based on containment. This was bad for a variety of reasons:

- It was difficult to separate the classes that responded to events from the classes that generated events.
- If you wanted to handle all events at the outermost container (such as the frame), you had to make the event hop the intermediate containers—in other words, the event was the water bucket, and the intermediate containers made up the bucket brigade. This was inefficient for deeply nested hierarchies.
- Noncontainer classes could not directly observe events, unless a container was gracious enough to provide such a class with the event.

Swing has always supported the newer event model, which allows event listeners (observers) to be registered to event sources (observables). The observers need not be containers; in fact, good design edicts dictate that they should not be containers. Any class that implements the appropriate event listener interface can be a listener for events of that type.

Table 11.1 summarizes the differences between Swing and AWT.

TABLE 11.1 How Swing Matches Up to AWT

Feature	Swing	AWT
Implementation language	Java	Java and native (OS-specific) implementation
Rendered by	UI class (such as `ButtonUI`)	Peer classes (not directly accessible in JDK 1.1 and above)
Display model	Based on MVC (with `Document` and `Model` classes)	Monolithic design with all parts of MVC tightly coupled

TABLE 11.1 Continued

Feature	Swing	AWT
Event model	Based on observer design pattern	Based initially on component containment, now the same as Swing
Event variety	Many events per component	Limited number of events per component
Property variety	Many properties per component	Limited number of properties per component

Design Guideline—Model View Controller Architecture

Model View Controller is a composite design pattern often used to partition user interface components into three related but separate concerns.

MVC is a combination of several other design patterns. In this section, we will look at MVC in some detail and see how Swing components implement a simplified version of MVC.

Simple MVC with Pull Semantics

MVC has been around for a while. It was originally conceived in the world of Smalltalk. Its motivation is to separate the following three concerns regarding a user interface:

- The underlying blob of information that is seen and possibly modified—the *Model*.
- The widget, graphical or textual, used to depict the model—the *View*.
- The glue to connect the two and provide the user with the ability to interact with the view and the model—the *Controller*.

In object-oriented languages such as Smalltalk and Java, these three participants naturally become three classes. In the original Smalltalk design, there was a fourth type class called the *Object*, which was the common ancestor (superclass) of all models. This allowed any class to act as a model. In Java, the presence of a common ancestor (`java.lang.Object`), which all classes extend, precludes the need for a separate object class.

Figure 11.1 shows the UML class diagram for the MVC design pattern.

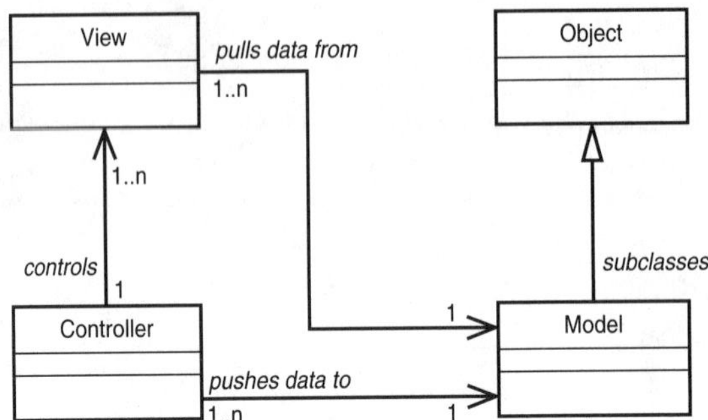

FIGURE 11.1 The classic Smalltalk MVC design pattern with a passive model.

Figure 11.1 shows MVC with a passive model. In this design, only one controller changes the model at a time. The model may have multiple views observing it simultaneously, though. Because the controller in effect owns the model, the controller can take charge and notify the views when they must refresh themselves by pulling the data from the model. Because of this, the design is said to have a passive model—the model just sits around doing nothing; its state is changed by the controller and observed when views pull data from it.

The MVC design pattern as described previously has the following implications:

- The model is unaware of both the view and the controller. This makes it possible to switch views and controllers on the same model to achieve effective user interfaces. For example, one UI may allow the user of a shopping cart application to type in her favorite color, another may allow her to select from a list, and a third may allow her to click on the colored swatches.
- Both the view and the controller are aware of the model. This is necessary, because, to observe or modify a class, the exact details of the class must be known.
- The controller is also aware of the view. This is necessary because the model tells the view to "go refresh yourself" after it changes the model.

MVC with Push Semantics

The passive model is no longer sufficient when more than one controller modifies the state of the model. In this case, the model needs to notify both the controller and the view of changes made to it. Figure 11.2 shows this solution.

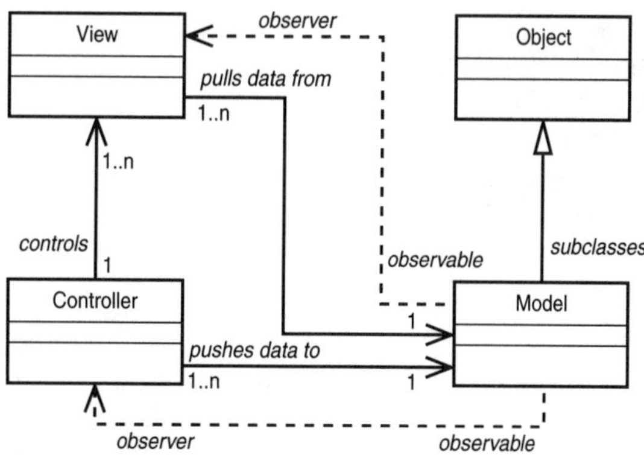

FIGURE 11.2 The MVC design pattern with an active model.

The differences between the pull and the push models are

- Multiple controllers can now modify the model. To do this safely, the model must provide some form of concurrency control. It should protect its state from being corrupted by simultaneous modifications from many controllers.
- The model can now notify the controllers and views attached to it that its state has changed. The view then refreshes itself, and the controller gets ready to provide user interactions with the modified state of the model.
- The model depends on the view and the controller to the minimum extent possible. In other words, the model doesn't expect much from the controller or the view, as long as it can prod them to say "ahem, I've been updated."

The last bulleted item describes an important point. The contract between the model and the view (and also between the model and the controller) is implemented by the observer design pattern. This decouples the actual implementation classes and thereby makes it easier to substitute one view for another, or have multiple views, possibly switched dynamically.

THE OBSERVER PATTERN

As mentioned earlier, MVC is a composite pattern. The observer is one of the patterns that comprise MVC.

The observer pattern strives to loosen the coupling between two objects that must share data and hence have to know about each other. The relationship is not symmetrical: One object publishes the data, and the other object subscribes to receive the data. Because of this, the observer pattern is also known as *publisher subscriber.*

> To realize this decoupling, the requirements made on the observable (publisher) and the observer (subscriber) must be minimal. All that is required of the observable is that it should allow observers to be attached to it. The only thing required from the observer is a way to notify it of changes to the observable.
>
> In Java, the observer usually implements a simple interface called a *listener interface* (such as `MouseListener` or `KeyListener`). The observable provides a pair of methods to add and remove observers (such as `addMouseListener()` and `removeMouseListener()`).

Figure 11.3 shows the detailed UML diagram for the model and view.

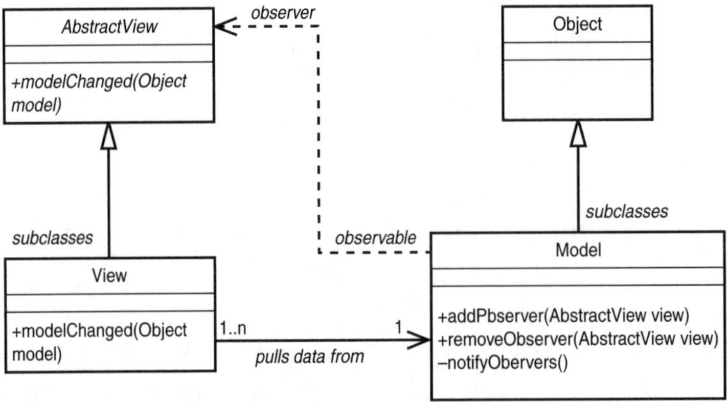

FIGURE 11.3 The model and view classes use the observer pattern.

MVC Meets Swing

Most Swing components implement MVC "in the small." Swing simplifies the MVC implementation by exposing most of the commonly used functions as public methods in one class (`JTextField`, `JButton`, and others). This means that most of the time, you have to work with only one object. However, the model and view are always there, easily accessible, so that you can use the full power of MVC whenever you feel the need.

Figure 11.4 shows a portion of the UML diagram for the `javax.swing.JTextField` class as generated by JBuilder. Only the relevant elements are shown.

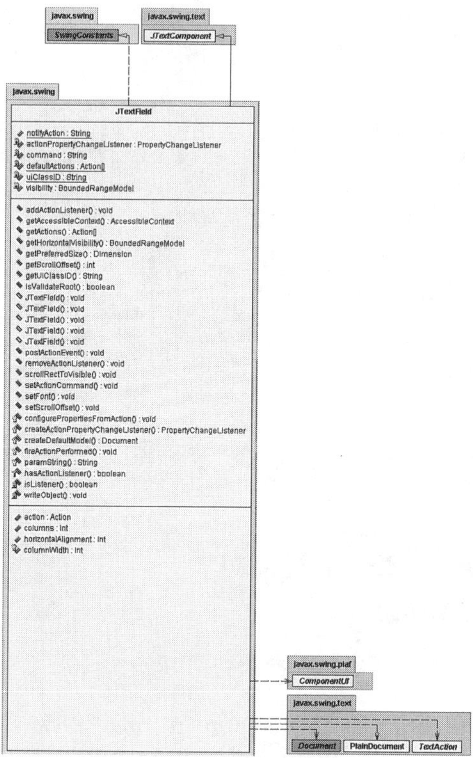

FIGURE 11.4 The `JTextField` and associated classes.

The `JTextField` properly corresponds to the controller. However, in Swing, it also acts as a proxy for the model and the view associated with the controller. This allows you to deal with a single `JTextField` object in most cases. `JTextField` provides methods such as `setText()` and `getText()` to interact with the underlying model (a `javax.swing.text.Document` object). However, both the model and the view are exposed through `getDocument()` and `getUI()` methods, respectively. This means that you can programmatically choose to interact directly with these other two parts of the MVC triad.

THE PROXY PATTERN

Swing uses a modification of the proxy pattern to expose most of the view- and model-related functions through the Swing classes (such as `JTextField`).

The proxy pattern is used to substitute one object, the proxy, for another, the subject. The proxy delegates all the real work to the subject. Proxies are used in many places: when the subject is a remote object; when operations on the subject are expensive and the proxy schedules them in batches; or, as in the case of Swing, to achieve simplicity in design so that most of the external interaction is through the proxy.

In Swing, classes such as `JTextField` may be thought of as proxies to `Document`. A method such as `setText()` defined in the `JTextField` has the effect of modifying the underlying model. The same effect can be produced by obtaining a reference to the document (`getDocument()`) and inserting the string at the desired location with the desired attributes (`insertString()`). The former approach is simpler; the latter one provides more control over the details of the design.

In an analogous manner, Swing uses controller classes such as `JTextField` as a proxy for views (`javax.swing.plaf.ComponentUI`).

As Figure 11.4 depicts, `JTextField` has dependencies on `Document` and `PlainDocument`, which constitute the model, and on `ComponentUI`, which is the view.

Swing Component Hierarchy

Figure 11.5 shows the UML diagram of a few Swing components.

Figure 11.5 shows that a majority of Swing components subclass `javax.swing.JComponent`. Subclasses of `JComponent` are called *lightweight components* because they do not use peer classes (unlike AWT components that subclass `java.awt.Component` but not `JComponent`). The most significant exceptions to this are `JDialog` and `JFrame`. These are Swing containers that represent free-standing windows—evident from the fact that they eventually subclass `java.awt.Window`.

Table 11.2 lists some of the common Swing components. It is not an exhaustive list. Its purpose is to compare the Swing component with the corresponding AWT component and point out some additional events and properties that the Swing components provide compared to their AWT counterparts.

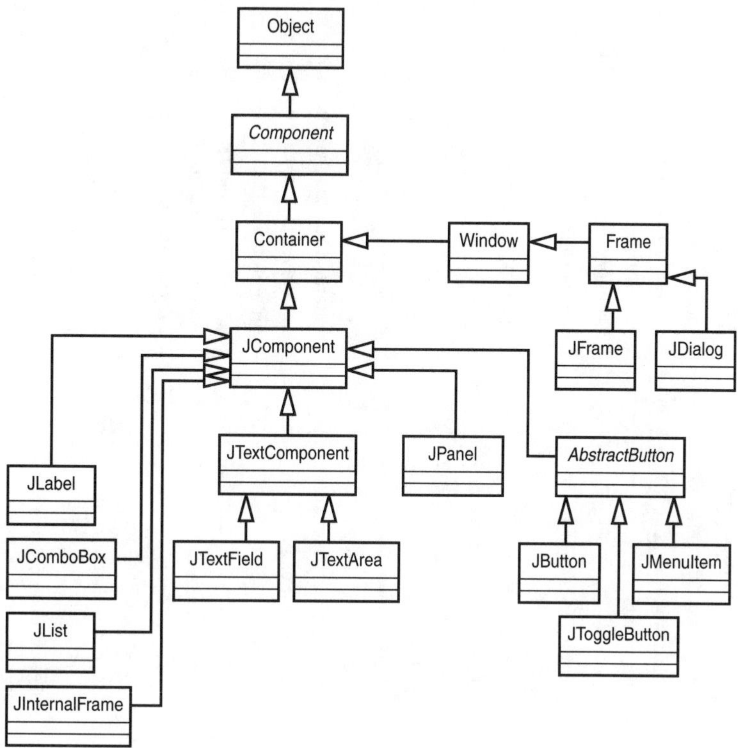

FIGURE 11.5 The class diagram of a sampling of Swing components.

Table 11.2 shows that by and large, Swing components have a richer variety of events and properties. Some of these properties (such as `ActionCommand` for `JTextField` and `CellRenderer` for `JList`) are a direct result of MVC support in Swing. Others (such as `Font` for `JTextArea` and the icon properties for `JToggleButton` subclasses) offer increased functionality not present in the corresponding AWT components.

TABLE 11.2 A Comparison of Features of Swing and AWT Components

Swing Component Name	Lightweight?	Corresponding AWT Component Name	Additional Properties and Events Compared to Corresponding AWT Component	
			Additional Properties	**Additional Events**
JComponent	Yes	Component	ActionMap, AlignmentX, AlignmentY, Autoscrolls, Border, and others	AncestorEvent, PropertyChangeEvent, VetoableChangeEvent
JLabel	Yes	Label	HorizontalAlignment, VerticalAlignment, Icon, and others	None (except those inherited from JComponent)
JButton	Yes	Button	Icon, DisabledIcon, DisabledSelectedIcon, RolloverIcon, Mnemonic, and others	ChangeEvent, ItemEvent
JMenuItem	Yes	MenuItem	All the above (via common superclass AbstractButton)	Inherited via AbstractButton
JToggleButton	Yes	None	Inherited via AbstractButton	Inherited via AbstractButton
JTextArea	Yes	TextArea	LineWrap, Font, WrapStyleWord, and others	CaretEvent, InputMethodEvent (inherited via JTextComponent)
JTextField	Yes	TextField	ActionCommand, ScrollOffset, HorizontalAlignment, and others	CaretEvent, InputMethodEvent (inherited via JTextComponent)
JList	Yes	List	CellRenderer, SelectionForeground, SelectionBackground, and others	ListSelectionListener
JComboBox	Yes	Choice		ActionEvent
JInternalFrame	Yes	None	DesktopIcon, Closable, Iconfiable, Maximizable, and others	InternalFrameEvent

TABLE 11.2 Continued

Swing Component Name	Lightweight?	Corresponding AWT Component Name	Additional Properties and Events Compared to Corresponding AWT Component	
			Additional Properties	**Additional Events**
`JFrame`	No	`Frame`	`DefaultCloseOperation`, `RootPane`, `GlassPane`, `ContentPane`, and others	None
`JDialog`	No	`Dialog`	`DefaultCloseOperation`, `RootPane`, `GlassPane`, `ContentPane`, and others	None

Working with Swing in JBuilder

To work with Swing components in a WYSIWYG manner, you need to be in Design mode (as opposed to Source mode). When the current file is a Java source file, click on the Design tab at the bottom of JBuilder's Content pane. This makes the Component Palette appear at the top of the Content pane.

The Component Palette contains two tabs dedicated to Swing. One of these has Swing components, and the other has Swing containers. These are shown in Figures 11.6 and 11.7, respectively.

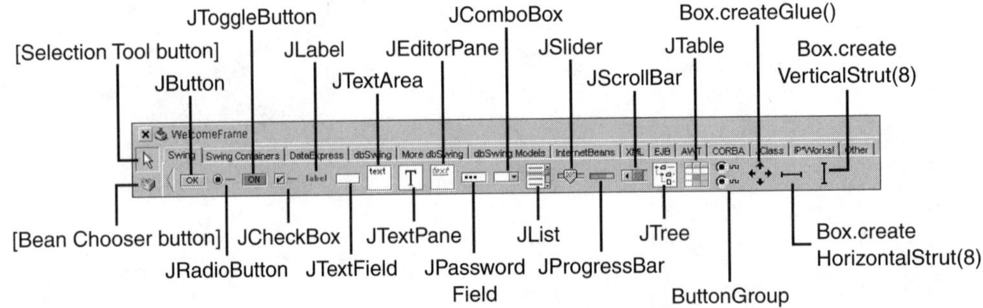

FIGURE 11.6 The Swing tab contains components that are not containers.

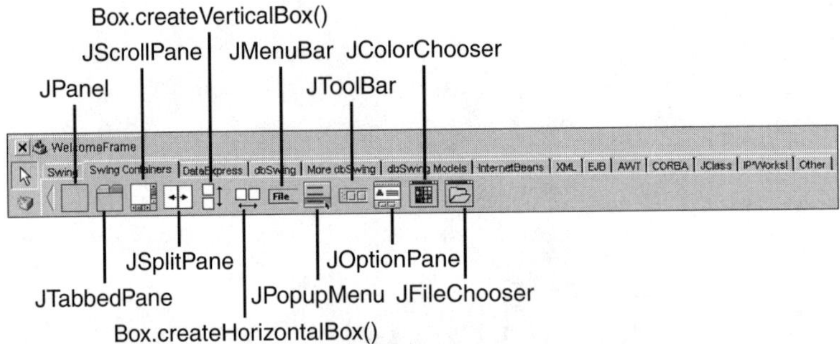

FIGURE 11.7 The Swing Containers tab on the Component Palette.

In JBuilder, you can add Swing components to your application in three primary ways:

- Top-level containers—`JFrames`, `JDialogs`, and `JApplets`—and `JPanels` are added through the Object Gallery (choose the File, New menu item). The `JFrame`, `JDialog`, and `JPanel` options are on the General tab of the Object Gallery; the

`JApplet` option is on the Web tab. Selecting any of these options brings up a wizard. On the first screen of the wizard, you can choose the appropriate class (`javax.swing.JFrame`, `javax.swing.JDialog`, `javax.swing.JPanel`, or `javax.swing.JApplet`) from the combo box.

- Swing containers and components can be selected from the Component Palette, shown in Figures 11.6 and 11.7, in Design view. Clicking on an icon on the Component Palette selects the corresponding component or container. After selecting, you can click on either the Content or the Structure pane to drop a new object of the selected type.
- If a Swing component does not appear on the Component Palette, you can select it individually by clicking on the Bean Chooser button on the Component Palette, shown in Figure 11.6. By clicking on this button and the Select option that then appears, you get the Bean Chooser dialog box, shown in Figure 11.8. From this dialog box, you can select the type of component you want. A component of the selected type can then be placed in your code by clicking in the Content or Structure panes.

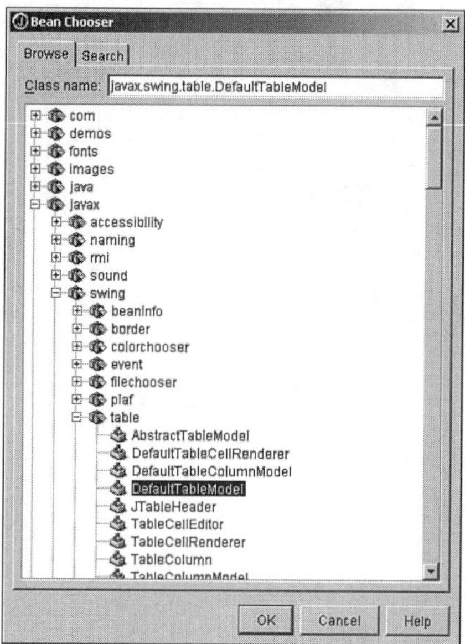

FIGURE 11.8 The Bean Chooser dialog box lets you select any valid component type known to JBuilder.

CAUTION

Be careful when you click and drop components on the Content pane. The component is "received" by the container directly underneath your cursor when you click. When containers are small and closely packed, you can easily put your component on the wrong container.

To make sure that you put your component in the container you intend, you can click on the container's name in the Structure pane (instead of the actual container in the Content pane). This way, you'll always target the correct, intended container—whether you have a jittery mouse or an itchy click-finger!

The Inspector shows the properties and events of the currently selected component. Figure 11.9 shows the Inspector with the properties of a `JTextField` component.

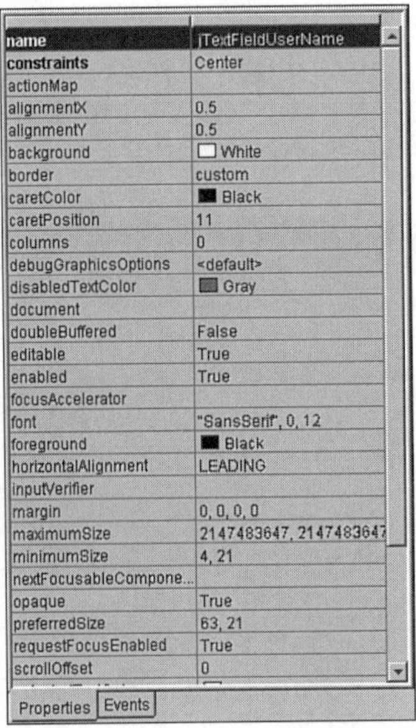

FIGURE 11.9 The properties of a `JTextField` component in the Inspector.

TIP

If you cannot see a property in the Inspector as expected, there could be one of two reasons: You have selected multiple disparate components, or you need to increase the property exposure level.

If you select multiple components of different types (say, a `JTextField` and a `JLabel`) by holding down the Shift key, the Inspector shows only the common properties for all the selected components. In this case, you need to deselect some components to make more properties show up in the Inspector.

If you have selected only one component (or multiple components of the same type) and you're still unable to see a property in the Inspector, you need to increase the property exposure level. Right-click anywhere on Properties tab in the Inspector, and select a higher value from the Property Exposure Level menu. The three values are Regular (commonly used properties are shown), Expert (additional properties are shown), and Hidden (all properties are shown).

In Practice

Now that we have looked at Swing components and how to use them in JBuilder, let's build a Swing-based user interface for the ChalkTalk application.

Chapter 4, "Modeling," introduced the UML diagrams for the various tiers of the ChalkTalk application. The diagram for the User Services tier is reproduced in Figure 11.10.

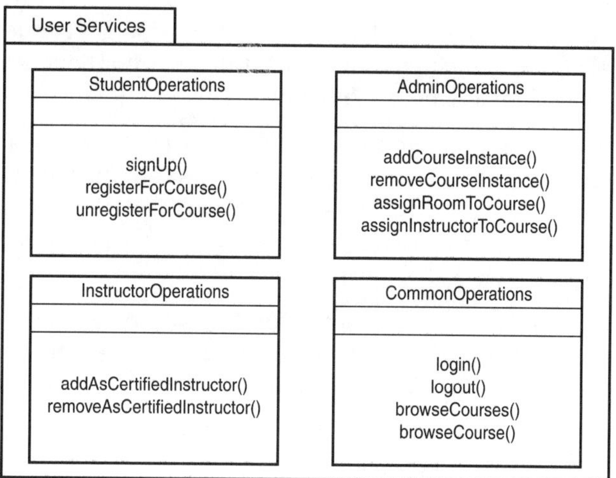

FIGURE 11.10 The User Services Tier classes and methods for the ChalkTalk application.

For now, we will create the basic framework of the application and support the `browseCourses` and `browseCourse` operations.

To give you an idea of where we are going, here is a summarized list of all the steps we will perform in this "In Practice" section:

1. Create a project and application.
2. Design the user interface of the `JFrame` and `JPanels`.

3. Design the `dataobjects` package and classes.
4. Design the `CommonOperations` class.
5. Connect the user interface to the `CommonOperations`.

Creating a Project and Application

Follow these steps to create a new project and application:

1. Select File, New Project.
2. On the first screen of the Project Wizard, enter **chap11** as the name of the project, and **C:\Projects\SAMS\Application\chap11** as the directory. Leave the type as jpx, leave the template as Default Project, and check the Generate project notes file check box. You can put your project in a different directory, but at least make sure that the last component is chap11. This will make it easier for you to run the files on the CD. Click Next.
3. On the second screen of the Project Wizard, no changes are needed. On the third screen, you can enter your name in the @author field, and your company name in the Company field. Click Finish.
4. Select File, New to bring up the Object Gallery. On the General tab, double-click on the Application icon to bring up the Application Wizard. On the first screen, enter **`com.sams.chalktalk.client.swing`** as the Package and **`ChalkTalkClient`** as the Class name. Check the Generate header comments check box. Click Next.
5. On the second screen of the Application Wizard, enter **`FrmMain`** as the Class and **`ChalkTalk`** as the Title of the frame. Check all the options (generate menu bar, toolbar, status bar, About dialog, and center frame onscreen). Click Next.
6. On the third and final screen, check the Create runtime configuration check box and enter **`ChalkTalkClient`** as the name.

You now have a basic application that you can run from the Run, Run Project menu (shortcut key is F9). Next we will design the user interface.

Designing the User Interface of the `JFrame` and `JPanels`

We will design the application in the Windows Explorer style—with one `JFrame`, which will have a `JTree` on the left and a `JPanel` on the right. However, we want to be able to plug different `JPanels` when different nodes in the tree are selected. This allows us to easily extend the application later to support `JPanels` for displaying and editing `CourseInstances`, for example. We will do this through polymorphism, by creating our own `JPanel` subclass.

1. Open the `FrmMain` frame and switch to the Design tab at the bottom of the AppBrowser.
2. Select the `statusBar` component and, in the Inspector, change its Border property to `LoweredBevel`. This adds the following line of code in the `jbInit()` method:

   ```
   statusBar.setBorder(BorderFactory.createLoweredBevelBorder());
   ```

3. In the toolbar, delete the second button (`jButton2`) by selecting it and pressing the Delete key. Rename `jButton1` to `jButtonBrowseCourses`.
4. From the Swing Containers tab on the Component Palette, select `JSplitPane` and drop it on the center of the frame in the Designer.
5. From the Swing tab on the Component Palette, select `JTree` and carefully drop it on the `JSplitPane`. (This is easier if you drop the `JTree` in the Structure pane rather than the Content pane of the AppBrowser.)
6. Select the `JTree` component to show its properties in the Inspector. Change the name to **`jTreeCourses`**.
7. In the Inspector for the `JSplitPane`, set the following properties: Name to **`jSplitPane`** and dividerLocation to **120.** This adds the following line to the `jbInit()` method:

   ```
   jSplitPane.setDividerLocation(120);
   ```

8. In the Inspector for `jTreeCourses`, set the constraints property to left. The following line is added to `jbInit()`:

   ```
   jSplitPane.add(jTreeCourses, JSplitPane.LEFT);
   ```

9. Next, create the menu. In the Designer, double-click on the `jMenuBar1` component to launch the Menu Designer.
10. Click on `jMenuFile` to open it in the Menu Designer. Add a new `JMenu` by simply typing **Browse Courses** in the Menu Designer.
11. Rename the newly created `JMenu` object to **`jMenuFileBrowseCourses`**. Drag it above `jMenuFileExit`. Insert a separator between `jMenuFileBrowseCourses` and `jMenuFileExit`. The completed menu should look like Figure 11.11.

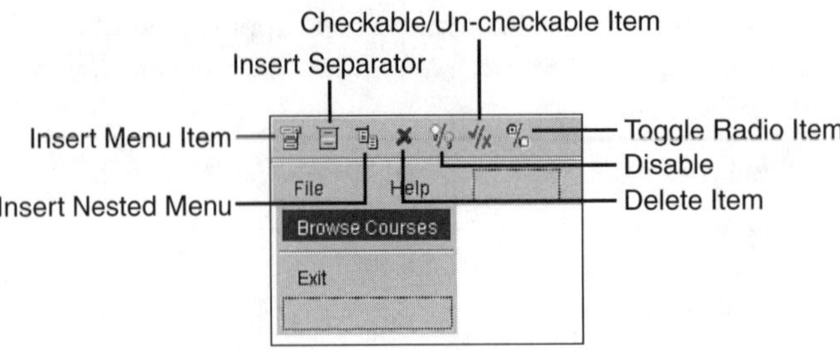

FIGURE 11.11 The finished menu for the `FrmMain` frame.

12. Now we'll create our own `JPanel` subclass. Select the File, New Class menu to launch the Class Wizard. Set the Package to be **`com.sams.chalktalk.client.swing`**, the Class name to be **`ContentPanel`**, and the Base class to be **`javax.swing.JPanel`**. In the Options box, select Public, Generate header comments, and Generate default constructor. Deselect Generate main method and override abstract methods. Click OK.

13. In the Designer, set the `toolTipText` for the `ContentPanel` to be **Content Panel**. The following line will be added to the `jbInit()` method:

```
this.setToolTipText("Content Panel");
```

14. In the Source tab, add the following `render` method to the `ContentPanel` class. The method does nothing. Subclasses of `ContentPanel` override this method to provide real behavior.

```
public void render(Object model) { }
```

15. Make the project (Ctrl+F9) to ensure that everything is as expected. If you find any compilation errors, use the Messages tab at the bottom and the Errors node in the Structure pane on the left to locate and fix your errors.

16. Create a subclass of `ContentPanel`. Launch the Class Wizard again (choose File, New Class). Set the Package to be **`com.sams.chalktalk.client.swing`**, the Class name to be **`CoursePanel`**, and the Base class to be **`com.sams.chalktalk.client.swing.ContentPanel`**. In the Options box, select Public, Generate header comments, and Generate default constructor. Deselect Generate main method and override abstract methods. Click OK.

17. In the Designer, set the layout property of the panel (this) to be **null**. The following line will be added to the `jbInit()` method:

```
this.setLayout(null);
```

18. From the Swing tab on the Component Palette, select the `JLabel` component and drop four of these on the `JPanel`. Then select the `JTextField` component and drop three of these. Finally, drop a `JScrollPane` from the Swing Containers tab and put a `JTextArea` (Swing tab) within the `JScrollPane`. Reposition and resize the components appropriately by dragging their edges so that your finished panel looks similar to Figure 11.12.

19. Save all your files by selecting the File, Save All menu option.

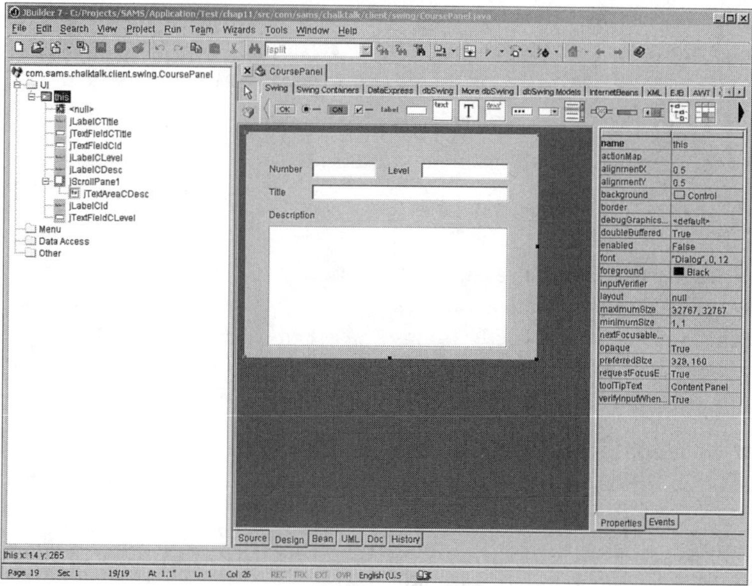

FIGURE 11.12 The finished `CoursePanel` after all the components have been placed on it.

CAUTION

You can drop multiple components of the same type quickly by pressing the Shift key, and then clicking on the appropriate component on the Component Palette. However, be careful not to drop more components than you need! After you are finished dropping multiple components, click on the Selection Tool on the Component Palette to deselect the component.

Designing the `dataobjects` Package and Classes

Now we will design the classes and interfaces that will assist us in representing the data model in ChalkTalk.

The one class that is easy to identify is `CourseData`. It represents the attributes of a `Course`. However, this is not all. We need a way to abstract all data classes so that we can get the display name (for the purpose of display in a tree node, for example) of any data object. This necessitates an interface, `Displayable`. `CourseData` (and any other class that must be displayed in a tree or some other user interface component) will implement this interface. Also, we will provide a `CourseFilter` class, which allows us to specify criteria when searching for courses.

1. Create the Displayable interface. Select File, New to bring up the Object Gallery. Select Interface from the General tab to launch the Interface Wizard. Enter **`com.sams.chalktalk.dataobjects`** as the Package, **`Displayable`** as the Interface name, **<none>** as the Base interface, and select Generate header comments. Click OK.

2. In the interface, add the following method:

```
public String getDisplayName();
```

3. Create the `CourseData` class. Launch the Class Wizard and enter **`com.sams.chalktalk.dataobjects`** as the Package, **`CourseData`** as the Class name, and **`java.lang.Object`** as the Base class. Select the Public, Generate header comments and Generate default constructor options and deselect the other options. Click OK.

4. On `CourseData`, switch to the Bean tab, and then the Properties tab within the Bean tab. Click on the Add Property button to launch the New Property dialog box, shown in Figure 11.13. Enter **description** in the Property name and **String** as the Type; select both Getter and Setter, and select none for the Binding. Deselect Expose through bean info. Your dialog box should look identical to Figure 11.13.

5. Click on the Apply button. The description property and the associated code are added to the `CourseData` class.

6. Keeping the New Property dialog box open, add the **`id`** property. The only difference is that the Property name is `id`. Everything else stays the same. Click Apply.

7. Add a third property with Property name **`title`**. Again, all other fields stay the same. This time, click OK to apply the property and dismiss the New Property dialog box.

8. Switch to the Source tab. Notice that JBuilder generated the property member variables as well as the getter and setter methods for the three properties.

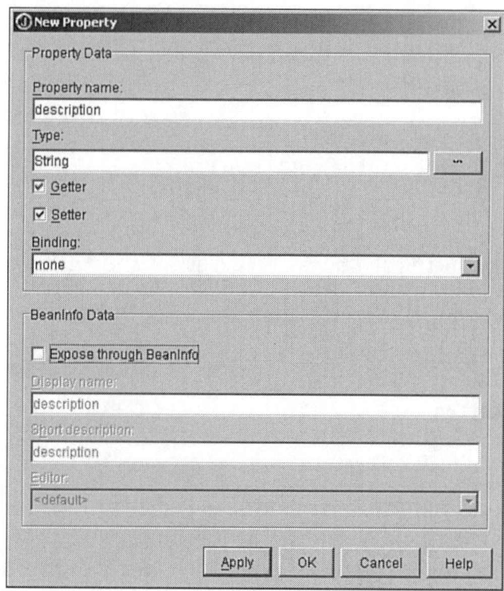

FIGURE 11.13 The New Property dialog box after the details for the description property of the `CourseData` class have been entered.

9. Now implement the `Displayable` interface. Select Wizards, Implement Interface to launch the Implement Interface Wizard dialog box shown in Figure 11.14.

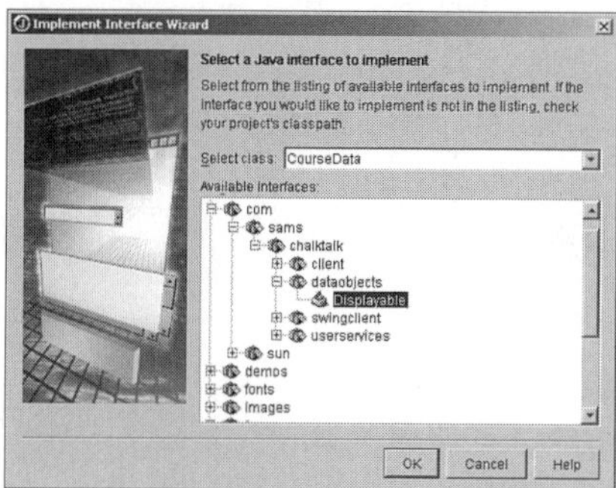

FIGURE 11.14 The Implement Interface Wizard dialog box.

10. On the wizard dialog box, navigate to the `Displayable` interface in the tree and select it. Click OK.

11. JBuilder places the `implements` clause in your class definition as well as the `getDisplayName` method in the class. Modify the body of this method so that it looks as shown here:

```
public String getDisplayName() {
  return getId() + ": \"" + getTitle() + '"';
}
```

12. Add a constructor to the `CourseData` class as shown here:

```
public CourseData(String title, String id, String description) {
  this.title = title;
  this.id = id;
  this.description = description;
}
```

13. Add a new class, named `StringData`, to the `com.sams.chalktalk.dataobjects` package. Use the Class Wizard to create the class and the Implement Interface Wizard to implement the `Displayable` interface. Listing 11.1 shows the entire class.

LISTING 11.1 StringData.java

```
package com.sams.chalktalk.dataobjects;

public class StringData implements Displayable {

  private String data;

  public StringData(String data) {
    this.data = data;
  }
  public String getDisplayName() {
    return data;
  }
  public String toString() {
    return data;
  }
}
```

14. Add another class, named `CourseFilter`, to the `com.sams.chalktalk.dataobjects` package. Use the New Property dialog box (accessible through the

Add Property button on the Properties tab within the Bean tab) to add a property named `ids` of type `String[]`. Make sure that you deselect the Expose through BeanInfo check box. Listing 11.2 shows the entire class.

LISTING 11.2 CourseFilter.java

```
package com.sams.chalktalk.dataobjects;

public class CourseFilter {
  private String[] ids;
  public String[] getIds() {
    return ids;
  }
  public void setIds(String[] ids) {
    this.ids = ids;
  }
}
```

15. Make the project.

Designing the `CommonOperations` Class

We are more than halfway through. In this section, we will add the `CommonOperations` class, and in the next section we will hook up the user interface to this class.

1. Create the new `CommonOperations` class by using the Class Wizard. The Package should be **`com.sams.chalktalk.userservices`**; the Class name, **`CommonOperations`**; and the Base class, **`java.lang.Object`**. Select the Public, Generate header comments, and Generate default constructor options, and deselect the other two options.

2. Add the four methods, `login`, `logout`, `browseCourses`, and `browseCourse`. At this point, there would be no implementation for the login and logout methods, and dummy implementations for the two browse methods. This is sometimes called *stubbing out* the methods. Because we haven't yet established connectivity to the database (or some other real data source), our browse methods will be merely stubs at this point. They will provide dummy data, but are otherwise fully functional. Listing 11.3 shows the complete `CommonOperations` class.

LISTING 11.3 CommonOperations.java

```
package com.sams.chalktalk.userservices;
import com.sams.chalktalk.dataobjects.*;
import java.util.*;

public class CommonOperations {

  public CommonOperations() {
  }

  public void login()  {
  // Currently unimplemented
  }

  public void logout() {
  // Currently unimplemented
  }

  public java.util.Collection browseCourses(CourseFilter courseFilter) {
    Vector v = new Vector();
    v.add(
      new CourseData(
        "Introduction to Java",
        "CS211",
        "This course will teach you the fundamentals of Java
➥using JDK 1.4. Topics include File I/O, AWT and Swing.
➥Student must have a grade of C or better in CS202 to
➥register for this course. Students who have obtained a
➥B or higher grade in CS201 may take this class
➥with Instructor's permission. There will be one mid-term
➥and one final exam with one substantial programming assignment.")
      );
    v.add(
      new CourseData(
        "Introduction to JBuilder",
        "CS251",
        "This course will teach you how to use JBuilder to
➥develop Java applications. Topics include developing,
➥JavaBeans, JSPs and Servlets. Student must have a grade of
➥C or better in CS211 to register for this course. There will
➥be one mid-term and one final exam with one substantial
➥programming assignment.")
```

LISTING 11.3 Continued

```
      );
    return Collections.unmodifiableCollection(v);
  }

  public CourseData browseCourse(String courseId) {
    return new CourseData(
      "Introduction to JBuilder",
      "CS251",
      "This course will teach you how to use JBuilder to develop
➥Java applications. Topics include developing, JavaBeans, JSPs
➥and Servlets.
➥Student must have a grade of C or better in CS211 to register
➥for this course. There will be one mid-term and one final exam
➥with one substantial programming assignment.");
  }
}
```

3. Make the project.

Connecting the User Interface to `CommonOperations`

In this section, we will create a simple class to encapsulate the nodes that can appear in the `jTreeCourses` in `FrmMain`. We will then add the event listeners that will connect the user interface to the `CommonOperations` class.

1. Create a new class, `ChalkTalkTreeNode`, that extends the `javax.swing.tree.DefaultMutableTreeNode` class. Listing 11.4 shows the entire class.

LISTING 11.4 ChalkTalkTreeNode.java

```
package com.sams.chalktalk.client.swing;

import javax.swing.tree.DefaultMutableTreeNode;
import com.sams.chalktalk.dataobjects.Displayable;

public class ChalkTalkTreeNode extends DefaultMutableTreeNode {
  Displayable contents;
  ContentPanel panel;

  public ChalkTalkTreeNode(Displayable contents) {
    this(contents, new ContentPanel());
```

LISTING 11.4 Continued

```
  }

  public ChalkTalkTreeNode(Displayable contents, ContentPanel panel) {
    this.contents = contents;
    this.panel = panel;
  }

  public String toString() {
    return contents.getDisplayName();
  }
  public Displayable getContents() {
    return contents;
  }
  public ContentPanel getPanel() {
    return panel;
  }
}
```

2. In the `FrmMain` class, add a new instance variable called `commonOps` as shown in the following line of code:

   ```
   CommonOperations commonOps = new CommonOperations();
   ```

3. Add the following `import` line at the top of the FrmMain.java, together with the other `import` statements:

   ```
   import java.util.*;
   ```

4. In the `FrmMain` class, implement the `javax.swing.event.TreeSelectionListener` interface by using the Implement Interface Wizard. JBuilder creates the `valueChanged` method for you. Implement this method as shown in Listing 11.5.

LISTING 11.5 `valueChanged` Event Handler in FrmMain.java

```
public void valueChanged(TreeSelectionEvent e) {
  ChalkTalkTreeNode node = (ChalkTalkTreeNode)e.getPath().
getLastPathComponent();
  node.getPanel().render(node.getContents());
  showContentPanel(node.getPanel());
}
private void showContentPanel(ContentPanel panel) {
  jSplitPane.add(panel, JSplitPane.RIGHT);
}
```

5. In the Designer, select the `jButtonBrowseCourses` button. In the Inspector, switch to the Events tab and click on the `actionPerformed` event (the first one in the list). Rename the event handler method to **`browseCourses_actionPerformed`**. Press Enter. JBuilder adds the event handler, and puts you back in the Source tab at the appropriate place. Modify the event handler so that it looks like Listing 11.6.

LISTING 11.6 `browseCourses_actionPerformed` Event Handler in FrmMain.java

```
void browseCourses_actionPerformed(ActionEvent e) {
  Collection courses = commonOps.browseCourses(null);
  showCourses(courses);
}
private void showCourses(Collection courses) {
  DefaultTreeModel model = (DefaultTreeModel)jTreeCourses.getModel();
  DefaultMutableTreeNode root = (DefaultMutableTreeNode) model.getRoot();
  for (Iterator iter = courses.iterator() ; iter.hasNext() ; ) {
    CourseData course = (CourseData)iter.next();
    if (course != null) root.add(new ChalkTalkTreeNode(course,
 new CoursePanel()));
  }
  jTreeCourses.repaint();
}
```

6. Now we will associate the above event handler with the Browse Courses menu item. In the Designer, select `jMenuFileBrowseCourses` and select the Events tab in the Inspector.

7. Select the `actionPerformed` event (first one in the list) and rename the event handler method to **`browseCourses_actionPerformed`**. Note that this is the same name used for the event handler method for `jButtonBrowseCourses` in step 3. Press Enter.

8. JBuilder switches to Source view and lands you in the `browseCourses_actionPerformed` method. But we already implemented this method in step 3. So we're all finished! The same event code will be executed whether the Browse Courses button is clicked or the Browse Courses menu item is selected.

Summary

Swing provides a lightweight and portable API for designing user interfaces. Not only this, the API uses the well-understood and time-tested MVC design pattern. JBuilder provides extensive facilities to use Swing components, some of which we used in this chapter.

Reflections

- How long did it take you to build the Swing application in the "In Practice" section in this chapter? How long do you think it would take you to do it without JBuilder?
- Can you think of improvements in the Swing application as designed previously? (Hint: using `javax.swing.Action` to share behavior between a `JMenuItem` and a `JButton`; reusing the same `CoursePanel` for all the course nodes.)
- Can you think of enhancements to the functionality of the Swing application designed previously? (Hint: providing undo facility by stacking `CoursePanels`; supporting other subclasses of `ContentPanels`.)

12

Understanding Layout Managers

IN THIS CHAPTER

- Uncovering Layout Managers
- Layout Managers Available
- Using a Layout Manager
- Using the `XYLayout` Manager
- Using the `BorderLayout` Manager
- Using the `FlowLayout` Manager
- Using `VerticalFlowLayout`
- Using the `BoxLayout2` Manager
- Using the `GridLayout` Manager
- Using the `CardLayout` Manager
- Using the `OverlayLayout2` Manager
- Using the `PaneLayout` Manager
- Using the `GridBagLayout` Manager
- Creating a Custom Layout Manager
- Design Guidelines

Every container, by default, has a layout manager associated with it. The layout managers have a singular responsibility: to determine where each new component is placed when it is added to the container. Technically, a layout manager is an object that implements the `LayoutManager` interface. Each container has a default layout manager assigned to it and an accessor and mutator to access or change the selected layout manager. Layout managers give you the following features:

- Correct positioning of each component independent of fonts, selected screen resolution, and desired platform
- Movement of components within containers dynamically resized at runtime
- Rearrangement of surrounding components as a given component resizes

Understanding layout managers does not just entail using a layout manger. For example, knowing how to drive a car does not necessarily mean that you know how to repair a car or diagnose what is wrong. We will cover the following aspects of a layout manager:

- Looking inside and understanding the basics of layouts
- Understanding the capabilities and selection criteria for different layout managers
- Building a custom layout manager

Uncovering Layout Managers

The layout manager is an integral part of all Java graphical user interface applications. Whether you are using Swing or AWT, a layout manager is still required. Many times, the default layout managers for the selected component are used, but these layout managers can be changed to gain the desired effect for the user interface design. For example, in the AWT environment, certain types of containers default to specific layout managers:

- All panels default to use `FlowLayout`. This also includes applets that extend a base panel.
- All windows, including frames and dialog boxes default to `BorderLayout`.

When you create a frame or panel for your application, the actual default layout manager can be seen only in the component window of the designer window. In the Inspector, it refers only to the `<default layout>` (see Figure 12.1). You will notice that for an AWT frame, the default indicated in the component window is `<border layout>`.

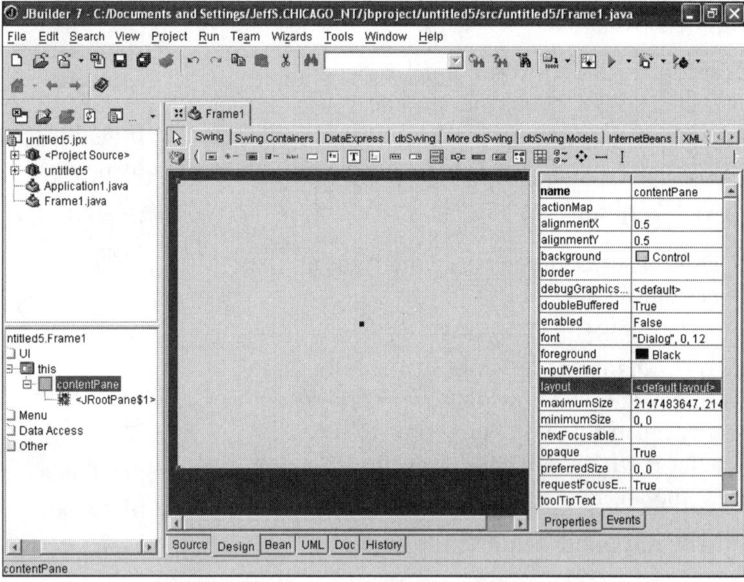

FIGURE 12.1 Design window showing the default layout manager chosen.

JBuilder's UI Designer assigns the default layout manager for each new container. If you want to change the default layout manager, simply change the layout property list in the Inspector. The Inspector then uses the mutator for the container and assigns the layout manager instance desired. Listing 12.1 demonstrates this.

LISTING 12.1 Changing the Default Layout Manager

```
public class Frame1 extends Frame {
  //Define an instance of the desired layout managers
  private BorderLayout borderLayout1 = new BorderLayout();
  private XYLayout xYLayout1 = new XYLayout();

...
  //Component initialization
  private void jbInit() throws Exception  {
    //setIconImage(Toolkit.getDefaultToolkit().createImage(
    ➥ Frame1.class.getResource("[Your Icon]")));
    this.setSize(new Dimension(400, 300));
    this.setTitle("Frame Title");
    //Assign the layout managers to the container
    this.setLayout(xYLayout1);
  }
...
```

Layout Managers Available

Each layout manager has some common characteristics, but the placement of components is typically what differs from one to another. Some layout managers are used to drive portable layouts, such as `FlowLayout` and `BorderLayout`. Others, such as `null` and `XYLayout`, are designed to quickly develop a user interface without much intervention from a layout manager. Table 12.1 describes in text the different layout managers.

TABLE 12.1 The Available Layout Managers in JBuilder

Layout	Description
`<Default Layout>`	This layout will always be one of the following layouts. The default layout for the container will be used. For example, a frame in AWT will select the `BorderLayout`.
`BorderLayout`	Components are placed in the directions of a compass: North—top of the container; South—bottom of the container; East—right of the container; West—left of the container; and Center—within the border areas. Components placed inside any of these coordinates expand as the container expands.

TABLE 12.1 Continued

Layout	Description
`BoxLayout2`	This layout manager is part of the Swing component libraries, but it also works with AWT. You can align components either vertically or horizontally. This differs from `FlowLayout`; components do not wrap to another row or column. This is the same as `BoxLayout` except that it is wrapped as a JavaBean so that it can be used in JBuilder's designers.
`CardLayout`	As you place components onto the container, they are stacked like a set of playing cards. As a card is selected, it moves to the top of the deck and becomes visible.
`FlowLayout`	Components line up in a horizontal row in the order they were added to the container. When a row is filled, the next row automatically starts. If the container is resized, the layout readjusts to display the child components.
`GridLayout`	This layout manager divides the container into a defined number of rows and columns. Each component is placed within a certain row and column. Every component placed within a cell fully occupies the cell, thus making all components equal size.
`GridBagLayout`	Just as in `GridLayout`, `GridBagLayout` divides the container into a grid. The difference is that each element within the grid can be a different size. All cells of the grid will be the same size, but each component can span multiple rows or columns.
`OverlayLayout2`	This component is Swing's `OverlayLayout`, wrapped as a Bean so that it can be selected as a layout in the Inspector. It is much like the `CardLayout` in that it places the components on top of each other. It differs from `CardLayout`, where only one component at a time is visible; the components can be visible at the same time if you make each component in the container transparent.
`PaneLayout`	The pane layout is a custom layout that comes with JBuilder. `PaneLayout` allows you to specify the size of a component with relation to its sibling component(s).
`XYLayout`	This is another custom layout manager provided by JBuilder. Each component is placed exactly where and to the size designed. The `XYLayout` uses a relative coordinate system with 0,0 being the left/topmost point within a container.
`VerticalFlowLayout`	This layout manager is provided as a custom layout available in JBuilder. It is similar to `FlowLayout` except that the components flow vertically rather than horizontally.
`<null>`	You can use the `null` layout, which leaves the components exactly where you place them and at the desired size. However, it differs from `XYLayout` by using a `setBounds()` method for each component. This method specifies the x,y and the width and height.

Using a Layout Manager

As a container is being placed on a frame, the default layout manager is selected. Often, the default layout manager does not produce the desired effect, so a change must be made. The following steps guide you in changing the default layout manager:

1. Select the desired container in either the component tree or the designer window.
2. Select the Properties tab of the Inspector.
3. Change the `layout` property to the desired layout manager.

Changing Layout Properties

Each container within your application will have a layout manager attached to it. Just like any other JavaBean, layout managers also have properties associated with them. These properties can be viewed only in the Inspector by selecting the attached layout manager in the component tree. Changing these properties affects the behavior of the selected layout manager, in turn changing the layout manager's behavior.

To modify the properties of any layout manager from the Inspector, follow these steps:

1. Select the layout from the component tree. JBuilder presents the properties defined for the select layout within the Inspector.
2. Change the property values you want to change. For example, in a `BoxLayout2`, you can modify the `axis` for which the components will be added to the frame.

Meeting of Components and Layout Managers

As you drop components onto a given container, the associated layout manager becomes important. JBuilder creates for each component a set of constraints required to specify to the layout manager where the component needs to be placed. The constraint property is then mapped to the `add()` method for the given layout manager to indicate component placement and size. To change a component's constraint, follow these steps:

1. Select the desired component.
2. Select the constraint property within the Inspector.
3. Change the properties within the associated property editor to receive the desired effect.

Using the `XYLayout` Manager

The `XYLayout` component is a JBuilder custom layout manager that comes only with the SE and Enterprise versions of JBuilder. It places components in a container at specific x and y coordinates relative to the top-left corner of the given container. Regardless of the deployment environment, the container always retains the relative x and y positions of the components (see Figure 12.2). Resizing a container with a `XYLayout`, however, does not resize or reposition the components within the container. For example, if you maximize the screen, the components stay the same relative distance from the top-left corner of the container.

NOTE

When you select the `XYLayout` in the Inspector, JBuilder in turn adds `com.borland.jbcl.layout.*` to your source code. If you change the layout manager from using the `XYLayout` manager, it will not remove the import.

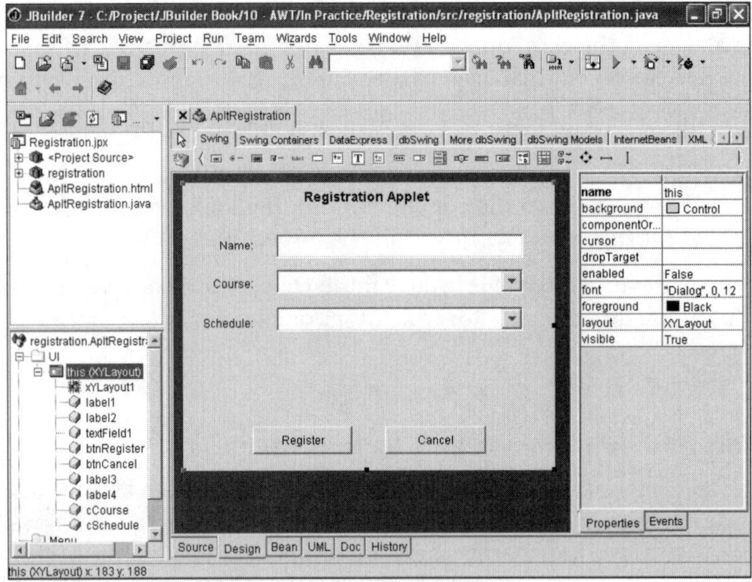

FIGURE 12.2 Layout demonstration using `XYLayout`.

When to Use `XYLayout` Manager

`XYLayout` is useful for designing your application. After you have the design worked out, you can choose from one of the standard layouts for the final design. It is easy to become mired in the details of the layout manager and lose focus of the requirements. The XYLayout manager is typically not deployed to production systems, and it is normally converted to a standard Swing or AWT layout manager. In fact, if you change the XYLayout to GridBagLayout, JBuilder creates a GridBagLayout using the same constraints placed when using the XYLayout. This is a great way to create a GridBagLayout also.

Aligning the Components

You must align components yourself because the layout manager places them wherever you drop them. Alignment does not work for any other layout managers because the layout manager controls the alignment. With JBuilder's alignment operations, within the designer, you can beautify your user interface. You can align either vertically or horizontally, and space or resize components in reference to each other. It is important to align all your components before you convert it to GridBagLayout, or you will create a complex grid rather than a simple grid.

An Example of Using XYLayout

As in any layout manager, each has its own requirements for adding a component to a container. The XYLayout requires an x,y, height, and width for each component within the given container. Listing 12.2 shows two buttons placed on a container. One uses the default size of the component, –1 height and width. The second has all four coordinates assigned to it.

LISTING 12.2 Add Components Using XYLayout

```
    //Add Component using the Default Height
    //and Width defined by component
    this.getContentPane().add(jButton2,
➥ new XYConstraints(56, 106, -1, -1));
    //Add Component with a specific and height and width
    this.getContentPane().add(jButton3,
➥ new XYConstraints(45, 27, 114, 53));
```

Using the BorderLayout Manager

A border layout lays out a container, arranging and resizing its components to fit in five different regions: north, south, east, west, and center. Each region is identified by a corresponding constant contained within the class: NORTH, SOUTH, EAST, WEST, and CENTER. When adding a component to a container with a border layout, use one of these five constants, as shown in Figure 12.3.

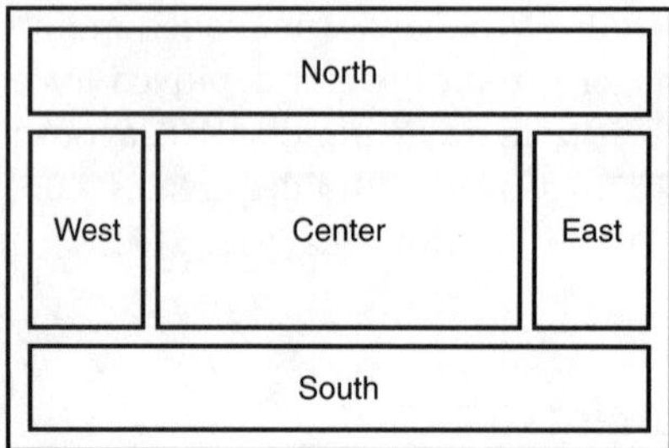

FIGURE 12.3 BorderLayout showing the five different regions.

When to Use BorderLayout

You will probably use BorderLayout the most. Although it is not normally used alone, BorderLayout is normally used in conjunction with nested containers and other layout managers. You will normally nest a Panel inside each region of the BorderLayout and then place each of the required components on each of the corresponding panels.

An Example of Using BorderLayout

You might want to put a toolbar on the top of your frame. The BorderLayout contains a Panel that has all the required buttons with its constraint placed in the NORTH. The following are the steps and results of building a toolbar on a frame:

1. Select the frame in which you want to have a toolbar.
2. Although the default for a Swing frame is BorderLayout, we prefer to specify the layout manager using the property layout in the Inspector.
3. Place a panel on the frame.
4. Change the constraint property of the new panel to NORTH using the Inspector.
5. Change the layout of the new panel to FlowLayout.
6. Drop buttons on the panel for the toolbar.
7. Evaluate the generated code in Listing 12.3.

LISTING 12.3 Building a Toolbar with BorderLayout

```
...
  private void jbInit() throws Exception  {
    //setIconImage(Toolkit.getDefaultToolkit().createImage
➥ (Frame1.class.getResource("[Your Icon]")));
```

LISTING 12.3 Continued

```
    this.setSize(new Dimension(400, 300));
    this.setTitle("BorderLayout");
    this.setLayout(borderLayout1);
    //Assign the layout managers to the container
    jPanel1.setLayout(flowLayout1);
    jButton1.setText("Close");
    jButton2.setText("Open");
    this.add(jPanel1, BorderLayout.NORTH);
    jPanel1.add(jButton2, null);
    jPanel1.add(jButton1, null);
  }
...
```

Using the `FlowLayout` Manager

`FlowLayout` draws components from left to right as they are added to the container. If a component will not fit on a row, a new row is added and the component is placed there, going from top to bottom. Each component takes on its `preferredSize`. For example, a `JButton` sizes to the width of text placed within it. `FlowLayout` provides a simple layout manager that is used, by default, for `JPanels`. For a demonstration of the layout manager's rules, see Figure 12.4.

NOTE

If you want to have a horizontal `FlowLayout`, use the layout manager `HorizontalFlowLayout`. This works exactly the same as the `FlowLayout` except that the components will be placed horizontally.

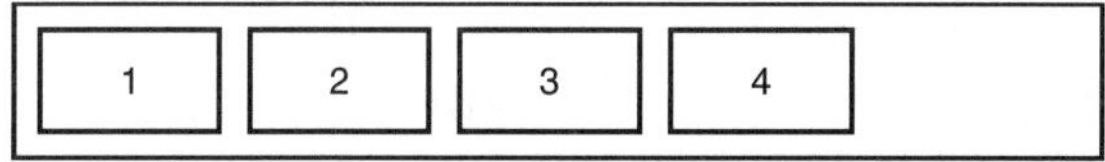

FIGURE 12.4 `FlowLayout` goes from left to right displaying components.

When to Use `FlowLayout`

The typical usage of `FlowLayout` is to display a group of buttons, such as a toolbar. The toolbar requires some features that are best suited by `FlowLayout`. For example, you normally want to have the first button located in the top-left section of the toolbar. As more components get added, they are drawn to the left of the prior object.

Important Properties

Typically, you might not want to use the default behaviors defined within the layout manager. `FlowLayout` contains a few properties to affect the behavior of the layout manager.

Alignment

The alignment of the layout manager specifies the placement of the first object, specifying in the Inspector an alignment of center, left, or right. For example, a toolbar normally is left aligned.

`hgap` and `vgap`

The `hgap` and `vgap` properties are used to inform the layout manager of the desired spacing gap between components both vertically and horizontally.

An Example of Using `FlowLayout`

When you need to create a toolbar with buttons, you will want to use `FlowLayout` for the placement and management of the components on the container. You also might want to make the horizontal gap between the objects very small, such as 1 or 2. Listing 12.4 demonstrates the implementation of a `JPanel` using `FlowLayout` layout manager.

LISTING 12.4 Building a Toolbar with `FlowLayout`

```
...
  //Component initialization
  private void jbInit() throws Exception  {
    //setIconImage(Toolkit.getDefaultToolkit().
➥ createImage(Frame1.class.getResource("[Your Icon]")));
    this.setSize(new Dimension(400, 300));
    this.setTitle("BorderLayout");
    this.setLayout(borderLayout1);
    //Assign the layout managers to the container
    pnlToolBar.setLayout(flowLayout1);
    btnClose.setText("Close");
    btnOpen.setText("Open");
    //Toolbar should start on the left
    flowLayout1.setAlignment(FlowLayout.LEFT);
    //Set the buttons to have no gap
    flowLayout1.setHgap(0);
    this.add(pnlToolBar, BorderLayout.NORTH);
    pnlToolBar.add(btnOpen, null);
    pnlToolBar.add(btnClose, null);
  }...
```

Using `VerticalFlowLayout`

`VerticalFlowLayout` arranges the components the same way as `FlowLayout`, except that it presents the components vertically rather than horizontally. The placement of each component starts at the top-left section of the containers and continues down until it reaches the bottom. After the components reach bottom, the layout manager creates a new column and starts again from the top.

When to Use `VerticalFlowLayout`

`VerticalFlowLayout` is typically used to display bottoms on a panel. For example, navigation bottoms may be displayed on a `JPanel` using this layout manager.

Properties

Using the Inspector you can change properties for the `VerticalFlowLayout`. These properties, which are discussed in the following sections, will then have mutators generated to apply them to the layout manager.

Alignment

The alignment of the layout manager specifies the placement of the first object, specifying in the Inspector an alignment of top, middle, or bottom. For example, a navigation bar normally is placed at the top.

`hgap` and `vgap`

The `hgap` and `vgap` properties are used to inform the layout manager of the desired spacing gap between components both vertically and horizontally.

Fill

`horizontalFill` and `verticalFill` make the objects fill the entire panel either vertically or horizontally. For example, if you set `horizontalFill` to `true`, the last component expands until it fills the remaining space of the container.

An Example of Using `VerticalFlowLayout`

You might want to put a navigation bar on the left of your frame. The `BorderLayout` contains a `Panel` that has all the required buttons with its constraint placed in `WEST`. The following are the steps and results of building a toolbar on a frame:

1. Select the frame in which you want to have a navigation bar.
2. Although the default for a Swing frame is `BorderLayout`, we prefer to specify the layout manager using the property `layout` in the Inspector.
3. Place a panel on the frame.

4. Change the constraint property of the new panel to `WEST` using the Inspector.
5. Change the layout of the new panel to `VerticalFlowLayout`.
6. Drop buttons on the panel for the toolbar.
7. Review the resulting code shown in Listing 12.5.

LISTING 12.5 Building a Navigation Bar Using a `VerticalFlowLayout`

```
...
  //Component initialization
  private void jbInit() throws Exception  {
    //setIconImage(Toolkit.getDefaultToolkit().
➥ createImage(Frame1.class.getResource("[Your Icon]")));
    this.setSize(new Dimension(400, 300));
    this.setTitle("BorderLayout");
    this.setLayout(borderLayout1);
    //Assign the layout managers to the container
    pnlToolBar.setLayout(verticalFlowLayout1);
    btnClose.setText("Close");
    btnOpen.setText("Open");
    this.add(pnlToolBar,  BorderLayout.WEST);
    pnlToolBar.add(btnOpen, null);
    pnlToolBar.add(btnClose, null);
  }
...
```

Using the `BoxLayout2` Manager

`BoxLayout2` is simply a wrapper for Java Swing `BoxLayout`. The `BoxLayout2` wraps the `BoxLayout` using the JavaBean specification. This allows JBuilder to use the Inspector to assign a layout manager. `BoxLayout2` combines the functionality of `FlowLayout` and `VerticalLayout` into one layout manager.

Creating a more lightweight container that uses `BoxLayout2`, you can achieve some layouts for which the more complex `GridBagLayout` is often used. `BoxLayout2` also can be used as a replacement for `GridLayout` or `BorderLayout`. The big difference between this layout manager and the others is that the `BoxLayout2` respects each component's maximum size and x,y alignment.

Using the `GridLayout` Manager

`GridLayout` places all components on the container in a grid specified by a row and column. `GridLayout` automatically expands all components to completely fill the cell. Each cell will be the same size, thus all components placed on the container will be the same size (see Figure 12.5).

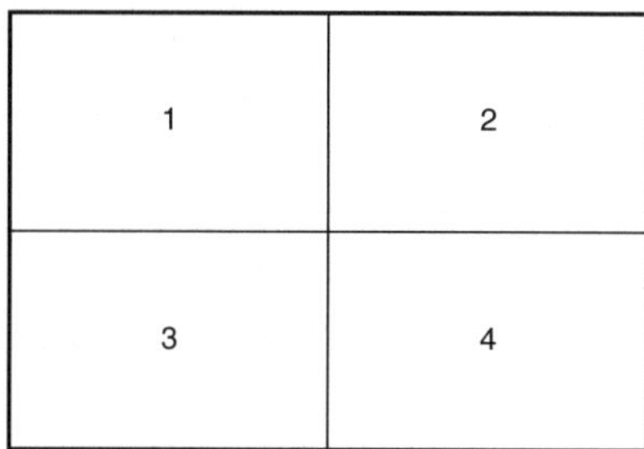

FIGURE 12.5 `GridLayout` displaying components within a defined set of rows and columns.

When to Use `GridLayout`

Use `GridLayout` when you want to have all the components the same size despite the size of the container. For example, when presented with a user interface that resembles a piece of graph paper or a spreadsheet, the `GridLayout` manager meets these requirements.

Properties

The `GridLayout` is not useful without setting the properties to indicate the number of rows and columns. Using the Inspector, these properties can be set.

Column and Rows

Specify the `columns` and `rows` for which a grid for components will be constructed. The number of columns and rows can also change at runtime as required.

`hgap` and `vgap`

The `hgap` and `vgap` properties are used to inform the layout manager of the desired spacing gap between components both vertically and horizontally.

An Example of Using `GridLayout`

An example for using `GridLayout` is creating a calculator. Each button on the calculator should have the same size, and as the container is resized, the requirement to resize the buttons is often also desired. The following steps are used to build a calculator using a GridLayout:

1. Create a frame.
2. Change the layout of the frame to GridLayout.
3. Assign a JPanel to both NORTH and CENTER.
4. Add a label to the panel placed on NORTH. This will be used to display the results.
5. Change the layout of the button panel to use GridLayout.
6. Assign properties of the GridLayout for columns and rows. columns=4 and rows=4.
7. Drop buttons for each number and operations for the calculator within each cell.

LISTING 12.6 Building a Calculator Using the GridLayout

```
...
  //Component initialization
  private void jbInit() throws Exception  {
    //setIconImage(Toolkit.getDefaultToolkit().
➥ createImage(Frame1.class.getResource("[Your Icon]")));
    contentPane = (JPanel) this.getContentPane();
    contentPane.setLayout(borderLayout1);
    this.setSize(new Dimension(400, 300));
    this.setTitle("Frame Title");
    lblResults.setText("Results:");
    jPanel1.setLayout(boxLayout21);
    pFunction.setLayout(gridLayout1);
    gridLayout1.setColumns(4);
    gridLayout1.setRows(4);
    jButton1.setText("1");
    jButton2.setText("3");
    jButton3.setText("4");
    jButton4.setText("5");
    jButton5.setText("2");
    jButton6.setText("6");
    jButton7.setText("-");
    jButton8.setText("7");
    jButton9.setText("8");
    jButton10.setText("9");
    jButton11.setText(".");
```

LISTING 12.6 Continued

```
    jButton12.setText(".");
    jButton13.setText("*");
    jButton14.setText("0");
    jButton15.setText("=");
    jButton16.setText("/");
    contentPane.add(jPanel1, BorderLayout.NORTH);
    jPanel1.add(lblResults, null);
    contentPane.add(pFunction,  BorderLayout.CENTER);
    pFunction.add(jButton1, null);
    pFunction.add(jButton5, null);
    pFunction.add(jButton2, null);
    pFunction.add(jButton13, null);
    pFunction.add(jButton3, null);
    pFunction.add(jButton4, null);
    pFunction.add(jButton6, null);
    pFunction.add(jButton7, null);
    pFunction.add(jButton8, null);
    pFunction.add(jButton9, null);
    pFunction.add(jButton10, null);
    pFunction.add(jButton11, null);
    pFunction.add(jButton14, null);
    pFunction.add(jButton12, null);
    pFunction.add(jButton15, null);
    pFunction.add(jButton16, null);
  }
...
```

Using the `CardLayout` Manager

`CardLayout` places components on top of each other like a deck of cards. Only one component will be visible at any given time. After the components are placed on the container, you must develop code to cycle through the given cards.

When to Use `CardLayout`

`CardLayout` is particularly good when you have an area that contains different components at different times. This gives you a way to manage many panels that need to share the same frame. You then will create a component that cycles the user through the components within the container. Figure 12.6 shows a sample of how `CardLayout` manages components.

With the introduction of `JTabbedPane`, `CardLayout` is not as useful as it used to be. `CardLayout` was normally used to emulate a tab display.

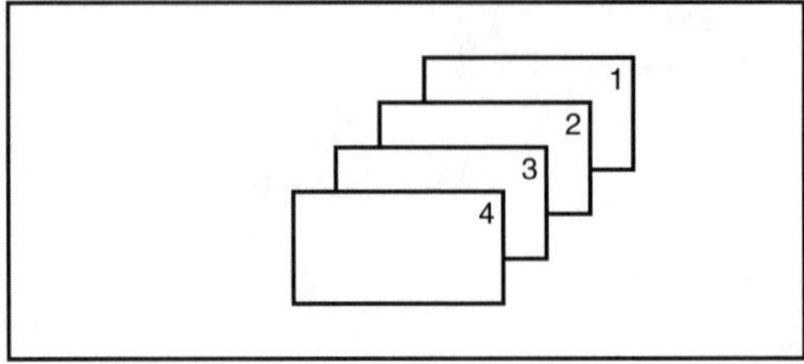

FIGURE 12.6 `CardLayout` sample display.

Properties

`CardLayout` has only a limited number of changes you can specify. The `hgap` and `vgap` properties are used to inform the layout manager of the desired spacing gap between components both vertically and horizontally.

Using the `OverlayLayout2` Manager

As with `BoxLayout2`, `OverlayLayout2` is Swing's `OverlayLayout`, wrapped as a Bean so that it can be used within JBuilder's Inspector. `OverlayLayout2` is similar to `CardLayout` because it places the components on top of each other. It differs from `CardLayout`, by allowing multiple components to be visible at the same time by setting the container transparency. As `CardLayout` has been replaced with `JTabbedPane`, the same fate has met the `OverlayLayout2`, which also is being replaced by `JTabbedPane`.

Using the `PaneLayout` Manager

`PaneLayout` gives you the ability to define the size of a component in relation to its sibling components. When `PaneLayout` is applied to a panel or frame, it lets you control the percentage of the container the components will have relative to each other. When using `PaneLayout`, the placement and size of each component are assigned relative to the components that have already been added to the container. Thus the order in which you add the components to the container is important.

Using the `GridBagLayout` Manager

Finally, we saved the most important and the most complicated layout manager for last. `GridBagLayout` divides the frame into rows and columns as it did with

GridLayout. Both GridLayout and GridBagLayout share the same definition of a cell—the intersection of a row and a column. Each component, however, is not restricted to be just the size of one cell, but can span multiple cells (see Figure 12.7). The area in which a component can span multiple cells is called its *display area*. This difference makes GridBagLayout the most flexible and the most portable of all the layout managers. Even though GridBagLayout is complex, it behaves best if you use a smaller number of nested panels.

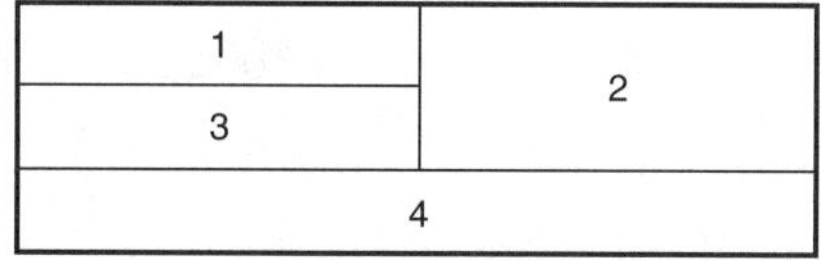

FIGURE 12.7 Using GridBagLayout for component placement.

When to Use GridBagLayout

GridBagLayout is the most predictable layout manager from platform to platform. It also has one of the best behaviors for resizing the frame. This is one of the most important layout managers in most of today's Swing and AWT applications.

NOTE

While doing research for this book, I discovered that many other books recommend not using GridBagLayout, whereas others just ignore it. Actually, you can create a user interface using a number of different layered panels and layout managers to accomplish a similar result. GridBagLayout is designed to behave correctly and predictably on multiple platforms. You should seriously consider the use of GridBagLayout because you have complete control over how a component's display behaves, regardless of platform or resizing requirements.

GridBagLayout Constraints

Many terms are introduced with GridBagLayout that you might not be familiar with when using other layout managers. These terms are important when using the layout to gain the desired effect. Before we look at how to set the constraints for a component, let's look at all the terms we are going to use:

- Display area—The area within a boundary of a defined number of rows and columns. This area ultimately will be occupied by a component.
- Insets—The vertical or horizontal spacing between the grid and the component. This produces a buffer of space between one component and another.

- GridBagConstraints—A class used to hold the constraints defined for a component's placement within the GridBagLayout.

GridBagLayout uses the GridBagConstraints object to define all the properties that the layout manager uses to display each object within the pane. Each component whose containership is specified for the given container must have an instance of GridBagConstraints defined for it. This object defines information for the component placement such as

- Absolute or relative position in reference to the container
- Absolute or relative size of the component
- Number of cells that the display area spans
- Rules for the unused portion of the display area
- Amount of padding between each component
- Weighting between similar components

When you design a user interface using the designer, JBuilder automatically builds the constraints based on the decisions made when graphically designing your interface. As each component is added, based on the relative location to another component, JBuilder builds the constraint automatically. The following code is a constraint built within JBuilder's designer:

```
   contentPane.add(jButton1, new
➥ GridBagConstraints(0, 0, 1, 1, 0.0, 0.0
            ,GridBagConstraints.CENTER, GridBagConstraints.NONE,
➥ new Insets(0, 0, 0, 0), 0, 0));
```

You can then modify these parameters within your source or use the GridBagConstraints Editor (see Figure 12.8).

Table 12.2 describes each of the GridBagConstraints properties. These properties are set either through the GridBagConstraints Editor or by changing the parameters on the construction of the GridBagConstraints object.

TABLE 12.2 GridBagLayout Constraint Properties as Encapsulated Within the GridBagConstraints Object

Property	Description
anchor	Whenever a component does not occupy the entire display area, this property informs the layout manager where to anchor the object. An example of anchor constraints would be GridBagConstraints.CENTER or GridBagConstraints.NORTHWEST.

TABLE 12.2 Continued

Property	Description
`fill`	Again, when the display area is larger than the component, the `fill` property informs the component to completely fill horizontally, vertically, both, or none. The `fill` parameter overrides the `anchor` property if they conflict. For example, if `fill` is set to `GridBagConstraints.BOTH`, it does not matter what the `anchor` is set to.
`insets`	External padding of the components. This is the space between a display area and the component.
`ipadx` and `ipady`	Defines the internal padding. The width of a component will be the minimum width + `ipadx`×2 pixels. The height is the minimum height + `ipady`×2.
`gridwidth` and `gridheight`	Defines the number of columns (`gridwidth`) or rows (`gridheight`) in the component's display area.
`gridx` and `gridy`	Defines the row and column at the upper left of the component. You may also define these properties as `GridBagConstraints.RELATIVE` to specify that the component should be placed to the right or below the component that was added to the container before this one.
`weigthx` and `weighty`	Defines how to distribute the space among the columns (`weightx`) and the rows (`weighty`). This behavior is important in controlling the size of a component as the frame resizes.

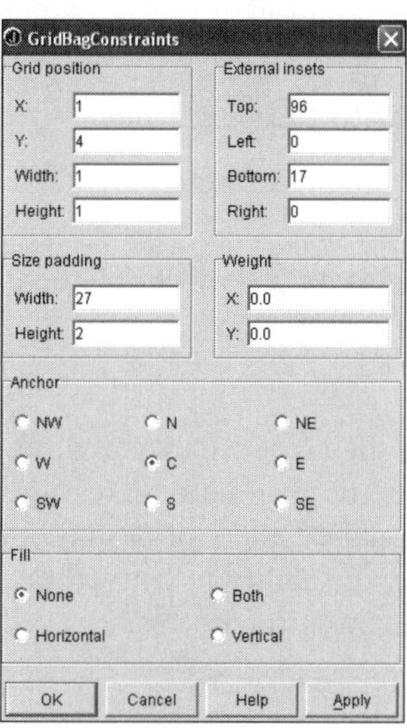

FIGURE 12.8 Modifying `GridBagLayout` with the `GridBagConstraints` Editor.

GridBagLayout Context Menu

Similar to XYLayout, a custom right-click menu is also available for GridBagLayout. This menu gives you quick and easy access to many of the GridBagLayout constraints. Table 12.3 lists the actions available with the right-click menu and their descriptions.

TABLE 12.3 Available Actions with GridBagLayout Menu

Menu Command	Description
Show Grid	Displays the current grid in the UI Designer window.
Constraints	Accesses the GridBagLayout constraints for the selected component.
Remove Padding	Sets the size padding values to zero.
Fill Horizontal	Assigns the fill property to HORIZONTAL. If fill is already VERTICAL, it changes to BOTH.
Fill Vertical	Assigns the fill property to VERTICAL. If fill is already HORIZONTAL, it also changes to BOTH.
Remove Fill	Changes the fill property to NONE.
Weight Horizontal	Sets the property weightx for the selected component to 1.0.
Weight Vertical	Assigns the property of weighty for the selected component to 1.0.
Remove Weights	Sets both weightx and weighty to 0.0.

An Example of Using GridBagLayout

You have two different methods for creating a user interface using GridBagLayout. Although GridBagLayout is complicated to use, JBuilder makes the process much easier with the UI Designer. The two methods for using GridBagLayout are as follows:

- Convert from XYLayout to GridBagLayout
- Start a new interface using GridBagLayout

As we look at this layout manager, we will implement the same sample using both methods of creating our user interface.

Conversion

To prevent the intrusion of the layout manager while creating a user interface, JBuilder provides two productivity-enhancing features within the designers. The first is XYLayout to allow for quick and efficient design of a user interface based on the requirements. The second is the ability to convert an XYLayout to a GridBagLayout. The following steps demonstrate this process:

1. Create a frame.
2. Change the layout property to use XYLayout.

3. Create the user interface as desired. See Listing 12.7 for the results of the user interface.

NOTE

Make sure that you align and size all your components to the desired specifications. This facilitates the conversion to produce a more efficient `GridBagLayout`. This also keeps the layout from becoming too complicated.

4. Change the `layout` property of the frame from `XYLayout` to `GridBagLayout`. Compare the results of the change in Listing 12.8.
5. Compile and test.

LISTING 12.7 Building the First Interface Using `XYLayout`

```
//Component initialization
private void jbInit() throws Exception  {
  //setIconImage(Toolkit.getDefaultToolkit().
➥ createImage(Frame1.class.getResource("[Your Icon]")));
  contentPane = (JPanel) this.getContentPane();
  btnTest.setPreferredSize(new Dimension(-1, -1));
  btnTest.setText("Test");
  contentPane.setLayout(xYLayout1);
  this.setSize(new Dimension(400, 300));
  this.setTitle("Frame Title");
  lblMessage.setFont(new java.awt.Font("Dialog", 0, 18));
  lblMessage.setText("Hello World!!!");
  btnExit.setText("Exit");
  contentPane.add(btnTest, new XYConstraints(81, 22, 101, 37));
  contentPane.add(lblMessage,  new XYConstraints(81, 113, 182, 36));
  contentPane.add(btnExit,  new XYConstraints(257, 200, 105, 36));
}
```

LISTING 12.8 Convert `XYLayout` to `GridBagLayout`

```
private void jbInit() throws Exception  {
  //setIconImage(Toolkit.getDefaultToolkit().
➥ createImage(Frame1.class.getResource("[Your Icon]")));
  contentPane = (JPanel) this.getContentPane();
  btnTest.setPreferredSize(new Dimension(-1, -1));
  btnTest.setText("Test");
```

LISTING 12.8 Continued

```
    contentPane.setLayout(gridBagLayout1);
    this.setSize(new Dimension(400, 300));
    this.setTitle("Frame Title");
    lblMessage.setFont(new java.awt.Font("Dialog", 0, 18));
    lblMessage.setText("Hello World!!!");
    btnExit.setText("Exit");
    contentPane.add(btnTest,  new GridBagConstraints(0, 0, 1, 1, 0.0, 0.0
            ,GridBagConstraints.CENTER,
➥ GridBagConstraints.NONE, new Insets(22, 81, 0, 0), 102, 38));
    contentPane.add(lblMessage,  new GridBagConstraints(0, 1, 2, 1, 0.0, 0.0
            ,GridBagConstraints.WEST,
➥ GridBagConstraints.NONE, new Insets(54, 81, 0, 137), 71, 12));
    contentPane.add(btnExit,  new GridBagConstraints(1, 2, 1, 1, 0.0, 0.0
            ,GridBagConstraints.CENTER,
➥ GridBagConstraints.NONE, new Insets(51, 75, 64, 38), 52, 9));
  }
```

Construction

Although not impossible, it can be challenging to create a GridBagLayout by hand. JBuilder's designers have a number of time-saving features that help the process. If we look at creating the same interface as in the conversion from XYLayout, we can get a fair comparison between the methods. The following rules and behaviors are important for you to know as you build a GridBagLayout using the designer:

- As you are adding the component, it will not be placed where you drop it, but will be placed in reference to the prior object and rules associated with GridBagLayout.
- Drop a component to the right of another and it creates a new column for that object.
- Drop a component below a component and it creates a new row to contain that component.
- GridBagConstraints can be changed with the GridBagConstraints Editor, changing source or using the speed menu. They will change the properties for the GridBagConstraints constructor for each component.

The following steps help you create a frame using GridBagLayout without converting from XYLayout:

1. Create a frame.
2. Change the layout property to use GridBagLayout.

3. Drop the Test `JButton` on the frame.
4. Click below the Test button to drop the `JLabel`. This creates a new row in the layout and places the `JLabel` within the row.
5. Place below the label another `JButton` to exit the system.
6. Right-click on all three components and choose Fill Vertical. This causes the column for these three objects to fill the frame completely.
7. Change the `GridBagConstraints` for all the components to `anchor = GridBagConstraints.CENTER`. This can be accomplished by right-clicking and selecting the editor, or you can change the constructor for `GridBagConstraints`.
8. Using the upper and lower inset nibs (blue boxes) of the label, increase the space between the upper boundary and the lower boundary. This can also be accomplished by right-clicking and selecting the editor, or you can change the constructor for `GridBagConstraints`.
9. Compile and test.

Creating a Custom Layout Manager

JBuilder allows the inclusion of layout managers other than the ones that ship with JBuilder. The layout manager is normally nothing more than a class that implements `LayoutManager`. You might want to have the layout manager also be available in the `layout` property within the Inspector.

To accomplish this, you must register the layout assistant. The registration step is simply one method call to the `initOpenTool()` method.

CAUTION

Before you start creating a new layout manager, verify that no other layout manager will work. You can also find a number of resources on the Internet for which you can download different layout managers.

Custom Layout Manager Implementation

To create a custom layout manager, you need to create a new class that implements the `LayoutManager` interface. Every new layout manager must implement the five methods defined in the interface. Table 12.4 defines the interface to be implemented. Listing 12.9 demonstrates the implementation of a custom layout manager.

TABLE 12.4 `LayoutManager` Interface Methods

Method	Description
`addLayoutComponent`	This method is called when the `Container add()` method is called.
`removeLayoutComponent`	This method is normally implemented but does noting.
`preferredLayoutSize`	This method should return the ideal size of the component.
`minimumLayoutSize`	This method should return the minimum size of the container.
`layoutContainer`	This method is called every time the container is sized or resized.

LISTING 12.9 Creating a New Layout Manager

```
package com.sams.diagonal;

import java.awt.*;
import java.util.Vector;

public class DiagonalLayout implements LayoutManager {
    private int vgap;
    private int minWidth = 0, minHeight = 0;
    private int preferredWidth = 0, preferredHeight = 0;
    private boolean sizeUnknown = true;

    public DiagonalLayout() {
        this(5);
    }

    public DiagonalLayout(int v) {
        vgap = v;
    }

    /* Required by LayoutManager. */
    public void addLayoutComponent(String name, Component comp) {
    }

    /* Required by LayoutManager. */
    public void removeLayoutComponent(Component comp) {
    }

    private void setSizes(Container parent) {
        int nComps = parent.getComponentCount();
        Dimension d = null;
```

LISTING 12.9 Continued

```
        //Reset preferred/minimum width and height.
        preferredWidth = 0;
        preferredHeight = 0;
        minWidth = 0;
        minHeight = 0;

        for (int i = 0; i < nComps; i++) {
            Component c = parent.getComponent(i);
            if (c.isVisible()) {
                d = c.getPreferredSize();

                if (i > 0) {
                    preferredWidth += d.width/2;
                    preferredHeight += vgap;
                } else {
                    preferredWidth = d.width;
                }
                preferredHeight += d.height;

                minWidth = Math.max(c.getMinimumSize().width,
                                    minWidth);
                minHeight = preferredHeight;
            }
        }
    }


    /* Required by LayoutManager. */
    public Dimension preferredLayoutSize(Container parent) {
        Dimension dim = new Dimension(0, 0);
        int nComps = parent.getComponentCount();

        setSizes(parent);

        //Always add the container's insets!
        Insets insets = parent.getInsets();
        dim.width = preferredWidth
                    + insets.left + insets.right;
        dim.height = preferredHeight
                     + insets.top + insets.bottom;
```

LISTING 12.9 Continued

```
        sizeUnknown = false;

        return dim;
    }

    /* Required by LayoutManager. */
    public Dimension minimumLayoutSize(Container parent) {
        Dimension dim = new Dimension(0, 0);
        int nComps = parent.getComponentCount();

        //Always add the container's insets!
        Insets insets = parent.getInsets();
        dim.width = minWidth
                    + insets.left + insets.right;
        dim.height = minHeight
                     + insets.top + insets.bottom;

        sizeUnknown = false;

        return dim;
    }

    /* Required by LayoutManager. */
    /*
     * This is called when the panel is first displayed,
     * and every time its size changes.
     * Note: You CAN'T assume preferredLayoutSize or
     * minimumLayoutSize will be called -- in the case
     * of applets, at least, they probably won't be.
     */
    public void layoutContainer(Container parent) {
        Insets insets = parent.getInsets();
        int maxWidth = parent.getSize().width
                       - (insets.left + insets.right);
        int maxHeight = parent.getSize().height
                        - (insets.top + insets.bottom);
        int nComps = parent.getComponentCount();
        int previousWidth = 0, previousHeight = 0;
        int x = 0, y = insets.top;
        int rowh = 0, start = 0;
        int xFudge = 0, yFudge = 0;
        boolean oneColumn = false;
```

LISTING 12.9 Continued

```
        // Go through the components' sizes, if neither
        // preferredLayoutSize nor minimumLayoutSize has
        // been called.
        if (sizeUnknown) {
            setSizes(parent);
        }

        if (maxWidth <= minWidth) {
            oneColumn = true;
        }

        if (maxWidth != preferredWidth) {
            xFudge = (maxWidth - preferredWidth)/(nComps - 1);
        }

        if (maxHeight > preferredHeight) {
            yFudge = (maxHeight - preferredHeight)/(nComps - 1);
        }

        for (int i = 0 ; i < nComps ; i++) {
            Component c = parent.getComponent(i);
            if (c.isVisible()) {
                Dimension d = c.getPreferredSize();

                 // increase x and y, if appropriate
                if (i > 0) {
                    if (!oneColumn) {
                        x += previousWidth/2 + xFudge;
                    }
                    y += previousHeight + vgap + yFudge;
                }

                // If x is too large,
                if ((!oneColumn) &&
                    (x + d.width) >
                    (parent.getSize().width - insets.right)) {
                    // reduce x to a reasonable number.
                    x = parent.getSize().width
                        - insets.bottom - d.width;
                }

                // If y is too large,
```

LISTING 12.9 Continued

```
                if ((y + d.height) >                   (parent.getSize().height
➥-insets.bottom)) {
                    // do nothing.
                    // Another choice would be to do what we do to x.
                }

                // Set the component's size and position.
                c.setBounds(x, y, d.width, d.height);

                previousWidth = d.width;
                previousHeight = d.height;
            }
        }
    }

    public String toString() {
        String str = "";
        return getClass().getName() + "[vgap=" + vgap + str + "]";
    }
}
```

Adding the New Layout Manager to JBuilder

The registration of new layout managers requires simply a one-line call to JBuilder's OpenTools. The method you must use is `initOpenTool()` static method. With this method, you need to inform the designer which layouts are available and which managers they are implementing. Listing 12.10 shows the implementation of the registration process with the OpenTools.

LISTING 12.10 Adding the Custom Layout Manager to JBuilder

```
package com.sams.diagonal;

import com.borland.jbuilder.designer.ui.*;

public class DiagonalLayoutAssistant extends BasicLayoutAssistant {

  /**
   * <p>Initializes and registers this OpenTool
   */
  public static void initOpenTool(byte majorVersion,
➥ byte minorVersion) {
```

LISTING 12.10 Continued

```
    UIDesigner.registerAssistant(
      DiagonalLayoutAssistant.class,
      "com.sams.diagonal.DiagonalLayout", //NORES
      true);
  }

}
```

Design Guidelines

Everyone seems to have an opinion on which layout manager to use and how to use it. The good news is that by following some simple guidelines, you will be able to create a user interface more efficiently. In addition to this efficiency, you will also gain a better design with flexibility and openness.

Do Not Be Afraid of `XYLayout` Conversion

Although `XYLayout` manager is a specific manager to JBuilder, it is important to realize that it is a great stepping stone to move you, ultimately to the `GridBagLayout`. In most cases, you will be able to create a user interface using `XYLayout` and conversion in a quarter of the time it would take you to create a `GridBagLayout`.

As long as you follow a few simple rules, your conversion to `GridBagLayout` should be uneventful:

- Align all components to their ultimate position and size before the conversion.
- Complete as much of the user interface as possible before conversion.
- Start converting the outer panels first and work your way in.
- Make minor changes to the constraints for the desired effect before attempting to check resizing requirements.
- Check resizing requirements by either running the application or expanding the frame within JBuilder Screen Designer.

Use Nesting of Panels

Most user interfaces should use more than one layout manager. Each layout manager has a specific purpose, and it is difficult, if not impossible, to make one layout manager work for all. You can garner the most control in building a user interface by nesting panels and different layouts within your main container. For example, most user interfaces will start with a `BorderLayout` and place panels within each region. The toolbar normally is a `BoxLayout2` or a `FlowLayout`. The Content pane, center panel of the `BorderLayout`, normally uses something like `GridLayout` or `GridBagLayout`.

You gain many benefits from nesting the panels and few drawbacks. The following is a list of many of the benefits:

- More control over the placement in a more granular area. For example, a completely different grid and cell structure can be defined for a different panel even though it may use the same layout manager.
- If you are using the `GridBagLayout`, it reduces the number of rows and columns required to display the user interface, ultimately making the `GridBagConstraints` easier to traverse and change.
- Helps reduce the ripple effect of changing one component in reference to another. For example, you may change the size of one cell, which in turn changes the size of the column or row, which in turn resizes other components.
- If you are using either `null` or `XYLayout` to convert to `GridBagLayout`, the frame will be more likely to convert without much modification required.
- Never, never, never attempt to use just one layout manager when you can get the benefits of all of them.

In Practice

Our practice exercise augments the user interface created in Chapter 11, "Swing." The user interface we created earlier used `XYLayout`. It is time to convert our layout to use `GridBagLayout` and various other layout managers that reach our requirements. Let's review the process again for converting `XYLayout` to `GridBagLayout`—for that matter, it works for any layout conversion:

- Align all components to their ultimate position and size before the conversion.
- Complete as much of the user interface as possible before conversion.
- Start converting the outer panels first and work your way in.
- Make minor changes to the constraints for the desired effect before attempting to check resizing requirements.
- Never, never, never attempt to use just one layout manager when you can get the benefits of all of them.

We'll start our exercise with the solution we created in Chapter 11. The following steps convert `null` to `GridBagLayout`:

1. Open the project completed in the "In Practice" section of Chapter 11.
2. Open the GUI Designer for the frame CoursePanel.java.
3. Make sure that all the components are aligned properly. This is accomplished by selecting two components that you want to align or make equal in size, as shown in Figure 12.9.

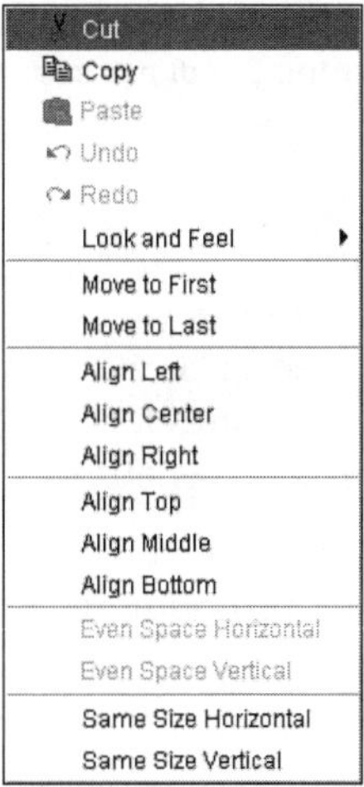

FIGURE 12.9 Alignment tool within the GUI Designer.

4. After the components are aligned to the desired size and location, it is time to convert the innermost panel to `GridBagLayout`. The innermost panel is identified by looking at the Structure panel in the lower-left corner of our IDE interface. The innermost panel in our case is `this`, which indicates the main frame of this screen.
5. Change the layout property from `null` to `GridBagLayout`. You will notice that the components shift a few pixels; this is normal behavior when converting to `GridBagLayout`.
6. Make any adjustments to the screen to obtain the same look and feel. For this frame, you should not have to make any adjustments.
7. Using the sizing nibs, expand the frame to be larger both vertically and horizontally. This verifies the desired behavior for screen expansion and contraction.
8. Compile and execute your project, as shown in Figure 12.10.

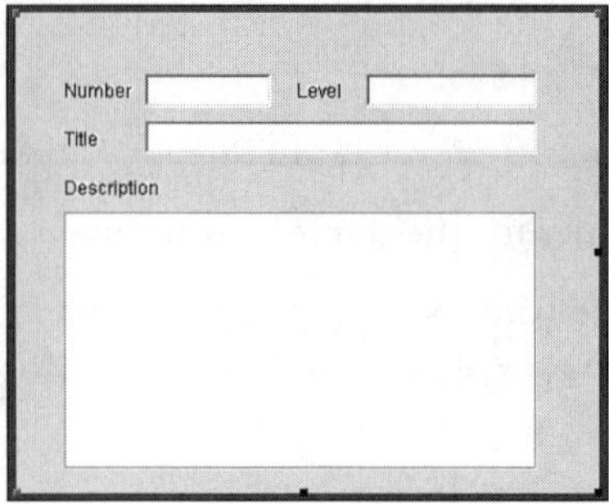

FIGURE 12.10 Final frame using the `GridLayoutManager`.

Summary

Every container must have a layout manager. If a layout manager does not fit your needs, do not attempt to make it work; choose a different layout manager. JBuilder provides a number of time-saving features for building a user interface. Do not be afraid or intimidated to use them. The benefit will pay for itself quickly and many times over.

JBuilder offers layout managers from the simple, such as `FlowLayout` or `BoxLayout`, to the complex, such as `GridBagLayout`.

Reflections

- Which layout manager is right for me?
- How does the layout manager I have chosen manage my components?
- Should I use one layout manager and standardize on it?

13 Drawing with Java

IN THIS CHAPTER

- Java2D API Overview
- Rendering Effects

Java offers a slew of graphics primitives that allow easy manipulation of graphical elements without extensive number crunching. This is useful because many graphical operations are usually performed as matrix transformations that can quickly become overwhelming.

In this chapter, we will review the Java2D API that provides these graphical operations. We will look at some of the rendering effects offered by the API. Finally, we'll put it all to work by adding printing capabilities to our ChalkTalk application.

Java2D API Overview

Historically, the Java framework was originally rather weak as far as its graphical capabilities were concerned. Most of the graphical functionality was exposed as methods in the `java.awt.Graphics` class. The drawing and filling of shapes, for example, was accomplished through `draw`*`XXX`* and `fill`*`XXX`* methods in the `Graphics` class (for instance, `drawLine`, `drawOval`, and `fillOval`). This was cumbersome because there was no shape type and hence no way to draw, fill, and otherwise manipulate shapes in a polymorphic manner.

This changed with the advent of the Java2D API, which introduced the `java.awt.Graphics2D` class and the shape hierarchy rooted in the `java.awt.Shape` interface.

In addition to the shape hierarchy, the Java2D API provides the following additional features:

- There are two coordinate systems: the user and the device coordinate systems. Transformations are possible between the two.

- Printing graphics is supported using the same primitives as displayed onscreen. In a way, printing is simply rendering on paper (as drawing is rendering on the screen).
- Complex shapes can be produced by clipping and compositing simple shapes. Figure 13.1 shows such a composite shape formed from simple ones.

FIGURE 13.1 Compositing and clipping simple shapes produces complex shapes like this pear formed from ovals and arcs (from the Java2D sample from Sun).

- It is possible to render text as graphical glyphs and thus treat text like shapes.

In the next section, we will look at the rendering and printing features provided by the Java2D API.

Rendering Effects

To understand the details involved in rendering a graphics object, it is important to know the two coordinate systems involved and the relationship between them.

The *user coordinate system* is the one you use to specify all the coordinates for your shapes. You can think of the origin in the user coordinate system anchored at the top-left corner of an imaginary rectangular piece of paper, with the positive x- and y-axes running toward the right and down, respectively.

The *device coordinate system* is the one used to actually render the shapes on the specific device (which could be paper if you're printing the shapes).

Java2D allows text to be rendered as graphical glyphs and treated like shapes.

It is possible to transform points from the user coordinate system into corresponding points in device coordinate systems using *affine transformations*.

AFFINE TRANSFORMS

An *affine transform* keeps the parallelness of lines intact. That is, parallel lines remain parallel and nonparallel lines stay that way after the transformation is applied. As a simple example, a transformation that changes the uppercase letter H to the italicized uppercase letter *H* is an affine transform. However, if the letter H is changed to an A after the transformation, it is clearly not an affine transform.

Mathematically, an affine transform can be represented by a 2×3 matrix, or equivalently by six constants as shown in the following equations:

$x' = m00\ x + m01\ y + m02$

$y' = m10\ x + m11\ y + m12$

The six m's are the constants that define the transformation from the point (x, y) to the point (x', y').

The `Graphics2D` class has an instance of the `java.awt.geom.AffineTransform` object that can be manipulated by calling its public methods. Here are some of the methods that the `Graphics2D` class exposes:

- `shear(double shx, double shy)`—Shearing causes the drawn shapes to be skewed along one or both axes. A simple example would be shearing the letter H along the x-axis, which would give something similar to the italicized letter *H*. Figure 13.2 shows another example of shearing.

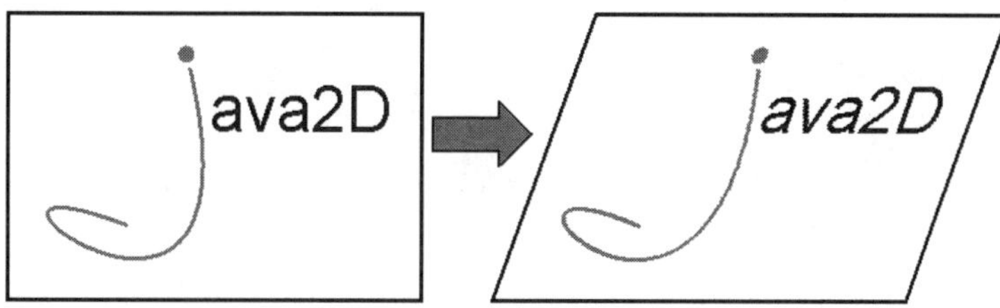

FIGURE 13.2 Horizontal shearing of the shape on the left side produces the shape on the right.

- `rotate(double theta)` and `rotate(double theta, double x, double y)`—These two methods rotate the drawn shapes by the angle theta radians. The second method rotates around the give point (x, y), whereas the former rotates around the origin (0, 0). As an example, rotating the letter p by Π radians around its center would give the letter d. Figure 13.3 shows another example.

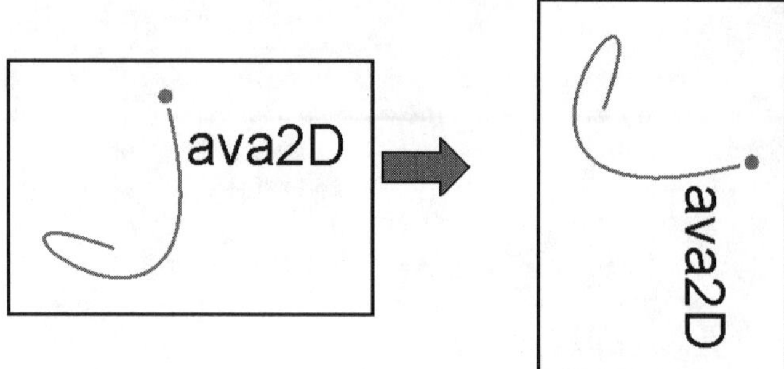

FIGURE 13.3 Rotating the shape on the left by Π/2 radians produces the shape on the right.

- `translate(double tx, double ty)`—Translation is simply sliding the drawn shapes along one or both axes, as shown in Figure 13.4.

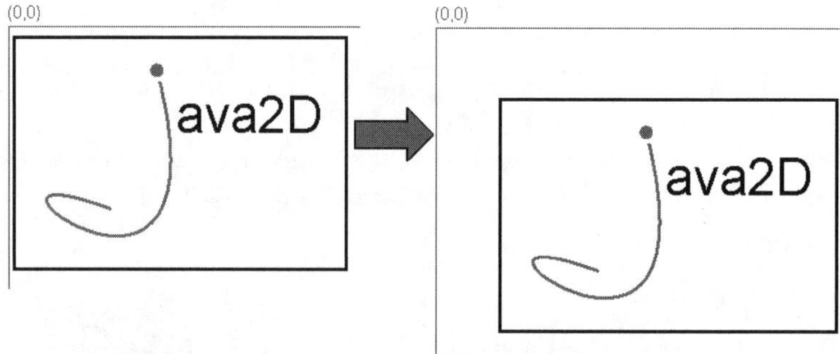

FIGURE 13.4 Translating the shape on the left along the positive direction in both axes produces the shape on the right.

It is important to realize that there is one `AffineTransform` object associated with each `Graphics2D` object. Therefore, successive calls to the preceding methods have a cumulative effect on the `AffineTransform` object. If you want to start fresh with a new transformation, you can use the corresponding `setTo`*`XXX`* methods in the `Graphics2D` object (`setToShear`, `setToRotate`, and `setToTranslate`).

Printing in Java2D

The `java.awt.print` package provides classes and interfaces related to printing. Two key interfaces are `Printable` and `Pageable`. A class must implement the `Printable` interface to print one page. The `Pageable` interface is implemented by a multipage document class.

Just as there is a callback method, `paint`, that is called whenever a component is to be drawn onscreen, there also is an analogous method `print` in the `Printable` interface that is called when a class needs to print something. The print method has the following signature:

```
public int print(Graphics2D graphics, PageFormat format, int pageIndex)
```

It is important to not confuse the preceding method with the parameterless `print()` method in the `PrinterJob` class. The latter method is used to trigger the actual printing. Here, again, there is an analogy between printing and painting: The `repaint` method in the `java.awt.Component` class is called to schedule a paint operation, and the `print` method in the `PrinterJob` class is called to schedule a print job.

In summary, you must do the following two things to allow an application to print:

1. Implement the `Printable` interface (and hence the `print` method).
2. Schedule the printing to be done by calling the `print` method of the `PrinterJob` class.

In Practice

Now that you have seen the Java2D API, we'll enhance our ChalkTalk application using some of what you learned in this chapter.

In this section, we will add a simple printing feature to the ChalkTalk application. This feature allows the user to print the title of the course—"Introduction to Java," for example—in large letters on a single sheet of paper. This is useful for printing signs that can be posted outside classrooms.

We will accomplish this in the following steps:

1. Copy the project from Chapter 11, "Swing," to create a new project.
2. Add a pop-up menu to `CoursePanel` to present the printing option to the user.
3. Add event handlers to the menu items in the pop-up menu.
4. Implement the `java.awt.Print` interface in the `CoursePanel` class.
5. Run the application.

So let's begin!

Copying Files

1. If you finished the "In Practice" section in Chapter 11, you can use that solution. Otherwise, you may use the provided solution from Chapter 11 as a starting point for the "In Practice" section. See the companion CD for the "In Practice" solutions.
2. Copy the entire contents of the chap11 directory into a new directory called chap13.
3. There should be three files called chap11 with different extensions. Rename these files so that they are named chap13.html, chap13.jpx, and chap13.jpx.local. If there are any files ending with a tilde (~) character, delete them. (These are backup files and will be re-created by JBuilder when needed.)
4. You now have a new project currently identical to the finished project for Chapter 11.

Adding a Pop-up Menu to `CoursePanel`

1. Open the `CoursePanel` class in the browser and switch to the Design tab.
2. Select `javax.swing.JPopupMenu` from the Swing Containers tab on the Component Palette and add it to the `CoursePanel` by clicking anywhere in the Structure pane on the bottom right.
3. The newly added pop-up menu, called `jPopupMenu1`, is visible under the Menu folder in the Structure pane. Double-click on the pop-up menu to launch the menu designer.
4. Select the pop-up menu in the Structure pane. Rename it to **`jPopupMenuCourse`** by changing the name property in the inspector.
5. Simply start typing into the menu designer to create a menu item. The text of the first menu item is **Print Title**.
6. Change the name of this menu item to **`jMenuItemPrintTitle`**.
7. Using the menu design toolbar that now appears immediately above the browser, add a separator. (Use the Insert Separator button.)
8. Add another menu item. The text of this menu item should be **Cancel** and the name should be **`jMenuItemCancel`**.
9. Save all your work (choose File, Save All).

Adding Event Handlers to Menu Items

1. While in the Design tab, select this (which represents this panel) under the UI folder in the Structure pane.
2. In the Inspector on the right side, switch to the Events tab.
3. Click on the `mouseReleased` event hander and press Enter. This gives you an event handler with the JBuilder-provided name `this_mouseReleased`. The browser should automatically switch to the Source tab and land you in the right spot.
4. In the event handler, add the following two lines of code:

   ```
   if (e.isMetaDown())
         jPopupMenuCourse.show(this,e.getX(), e.getY());
   ```

5. Still in the Design tab, select `jMenuItemPrintTitle` in the Structure pane.
6. In the Inspector, switch to the Events tab.
7. Select the `actionPerformed` event handler (the first one in the list). The suggested name for the event handler appears in the second (right) column. Change this name to **`printTitle_actionPerformed`**. Press Enter.
8. JBuilder switches to the Source tab and lands the cursor in the newly created `printTitle_actionPerformed` method. At this point, we do not have the printing code to call, so leave this method as is for now. We will modify it later.
9. Switch back to the Design tab. Add an `actionPerformed` event handler named **`printCancel_actionPerformed`** for the `jMenuItemCancel` menu item. Press Enter to switch to the Source tab.
10. Add the following single line of code to the event handler method (the cursor should already be in the right spot):

    ```
    jPopupMenuCourse.setVisible(false);
    ```

11. Save all files.

Implementing the `Print` Interface in `CoursePanel`

1. With the `CoursePanel` file selected in the browser, select the Wizards, Implement Interface menu item.
2. In the dialog box that appears, select the `java.awt.print.Printable` interface and click, as shown in Figure 13.5.

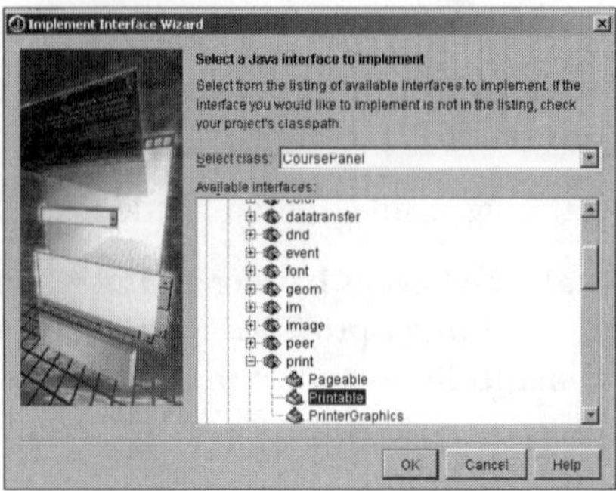

FIGURE 13.5 Implementing the `java.awt.print.Printable` interface through the Implement Interface Wizard.

3. In the `print()` method generated by JBuilder, delete the line that throws the exception and add the code shown in Listing 13.1.

LISTING 13.1 `print()` Method in CoursePanel.java

```
public int print(Graphics graphics, PageFormat pageFormat,
➥ int pageIndex) throws PrinterException {
    if (pageIndex >= 1) {
        return Printable.NO_SUCH_PAGE;
    }
    Graphics2D g = (Graphics2D)graphics;
    FontMetrics fm = jTextFieldCTitle.getFontMetrics(
➥ jTextFieldCTitle.getFont());
    int maxAscent = fm.getMaxAscent();
    Dimension d = fm.getStringBounds(
➥ jTextFieldCTitle.getText(), g).getBounds().getSize();
    double scalex = pageFormat.getImageableWidth() / d.width ;
    double scaley = pageFormat.getImageableHeight() / d.height;
    double scale = Math.min(scalex, scaley);
    g.translate(pageFormat.getImageableX(),
➥ (pageFormat.getImageableHeight() - (maxAscent))/2D);
    g.scale(scale, scale);
    g.drawString(jTextFieldCTitle.getText(), 0, maxAscent);
    return Printable.PAGE_EXISTS;
}
```

4. In the `printTitle_actionPerformed` method, add code as shown in Listing 13.2.

LISTING 13.2 `printTitle_actionPerformed()` Method in CoursePanel.java

```
void printTitle_actionPerformed(ActionEvent e) {
    PrinterJob printJob = PrinterJob.getPrinterJob();
    printJob.setPrintable(this);
    if (printJob.printDialog()) {
        try {
            printJob.print();
        } catch (Exception ex) {
            ex.printStackTrace();
        }
    }
    return;
}
```

5. Save all files in your project.

Running the Finished Application

1. Run the `ChalkTalkClient` by pressing F9.
2. Navigate to the `CoursePanel` by clicking on the Get Courses button, and then clicking on one of the courses that appear.
3. Right-click anywhere on the `CoursePanel` and select the Print item from the menu.
4. You should get the printer dialog box shown for your operating system. The Windows dialog box looks similar to that shown in Figure 13.6.

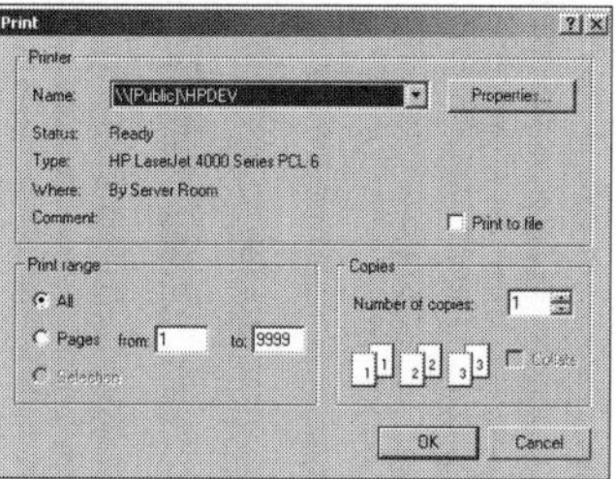

FIGURE 13.6 The printer dialog box on the Microsoft Windows operating system.

5. If you have a printer correctly set up, selecting that printer and clicking OK prints the course name in large letters on a single piece of paper.

Summary

This chapter showed how you can use Java to create robust graphical applications. The Java2D API provides easy-to-use transformation and printing functions, enabling you to make your application come to life! The Java2D API is used by commercial packages to provide reporting and simple graphic applications. If you want to create your own reporting or graphic application, the Java2D API is one way to go.

Reflections

- How would you compare the Java2D API's graphical manipulation features with that of some other language?
- Printing and painting are treated similarly in Java2D. Can you think of any disadvantages of this approach?
- How would you change Listing 13.1 to print the title of the class in landscape orientation on paper? (Hint: `java.awt.print.PageFormat`.)

14 Files, Streams, and Serialization

IN THIS CHAPTER

- `File` Class
- Input and Output Streams
- `Reader` and `Writer` Classes
- `StreamTokenizer` Class
- Object Serialization

Java provides an Input/Output package, `java.io`, that contains the functionality needed to read and write data from files and streams. Learning how to use files and streams is a primary requirement in modern languages.

In Java, learning how to work with files and streams gives you a better understanding of distributed application design, which requires that information be passed from one system to another. Java streams provide a way to move data and objects from one virtual machine to another virtual machine with little coding effort. The ability to move an object by value over a network and reconstitute that object made Java a big player in distributed computing.

Object serialization means reading and writing an object to a stream. The stream can be a connection between two machines allowing an object to move locations.

In this chapter, we will learn about

- The `File` class
- Input and output streams
- `Reader` and `Writer` classes
- The `StreamTokenizer` class
- Object serialization

`File` Class

The `File` class hides the differences of a variety of operating systems and file systems. The `File` class provides a common interface for handling files and directories. The `File` class does not manage the reading and writing of data to files. The stream classes are used to read and write data to a file.

Suppose that you are writing an application that needs to run on Unix and Windows. Unix and Windows have fundamental differences in the representation of filenames and locations.

Unix path- and filenames use the path separator "/" and do not include a drive location. All file locations are created off the root directory location, which is represented by the character "/". For example, the filename class.dat is stored in the usr directory off the root directory. The filename class.dat is represented as /usr/class.dat.

In Unix, the concept of drive names is replaced with directory mounts locations. A floppy drive in the Windows world is typically referred to as drive A:, whereas in the Unix world, the floppy drive would be mounted off the root directory. So, the location might be something like /drives/floppyA. The Unix operating system handles the accessing of the floppy drive as just another directory on the system.

In Windows, the path separator is "\", and the filename can have two different representations. The typical representation of a file in Windows uses a drive letter and a colon. For example, the filename class.dat is stored in the usr directory off the root directory on drive C:. The filename class.dat is represented as C:\usr\class.dat.

The advancement of the Internet and peer-to-peer computing has led to the Universal Naming Convention (UNC) standards. The UNC represents a file location using the hostname and the sharename of the path in the following representation \\hostname\sharename\filename. Taking the previous example, the filename class.dat is stored in the usr directory off the root directory on drive C:. The machine name is ORION, and the sharename is classroom. The UNC format of the filename class.dat is \\ORION\classroom\class.dat.

Java accounts for the different methods of locating a file. Included in the `File` class are static parameters for name separators and path separators. Java also provides methods for finding files, deleting files, renaming files, creating directories, and other file-manipulation tasks.

The location of a directory or file can be an *absolute location* or a *relative location*. An absolute location does not need additional information to find the file or directory. A relative location needs a starting point before finding a file. The starting location is based on the system property `user.dir` setting. Relative addressing prevents the hard coding of machine-specific file locations, allowing an application to be moved from directory to directory and from system to system.

Listing 14.1 displays some of the more interesting system properties. Notice that the file separator and path separator properties are available as system settings.

LISTING 14.1 System Properties (SystemFun101.java)

```
public class SystemFun101 {
  public static void main(String[] args) {
    System.out.println("user.dir:" + System.getProperty("user.dir"));
     System.out.println("user.home:" + System.getProperty("user.home"));
     System.out.println("user.name:" + System.getProperty("user.name"));
     System.out.println("path.separator:" +
➥System.getProperty("path.separator"));
     System.out.println("file.separator:" +
➥System.getProperty("file.separator"));
     System.out.println("os.name:" + System.getProperty("os.name"));
     System.out.println("os.version:" + System.getProperty("os.version"));
     System.out.println("java.version:" + System.getProperty("java.version"));
     System.out.println("java.home:" + System.getProperty("java.home"));
     System.out.println("java.vm.version:" +
➥System.getProperty("java.vm.version"));
     System.out.println("java.vm.name:" + System.getProperty("java.vm.name"));
     System.out.println("java.vm.vendor:" +
➥System.getProperty("java.vm.vendor"));
    System.out.println("java.class.path:" +
➥System.getProperty("java.class.path"));  }
}
```

The output of the code in Listing 14.1 is shown in Listing 14.2 for Windows and Listing 14.3 for Unix. Notice the path and file separators on the different operating systems. The output from your system may be different from the output in Listings 14.2 and 14.3.

LISTING 14.2 Output of the System Properties on a Windows-based Machine (SystemFun101.java)

```
user.dir:C:\jbbook\ch14\FilesAndStreams
user.home:C:\Documents and Settings\mikel
user.name:mikel
path.separator:;
file.separator:\
File.pathSeparator:;
File.separator:\
os.name:Windows 2000
```

LISTING 14.2 Continued

```
os.version:5.1
java.version:1.3.1
java.home:C:\JBuilder7\jdk1.3.1\jre
java.vm.version:1.3.1-b24
java.vm.name:Java HotSpot(TM) Client VM
java.vm.vendor:Sun Microsystems Inc.
java.class.path:C:\jbbook\ch14\FilesAndStreams\classes;
```

LISTING 14.3 Output of the System Properties on a Unix-based Machine (SystemFun101.java)

```
user.dir/export/home/mikel
user.home:/export/home/mikel
user.name:mikel
path.separator::
file.separator:/
os.name:SunOS
os.version:5.8
java.version:1.4.0
java.home:/usr/j2sdk1.4.0/jre
java.vm.version:1.4.0-b92
java.vm.name:Java HotSpot(TM) Client VM
java.vm.vendor:Sun Microsystems Inc.
java.class.path:.
```

The `user.dir` system property setting provides a context for relative file addressing. This is important in situations where more than one user may have access to a machine and want to keep their custom settings. Unix started in a world where a single machine was used by multiple users. Each user would get his own system settings and preferences. Windows began as a single-user-per-computer operating system. All users of the Windows machine used the system settings and preferences. As Windows matured, it added support for multiple users for a single Windows machine. The latest versions of Windows provide for the separation of user system settings and preferences.

Building an application that supports individual-user system settings and preferences is a requirement. Using the system properties and the `File` class, creating a flexible application that can support multiple-user settings is easier than ever.

To learn how to support custom preferences and settings, you must first learn more about the `File` class. The Java `File` class provides methods for managing an abstract hierarchy of files and directories. The abstract hierarchy is then translated to the file system being used by the application.

The `java.io.File` class does not make a distinction between filenames and directory names. Filenames and directory names are markers in a hierarchy of a file system. The `java.io.File` class encapsulates these hierarchical markers, treats them identically, and calls them *pathnames*. The properties of these markers or pathnames determine whether the object is representing a file or a directory name.

NOTE

Because a filename and a directory name are treated the same, you must be careful in examining the results of the `File` class methods. One method of the `File` class that may be confusing is the `getPath` method.

Suppose that you have a file object that represents the filename c:\temp\class.tmp. In common terms, the path c:\temp holds the file class.tmp. However, the `java.io.File` class does not distinguish between files and directories. Therefore, the file object tells you that the path is c:\temp\class.tmp rather than c:\temp.

The `java.io.File` class has three constructors and three static methods. The following sections describe the constructors and the static methods of the `java.io.File` class.

`File(File` *`parent`*`, String` *`child`*`)`

The `File` constructor creates a file object using an existing `File` object to represent the parent pathname and a string to represent the pathname to append.

For example, the following code creates a file object for a file class.tmp using the pathname of a file object created earlier:

```
... //fileTemp is created and has a pathname of c:\temp
fileClass = new File( fileTemp, "class.tmp");
```

The `fileClass` variable represents the pathname c:\temp\class.tmp. The pathname does not have to exist prior to creating a file object.

`File(String` *`pathname`*`)`

The `File` constructor creates a file object using the pathname provided. For example, the following code creates a file object for a file class.tmp located in the c:\temp directory:

```
fileClass = new File("c:\\temp\\class.tmp");
```

The `fileClass` variable represents the pathname c:\temp\class.tmp. The pathname does not have to exist prior to creating a file object.

File(String *parent*, String *child*)

The `File` constructor creates a file object using a string to represent the parent pathname and a string to represent the child pathname to append.

For example, the following code creates a file object for a file class.tmp using a parent pathname:

```
fileClass = new File( "c:\\temp", "class.tmp");
```

The `fileClass` variable represents the pathname c:\temp\class.tmp. The pathname does not have to exist prior to creating a file object.

static File createTempFile(String *prefix*, String *suffix*)

The `createTempFile` method creates an empty file in the default system temporary directory. The default system temporary directory is identified by the system property `java.io.tmpdir`.

The prefix must be a minimum of three characters. The suffix can be null. If the suffix is null, the suffix .tmp is used by default. The remainder of the temporary filename uses five or more system-generated characters.

If the temporary filename exceeds the platform-specific file naming conventions, the prefix is truncated to the first three characters. In addition, the suffix is truncated. If the suffix begins with a period, the suffix is truncated after the first three characters following the period.

This method throws three exceptions. If the prefix contains fewer than three characters, an `IllegalArgumentException` is thrown. If the file cannot be created, an `IOException` is thrown. If the security manager prevents a file from being created, a `SecurityException` is thrown.

static File createTempFile(String *prefix*, String *suffix*, File *directory*)

The `createTempFile` method creates an empty file in the specified directory. If the specified directory is null, the default system temporary directory is used.

The prefix and suffix parameters are identical to the `createTempFile(String` *`prefix`*`, String` *`suffix`*`)`.

static File[] listRoots()

The `listRoots` method returns an array of `File` objects that contain the root name of all file systems. In Unix, there is only one root file system. In Windows, each device is considered to have its own root directory. For example, the floppy drive typically has a root A:\, and the main hard drive typically has a root C:\.

The file systems included in the `listRoots` are local or mapped to the machine. The `listRoots` method does not return file systems that use the UNC.

The `listRoots` method handles security exceptions by not listing a file system that cannot be accessed due to security restrictions.

Listing 14.4 shows an example of using the `listRoots` method to display all the accessible file systems.

LISTING 14.4 Show All Root File Systems (FileFun101.java)

```
  private void showRoots() {
    File[] sList;
    int i;

    sList = File.listRoots();

    for(i=0;i<sList.length;i++)
      System.out.println("File System Roots: " + sList[i].toString());
  }

  public static void main(String[] args) {
    FileFun101 ff = new FileFun101();

    ff.showRoots();
... // other code
    }
}
```

Depending on which operating system you are running, the output in Listing 14.5 will be different.

LISTING 14.5 Output from `listRoot` Method Call on Windows

```
File System Roots: A:\
File System Roots: C:\
File System Roots: D:\
File System Roots: F:\
File System Roots: Y:\
File System Roots: Z:\
```

Listing 14.5 displays the root file systems available on my computer. If you run the `listRoots` method on your machine, you can expect a different output.

A list of the more interesting `File` class methods is found in Table 14.1. For a complete list of all methods, refer to the Java SDK documentation. Because file system access can be controlled by a security manager, most of the `File` class methods can throw the `SecurityException`.

TABLE 14.1 `java.io.File` Class Methods

Method	Description
`boolean canRead()`	Returns true if the pathname can be read.
`boolean canWrite()`	Returns true if the pathname is marked as read-only.
`boolean delete()`	Returns true if it succeeds in erasing the pathname. If the pathname is a directory, the directory must be empty to be deleted.
`void deleteOnExit()`	Attempts to erase the pathname on a normal termination of the virtual machine. If the pathname represents a directory, the directory must be empty before the deletion will succeed.
`boolean exists()`	Returns true if the pathname exists on the file system.
`File getAbsoluteFile()`	Returns a `File` object that provides the complete pathname including all relative references. A pathname that consists of ..\data\class.dat will have an absolute pathname consisting of the user directory name concatenated with the pathname. The user directory is retrieved from the system property `user.dir`. In this example, suppose that the `user.dir` setting has a value of c:\javabook\chapter14, and the pathname has a value of ..\data\class.dat. The returned `File` object will have a pathname of c:\javabook\chapter14\..\data\class.dat.
`File getCanonicalFile()`	Returns a `File` object that has the complete pathname with all relative references resolved. Suppose that the `user.dir` system setting has a value of c:\javabook\chapter14, and the pathname has a value of ..\data\class.dat. The returned `File` object will have a pathname of c:\javabook\data\class.dat. Notice that the relative references have been resolved.
`String getName()`	Returns the last name in the pathname sequence. For example, if the pathname is c:\temp, the method returns temp. If the pathname is c:\temp\abc.doc, the method returns abc.doc.
`String getParent()`	Returns the immediate parent in the pathname sequence. For example, if the pathname is c:\temp, the method returns c:\. If the pathname is c:\temp\abc.doc, the method returns c:\temp.

TABLE 14.1 Continued

Method	Description
String getPath()	Returns the pathname sequence using the default name separator. The default name separator is platform specific and a static property of the File class. Remember that getPath() should not be confused with getting the path location to a file. If the pathname represents a file, the getPath method returns the complete pathname, which includes the filename.
boolean isAbsolute()	Returns true if the pathname does not contain relative references.
boolean isDirectory()	Returns true if the pathname represents a directory name.
boolean isFile()	Returns true if the pathname represents a file.
boolean isHidden()	Returns true if the pathname represents a hidden file object.
long lastModified()	Returns the time and date stamp that the file was last modified. The time is measured in milliseconds from GMT, January 1, 1970.
long length()	Returns the number of bytes of the file. If the file does not exist and is not a directory, the length will be 0.
String[] list()	Returns an array of String objects that contain all the files and directories based on the pathname. The files and directories appear in the array in no particular order. If no files or directories are in the pathname, the array will be empty. If the pathname is invalid, the array will be null.
File[] listFiles()	Is identical to the list() method except that the array is composed of File objects rather than strings. The File objects are constructed using the File(File, String) constructor.
String[] list (FilenameFilter *filter*)	Returns an array of String objects that contain all the files and directories based on the pathname that match the filename filter. If a filename does not match the filter, it will not be returned in the array. If no names are found, the array will be empty. If the pathname is invalid, the array will be null.
boolean mkdir()	Creates a new directory based on the pathname. If the parent pathname directories do not exist, the mkdir fails and returns false. If successful, mkdir returns true.
boolean mkdirs()	Creates a new directory based on the pathname. If the parent pathname directories do not exist, they will be created. If successful, mkdirs returns true.
boolean renameTo(File *dest*)	Renames the current pathname to the dest pathname. renameTo returns true if successful.
String toString()	Returns the pathname. The methods toString and getPath perform the same function.
URL toURL()	Converts the pathname into a file URL. If the pathname refers to a directory, the URL ends with a slash.

Listing 14.6 examines the method calls in more detail and displays all the files in the root directory using the `list` method call.

LISTING 14.6 Listing Out a Directory (FileFun101.java)

```
private void showDirectory( String sFilePath )
{
  File fInput;
  String[] sList;
  int i, nFiles;

  System.out.println("Directory Listing of " + sFilePath );

  fInput = new File(sFilePath);

  sList = fInput.list();
  nFiles = sList.length;

  for (i = 0; i<nFiles; i++)
    System.out.println("Files: " + sList[i]);

}
```

Listing 14.6 creates a `java.io.File` object based on the filename or pathname passed in as a parameter. After the file object is created, the `list` method is called and returns an array of strings. The array is filled with all the files and directories that exist in that pathname.

Listing 14.7 places a filter on the `list` method to limit the array to all files. Directories will not be listed based on the implementation of the `FilenameFilter` class. The `FilenameFilter` class uses the `isDirectory` method to determine whether the pathname is a directory.

LISTING 14.7 Listing Out Files Only (FileFun101.java)

```
private void showAllFiles( String sFilePath )
{
  File fInput;
  String[] sList;
  int i, nFiles;

  System.out.println("Directory Listing of " + sFilePath );

  fInput = new File(sFilePath);
```

LISTING 14.7 Continued

```
    System.out.println("Filter: No Directories");
    FilenameFilter fFilter = new FilenameFilter() {
        public boolean accept(File dir, String name) {
          return !(new File(dir,name).isDirectory());
        }
      };
    sList = fInput.list( fFilter );
    nFiles = sList.length;

    for (i = 0; i<nFiles; i++)
      System.out.println("Files:" + sList[i]);
  }
```

It then displays all the files that are not directories.

`FilenameFilter` is an interface that needs to be created to support the filtering of filenames. The `list` method forwards the directory name and filename to the `FilenameFilter` class for processing. The `accept` method implementation of the `FilenameFilter` class checks to see whether the file is a directory. If the file is a directory, the method returns false. If the file is not a directory, the method returns true. The `list` method then adds all the files that return true to the string array.

Listing 14.8 provides more detailed information on a particular pathname and displays the statistics of a pathname.

LISTING 14.8 Show Statistics on a Pathname (FileFun101.java)

```
  private void showStats(String sName)
  {
  File fInput;

  System.out.println("Information on :" + sName );
  fInput = new File(sName);

  try {
    System.out.println("Can read:" + fInput.canRead());
    System.out.println("Can write:" + fInput.canWrite());
    System.out.println("Exists: " + fInput.exists());
    System.out.println("AbsoluteFile:" + fInput.getAbsoluteFile().toString());
    System.out.println("Canonical File:" +
➥ fInput.getCanonicalFile().toString());
    System.out.println("Name:" + fInput.getName());
```

LISTING 14.8 Continued

```
    System.out.println("Parent:" + fInput.getParent());
    System.out.println("Path:" + fInput.getPath());
    System.out.println("Absolute:" + fInput.isAbsolute());
    System.out.println("Directory:" + fInput.isDirectory());
    System.out.println("File:" + fInput.isFile());
    System.out.println("Hidden:" + fInput.isHidden());
    System.out.println("Last modified:" +
➥new java.util.Date(fInput.lastModified()).toString());
    System.out.println("Length:" + fInput.length());
    System.out.println("toString:" + fInput.toString());
    System.out.println("toURL:" + fInput.toURL());
    }
  catch( Exception e)
    {
    System.out.println(e.toString());
    }
  }
```

Most of the code that provides the statistics on a pathname is enclosed in a `try...catch` block. This is because most of these methods call the `SecurityException` or `IOException` if the pathname cannot be read.

TIP

Two of the most common steps in accessing a file are determining whether the file exists and determining how big the file is. The `exists` method determines whether the file exists. The `length` method returns the size in bytes of the file.

Finally, the `java.io.File` object has methods to create a temporary file and create a new file. Listing 14.9 shows how to create a temporary file.

LISTING 14.9 Creating Temporary Files (FileFun101.java)

```
    private String createTempFile()
  {
    File fTemp;
    try {
      fTemp = File.createTempFile("dsg",".tmp");
      System.out.println("Temporary File Name: " + fTemp.toString());
      return fTemp.toString();
    }
```

LISTING 14.9 Continued

```
    catch (Exception e) {
      System.out.println("Exception: " + e.toString());
    }
    return "";
  }
```

Listing 14.9 creates a temporary file and returns the pathname. The temporary file is actually created with a length of 0 bytes.

NOTE

In many multiuser applications, the user is given the ability to generate reports or create custom *dataset downloads*. These reports or dataset downloads are generated by the system and written to a file. Each user would require a unique filename for his information so that it can be made available to him. In addition, you do not want the filename to be easily guessed by other users, thereby allowing them to download the wrong information. The filename should be unique and random enough to provide security. The `java.io.File.createTempFile` method makes filenaming easy, random, and quick.

Input and Output Streams

Streams is the term used for reading and writing of information to an object, audio, OS pipe command, and file. This section focuses on the reading and writing of files using the many different stream classes. The stream for objects will be covered in the "Object Serialization" section later in the chapter. The streams for audio and piping will not be covered.

Streams flow in a single direction from one entity to another. To read and write from one entity to another requires two streams: one stream for reading and one stream for writing.

The `System` package has a predefined input stream, output stream, and error stream. The predefined streams are `System.in`, `System.out`, and `System.err`. `System.in` represents an input stream typically set to the keyboard input. `System.out` and `System.err` represent write streams typically set to the console for output. `System.out` is the most familiar stream because it is primarily used for displaying output. The predefined streams can be redirected. For example, the `System.in` can be set to get the input from a file or a communications port.

Table 14.2 contains a list of the common stream classes in the `java.io` and `java.util.zip` packages and a brief description of their use.

TABLE 14.2 List of Common Stream Classes

Stream Class Names	Descriptions
`InputStream/OutputStream`	The superclasses of all byte streams.
`FileInputStream/FileOutputStream`	Read and write bytes in a file. These streams are unidirectional in reading and writing bytes.
`BufferedInputStream/BufferedOutputStream`	Read and write bytes in a file using a buffer stream. The input stream buffer allows a stream of bytes to be read in two directions. Stream data can be read, have its position marked, read some more, reset to the marked point, and read again. The output stream writes data to a buffer prior to writing out the buffer. This allows for more efficient write operations.
`GZIPInputStream/GZIPOutputStream`	Read and write bytes in a file using the gzip compression routines. These streams are found in the `java.util.zip` package.
`ZipInputStream/ZipOutputStream`	Read and write bytes in a file using the zip compression routines. These streams are found in the `java.util.zip` package.
`ObjectInputStream/ObjectOutputStream`	Read and write objects to a file. By allowing persistent storage of an object, it can be re-created on another virtual machine with the exact same state. The `ObjectInputStream` and `ObjectOutputStream` are covered in the "Object Serialization" section later in the chapter.

A stream's typical use is to read and write bytes to a file. Reading and writing bytes are primarily used for binary files where special characters need to be at specific locations. This differs from text files where data is usually read and written on a carriage return and line feed basis.

Listing 14.10 uses the `FileInputStream` and `FileOutputStream` classes to create a file, write data to the file, close the file, open the file, and read the data.

LISTING 14.10 Create, Write, and Read a Stream (StreamFun101.java)

```
import java.io.*;

public class StreamFun101 {
  public static void main(String[] args) {

    try {
```

LISTING 14.10 Continued

```
      // Create a unique name
      File fNew = File.createTempFile("mjl",".tmp");

      // Open the file for writing
      FileOutputStream fOut = new FileOutputStream(fNew);
      System.out.println("Created file:" + fNew.toString() );

      // Write data to the file
      fOut.write("Writing data should be bytes.".getBytes());
      fOut.write(42); // ascii character for asterisk
      fOut.write("Write only part of this string".getBytes(),0,5);

      // Close the file
      fOut.close();
      System.out.println("Data has been written to: " + fNew.toString());

      // Open the file
      FileInputStream fIn = new FileInputStream(fNew);
      System.out.println("Opening file:" + fNew.toString());

      // Read all data from file and output to screen
      int data;
      data = fIn.read();
      // read data until end of file (-1)
      System.out.println("Data in file:");
      while (data != -1 ) {
        System.out.print((char)data);
        data = fIn.read();
      }
      System.out.println("");

      // Close the file
      fIn.close();
      System.out.println("File closed.  Success");
    }
    catch (IOException ex) {
      System.out.println("Error:" + ex.toString() );
    }

  }
}
```

In Listing 14.10, a `File` object is created to generate a temporary filename. That filename is opened for writing. The write methods take a byte, an array of bytes, or a portion of an array of bytes. Listing 14.10 uses all three write methods. The first write method outputs a string. The second write method writes out an integer value of 42. The third write method writes out the first five characters of the string using the offset and length parameters.

After the file is written to and closed, it is opened for reading. `FileInputStream` has three different read methods that return a byte, an array of bytes, and a select array of bytes using an offset and length. In addition, the input stream has the capability to skip over bytes and move to a new position. If any of the read methods return a –1, this indicates that the end of the file has been reached. Listing 14.10 reads only one byte at a time, displays the byte as a character, and then gets the next byte.

TIP

Reading a file one byte at a time is not efficient because it causes many file I/O method calls. A more efficient way to read in a file is to use an array of bytes as a buffer. Operations should then work on the buffer, which can be hundreds of times faster than single-byte operations.

Listing 14.10 generates the output shown in Listing 14.11. The output contains the asterisk that was written using its ASCII representation.

LISTING 14.11 Output from Streams (StreamFun101.java)

```
Created file:C:\DOCUME~1\mikel\LOCALS~1\Temp\mjl57352.tmp
Data has been written to: C:\DOCUME~1\mikel\LOCALS~1\Temp\mjl57352.tmp
Opening file:C:\DOCUME~1\mikel\LOCALS~1\Temp\mjl57352.tmp
Data in file:
Writing data should be bytes.*Write
File closed.  Success
```

Most input and output streams work the same with slight differences. For example, the buffered streams allow you to move backward in a stream, whereas the zip and gzip streams allow you to compress files and directories.

Listing 14.12 compresses a file and then uncompresses the file using the gzip streams. Notice that the gzip streams require an input and output stream as constructor parameters. The input and output streams are provided using the `FileInputStream` and `FileOutputStream`.

LISTING 14.12 Compress and Uncompress a File (ZipFun101.java)

```
import java.io.*;
import java.util.zip.*;

public class ZipFun101 {
  public static void main(String[] args) {
    if (args.length != 1 ) {
      System.out.println("Please pass the name of a file to compress.");
      System.exit(0);
    }
    // Compress the file with a ".Z" extension
    CompressFile(args);
    // Uncompress the file with a ".orig" extension
    UnCompressFile(args);
  }

  private static void CompressFile(String[] args) {
    try {
      FileInputStream fIn = new FileInputStream(args[0]);
      FileOutputStream fOut = new FileOutputStream(args[0] + ".Z");
      try {
        GZIPOutputStream fGOut = new GZIPOutputStream( fOut );
        byte[] data = new byte[8192];
        int nBytes;
        while( (nBytes = fIn.read(data)) != -1) {
          fGOut.write(data,0,nBytes);
        }
        fIn.close();
        fGOut.close();
        fOut.close();
      }
      catch (IOException ex) {
        System.out.println("GZIP Error: " + ex.toString());
        System.exit(0);
      }
    }
    catch (FileNotFoundException ex) {
      System.out.println("File is not found. File:" + args[0] );
      System.exit(0);
    }
  }
```

LISTING 14.12 Continued

```
  private static void UnCompressFile(String[] args) {
    try {
      FileInputStream fIn = new FileInputStream(args[0] + ".Z");
      FileOutputStream fOut = new FileOutputStream(args[0] + ".orig");
      try {
        GZIPInputStream fGIn = new GZIPInputStream(fIn);
        byte[] data = new byte[8192];
        int nBytes;
        while( (nBytes = fGIn.read(data)) != -1) {
          fOut.write(data,0,nBytes);
        }
        fGIn.close();
        fIn.close();
        fOut.close();
      }
      catch (IOException ex) {
        System.out.println("Uncompress GZIP Error: " + ex.toString());
        System.exit(0);
      }
    }
    catch (FileNotFoundException ex) {
      System.out.println("File is not found. File:" + args[0] );
      System.exit(0);
    }
  }
}
```

A filename must be passed when you run the code in Listing 14.12. The file is opened, read from, and passed to the `GZIPOutputStream` object. The gzip output stream compresses the data and writes it to a file with the same name and a .Z extension.

The compressed file is then opened using the `GZIPInputStream` object. The gzip input stream is created with a normal input stream and then uncompresses the data as it is read. The data is then written to a file with the same name and a .orig extension.

In our example, the streams were file-based streams and easy to see. The streams could have easily been pipe based or memory based. The gzip routines compress any input stream and uncompress any output stream. Compressing data on-the-fly reduces the amount of data sent across the wire resulting in more efficient transfer methods.

Most streams raise the IOException and the FileNotFoundException. The IOException can occur for any number of reasons, from file access denied to failure of the hard drive. FileNotFoundException results from an attempt to open a file that does not exist. JBuilder does a good job of informing you when you need to handle an exception by putting the error information in the Errors folder in the Structure pane.

Finally, it is important to note that streams are based on bytes of data being moved around. If you are working with textual data such as Unicode, the Reader and Writer classes provide improved functionality.

Reader and Writer Classes

Reader and Writer classes provide the capability to read and write 16-bit streams. Java's international appeal has required that Java support international languages and character sets. Unicode is a 16-bit character set that provides for more than 65,000 characters, making it an international standard.

The Reader and Writer classes were created to access data in Unicode format. Similar to the input and output streams, there are many different Reader and Writer classes. Table 14.3 lists some of the more popular Reader and Writer classes.

TABLE 14.3 Common Reader/Writer Classes

Reader/Writer **Names**	**Description**
Reader/Writer	The base classes from which other Reader and Writer classes are derived. These are the counterparts to the InputStream and OutputStream classes.
InputStreamReader/OutputStreamWriter	InputStreamReader constructs an object that reads in a character stream. OutputStreamWriter writes out a character stream.
FileReader/FileWriter	Used to read and write characters to a text file.
BufferedReader/BufferedWriter	Buffers character data so that reads and writes are more efficient. The buffered classes also provide routines that read and write strings.

An important aspect of any application is getting information from the user and saving that information. The information can then be read back at a later time.

Listing 14.13 reads in a string of data from the user and writes it to a file. The file is then opened, and the output is displayed. The code uses a number of the available reader and writer classes.

LISTING 14.13 Compress and Uncompress a File (ReaderFun101.java)

```
import java.io.*;

public class ReaderFun101 {
  public static void main(String[] args) {
    int data;
    String readData;

    // Get input from the user
    InputStreamReader inKeyboard = new InputStreamReader(System.in);
    OutputStreamWriter outConsole = new OutputStreamWriter(System.out);

    try {
      // Open a file for output.
      FileWriter fileOut = new FileWriter("User.txt");

      // It is much easier to user System.out, but for our example
      // we use the OutputStreamWriter
      outConsole.write("Please type in a sentence. Hit enter when done.\n");
      outConsole.flush();

      while((data = inKeyboard.read()) != '\n') {
        // Save the input to a file
        fileOut.write((char) data);
      }
      // close the file
      fileOut.close();
      System.out.println("Data has been captured.");

      FileReader fileIn = new FileReader("User.txt");
      BufferedReader bufIn = new BufferedReader( fileIn );
      while ((readData = bufIn.readLine())!=null) {
        outConsole.write(readData);
        outConsole.flush();
      }
      bufIn.close();
      fileIn.close();

      System.out.println("\nDone.");
    }
    catch (IOException ex) {
      System.out.println("Error: " + ex.toString());
```

LISTING 14.13 Continued

```
            System.exit(0);
        }

    }
}
```

The keyboard input is captured using the `System.in` stream. The console output is captured using the `System.out` stream. In most situations, the `System.out.println` is more efficient than creating an output writer class. Using the output writer class requires the use of the `flush` method to make sure that the information in the buffer is sent to the stream.

The `FileWriter` class is used to output the data to a file named User.txt. The `FileReader` class is wrapped inside a `BufferedReader` class for reading the file back in a line at a time.

Reading and writing text files for an international audience is best handled using the reader and writer classes. Although the same can be accomplished using the stream classes, more work must be done to accomplish the same results.

`StreamTokenizer` Class

The `StreamTokenizer` class allows a stream to be interpreted as it is being read. The stream can strip out words, numbers, end-of-line markers, and end-of-file markers. The tokenizer works on `InputStream` classes and `Reader` classes.

Table 14.4 lists some of the available fields and methods in the `StreamTokenizer` class. The stream tokenizer reads a token at a time allowing you to perform actions based on the token.

TABLE 14.4 `StreamTokenizer` Fields and Methods

Field/Method	Description
`int ttype`	Contains the type of token. A token can be one of the following constants: `static int TT_EOF`—End of stream `static int TT_EOL`—End of line `static int TT_NUMBER`—Numeric token `static int TT_WORD`—Word token
`double nval`	Value of the numeric token.
`String sval`	String value of the word token.
`int lineno()`	Get the current line number.
`int nextToken()`	Get the next token.

TABLE 14.4 Continued

Field/Method	Description
`void parseNumbers()`	Specifies that numbers should be parsed as doubles and not words. If the token can be formatted as a double precision number, it sets the `nval`.
`void pushBack()`	Puts the current token back so that a call to `nextToken` returns the current token again.

In addition to these more popular fields and methods, the tokenizer contains fields and methods that specify valid character ranges, quote delimiters, comment characters, and slash characters.

Listing 14.14 creates a stream tokenizer for a file. The tokenizer parses the file and displays words and numeric values as they are parsed.

LISTING 14.14 Tokenize a File (TokenFun101.java)

```
import java.io.*;

public class TokenFun101 {
  public static void main(String[] args) {
    try {
      FileReader fIn = new FileReader("TokenFun.txt");
      StreamTokenizer stToken = new StreamTokenizer(fIn);

      String sData;
      double dData;

        while(stToken.nextToken() != stToken.TT_EOF) {
          if (stToken.ttype == stToken.TT_NUMBER) {
            System.out.print("Line: " + stToken.lineno() );
            System.out.println(" Number: " + stToken.nval);
          }
          if (stToken.ttype == stToken.TT_WORD) {
            System.out.print("Line: " + stToken.lineno() );
            System.out.println(" Word: " + stToken.sval );
          }
        }
        fIn.close();
    }
    catch (FileNotFoundException ex) {
      System.out.println("File Not Found Error: " + ex.toString());
      System.exit(0);
    }
```

LISTING 14.14 Continued

```
    catch (IOException ex) {
      System.out.println("Error: " + ex.toString());
      System.exit(0);
    }

  }
}
```

The input file TokenFun.txt (see Listing 14.15) contains four lines with a mixture of punctuation and characters.

LISTING 14.15 Input File TokenFun.txt

```
How hard can it be to add 2 plus 2?
This is a sentence with 3 lines.
23 45.6 34.5 are all numbers
Can you see me?
```

The output from Listing 14.14 using the TokenFun.txt file in Listing 14.15 can be seen in Listing 14.16.

LISTING 14.16 Output from Listing 14.14

```
Line: 1 Word: How
Line: 1 Word: hard
Line: 1 Word: can
Line: 1 Word: it
Line: 1 Word: be
Line: 1 Word: to
Line: 1 Word: add
Line: 1 Number: 2.0
Line: 1 Word: plus
Line: 1 Number: 2.0
Line: 2 Word: This
Line: 2 Word: is
Line: 2 Word: a
Line: 2 Word: sentence
Line: 2 Word: with
Line: 2 Number: 3.0
Line: 2 Word: lines.
Line: 3 Number: 23.0
Line: 3 Number: 45.6
```

LISTING 14.16 Continued

```
Line: 3 Number: 34.5
Line: 3 Word: are
Line: 3 Word: all
Line: 3 Word: numbers
Line: 4 Word: Can
Line: 4 Word: you
Line: 4 Word: see
Line: 4 Word: me
```

The stream tokenizer is easy to use and can be powerful when parsing through streamed data. Another way to parse and tokenize data is by using an XML-formatted stream and the Java XML libraries. A file that conforms to an XML standard can be quickly parsed using the Java XML feature discussed in Chapter 20, "XML."

Object Serialization

Object serialization is the capability of an object to write out its state to a stream and read it back in again. An object that is serialized writes out all its public and private fields including all fields inherited from all superclasses.

When an object is being serialized and it finds a field that refers to an object or array, serialization will be invoked on that object or array. Serialization is recursive until all fields of an object have been serialized. If an object does not implement the serialization interface, a `NotSerializableException` exception is thrown.

The `java.io` package provides for object serialization through the `ObjectOutputStream` and the `ObjectInputStream`. These streams provide the methods `writeObject` and `readObject`, respectively. In addition, the object streams provide methods for reading and writing bytes, booleans, characters, doubles, floats, long integers, short integers, and integers.

An object that wants to be serializable must implement the `Serializable` or `Externalizable` interfaces. These interfaces provide the Java Virtual Machine a framework to persist an object to a stream.

The `Serializable` interface is a *tagging interface* and does not define any methods to implement. A tagging interface is used to simply mark the object as being capable of serializing. The `Externalizable` interface defines methods that must be implemented. `Externalizable` is used if you want to have control over the way the object is serialized.

NOTE

The way in which an object is serialized can still be overridden even though the `Serializable` interface is a marker interface with no method defined. The methods have the following signatures: `private void writeObject(...)` and `private void readObject(...)`.

Serializable has no methods to be overridden, but somehow a private method of an object can be used. So, how does one object such as `ObjectOutputStream` access the private internal serialization function of another object? Magic! The Java Virtual Machine takes care of this glaring issue and as such we ignore it.

One benefit of overriding the `readObject` method can be seen in object initialization. Suppose that the object that had been persisted needs connections to a database. Prior to the object being ready for use, those database connections would need to be reestablished. By overriding the `readObject` method, you can write code that reinitializes the database connection prior to the object being ready for use!

Not all objects should be serialized. For example, platform-specific objects, such as low-level file descriptors, would have no meaning if they were created in another virtual machine. Therefore, serialization of these objects could be disastrous.

In addition to objects, some fields in an object should not be serialized. For example, temporary or working variables that hold data that is not relevant should not be serialized. Although there are no problems with serializing an object with meaningless temporary and working variables, it does save space when they are removed from serialization. This becomes important when an object is serialized and passed to another virtual machine. The less data that is passed the better the performance because processing can begin sooner.

The `transient` keyword modifier is used to prevent a field from being serialized. Consider a `transient` field that represents the number of days that have elapsed since your last visit to the doctor:

```
private transient int nDaysSinceLastVisit;
```

The value is calculated based on today's date minus your last doctor visit. Storing the number of days would be useless if the object was deserialized a week later. The field would contain an invalid value. The `transient` modifier tells serialization to skip this field.

Listing 14.17 creates a class that implements the `Serializable` interface. The class contains `transient` fields that will not be persisted.

LISTING 14.17 Serializing and Deserializing an Object (ObjectFun101.java)

```
import java.io.*;

public class ObjectFun101 implements Serializable{
  public int nMaxObjects;
  private String sObjectName;
  protected boolean bObjectValid;

  public transient int nNumberOfObjects;

  // Initialize the object
  public ObjectFun101( String name ) {
    bObjectValid = true;
    nNumberOfObjects = 0;
    sObjectName = name;
    nMaxObjects = 15;
  }

  // Display the object in a meaningful way
  public String toString() {
    return sObjectName + " - Max=" + nMaxObjects +
           " Current=" + nNumberOfObjects + " Valid:" + bObjectValid;
  }

  public static void main(String[] args) {
    String sDate;
    // Initialize the object
    ObjectFun101 oFun = new ObjectFun101("Bank Account");
    oFun.nMaxObjects = 20;
    oFun.nNumberOfObjects ++;
    System.out.println("Object Created: " + oFun.toString());

    // Persist the object to a file
    try {
      // Create the output file and output stream for the object
      FileOutputStream fOut = new FileOutputStream("Object.dat");
      ObjectOutputStream oFOut = new ObjectOutputStream( fOut);

      // write the object out to the file
      oFOut.writeObject(oFun);
```

LISTING 14.17 Continued

```
        // write the date and time the object was written to the file
        sDate = new java.util.Date().toString();
        oFOut.writeObject(sDate);
        oFOut.flush();

        // close the file
        oFOut.close();
        fOut.close();
        System.out.println("Object was persisted at: " + sDate);

        // open the file and create the object stream
        FileInputStream fIn = new FileInputStream("Object.dat");
        ObjectInputStream oFIn = new ObjectInputStream( fIn);

        // create a place for the object to be read into
        ObjectFun101 oNewFun;

        // read in the object from the file and convert it to
        // the proper type.
        oNewFun = (ObjectFun101) oFIn.readObject();

        // read in the object that contains the date the object
        // was persisted to the file
        sDate = (String) oFIn.readObject();

        // close the file and stream
        oFIn.close();
        fIn.close();

        // waste time waiting for the time to change
        while(sDate.equals(new java.util.Date().toString()));

        // write out the new de-serialized object and the date
        // it was persisted.
        System.out.println("New Object: " + oNewFun.toString());
        System.out.println("Object was originally persisted at: " + sDate);
        System.out.println("Object has been re-created at:" +
                           new java.util.Date().toString());
    }
    catch (Exception ex) {
```

LISTING 14.17 Continued

```
        System.out.println("Error:" + ex.toString());
        System.exit(0);
      }

  }
}
```

Notice how the class in Listing 14.17 implements the `Serializable` interface. A review of the object's fields shows that it has three fields and a `transient` field.

The object constructor sets the name and sets the other fields to default values. The `main` method creates the object, changes the number of maximum object fields to 20, and increments the number of objects.

The next part of the `main` method opens a file and object stream so that the object can be persisted to a file. The `writeObject` method is called on the object as well as the current date and time the object was persisted. The output file is now closed.

The `main` method goes on to open the file and create the object input stream. The objects are read from the file and cast to the correct data type. The objects are retrieved in the same order that they were written. Therefore, the main object is retrieved first, and the date the object was persisted is read next.

Notice in the output shown in Listing 14.18 that the deserialized object has a different value for number of objects than the persisted object. This was expected because the field for number of objects is transient.

LISTING 14.18 Output from Listing 14.17

```
Object Created: Bank Account - Max=20 Current=1 Valid:true
Object was persisted at: Thu Jun 06 23:43:49 CDT 2002
New Object: Bank Account - Max=20 Current=0 Valid:true
Object was originally persisted at: Thu Jun 06 23:43:49 CDT 2002
Object has been re-created at:Thu Jun 06 23:43:50 CDT 2002
```

Serialization is an important concept because it allows an object to be persisted and then re-created with the same state information.

When an object is serialized, it is given a unique identifier to control its version. The serialization features provide a built-in method for the versioning of objects. If there is a version mismatch in a persisted object and the runtime object, the persisted object cannot be re-created in the runtime object.

In Practice

This lab focuses on reading key pairs from a file. The file will be used to hold configuration settings for the current user.

You will enhance a class named `ConfigFile` based on the following requirements:

- The `Properties` class found in the `java.Util` package will be used to set properties, get properties, load properties, and restore properties.
- The `Properties` class contains methods that will read and write the properties to a stream.
- If the configuration file does not exist, create it.
- If the configuration file does exist, load in the key pairs.
- Implement methods to read a property, set a property, and save a property.
- Allow the configuration file to be passed in the constructor of the class.

Step 1: Opening the Example and Reviewing the Class

In this step, you open the example project and review the source code file.

To open the example project

1. Select File, Open Project from the JBuilder menu.
2. Locate the jbbook/ch14/ConfigurationFiles.jpx and click OK.
3. The project opens in the Project pane. The project contains a single file, ConfigFile.java.
4. Double-click on ConfigFile.java. The Content pane displays the file.

Listing 14.19 contains the code in ConfigFile.java. The code contains the shell that you will fill in using the following exercises.

LISTING 14.19 Initial Code Skeleton for ConfigFile.java

```
import java.io.*;
import java.util.*;

public class ConfigFile {
  private String sConfigFilename;
  private Properties mProperties;
```

LISTING 14.19 Continued

```
public ConfigFile( String sFileName) {
  // Create a properties object
  mProperties = new Properties();

  // Create a file object for the filename

  // Save the configuration filename

  // Determine if the file exists, if not, create the file.
  if () {
    try {
      // file does not exist, so create the file
    }
    catch (IOException ex) {
      System.err.println("Cannot create" + sConfigFilename +
                         " file:" + ex.toString());
    }
  }
  else
  {
    try {
      // Open the existing configuration files and read information
      // into the properties object
    }
    catch (IOException ex) {
      System.err.println("Cannot open and read " + sConfigFilename +
                         " file:" + ex.toString());
    }

  }
}

public String readKey( String key) {
  return mProperties.getProperty(key, "");
}

public void writeKey( String key, String value) {
  mProperties.setProperty(key, value);
}
```

LISTING 14.19 Continued

```
  public void saveKey( ) {
    try {
      // Open up the configuration file for output and store the
      // properties to the output stream
    }
    catch (IOException ex) {
      System.err.println("Cannot write to " + sConfigFilename +
                         " file:" + ex.toString());

    }
  }

  public void listKeys() {
    // PrintWriter is a type of java.io.Writer class.
    // For more information, look up PrintWriter in the
    // on-line help guides
    PrintWriter pw = new PrintWriter( System.out, true);
    mProperties.list(pw);
    pw.close();
  }

  public static void main(String[] args) {
    // Open or create the configuration file
    ConfigFile cf = new ConfigFile("info.config");

    // write keys to the Properties class
    cf.writeKey("gofast","true");
    cf.writeKey("NewItem", "false");

    // look up values from the file
    System.out.println("Looking for gofast..." + cf.readKey("gofast"));
    System.out.println("Looking for nobugs..." + cf.readKey("nobugs"));
    System.out.println("Looking for highlight..." + cf.readKey("highlight"));

    // Save the keys
    cf.saveKey();
    // List the keys
    cf.listKeys();
  }
}
```

Step 2: Writing the Constructor to Open or Create the Configuration File

The first method you want to complete is the constructor. The constructor creates a new `Properties` object and assigns it to a private class variable named `mProperties`.

You need to write the code that creates a file object in the user's home directory named `info.config`. The filename and path are stored in the private variable `sConfigFilename`. The file object allows you to test whether the file exists. If the file exists, then the file should be opened and the information placed in the properties object. If the file does not exist, it should be created. Listing 14.20 shows the added code in bold.

LISTING 14.20 ConfigFile Constructor Method

```
public ConfigFile( String sFileName) {
  // Create a properties object
  mProperties = new Properties();

  // Create a file object for the filename
  File fConfigFile = new File(System.getProperty("user_home"),
➥ "info.config");

  // Save the configuration filename
  sConfigFilename= fConfigFile.toString() ;

  // Determine if the file exists, if not, create the file.
  if (fConfigFile.exists() == false ) {
    try {
      // file does not exist, so create the file
      fConfigFile.createNewFile();
    }
    catch (IOException ex) {
      System.err.println("Cannot create" + sConfigFilename +
                         " file:" + ex.toString());
    }
  }
  else
  {
    try {
      // Open the existing configuration files and read information
      // into the properties object
      FileInputStream fIn = new FileInputStream(sConfigFilename);
      mProperties.load(fIn);
```

LISTING 14.20 Continued

```
        fIn.close();
        listKeys();
      }
      catch (IOException ex) {
        System.err.println("Cannot open and read " + sConfigFilename +
                           " file:" + ex.toString());
      }

    }
  }
```

The first line of code added creates a file object based on the user's home directory and the filename `info.config`. The class and method to get a user's home directory is

```
System.getPropery("user.home")
```

The `File` constructor `File(String Parent, String Child)` creates an object based on a parent path and a child filename. Combine this with the preceding code line, and the file object is created as follows:

```
    File fConfigFile = new File(System.getProperty("user.home"),
➥ "info.config");
```

The `toString` method is then used to set the complete filename, including the parent path, to the private variable `sConfigFilename`. The full filename and path will be needed to open the file for reading and writing.

The file object can be used to test whether a file exists using the `exists` method. If the file does not exist, it can be created using the `createNewFile` method of the file object.

If the file does exist, the `Properties` object's `load` method reads in a stream and creates the key pairs. The load signature of the `Properties` class is `load(InputStream)`. The `load` method requires an input stream to create the properties. Because we are working with a file, the `FileInputStream` class is used. Here is the code added to open a file, read in the properties, and display the properties created:

```
FileInputStream fIn = new FileInputStream(sConfigFilename);
mProperties.load(fIn);
fIn.close();
listKeys();
```

The private listKeys method creates a PrintWriter and then calls the Properties class list method. The PrintWriter class is redirected to display the list to the System.out stream. System.out is typically set to the console display.

Step 3: Opening an Output Stream and Storing the Properties to a File

Locate the saveKey method. This method uses the store method of the Properties class. The store method takes an output stream and a comment to write information to a stream. The comment can be anything you want.

Listing 14.21 details the added code for the saveKey method. The code in bold has been added to the current saveKey method.

LISTING 14.21 saveKey Method

```
public void saveKey( ) {
  try {
    // Open up the configuration file for output and store the
    // properties to the output stream
    FileOutputStream fOut = new FileOutputStream( sConfigFilename);
    mProperties.store( fOut, "Configuration File" );
    fOut.close();
  }
  catch (IOException ex) {
    System.err.println("Cannot write to " + sConfigFilename +
                       " file:" + ex.toString());


  }
}
```

The first line of added code creates a file output stream based on the filename. After the output stream is created, the store method of the Properties class is called to write out the comment and all the properties to the stream. Finally, the file is closed.

Step 4: Running the Application and Reviewing the Configuration File

Now that the code has been added and is error free, you can run the file. If your application successfully executes, you receive the output shown in Listing 14.22.

LISTING 14.22 Output from the Configuration Class

```
Looking for gofast...true
Looking for nobugs...
Looking for highlight...
-- listing properties --
NewItem=false
gofast=true
```

Locate the `info.config` file in your user home directory. Open up the file and you should see the output shown in Listing 14.23.

LISTING 14.23 Contents of the `info.config` File

```
#Configuration File
#Thu Jun 13 22:53:58 CDT 2002
NewItem=false
gofast=true
```

Try adding your own key pairs to the file and run the application again.

Summary

Java provides a class to encapsulate the underlying file system of many platforms. The class provides you with the ability to manipulate files and directories without knowledge of the underlying file system.

Besides manipulation of files and directories, Java provides many different classes to read and write files. The stream classes are used to read and write bytes of data, whereas the reader classes are used to read and write text data.

Java provides stream classes that compress and decompress data on-the-fly, allowing for unique file management opportunities. In addition, the reader classes support internationalization by reading and writing Unicode.

Finally, Java introduced the concept of object state persistence. A persisted state can be transferred over the wire to another machine. On the other machine, the object can then be re-created with the exact same state as the original machine.

Reflections

- How will you maintain user settings in your application?
- How will your application turn on and off configuration options?

15

Database Connectivity

IN THIS CHAPTER

- Overview of Databases, SQL, JDBC, and DataExpress
- Using the JDBC API
- Using JBuilder's DataExpress
- Using Data Modules

Using a database has become essential in today's business environment. A database provides an efficient way to store and retrieve information based on a Structured Query Language (SQL). Java supports connectivity to a database and the SQL through the Java DataBase Connectivity (JDBC) API.

JBuilder supports the JDBC API and has created a complete database framework named DataExpress. DataExpress extends the JDBC API to support enterprise and mobile database solutions. The DataExpress framework has created a set of database components and visual components that are data aware.

JBuilder's DataExpress partitions your database access logic from your business and presentation logic. The partitioning of this access makes it easier to create multitier applications with high scalability and failover.

This chapter introduces you to the JDBC API and DataExpress. The following topics will be covered:

- Overview of databases, SQL, JDBC, and DataExpress
- Using the JDBC API
- Using JBuilder's DataExpress
- Using data modules

Overview of Databases, SQL, JDBC, and DataExpress

In almost every business situation, for better or for worse, the use of a database has become the silver bullet. In particular, relational databases such as Oracle, SQL Server,

Sybase, Informix, DB2, and MySQL have become the corporate solution for storing and retrieving data.

Databases have become so popular that future versions of some operating systems are rumored to have their file systems replaced with a database system. After all, a file system is a type of database that allows you to store and retrieve files.

Databases

In the early days of databases, communicating with a database required a proprietary set of libraries provided by the database vendor. These proprietary libraries provided unique ways to connect to the database and issue commands. The way data was retrieved and the capabilities of a particular database vendor were weaved through their proprietary libraries.

Many database vendors realized that there was a need to standardize the language by which commands are issued to a database. The language acts as a common thread so that commands written in one database could be executed on a database from a different vendor. The common language became known as SQL.

SQL

SQL is supported by most relational databases although the exact implementations vary based on the features of the database. SQL is broken down into two main categories: the database definition language (DDL), and the data manipulation language (DML).

The DDL is a standard set of commands that manage the creation, manipulation, and destruction of database objects. The database objects include tables, indexes, views, triggers, stored procedures, and security commands.

The DML handles the selecting, inserting, updating, and deleting of data. DML is used to query the database for data matching certain criteria. DML is also used to modify existing data or insert new data.

SQL provides a way for developers to learn one common language for manipulating a database's objects and data. What SQL does not specify is the manner in which the database communicates with the client issuing the commands. The communication layer is completely proprietary.

JDBC

The proprietary communication libraries provided by each vendor made it difficult for a developer to build an application that worked on a wide variety of database platforms. In the late 80s and early 90s, Microsoft pushed a standard for communicating with databases on the Windows platform. The communication interface became known as Open Database Connectivity (ODBC). ODBC was based on the SQL X/Open Call Level Interface standard.

The common API provided by ODBC allowed developers to write applications that worked with a variety of database vendors. ODBC is extremely popular and is used by many systems for communications. As applications grew larger in scope and size, ODCB revealed limitations. ODBC is a heavy-weight process that has performance problems for large databases and cannot handle nonrelational data stores. In addition, ODBC is a C language interface that is primarily Windows based.

Over time, Microsoft developed new standards that provide lightweight processes for database connectivity and nonrelational data stores. These standards are very popular and work extremely well, if you are on the Windows operating system.

In the mid 90s, Java hit the street with the promise of "write once and run anywhere." Although this tag line never lived up to its hype, Java presented an alternative, cross-platform programming language. To make it as a corporately accepted language, Java needed to be able to connect to corporate databases.

Java learned from the success and failure of ODBC when the JDBC API was released. JDBC provides an operating system-independent method of connecting to databases.

To capitalize on the number of ODBC drivers to various databases, Java came out with a series of driver types numbered 1 through 4. The goal of these driver types is to provide a way to leverage existing database libraries while developing all Java versions of the same drivers. Figure 15.1 shows an overview of JDBC and the different driver types.

Type 1 drivers provide a JDBC to ODBC gateway that leverages the existing database driver market. Java applications could now be written to access non-Java-based database drivers. Typically, this driver is not used due to the wide availability of pure Java-based database drivers.

Type 2 drivers are slightly better than Type 1 drivers because they convert the JDBC calls into native database driver calls. Where ODBC wrapped the native drivers in an interface, Type 2 drivers required the native driver libraries. Type 2 drivers have notable performance improvements over Type 1 drivers by eliminating the ODBC wrapper.

Type 3 drivers are all Java-coded network protocols that route requests to a middle tier that executes the database requests against the native libraries. The all-Java drivers allow an application to be operating system independent. The middle tier receives the database requests and translates them to the appropriate native database drivers.

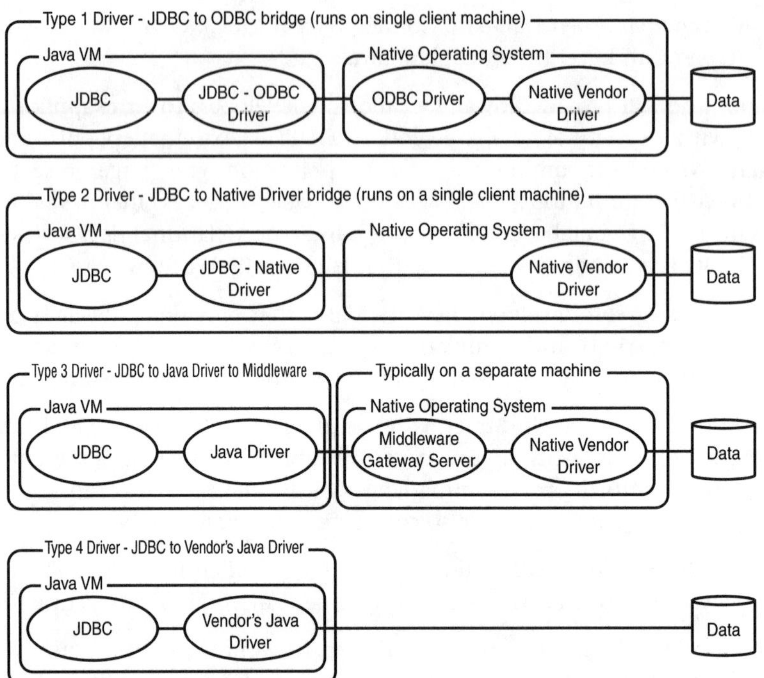

FIGURE 15.1 Overview of JDBC and database driver types.

Type 4 drivers are Java-based drivers that natively connect to the database using the database's protocol. These drivers are typically developed by the database vendor and are the best for cross-platform requirements and performance considerations. Because Type 4 drivers were not readily available when Java was maturing, driver Types 1, 2, and 3 were stopgap measures.

Today, JDBC Type 4 drivers can be found for most databases, including Microsoft's SQL Server, Oracle, Sybase, and DB2.

As Java worked its way into the enterprise with database drivers, the need for a robust database framework grew. JBuilder added a framework on top of JDBC called DataExpress.

DataExpress

DataExpress provides two sets of components for JDBC and database functionality. DataExpress is a set of wrapper classes for the Swing UI components making them data aware. DataExpress also provides wrapper classes for the database connection and query objects to facilitate a data-aware framework.

DataExpress encapsulates many of the database technical requirements into simple method calls and properties. JDBC is a powerful and complex set of methods that force a developer to really understand all the inner workings of databases. Methods have to be called in a certain order to get the desired effect. DataExpress allows less-knowledgeable developers to create robust and powerful database applications.

Using the JDBC API

The JDBC API is a set of interfaces that a database vendor implements for its database server. The set of interfaces describes connection, statement, and resultset objects. These three objects are the crux of a JDBC driver and must be implemented by the vendor for JDBC compliance. JDBC version 2.0 specifications have been released and provide added support for connection pooling, bidirectional cursors, and other more advanced features.

After a driver has been implemented to the JDBC specification, it must be registered with the `DriverManager` before it can be used by your application. The `DriverManager` coordinates the JDBC calls with the driver implementation to satisfy requests for connection, statement execution, and resultset.

There are different ways to register a JDBC driver with the `DriverManager`. The most common and flexible way is to load the class at runtime. The driver name can be stored in a properties file to make it even more flexible. JDBC drivers have a static initializer that automatically calls the `DriverManager.registerDriver()` method. Listing 15.1 shows how to dynamically load a JDBC driver at runtime for the JDataStore database that ships with JBuilder.

LISTING 15.1 Dynamic Load of JDBC Driver

```
// The driver name is stored in a string, but it could have
// been loaded from a properties file.
String DRIVER = "com.borland.datastore.jdbc.DataStoreDriver";
Class.forName(DRIVER);
```

Another way of loading the JDBC driver is to explicitly load the object using the standard Java new operator. The problem with this method is that the driver name is hard coded in the application, and if you want to update the driver or change drivers, you will be forced to recompile the application.

The final way to load a driver is to pass the driver name on the `java` command line. Using the parameter setting `jdbc.drivers`, the command line would look like this:

```
java -Djdbc.drivers=DRIVER  program
```

In the preceding line of code, the DRIVER would be replaced with the name of the JDBC driver, such as com.borland.datastore.jdbc.DataStoreDriver. This method requires that you specify the driver every time you run the application.

After the JDBC driver has been registered with the DriverManager, it is time to work with the database. The normal course followed is to connect to the database using the Connection object. After connecting to the database, statements are executed against the database using the Statement object. Statements may return a resultset of data using the ResultSet object. Finally, the application disconnects from the database.

Listing 15.2 shows an application that connects to a JDataStore database, creates a table, executes a couple of commands against the table, iterates through a resultset, and then disconnects from the database. The sample application assumes that a JDataStore database named JDBCFun.jds has been created and placed in the application directory.

LISTING 15.2 Sample JDBC Application (jbbook/ch15/JDBCSample/JDBCFun.java)

```
// Remember to make sure the jds.jar file is in the CLASSPATH

// Remember to import the java.sql package
import java.sql.*;

public class JDBCFun {

  public static void main(String[] args) {
    // Use the JDataStore database driver.
    // You may replace this with your own database driver, see your
    // database's documentation for the correct format
    String DRIVER =   "com.borland.datastore.jdbc.DataStoreDriver";

    // The format of the connection string is different for each
    // database. Review your database's documentation for the
    // connection string.

    String CONNECTIONURL    =    "jdbc:borland:dslocal:JDBCFun";

    // Initialize the connection and statement objects
    Connection connect = null;
    Statement stmtCommand = null;

    try
    {
```

LISTING 15.2 Continued

```
        // Dynamically load the database driver
        Class.forName(DRIVER);
        // Get a connection to the database
        connect = DriverManager.getConnection(CONNECTIONURL, "user", "");

        // Create a statement for the connection
        stmtCommand = connect.createStatement();

        // Execute a DDL command to create a table
        stmtCommand.executeUpdate("create table JDBCSample" +
            "(Name varchar(15), Age int )");

        // Execute DML commands to fill the table with data
        stmtCommand.executeUpdate("insert into JDBCSample values('Michael',
➥ 45)");
        stmtCommand.executeUpdate("insert into JDBCSample values('Jeff',
➥ 22)");
        stmtCommand.executeUpdate("insert into JDBCSample values('Saleem',
➥ 36)");

    // Execute a DML command to return a result set with data
    ResultSet rsData = stmtCommand.executeQuery("select * from JDBCSample");

        // Iterate through the result set and print out the data
        while (rsData.next()) {
          System.out.print( "Name: " + rsData.getString("Name"));
          System.out.println( "   Age: " + rsData.getInt("Age"));
        }

        // Execute a DDL statement to delete the table
        stmtCommand.executeUpdate("drop table JDBCSample");
      }
      catch(Exception e)
      {
        if (e instanceof SQLException) {
        System.out.println("Error with database: " + CONNECTIONURL + ": "
                           + e.getMessage() + "\nState:"
                           + ((SQLException) e).getSQLState());
        }
        else
        {
```

LISTING 15.2 Continued

```
        System.out.println("Error with database: " + CONNECTIONURL + ": "
                             + e.getMessage() );
      }
    }
    finally
    {
      // It is always good practice to clean up statements and connections
      // before you finish a routine.
      try {
        if (stmtCommand != null ) stmtCommand.close();
        if (connect !=null) connect.close();
      }
      catch (SQLException ex) {
        System.out.println("Error shutting down database: " + CONNECTIONURL
                             + ": " + ex.getMessage() + "\nState:"
                             + ex.getSQLState());
      }
    }
  }
}
```

Listing 15.2 can be broken down into the following logical steps.

Step 1: Register the Driver with the `DriverManager`

In Listing 15.2, the database driver is dynamically loaded. After the class is loaded, it implicitly registers itself with the `DriverManager`:

```
    String DRIVER =   "com.borland.datastore.jdbc.DataStoreDriver";
...
    Class.forName(DRIVER);
```

Using the `Class.forName` method loads the class file passed in as the parameter. Another way of registering the driver explicitly would be

```
com.borland.datastore.jdbc.DataStoreDriver dbDriver = new
➥ com.borland.datastore.jdbc.DataStoreDriver();
DriverManager.registerDriver( dbDriver );
```

The library `com.borland.datastore.jdbc.DataStoreDriver` is a Type 4 driver for the JDataStore database included with JBuilder. If you do not want to connect to JDataStore, you can use the built-in Java to ODBC bridge supplied by Sun. The driver name is `sun.jdbc.odbc.JdbcOdbcDriver`.

Here is a list of the more popular database driver classes. Remember that you must place the database driver in the `CLASSPATH` to use these drivers.

- JDBC-ODBC bridge—`sun.jdbc.odbc.JdbcOdbcDriver`
- Oracle JDBC—`oracle.jdbc.driver.OracleDriver`
- SQL Server—`com.microsoft.jdbc.sqlserver.SQLServerDriver`
- MySQL—`org.gjt.mm.mysql.Driver`

Step 2: Get a Connection to the Database

The `getConnection` method of the `DriverManager` object is used to get a connection to a database using a driver you just registered. The `getConnection` method takes the database URL, username, and password parameters. A `Connection` object is returned if the driver connects to the database using the database URL, username, and password.

```
String CONNECTIONURL    =    "jdbc:borland:dslocal:JDBCFun";
connect = DriverManager.getConnection(CONNECTIONURL, "user", "");
```

The database URL has the following format:

```
jdbc:DriverManager:database
```

All vendor implementations start with `jdbc`, but after that, it is vendor dependent. Some of the more common URL formats for popular databases are

- JDBC-ODBC bridge—`jdbc:odbc:datasource;param=value;`
- Oracle—`jdbc:oracle:thin:@hostname:port:database`
- SQL Server—`jdbc:microsoft:sqlserver://`*`hostname`*`:`*`port`*`[;`*`property=value`*`...]`
- MySQL—`jdbc:mysql://[hostname][:port]/[dbname][?param1=value1][¶m2=value2]`

Step 3: Create a Statement to Issue Commands

After a connection has been established to the database, you need a `Statement` object to issue commands. The `Statement` object can only have one resultset associated with it. Therefore, if you need to iterate through two resultsets, they must be created with two different statements.

```
stmtCommand = connect.createStatement();
```

The `Connection` object acts like an operator making a phone call to the database on your behalf. The `Statement` object is the operator giving you the phone after the call has been answered by the database.

Step 4: Execute SQL Statements

The `Statement` object allows you to send commands to the database and receive information back. The `Statement` object supports the methods listed in Table 15.1.

TABLE 15.1 `Statement` Object Methods

Method	Description
`boolean execute(String sql)`	Executes a single SQL statement that may return one or more results.
`ResultSet executeQuery(String sql)`	Executes a single SQL select statement that returns a `ResultSet` object.
`int executeUpdate(String sql)`	Executes a single SQL `Insert`, `Update`, or `Delete` statement and returns the number of rows affected. This method can also be used to execute DDL commands such as `create` and `drop` statements. When executing DDL commands, the method returns a `0`.

In Listing 15.3, the code executes a `create table` command, fills the table with data, and then generates a resultset based on the data.

LISTING 15.3 Executing Commands (Subset of Listing 15.2)

```
    // Execute a DDL command to create a table
    stmtCommand.executeUpdate("create table JDBCSample" +
        "(Name varchar(15), Age int )");

    // Execute DML commands to fill the table with data
    stmtCommand.executeUpdate("insert into JDBCSample values('Michael',
➥ 45)");
    stmtCommand.executeUpdate("insert into JDBCSample values('Jeff',
➥ 22)");
    stmtCommand.executeUpdate("insert into JDBCSample values('Saleem',
➥ 36)");

    // Execute a DML command to return a result set with data
    ResultSet rsData = stmtCommand.executeQuery("select * from JDBCSample");
```

The SQL statements can contain database vendor-specific commands for optimizing performance. If you want to make your code more database neutral, the `Statement` object supports SQL escape sequences. SQL escape sequences are not supported by all database driver implementations and should be used with care.

TIP

If you want to support multiple database vendors, consider placing your SQL statements in a properties file or a class containing string constants. By doing this, you can make changes to the statements without recompiling your application.

Step 5: Return a Resultset

The `ResultSet` object contains a set of data with a cursor at the beginning of the set. The cursor points to the active row of data. When a resultset is created, the cursor is located before the first row of data. By default, you can only move forward through the resultset, and the data is not updateable.

NOTE

If your database driver is JDBC 2 compliant, you can make bidirectional resultsets that can be updatable. The `Statement` object is used to set the `ResultSet` object parameters. The following line of code creates resultset objects that are bidirectional and updatable:

```
Statement stmt = con.createStatement( ResultSet.TYPE_SCROLL_INSENSITIVE,
➥ ResultSet.CONCUR_UPDATABLE);
```

Not all SQL statements allow an updatable resultset. Typically, `select` statements that perform a join across tables will not be updatable.

The `ResultSet` object does not know how many rows, columns, and data types to expect until the SQL command is issued. To account for these unknowns, the `ResultSet` object provides multiple `getXXX` methods for retrieving column values. Each database driver maps the database's data types to Java data types.

Remember that only one row of data can be accessed at a time. Therefore the `getXXX` method executes on the current row of data. To specify the column value to return, the name or index of the column must be passed to the `getXXX` method. The columns are numbered starting with 1 and are read in left-to-right order. Performance is improved using the column numbers, whereas code readability and maintainability are better using the column names.

In Listing 15.4, the result is created from a `select` statement. The resultset cursor points to just before the first row of data. Therefore, the `next` method is called on the `ResultSet` object to get the first row of data. If there are no rows of data, the `next` method returns false. This makes the `next` method ideal for a `while` loop:

LISTING 15.4 Resultset Iterations (Subset of Listing 15.2)

```
while (rsData.next()) {
  System.out.print( "Name: " + rsData.getString("Name"));
  System.out.println( "   Age: " + rsData.getInt("Age"));
}
```

TIP

The SQL statement used to generate the resultset is `Select * from JDBCSample`. Without explicitly listing the column names, it is difficult to use the column indexes to retrieve the data. It is ambiguous by the SQL statement used to determine whether the `Name` column is the first or second index.

Even if I test this program and find that in my situation the `Name` column is the first index, there is no guarantee that it will always be that index.

Therefore, if you plan on using index values to access your data, you should explicitly list the column names in your `select` statements and avoid the use of *.

Step 6: Disconnect from the Database

As good programming practice, you should always close your connections and statement. If you reuse a statement, any resultsets created by the statement are implicitly closed.

```
if (stmtCommand != null ) stmtCommand.close();
if (connect !=null) connect.close();
```

The `Statement.close` and `Connection.close` methods are used to close connections to a database.

Step 7: Catch `SQLExceptions`

Most JDBC commands raise a `SQLException`. `SQLException` is a subclass of the `Exception` class and contains an additional method named `getSQLState`.

The `SQLState` is defined by the X/Open and SQL Access Group SQL CAE specification. `SQLState` is a string of five character values that provide the result status of an executed SQL statement.

```
catch(Exception e)
{
  if (e instanceof SQLException) {
  System.out.println("Error with database: " + CONNECTIONURL + ": "
                   + e.getMessage() + "\nState:"
                   + ((SQLException) e).getSQLState());
  }
  else
  {
    System.out.println("Error with database: " + CONNECTIONURL + ": "
                     + e.getMessage() );
  }
}
```

As you can see by Listing 15.2, JDBC provides many different methods for each of its core objects. Many of these methods can be used to optimize the behavior of the database connection.

JDBC has released a specification for version 2 and version 3 compliant drivers. JDBC 3 compliant drivers are not widely available as of this writing. Many popular databases have released JDBC 2 compliant drivers. JDBC 2 provides additional methods to take advantage of database features such as bidirectional resultset processing.

The previous Table 15.1 and the following subsections show the more common JDBC and JDBC 2 methods. These methods apply to the `Statement`, `Connection`, `PreparedStatement`, and `ResultSet` objects, respectively.

Common Methods for `java.sql.Connection`

Statement `createStatement()`
The `createStatement` object creates a `Statement` object for the given database connection. A `Statement` object may be used to execute SQL statements against the database as shown in Table 15.1.

The `ResultSet` object will have forward-only type and read-only concurrency. Forward-only type means that the resultset can only be moved forward so that you cannot go back to the previous record. Read-only concurrency means that you cannot modify the resultset records.

Statement `createStatement(int` *`type`*`, int` *`concurrency`*`)`
If the database driver is JDBC 2 compliant, you can use this form of the `createStatement`. It takes the following type and concurrency parameters:

- static int TYPE_FORWARD_ONLY—Creates a resultset that can only move forward.
- static int TYPE_SCROLL_INSENSITIVE—Creates a resultset that is bidirectional and does not show changes made by others.
- static int TYPE_SCROLL_SENSITIVE—Creates a resultset that is bidirectional and shows changes made by others.
- static int CONCUR_UPDATABLE—The resultset should be made updatable.
- static int CONCUR_READ_ONLY—The resultset should be made read-only.

PreparedStatement prepareStatement(String *SQL*)
Prepared statements are precompiled SQL statements that use question marks as placeholders for variables. The question marks are assigned to variables in the application. Prior to executing the query, the prepared statement gets the values of the variables and replaces the question marks with their values.

There are two main reasons why you should use prepareStatement over the createStatement method.

The first reason is performance. If a SQL statement is in a loop and the SQL statement condition is static or changing, a prepared SQL statement will outperform a regular SQL statement.

The second reason is the capability to bind variables to the SQL statement. Consider the SQL statement that is built based on a string named sLastName:

```
sSQL = "Select * from STUDENT where LASTNAME = '" + sLastName + "' ";
```

If sLastName contained the string "Smith", the sSQL statement would be a valid SQL statement. If the sLastName contained the string "O'Neal", the preceding SQL statement would be incorrect and raise an error. The embedded apostrophe in the name "O'Neal" causes the SQL statement to have invalid matching quotes. A SQLException will be raised when the statement is executed. You would need to write code that validated every data type for characters that would not cause errors in your SQL statement.

If a prepared statement is used, the SQL statement would be

```
sSQL = "Select * from STUDENT where LASTNAME = ? ";
PreparedStatement preparedQuery = connection.prepareStatement(sSQL);
preparedQuery.setString( 1, sLastName);
```

The "?" is a placeholder variable the string variable sLastName. The prepared statement replaces the "?" with the value of sLastName when the statement is executed.

`PreparedStatement prepareStatement(String` *`SQL`*`, int` *`type`*`, int` *`concurrency`*`)`
If the database driver is JDBC 2 compliant, you can use this form of the `prepareStatement`. It takes the same parameters as the preceding `createStatement` method for creating resultsets.

`void setAutoCommit( boolean` *`b`*`)`
By default, all statements are autocommitted to the database. For transactional support, you would need to set the autocommit for a connection to false.

When autocommit is set to false, the `commit` and `rollback` methods control the transaction.

`void commit()`
The `commit` method commits all changes to the database from the beginning of the transaction.

`void rollback()`
The `rollback` method rolls back all changes to the database from the beginning of the transaction.

`void close()`
The `close` method closes the connection to the database immediately.

Common Methods for `java.sql.PreparedStatement`

The following are common methods for `java.sql.PreparedStatement`:

- `void setString( int` *`parameterIndex`*`, String` *`x`*`)`
- `void setInt(int` *`parameterIndex`*`, int` *`x`*`)`
- `void set`*`Nnn`*`(int` *`parameterIndex`*`,` *`Nnn x`*`)`—Because a database can handle many different data types, the `PreparedStatement` has many different setter methods. The setter methods take the form of `set`*`Nnn`*`(int` *`parameterIndex`*`,` *`Nnn x`*`)` where *`Nnn`* is replaced by `Date`, `Int`, `Long`, `Double`, `Byte`, `Array`, `Blob`, `Time`, `Short`, and so on.
- `void setNull(int` *`parameterIndex`*`, int` *`SQLType`*`)`—If a parameter needs to be represented as null, use the `setNull` method and pass the appropriate SQL type code. The SQL type codes are enumerated in the `java.sql.Types` class.
- `void clearParameters()`—Clears the current parameter values.
- `ResultSet executeQuery()`—Executes a SQL `SELECT` statement that returns 0 or more rows of data in a `ResultSet` object. This is identical to the `executeQuery` method of the `Statement` class.

- `int executeUpdate()`—Executes a SQL statement that does not return a resultset but does return the number of rows affected by the command. Typically, this is used to return the number of rows affected by an `Update`, `Delete`, or `Insert` command.
- `void close()`—Closes the prepared statement and the resultset associated with the statement.

Common Methods for `java.sql.ResultSet`

When a `ResultSet` object is created, it is filled with the data results of a query. The resultset has a cursor that points to the current row being processed. The cursor points to a place right before the first row of data.

Prior to JDBC 2, the only direction the cursor could move through the resultset was forward. In addition, the data could not be updated. JDBC 2 specifications support bidirectional cursors and updatable resultsets.

The common methods are

- `boolean next()`—Moves the cursor to the next row in the resultset. A `false` is returned when attempting to move past the last row in the resultset. Remember that when a resultset is created, the cursor points to a row before the first record of data. Therefore, the `next` method must be called get the first row of data.
- `boolean previous()`—Moves the cursor to the previous row in a resultset. A `false` is returned if the beginning of the resultset has been reached.
- `String getString(String` *`columnName`*`)`
- `String getString(int` *`columnNumber`*`)`
- `int getInt(String` *`columnName`*`)`
- `int getInt(int` *`columnNumber`*`)`
- *`Nnn`* `get`*`Nnn`*`(String` *`columnName`*`)`
- *`Nnn`* `get`*`Nnn`*`(int` *`columnNumber`*`)`—To retrieve data from a resultset, there are many getter methods. Each of the getter methods takes either the column name or the column index. The first column in a resultset has an index of 1.

  The methods convert the SQL data types to the appropriate Java equivalents. Review the Java to SQL mappings provided by the vendor's database driver. The *`Nnn`* can be replaced with the other Java data types such as `Double`, `Long`, `Boolean`, `Blob`, and so on.

- `void updateString(String columnName, String x)`
- `void updateString(int columnNumber, String x)`
- `void updateInt(String columnName, int x)`
- `void updateInt(int columnNumber, int x)`
- `void updateNnn(String columnName, Nnn x)`
- `void updateNnn(int columnNumber, Nnn x)`—In JDBC 2, a resultset may be updatable. To update data in a resultset, there are many update methods. Each of the update methods takes either the column name or the column index and the data value to persist. The first column in a resultset has an index of 1.

  The database will not be updated until the method `updateRow` or `insertRow` is called.

  The methods convert the Java data types to the appropriate SQL data type equivalents. Review the SQL to Java mappings provided by the vendor's database driver. The *Nnn* can be replaced with the other Java data types such as `Double`, `Long`, `Boolean`, `Blob`, and so on.
- `void updateNull(int columnNumber)`
- `void updateNull(String columnName)`—In JDBC 2, a resultset may be updatable. The columns in the database may accept a null value. The `updateNull` methods are used in cases where a null value needs to be sent to the database. The `updateNull` takes a column name or column index.
- `void updateRow()`
- `void insertRow()`
- `void deleteRow()`—In JDBC 2, a resultset may be updatable. This allows rows to be added, updated, and deleted from the resultset and database.

  If the cursor is on a valid resultset row, the current row can be updated using the `updateNnn` methods. After the updates to the resultset are made, the current row can be updated in the database by calling the `updateRow` method.

  If the cursor is on a valid resultset row, the current row can be deleted from the database using the `deleteRow` method.

  If the cursor has been moved to the special insert row, the new row can be updated using the `updateNnn` methods. After the updates to the new row are complete, the `insertRow` method adds the row to the database.
- `void moveToInsertRow()`

- `void moveToCurrentRow()`—In JDBC 2, a resultset may be updatable. The `moveToInsertRow` method moves the cursor to a special insert row. The previous cursor position will be remembered prior to moving to the special insert row.

  The `moveToCurrentRow` method moves the cursor back to the previous row that was remembered when the `moveToInsertRow` was called. This method does not do anything unless the cursor is on the special insert row.

- `void close()`—The close method immediately closes the resultset.

JDBC and JDBC 2 provide for robust control of the database. Learning to use the JDBC class framework can be a monumental task. JBuilder makes it easier to use JDBC by encapsulating the power in a framework called DataExpress.

Setting Up JBuilder Database Drivers

The JBuilder environment is a Java application itself and has a classpath it uses to load database and application server drivers. JBuilder adds the path of these libraries to its classpath so that JBuilder tools such as Database Pilot can find it.

When JBuilder is loading, it looks in the \JBuilder7\lib\ext for .config files. The .config files contain information on additional classpaths to be added to the JBuilder environment. The easiest way to create these .config files is to use the Tools, Enterprise Setup menu. Figure 15.2 shows the Enterprise Setup dialog box with the Database Drivers tab selected.

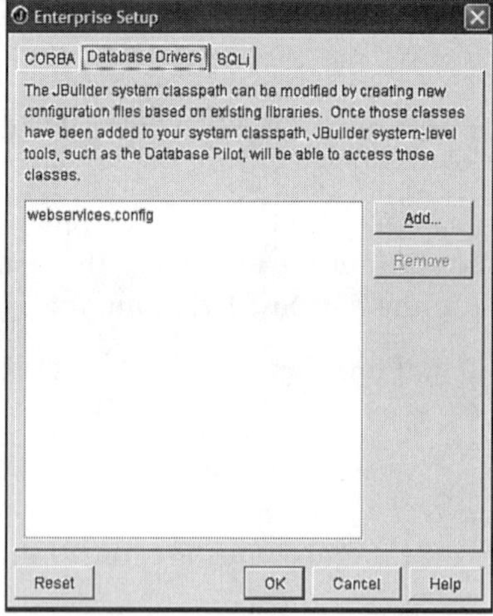

FIGURE 15.2 The Enterprise Setup dialog box.

To create a new .config entry, you must have a library set up with the database drivers. When you click the Add button on the Database Drivers tab, the dialog box in Figure 15.3 displays a list of libraries.

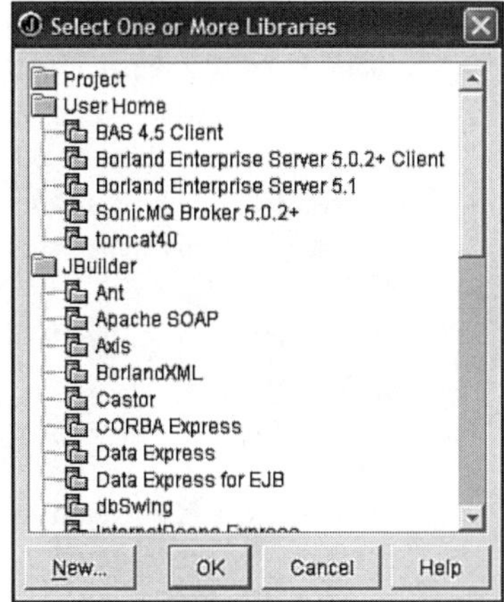

FIGURE 15.3 The Select One or More Libraries dialog box.

If your database drivers have not been placed into a JBuilder library file, you would select the New button and create the new library entry. After the library entry is created, you must select it and click OK.

JBuilder automatically creates the .config file in the \JBuilder7\lib\ext directory. JBuilder must be restarted for the classpath to be integrated into the JBuilder environment. After JBuilder is restarted, your database driver's classpath is available to Jbuilder's Database Pilot and other tools.

Table 15.2 shows the common database driver connection strings.

TABLE 15.2 Common Database, Driver Name, and URLs

Database	Driver Name and URL

Microsoft SQL Server 2000	`com.microsoft.jdbc.sqlserver.SQLServerDriver`
	URL: `jdbc:microsoft:sqlserver://`*`hostname`*`:`*`port`*
	`[;`*`property=value...`*`]`
	where:
	`hostname` is the TCP/IP name of the server.
	`port` is the number of the TCP/IP port
	property:
	`DatabaseName` is the name of the database.
	`Password` is the database password.
	`User` is the database username.

TABLE 15.2 Continued

Database	Driver Name and URL
Oracle	`oracle.jdbc.driver.OracleDriver` URL: `jdbc:oracle:thin:@`*`myhost:port:SID`* where: *`myhost`* is the TCP/IP name of the server. *`port`* is the number of the TCP/IP port. *`SID`* is the name of the Oracle instance.
IBM DB2	`COM.ibm.db2.jdbc.app.DB2Driver` URL: `jdbc:db2:dbname` where: *`dbname`* is the name of the database.
MySQL	`org.gjt.mm.mysql.Driver` URL: `jdbc:mysql:`*`//[hostname][:port]/dbname`* where: *`hostname`* is the TCP/IP name of the server. *`port`* is the number of the TCP/IP port. *`dbname`* is the name of the database.

The JDBC drivers for these databases and many more are constantly being updated and improved. Check with the current documentation on your JDBC driver for new parameters, URL formats, and driver names.

Using JBuilder's DataExpress

JBuilder created a database framework named DataExpress, which is built on top of JDBC and provides a visual framework for building database applications. DataExpress is composed of visual and nonvisual controls.

DataExpress provides for offline data stores for mobile applications. This allows an application to download data, work on the data offline, and then synchronize it back to the original data source handling any data conflicts.

The key classes we will review in DataExpress are the following:

- DataExpress overview
- Connect to the database
- Database component methods and properties
- Query the database
- Build SQL statements

- Build a database UI
- Update the database

DataExpress Overview

The DataExpress architecture can be broken down into four distinct class groups: provider, resolver, data set, and visual.

The provider classes retrieve data from a data source. A data source can be a database, file, or custom application.

The resolver classes save data to a data source and resolve any conflicts. The data source can be a database, file, or custom application.

By breaking down the data access into provider and resolver classes, an application can be scaled across multiple tiers. The separation of these two facilities created the third set of class groups named data sets.

The data set classes allow the local manipulation of a resultset. The manipulation can be done independent of a live connection back to the data source. After the data has been provided, it can be manipulated locally. After it has been manipulated locally, it can be resolved back to the data store.

Figure 15.4 shows the toolbar for the DataExpress components. These components are further described in Table 15.3. The components can be found in the `com.borland.dx`, `com.borland.javax`, and `com.borland.datastore` packages.

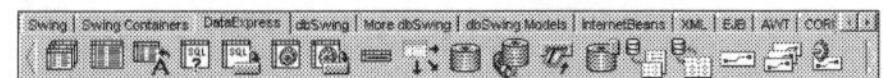

FIGURE 15.4 Overview of DataExpress components.

TABLE 15.3 DataExpress Component Overview

Component	Description
`Database`	Establishes and maintains a JDBC connection to a database. The username, password, and database URL are passed as connection parameters.
`TableDataSet`	When used with `TextDataFile`, the `TableDataSet` allows the import and manipulation of file-based data. `TableDataSet` provides SQL-like functionality such as sorting and master-detail relationships for file-based data sources. `TableDataSet` can be attached to the dbSwing controls.
`TextDataFile`	Imports and exports data to a file using the specified delimiters, field separators, and file format. This component is used to populate a `TableDataSet` from a file and write `TextDataFile`.

TABLE 15.3 Continued

Component	Description
`QueryDataSet`	The resultset of a database query is stored in a `QueryDataSet`. Unlike a JDBC `ResultSet`, you can work with a `QueryDataSet` while it is not attached to the data source. `QueryDataSet` provides methods to move through the data records in both directions, update the underlying data, and post the updates back to the data source at a later time.
`QueryResolver`	The default resolver for the Database component. The resolver can be used to customize the behavior of storing SQL data.
`ProcedureDataSet`	Calls a stored procedure passing in parameters and expects a resultset as a return. The `ProcedureDataSet` does not work on all databases. It depends on your database vendor and the implementation of the JDBC driver.
`ProcedureResolver`	Can be used to provide a custom resolver using stored procedures for insert, update, and delete.
`ParameterRow`	Allows the creation of a parameter array that can be used with a parameterized query using the `QueryDataSet` and `ProcedureDataSet`.
`DataSetView`	Gives you the ability to have an alternate view of an existing `QueryDataSet` without creating a new data set. The view can have different sort orders and independent navigation.
`DataStore`	A persistent storage implementation for a data set. `DataStore` supports indexes, data, files, and other data formats. Normally, data sets are stored in memory and are not persistent.
`DataStoreConnection`	Allows the support of one or more transaction connections to a `DataStore`.
`TxManager`	Enables crash recovery and transaction support for a `DataStore`.
`DataStoreServer`	Creates a server `DataStore` process that listens for connections from a remote `DataStore` JDBC driver.
`DataStorePump`	Provides utility functions to move data into a `DataStore` file.
`DataStoreSync`	Works with the `DataStorePump` to synchronize the copying of data from a JDBC source into a `DataStore`.
`JdbcDataSource`	An implementation of the JDBC 2.0 `javax.sql.DataSource` interface. A JDBC 2.0 data source can be registered with a JNDI naming service.
`JdbcConnectionPool`	An implementation of the `javax.sql.DataSource` connection pooling interface. It can be registered with a JNDI naming service.
`JdbcConnectionFactory`	Provides custom implementations of a connection factory for the `JdbcConnectionPool` component.

The fourth set of components is visual and built on top of the Java Swing classes. These `dbSwing` classes provide a visual interpretation of the data set to the user interface. User interface objects include fields, check boxes, radio buttons, grids, and other swing elements. Also provided is a set of visual navigation components that allow the data set to be transversed, manipulated, and resolved back to the data source.

Connect to the Database

DataExpress includes a set of designers that help you create database connections, queries, and interfaces. The designers write code that sets properties and calls methods of the DataExpress components.

When building a database application, the first step is to make a connection to the database. To do this, bring up a frame and drop the `Database` component from the DataExpress tab onto the frame. The `Database` component is an invisible component and does not appear on the frame. It appears in the Structure pane as shown in Figure 15.5.

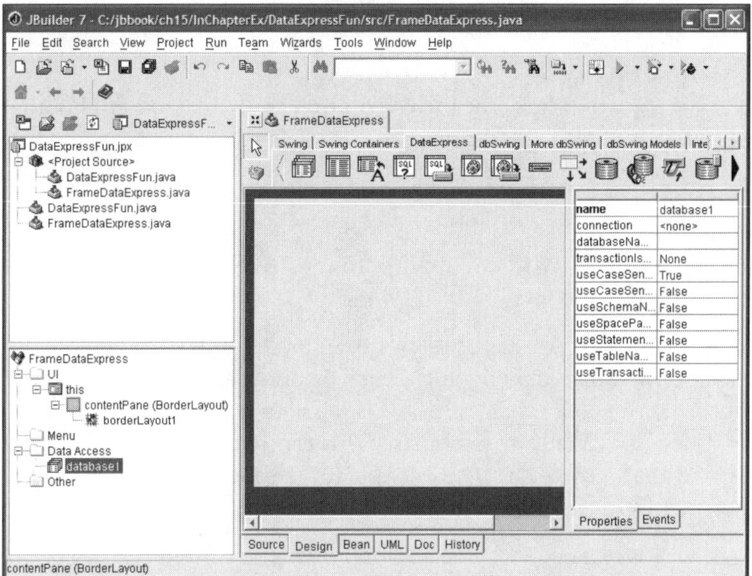

FIGURE 15.5 Database components on a frame.

In the Structure pane, the `Database` component `database1` has been created. The class variable `database1` is added to the class as shown in the following line of code:

```
private Database database1 = new Database();
```

The `Database` component has methods and properties that control the different database connection features. These methods and properties are listed in the following subsections.

Database Component Methods and Properties

This section covers database component methods and properties.

`boolean getAutoCommit()`

This returns the current setting of the autocommit flag. If set to `true`, all commands are committed automatically. If set to `false`, all commands are not committed, and a transaction is created. The transaction ends with a `commit()` or `rollback()` being called.

`void setAutoCommit(boolean)`

This sets the autocommit flag. If set to `true`, all commands are committed automatically. If set to `false`, all commands are not committed, and a transaction is created. The transaction ends with a `commit()` or `rollback()` being called.

`databaseName`

This is the JNDI name associated with this connection.

`TransactionIsolation`

This sets the transaction level for the connection to the database. This affects the way the connection locks the database records and what data is available to the user. If the database does not support transactions, the `SQLException` is thrown.

The valid transaction isolation levels are

- `TRANSACTION_NONE`—Do not attempt to set a transaction level. Use the database default transaction level.
- `TRANSACTION_READ_UNCOMMITTED`—Allows uncommitted data to be read. Uncommitted data may be rolled back by another user, resulting in a different resultset if the data is read again. It is possible that a row in the resultset may not reflect the data in the database. This can happen if another user has updated that record. It is also possible for the resultset to grow and pick up rows that were not there when the data was originally read.
- `TRANSACTION_READ_COMMITTED`—Allows only committed rows to be read. It is possible that the record read may not reflect the data in the database. This can happen if another user has updated that record. The resultset may change on subsequent reads as more data is committed to the database.
- `TRANSACTION_REPEATABLE_READ`—Reads only committed rows. The connection prevents other users from changing the data so that the resultset always reflects the data in the database. The resultset can pick up records that were not there when the original data set was created.

- TRANSACTION_SERIALIZABLE—Only committed data is to be read. The resultset does not change on subsequent reads, providing a stable and consistent resultset.

The connection property of database1 brings up the dialog box shown in Figure 15.6. The Connection dialog box sets the database URL, username, password, and any additional database-specific parameters that you want to set.

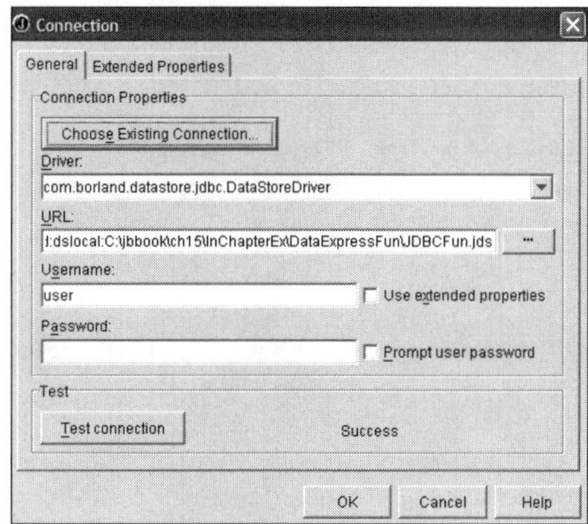

FIGURE 15.6 The Connection dialog box.

The Connection dialog box allows you to choose an existing connection that the IDE stored from an earlier data connection setup. If you do not have an existing connection created, you can select the database driver from a drop-down list.

The Driver drop-down lists the available drivers identified by JBuilder. The driver names appear in black and red. The driver names in black represent database connections whose libraries are already set up. The red driver names require that the database library be added to the project library files so that it can be found.

After the database driver has been chosen, the database URL must be entered. You can type in the database URL, or you can select it from a database list. The ... button at the end of the field displays a dialog box that is sensitive to the database driver you have chosen. The dialog box helps you create the proper database URL.

After the database has been selected, you can enter an authorized database user in the Username and Password fields. If the Prompt User Password check box is selected, a dialog box pops up anytime a connection to the database is attempted by the application or the IDE.

If you would like to set additional connection parameters that are database specific, you must select the Use Extended Properties check box and enter the parameters on the Extended Properties tab.

Finally, click the Test Connection button to make sure that you can connect to the database. Failure to connect to the database makes it more difficult to use the JBuilder designers in creating your application. Without a valid connection, the application will not show you live data in a grid or column name values when using the `dbSwing` components.

When you finish setting up the connection, click OK. The `connection` property you just set adds the following line of code to your class in the `jbInit` method:

```
database1.setConnection(new com.borland.dx.sql.dataset.ConnectionDescriptor
➥("jdbc:borland:dslocal:C:\\jbbook\\ch15\\InChapterEx\\DataExpressFun
➥\\JDBCFun.jds", "user", "", false,
➥"com.borland.datastore.jdbc.DataStoreDriver"));
```

If you set any other `Database` component properties, the IDE generates the appropriate code for them in the `jbInit` method.

Query the Database

After the database connection has been created, the next step is to create a query that returns data from the database. The `QueryDataSet` component provides functionality to run a query statement that might not contain parameters.

Like the `Database` component, the `QueryDataSet` does not have a visible display on the frame, but it is added to the Structure pane. The `QueryDataSet` has a designer that allows you to set up the SQL statement for executing a query.

Figure 15.7 shows the `QueryDataSet` designer window. The designer enables design-time connection and execution of a SQL query.

The `QueryDataSet` must attach to an existing `Database` component. In Figure 15.7, the `QueryDataSet` is attached to the `database1` component.

After the Database field has been set, the designer gives two options for creating a SQL statement. These options are discussed in the following "Build SQL Statements" section.

The SQL statement that is generated or manually typed in is located in the SQL statement text box.

The Query dialog box provides two check boxes that control when the SQL statement is executed and the location of the text for the SQL statement.

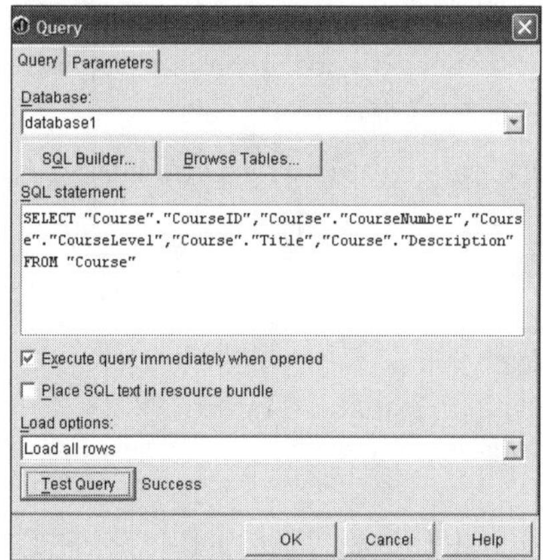

FIGURE 15.7 `QueryDataSet` component designer.

The first check box, Execute Query Immediately when Opened, executes the query during the design-time environment allowing for database UI controls to show the data from the `QueryDataSet`.

The second check box, Place SQL Text in Resource Bundle, places the SQL statement text in a separate resource file. The resource file can then be loaded at runtime, allowing the SQL statements to be modified outside the code. This is a good option to choose when supporting many different database brands.

You have the option to specify how the `DataResultSet` will be filled with data from the SQL statement. The Load Options combo box has the values shown in Table 15.4.

TABLE 15.4 Load Options

Option	Description
Load All Rows	All data rows are loaded, and then control is returned to the application. For large resultsets, this may cause exceptional delays and user frustration.
Load Rows Asynchronously	Data is returned, and a separate thread continues to retrieve data.
Load As Needed	Data is loaded to fulfill the UI elements. When more data is required, it is loaded. For example, a grid is a control that shows a number of rows until the user presses the down arrow. When the control requests more data, it is loaded from the database as needed.
Load 1 Row at a Time	Data is loaded one row at a time.

When the SQL statement is ready, the Test Query button determines whether your SQL statement can be processed. If your statement returns success, the OK button saves this information to your application.

The following lines of code are created when you customize a `QueryDataSet`:

```
queryDataSet1.setQuery(new com.borland.dx.sql.dataset.QueryDescriptor(
    database1, "SELECT \"Course\".\"CourseID\",\"Course\".\"CourseNumber\",
    \"Course\".\"CourseLevel\",\"Course\".\"Title\",\"Course\".\"" +
  "Description\" FROM\"Course\"
    WHERE \"Course\".\"Title\"LIKE\'Intro%\'ORDER " +
  "BY\"Course\".\"CourseLevel\"DESC", null, true, Load.ALL));
```

If you had chosen to place your SQL text into a resource bundle or properties file, JBuilder would add the appropriate files, variables, and method calls to get the SQL data.

Build SQL Statements

Earlier we saw that the Query dialog box provides for two ways to build your SQL statement for the SQL statement text box.

The first option is to dynamically build your SQL statement using the SQL Builder button. SQL Builder allows you to click and choose your tables, conditions, sort order, and group order. SQL Builder tests the SQL statements you build and returns data. Figure 15.8 shows the SQL Builder interface.

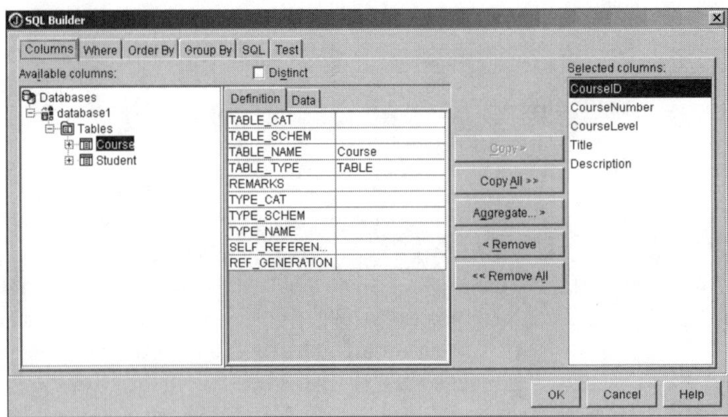

FIGURE 15.8 SQL Builder interface.

The second option for creating SQL statements is to hand code your own SQL statements. The Browse Tables button displays the tables and columns for the database connection. You can select a table or column name and have it automatically passed into the SQL Statement window in the `QueryDataSet` Designer. Figure 15.9 shows the Available tables and columns dialog box.

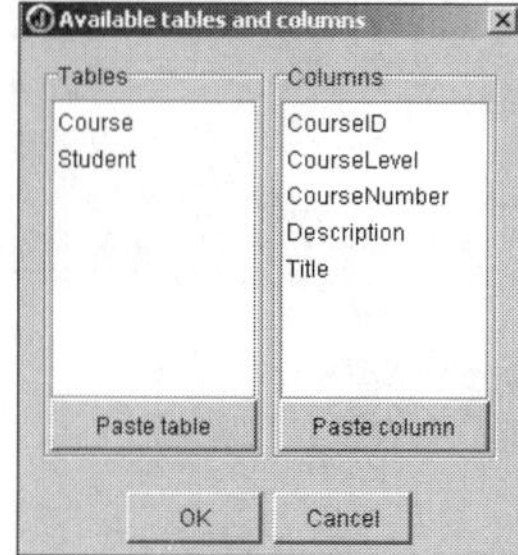

FIGURE 15.9 Browse Table interface.

SQL Builder Interface

The SQL Builder interface is typical of most database query tools. Writing a SQL statement can be difficult and time consuming. This affects all levels of developers because you cannot remember all the exact spelling of column names, their data types, and other properties. SQL Builder frees you to quickly put together SQL statements that can be optimized later.

Figure 15.8 shows the Columns tab of the SQL Builder dialog box. The available columns show the database connection that you chose on the Query dialog box in Figure 15.7. The Distinct check box gives you the option to add the distinct SQL keyword to your SQL statement.

When you expand out the database connection, you will see all the tables available for that database connection. You may select a column for the table or the table itself and press the Copy or Copy All button. This copies the column name into the Selected column list.

The order that they appear in the Selected column list is the order that they will appear in the resultset. If you want to change the order of the columns, you must add them in order or manually change the SQL statement on the SQL tab.

If you press the Aggregate button in Figure 15.8, JBuilder displays a dialog box, shown in Figure 15.10, with the standard SQL aggregates. You can select a column and aggregate to add to the Selected columns list. The Distinct check box adds the SQL keyword `distinct` inside the aggregate. The Add Aggregate button puts the aggregate column in the Selected column list.

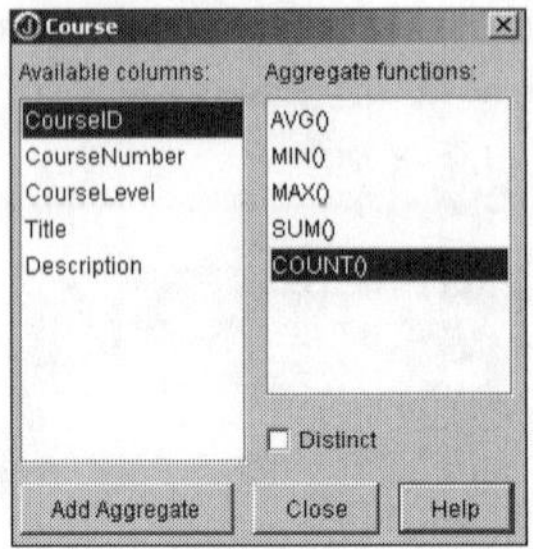

FIGURE 15.10 Add Aggregate interface.

After you choose the columns you want in your SQL statement, you must set up any filtering criteria. Filtering criteria is known as the Where clause and is shown on the Where tab in Figure 15.11.

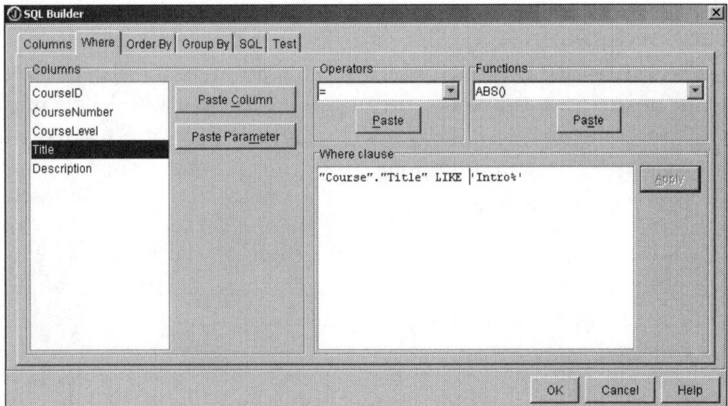

FIGURE 15.11 Where tab interface.

The Where tab provides many different helper options to create the `where` clause. Each of the helper options provides a Paste button to copy your selection into the Where clause text box.

There are four helper options. The first helper option allows you to select a column name and paste it into the Where clause text box. The second helper option allows you to select a column and paste in a named parameter based on the selected column name. The third helper option displays the operators you can paste into the `where` clause. The fourth and final option allows you to paste functions into the `where` clause.

NOTE

It is easy to make mistakes when pasting text into the Where clause text box. There is no syntax checking to make sure that you correctly formatted your `where` statement. Always go to the Test tab to make sure that your SQL statement is valid and working.

You have the option to hand code `where` conditions by manually typing in the Where clause text box.

After you click the Apply button on the Where clause text box, the `where` condition is copied into the SQL statement on the SQL tab. If you incorrectly created a SQL statement, the SQL statement may bring up errors when you test it.

The next tab is the Order By tab, which allows you to set one or more sort orders to the data being returned. Figure 15.12 shows the Order By tab with the Available columns for sorting by and the Order By columns that will be used.

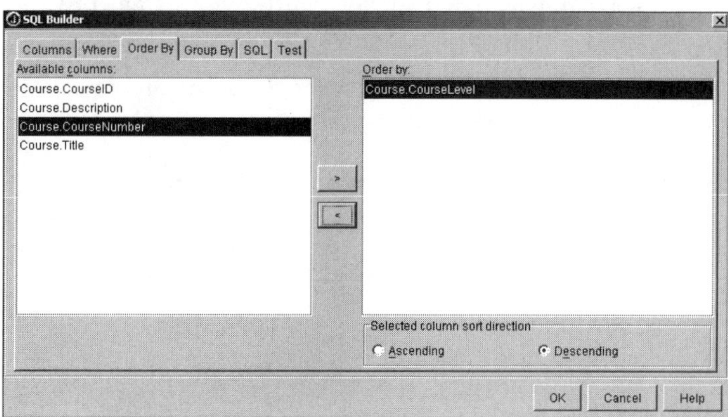

FIGURE 15.12 Order By tab interface.

For each selected column in the Order By list, you may choose an ascending or descending sort order. Select the column from the Order By list, change the sort order, and then move to the next column.

In addition to Order By settings, SQL Builder allows for Group By settings on the Group By tab. The Group By tab, shown in Figure 15.13, allows you to set the SQL grouping.

If you want to add additional conditions to the Group By settings, you must add them manually in the SQL tab.

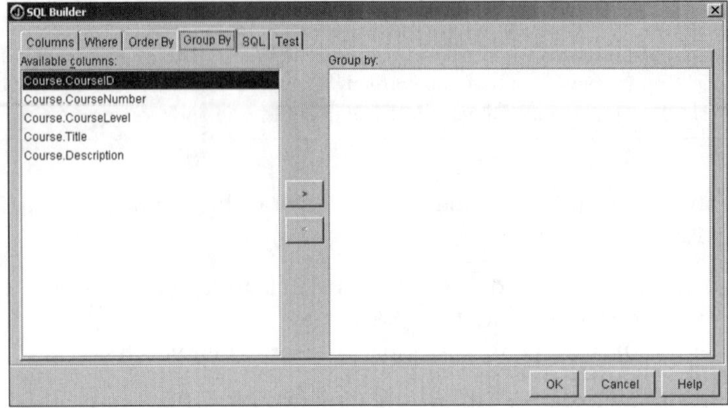

FIGURE 15.13 Group By tab interface.

By selecting the SQL tab in SQL Builder, you get the SQL statement you generated by making your previous selections.

Figure 15.14 shows the SQL tab and the generated SQL statement based on the Columns, Where, Order By, and Group By settings that have been chosen.

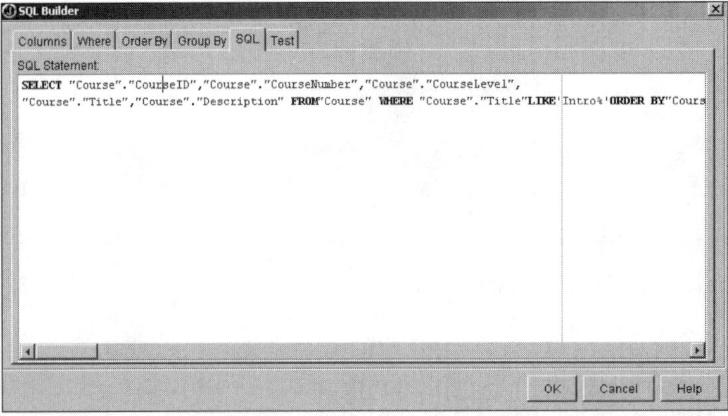

FIGURE 15.14 SQL tab interface.

The SQL tab allows you to modify the SQL statement—for example, adding a calculated column to your SQL statement. After you add the calculated column, it shows up in the Selected column list on the Columns tab, but you cannot add it from that tab. Therefore, calculated columns are added from the SQL tab.

Finally, after you have tweaked your SQL statement to your liking, you can test it from the Test tab. The Test tab, shown in Figure 15.15, executes your query against the database connection and returns the resultset in a grid.

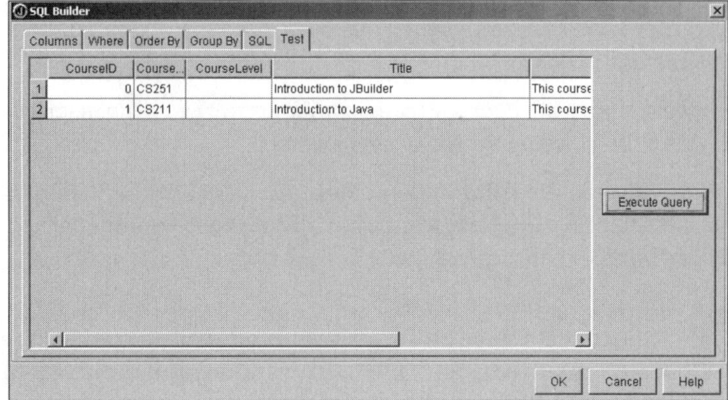

FIGURE 15.15 Test tab interface.

If the query returns an error, you are notified by an error dialog box. Correct the error and try again. If you used parameters in your SQL statement, the Execute query suppresses the error messages, and no results are returned.

CAUTION

It is really easy to get SQL Builder out of sync and return error messages on your SQL statement. SQL Builder is a quick and dirty tool to help you copy and paste simple SQL statements.

If you try to do complicated queries, it is almost better to write them by hand and test them in the vendor-supplied query tool.

Build a Database UI

After the `QueryDataSet` has been set up to return data, it is time to do something with that data. Data is typically given a visual appearance either showing a single data record at a time or all the data records at once.

JBuilder provides three different data-aware component palettes named `dbSwing`, `More dbSwing`, and `dbSwing Models`. We will discuss some of the data-aware components in this chapter, whereas a majority of them can be reviewed using the online help.

The dbSwing controls inherit from the Swing classes and add dataSet and columnName properties. To enable the controls to become data aware, you must set both properties when required.

The dataSet property can be set from a drop-down list when a data set has been created. In our previous example, when the QueryDataSet is created, it shows up in the dataSet list of the control.

After you have selected the QueryDataSet component, the columnName property lists the names of all the columns in the QueryDataSet.

After you have selected the column name from the data set, the field displays the value from the database. The data will not be displayed if you unchecked the Execute Query Immediately when Opened check box.

Figure 15.16 shows the property window for a dbSwing component of type jdbTextField. Notice that the dataSet property is set to queryDataSet1, and the columnName property is set to Title. The design window shows the real-time access to the database to display the title data.

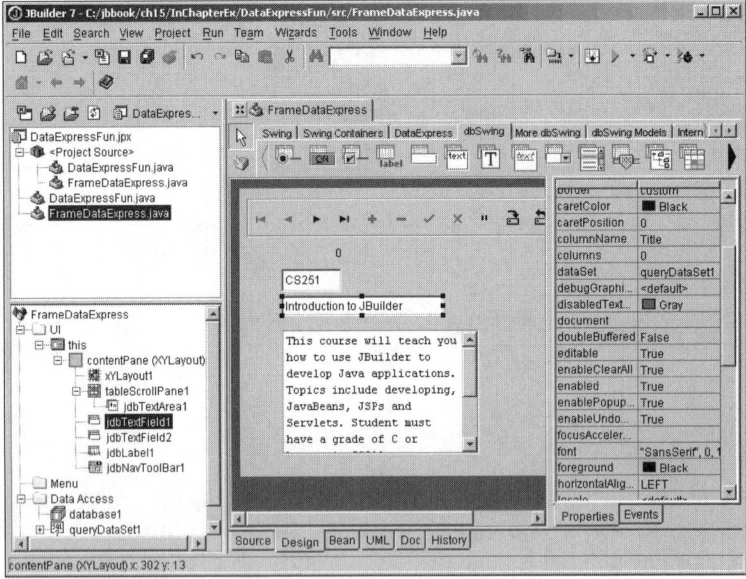

FIGURE 15.16 dbSwing components.

In Figure 15.17, the application has a TableScrollPane component with a jdbTable inside. The jdbTable component has only the dataSet property. The table creates columns for all the columns in the dataSet.

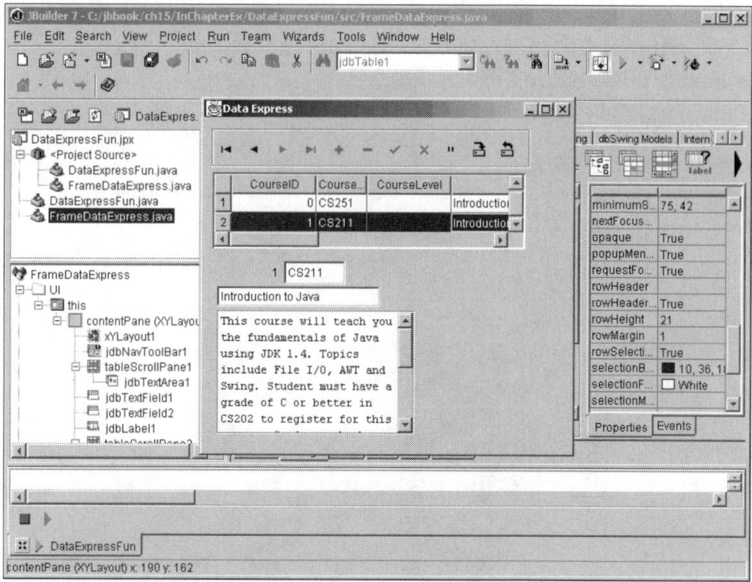

FIGURE 15.17 `jdbTable` application.

Figure 15.17 has one `QueryDataSet` defined, and all the `dbSwing` classes are attached to it. As the current row of the table is moved, all the UI controls on the form stay in sync with the current row. Remember that a `QueryDataSet` has only one cursor to the current row. Use the `DataSetView` component to support multiple cursors into a single resultset. This allows the table to scroll independently from the other UI controls.

Update the Database

A `QueryDataSet` can update your database depending on how complicated your query. If your query is updatable, you can control the update programmatically using the `saveChanges` method of the `QueryDataSet`.

To get an update or insert to work, you may need to tell the `QueryDataSet` more about some of the columns in the database. Normally, the `QueryDataSet` issues two queries when opening.

The first query is to get the metadata on the columns in the query. The metadata includes data type, scale, precision, row ID, and searchable information. The metadata is used to dynamically create the columns at runtime.

The second query actually retrieves the data for the resultset. Subsequent calls to retrieve data will not reissue the first query for metadata.

If the QueryDataSet cannot identify the column or columns that uniquely identify the row, you will not be able to update the data. Therefore, you must manually tell the QueryDataSet the unique row identifier.

To tell the QueryDataSet what the unique row identifier is, you have to tell the QueryDataSet to stop trying to resolve it from the metadata. Select the QueryDataSet and modify the property MetaDataUpdate. By clicking on the ... part of the MetaDataUpdate property, the dialog box shown in Figure 15.18 is displayed. Deselect the RowId check box so that the QueryDataSet does not try to determine the unique row identifier.

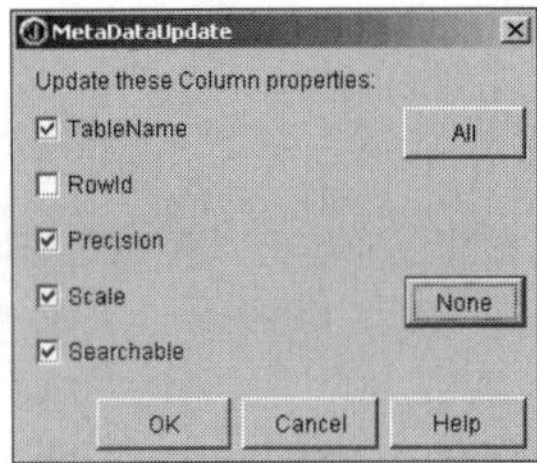

FIGURE 15.18 MetaDataUpdate property.

After the QueryDataSet has been told not to find the row ID, the row ID column in the QueryDataSet must be statically created. To do this, expand the QueryDataSet component in the Structure pane to reveal the columns. Select the column that represents the row ID and set the rowId property to true.

After the rowId property of a column has been set to true, that column is statically created. The code in Listing 15.5 is added to your class.

LISTING 15.5 Static Column Code

```
column1.setColumnName("CourseID");
column1.setDataType(com.borland.dx.dataset.Variant.LONG);
column1.setRowId(true);
column1.setTableName("Course");
column1.setServerColumnName("CourseID");
column1.setSqlType(-5);
queryDataSet1.setColumns(new Column[] {column1});
```

By statically creating columns, you must maintain this code if your database schema changes.

TIP

The performance of an application can be significantly improved if all the columns are created statically and the `MetaDataUpdate` is set to none.

The trade-off is performance for maintainability.

Using Data Modules

A *data module* is an interface specification that allows data components to be centralized. By centralizing the data components, and in theory, centralizing the business rules, a data module can be shared across forms and projects.

A data module is created from the File, New menu. This brings up the Object Gallery. Select the General tab and click on Data Module. Click OK.

Figure 15.19 displays the Data Module Wizard that is invoked when you add a data module to your project.

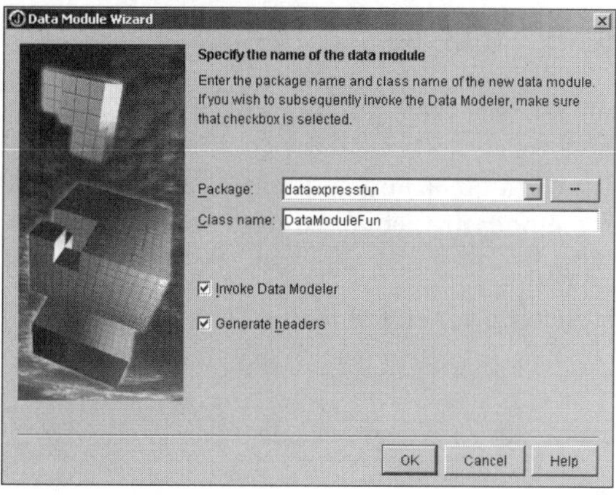

FIGURE 15.19 Data Module Wizard.

The Data Module Wizard prompts you for the package and class name for the data module. The package does not have to be the same package as your application. This is beneficial when you want to share your data module with other applications.

The wizard optionally launches the Data Modeler tool to build your queries. The other option is to generate headers in the class it is about to dynamically create.

Data Modeler is identical to SQL Builder except that Data Modeler allows the management of multiple queries and has the capability to link queries in a master-detail relationship.

Figure 15.20 shows the Data Modeler with two queries created for Course and Student.

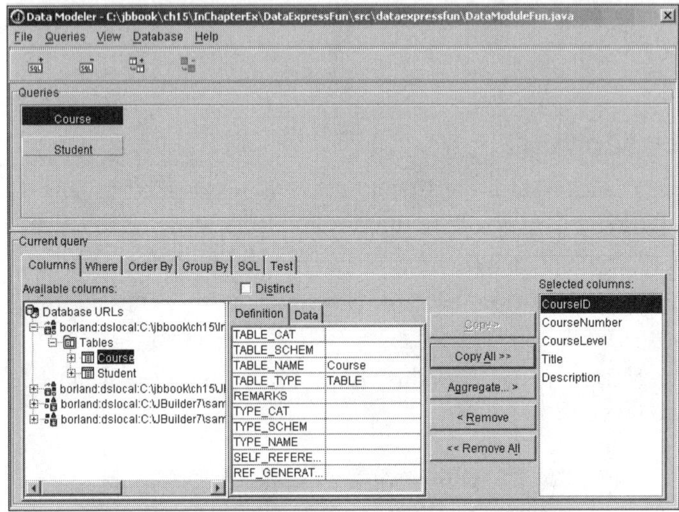

FIGURE 15.20 Data Modeler tool.

The Data Modeler tool is a quick and easy way to generate simple queries in a data module. The getter methods are generated in the data module by using the Data Modeler tool.

Listing 15.6 shows the code generated by the Data Modeler tool using two simple queries.

LISTING 15.6 Data Modeler Generated Code

```
package dataexpressfun;

import java.awt.*;
import java.awt.event.*;
import com.borland.dx.dataset.*;
import com.borland.dx.sql.dataset.*;

public class DataModuleFun implements DataModule {
  static private DataModuleFun myDM;
  private Database database1 = new Database();
  private QueryDataSet course = new QueryDataSet();
  private QueryDataSet student = new QueryDataSet();
```

LISTING 15.6 Continued

```
  public static DataModuleFun getDataModule() {
    if (myDM == null) {
      myDM = new DataModuleFun();
    }
    return myDM;
  }

  public DataModuleFun() {
    try {
      jbInit();
    }
    catch(Exception e) {
      e.printStackTrace();
    }
  }
  private void jbInit() throws Exception {
    student.setQuery(new com.borland.dx.sql.dataset.QueryDescriptor(
        database1, "SELECT \"Student\".\"StudentID\",\"Student\".\"LastName\",
        \"Student\".\"FirstName\",\"Student\".\"eMail\" " +
      "FROM\"Student\"", null, true, Load.ALL));
    course.setQuery(new com.borland.dx.sql.dataset.QueryDescriptor(
        database1, "SELECT \"Course\".\"CourseID\",\"Course\".\"CourseNumber\",
        \"Course\".\"CourseLevel\",\"Course\".\"Title\",\"Course\".\"" +
      "Description\" FROM\"Course\"", null, true, Load.ALL));

    database1.setConnection(new
        com.borland.dx.sql.dataset.ConnectionDescriptor(
        "jdbc:borland:dslocal:C:\\jbbook\\ch15\\InChapterEx\\
        ➥DataExpressFun\\JDBCFun.jds"
        , "user", "", false, "com.borland.datastore.jdbc.DataStoreDriver"));
  }
  public Database getDatabase1() {
    return database1;
  }
  public QueryDataSet getCourse() {
    return course;
  }
  public QueryDataSet getStudent() {
    return student;
  }

}
```

Notice how the data module is created using the Singleton pattern. If the data module already exists, it returns itself. Otherwise, the data module creates a new instance. All objects will use the same data module class.

The Data Modeler tool created the `getCourse` and `getStudent` methods to return `QueryDataSet` objects.

After the data module has been created, the frames in the application have to be told to use the data module. Select Wizards, Use DataModule from the menu. The Use DataModule Wizard shown in Figure 15.21 appears.

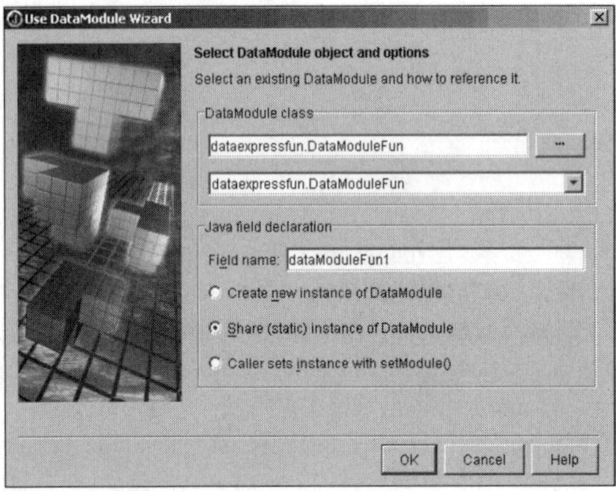

FIGURE 15.21 Using a data module.

The Use DataModule Wizard lets the selected frame access the data module. The first field allows you to choose the package where the DataModule exists. The package is then searched for all `DataModules` available and provided in the drop-down box in the `DataModule` class section.

The Java field declaration section explains the usage of the `DataModule` by the frame. The Field name represents the variable name to assign the `DataModule`. This field name is used by the data-aware controls as part of the data set name.

The next option determines how to create the DataModule for use by the frame. The DataModule can be created by three different methods.

The first method is Create New Instance of DataModule. This method creates a new instance of the DataModule for the frame. The view of the data module will be independent of any other frame in the application. Therefore, different frames can be looking at different records in the data module.

The second method is to Share (Static) Instance of DataModule. This method has the frame share the same instance of the DataModule as other frames. Therefore, moving the record in one frame automatically moves it on the other frames keeping them in sync.

The final method of creating the DataModule is Caller Sets Instance with `setModule()`. This method lets the caller set the instance of the DataModule by implementing the `setModule` method. This allows a runtime decision on sharing data modules.

After the DataModule has been set up for use by a frame, the control on that frame will now see the DataModule as a data set. The JBuilder environment opens the DataModule and shows a list of available data sets to choose from. After a selection has been made, the column names appear.

In Practice

In our lab exercise, we are going to take our swing application for course maintenance and make it database aware.

We will first remove the existing code for statically retrieving the course description, title, and ID. The architecture of the application requires that the data be passed back as Java collection objects.

Step 1: Opening the Example and Reviewing the Class

In this step, you open the example project and review the source code file.

To open the example project

1. Select File, Open Project from the JBuilder menu.
2. Locate the jbbook/ch15/swing/ChalkTalk.jpx and click on OK.
3. The project opens in the Project pane. The project contains many files. Select the file CommonOperations.java located in the userservices folder.
4. Double-click on CommonOperations.java. The Content pane displays the file.

Step 2: Locating the Method `browseCourses`

Search the file and locate the method `browseCourses`. Listing 15.7 shows the current code for `browseCourses`.

LISTING 15.7 `browseCourses` Method

```
public java.util.Collection browseCourses(CourseFilter courseFilter) {
  Vector v = new Vector();

  v.add(
    new CourseData(
      "Introduction to Java",
      "CS211",
      "This course will teach you the fundamentals of Java using JDK 1.4.
➥Topics include File I/O, AWT and Swing. Student must have a grade
➥of C or better in CS202 to register for this course. Students who
➥have obtained a B or higher grade in CS201 may take this class with
➥Instructor's permission. There will be one mid-term and one final
➥exam with one substantial programming assignment.")
    );
  v.add(
    new CourseData(
      "Introduction to JBuilder",
      "CS251",
      "This course will teach you how to use JBuilder to develop Java
➥applications. Topics include developing, JavaBeans, JSPs and
➥Servlets. Student must have a grade of C or better in CS211 to
➥register for this course. There will be one mid-term and one
➥final exam with one substantial programming assignment.")
     );

  return Collections.unmodifiableCollection(v);
}
```

Notice that this method creates a vector, statically adds data to the vector, and then returns a collection back to the calling method.

Step 3: Removing Existing Code

Delete the code in the method `browseCourses` leaving the creation of the vector and the return of the collection. The `browseCourses` method should now look like Listing 15.8.

LISTING 15.8 Skeleton Code for `browseCourses`

```
public java.util.Collection browseCourses(CourseFilter courseFilter) {
  Vector v = new Vector();

  return Collections.unmodifiableCollection(v);
}
```

Step 4: Adding `Database` and `QueryDataSet`

Click on the Design tab for the CommonOperations.java file. Drop the `Database` component and `QueryDataSet` objects on the form. Figure 15.22 should now be displayed.

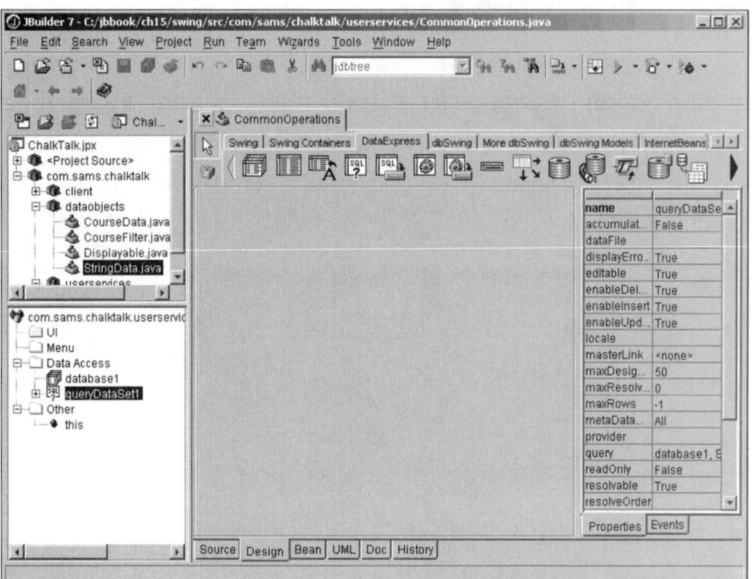

FIGURE 15.22 CommonOperations.java Design tab.

Select the `Database` component and set the `connection` property. The Connection dialog box shown in Figure 15.23 appears. Set the following properties:

Property	Value
Driver	**`com.borland.datastore.jdbc.DataStoreDriver`**
URL	**`jdbc:borland:dslocal:C:\jbbook\ch15\swing\JDBCFun.jds`**
Username	**`user`**

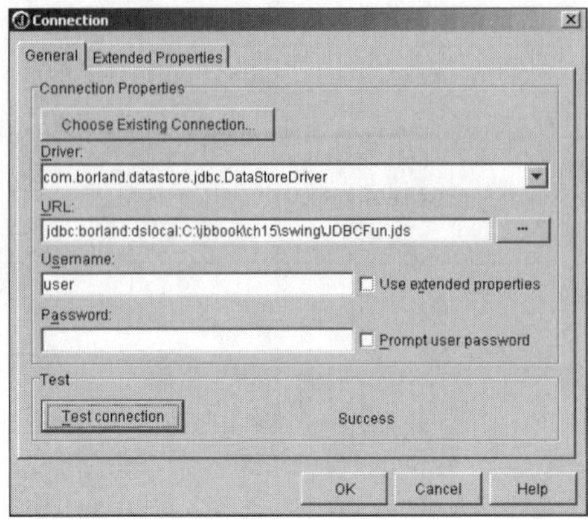

FIGURE 15.23 Connection dialog box.

Click on the Test Connection button. Make sure that the result displays Success. If the connection returns success, click OK. If the result does not display Success, verify the previous properties.

After the connection has been set, select the `queryDataSet1` and set the `query` property. The `query` property brings up the Query dialog box shown in Figure 15.24.

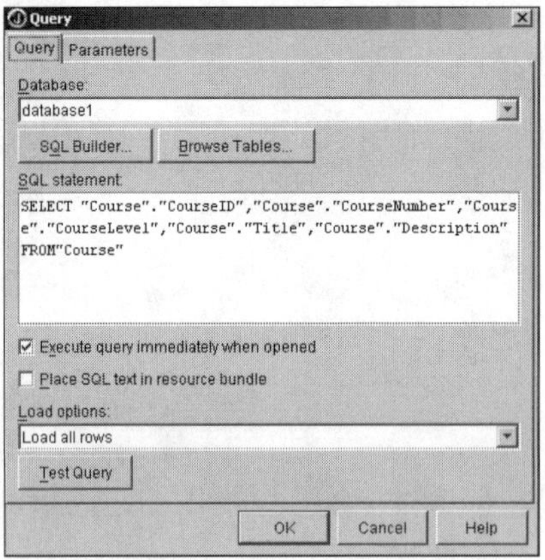

FIGURE 15.24 Query dialog box.

Set the Query dialog box properties to the following:

Property	Value
Database	**Database1**
SQL Statement	**SELECT "Course"."CourseID", "Course"."CourseNumber", "Course"."CourseLevel", "Course"."Title", "Course"."Description" FROM "Course"**
Execute Query Immediately when Opened	Check box is checked.
Load Options	Load all rows.

After the properties have been set, click the Test Query button to validate the query. If the query returns success, click OK. If the query does not return success, verify the property settings.

After setting the query property, switch to the Source tab. Listing 15.9 shows the code generated after the properties are set. A constructor and `jbInit` methods have been added to the code.

LISTING 15.9 New Methods Added to the CommonOperations.java Class

```
public CommonOperations() {
  try {
    jbInit();
  }
  catch(Exception e) {
    e.printStackTrace();
  }
}
private void jbInit() throws Exception {
  queryDataSet1.setQuery(new com.borland.dx.sql.dataset.QueryDescriptor(
➥database1, "SELECT \"Course\".\"CourseID\",\"Course\".\"CourseNumber\",
➥\"Course\".\"CourseLevel\",\"Course\".\"Title\",\"Course\".\"" +
     "Description\" FROM\"Course\"", null, true, Load.ALL));
  database1.setConnection(new com.borland.dx.sql.dataset.ConnectionDescriptor(
➥"jdbc:borland:dslocal:C:\\jbbook\\ch15\\swing\\JDBCFun.jds",
➥"user", "", false, "com.borland.datastore.jdbc.DataStoreDriver"));
}
```

Step 5: Adding Code to the `browseCourses` Method

Now that the database and query components have been set, the `browseCourses` method needs to be written to retrieve the data into a collection.

Listing 15.10 shows the new `browseCourses` method. The code executes the query, validates that data exists, and loops through the resultset to process the data.

LISTING 15.10 Updated `browseCourses` Method

```
public java.util.Collection browseCourses(CourseFilter courseFilter) {
  Vector v = new Vector();

  queryDataSet1.executeQuery();
  if (queryDataSet1.getRowCount() > 0)
  {
   do {
    v.add(new CourseData(queryDataSet1.getString("Title"),
                         queryDataSet1.getString("CourseNumber"),
                         queryDataSet1.getString("Description")));

  } while (queryDataSet1.next());
  }
  queryDataSet1.close();

  return Collections.unmodifiableCollection(v);
}
```

Step 6: Running the Application

Run the application. The application now gets the data from the database. The final application appears in Figure 15.25.

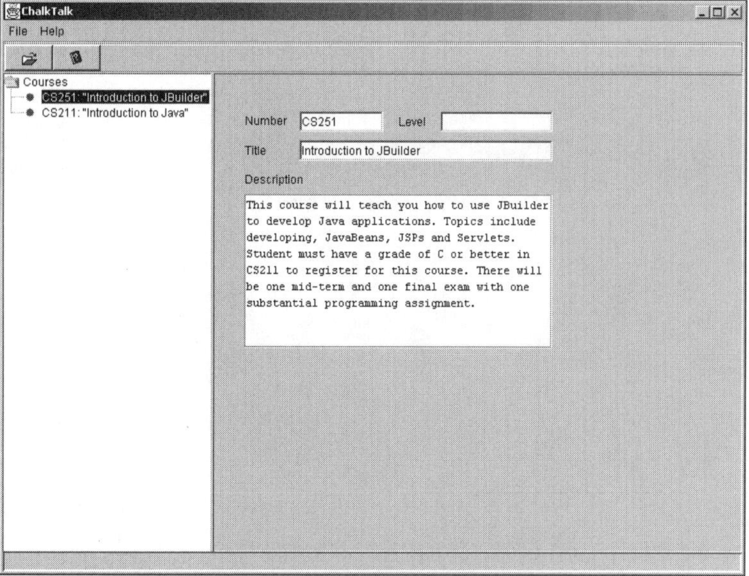

FIGURE 15.25 ChalkTalk application in action.

Summary

This chapter covered the tip of the iceberg known as DataExpress. DataExpress provides a complete and complex framework for database access. DataExpress provides many helper functions and components that make data-aware applications easier to create.

The DataExpress framework supports client/server applications to n-tier applications using the same components. The component framework is built on top of JDBC to provide maximum compatibility with existing applications.

Reflections

- Why would you want to use a component framework for database access?
- Why would you not want to use a component framework for database access?

PART IV

JBuilder for Web-based Applications

IN THIS PART

16

Servlets

IN THIS CHAPTER

- What Is a Web Application?
- What Are Servlets?
- Why Servlets?
- The Java Servlet API
- Debugging
- Deployment

In the development of Web-based applications using Java, servlets are a key technology that can simplify the delivery and construction of dynamic content. The focus over the years has shifted from primarily a delivery mechanism for dynamic HTML content, to being the centerpiece of Web applications designed to deliver dynamic content in various formats (WML, HTML, XML) that are self-contained and easily deployed.

A Web application defines a rigid directory organization containing the following components that can be read by any server that understands the defined structure:

- Java servlets
- Java Server Pages (JSP)
- Java Custom Tag Libraries
- Java class libraries
- Deployment descriptor
- Static content (HTML pages, images, and so on)
- Any other resources required

If the Web application contains any servlets, JSP, or Custom Tag Libraries, the Web server requires that a Java Servlet/JSP container be available in the code to be executed. This can be a container targeted at only Java servlets and JSPs such as the Apache Tomcat server, or a full J2EE (Java 2, Enterprise Edition) application server such as the Borland Enterprise Application Server.

With the installation of JBuilder 7 Enterprise, Apache Tomcat 3.3 and 4.0 are installed and may be used for both the development and debugging of Java servlets and JSP code.

In this chapter, we will examine the basic structure of Java servlets and how JBuilder 7 assists in the development of our servlets. In subsequent chapters, we will examine JSP and Custom Tag Libraries as part of Web-based applications. We will put what we learn to good use by designing a simple user interface for our ChalkTalk application.

In JBuilder, the servlets are created within a structure called a Web application that provides a structure for deployment and maintenance of a Web-based application. Before discussing servlets, we will begin by discussing the concept of a Web application as a framework for the servlets.

What Is a Web Application?

A key benefit of programming in Java is the capability to write and compile code on one platform and expect it to run on another platform with similar results.

The Web application attempts to define a self-contained directory structure containing all the files and definitions on how to deploy and execute the application. This attempts to expand on the portability of the Java language to an entire Web-based application encompassing static HTML pages, images, and dynamic content generation to provide a consistent presentation across various server platforms.

The Web application infrastructure requires the creation of a specific root directory to contain all the resources required for execution. All the HTML pages, JSP, images, and other resources except for Java classes/libraries that make up the Web application are to be placed below the root in a directory structure appropriate for the content.

Below the root directory, a special directory called WEB-INF is to be created that contains the following elements:

- File: web.xml—This is the deployment descriptor file for the Web application in XML format describing the various details required by the server for proper consistent deployment.
- Subdirectory: classes/—This directory contains all the individual Java classes required by the Web application for execution. This includes all the servlet class files along with the supporting class files.
- Subdirectory: lib/—This directory contains all the class libraries in JAR format that are required for the operation of the Web application.

As an example of the preceding structure, Listing 16.1 shows a partial Web application directory structure containing the Web interface for the ChalkTalk application to be developed within this chapter. This example is named chalktalkweb.

LISTING 16.1 Web Application Directory Structure

```
(Document Root)
    chalktalkweb/
    chalktalkweb/index.html
    chalktalkweb/WEB-INF/
    chalktalkweb/WEB-INF/web.xml
    chalktalkweb/WEB-INF/classes/
    chalktalkweb/WEB-INF/classes/com/sams/chalktalk/client/web/courselist.class
    chalktalkweb/WEB-INF/classes/com/sams/chalktalk/client/web/login.class
    chalktalkweb/WEB-INF/lib/
```

This directory structure either can be left expanded, or can be compressed into a single file known as a Web Application Archive (WAR) file. Whether the Web application is compressed to a single file or left expanded, deployment should consist of simply copying it to the deployment location specific to your servlet or J2EE server.

JBuilder automates the development of Web applications by providing wizards and screens that aid in setting up the required directories and the configuration of the web.xml file.

What Are Servlets?

Web sites and related Web-based applications often consist of a combination of static content (does not change) and dynamic content. Web servers are well suited for the presentation of static content in the form of HTML pages to an individual Web browser on request. In many Web applications and sites, there are requirements to display content customized for a particular user, a specific request, or to reflect changing information in a database.

Over the years, a number of techniques and methodologies have been developed using various technologies to provide the dynamic content alongside static content. One such technique has been the creation of the Servlet API as an extension to the Java language.

In many Web sites, the user submits a request for a page of content from a Web server. The Web server reads the request and any associated parameters submitted with the request, and then sends the requested content back to the user in a response. It either returns an already existing file or uses information both in the request and on the server to generate a custom response. Within this architecture, servlets are executed on the Web server to parse the client request and dynamically assemble a response appropriate to the request.

Figure 16.1 shows the request/response architecture.

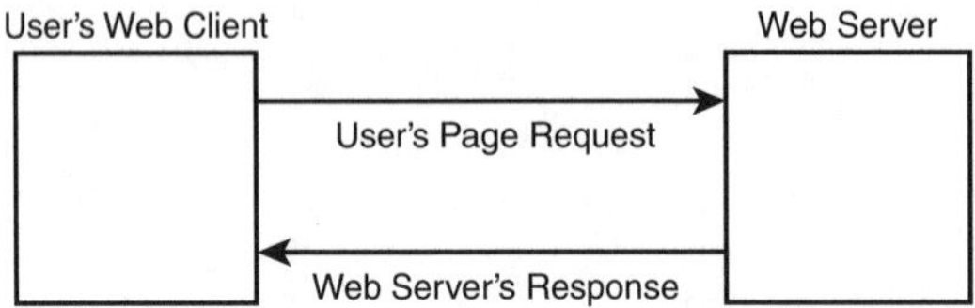

FIGURE 16.1 The request/response architecture.

To use Java servlets to process client requests, the Web server must support the Java Servlet API. This is accomplished either through a Web server that has built-in support or through the integration of an external engine to the Web server that supports the execution of Java servlets. In either case, after a Web application has been created and tested within JBuilder using servlets, copy the WAR file or the directory structure, beginning at the application root, to the location specific to your server set up to deploy them.

When the Web server receives the requests for a specified resource, if the resource represents a servlet, the servlet is executed and the request is passed to it. The servlet processes the request and creates a response that is returned to the Web server. The Web server then sends the response on to the user's Web client that made the request.

Why Servlets?

With an understanding of the role of Java servlets, the next decision is whether they are the right option for the Web-based application. We will review several benefits of using Java servlets to handle requests from Web clients.

As with most Java applications and classes, Java servlets are portable between various platforms. As long as a server, supporting the Java Servlet API, exists on the desired platform, the servlets written and designed in one environment should execute the same on a second environment. This assumes that the supporting Java class libraries used by the servlets are available on both platforms. As long as this remains the case, the servlets should be portable without any difficulties.

Because Java servlets are written in Java code, they have access to use all functionality implemented in Java class libraries and any custom class libraries developed. This includes the entire Java 2 Standard Edition (J2SE) as well as the entire Java 2

Enterprise Edition (J2EE). As additional APIs become available, a servlet will have the capability to take advantage of them, as long as the class library is made available to the servlet, both at development and runtime.

The structure of the Java servlet code is straightforward and lends itself to the implementation of many different client/server communication protocols. The Servlet API was designed as protocol neutral and only assumes the basic request/response architecture. This means that no matter what protocol your Web-based application uses to communicate to the Web client, chances are that the servlets can be used as the basis for the communication.

The Java Servlet API

When an application architect decides to begin using Java servlets to provide the dynamic content generation in your Web-based application, it is important to learn the Java Servlet API. All servlets that are developed must inherit functionality and use structures defined within the `javax.servlet` and the `javax.servlet.http` packages. We will begin by reviewing the classes and interfaces defined within these packages and briefly define the role that they play in servlet development.

The `javax.servlet` package contains the classes and interfaces required to create protocol-independent servlets. Any servlet can be created from the `javax.servlet` including support for various communication protocols. Using this package, other classes and packages can be created that implement servlets supporting specific protocols. The `javax.servlet.http` is a package of classes and interfaces defined to facilitate the creation of servlets that communicate using HTTP.

For the purpose of learning the Servlet API, the following sections primarily focus on the creation of HTTP protocol-based servlets using the `javax.servlet.http` package. We will begin by listing the classes and interfaces that make up the `javax.servlet` package that serves as a basis for the Servlet API in Table 16.1.

TABLE 16.1 The `javax.servlet` Package

Name	Purpose
`Servlet`	All servlets must implement this interface. The servlet container uses this interface to communicate and call methods to initialize, respond to requests, and destroy the servlet.
`GenericServlet`	An implementation of the `Servlet` interface for a protocol-independent servlet. This class serves as a starting point to make the creation of servlets easier but is not required.
`SingleThreadModel`	Implementing this interface guarantees that this servlet will serve a single request at a time.

TABLE 16.1 Continued

Name	Purpose
`ServletConfig`	This interface is implemented by the servlet container and not by the creator of the servlet. The object implementing this interface is used by the servlet to obtain initialization information such as parameters. A reference to this object is obtained through the `Servlet` interface.
`ServletContext`	This interface is implemented by the servlet container and not by the creator of the servlet. The object implementing this interface is used by the servlet to communicate to the servlet container. A reference to this object is obtained through the `ServletConfig` interface.
`RequestDispatcher`	This interface is implemented by the servlet container and not by the creator of the servlet. The object implementing this interface is used by the servlet to either forward the request onto another known resource or include the results of another resource in the response. A reference to this object is obtained by a call to the `getRequestDispatcher` method of the `ServletContext` interface.
`ServletRequest`	This interface is implemented by the servlet container and not by the creator of the servlet. The object implementing this interface is used by the servlet to retrieve the request information submitted to the servlet by the Web user. A reference to this object is obtained when the servlet container makes a call to the service method of the `Servlet` interface.
`ServletResponse`	This interface is implemented by the servlet container and not by the creator of the servlet. The object implementing this interface is used by the servlet to create the response to be returned to the Web user submitting the request. A reference to this object is obtained when the servlet container makes a call to the service method of the `Servlet` interface.
`ServletRequestWrapper`	This class is an implementation of the `ServletRequest` interface that can be used to wrap the `ServletRequest` object with custom functionality. To use this class, pass the existing `ServletRequest` object as a parameter to the class constructor.

TABLE 16.1 Continued

Name	Purpose
`ServletResponseWrapper`	This class is an implementation of the `ServletResponse` interface that can be used to wrap the `ServletResponse` object with custom functionality. To use this class, pass the existing `ServletResponse` object as a parameter to the class constructor.
`ServletInputStream`	This class is implemented by the servlet container and not by the creator of the servlet. The object implementing this abstract class is used by the servlet to read binary data submitted by the Web user. A reference to this object is obtained by a call to the `getInputStream` method of the `ServletRequest` interface.
`ServletOutputStream`	This class is implemented by the servlet container and not by the creator of the servlet. The object implementing this abstract class is used by the servlet to write binary data to be returned to the Web user submitting the request. A reference to this object is obtained by a call to the `getInputStream` method of the `ServletResponse` interface.
`Filter`	An object implementing this interface is designed to allow interception of the `ServletRequest` and the `ServletResponse` objects destined for a specified resource on the server. The filter can process a request and pass it on or keep it from reaching the targeted resource.
`FilterConfig`	This interface is implemented by the servlet container and not by the creator of the filter. The filter uses the object that implements this interface to obtain initialization information and parameters. A reference to this object is obtained when the servlet container makes a call to the `init` method of the `Filter` interface.
`FilterChain`	This interface is implemented by the servlet container and not by the creator of the filter. The filter uses the object that implements this interface to pass the `ServletRequest` and `ServletResponse` objects to the resource originally requested by the Web user. A reference to this object is obtained when the servlet container makes a call to the `doFilter` method of the `Filter` interface.

TABLE 16.1 Continued

Name	Purpose
`ServletContextListener`	If notification is required when the servlet context is ready to receive requests or it has been shut down, a class implementing this interface must be registered to listen for the events in the deployment descriptor (web.xml) for the Web application.
`ServletContextAttributeListener`	If notification is required when an attribute is added, removed, or replaced on the servlet context, a class implementing this interface must be registered to listen for the events in the deployment descriptor (web.xml) for the Web application.
`ServletContextEvent`	An object of this class type is sent to all registered listeners implementing the `ServletContextListener` interface. This object contains a reference to the `ServletContext` object that triggered the event.
`ServletContextAttributeEvent`	An object of this class type is sent to all registered listeners implementing the `ServletContextAttributeListener` interface. This object contains a reference to the `ServletContext` and the name and value of the attribute that triggered the event.
`ServletException`	When a servlet encounters a problem that is not completely handled, it can throw a `ServletException` to indicate the situation.
`UnavailableException`	When a servlet is unavailable either permanently or temporarily, this exception is thrown to indicate the situation.

As an example of how to support specific communication protocols on top of the basic Servlet API, Table 16.2 lists the classes and interfaces available within the `javax.servlet.http` package. The classes and interfaces within this package extend many of the classes and interfaces defined as part of the `javax.servlet` package.

TABLE 16.2 The `javax.servlet.http` Package

Name	Purpose
`HttpServlet`	An implementation of the `Servlet` interface that can be used to support receiving and responding to the HTTP protocol-based communication such as with Web sites. This class serves as a starting point for the creation of HTTP protocol-based servlets and has defined methods for each of the HTTP commands that can be overwritten.
`HttpServletRequest`	This interface extends the `ServletResponse` interface and is implemented by the servlet container and not by the creator of the servlet. The object implementing this interface is used by the servlet to create the response to be returned to the Web user submitting the request. A reference to this object is received as a parameter to one of the `do` methods in the `HttpServlet` class through a call from the servlet container.
`HttpServletResponse`	This interface extends the `ServletRequest` interface and is implemented by the servlet container and not by the creator of the servlet. The object implementing this interface is used by the servlet to retrieve the request information submitted by the Web user. A reference to this object is received as a parameter to one of the `do` methods in the `HttpServlet` class through a call from the servlet container.
`HttpServletRequestWrapper`	This class is an implementation of the `HttpServletRequest` interface that can be used to wrap the `HttpServletRequest` object with custom functionality. To use this class, pass the existing `HttpServletRequest` object as a parameter to the class constructor.
`HttpServletResponseWrapper`	This class is an implementation of the `HttpServletResponse` interface that can be used to wrap the `HttpServletResponse` object with custom functionality. To use this class, pass the existing `HttpServletResponse` object as a parameter to the class constructor.
`HttpSession`	This interface is implemented by the servlet container and not by the creator of the servlet. The object implementing this interface is used by the servlet to preserve information for a particular Web user across HTTP calls. A reference to this object is obtained through a call to the `getSession` method on the `HttpServletRequest` interface.
`Cookie`	This class contains small bits of information to be sent to the Web user as part of the response and be retrieved from the Web user as part of the request. This class is used in conjunction with the `HttpSession` to preserve the identity of a particular Web user from request to request.

TABLE 16.2 Continued

Name	Purpose
`HttpSessionListener`	If notification is required when HTTP sessions are added or destroyed, a class implementing this interface must be registered to listen for the events in the deployment descriptor (web.xml) for the Web application.
`HttpSessionAttributeListener`	If notification is required when a session attribute is added, removed, or replaced, a class implementing this interface must be registered to listen for the events in the deployment descriptor (web.xml) for the Web application.
`HttpSessionBindingListener`	Any object that implements this interface will be notified when it is bound and unbound from an HTTP session.
`HttpSessionActivationListener`	Any object bound to an HTTP session that implements this interface will be notified before the session is deactivated and after the session is activated. At various times, the servlet container may choose to remove the session from memory temporarily and later reactivate it for use.
`SessionEvent`	This object is sent with all notifications to registered listeners implementing the `HttpSessionActivationListener` or the `HttpSessionListener` interface. This object contains a reference to the `HttpSession` object that triggered the event.
`SessionBindingEvent`	This object is sent with all notifications to registered listeners implementing the `HttpSessionAttributeListener` or the `HttpSessionBindingListener` interface. This object contains a reference to the `HttpSession` and the name and value of the attribute that triggered the event.
`HttpUtils`	Deprecated. This object has been removed from the API, and its use should be avoided.
`HttpSessionContext`	Deprecated. This object has been removed from the API, and its use should be avoided.

Servlet Life Cycle

The execution of servlets occurs within the context of a container whose responsibility it is to manage the life cycle. The life cycle of a servlet consists of the following sequence of events that entail calls to individual methods on the `Servlet` interface of each servlet:

- Create an instance of the servlet and initialize it—When the servlet container receives a request for a particular servlet and an available servlet has not been initiated, an instance of the servlet must be created and initialized. After the servlet has been created, the servlet container makes a call to the `init` method on the `Servlet` interface. The `init` method provides the servlet an opportunity to perform preparation or initialization tasks that need to be completed before processing requests and only executes once. If the `init` method fails for any reason, the servlet should throw the `ServletUnavailable` exception to the servlet container indicating not to use it for processing requests.

- Handle client requests—After a servlet has been created and successfully initialized, it is ready to receive and process requests. For each request received, the servlet container makes a call to the `service` method on an available instance of the requested servlet. If the normal operation of the `service` method fails, the `ServletException` exception is thrown to the servlet container. If an input or output exception occurs, the servlet throws the `java.io.IOException` to the servlet container.
- Remove and destroy the servlet—When the servlet container decides to remove the servlet, it calls the `destroy` method on the `Servlet` interface. This gives the servlet an opportunity to clean up any resources being used and is only executed once before destroying the servlet.

In addition to the sequence of life cycle events, the servlet container is designed to send notifications of the following events to the appropriate registered listener objects throughout the life of the servlet. The classes implementing these listener interfaces must be registered in the deployment descriptor (web.xml) of the Web application.

- The servlet context for the Web application is ready to receive requests. (`ServletContextListener`)
- The servlet context for the Web application is ready to be shut down. (`ServletContextListener`)
- An attribute is added, removed, or replaced in the servlet context for the Web application. (`ServletContextAttributeListener`)
- An HTTP session has been added or destroyed for the Web application. (`HttpSessionListener`)
- An attribute is added, removed, or replaced in an HTTP session for the Web application. (`HttpSessionAttributeListener`)

Individual objects bound to an HTTP session receive the following notifications from the servlet container if they have implemented the appropriate listener interface:

- The object is bound or unbound from the HTTP session. (`HttpSessionBindingListener`)

- The HTTP session is about to be passivated. (`HttpSessionActivationListener`)
- The HTTP session has just been activated. (`HttpSessionActivationListener`)

Handling Client Requests

In this section we will focus on handling HTTP requests within a servlet with a focus on the following interfaces:

- `javax.servlet.http.HttpServletRequest`
- `javax.servlet.http.HttpServletResponse`
- `javax.servlet.RequestDispatcher`
- `javax.servlet.Filter`

In subsequent sections we will discuss additional classes and interfaces within the Java Servlet API.

The majority of the work performed by a servlet occurs when the servlet container receives a client request and forwards it to the servlet through a call to the `service` method. For servlets extended from the `HttpServlet` class, the call to the `service` method is translated into calls to specific methods corresponding to HTTP commands submitted by the client. These methods along with the corresponding HTTP command are as follows:

- `doDelete`—Corresponds to the HTTP `DELETE` command
- `doGet`—Corresponds to the HTTP `GET` command
- `doHead`—Corresponds to the HTTP `HEAD` command
- `doOptions`—Corresponds to the HTTP `OPTIONS` command
- `doPost`—Corresponds to the HTTP `POST` command
- `doPut`—Corresponds to the HTTP `PUT` command
- `doTrace`—Corresponds to the HTTP `TRACE` command

For most servlets extending the `HttpServlet` class, there is only a need to override one of these seven methods to create a properly functioning servlet. The signature of each of the preceding methods contains both an `HttpServletRequest` and an `HttpServletResponse` object. The `HttpServletRequest` object provides access to the contents of the actual request submitted to the servlet. The `HttpServletResponse` object provides an object to contain the contents of the response to be returned to the client.

HttpServletRequest

The `HttpServletRequest` object provides numerous methods for parsing through the request submitted by the client. The following is a partial list of some common methods used to process the HTTP request:

- `getParameter(java.lang.String)`—Retrieves the value of a named parameter.
- `javax.servlet.http.HttpSession getSession()`—Retrieves the HTTP session for this request. This creates a new session if there is none. This is used for session tracking, which is discussed later.
- `java.lang.StringBuffer getRequestURL()`—Retrieves the URL to which the request was submitted. Does not include any characters passed as part of a query string at the end of the URL.
- `java.lang.String getHeader(java.lang.String)`—Retrieves the value associated with the specified header.
- `javax.servlet.ServletInputStream getInputStream()`—Retrieves the body of the raw HTTP request as binary data. This method is useful for retrieving data from the HTTP `POST` and `PUT` commands if the data is not character based.
- `javax.servlet.RequestDispatcher getRequestDispatcher(java.lang.String)`—Retrieves a reference to a specified resource such as another servlet. This request can be forwarded to the resource, or the output of the resource can be included in the response to this request.
- `java.io.BufferedReader getReader()`—Retrieves the body of the HTTP request as character data.

Many other methods are available that deal with further parsing of the parameters, headers, URLs, and authentication. For further information on these additional methods, refer to the help files available within JBuilder.

HttpServletResponse

The `HttpServletResponse` object provides numerous methods to assist in assembling the response to be returned to the client. The following is a partial list of some common methods used to process the HTTP request:

- `javax.servlet.http.HttpSession sendError(int sc, java.lang.String msg)`—Indicates that the server should create an HTML page with the specified HTTP status code and the indicated message to be returned as the response.
- `void sendRedirect(java.lang.String location)`—Sends a response to the client indicating that the browser should load the URL returned as the location.

- `void setHeader(java.lang.String name, java.lang.String value)`—Sets the value header to the response to be returned to the client.
- `javax.servlet.ServletOutputStream getOutputStream()`—Retrieves an instance of the `ServletOutputStream` object that can be used for sending binary data in the response back to the client. This can be useful for sending images back to the client.
- `java.io.BufferedReader getWriter()`—Retrieves a `java.io.PrintWriter` object that can be used to send character data back to the client.

Several other methods are available that deal with more precisely controlling the header values and with session tracking. We will discuss the session tracking later in this chapter, but for information on the other available methods, refer to the help available in JBuilder.

Listing 16.2 contains a simple servlet named `DisplayParameter`, which reads a parameter from the `HttpServletRequest` object and assembles an HTML page using the `HttpServletResponse` object to be returned to the client. Notice that only the `doGet` method has been defined to create a fully functional servlet.

LISTING 16.2 DisplayParameter.java

```
package test;

import javax.servlet.*;
import javax.servlet.http.*;
import java.io.*;
import java.util.*;

public class DisplayParameter extends HttpServlet {
  static final private String CONTENT_TYPE = "text/html";

  //Process the HTTP Get request
  public void doGet(HttpServletRequest request, HttpServletResponse response)
                                  throws ServletException, IOException {
    response.setContentType(CONTENT_TYPE);
    PrintWriter out = response.getWriter();
    out.println("<html>");
    out.println("<head><title>Parameter Display</title></head>");
    out.println("<body>");
    out.println("<p>The parameter  is " +
                request.getParameter("param1") +
                "</p>");
```

LISTING 16.2 Continued

```
    out.println("</body></html>");
  }

}
```

Figure 16.2 displays the results of submitting the following URL to the `DisplayParameter` servlet in Listing 16.2:

`http://localhost:8082/displayparameter?param1=testing`

Notice the query string `param1=testing` that has been submitted as part of the URL. The servlet retrieved the value of `param1` as a parameter and placed it into the HTML page created for the response.

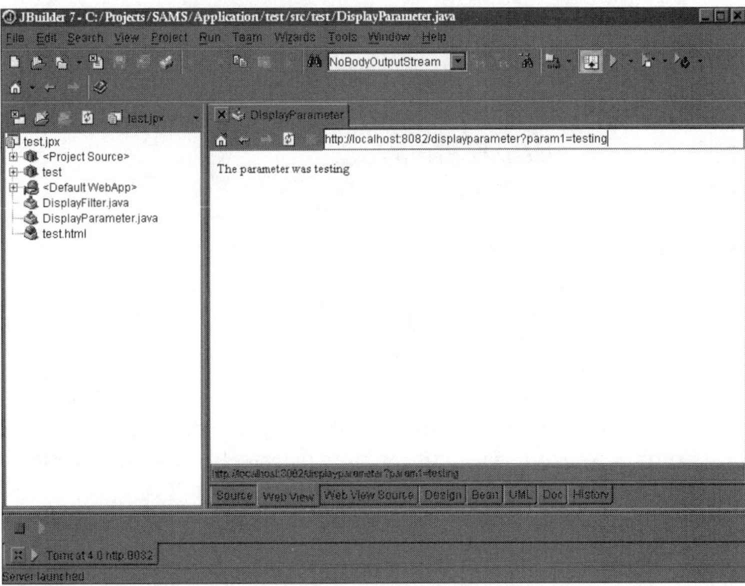

FIGURE 16.2 The result of running the `DisplayParameter` servlet in Listing 16.2.

`RequestDispatcher`

The `RequestDispatcher` object allows the reuse of servlets, JSP, HTML pages, and other resources in the generation of content in response to client requests. The request can be forwarded to the other resource to generate the response through a call to the `forward` method. Through a call to the `include` method, the output generated from the other resource can be used in the generation of the response. The other resource is typically another servlet within the context of the same Web application, but can be any resource accessible either by name (specified in the deployment descriptor file web.xml) or by URL within the context of the Web application.

A `RequestDispatcher` object can be obtained through the following methods:

- `ServletContext.getNamedDispatcher(java.lang.String)`
- `ServletRequest.getRequestDispatcher(java.lang.String)`

Filters

A `Filter` object can be any Java class as long as it implements the `Filter` interface and is registered in the deployment descriptor (web.xml) for the Web application. Listing 16.3 shows the syntax for registering a filter named `test.DisplayFilter` that intercepts any client requests targeted at the `test.DisplayParameter` servlet for additional processing.

LISTING 16.3 Filter Declaration in web.xml

```
<filter>
  <filter-name>displayfilter</filter-name>
  <filter-class>test.DisplayFilter</filter-class>
</filter>
<filter-mapping>
  <filter-name>displayfilter</filter-name>
  <servlet-name>displayparameter</servlet-name>
</filter-mapping>
```

The servlet container can pass the request through any number of registered filters prior to handing it to the servlet. All filters registered for the same servlet become part of a filter chain with the servlet being the end point. The order of the filters in the chain is the same as the declaration order in the deployment descriptor.

Similar to the life cycle of a servlet, the servlet container calls the `init` method on the `Filter` interface once before it is used the first time to perform any necessary initialization. Prior to the servlet container destroying the `Filter` object, it calls the `destroy` method on the interface only once to allow any necessary cleanup to be performed. Each time a client request is passed to this filter, a call to the `doFilter` method is called to process the `ServletRequest` object.

Each call to the `doFilter` method on the filter receives a reference to the next filter or servlet in the filter chain for the targeted servlet. To pass the client request down the filter chain toward the servlet, a call needs to be made to the `doFilter` method of the `FilterChain` object.

Listing 16.4 contains the code for the DisplayFilter.java class as created by the Servlet Wizard in JBuilder. We added two lines of code to the `doFilter` method to include the words `Hello World` at the top of the HTML page returned from the targeted servlet, in this case `test.DisplayParameter`. Note that the Servlet Wizard within JBuilder creates the `Filter` object as a servlet extended from the `HttpServlet` class. The `test.DisplayFilter` class could have been extended from any class including the `java.lang.Object` because the only requirement for a filter is that it implement the `Filter` interface.

LISTING 16.4 DisplayFilter.java

```
package test;

import javax.servlet.*;
import javax.servlet.http.*;
import java.io.*;
import java.util.*;

public class DisplayFilter extends HttpServlet implements Filter {
  private FilterConfig filterConfig;
  //Handle the passed-in FilterConfig
  public void init(FilterConfig filterConfig) {
    this.filterConfig = filterConfig;
  }
  //Process the request/response pair
  public void doFilter(ServletRequest request,
                       ServletResponse response,
                       FilterChain filterChain) {
    try {
      PrintWriter out = response.getWriter();
      out.println("<html><body>Hello World</html></body>");
      filterChain.doFilter(request, response);
    }
    catch(ServletException sx) {
      filterConfig.getServletContext().log(sx.getMessage());
    }
    catch(IOException iox) {
      filterConfig.getServletContext().log(iox.getMessage());
    }
  }
  //Clean up resources
  public void destroy() {
  }
}
```

Session Tracking

Most Web-based applications depend on the capability to have interactive conversations with a user. To provide the necessary interactions, the application needs to preserve various values related to the state of the conversation. The HTTP protocol, common in many Web-based applications, does not inherently provide support for interactive conversations and thus is limited in the capability to support business transactions without external support. In the case of the Servlet API, this preservation of state information is called *session tracking* and is supported through the creation of an `HttpSession` object by the servlet container.

Every client request received by the servlet container is associated with a session object with a unique identifier. The session object is available for the storage and maintenance of information about the user or the conversation such as a shopping cart that tracks items for purchase. When the conversation is completed, either the session object is destroyed, or the content is preserved until the next time a conversation with the same user occurs.

We will review two methods commonly supported within servlet containers (other methods are available):

- Cookies
- URL rewriting

Both methods assume that the client submits identifying information with each request that allows the servlet container to match it with an existing session or to create a new session. These mechanisms differ primarily in how this identifying information is communicated to the client and how it is passed to the servlet with each request.

Cookies are small pieces of information that can be passed as part of the response to the client. The client can store the cookie and submit it with each subsequent request back to the server until the cookie expires. To support session tracking, the servlet container creates a small cookie containing the session ID for the session on the server, which is sent to the client within the response headers. When a subsequent request is received from the client, the session ID is retrieved from the cookie and used to associate the request with the `HttpSession` object already on the server.

When the client does not support cookies or refuses to accept them, they cannot be used for session tracking. In the cases when cookies cannot be used, the strategy of URL rewriting is often employed. URL rewriting requires that URLs returned to the client be encoded with the session ID. When the user submits a subsequent request using the encoded URL, the servlet container extracts the session ID from the URL and associates it with an existing session on the server.

To establish session tracking with the servlet container, a call should be made to the `getSession` method on the `HttpServletRequest` object prior to returning the response to the client. The following statement creates a variable called `sess` that contains the `HttpSession` object:

```
HttpSession sess = request.getSession();
```

This method initiates the session if it does not exist and refreshes the session if it already exists so as to keep the session from being destroyed due to the age extending beyond a set timeout period. If there is a need to support session tracking and a possibility that the clients might not accept cookies, each of the URLs returned to the client in the response should be encoded through a call to one of the following methods of the `HttpServletResponse` object:

- `encodeURL(java.lang.String)`
- `encodeRedirectURL(java.lang.String)`

A call to these methods returns the URL encoded with the session ID. If the client accepts cookies and they are to be used for session tracking, the URLs shall remain unchanged by the calls to the previous methods.

Handling Cookies

Within session tracking as described in the preceding section, a cookie can be created and added to the response headers from the servlet without requiring the developer to explicitly deal with cookies. There are times when a cookie is needed for other purposes beyond simple session tracking. For these times, the Servlet API provides a `javax.servlet.http.Cookie` class that can be used to create additional cookies to be returned to the client. Prior to the response being returned to the client, the servlet may create additional cookies using this class:

```
Cookie newcookie = new Cookie("Name","Value")
```

This statement creates a new cookie with a name of `"Name"` and a value of `"Value"`. This cookie can then be added to the response by calling the `HttpServletResponse.addCookie` method and is returned as an additional header value to the client to be returned in a subsequent request. A list of cookies submitted as part of a client request can be obtained through a call to the `HttpServletRequest.getCookies` method.

Table 16.3 lists the various attributes that can be set as part of a cookie and the purpose of the attribute.

TABLE 16.3 Properties of Cookies in the Servlet API

Properties of a Cookie	Purpose
`Comment`	A string containing desired string information to be included with the cookie. This is often a description of the purpose of the cookie.
`Domain`	The domain name of the servers to which the client should submit this cookie. By default the cookie is returned only to the server that passed it to the client.
`MaxAge`	The number of seconds this cookie should exist before expiring. If the `MaxAge` is negative, the cookie expires as soon as the client is shut down.
`Name`	Name of the cookie. This is set at the time of creation.
`Path`	The path on the server identifying the resources to which this cookie should be submitted as part of the request.
`Value`	The value associated with the cookie. This is set at the time the cookie is created and can be changed when needed.
`Version`	The version of the specifications that this cookie complies with.
`Secure`	This is a Boolean property indicating to the client whether this cookie should be sent only through a secure protocol.

Debugging

After we have at least one servlet created within our project, we are ready to run or debug it. The execution and debugging of a Web-based application within JBuilder is similar to that used for any other Java development. Several items differ and must be noted.

To begin with, the server that JBuilder uses to execute the servlets must be configured. Figure 16.3 shows the Server tab on the Project Properties window.

The Server tab allows the user to configure the servers used by JBuilder to execute the various components of the project. In this case, we will discuss the debugging of servlets within JBuilder requiring that we specify a JSP/Servlet server that should be used to run our servlets. JBuilder is installed with Apache Tomcat preconfigured for use in running servlets, thus we need to verify that Tomcat 4.0 is the configured server for our servlets. Looking at Figure 16.3, that is the case. If other servers were available, we could certainly choose to use them. Because Tomcat 4.0 is the reference implementation for the Servlet API 2.3 and comes installed with JBuilder, it is easily used and available for our development and testing.

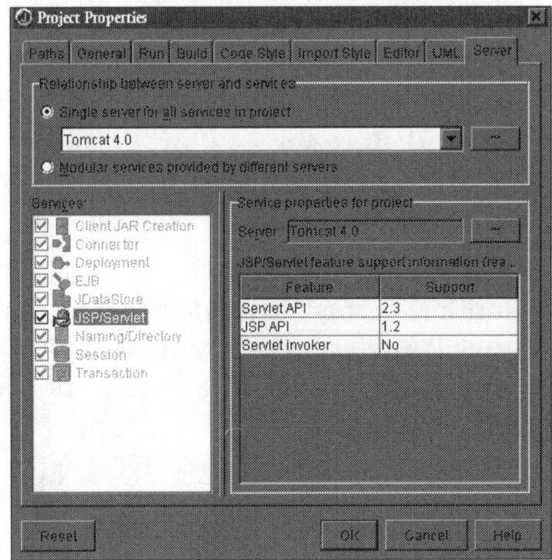

FIGURE 16.3 Project Properties: Configure servers.

After we set the servers to use for our project, we need to set the default runtime configuration for our application. The runtime configuration provides a mechanism to set the code to be executed within our application upon startup during runtime or debugging within JBuilder and does not affect execution outside JBuilder.

Figure 16.4 shows a picture of the Run tab on the Project Properties window listing all the runtime configurations set up for this project. There is only one named chalktalkweb displayed in Figure 16.4.

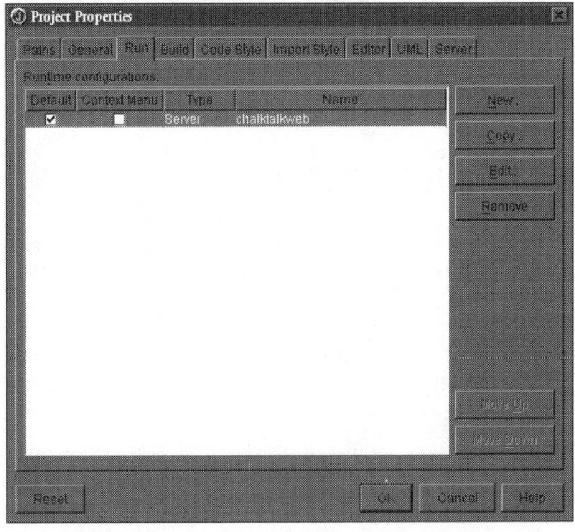

FIGURE 16.4 Project Properties: Runtime configuration.

Multiple runtime configurations can be defined for each project. Figure 16.4 shows two check boxes to the left of the server type in the list of runtime configurations. If there are multiple configurations, the one marked as default will be the one used when the application is run. There is also a Context Menu check box. Each configuration marked with Context Menu will be listed in a dialog box for the user to choose the configuration to use for execution when there are no default configurations.

Figure 16.5 shows the Runtime Properties window for the chalktalkweb runtime configuration. Selecting the desired runtime configuration and clicking the Edit button on the Run tab displayed in Figure 16.4 accesses this window.

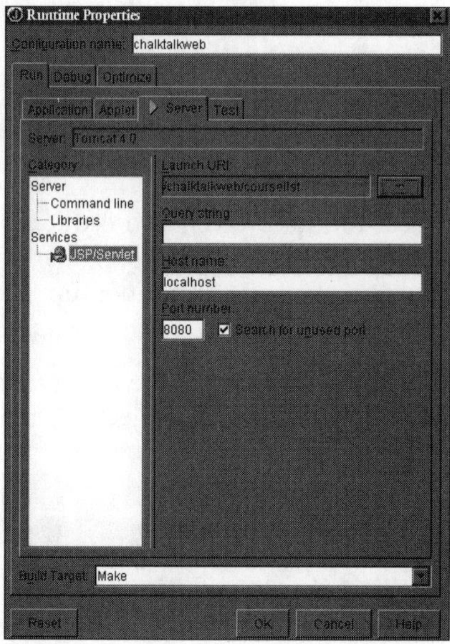

FIGURE 16.5 Project Properties: Runtime Properties.

Note in Figure 16.5 that the Server tab is selected and that the JSP/Servlet item is selected in the Category list. The text boxes to the right of the Category list provide the port number to use for the Tomcat 4.0 execution along with the initial URI to access the initial page in our application. This allows us to control what servlet or Web page should initially be displayed when debugging or running our project within JBuilder.

After the runtime configuration and the JSP/Servlet server are set up, we may run the application or debug the application just as we would any other project within

JBuilder by selecting either Run or Debug from the Project menu. Figure 16.6 shows a project running within the Tomcat 4.0 JSP/Servlet server, which accesses a servlet that generates the message `The servlet has received a GET. This is the reply.`

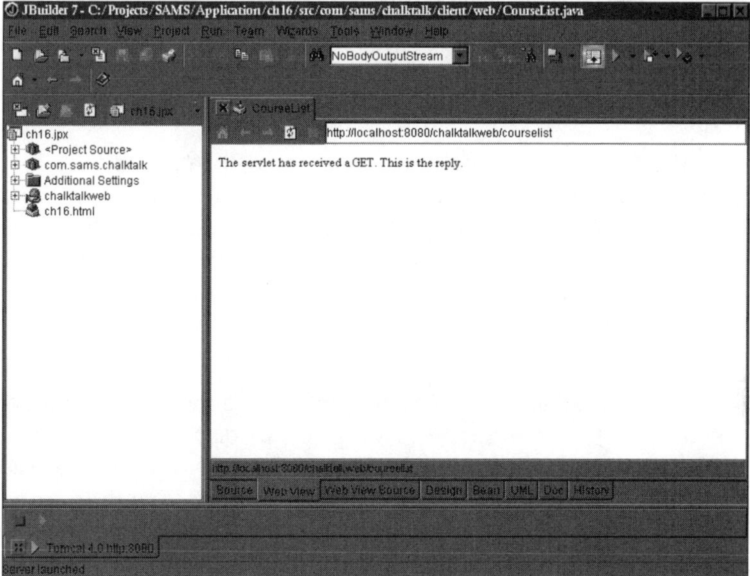

FIGURE 16.6 JBuilder running a Web application in Tomcat 4.0.

The tab at the bottom of the screen labeled Tomcat 4.0 http:8080 represents the Web server through which the Web-based application will be accessed. The red button just above the tab can be clicked at anytime to stop the server.

The CourseList tab shown in Figure 16.6 represents the application that is running or being debugged. The Web View tab within that tab is a functioning Web browser that can be used to test the functionality of the entire application including all the servlets. The Web View Source tab next to the Web View tab contains a listing of the source code currently displayed in the Web view.

If there is a need to debug a servlet, simply place a breakpoint in the source file of the desired servlet and debug as normal. It is important to note that if the source code of the servlets changes, the Tomcat server must be stopped before rerunning the project to account for the changes.

Deployment

After the Web-based application has been created and debugged, it is time to deploy into a Web server outside JBuilder. As a Web application, there are two ways to deploy it as discussed at the beginning of the chapter:

- Expanded directories beginning at the root
- A single Web Application Archive (WAR) file

The first method requires the root directory of the Web application to be copied with all associated subdirectories to a location specified by the targeted Web server. The second method requires the root directory and the subdirectories to be collapsed into a single file with the file extension .war. Depending on your deployment method, either the single WAR file or the expanded directory hierarchy needs to be copied to the location specified according to the deployment instructions for your particular Web server.

JBuilder provides a mechanism to automatically create the WAR file for deployment purposes whenever the project is rebuilt. Figure 16.7 displays the Properties screen for the Web application. Clicking with the right mouse button on the Web application node named "chalktalkweb" in the Project window of Figure 16.6 and selecting the Properties item in the pop-up menu accesses this Properties screen.

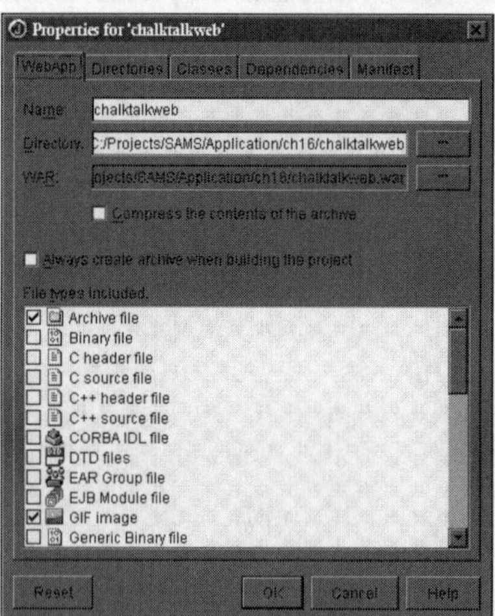

FIGURE 16.7 Web application Properties window.

The window in Figure 16.7 lists the name of the WAR to be created along with the path to the root directory of the targeted Web application. The location to place the created WAR file is indicated in the WAR text box. Two check boxes deal with whether to create the WAR file for the application.

The Compress the contents of the archive check box indicates whether the contents should be compressed to save space.

The Always create archive when building the project check box controls whether JBuilder creates the WAR file. If this check box is checked when the project is built, the WAR file will be created in the location specified.

In Practice

Now that we have looked at the structure of the Java Servlet API and what servlets are, we'll build a Web-based user interface for our ChalkTalk application.

We will create the Web interface as a simple Web application called chalktalkweb that demonstrates the steps involved in creating a Web-based application in JBuilder using servlets. This application simply provides a Web page to display the results of the `browseCourses` method in the `com.sams.chalktalkuserservices.CommonOperations` class. To demonstrate the implementation of session tracking, a servlet will be created that makes calls to both the `Login` and `Logout` methods of that class.

To give you an idea of where we are going, here is a summarized list of all the steps we will perform in this "In Practice" section:

1. Create a project and Web application.
2. Design a View Course List servlet.
3. Design a Login servlet.
4. Design a filter.
5. Configure the Web application to use the filter.

Creating a Project and Web Application

We will begin by creating a new JBuilder project and inserting a new Web application to be named chalktalkweb. The servlets and the Java classes created as part of our discussion will be placed within the context of this Web application.

1. Copy the directory named chalktalkapp from the Chapter 16 source code to your hard drive. The Java packages in the chalktalkapp directory represent the class library that our Web-based application will be using to provide the business logic.

2. Select File, New Project.
3. On the first screen of the Project Wizard, enter **`ch16`** as the name of the project and **`C:\Projects\SAMS\Application\ch16`** as the directory. Leave the type as jpx, leave the Template as (Default Project), and check the Generate project notes file check box. You can put your project in a different directory, but at least make sure that the last component is chap16. This makes it easier for you to run the files. Click Next.
4. On the second screen of the Project Wizard, add a reference to include the source files from the existing ChalkTalk application. Click on the Add button next to the Source tab to bring up a dialog box and search for the location where the chalktalkapp directory was copied in step 1. After the directory has been located, click on OK to close the dialog box. The chalktalkapp directory should be listed in the list box on the Source tab. Click Next.
5. On the third screen, enter your name in the @author field, and your company name in the Company field. Click Finish.
6. Select File, New to bring up the Object Gallery. On the Web tab, double-click on the Web Application icon to bring up the Web Application Wizard. The Web Application icon will be disabled if a server has not been set up to run the JSPs and servlets for the project. In the "Debugging" section earlier in the chapter, we looked at the process needed to configure the JSP/Servlet server for a project.
7. On the screen, enter **`chalktalkweb`** as the name and **`C:/Projects/SAMS/Application/ch16/chalktalkweb`** as the directory name. Click OK.

We now have an empty Web application available that serves as the basis to create our Web interface for the existing ChalkTalk application. Next we will create a servlet to display the results of the `browseCourses` method in the `com.sams.chalktalk.userservices.CommonOperations` class.

Designing a View Course List Servlet

We will design the View Course List to contain two sections. The top section shows a menu of links to the other aspects of our Web application, and the bottom section displays the list of courses. For the purposes of our ChalkTalk application, we will design only a single page of our Web interface, leaving our menu to only contain the View Course List link.

1. Select File, New to bring up the Object Gallery. On the Web tab, double-click on the Servlet icon to bring up the Servlet Wizard.

2. On the first screen of the Servlet Wizard, enter **com.sams.chalktalk.client.web** as the name of the package and **CourseList** as the name of the servlet class. Check the Generate header comments check box. Check the Single Thread Model check box. Make sure that chalktalkweb is specified as the Web App for this servlet. Choose the Standard Servlet radio button and not the Filter or Listener Servlet. Click Next.

3. On the second screen of the Servlet Wizard, no changes are needed. Click Next.

4. On the third screen of the Servlet Wizard, no changes are needed. Click Next.

5. On the fourth screen of the Servlet Wizard, no changes are needed. Click Next.

6. On the fifth screen of the Servlet Wizard, no changes are needed. Click Finish.

7. Attempt to run the project from the Run, Run Project menu (shortcut key is F9) to verify that all the settings have been correctly set up and are working. The output is simply that of the default `CourseList` servlet that we just created.

8. After reviewing the output and confirming that it works, stop the Web application from running before moving to the next step. This can be accomplished by clicking on the red button in the bottom left of the screen just above the words "Tomcat 4.0."

We now have a basic Web application that can run. Next we will customize this servlet to display the list of courses:

1. Open the `CourseList` servlet file in the Content pane and switch to the Source tab at the bottom.

2. Add the following statements just below the existing `import` statements. These classes provide the servlet access to the existing ChalkTalk application business logic.

```
import com.sams.chalktalk.userservices.CommonOperations;

import com.sams.chalktalk.dataobjects.CourseData;
```

3. Add the following statement just below the declaration of the `CONTENT_TYPE` variable:

```
private CommonOperations commonOps;
```

4. Modify the body of the `init` method so that it looks as follows:

```
public void init() throws ServletException {
   commonOps = new CommonOperations();
}
```

5. Modify the body of the `doGet` method so that it looks as shown in Listing 16.5. (Note: The `Login` servlet will be created in the next section.)

LISTING 16.5 `doGet` Method Within the File CourseList.java

```
public void doGet(HttpServletRequest request, HttpServletResponse response)
                                throws ServletException, IOException {
  response.setContentType(CONTENT_TYPE);

  PrintWriter out = response.getWriter();
  out.println("<html>");
  out.println("<head><title>courselist</title></head>");
  out.println("<body>");

  //Create Menu of Operations
  out.println("<A HREF=\"" +
              response.encodeURL("login?Submit=Logout") +
              "\">Logout</A> ");
  out.println("<A HREF=\"" +
              response.encodeURL("courselist") +
              "\">View Course List</A>");
  out.println("<HR>");

  //Build List of Courses
  out.println("<table border=1>");
  out.println("<tr><td>Id</td>");
  out.println("<td>Title</td>");
  out.println("<td>Description</td></tr>");
  for (Iterator iter = commonOps.browseCourses(null).iterator() ;
       iter.hasNext() ; ) {
    CourseData course = (CourseData)iter.next();
    if (course != null) {
      out.println("<tr><td>"+ course.getId() +"</td>");
      out.println("<td>"+course.getTitle()+"</td>");
      out.println("<td>"+course.getDescription()+"</td></tr>");
    };
  }
  out.println("</table>");
  //End of Course List

  out.println("</body></html>");
}
```

6. Run the project to verify that the changes are working. Figure 16.8 shows the output of the `CourseList` servlet while running the project within JBuilder.

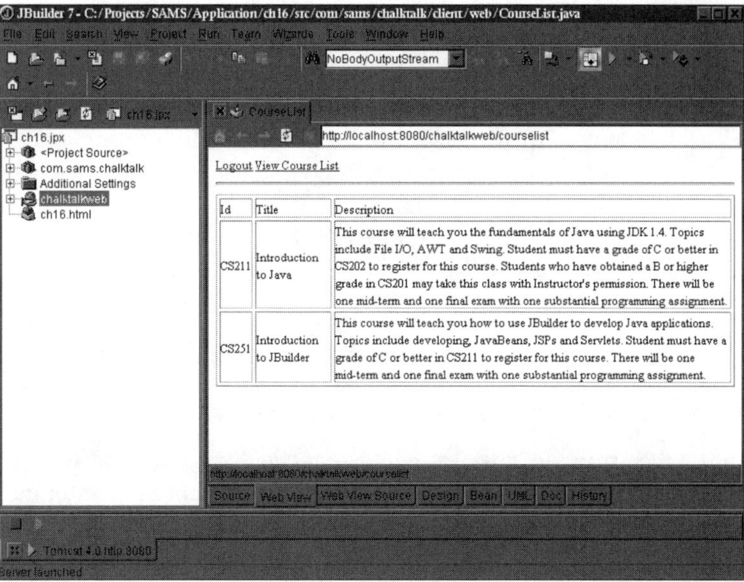

FIGURE 16.8 Output of the CourseList.java servlet.

7. After reviewing the output and confirming that it works, stop the Web application from running before moving to the next step. This can be accomplished by clicking on the red button in the bottom left of Figure 16.8 just above the words "Tomcat 4.0."

The Web application now serves to display the results of the call to the `browseCourses` method of the `CommonOperations` class.

Designing a Login Servlet

We will design the `Login` servlet to implement both the `Login` and the `Logout` methods of the `CommonOperations` class. In implementing these methods, we will demonstrate the use of session tracking to preserve state information across servlet calls and to preserve the URL that will be accessed upon a successful login. The `Login` servlet will be designed to perform the following tasks:

- Process requests to log in or log out.
- Display a login page.

When the request is received by the servlet, if the `submit` parameter is set to either `Login` or `Logout`, the servlet performs the operation; otherwise, the servlet responds with the login HTML page.

1. Select File, New to bring up the Object Gallery. On the Web tab, double-click on the Servlet icon to bring up the Servlet Wizard.
2. On the first screen of the Servlet Wizard, enter **`com.sams.chalktalk.client.web`** as the name of the package and **`Login`** as the name of the servlet class. Check the Generate header comments check box. Check the Single Thread Model check box. Make sure that chalktalkweb is specified as the Web App for this servlet. Choose the Standard Servlet radio button and not the Filter or Listener Servlet. Click Next.
3. On the second screen of the Servlet Wizard, no changes are needed. Click Next.
4. On the third screen of the Servlet Wizard, no changes are needed. Click Next.
5. On the fourth screen of the Servlet Wizard, no changes are needed. Click Next.
6. On the fifth screen of the Servlet Wizard, check the Create a runtime configuration check box. Enter **`Login`** as the name of the runtime configuration and leave the Base configuration as **`none`**. Click Finish.
7. Open the `Login` servlet file in the Content pane and switch to the Source tab at the bottom.
8. Add the following statement just below the existing `import` statements. These classes provide the servlet access to the existing ChalkTalk application business logic.

   ```
   import com.sams.chalktalk.userservices.CommonOperations;
   ```

9. Add the following statement just below the declaration of the `CONTENT_TYPE` variable:

   ```
   private CommonOperations commonOps;
   ```

10. Modify the body of the `init` method so that it looks as follows:

    ```
      public void init() throws ServletException {
         commonOps = new CommonOperations();
      }
    ```

11. Modify the body of the `doGet` method so that it looks as shown in Listing 16.6.

LISTING 16.6 doGet Method Within the File Login.java

```
public void doGet(HttpServletRequest request, HttpServletResponse response)
                      throws ServletException, IOException {
  response.setContentType(CONTENT_TYPE);
  PrintWriter out = response.getWriter();

  //Setup Session Variable
  HttpSession sess = request.getSession();

  //Determine operation performed by user
  String sOperation = (String)request.getParameter("Submit");

  if (sOperation == null) {
  }
  else if (sOperation.equals("Login"))  {
     commonOps.login();
     response.sendRedirect(
          response.encodeRedirectURL((String)sess.getAttribute("target")));
     sess.setAttribute("LoggedIn", new Boolean(true));
     return;
  }
  else if (sOperation.equals("Logout")) {
    commonOps.logout();
    response.sendRedirect(
         response.encodeRedirectURL((String)sess.getAttribute("target")));
    sess.invalidate();
    return;
  }
  else {
  }

  //Create HTML page
  out.println("<html>");
  out.println("<head><title>Course Registration Login</title></head>");
  out.println("<body>");

  //Create Menu of Operations
  out.println("<form action=\"" +
             response.encodeURL(request.getRequestURI()) +
             "\" method=\"GET\">");
  out.println("UserName: <input name=\"username\"><br>");
```

LISTING 16.6 Continued

```
    out.println("Password: <input type=\"password\" name=\"password\"><br>");
    out.println("<input type=\"submit\" name=\"Submit\" value=\"Login\">");
    out.println("<input type=\"reset\" value=\"Reset\">");
    out.println("</form>");

    out.println("</body></html>");
  }
```

12. Run the project to verify that the `Login` servlet can be executed and is correct. Choose the Login Runtime Configuration from the Choose Runtime Configuration dialog box to view the output of the `Login` servlet. The output from the `Login` servlet is shown in Figure 16.9.

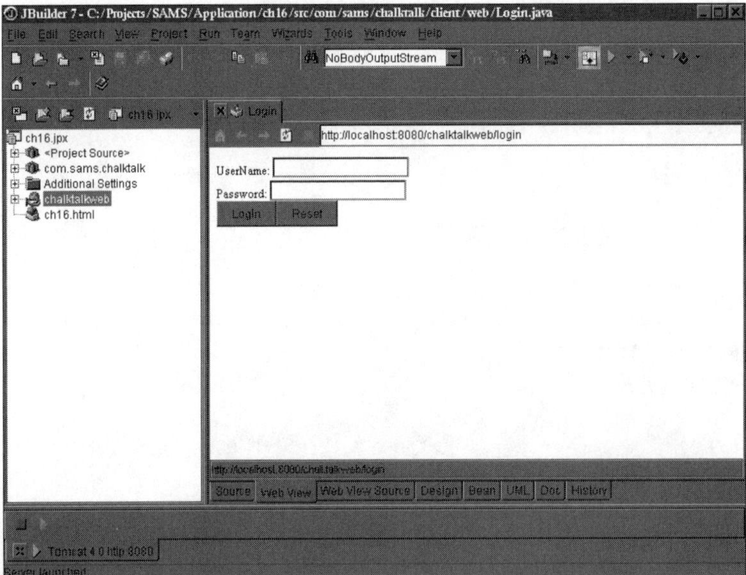

FIGURE 16.9 Output of the Login.java servlet.

13. After reviewing the output and confirming that it works, stop the Web application from running before moving to the next step. This can be accomplished by clicking on the red button in the bottom left of Figure 16.9 just above the words "Tomcat 4.0."

The Web application now consists of two servlets that together execute the methods within the `CommonOperations` class.

Designing a Filter

With our Web application, we will design a filter that can be used to redirect the user to a login screen if the user is not logged in when attempting to access the `CourseList` servlet:

1. Select File, New to bring up the Object Gallery. On the General tab, double-click on the Class icon to bring up the Class Wizard.
2. On the first screen of the Class Wizard, enter **`com.sams.chalktalk.client.web`** as the name of the package and **`LoginFilter`** as the name of the class. Leave `java.lang.Object` as the base class. Leave the remaining check boxes with the default values. Click OK.
3. Open the `LoginFilter` class in the Content pane and switch to the Source tab at the bottom.
4. Add the following statements just below the existing `import` statements:

    ```
    import javax.servlet.*;
    import javax.servlet.http.*;
    import java.io.*;
    ```

5. Modify the `LoginFilter` class definition to match the following signature in Listing 16.7.

LISTING 16.7 `LoginFilter` Class Within File LoginFilter.java

```
public class LoginFilter implements Filter {
  private FilterConfig filterConfig;
  //Handle the passed-in FilterConfig
  public void init(FilterConfig filterConfig) {
    this.filterConfig = filterConfig;
  }
  //Process the request/response pair
  public void doFilter(ServletRequest request,
                       ServletResponse response,
                       FilterChain filterChain) {
  }
  //Clean up resources
  public void destroy() {
  }
}
```

6. Modify the `doFilter` method to match the code in Listing 16.8.

LISTING 16.8 `doFilter` Method Within File LoginFilter.java

```
public void doFilter(ServletRequest request,
                     ServletResponse response,
                     FilterChain filterChain) {
  try {
    HttpServletRequest req = (HttpServletRequest) request;
    HttpServletResponse res = (HttpServletResponse) response;

    //Setup Session Variable
    HttpSession sess = req.getSession();

    //Determine whether logged in
    Boolean bLoggedIn = (Boolean)sess.getAttribute("LoggedIn");

    //if not logged in redirect to the login servlet
    if ((bLoggedIn == null) || !bLoggedIn.booleanValue()) {
        sess.setAttribute("target",req.getRequestURL().toString());
        res.sendRedirect(res.encodeRedirectURL("login"));
        return;
    }

    filterChain.doFilter(request, response);
  }
  catch(ServletException sx) {
    filterConfig.getServletContext().log(sx.getMessage());
  }
  catch(IOException iox) {
    filterConfig.getServletContext().log(iox.getMessage());
  }
}
```

Configuring the Web Application to Use the Filter

In this section we will modify the deployment descriptor for the Web application to ensure that the `LoginFilter` filter intercepts every request to the `CourseList` servlet that we created.

1. Open the deployment descriptor file for the Web application. Figure 16.10 shows the WebApp DD Editor.

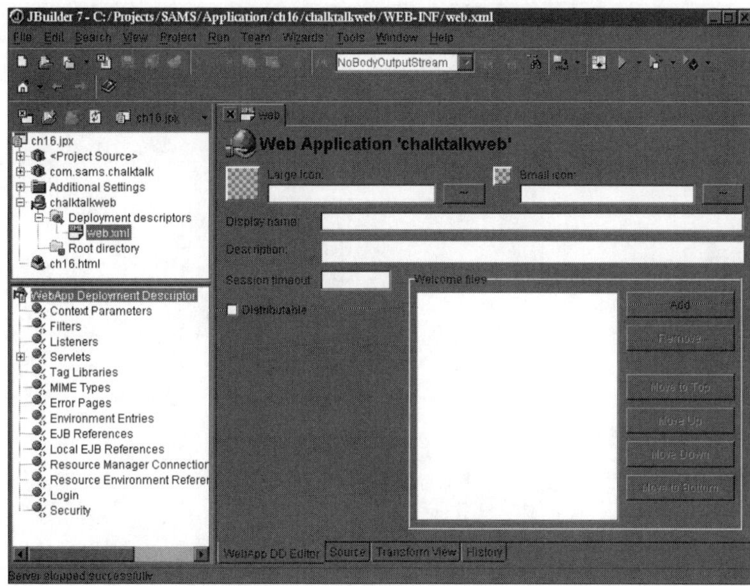

FIGURE 16.10 WebApp DD Editor.

2. Right-click in the Structure pane and select the Add Filter item from the pop-up menu. Enter **`LoginFilter`** as the filter name in the New Filter dialog box. This creates a node labeled LoginFilter below the Filters node.

3. Set the mappings that indicate what client requests will be intercepted by this filter. Click on the Filters node in the Structure pane to bring up the Filter Mappings list in the Content pane as shown in Figure 16.11. Click on the Add button in the Content pane to create a new filter mapping. Enter **`CourseList`** for the servlet name and **`LoginFilter`** for the filter.

4. Set the properties for the filter. Click on the LoginFilter node in the Structure pane to bring up the filter properties in the Content pane as shown in Figure 16.12. Enter **`com.sams.chalktalk.client.web.LoginFilter`** for the Filter class.

5. Create an additional servlet mapping to indicate the default servlet to be executed. This will be executed when the URL does not map to any servlets or resources in the chalktalkweb context. Click on the Servlets node in the Structure pane to bring up the Servlet Mappings list in the Content pane as shown in Figure 16.13. Click on the Add button to create an additional mapping and enter `/` as the URL pattern and **`courselist`** as the servlet.

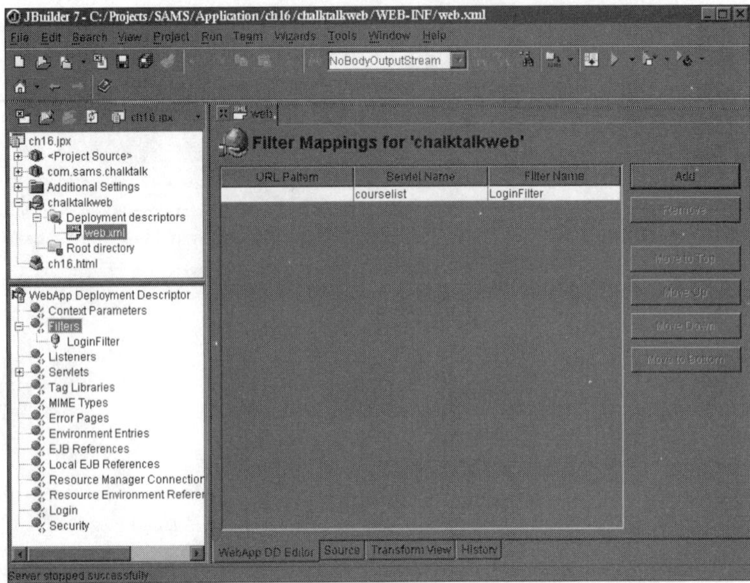

FIGURE 16.11 WebApp DD Editor: Filter mappings.

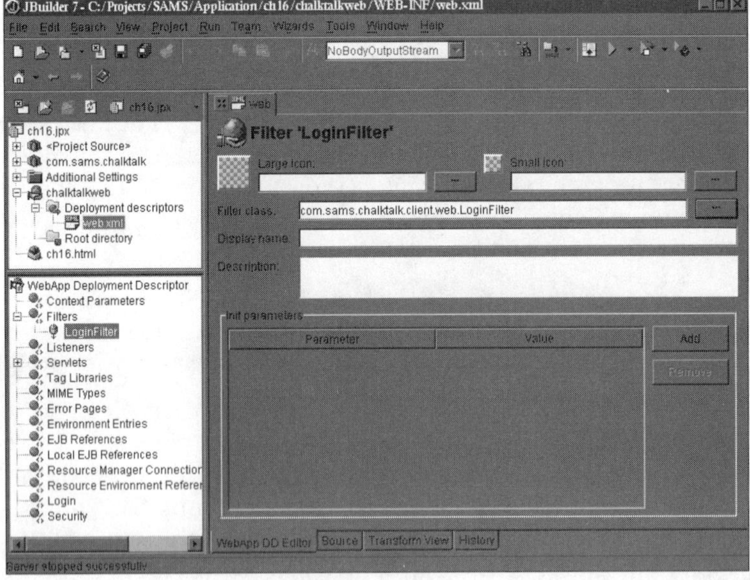

FIGURE 16.12 WebApp DD Editor: Filter properties.

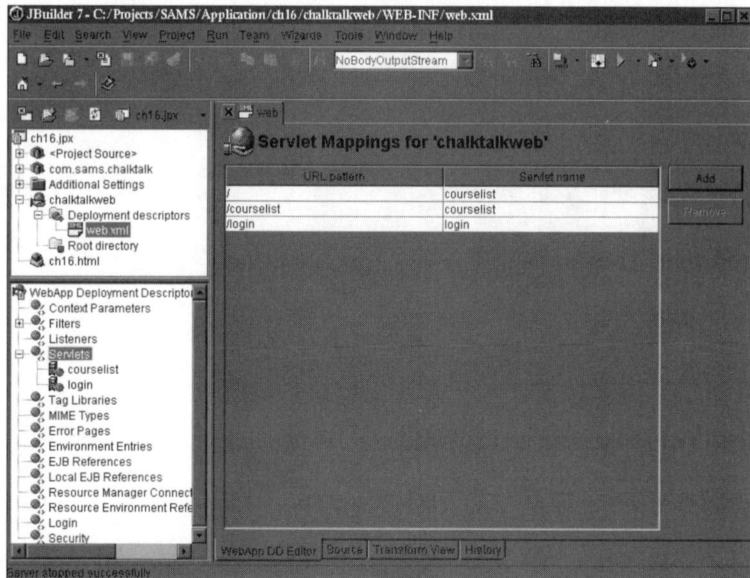

FIGURE 16.13 WebApp DD Editor: Servlet mappings.

6. Rebuild the project by selecting Project, Rebuild Project "ch16.jpx" from the menu.

7. Run the project to verify that the filter works. Choose the `courselist` Runtime Configuration from the Choose Runtime Configuration dialog box. Any attempt to access the `CourseList` servlet should be redirected to the `Login` servlet if the user has not logged in during the session.

SESSION PERSISTENCE

In our chalktalkweb application, we are using session tracking to maintain whether the Web client has logged in. By maintaining whether a user has logged in, we can limit access to a protected resource only to those Web clients that have permission. As demonstrated in chalktalkweb, this works.

When testing the chalktalkweb application, you might find that when the application is run, the Web client does not always redirect to the Login JSP as intended. The Tomcat 4.0 server and JBuilder work to preserve the session information across runs of the application and separate instances of the Tomcat 4.0 server. When the Web application is stopped or the Tomcat 4.0 server is shut down, a file named session.ser is generated containing the contents of the current sessions in serialized format. JBuilder and the Tomcat server use the information within this file to preserve the session information associated with the application you are running.

> This results in unexpected behavior in testing our chalktalkweb application. If the chalktalkweb application is shut down while the user is logged in, the next time it is run, the Web client will appear to be logged in at the time the application starts. This means that the Web client will not be automatically redirected to the Login Java server page as expected, but will be allowed access to the `CourseList` Java server page.
>
> The session information is preserved for runs while the same instance of JBuilder remains open. When a new instance of JBuilder is opened, the session information from the previous executions will not be reused. Within the same instance of JBuilder, if the Tomcat directory within the chalktalkweb project is removed, the session information will not be preserved.

Summary

The Java Servlet API is a powerful paradigm for creating Web-based applications with features that facilitate their deployment and portability as Web applications. JBuilder provides a number of wizards and editors to facilitate the development of Web-based applications, many of which we looked at in this chapter.

Reflections

- As we have discussed, servlets can be powerful in the generation of dynamic content for Web applications. What are some applications for servlets in addition to the generation of HTML code?
- In the "In Practice" section, we used a filter as a means to protect the `CourseList` servlet from unapproved access. What other uses are there for a filter or series of filters?
- The Servlet API provides a `RequestDispatcher` that can be used to forward client requests to another resource or to include the content of another resource in a response. What potential uses can this provide?

17

Java Server Pages

IN THIS CHAPTER

- Where Do JSPs Fit into a Web Application?
- The Java Server Pages API
- Debugging
- Deployment

As discussed in the preceding chapter, Java servlets are an effective technology for the development and delivery of dynamic Web-based applications. Many Web sites consist mostly of textual documents such as HTML pages interspersed with dynamic content generated as needed. A drawback of using servlets as the infrastructure for the dynamic content for the Web site is the requirement to translate many of the design and static aspects into Java code. This requires that the layout/content designer understand programming to effectively translate the designs into Java code in the form of Java servlets. In an attempt to address this issue and separate the layout and design of a Web site from the programming required to provide the dynamic data to be displayed, Java Server Pages (JSP) were developed.

JSPs were created to allow the Web site designer to define the content, both dynamic and static, using textual documents. Because these pages are textual documents and not Java class files, the designer can be more concerned with the design and layout rather than how to program Java class files. The programming required to generate the data used by the Web site can be further relegated to Java classes maintained by a programmer.

JSPs are an extension to the Servlet API and use it as the underlying architecture. Each JSP created for a Web site is translated into a servlet for execution within a JSP container available to the Web server. When a Web client first requests a JSP from a Web server, the page is automatically translated into a servlet that handles the client request. Each subsequent request for the same JSP is forwarded to the already existing servlet for the JSP. The dynamic content for the response is assembled during the execution of the servlet.

If the designer of the Web site needs to adjust the layout of the Web pages, modifications need to be made only to the textual documents describing where and how to integrate the dynamic content. It is the responsibility of the JSP container to translate the textual document into a Java servlet capable of assembling the required content at runtime and retrieving the data as needed. The Java classes used by the servlet to access data are programmed by a Java programmer and may not be modified by the Web site designer, only used.

This technique requires the Web designer to be familiar with some Java structures to properly define how to integrate the dynamic content with the static content. In Chapter 18, "Tag Libraries," we will discuss the creation of custom tag libraries that can serve to encapsulate the Java structures used by the JSPs in a set of XML tags. This further separates the Web page designer from the Java programmer by hiding all the Java code behind a set of XML tags similar to the markup tags already contained within the Web pages.

This chapter describes the basic structure of JSPs and how to create them within JBuilder.

Where Do JSPs Fit into a Web Application?

The JSPs need to be placed below the root directory of the Web application, in a manner similar to HTML pages as shown in Listing 17.1. The JSP placed below the WEB-INF directory will not be directly accessible by the Web client, but servlets or other JSPs can still forward client requests to them as needed. After the JSP files are added, the Web application can be used with the additional requirement that the Web server have access to submit the JSPs to a JSP container for execution and translation into servlets.

LISTING 17.1 Web Application Containing a JSP

```
(Document Root)     chalktalkweb/
chalktalkweb/login.jsp
chalktalkweb/index.html
chalktalkweb/WEB-INF/
chalktalkweb/WEB-INF/web.xml
chalktalkweb/WEB-INF/classes/
chalktalkweb/WEB-INF/classes/com/sams/chalktalk/client/web/LoginFilter.class
chalktalkweb/WEB-INF/classes/com/sams/chalktalk/client/web/Login.class
chalktalkweb/WEB-INF/lib/
```

The JSP API

The JSP API is based on the infrastructure created for Java servlets and thus has been given the package name `javax.servlet.jsp`.

The `javax.servlet.jsp` package contains the classes and interfaces required to use JSPs to generate both static and dynamic content. Table 17.1 contains a list of the classes and interfaces defined within the JSP API 1.2.

TABLE 17.1 The `javax.servlet` Package

Name	Purpose
`JspPage`	The JSP container implements this interface. When a JSP is translated into a servlet for execution within the JSP container, the created servlet must implement this interface, which defines the interactions between the container and the servlet.
`HttpJspPage`	The JSP container implements this interface when a JSP using HTTP is translated into a servlet for execution within the JSP container. The created servlet must implement this interface, which defines the interactions between the container and the servlet for HTTP.
`JspEngineInfo`	The JSP container implements this abstract class. A reference to this object is obtained through the `JspFactory` object and should not be used by the JSP designer.
`JspFactory`	The JSP container implements this abstract class. A reference to this object is obtained through the static `getDefaultFactory` method of the `JspFactory` class and should not be used by the JSP designer.
`JspWriter`	The JSP container implements this abstract class. A reference to this object is obtained through the `getOut` method of the `PageContext` object and may be used by the JSP designer to effect the response to be sent to the Web client. A reference to this object is also available as the implicit object `Out`.
`PageContext`	The JSP container implements this abstract class. A reference to this object is obtained through the implicit object `pageContext`, which is always available within a JSP. The `pageContext` object is used for interacting with other servlets and JSPs within the Web application through various methods.
`JspException`	When a JSP encounters a problem that is not completely handled, it can throw a `JspException` to indicate the situation. The JSP container has been designed to intercept this exception and return an error page to the Web client in response to the request.
`JspTagException`	When a JSP custom tag handler (to be discussed in Chapter 18) encounters a problem that is not completely handled, it can throw a `JspTagException` to indicate the situation. The JSP container has been designed to intercept this exception and return an error page to the Web client in response to the request.

The JSP Life Cycle

The execution of a JSP occurs within the context of a container whose responsibility it is to manage the life cycle. The life cycle of a JSP consists of the following sequence of events:

- Translation phase—Prior to the JSP handling requests, it must be translated into a Java class file implementing the `javax.servlet.jsp.JspPage` interface. This class may then be instantiated by the JSP container to handle the requests for the JSP. This is done only once for each JSP, either at the time the page is requested or prior to the request being received.

- Request phase—When the JSP container receives a request for a specific JSP, the Java class created during the translation phase will be instantiated to handle it. This is done once for each request that the JSP container receives. Instances of the servlet class may be reused by multiple requests, but that is determined and handled by the JSP container.

- Initialization—After the JSP has been instantiated by the JSP container, the JSP container calls the `jspInit` method on the JSP before sending a request to it. The `jspInit` method allows the JSP to prepare itself to handle a request, but it is optional and does not need to be defined.

- Destruction—When a JSP container determines that it is necessary to destroy an instance of a JSP, the `jspDestroy` method is called. The `jspDestroy` method provides the JSP the opportunity clean up any resources it used. This method is optional and does not need to be implemented by the JSP designer.

Handling Client Requests

This section discusses handling HTTP requests within a JSP with a focus on the following elements provided by the JSP specification:

- Objects
- Directives
- Scripting element: Declarations
- Scripting element: Expressions
- Scripting element: Scriptlets
- JSP comments
- Standard actions

The combination of the preceding elements interspersed with template data constitutes the JSP. *Template data* is the text that should be ignored by the JSP container and passed straight through as part of the response to the client request. During the translation phase of each JSP, the preceding elements along with the template data are translated into Java code and placed into a servlet. The JSP container executes the corresponding servlet to process each request received for a JSP and generate the content to be returned to the client.

Objects

While processing a request, the JSP can create any number of objects and variables. The JSP specification defines four scopes to which the objects can be associated. Each scope reflects the extent that the objects will be preserved between pages within the Web application. Table 17.2 lists the scopes available to the objects and their definitions.

TABLE 17.2 JSP Scope Definitions

Name of Scope	Definition
Page	All objects created with a Page scope are available only during the processing of the current JSP. The references to the object will be released when the response is returned to the client or the processing of the request is forwarded to another resource.
Request	All objects created with a Request scope are available during the processing of the current client request. The objects will be available until the response is sent back to the client even if the current request is forwarded to another resource for processing. The references to the object will be released when the response is returned to the client.
Session	All objects created with a Session scope are used in session tracking. The objects will be available to the user associated with the session until the session either times out or is invalidated. The references to the object will be released when the session is destroyed.
Application	All objects created with an Application scope are available throughout the entire Web application. An object with application scope is often used for the maintenance of limited resources that are to be available applicationwide, such as database connections. The references to the object will be released when the Web application is unloaded from the container.

Implicit objects are automatically provided to the JSP designer to assist in processing the client request. They represent local variables that can be used throughout the JSP. Table 17.3 lists the implicit objects that the JSP container provides along with the scope associated with each.

TABLE 17.3 JSP Implicit Objects

Name	Scope	Purpose
`Page`	Page	The `Page` object represents the servlet class that implements the JSP. This provides direct access to the methods and variables declared as part of the servlet class or any of its parents.
`Config`	Page	The `Config` object implements the `javax.servlet.ServletConfig` interface. This object provides access to retrieve any servlet initialization parameters and the servlet context.
`Request`	Request	The `Request` object implements the `javax.servlet.ServletRequest` interface. If the HTTP is being used, it implements the `javax.servlet.http.HttpServletRequest` interface. This object contains the request received by the JSP.
`Response`	Page	The `Response` object implements the `javax.servlet.ServletResponse` interface. If the HTTP is being used, it implements the `javax.servlet.http.HttpServletResponse` interface. This object contains the response object to be returned to the client making the request.
`Out`	Page	The `Out` object is an instance of the `javax.servlet.jsp.JspWriter` class. This represents the output stream that will be sent from the JSP back to the client making the request.
`Session`	Session	The `Session` object implements the `javax.servlet.http.HttpSession` interface and represents the session associated with a single user. This object allows for the storing and retrieval of attributes/objects between pages accessed by the individual user.
`Application`	Application	The `Application` object implements the `javax.servlet.ServletContext` interface. This object represents the context of the entire application. This object allows for the storing and retrieval of attributes/objects that will be available to all pages in the entire application. This could be a resource such as a database connection pool that should be accessible by the entire application.
`PageContext`	Page	The `PageContext` object implements the `javax.servlet.jsp.PageContext` interface. This object represents the individual JSP being processed. Because this object represents the individual page, it provides methods to retrieve and work with all attributes and objects available to the page whether the scope is Page, Request, Session, or Application.

TABLE 17.3 Continued

Name	Scope	Purpose
`Exception`	Page	The `Exception` object is an instance of the `java.lang.Throwable class`. This object is available only to those JSPs that have the `isErrorPage` directive set to True. This object is used to retrieve information regarding a particular exception that occurred.

Directives

Directives are a set of markup tags that serve as messages and information to the JSP container to control the various aspects of how the JSP is to be processed. Three types of directives are available for use:

- Tag library
- Page
- Include

The tag library directive permits additional libraries of custom actions in the form of markup tags to be available to the page designer beyond the standard actions defined in the JSP specification. These custom tag libraries will be discussed in Chapter 18. The following shows the syntax of the tag library directive.

```
<%@ taglib uri="tagLibraryURI" prefix="tagPrefix" %>
```

`tagLibraryURI` contains a resource path where the JSP container can find the tag library.

`tagPrefix` is a set of characters that will serve as an alias to identify the tags in the JSP that use this tag library.

The page directive provides a mechanism for a number of properties regarding the JSP to be communicated to the JSP container. Each of the properties takes a single value that controls a specific aspect of the processing of the JSP by the container. The following shows the syntax of the page directive. The page directive has 12 properties that are considered attributes of the page directive. Multiple properties may be set in a single page directive by listing all the properties as additional attributes within the tag. The following shows the syntax of the tag library directive setting a single property, but simply listing them as additional attributes can set additional properties.

```
<%@ page propertyName="value1" %>
```

propertyName represents one of 12 properties to be set.

value1 represents the value to set the named property to.

Table 17.4 lists the 12 page properties that can be set with the page directive.

TABLE 17.4 Page Directive Properties (Attributes)

Property	Definition
info	Allows a documentation string to be set for the JSP. After the page has been translated to a servlet, this information can be retrieved using the getServletInfo method of the Page object.
language	Specifies the scripting language to be used within the JSP. This is typically only Java.
contentType	Specifies the MIME type of the content of the response generated by the JSP. If the output generated from the JSP is HTML, this property takes the format of the following example: `<%@ page contentType="text/html" %>` If this property is not set, the JSP container assumes that the MIME should be "text/html".
pageEncoding	Specifies the character set that will be used in the response generated from this JSP. The character set is ISO-8859-1 by default.
extends	When the JSP is translated into a servlet, this property specifies the class from which the servlet should be extended. If the JSP is to handle the HTTP, the specified class must implement the javax.servlet.jsp.HttpJspPage interface. For any other protocol, the specified class should implement the javax.servlet.jsp.JspPage interface. When this property is not set, the JSP container extends a class of its choosing for the resultant servlet.
import	Specifies the list of Java packages and classes that the JSP is to import. This property serves the same purpose as the import statement in Java class files.
session	Specifies whether this JSP should participate in session tracking. If this property is set to false, the implicit session object will not be available on this page.
buffer	Controls whether and how buffering will be implemented on this JSP. If buffering is not used, the output is immediately sent to the client as the response is generated instead of waiting until after it is generated. This also controls the minimum size of the buffer by specifying a size.
autoFlush	Specifies whether the JSP container should automatically send the contents of the response buffer if it reaches capacity. If this property is set to false and the response buffer reaches capacity, an exception is raised instead of sending the response to the client.
isThreadSafe	Specifies whether the JSP should be considered capable of handling processing by multiple threads simultaneously. Setting this property to true is similar to having a servlet implement the javax.servlet.SingleThreadModel interface.

TABLE 17.4 Continued

Property	Definition
errorPage	Specifies a page to be displayed if an uncaught exception occurs while processing a request on the page. The value represents either an absolute or a relative URL within the context of the Web application.
isErrorPage	Specifies whether this JSP should be considered an error page. If the value is true, the implicit exception object will be available for use on the page.

The include directive permits a JSP to include the text of additional files into its own page. The raw text of the file is included into the main JSP without translation or processing prior to the translation phase. This means that the file to be included does not even have to be a JSP; it could simply be a file containing plain text, a JSP fragment, or anything else that is desired. This is useful in that common textual constructs, such as headers or footers, can be portioned off into their own JSP fragments that can be included as needed in constructing a JSP. The following shows the syntax of the include directive:

```
<%@ include file="relativeURL" %>
```

The `relativeURL` contains a reference to the file to be included relative to the location of the current JSP.

Scripting Elements

For the JSP to process the client request and to assemble dynamic content, it is often necessary to manipulate the implicit objects discussed previously as well as other Java APIs and custom code. To facilitate this, the JSP specification provides three types of scripting elements—declarations, expressions, and scriptlets—that are executed in response to a client request. The most common language used for the scripting is Java, but other scripting languages can be made available through the JSP container. For the purpose of this book, we will assume Java is the scripting language because that is available in JBuilder.

Declarations

Declarations provide a means for variables, methods, and other constructs to be declared that can be used in the scripting elements throughout the entire JSP. The declarations are processed and made available to the rest of the JSP prior to the JSP container passing a client request to it for processing. The declarations can even be used by other declarations on the same page. The following shows the syntax of the declaration scripting element:

```
<%! declaration(s) %>
```

The `declaration(s)` contains one or more statements that declare a variable or method. A declaration for an integer variable called `iCount` follows:

```
<%! private int iCount = 0 %>
```

The variable `iCount` then is available to be used in expressions, scriptlets, and even other declarations. A method could be declared with the name of `jspInit` or `jspDestroy` to respond to the corresponding life cycle events discussed previously.

Expressions

Expressions provide a means to generate dynamic content to be output with the rest of the template data. When the client request is processed, the expression tag is replaced by a string representation of the results of the expression. The following shows the syntax of the expression scripting element:

```
<%= expression %>
```

If the value of one of the request parameters is needed as output in the response, the following expression could be used to generate it:

```
<%= request.getParameter("param1") %>
```

The output of the call to the `getParameter` method is placed at the precise location in the response that the expression tag is placed. The white space surrounding the tag is preserved.

Scriptlets

Scriptlets can represent any code fragment valid for the scripting language, in this case Java. Any Java code can be placed into a scriptlet on a JSP. The code is executed when it is processing a client request and can serve to implement any valid logic for handling the request. The following shows the syntax of the scriptlet scripting element:

```
<% scriptlet %>
```

The scriptlet defined within the preceding tag can be a partial statement or a complete statement. It is required that all the code fragments within the various scriptlets on a JSP combine to be a series of complete statements. This is an important feature that is used when implementing if/then/else statements or loops within the scriptlets. Listing 17.2 shows a fragment of a JSP that generates a table using a `for` loop encapsulated between scriptlet tags. As an alternative to using scriptlets as shown, custom tag libraries can be developed to encapsulate the code as explained in Chapter 18.

LISTING 17.2 JSP Fragment Containing a `for` Loop

```
<table border=1>
<tr><td>Id</td><td>Title</td><td>Description</td></tr>
<%
  for (Iterator iter = oOperation.browseCourses(null).iterator() ;
       iter.hasNext() ; ) {
      CourseData course = (CourseData)iter.next();
      if (course != null) {
%>
<tr><td><%= course.getId() %></td>
    <td><%= course.getTitle() %></td>
    <td><%= course.getDescription() %></td></tr>
<%
      };
  }
%>
</table>
```

The `for` loop within Listing 17.2 loops through a list of courses and generates an HTML table with one row for each course. The `for` loop begins in one scriptlet, and the closing bracket is placed in a second scriptlet. The HTML code that is to be repeated is placed between the scriptlets. Each time through the `for` loop, the HTML code for the row is output in the response. This results in a table containing a dynamic number of rows based on the number of courses in the list.

JSP Comments

At times, it is necessary to introduce comments into the JSP that are to be ignored by the JSP container and not sent to the client in the response. The following shows the syntax of the of a JSP comment:

```
<%-- comment --%>
```

Any text placed within this tag will be completely ignored by the JSP container at translation time and as a result will not exist in the created servlet and will not show up in the generated output to the client.

Standard Actions

The scriptlet scripting element discussed previously provides a means to create dynamic content generation, but requires the inclusion of Java code directly in the JSP. The JSP specification provides a mechanism called *actions* that attempts to minimize the amount of Java code inserted into the JSP. The actions are sets of XML tags that encapsulate logic used to generate the dynamic content for sending back to the client. There are two types of actions: *standard actions* and *custom actions*. The custom actions are defined within custom tag libraries and will be discussed in Chapter 18. The standard actions are available by default and implement several functionalities commonly required within JSPs.

All the logic implemented by actions, both custom and standard, can be implemented using the scripting elements discussed previously. To reduce and possibly eliminate the need to place any Java code within the JSP, it is recommended to use the standard actions where possible and, if appropriate, custom actions.

Table 17.5 lists the nine standard actions, each with its own tag, that all fall within the XML namespace associated with the `jsp` prefix.

TABLE 17.5 JSP Standard Actions

Standard Action	Purpose
`jsp:useBean`	Makes a Bean accessible to the JSP either by retrieving it from the specified scope or by creating an instance if it does not exist
`jsp:setProperty`	Sets properties on a Bean either from the request parameters or with specified values
`jsp:getProperty`	Retrieves the value of a specified property from a Bean for inclusion in the generated output
`jsp:include`	Includes the output of one resource into the generated content of another JSP
`jsp:forward`	Forwards the client request onto a second resource for further processing
`jsp:param`	Allows additional parameters to be added to the client request for both include and forward actions
`jsp:plugin`	Generates the HTML required to allow a Java applet to be executed using the Sun Microsystems Java plug-in on the client
`jsp:params`	Allows parameters to be submitted to the applet that is to be run using the Java plug-in
`jsp:fallback`	Provides text that should be displayed if the Java plug-in cannot be started to run the applet

JSP and JavaBeans

While processing a request, it is often necessary to use logic that has already been implemented in existing Java APIs and other JavaBeans. One way to use these existing Java classes is to directly embed the required Java code in the JSP using the scriptlets previously discussed.

To limit the amount of Java code directly placed into a JSP, you can use the following standard actions designed to work with JavaBeans:

- `jsp:useBean`
- `jsp:setProperty`
- `jsp:getProperty`

As long as the names of the properties on the Bean follow the JavaBeans specification, these actions will work. After a Bean is associated with the JSP, the Bean can be accessed directly through scriptlets or using the `jsp:setProperty` and the `jsp:getProperty` standard actions.

We will review the functionality of each of the preceding actions followed by an example of their usage.

`jsp:useBean`

The `jsp:useBean` action encapsulates the logic required to make an instance of the JavaBean accessible to the rest of the JSP. Several attributes are available to the action:

- `id`
- `scope`
- `class`
- `type`
- `beanName`

Essentially, the JSP attempts to access an object with the `id` and the `scope` specified. If the object does not exist, the object will be created using either the `beanName` or the `class` depending on which is provided and associated with the specified scope. After a reference to the Bean is created, the Bean will be cast to the interface or class specified in the `type` attribute. This Bean will now be accessible throughout the rest of the JSP. The following shows the syntax of the `jsp:useBean` action tag:

```
<jsp:useBean id="LoginId" scope="session"
  class="com.sams.ch17.Login" />
```

This command creates an object named `LoginId` with a session scope using the class `com.sams.ch17.Login`. Because this object has the scope set as session, after the object is created, it will be accessible to users associated with the session from any JSP.

`jsp:setProperty`

The `jsp:setProperty` action encapsulates the logic required to set any public property on the Bean created with the `jsp:useBean` action. Several attributes are available:

- name
- property
- param
- value

The jsp:setProperty action attempts to set a property on the existing Bean with the specified name. This Bean can be used to simply set the properties of the Bean with the values passed to the JSP as parameters. The name attribute contains the name of the Bean to set properties on. This matches the id attribute of the jsp:useBean action. The property attribute contains the property that is to be set on the Bean. The param attribute specifies the request parameter received by the JSP whose value should be used to set the property. The value attribute contains the specific value to be set on the property.

If the property attribute is specified with a * rather than the exact property name, the action attempts to set any public property that matches a parameter of the same name with the value of the parameter. Neither the param nor the value attribute should be provided in this case.

If the property attribute is specified, only that property on the Bean will be set. If neither the param nor the value attribute is provided, the property will be set with a request parameter of the same name. If the value attribute is set, the property will be set to the value specified. If the param attribute is specified, the property will be set to the value of the matching request parameter name.

The following shows the syntax of the jsp:setProperty action tag:

```
<jsp:setProperty name="LoginId" property="username" value="myname" />
```

This action tag sets the username property on the LoginId Bean to the value myname.

jsp:getProperty

The jsp:getProperty action encapsulates the logic required to set any public property on the Bean created with the jsp:useBean action. Two attributes are available:

- name
- property

The jsp:getProperty action attempts to retrieve the value of the specified property from the specified Bean. The entire tag is replaced by the value retrieved when processed, sending only the value as the generated content. The following shows the syntax of the jsp:getProperty action tag:

```
<jsp:getProperty name="LoginId" property="username"/>
```

This action tag retrieves the value of the `username` property on the `LoginId` Bean.

Listing 17.3 and Listing 17.4 contain code for a complete JSP and JavaBean that simply displays the initial values for the `username` and `password` properties retrieved from the Bean.

LISTING 17.3 Login.jsp

```
<html>
<head>
<title>
Login
</title>
</head>
<jsp:useBean id="LoginId" scope="session" class="com.sams.ch17.Login" />
<body>
<form action="Login.jsp" method="POST">
UserName:
<input name="username"
       value="<jsp:getProperty name="LoginId" property="username"/>"><br>
Password:
<input type="password"
       name="password"
       value="<jsp:getProperty name="LoginId" property="password"/>"><br>
<input type="submit" name="Submit" value="Login">
<input type="reset" value="Reset">
</form>
</body>
</html>
```

Listing 17.4 contains the code for the JavaBean used by the JSP file in Listing 17.3.

LISTING 17.4 Login.java

```
package com.sams.ch17;

public class Login {
  private String username = "MyName";
  private String password = "MyPassword";

  public String getUsername() {
```

LISTING 17.4 Continued

```
    return username;
  }
  public void setUsername(String newValue) {
    if (newValue!=null) {
      username = newValue;
    }
  }
  public String getPassword() {
    return password;
  }
  //Access sample property
  public void setPassword(String newValue) {
    if (newValue!=null) {
      password = newValue;
    }
  }
}
```

Reviewing the code between Listings 17.3 and 17.4, you will notice that the JSP (Login.jsp) can use the functionality provided by the JavaBean (Login.java) using only the standard action tags and no Java code. This is significant in that it demonstrates the capability to minimize the mixing of Java code within the HTML code created by the Web designer.

JSP and Servlets

Servlets can forward requests to other servlets and include the output of other servlets in their responses. Similarly, JSPs can forward requests to other servlets for additional processing and generation of the final content. JSPs also can include content generated in other resources as part of their own generated content.

Because JSPs are based on the Servlet API, the mechanisms available to servlets have been inherited and are available. Both forwards and includes can be implemented using scriptlets and explicitly calling the `RequestDispatcher` methods from the Servlet API. To simplify the capability for JSPs to forward requests or include content, the following standard actions were created as part of the JSP API:

- `jsp:forward`
- `jsp:include`
- `jsp:param`

This section discusses how these standard actions work and shows examples of syntax.

jsp:forward

The jsp:forward action encapsulates the logic required to forward the request to another resource within the Web application. The only attribute is the page to which the request should be forwarded. If additional parameters need to be added to the request prior to being forwarded, the jsp:param should be used. The following shows the syntax of the jsp:forward action tag:

```
<jsp:forward page="Login.jsp" />
```

This statement forwards the client request to the Login.jsp page for further processing. In addition to the original request object being available to the Login.jsp page, the implicit Application and Session objects will be available to the targeted resource.

jsp:include

The jsp:include action encapsulates the logic required to include the content generated by a specified resource within the Web application. Two attributes are available:

- page
- flush

The page attribute specifies the resource whose generated content should be included in the originating JSP. If the flush attribute is set to true, the currently generated content will be sent to the client prior to the content being received from the included resource. If additional parameters need to be added to the request prior to being passed to the included resource, the jsp:param action should be used.

The following shows the syntax of the jsp:include action tag:

```
<jsp:include page="Header.jsp" flush="false" />
```

This includes the content generated from the Header.jsp page into the output from the main JSP. The generated content from the initial JSP will not be sent to the client until after the content from Header.jsp is received. The original client request, as well as the Application and the Session objects that had been available to the initial JSP will continue to be available to the targeted resource.

jsp:param

The jsp:param action encapsulates the logic required to append additional request parameters to a request prior to performing the jsp:include or jsp:forward action. Two attributes are available:

- name
- value

The name attribute specifies the name of the parameter to be added to the request, and the value attribute specifies the value for the parameter.

The following example shows the syntax of the jsp:param action tag as used by the jsp:include action:

```
<jsp:include page="Login.jsp" flush="false">
    <jsp:param name="username" value="myname" />
</jsp:include>
```

The following example shows the syntax of the jsp:param action tag as used by the jsp:forward action:

```
<jsp:forward page="Login.jsp" >
    <jsp:param name="username" value="myname" />
</jsp:forward>
```

In both the preceding examples, the jsp:param action adds the parameter "username" to the request prior to passing it to the Login.jsp page.

Usage

The capabilities to forward requests to other resources or to include the content from other resources can be powerful design tools in the architecture of Web-based applications. The application of JSPs to the MVC design pattern, as discussed in previous chapters, provides a strategy for separating the logic from the presentation. A servlet often serves as the controller mechanism that receives and processes all the Web requests and redirects or forwards the request to a JSP for the generation of the Web interface. We will use this strategy at the end of the chapter as we redesign the Login servlet from the Chapter 16 "In Practice" section to use JSPs.

Debugging

The JSP API is based on the Servlet API discussed in Chapter 16. Because of this dependence, the process of debugging a Web-based application using JSPs is practically identical to that of debugging a Web-based application that does not use JSPs.

Several items are important when it comes to building the JSP and the subsequent execution within the JBuilder environment. JSPs are typically not translated into servlets until the first time the Web application attempts to access the page. Errors can occur during the translation phase from the text document into the servlet. To catch defects during the development process, JBuilder allows the developer to force the translation of JSPs into servlets during the build process as a means to check for errors. Figure 17.1 shows the JSP configuration tab that controls various aspects of how JBuilder builds JSPs during development. The JSP Build tab is available from the Project Properties window.

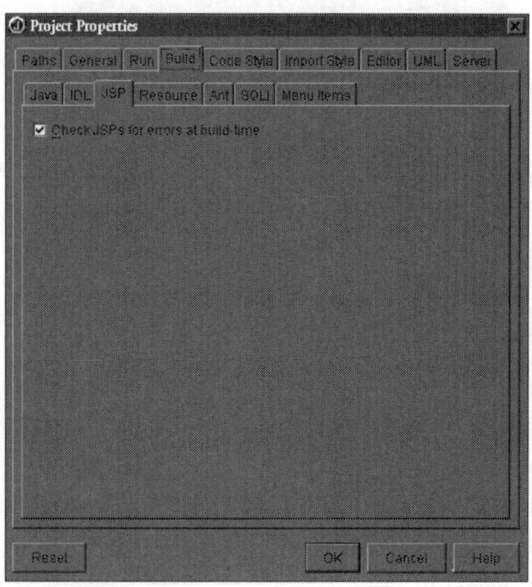

FIGURE 17.1 JSP Build Project Properties.

If you want the JBuilder environment to force translation of the JSP into a servlet during development, the Check JSPs for errors at build-time check box should be checked. This property is applied to all JSPs within the project.

If a file is a partial JSP and is intended to be included in another JSP using the include directive, it should not be translated into a servlet during the build process. It will generate unnecessary errors. JBuilder provides a means to mark individual JSPs as not needing to be checked for errors while still maintaining the projectwide setting. Figure 17.2 shows the properties window for an individual JSP file in the project.

If the JSP file should not be checked for errors during the build process, the Check JSPs for errors at build-time check box should not be checked.

During the debug process for a particular JSP, breakpoints can be added in the same way as is done with other Java classes. The main difference is that breakpoints can be added only to lines that contain either scriptlet or expression scripting elements. Other than that, they will behave as in any other Java source file.

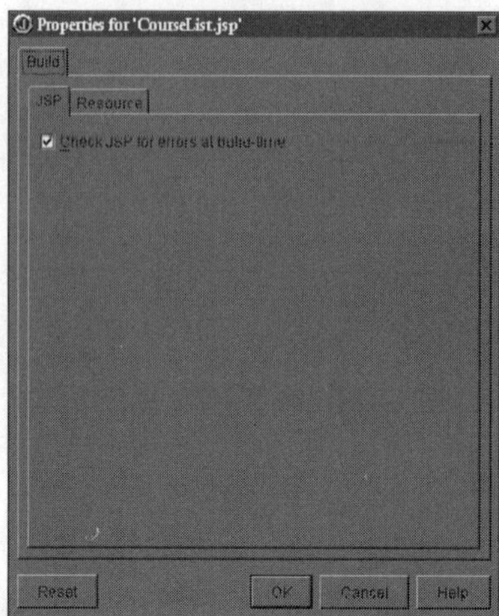

FIGURE 17.2 Properties window for a specific JSP file.

Deployment

The deployment for a Web application, whether it includes any JSPs or not, is essentially the same as that described in Chapter 16. When the JSP Wizard is used in JBuilder to create the framework for a JSP, the JSP is not registered with the deployment descriptor for the Web application. The identification of the JSP is not required in the deployment descriptor unless there is a need to define initialization parameters, filters, and other settings specific to the JSP. The configuration entries for a JSP are essentially the same as that for a servlet with only slight differences. We will look at the technique in JBuilder to register a JSP in the deployment descriptor.

After the JSP is created, it can be registered in the deployment descriptor. We will look at the process for registering a JSP by the name of CourseList.jsp. Figure 17.3 shows the WebApp Deployment Descriptor editor for the ChalkTalk application.

A new servlet must be added to the deployment descriptor by right-clicking on the Servlets node in the Structure pane as shown in Figure 17.4.

The Add Servlet menu item should be chosen and a name given to the servlet. In this case, the name is `CourseList`. At this point, we need to associate the `CourseList` servlet entry with the JSP that it belongs to. Figure 17.5 displays the servlet configuration screen in the Content pane.

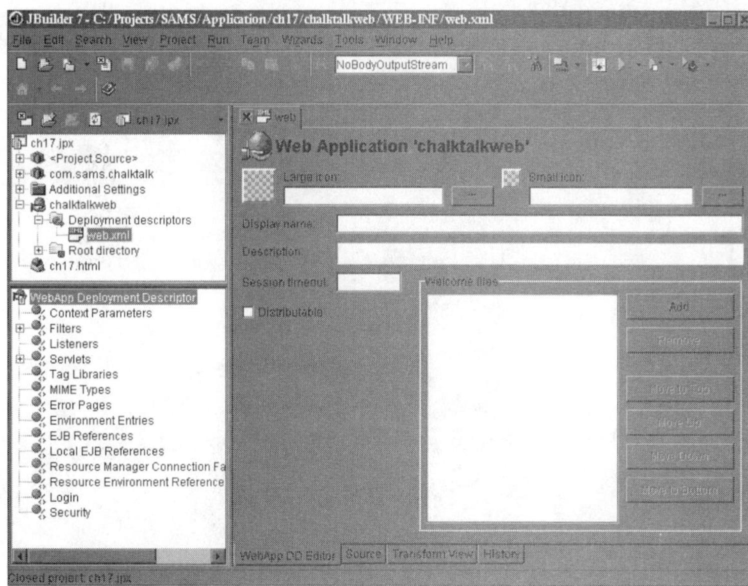

FIGURE 17.3 JSP registration: WebApp DD editor.

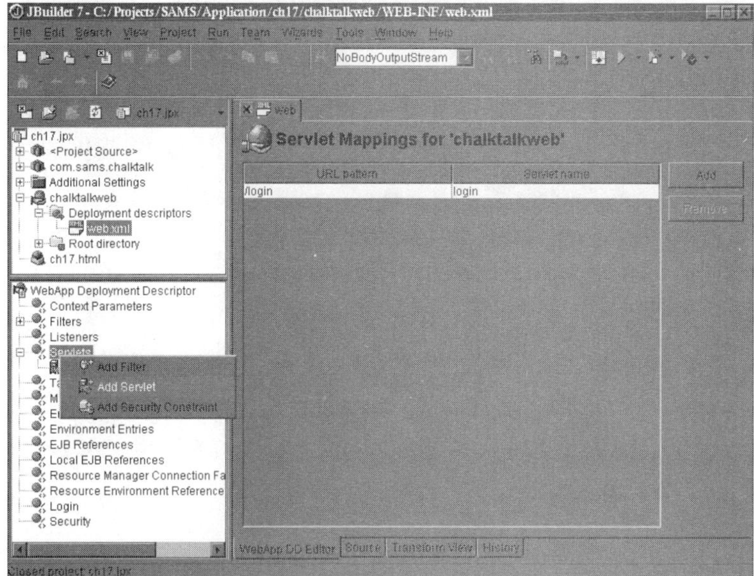

FIGURE 17.4 JSP registration: Add Servlet context menu.

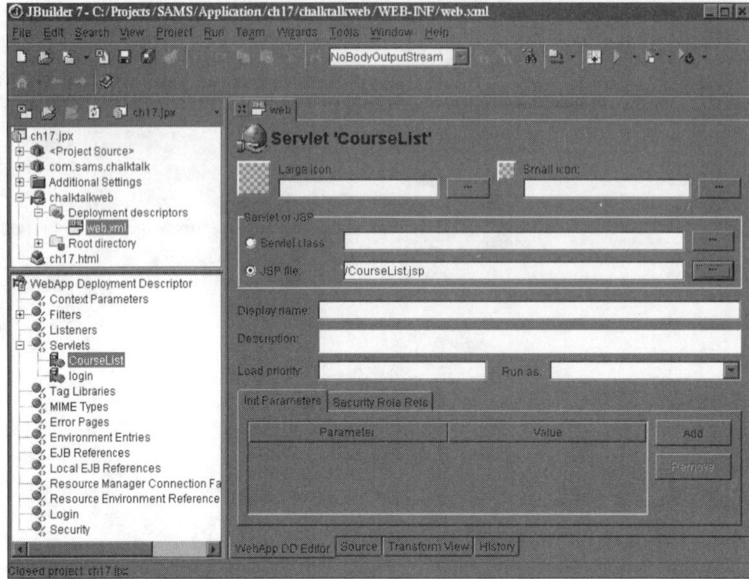

FIGURE 17.5 JSP registration: Servlet configuration screen.

As shown in Figure 17.5, we click on the JSP File radio button and enter the value `/CourseList.jsp` in the text box. At this point, the JSP is registered in the deployment descriptor allowing for filters, initialization parameters, and other settings to be chosen.

In Practice

Now that we have looked at the structure of the JSP API and what JSPs are, we'll adjust the Web-based interface for the ChalkTalk application to use JSPs as the Web interface.

The chalktalkweb application from Chapter 16 uses two Web pages generated from servlets. We will redesign the chalktalkweb application to perform the same functionality but have the HTML pages generated from JSPs rather than the servlets. The redesign of the chalktalkweb interface demonstrates the facilities within JBuilder to work with JSPs.

We will create the Web interface as a simple Web application called chalktalkweb, which demonstrates the steps involved in creating JSPs. The new chalktalkweb application simply provides a Web page to display the results of the `browseCourses` method in the `com.sams.chalktalkuserservices.CommonOperations` class. The Login process from the previous chalktalkweb application will be divided into a JSP and an accompanying servlet to process the logic.

To give you an idea of where we are going, here is a summarized list of all the steps we will perform in this "In Practice" section:

1. Create a project and Web application.
2. Design a View Course List JSP.
3. Design a Login JSP.
4. Design the Login servlet.
5. Configure the Web application.

Creating a Project and Web Application

We begin by creating a new JBuilder project and inserting a new Web application to be named chalktalkweb. The JSPs and the Java classes created as part of our discussion will be placed within the context of this Web application.

1. Copy the directory named chalktalkapp from the Chapter 17 source code to your hard drive. The Java packages in the chalktalkapp directory represent the class library that our Web-based application will be using to provide the business logic.
2. Select File, New Project.
3. On the first screen of the Project Wizard, enter **`ch17`** as the name of the project and **`C:\Projects\SAMS\Application\ch17`** as the directory. Leave the type as jpx, the Template as (Default Project), and check the Generate project notes file check box. You can put your project in a different directory, but at least make sure that the last component is `ch17`. This simplifies the process of following the steps outlined in this section. Click Next.
4. On the second screen of the Project Wizard, add a reference to include the source files from the existing ChalkTalk application. Click on the Add button next to the tab labeled as Source to bring up a dialog box and search for the location where the chalktalkapp directory was copied in step 1. After the directory is located, click on the OK button to close the dialog box. The chalktalkapp directory will be listed in the list box on the Source tab. Click Next.
5. On the third screen, enter your name in the @author field and your company name in the Company field. Click Finish.
6. Select File, New to bring up the Object Gallery. On the Web tab, double-click on the Web Application icon to bring up the Web Application Wizard. The Web Application icon might be disabled if a server has not been set up to run the JSPs and servlets for the project. In the section "Debugging" in Chapter 16, we looked at the process needed to configure the JSP/Servlet server for a project.

7. On the screen, enter **`chalktalkweb`** as the name and **`C:/Projects/SAMS/Application/ch17/chalktalkweb`** as the directory name. Uncheck the Generate WAR check box. This controls whether JBuilder generates a WAR file for our Web application during each build of the application. For the purposes of our discussion, leave this check box unchecked. Click OK.

We now have an empty Web application available that will serve as the basis to create the new Web interface for the existing ChalkTalk application. Next, we will create a JSP to display the results of the `browseCourses` method in the `com.sams.chalktalk.userservices.CommonOperations` class.

Designing a View Course List JSP

We will design the View Course List Web page to contain two sections. The top section shows a menu of links to the other aspects of our Web application, and the bottom section displays the list of courses. For the purposes of our ChalkTalk application, we will design only a single page of our Web interface leaving our menu to contain only the View Course List link.

1. Select File, New to bring up the Object Gallery. On the Web tab, double-click on the Java Server Page icon to bring up the JSP Wizard.
2. On the first screen of the JSP Wizard, make sure that chalktalkweb is specified as the Web App for this JSP. Enter **`CourseList`** as the name of the JSP. Uncheck the Generate Submit Form check box. Uncheck the Declare InternetBeans tag library check box. Uncheck the Generate Error Page and the Generate Sample Bean check boxes. Click Next.
3. On the second screen of the JSP Wizard, no changes are needed. Click Next.
4. On the third screen of the JSP Wizard, check the Create a runtime configuration check box. Enter **`CourseList - JSP`** as the name of the runtime configuration and leave the base configuration as none. Click Finish.
5. Attempt to run the project from the Run, Run Project menu (shortcut key is F9) to verify that all the settings have been correctly set up and are working. The output is simply that of the CourseList JSP that we have created, displaying the message "JBuilder Generated JSP."

We now have a basic Web application that can run containing the default JBuilder generated JSP. Next we will customize this JSP to display the list of courses:

1. Open the CourseList JSP file in the Content pane and switch to the Source tab at the bottom. The code should look like a plain HTML file.

2. Replace the existing HTML code with the code in Listing 17.5. The new logic creates a reference to an instance of the `CommonOperations` class, using the Application scope. This object is used to retrieve the list of courses to be displayed on the Web page.

LISTING 17.5 In Practice: CourseList.jsp

```
<html>
<head>
<title>
CourseList
</title>
</head>
<%@ page import="com.sams.chalktalk.userservices.CommonOperations" %>
<%@ page import="com.sams.chalktalk.dataobjects.CourseData" %>
<%@ page import="java.util.Iterator" %>
<jsp:useBean id="oOperation"
             scope="application"
             class="com.sams.chalktalk.userservices.CommonOperations" />
<body>
<A HREF="<%= response.encodeURL("login?Submit=Logout")%>">Logout</A>
<A HREF="<%= response.encodeURL("CourseList.jsp")%>">View Course List</A>
<HR>

<table border=1>
<tr><td>Id</td><td>Title</td><td>Description</td></tr>
<%
  for (Iterator iter = oOperation.browseCourses(null).iterator() ;
       iter.hasNext() ; ) {
      CourseData course = (CourseData)iter.next();
      if (course != null) {
%>
<tr><td><%= course.getId() %></td>
    <td><%= course.getTitle() %></td>
    <td><%= course.getDescription() %></td></tr>
<%
      };
  }
%>
</table>

</body>
</html>
```

3. Run the project to verify that the changes are working. Figure 17.6 shows the output of the CourseList JSP while running the project within JBuilder.

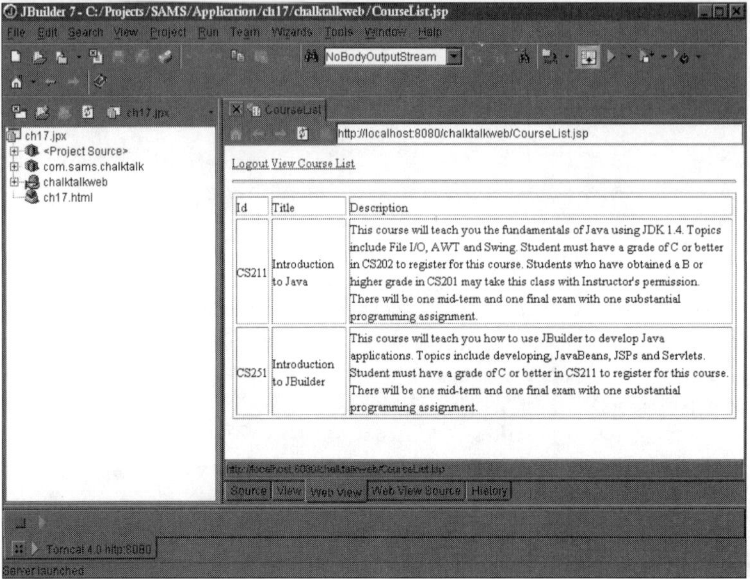

FIGURE 17.6 Output of the CourseList.jsp page.

4. After reviewing the output and confirming that it works, stop the Web application from running before moving to the next section. This can be accomplished by clicking on the red button in the bottom left of Figure 17.6 just above the words "Tomcat 4.0."

The Web application now displays the results of the call to the `browseCourses` method of the `CommonOperations` class.

Designing a Login JSP

We will design the Login JSP to provide a screen that allows the user to enter his username and password:

1. Select File, New to bring up the Object Gallery. On the Web tab, double-click on the Java Server Page icon to bring up the JSP Wizard.

2. On the first screen of the JSP Wizard, make sure that chalktalkweb is specified as the Web application for this JSP. Enter **`Login`** as the name of the JSP. Uncheck the Generate Submit Form check box. Uncheck the Declare

InternetBeans tag library check box. Uncheck the Generate Error Page and the Generate Sample Bean check boxes. Click Next.

3. On the second screen of the JSP Wizard, no changes are needed. Click Next.

4. On the third screen of the JSP Wizard, check the Create a runtime configuration check box. Enter **`Login - JSP`** as the name of the runtime configuration and leave the base configuration as none. Click Finish.

5. Open the Login.jsp file in the Content pane and switch to the Source tab at the bottom.

6. Replace the existing HTML code with the code in Listing 17.6. The new logic provides a screen allowing the user to enter a username and password for login to the application. Additionally, session tracking has been supported through a call to the `encodeURL` method to perform URL rewriting if necessary.

LISTING 17.6 In Practice: Login.jsp

```
<html>
<head><title>Course Registration Login</title></head>
<body>
<form action="<%= response.encodeURL("login")%>" method="POST">
UserName: <input name="username"><br>
Password: <input type="password" name="password"><br>
<input type="submit" name="Submit" value="Login">
<input type="reset" value="Reset">
</form>
</body>
</html>
```

7. Run the project to verify that the Login.jsp page can be executed and is correct. Choose the Login - JSP Runtime Configuration from the Choose Runtime Configuration dialog box to view the output of the Login JSP. Figure 17.7 shows the output of the Login JSP while running the project within JBuilder.

8. After reviewing the output and confirming that it works, stop the Web application from running before moving to the next section. This can be accomplished by clicking on the red button in the bottom left of Figure 17.7 just above the words “Tomcat 4.0.”

The Web application now consists of two JSPs that make up the user interface of the redesigned chalktalkweb application.

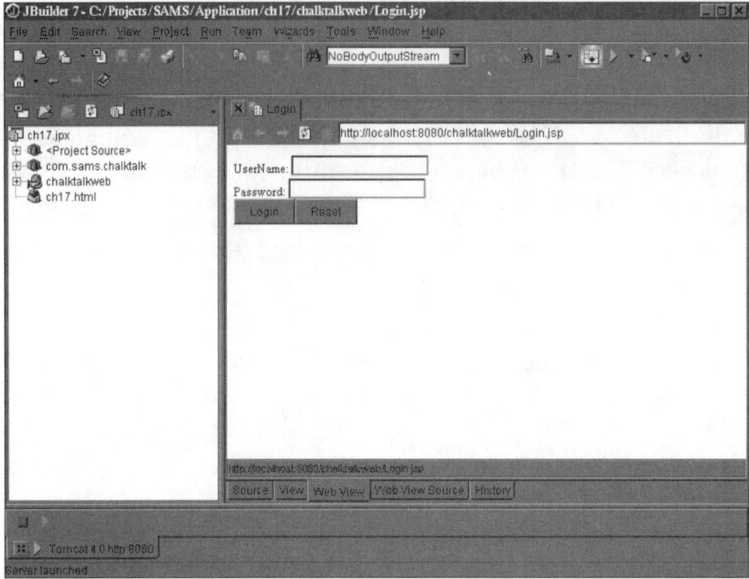

FIGURE 17.7 Output of the Login.jsp page.

Designing the Login Servlet

We will design the Login servlet to implement both the `Login` and the `Logout` methods of the `CommonOperations` class. In implementing these methods, we will demonstrate the use of session tracking to preserve state information across servlets and JSPs. The Login servlet will be designed to perform the following tasks:

- Process requests to log in or log out.
- Redirect the user to the next page.

When the request is received by the servlet, if the `Submit` parameter is set to either Login or Logout, the servlet should perform the operation; otherwise, the servlet should simply redirect the user to the Login.jsp page.

1. Select File, New to bring up the Object Gallery. On the Web tab, double-click on the Servlet icon to bring up the Servlet Wizard.
2. On the first screen of the Servlet Wizard, enter **`com.sams.chalktalk.client.web`** as the name of the package and **`Login`** as the name of the servlet class. Check the Generate header comments check box. Check the Single Thread Model check box. Make sure that chalktalkweb is specified as the Web

application for this servlet. Choose the Standard Servlet radio button and not the Filter or Listener Servlet. Click Next.

3. On the second screen of the Servlet Wizard, check the doGet and the doPost check boxes. This ensures that both a `doGet` and a `doPost` method handler exist in the default servlet. Uncheck the Generate SHTML file check box. Click Next.

4. On the third screen of the Servlet Wizard, no changes are needed. Click Next.

5. On the fourth screen of the Servlet Wizard, no changes are needed. Click Next.

6. On the fifth screen of the Servlet Wizard, check the Create a runtime configuration check box. Enter **`Login - Servlet`** as the name of the runtime configuration and leave the Base configuration as none. Click Finish.

7. Open the Login.java servlet file in the Content pane and switch to the Source tab at the bottom.

8. Add the following statement just below the existing import statements. These classes provide the servlet access to the existing ChalkTalk application business logic.

```
import com.sams.chalktalk.userservices.CommonOperations;
```

9. Add the following statement just below the declaration of the `CONTENT_TYPE` variable.

```
private CommonOperations commonOps;
```

10. Modify the body of the `init` method so that it looks as follows. The `init` method creates a new instance of the `CommonOperations` class if it does not already exist in the application; otherwise, it will be reused.

```
public void init() throws ServletException {
   commonOps =
        (CommonOperations)getServletContext().getAttribute("oOperation");
   if (commonOps == null) {
     commonOps = new CommonOperations();
     getServletContext().setAttribute("oOperation",commonOps);
   }
}
```

11. Modify the body of the `doGet` method so that it looks as shown in Listing 17.7.

LISTING 17.7 In Practice: doGet Method of the Login.java Class

```
public void doGet(HttpServletRequest request, HttpServletResponse response)
                         throws ServletException, IOException {
  response.setContentType(CONTENT_TYPE);

  //Determine operation performed by user
  String sOperation = (String)request.getParameter("Submit");
  if (sOperation == null) {
    sOperation = "";
  }

  //Setup Session Variable
  HttpSession sess = request.getSession();

  //Determine for target after this page
  String sTarget = (String)sess.getAttribute("target");
  if (sTarget == null) {
    sTarget = "CourseList.jsp";
  }

  if (sOperation.equals("Login"))  {
     commonOps.login();
     sess.setAttribute("LoggedIn", new Boolean(true));
     sTarget = response.encodeRedirectURL(sTarget);
  }
  else if (sOperation.equals("Logout")) {
    commonOps.logout();
    sess.invalidate();
  }
  else {
    sTarget = "Login.jsp";
    if (!sess.isNew()) {
      sTarget = response.encodeRedirectURL(sTarget);
    }
  }
  response.sendRedirect(sTarget);
}
```

12. Modify the body of the doPost method so that it looks as follows:

```
public void doPost(HttpServletRequest request,
➥HttpServletResponse response)
```

```
                                  throws ServletException, IOException {
        doGet(request,response);
    }
```

13. Run the project to verify that the Login servlet can be executed and is correct. Choose the Login—Servlet Runtime Configuration from the Choose Runtime Configuration dialog box to view the output of the Login servlet. Figure 17.8 shows the output of the Login servlet while running the project within JBuilder.

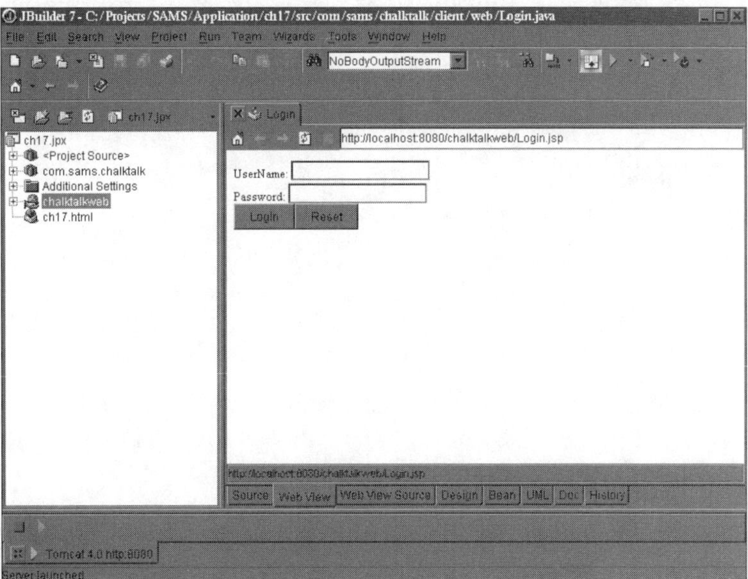

FIGURE 17.8 Output of the Login.java servlet.

14. After reviewing the output and confirming that it works, stop the Web application from running before moving to the next section. This can be accomplished by clicking on the red button in the bottom left of Figure 17.8 just above the words "Tomcat 4.0."

The Web application now consists of two JSPs and a servlet that processes the login and logout logic. When the Login.java servlet was executed previously, the request was redirected to the Login.jsp to generate the Web page for display. If the Login button is clicked, the CourseList.jsp page will be displayed indicating that a successful login occurred. The servlet has been designed to control the login and logout operations of the application. If the client request includes a `Submit` parameter with a value of `Login` or `Logout`, the corresponding action will be processed, followed by a redirection of the client to the appropriate page. If the client request does not include the `Submit` parameter or the parameter contains a value other than `Login` or `Logout`, then the client will be redirected to the Login.jsp to permit the user to log in. The redirection is produced by a call to the `response.sendRedirect` method that forces the client to display the specified URL.

Configuring the Web Application

In Chapter 16, we created a filter with the purpose of intercepting every request to the `CourseList` servlet to require login prior to access. In this section, we will reuse the same `LoginFilter` filter to require login to the application prior to accessing the `CourseList` JSP. We will modify the deployment descriptor for the Web application to ensure that every client request to the `CourseList` JSP is intercepted.

1. Open the deployment descriptor file for the Web application. Figure 17.3 shows the WebApp DD Editor.

2. Right-click in the Structure pane of the WebApp DD Editor and select the Add Filter item from the pop-up menu. Enter **`LoginFilter`** as the filter name in the New Filter dialog box. This creates a node labeled LoginFilter below the Filters node.

3. Set the mappings that indicate what client requests will be intercepted by this filter. Click on the Filters node in the Structure pane to bring up the Filter Mappings list in the Content pane as shown in Figure 17.9. Click on the Add button in the Content pane to create a new filter mapping. Enter **`/CourseList.jsp`** for the URL Mapping and **`LoginFilter`** for the filter.

4. Set the properties for the filter. Click on the LoginFilter node in the Structure pane to bring up the filter properties in the Content pane as shown in Figure 17.10. Enter **`com.sams.chalktalk.client.web.LoginFilter`** for the `Filter` class.

5. Run the project to verify that the filter works. Choose the CourseList—JSP Runtime Configuration from the Choose Runtime Configuration dialog box. Any attempt to access the CourseList.jsp should be redirected to the Login.jsp for authentication if the user has not logged in during the session. When running this application, it may not always force a login before accessing the CourseList.jsp file. This is due to an attempt to persist session information across various runs of the application. A more extensive explanation of the issue is included in the "Session Persistence" sidebar at the end of the Chapter 16 "In Practice" section.

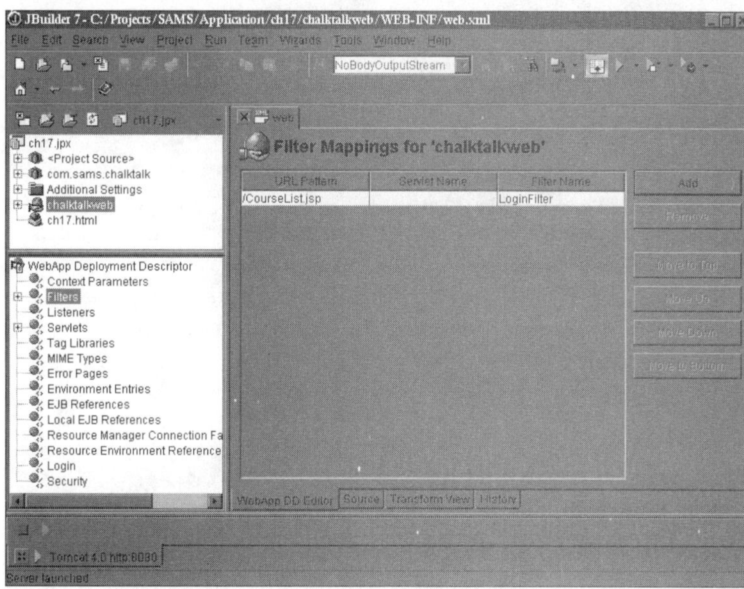

FIGURE 17.9 WebApp DD Editor: Filter Mappings.

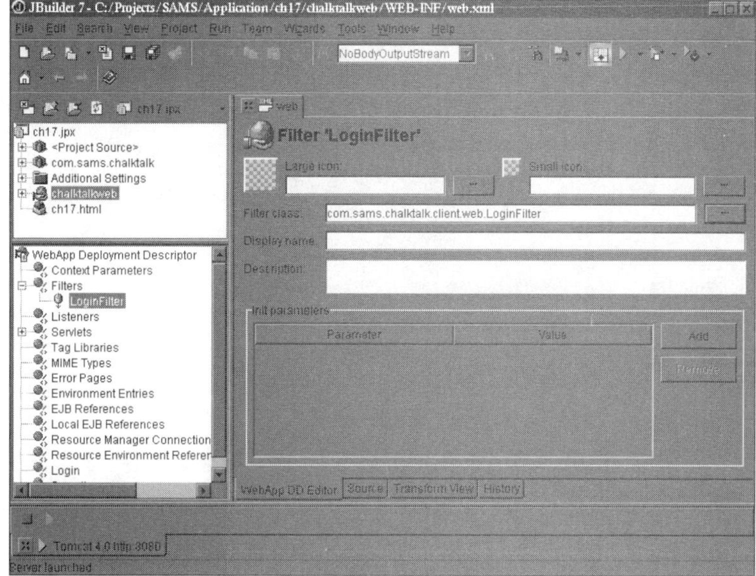

FIGURE 17.10 WebApp DD Editor: Filter Properties.

Summary

The JSP API depends on the strength of Java servlets for creating Web-based applications. As we discussed, JSPs provide a means to support the addition of Java programming to the generation of dynamic content. Unlike servlets, JSPs do not require the Web designer to work in a Java IDE like JBuilder and to compile the page designs into Java classes. With the support for standard and custom actions, JSPs can significantly reduce the amount of Java code intertwined with the page layout and possibly eliminate it completely. As extensions of the Java servlets, JSPs can be intermixed within a Web application to provide flexible content generation while maintaining the power of Java programming. JBuilder provides several wizards and editors to facilitate the development of JSPs.

Reflections

- In Listing 17.5, we set up the `oOperation` variable reference as having application scope. We could also have assigned page, session, or request scope. What are the benefits of using each of these scopes and when would they be used?
- In the "In Practice" section, we used a filter to intercept client requests to the CourseList.jsp to require login access to our protected resource. This requires the addition of a Filter Mapping to the deployment descriptor to enforce this relationship. Is there another way that this could have been implemented using the standard actions and the scriptlets?
- How does the usage of JSPs to implement user interfaces in combination with servlets relate to the Model-View-Controller design pattern often applied in Java programming?

18

Tag Libraries

IN THIS CHAPTER

In Chapter 17, "Java Server Pages," we looked at how custom Java code can be used to create dynamic content using the Java Server Pages (JSP) API. As discussed, the JSP API allows Web content to be designed in a similar fashion to an HTML/XML page, but with the power and the functionality of the Java language to assemble dynamic content. This is an improvement over using servlets in that it does not require the content and design to be translated by a programmer into a servlet for compilation prior to use. In our discussion of JSPs, we reviewed the markup tags and actions that allow for the dynamic content to be included in the pages viewed by the Web client. At times, this requires Java code to be embedded directly into the Web page alongside the static text. In addition to the standard actions provided in the JSP API, custom actions called *tag libraries* can be developed.

In this chapter we will describe the basic structures of tag library development and one way to create a tag library within JBuilder. At the end of the chapter, we will create a simple tag library to encapsulate some of the functionality of our chalktalkweb application and modify the application to use our newly developed tags.

What Is a Tag Library?

A tag library is a set of custom XML tags encapsulating any logic or processing that may be developed in the Java language. The developer of a tag library implements the functionality behind the XML tags using Java classes, called *tag handlers*. The Web page designer will be presented with the set of custom XML tags to be included in any JSP with only an understanding of how to use the tags and not the underlying Java programming.

A tag library can be any set of commonly performed actions such as loops and if-then logic, or it can be highly customized to a particular Web site or business. Using a tag library customized for a particular Web application has the potential of eliminating all Java code from a Web page, yet still supplying the functionality and power of Java to the generation of dynamic content.

A tag library consists of the following two components that may be stored as a single Java archive (JAR) file or maintained as separate files:

- Tag library descriptor (TLD) file
- Tag handler class files

For each XML tag in a tag library, a tag handler must be written in the Java language that implements the `javax.servlet.jsp.tagext.Tag` interface. All tag handlers must implement this interface or subclasses of this interface to allow the JSP container to interact with the Java code while processing a JSP.

As each JSP is translated into a servlet by the JSP container, it is necessary for the JSP container to recognize the custom XML tags and to locate the associated tag handlers. Each tag library must include a TLD file listing the available tags and their usage along with their associated tag handlers. The TLD file is an XML document with the filename extension of .tld, such as chalktalktaglib.tld.

Integrating a Tag Library into a Web Application

We will begin by discussing the basics for integrating a tag library into our Web application; later in the chapter we will discuss how to create the tag library. An understanding of where tag libraries fit into the Web application structure introduced in Chapter 16, "Servlets," and Chapter 17 will provide context to how the code that we develop applies to JSPs. For our discussion, we will assume that a tag library named chalktalktaglib has been developed consisting of two custom XML tags implementing the functionality needed by our chalktalkweb Web application.

For a JSP to use the tag library as a resource for our Web application, four elements need to be set up:

- Deployment of the tag library
- Inclusion of the tag library into a Web application
- Web application deployment descriptor (web.xml)
- Inclusion of a tag library on a JSP

Deployment of the Tag Library

A tag library may either be deployed as a single JAR file or as a set of files to be included within the Web application. If the tag library is to be deployed as a single JAR file, the requirements are the same as for a standard JAR file with the addition of the TLD file to the META-INF directory. Listing 18.1 shows the structure of the contents of the tag library JAR file containing two tag handlers and the TLD file called chalktalktaglib.tld.

LISTING 18.1 Tag Library JAR File

```
/META-INF/MANIFEST.MF
/META-INF/chalktalktaglib.tld
/com/sams/chalktalk/client/taglib/ListTag.class
/com/sams/chalktalk/client/taglib/CourseTag.class
```

Inclusion of the Tag Library into a Web Application

After the tag library has been developed and prepared for deployment, it is necessary to include it as part of the Web application. The location for placing the files is different depending on whether it is contained within a single JAR file or maintained as separate files. Listing 18.2 shows the structure of the Web application contents if the tag library has been maintained as multiple files. For the purpose of comparison, we are using the same two tag classes used in Listing 18.2.

LISTING 18.2 Web Application with Tag Library As Multiple Files

```
(Document Root) chalktalkweb/
 chalktalkweb/courselist.jsp
 chalktalkweb/index.html
 chalktalkweb/WEB-INF/
 chalktalkweb/WEB-INF/web.xml
 chalktalkweb/WEB-INF/tlds/chalktalktaglib.tld
 chalktalkweb/WEB-INF/classes/
 chalktalkweb/WEB-INF/classes/com/sams/chalktalk/client/taglib/ListTag.class
 chalktalkweb/WEB-INF/classes/com/sams/chalktalk/client/taglib/CourseTag.class
 chalktalkweb/WEB-INF/classes/com/sams/chalktalk/client/web/CourseList.class
 chalktalkweb/WEB-INF/lib/
```

Notice in Listing 18.2 that the tag handler classes are placed below the WEB-INF/classes directory alongside the other Java class files in the Web application. The TLD file may be placed in any directory below the WEB-INF directory tree; in Listing 18.2 it was placed in the WEB-INF/tlds directory. Listing 18.3 shows the structure of the same Web application if the tag library had been deployed as a single JAR file named chalktalktaglib.jar. If the decision is made to deploy the tag library as multiple files, it is often good practice to create a subdirectory below WEB-INF to contain all the TLD files, as in Listing 18.2. This is done mainly as a way of organizing the files within the Web application.

LISTING 18.3 Web Application with Tag Library As a JAR File

```
(Document Root) chalktalkweb/
 chalktalkweb/courselist.jsp
 chalktalkweb/index.html
 chalktalkweb/WEB-INF/
 chalktalkweb/WEB-INF/web.xml
chalktalkweb/WEB-INF/classes/
chalktalkweb/WEB-INF/classes/com/sams/chalktalk/client/web/CourseList.class
 chalktalkweb/WEB-INF/lib/chalktalktaglib.jar
```

Notice in Listing 18.3 that the tag library JAR file has been placed within the WEB-INF/lib directory, and there is no separate TLD file. The TLD file is stored within the tag library JAR file and is thus accessible to the Web application. We have looked at two methods for deploying a tag library; each method has its benefits. In development of the tag library, it can be useful to deploy it as multiple files to facilitate the modification and testing of the tag classes. In the actual usage of the tag library in a Web application, it is good practice to create a single JAR containing the TLD file along with all supporting Java class files. This provides a straightforward way of including the tag library in a Web application and to tag class files isolated from the rest of the files in the Web application.

Web Application Deployment Descriptor (web.xml)

A `taglib` element exists within the web.xml file that allows for an explicit listing of all tag libraries contained within the Web application. The `taglib` element is not required, but it is highly recommended as a good way to document all the tag libraries that are to be available for the JSPs in the Web application. The `taglib` element consists of two parts: the location of the TLD file for the tag library and a Universal Resource Identifier (URI) that JSPs are to use for referring to the library. If the `taglib` element is not included in the web.xml file, the JSP can refer to the tag library by specifying the location in the Web application in which the TLD file or the tag library JAR file resides. Listing 18.4 is an excerpt from a web.xml file showing the syntax for the `taglib` element explicitly naming the TLD file as it would be used if the tag library was deployed as individual classes.

LISTING 18.4 Excerpt from a web.xml File: `taglib` Element Referencing a Tag Library JAR

```
<taglib>
<taglib-uri>/chalktalktaglib.tld</taglib-uri>
<taglib-location>/WEB-INF/chalktalktaglib.tld</taglib-location>
</taglib>
```

Listing 18.5 is an excerpt from a web.xml file showing the syntax for the `taglib` element that identifies the tag library JAR file as the location of the TLD file.

LISTING 18.5 Excerpt from a web.xml File: `taglib` Element Referencing the Tag Library JAR

```
<taglib>
<taglib-uri>/chalktalktaglib.tld</taglib-uri>
<taglib-location>/WEB-INF/lib/chalktalktaglib.jar</taglib-location>
</taglib>
```

No two `taglib` elements in a web.xml file are allowed to have the same `taglib-uri` value.

Inclusion of a Tag Library on a JSP

Assuming that the first three elements have been set up within the Web application, any JSP in the Web application can access the tag library. Each JSP that needs to use a custom tag must include a tag library directive identifying the tag library to which the tag belongs. When translating the JSP into a servlet, the JSP container uses the directive to locate the TLD file for the required tag library and identify the custom tags used on the page. Listing 18.6 shows the syntax for the tag library directive.

LISTING 18.6 Tag Library Directive

```
<%@ taglib uri="/chalktalktaglib.tld" prefix="chalk" %>
```

The tag library directive as shown in Listing 18.6 contains two attributes. The `uri` attribute represents either the `taglib-uri` value in the web.xml file as shown in Listing 18.4 and 18.5, or the specific location of the TLD file for the tag library. The prefix attribute represents the XML namespace assigned to all tags from the library that is used in the JSP. If a tag called `singlecourse` were used, it would be identified as `<chalk:singlecourse></chalk:singlecourse>`.

Tag Library Descriptor (TLD) File

Every tag library is required to have a TLD file associated with it. The TLD file serves as a contract describing how the JSP container should interact with it along with a list of the available custom tags. The TLD file is an XML document with its own DTD file specifying its format. Each TLD file has two main sections: the header and the `<taglib>` root element. The header section must include the definition of the XML version and the encoding format along with the appropriate `DOCTYPE` statement identifying the governing DTD. Listing 18.7 is an example of a valid header section for a TLD file. The next section consists of the `<taglib>` root element containing the following 11 subelements listed in Table 18.1.

LISTING 18.7 TLD File Header

```
<?xml version="1.0" encoding="UTF-8"?>
<!DOCTYPE taglib PUBLIC
"-//Sun Microsystems, Inc.//DTD JSP Tag Library 1.2//EN"
"http://java.sun.com/dtd/web-jsptaglibrary_1_2.dtd">
```

TABLE 18.1 TLD File: `taglib` Subelements

Name of Subelement	Role
`tlib-version`	Version number for this Custom Tag library. This number should be incremented by the tag library author as adjustments are made to the library.
`jsp-version`	Contains the JSP specification version number that this tag library requires for proper operation.
`short-name`	Shortened name intended for use by various authoring tools to identify the tag library. This should not contain any spaces and should begin with an alphabetic character.
`uri`	Intended to be a unique identifier for the tag library.
`display-name`	The name of the tag library to be displayed by JSP authoring tools.
`small-icon`	An icon that can be used by JSP authoring tools to identify the tag library.
`large-icon`	An icon that can be used by JSP authoring tools to identify the tag library.
`description`	A textual description detailing the purpose and usage for the tag library.
`validator`	A `TagLibraryValidator` class intended for use by the JSP container for validation of the JSP using this tag library. This class is used during the translation phase of the JSP into a servlet. The `Validator` element contains subelements identifying the Java class along with the associated initialization parameters.

TABLE 18.1 Continued

Name of Subelement	Role
`listener`	The tag library author can specify certain Java classes that should be instantiated by the JSP container to listen for various JSP life cycle events. This element has a single subelement containing the Java class implementing the listener interfaces.
`tag`	Each custom tag in the tag library must have a corresponding `tag` element in this TLD file. This provides the authoritative list of custom tags in the tag library. This element has 11 subelements, listed in Table 18.2.

The `tag` element listed in Table 18.1 contains 11 subelements that describe each custom tag in the library and its intended use. Table 18.2 lists these subelements along with a definition of each subelement's purpose.

TABLE 18.2 TLD File: `tag` Subelements

Name of Subelement	Role
`name`	The name of the custom tag. This is the name that will be used in the JSP to refer to the tag.
`tag-class`	Name of the Java class that handles this custom tag. The class is often referred to as the tag handler.
`tei-class`	`TagExtraInfo` class defined for this custom tag. This class is used for additional validation information for the tag as well as variable definitions.
`body-content`	A value of `empty` means that the tag never contains a body. A value of `JSP` means that the JSP container should interpret the body as JSP markup tags. A value of `tagdependent` means that the JSP container should pass the body to the tag handler without any processing or adjustments.
`display-name`	This is the name of the custom tag to be displayed by JSP authoring tools.
`small-icon`	An icon that can be used by JSP authoring tools to identify the custom tag.
`large-icon`	An icon that can be used by JSP authoring tools to identify the custom tag.
`description`	A textual description detailing the purpose and usage for the custom tag.
`variable`	A custom tag may generate variables that are to be made available to the `PageContext` of the JSP. Each variable listed for a tag will be made available for additional processing from the JSP. There can be multiple variable elements for a tag. This element has six subelements listed in Table 18.3.

TABLE 18.2 Continued

Name of Subelement	Role
`attribute`	A custom tag may have several associated attributes. Each attribute for a tag must be listed here with an `attribute` element. There can be multiple attribute elements for a tag. This element has five subelements listed in Table 18.4.
`example`	The `example` tag is intended to contain an example of the proper usage of this tag.

The `variable` element in Table 18.2 contains six subelements defining its usage. Table 18.3 lists the six subelements associated with each `variable` along with a definition of their purpose.

TABLE 18.3 Variable Element: Subelements

Name of Subelement	Role
`name-given`	Either `name-given` or `name-from-attribute` must have a value but not both. The `name-given` specifies a fixed name to be used for this variable. This is the name to be used on the JSP to access this variable.
`name-from-attribute`	Either `name-given` or `name-from-attribute` must have a value but not both. The `name-from-attribute` states that the value of the specified attribute should be used for the name of the variable. This is the name to be used on the JSP to access this variable.
`variable-class`	The Java class that represents the data type for this variable.
`declare`	`True` or `False` depending on whether this variable needs to be declared prior to use. A value of `False` means that the variable has been declared prior to this custom tag being used.
`scope`	A value of `AT_BEGIN` means that the variable will be in scope immediately following the completion of the `doStartTag` method during the execution of the tag handler for this custom tag. A value of `AT_END` means that the variable will not be in scope until after the `doEndTag` method is called on the tag handler. A value of `NESTED` means that the variable will only be in scope following the execution of the `doStartTag` until the completion of the `doEndTag` method of the tag handler.
`description`	Documentation of the purpose and usage of this variable.

The `attribute` element in Table 18.2 contains five subelements defining its usage. Table 18.4 lists the five subelements associated with each `attribute` along with a definition of their purpose.

TABLE 18.4 Attribute Element: Subelements

Name of Subelement	Role
`name`	The name of the attribute.
`required`	`True` or `False` depending on whether this attribute is required.
`rtexprvalue`	`True` or `False` depending on whether the attribute can be set at request time for the JSP. The attribute value may set using a scriptlet rather than a constant value.
`type`	The Java class representing the value to be submitted from the JSP. This is an optional field unless `rtexprvalue` is set to `True`. The default value for this field is `java.lang.String`.
`description`	Documentation as to the purpose of this attribute.

The Custom Tag Library API

The Custom Tag library API is designed as an extension to the JSP specification and is maintained in the package name `javax.servlet.jsp.tagext`. The `javax.servlet.jsp.tagext` package contains the classes and interfaces required to implement custom XML tags to be used within the JSP. Table 18.5 lists the classes and interfaces defined within the JSP API 1.2 to support the extensions for development of tag libraries.

TABLE 18.5 The `javax.servlet.jsp.tagext` Package

Name	Role
`Tag`	All tag handlers must implement this interface. The JSP container uses this interface to communicate and call methods to initialize and process body content for the tag and to release acquired resources. This interface allows for the body of the tag to be processed by the JSP container only a single time. The tag itself has no access to the body content.
`IterationTag`	(Added as part of JSP 1.2) This interface extends the `Tag` interface. This interface allows for the body of the tag to be processed by the JSP container multiple times. The tag itself has no access to the body content. This is useful in processing an array of data or a collection.
`TagSupport`	An implementation of the `IterationTag` interface for a basic tag not requiring access to the content of the tag body. This class serves as a starting point to make the creation of tag handlers easier but is not required.
`BodyTag`	This interface extends the `IterationTag` interface. This interface allows for the body of the tag to be processed by the JSP container multiple times. The tag itself also has access to the body content between the start and the end tag.

TABLE 18.5 Continued

Name	Role
BodyTagSupport	An implementation of the BodyTag interface for a tag requiring access to the content of the tag body. This class serves as a starting point to make the creation of tag handlers easier but is not required.
BodyContent	This class is implemented by the JSP container. The JSP container makes an instance of the class available to all tag handlers implementing the BodyTag interface. This class provides the tag handler access to read and process the body content of the tag.
TryCatchFinally	(Added as part of JSP 1.2) This interface provides a mechanism for the JSP container to forward uncaught exceptions to the tag handler for processing. Without implementing this interface, all exceptions will be passed through the standard JSP error handling. That is, the exception will be sent to the client as a special Exception page. This interface also provides a mechanism to allow the tag handler to ensure that all resources are cleaned up after each invocation whether an exception occurs or not.
TagLibraryValidator	(Added as part of JSP 1.2) This class is intended to provide a means for the validation of the custom tags used in a JSP. The JSP container calls methods on this class to validate the custom tags on a JSP during translation.
PageData	This class is implemented by the JSP container. An instance of this class is passed to the TagLibraryValidator from the JSP container. The TagLibraryValidator class uses the PageData class to access the text of the entire page for validation.
ValidationMessage	(Added as part of JSP 1.2) This class is intended to contain the resulting messages of the JSP validation performed by the TagLibraryValidator class. The JSP container uses the messages to generate a response warning of the invalid JSP.
TagExtraInfo	This class is created by the author of the tag library to provide additional information to the JSP container regarding scripting variables and tags. The JSP container uses this class only during page translation.
VariableInfo	This class contains various attributes regarding a scripting variable. This class is returned to the JSP container in response to calls to the TagExtraInfo.getVariableInfo method.
TagData	This class contains attribute and value information regarding a specific tag. This class is used by the JSP container for calls to the TagExtraInfo class during JSP translation.
TagInfo	This class is used by the JSP container to obtain information about the Tag instance during page translation. This class is normally not accessed by the tag library author. An instance of this class can be obtained by calling the TagExtraInfo.getTagInfo method if needed.

TABLE 18.5 Continued

Name	Role
TagLibraryInfo	This class is used by the JSP container to obtain information about the tag library during page translation. This class is normally not accessed by the tag library author. An instance of this class can be obtained by calling the `TagInfo.getTagLibraryInfo` method if needed.
TagVariableInfo	This class is used by the JSP container to obtain information about scripting variables related to a specific tag during page translation. This class is normally not accessed by the tag library author. An instance of this class can be obtained by calling the `TagInfo.getTagVariableInfo` method if needed.
TagAttributeInfo	This class is used by the JSP container to obtain information about the attributes related to a specific tag during page translation. This class is normally not accessed by the tag library author. An instance of this class can be obtained by calling the `TagInfo.getAttributes` method if needed.

Custom Tag Validation

During the Translation phase of the JSP life cycle, the JSP container performs several validations on the custom tags included on the JSP. When the JSP container translates the JSP into a servlet, it needs to validate the syntax and the structure of any custom tags on the page. The JSP specification includes a sequence of three levels of validations, each resulting in the generation of error notifications when errors are found during the Translation phase. During the development of the JSPs, it is possible to force compilation of the pages and thus help to eliminate the potential errors that occur in response to actual page requests. The following list identifies the three stages and describes the purpose of the validation:

- Validation against the TLD file
- Validation using a `TagLibraryValidator`
- Validation of individual tags

The first step in translating a JSP is to verify that the basic syntax of the custom tags is correct. This requires verifying that all the custom tags on a JSP have an associated tag library and that it is used appropriately. The JSP container reads the TLD files for each tag library associated with the JSP and validates that the usage of the custom tags matches its definition. If any tag does not match its definition in the TLD file, the JSP container reports the error.

Each tag library may optionally implement a `TagLibraryValidator` class for the purpose of validation, but it can be useful in minimizing runtime errors using the library. If the JSP passes the syntactical validation against the TLD file and there is a `TagLibraryValidator` class associated with the tag library, the JSP will be passed to the class for validation. This validation is intended to allow the tag library author to perform an overall review, making sure that the tag library has been correctly used and meets all stipulated requirements. If a JSP references multiple tag libraries, the JSP will be submitted to the `TagLibraryValidator` class in each tag library.

Each tag library may optionally implement a `TagExtraInfo` class for each custom tag in the library for the purpose of validating individual tags. This validation is limited in scope and only supports checking that the attribute and values associated with the tag are valid combinations. Generally, if a `TagLibraryValidator` class has been implemented, there is no need to use the `TagExtraInfo` class for tag validation.

On the completion of these validations, the JSP container finishes the translation of the JSP into a servlet. This does not ensure that errors will not occur in handling client requests, but it helps eliminate many potential usage problems.

The Tag Handler Life Cycle

The execution of a tag handler occurs within the context of the Request phase of the JSP life cycle discussed in Chapter 17. It is the responsibility of the JSP container to manage the life cycle events to ensure that the custom tags are processed. Three interfaces may be implemented by a tag handler: `Tag`, `IterationTag`, and `BodyTag`. Depending on which interface is implemented, the tag handler experiences a slightly different sequence of events initiated by the JSP container. We will begin by reviewing the full list of life cycle events of a tag handler, all of which occur for a tag handler implementing the `BodyTag` interface:

1. Obtain instance of tag handler.
2. Call to `setPageContext()` and `setParent()` methods.
3. Process tag attributes.
4. Call to `doStartTag()` method.
5. Call to `setBodyContent()` method.
6. Call to `doInitBody()` method.
7. Process tag body.
8. Call to `doAfterBody()` method.
9. Call to `doEndTag()` method.
10. Call to `release()` method.

The preceding sequence of life cycle events will be controlled by the JSP container and followed for each custom tag within the JSP. The deviations in the life cycle events for tag handlers implementing the `Tag` or the `IterationTag` interface will be identified.

Obtain Instance of Tag Handler

When the JSP container handles a request for a JSP that includes a custom tag, an instance of the corresponding tag handler class is required to process the tag. The JSP container either creates a new instance of the class or obtains a reference to an existing instance for use on the JSP. The remaining life cycle events will be executed upon the tag handler class instance to fully process the custom tag.

Call to the `setPageContext()` and `setParent()` Methods

After a reference to the tag handler class is obtained, the JSP container must prepare the class for processing the custom tag. The methods `setPageContext` and `setParent` are called on the tag handler class. The `setPageContext` method provides the tag handler with a reference to the `javax.servlet.jsp.PageContext` object for the JSP being processed. If the current tag is placed within the body of another custom tag, the `setParent` method provides a reference to the tag handler of that outer custom tag. This information is then available to the tag handler in processing the current custom tag.

Process Tag Attributes

Every XML tag may contain attributes listed within the tag syntax. For each attribute listed for the tag in the JSP, the JSP container executes the setter method for the corresponding property on the tag handler class. Each of the properties is required to follow the JavaBean syntax for properties to allow the JSP container to appropriately transfer the attribute values to the tag handler properties.

Call to `doStartTag()` Method

At this point, the tag handler class is ready to begin processing the custom tag on the JSP. The JSP container executes the `doStartTag()` method on the handler class and expects a return value indicating whether to process the body of the tag or to skip the body. For each instance of the custom tag on the JSP, the JSP container calls this method once immediately prior to processing the tag body. Depending on the return value, the tag body may or may not be processed. Three constants are defined that correspond to the three options for the return value:

- `BodyTag.EVAL_BODY_BUFFERED`
- `Tag.EVAL_BODY_INCLUDE`
- `Tag.SKIP_BODY`

A return value of BodyTag.EVAL_BODY_BUFFERED indicates that the tag handler needs to have access to the results of processing the tag body by the JSP container. The JSP container should move forward to the setBodyContent life cycle event.

A return value of Tag.EVAL_BODY_INCLUDE indicates that the JSP container should process the content of the tag body, and the tag handler does not need access to the output. The JSP container should move forward to the Process Body life cycle event.

A return value of Tag.SKIP_BODY indicates that the content of the tag body should not be processed. The JSP container should move forward to the doEndTag() life cycle event because the processing of the custom tag is complete.

For tag handlers implementing the Tag or the IterationTag interface, only the Tag.EVAL_BODY_INCLUDE and the Tag.SKIP_BODY constants may be returned.

Call to the setBodyContent() Method

The JSP container makes a call to the setBodyContent() method to provide the tag handler class a reference to the BodyContent object. The BodyContent object serves as a wrapper providing access to the contents of the tag body.

Call to the doInitBody() Method

The JSP container makes a call to the doInitBody() method of the tag handler class to permit any required initialization before the JSP container begins processing the contents of the tag body.

Process Tag Body

The JSP container processes the content tag body as appropriate. If the body-content element in the TLD file has a value of JSP, the content of the tag body will be processed as additional JSP elements. If the body-content element in the TLD file has a value of tagdependent, the tag handler and not the JSP container will interpret the content of the tag body.

Call to the doAfterBody() Method

The JSP container makes a call to the doAfterBody() method to indicate to the tag handler that the tag body has been processed. One of the following constants must be returned indicating whether to process the tag body again:

- IterationTag.EVAL_BODY_AGAIN
- Tag.SKIP_BODY

A return value of IterationTag.EVAL_BODY_AGAIN indicates that the JSP container should process the tag body again. The JSP container should re-execute the Process Tag Body life cycle event again.

A return value of `Tag.SKIP_BODY` indicates that the content of the tag body should not be processed again. The JSP container should move forward to the `doEndTag()` life cycle event because the processing of the custom tag is complete.

For tag handlers implementing the `Tag` interface, the JSP container will not call the `doAfterBody()` life cycle event.

Call to the `doEndTag()` Method

The JSP container calls the `doEndTag()` method to give the tag handler the opportunity to determine whether to continue processing the remainder of the JSP. One of the following constants must be returned:

- `Tag.EVAL_PAGE`
- `Tag.SKIP_PAGE`

A return value of `Tag.EVAL_PAGE` indicates that the processing of the JSP should continue.

A return value of `Tag.SKIP_PAGE` indicates that the JSP container should not process the remainder of the JSP.

The processing of this custom tag on the JSP has been completed. The instance of the tag handler is no longer needed and is available for reuse to process another custom tag on the same JSP.

Call to the `release()` Method

The JSP container makes a call to the `release()` method to indicate to the tag handler to clean and remove all state information in preparation for reuse or for elimination by the garbage collector.

Tag Handler Design

Custom tag handlers are designed to run within the context of the JSP container being controlled from initialization to completion through calls to the life cycle events described previously. When a JSP container receives a request for a JSP that uses a custom tag, the JSP container locates an instance of the tag handler and executes the appropriate life cycle methods at the appropriate times to fully process the tag and any associated body content. We will discuss the process of designing three custom tags.

Depending on whether the custom tag needs to process the contents of the body of the tag, the tag handler class can use one of two base classes as a simplified starting point:

- `javax.servlet.jsp.tagext.TagSupport`
- `javax.servlet.jsp.tagext.TagBodySupport`

These classes contain default implementations of the `Tag`, `IterationTag`, and `BodyTag` interfaces that can be used for implementing only the life cycle event methods needed for the specific tag.

A Basic Tag

We will begin by looking at the setup and design of a custom tag that simply displays today's date on the JSP using the format MM/dd/yyyy. This basic tag demonstrates how to create a tag handler.

The process of placing the current date on the JSP only requires the custom tag to be replaced with the output of the tag handler during the JSP Request phase. We will name the tag `showDate`, and because there is no need for a tag body to be processed by the tag handler, we will extend the `TagSupport` class as a starting point. Listing 18.8 contains the Java code for the `showDate` custom tag.

LISTING 18.8 ShowDateTag.java

```
package com.sams.chalktalk.client.taglib;

import javax.servlet.jsp.tagext.TagSupport;
import javax.servlet.jsp.JspWriter;
import javax.servlet.jsp.JspTagException;
import java.io.IOException;
import java.util.Date;
import java.text.SimpleDateFormat;

public class ShowDateTag extends TagSupport {

  public int doStartTag() throws JspTagException {
    JspWriter out = pageContext.getOut();
    SimpleDateFormat dt = new SimpleDateFormat("MM/dd/yyyy");
    try {
        out.print(dt.format(new Date()));
    } catch(IOException e) {
      throw new JspTagException(e.getMessage());
    }
    return SKIP_BODY;
  }
}
```

The `showDate` tag only requires the generation of a string containing the current date. To accomplish this, we overwrite the `doStartTag` method to actually obtain the date and to output it as a string. The `TagSupport` class provides the `pageContext` variable that can be used to obtain the available information from the JSP container. This is an instance of the `javax.servlet.jsp.PageContext` class discussed in Chapter 17 and provides access to information regarding the client request, client response, application, current HTTP session, and other information regarding the JSP being processed. In Listing 18.8, a reference to the `PageContext` out object is obtained to permit the tag handler to write out the date string as part of the page response.

For the `showDate` tag handler to be accessible to the JSP container, a TLD file must exist that includes a `tag` element describing the custom tag. Listing 18.9 shows an excerpt from the chalktalktaglib.tld file containing the definition for the `showDate` custom tag.

LISTING 18.9 `showDate` Custom Tag Element

```
<tag>
   <name>showDate</name>
   <tag-class>com.sams.chalktalk.client.taglib.ShowDateTag</tag-class>
   <body-content>empty</body-content>
   <description>Prints out the current Date Time</description>
</tag>
```

A Custom Tag with Attributes

To demonstrate the addition of attributes to the preceding `showDate` example, we will create a new custom tag called `showFormattedDate` that will accept a format string as an attribute. The new custom tag will display the current date in the format that we specify as an attribute to the tag.

For our example we will define a single attribute named `format`. For our tag handler to receive the attribute value, we must add a JavaBean-style property called `Format` with only a setter method. For this example, there is no need for the corresponding getter method, but we could include it for completeness or potential use in the future. Listing 18.10 shows the source code for the `showFormattedDateTag` class with the additional `Format` property.

LISTING 18.10 ShowFormattedDateTag.java

```
package com.sams.chalktalk.client.taglib;

import javax.servlet.jsp.tagext.TagSupport;
import javax.servlet.jsp.JspWriter;
```

LISTING 18.10 Continued

```
import javax.servlet.jsp.JspTagException;
import java.io.IOException;
import java.util.Date;
import java.text.SimpleDateFormat;

public class ShowFormattedDateTag extends TagSupport {

  private String sFormat;

  public void setFormat(String sFormat) {
      this.sFormat = sFormat;
  }
  public int doStartTag() throws JspTagException {
    JspWriter out = pageContext.getOut();
    SimpleDateFormat dt = new SimpleDateFormat(sFormat);
    try {
        out.println(dt.format(new Date()));
    } catch(IOException e) {
      throw new JspTagException(e.getMessage());
    }
    return EVAL_PAGE;
  }
}
```

Listing 18.11 shows an excerpt from the chalktalktaglib.tld file containing the definition for the new `showFormattedDate` custom tag that includes a `format` attribute. We are specifying the attribute to be a required value that has to be a fixed value. The `format` attribute will contain a string value specifying the date format. The `type` element controls the data type to be submitted for the attribute; in this case, it is `java.lang.String`.

LISTING 18.11 `showFormattedDate` Custom Tag Element

```
  <tag>
     <name>showFormattedDate</name>
     <tag-class>
         com.sams.chalktalk.client.taglib.ShowFormattedDateTag
     </tag-class>
     <body-content>empty</body-content>
     <description>
         Prints out the current Date Time in the specified format
```

LISTING 18.11 Continued

```
    </description>
    <attribute>
      <name>format</name>
      <required>true</required>
      <rtexprvalue>false</rtexprvalue>
      <type>java.lang.String</type>
      <description>Format to use for displaying the date</description>
    </attribute>
  </tag>
```

A Custom Tag Using the Tag Body

The next custom tag uses the capability of tag handlers to read and process the tag body. For a Web page to support session tracking, it is necessary to preserve the session ID across page accesses. When the client does not accept cookies, it is necessary to encode the session ID in the URL. On a JSP this requires the use of Java code to encode the URL that is returned to the client. We will design a custom tag that will encode whatever URL is found in the tag body with the session ID using the `HttpServletResponse.encodeURL()` method. This is called *URL rewriting* as discussed in Chapter 16 in the section "Session Tracking."

In the previous two examples, we used the `TagSupport` class as the starting point for our tag handler. In this example, we need access to the contents of the tag body, so we will use the `TagBodySupport` class as our starting point. We will place our logic in the `doAfterBody` life cycle event method to allow us to use the contents of the tag body. Listing 18.12 shows the source code for the `encodeURLTag` class.

LISTING 18.12 EncodeURLTag.java

```
package com.sams.chalktalk.client.taglib;

import java.io.*;
import javax.servlet.http.*;
import javax.servlet.jsp.*;
import javax.servlet.jsp.tagext.*;


public class EncodeURLTag extends BodyTagSupport {

  public int doAfterBody() throws JspTagException {
    JspWriter out = getPreviousOut();
    String sURL = getBodyContent().getString();
    HttpServletResponse res = (HttpServletResponse) pageContext.getResponse();
```

LISTING 18.12 Continued

```
    try {
        out.print(res.encodeURL(sURL));
    } catch(IOException e) {
      throw new JspTagException(e.getMessage());
    }
    return SKIP_BODY;
  }
}
```

In Listing 18.12, we use the `BodyTagSupport.getPreviousOut` method to obtain the `JspWriter` rather than the `PageContext.getOut` method as used in the other examples. If the constant `BodyTag.EVAL_BODY_BUFFERED` is returned from the `doStartTag` method, as is the case here, the implicit out object for the `PageContext.getOut` method returns the `BodyContent` object for the current tag rather than the `JspWriter` object for the client response. After the `doEndTag` method is executed, the `PageContext.getOut` method again returns the `JspWriter` object for the client response.

In Listing 18.12, we also make a call to the `getBodyContent` method to retrieve the body of the tag being processed. The tag body contains the URL to be encoded, thus allowing us to accomplish the URL rewriting operation.

Listing 18.13 shows an excerpt from the chalktalktaglib.tld file containing the definition for the `encodeURL` custom tag. We changed the `content-body` element to specify `JSP` rather than `empty` as in the previous examples. We could have also set it to `tagdependent`. Either value indicates to the JSP container that the custom tag may contain a body. A value of JSP tells the JSP container to process the content of the body before passing it to the tag handler, whereas a value of `tagdependent` tells the JSP container not to touch the tag body and simply pass it to the tag handler.

LISTING 18.13 `encodeURL` Custom tag Element

```
<tag>
   <name>encodeURL</name>
   <tag-class>com.sams.chalktalk.client.taglib.EncodeURLTag</tag-class>
   <body-content>JSP</body-content>
   <description>Encodes the URL with the session id if needed</description>
</tag>
```

Using the Example Tags in a JSP

Finally, as part of our discussion on tag design, we will look at a JSP that references the three custom tags. Each tag library in our Web application should be identified by a URI value within the web.xml deployment descriptor; in this case, the tag library has been assigned a URI value of /sampletaglib. For each tag library used on a JSP, a `taglib` directive must be placed on the JSP identifying both the URI of the tag library and an XML namespace prefix to identify the tags used from the library. Listing 18.14 shows the completed TLD file identifying all three of our custom tags.

LISTING 18.14 sampletaglib.tld

```
<?xml version="1.0" encoding="UTF-8"?>
<!DOCTYPE taglib PUBLIC
"-//Sun Microsystems, Inc.//DTD JSP Tag Library 1.2//EN"
"http://java.sun.com/dtd/web-jsptaglibrary_1_2.dtd">
<taglib>
  <tlib-version>1.0</tlib-version>
  <jsp-version>1.2</jsp-version>
  <short-name>chalktalktaglib</short-name>
  <uri>/chalktalktaglib</uri>
  <tag>
     <name>showDate</name>
     <tag-class>com.sams.chalktalk.client.taglib.ShowDateTag</tag-class>
     <body-content>empty</body-content>
     <description>Prints out the current Date Time</description>
  </tag>
  <tag>
     <name>encodeURL</name>
     <tag-class>com.sams.chalktalk.client.taglib.EncodeURLTag</tag-class>
     <body-content>JSP</body-content>
     <description>Encodes the URL with the session id if needed</description>
  </tag>
  <tag>
     <name>showFormattedDate</name>
     <tag-class>
         com.sams.chalktalk.client.taglib.ShowFormattedDateTag
     </tag-class>
     <body-content>empty</body-content>
     <description>
         Prints out the current Date Time in the specified format
     </description>
     <attribute>
        <name>format</name>
        <required>true</required>
        <rtexprvalue>false</rtexprvalue>
        <type>java.lang.String</type>
        <description>Format to use for displaying the date</description>
```

LISTING 18.14 Continued

```
    </attribute>
  </tag>
</taglib>
```

Listing 18.15 shows a JSP that uses all three of our custom tags including the `taglib` directive at the top of the page.

LISTING 18.15 SampleTags.jsp

```
<%@ taglib uri="/sampletaglib" prefix="chalk" %>
<html>
<head>
<title>
Display Date
</title>
</head>
<body>
<h1>
Display Date -- showDate tag (MM/dd/yyyy)
</h1>
The current date is <chalk:showDate />
<p>
<h1>
Display Date -- showFormattedDate tag (E, MMM d, yyyy)
</h1>
The current date is <chalk:showFormattedDate format="E, MMM d,yyyy" />
<p>
<h1>
encodeURL tag -- include session id when cookies are not supported
</h1>
Encoded URL -- <chalk:encodeURL>SampleTags.jsp</chalk:encodeURL>
<p>
<a href="<chalk:encodeURL>SampleTags.jsp</chalk:encodeURL>">SampleTags.jsp</a>
</body>
</html>
```

Figure 18.1 shows the output of the JSP in Listing 18.15 when the Web browser does not accept cookies and thus requires URL encoding to support session tracking. The output of the `encodeURL` tag including the session ID is displayed above the link.

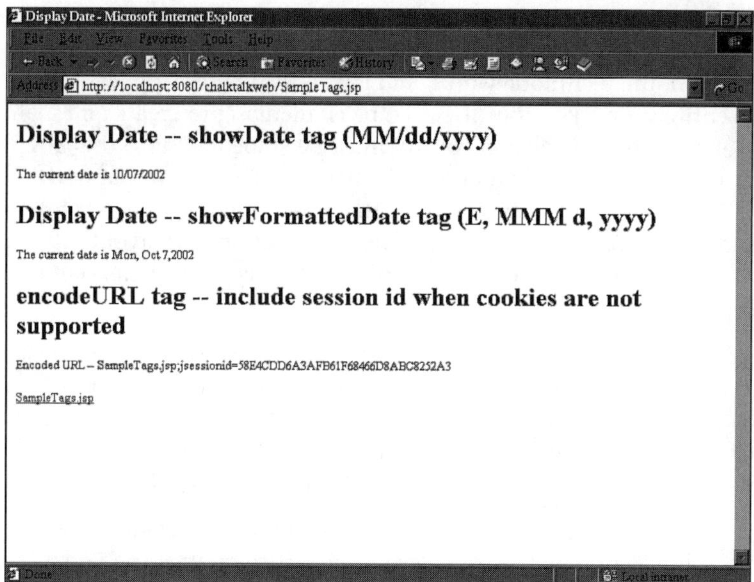

FIGURE 18.1 Output of SampleTags.jsp.

Servlet and JSP Development Guidelines

We have looked at three techniques for developing Web-based applications that all have symbiotic relationships in their structure and usage:

- Chapter 16, "Servlets"
- Chapter 17, "Java Server Pages"
- Chapter 18, "Tag Libraries"

You learned about how servlets can be used for applying the flexibility of Java to the processing and generation of dynamic content for Web applications. It is a server-centric approach that requires the translation of the user interface and layout into a series of `println` statements. This technique works and provides a lot of flexibility and power in assembling dynamic content, but it can be challenging to use for the design and maintenance of user-friendly interfaces. Servlets are useful and efficient for processing HTTP requests and executing the required business/application logic, but not very useful for the actual presentation of the resulting content.

You learned about Java Server Pages (JSPs) and the flexibility they provide for the development and maintenance of Web application user interfaces. JSPs are user-interface centric in that they target the Web designer in providing an easily maintained set of Web pages for the presentation and layout of dynamic Web content. Again, the technique works, and entire Web-based applications can be designed entirely with JSPs, but they can be challenging to create and maintain when a lot of business logic and control must be embedded into the JSPs. For complex applications, they can become difficult to manage in that both the Java code and the markup languages used for the presentation of the user interface become intertwined. JSPs are useful for the construction and layout of the presentation of content to the user, but they do not work as well for the execution of complex application logic.

The extension of the JSP technology to include the creation of Custom Tag libraries serves to help separate the business/application logic from the presentation. The application of Custom Tag libraries to the development of Web-based applications takes advantage of the user-interface centric JSPs for the presentation while providing a means of replacing Java code in the JSPs with custom XML tags.

The better approach to the development of Web-based applications using Java technology is to use a combination of JSPs and servlets to control the flow of the application and the interactions with the user. This allows the application to use the best features of each technique and avoid many of the negatives of using only servlets or only JSPs. Following the guiding principles of the Model-View-Controller (MVC) pattern prevalent in the development of Java applications, we can apply each technique to the area in which it excels. The flexibility of servlets to listen for HTTP requests and to respond makes servlets a good fit for the implementation of the controller functions that direct the flow of the user through the application. The JSPs are good at providing the capability to lay out and maintain the actual presentation of information to the user, making JSPs a good fit to fill the View functions within the Web application. The model can be implemented by encapsulating the content/logic for the Web page within various Java classes and structures to be accessed by both the servlets and the JSPs. When appropriate, the tag libraries can serve to provide a means for the JSPs to access the model. Tag libraries are useful for encapsulating Java code that can be reused on JSPs by replacing the code with an XML tag. These custom XML tags can simplify the creation of new JSPs and reduce the potential defects by requiring the testing and development of the tags apart from the application and fostering their reuse.

The extent that each of these techniques can be used to implement the MVC pattern in Web applications changes and differs based on the actual business/applications to be implemented. The use of servlets, JSPs, and tag libraries are symbiotic in how they work together and can be used in ways that benefit from the strengths of each technique.

In Practice

Now that we have looked at what tag libraries are and how they work, let's create a tag library that encapsulates some of the application logic of the ChalkTalk application.

The chalktalkweb application from Chapter 17 used two JSPs as the user interface, while using a servlet to process the login/logout functions. The logic for retrieving the course listing was embedded into the JSP. We will create several custom tags as part of the ChalkTalk tag library for retrieving and displaying the course listing and a couple of other functions. This allows us to pull most of the Java code out of the JSPs and demonstrates how to create a tag library using JBuilder.

We will create our Custom Tag library to be deployed as a set of files rather than a single JAR file. This provides the benefit of allowing us to test and debug our tag handlers in the same project as our Web application. After the tag library has been developed and tested, a JAR file can be created that contains the tag handlers and the TLD file.

To give you an idea of where we are going, here is a summarized list of all the steps we will perform in this "In Practice" section:

- Create a project and Web application.
- Create tag handlers for the tag library.
- Create a tag library descriptor (TLD) file.
- Configure the WebApp deployment descriptor (web.xml) file.
- Design the View Course List JSP.
- Design the Login JSP.

Creating a Project and Web Application

1. Copy the directory named chalktalkapp from the Chapter 18 source code to your hard drive. The Java packages in the chalktalkapp directory represent the class library that our Web-based application will use to provide the business logic.
2. Select File, New Project.
3. On the first screen of the Project Wizard enter **ch18** as the name of the project and **C:\Projects\SAMS\Application\ch18** as the directory. Leave the type as jpx, leave the Template as (Default Project), and check the Generate Project Notes File check box. You can put your project in a different directory, but at

least make sure that the last component is ch18. This makes it easier for you to run the sample application. Click Next.

4. On the second screen of the Project Wizard, a reference needs to be added to include the source files from the existing ChalkTalk application. Click on the Add button next to the Source tab to bring up a dialog box and search for the location where the chalktalkapp directory was copied in step 1. After the directory has been located, click OK to close the dialog box. The chalktalkapp directory should be listed in the list box on the Source tab. Click Next.

5. On the third screen, enter your name in the Author field and your company name in the Company field. Click Finish.

6. Select File, New to bring up the Object Gallery. On the Web tab, double-click on the Web Application icon to bring up the Web Application Wizard.

7. On the screen, enter **chalktalkweb** as the Name and **C:/Projects/SAMS/Application/ch18/chalktalkweb** as the Directory name. Click OK.

We now have an empty Web application available that serves as the basis to create our tag library for the ChalkTalk application. Next we will create the four custom tags for the tag library to be used by the JSP to display the results of the `browseCourses` method in the `com.sams.chalktalk.userservices.CommonOperations` class.

Creating Tag Handlers for the Tag Library

We will begin by creating the class files that will contain the tag handlers for our custom tags. The first custom tag called `encodeURL` will be used to facilitate session tracking by exposing the `HttpServletResponse.encodeURL` method.

1. Select File, New Class to bring up the Class Wizard.

2. On the first screen of the Class Wizard, enter **`com.sams.chalktalk.client.taglib`** as the name of the package and **`EncodeURLTag`** as the name of the class. Enter **`javax.servlet.jsp.tagext.BodyTagSupport`** as the base class. Check the Public check box and uncheck the remaining check boxes. Click OK.

3. Open the `EncodeURLTag` class in the Content pane and switch to the Source tab at the bottom.

4. Modify the `EncodeURLTag` class definition to match the code in Listing 18.16.

LISTING 18.16 EncodeURLTag.java

```
package com.sams.chalktalk.client.taglib;

import java.io.*;
import javax.servlet.http.*;
import javax.servlet.jsp.*;
import javax.servlet.jsp.tagext.*;

public class EncodeURLTag extends BodyTagSupport {

  public int doAfterBody() throws JspTagException {
    JspWriter out = getPreviousOut();
    String sURL = getBodyContent().getString();
    HttpServletResponse res = (HttpServletResponse) pageContext.getResponse();
    try {
         out.print(res.encodeURL(sURL));
    } catch(IOException e) {
      throw new JspTagException(e.getMessage());
    }
    return SKIP_BODY;
  }
}
```

5. Save the changes and close the `EncodeURLTag` class in the Content pane.

The second custom tag called `checksecurity` will be used to perform a security check when the client has logged in to the Web application. If the client has not logged in, the client will be redirected to the `Login` servlet to handle user validation. This tag handler performs the same purpose as the `LoginFilter` in the previous version of the chalktalkweb application. The JSP designer only needs to place the `checksecurity` tag at the top of any page that has security restrictions. This forces the user to log in to the application before viewing the JSP.

1. Select File, New Class to bring up the Class Wizard.
2. On the first screen of the Class Wizard, enter **`com.sams.chalktalk.client.taglib`** as the name of the package and **`CheckSecurityTag`** as the name of the class. Enter **`javax.servlet.jsp.tagext.TagSupport`** as the base class. Check the Public check box and uncheck the remaining check boxes. Click OK.

3. Open the `CheckSecurityTag` class in the Content pane and switch to the Source tab at the bottom.

4. Modify the `CheckSecurityTag` class definition to match the code in Listing 18.17.

LISTING 18.17 CheckSecurityTag.java

```
package com.sams.chalktalk.client.taglib;

import java.io.*;
import javax.servlet.http.*;
import javax.servlet.jsp.*;
import javax.servlet.jsp.tagext.*;


public class CheckSecurityTag extends TagSupport {
  private HttpServletRequest req;
  private HttpServletResponse res;
  private HttpSession sess;
  private Boolean bLoggedIn;
  private String sTarget;

  public int doStartTag() throws JspTagException {
    return SKIP_BODY;
  }

  public int doEndTag() throws JspTagException {
    try {
      req = (HttpServletRequest) pageContext.getRequest();
      res = (HttpServletResponse) pageContext.getResponse();

      //Determine whether logged in
      bLoggedIn =
       (Boolean)pageContext.getAttribute("LoggedIn",PageContext.SESSION_SCOPE);

      //Set Target Page
      sTarget = req.getRequestURL().toString();

      //if not logged in redirect to the login servlet
      if ((bLoggedIn == null) || !bLoggedIn.booleanValue()) {
        pageContext.setAttribute("target",sTarget,PageContext.SESSION_SCOPE);
        res.sendRedirect(res.encodeRedirectURL("login"));
```

LISTING 18.17 Continued

```
        return SKIP_PAGE;
      } else {
        return EVAL_PAGE;
      }

    }
    catch(IOException iox) {
      pageContext.getServletContext().log(iox.getMessage());
      throw new JspTagException(iox.getMessage());
    }
    finally {
      sTarget = null;
      bLoggedIn = null;
      sess = null;
      res = null;
      req = null;
    }
  }
}
```

5. Save the changes and close the `CheckSecurityTag` class in the Content pane.

The third custom tag called `courselist` will be created to display the list of courses retrieved from the `browseCourses` method in the `com.sams.chalktalk.userservices.CommonOperations` class. The tag handler simply iterates over the list of courses. A second tag handler called `coursefield` will be created that permits retrieval of the field values for each course.

1. Select File, New Class to bring up the Class Wizard.
2. On the first screen of the Class Wizard, enter **`com.sams.chalktalk.client.taglib`** as the name of the package and **`CourseListTag`** as the name of the class. Enter **`javax.servlet.jsp.tagext.TagSupport`** as the base class. Check the Public check box and uncheck the remaining check boxes. Click OK.
3. Open the `CourseListTag` class in the Content pane and switch to the Source tab at the bottom.
4. Modify the `CourseListTag` class definition to match the code in Listing 18.18.

LISTING 18.18 CourseListTag.java

```
package com.sams.chalktalk.client.taglib;

import javax.servlet.jsp.tagext.TagSupport;
import javax.servlet.jsp.PageContext;
import javax.servlet.jsp.JspTagException;
import com.sams.chalktalk.userservices.CommonOperations;
import com.sams.chalktalk.dataobjects.CourseData;
import java.util.Iterator;

public class CourseListTag extends TagSupport {
      private CommonOperations op;
      private CourseData oCourse;
      private Iterator iter;

   public int doStartTag() throws JspTagException {
      op = (CommonOperations)
                     pageContext.getAttribute("oOperation",
                                          PageContext.APPLICATION_SCOPE);
      if (op == null) {
         op = new CommonOperations();
         pageContext.setAttribute("oOperation",
                                 op,PageContext.APPLICATION_SCOPE);
      }
      iter = op.browseCourses(null).iterator();
      if (iter.hasNext() == true) {
          oCourse = (CourseData)iter.next();
          pageContext.setAttribute("CourseData",
                                 oCourse,PageContext.PAGE_SCOPE);
          return EVAL_BODY_INCLUDE;
      }
      else {
        return SKIP_BODY;
      }
   }

   public int doAfterBody() {
      if (iter.hasNext() == true) {
          oCourse = (CourseData)iter.next();
          pageContext.setAttribute("CourseData",
                                 oCourse,PageContext.PAGE_SCOPE);
          return EVAL_BODY_AGAIN;
```

LISTING 18.18 Continued

```
      }
      else {
        return SKIP_BODY;
      }
  }

  public int doEndTag() throws JspTagException {
      iter = null;
      oCourse = null;
      op = null;
      return EVAL_PAGE;
  }
}
```

5. Save the changes and close the `CourseListTag` class in the Content pane.

The fourth custom tag called `coursefield` will be designed to allow the page designer to specify which fields to display for each course in the list. The tag handler will simply replace the tag with the value of the specified course field.

1. Select File, New Class to bring up the Class Wizard.
2. On the first screen of the Class Wizard, enter **`com.sams.chalktalk.client.taglib`** as the name of the package and **`CourseFieldTag`** as the name of the class. Enter **`javax.servlet.jsp.tagext.TagSupport`** as the base class. Check the Public check box and uncheck the remaining check boxes. Click OK.
3. Open the `CourseFieldTag` class in the Content pane and switch to the Source tab at the bottom.
4. Modify the `CourseFieldTag` class definition to match the code in Listing 18.19.

LISTING 18.19 CourseFieldTag.java

```
package com.sams.chalktalk.client.taglib;

import javax.servlet.jsp.tagext.TagSupport;
import javax.servlet.jsp.PageContext;
import javax.servlet.jsp.JspTagException;
import java.io.IOException;
import javax.servlet.jsp.JspWriter;
import com.sams.chalktalk.dataobjects.CourseData;
```

LISTING 18.19 Continued

```
public class CourseFieldTag extends TagSupport {
      private CourseData oCourse;
      private JspWriter out;
      private String sField;

  public void setField(String sField) {
      this.sField = sField;
  }

  public int doStartTag() throws JspTagException {
      out = pageContext.getOut();
      oCourse = (CourseData)pageContext.getAttribute("CourseData",
                                                    PageContext.PAGE_SCOPE);
      try {
          if (sField == "Id") {
            out.print(oCourse.getId());
          } else if (sField == "Title") {
            out.print(oCourse.getTitle());
          } else if (sField == "Description") {
            out.print(oCourse.getDescription());
          }
      } catch(IOException e) {
        throw new JspTagException(e.getMessage());
      }

      return SKIP_BODY;
  }

  public int doEndTag() {
      oCourse = null;
      out = null;
      return EVAL_PAGE;
  }
}
```

5. Save the changes and close the `CourseFieldTag` class in the Content pane.

The tag handlers for the four custom tags have been created. The next step is to create the TLD file to expose our tag handlers to the JSP container.

Creating a TLD File

In this section we will create the TLD file for our custom tags. The TLD file will be placed in the \WEB-INF\tlds subdirectory, which by default will not be included in the WAR file generated for the Web application by JBuilder. If the TLD file is stored in the /WEB-INF subdirectory instead, it would be included in the WAR file. Steps 2 and 3 show how to include the TLD files in the WAR file, when stored in the WEB-INF/tlds directory.

1. Select Project, Add Files/Packages to bring up the Add File or Packages to Project dialog box. Enter **`C:\Projects\SAMS\Application\ch18\chalktalkweb\WEB-INF\tlds\chalktalktaglib.tld`** into the Filename field. Click OK to create the file. A message box appears warning that the file does not exist and asking whether you want to create it. Click OK to create the file.

2. Right-click on the chalktalkweb node in the Project pane of the JBuilder IDE. Select the Properties menu option on the pop-up menu that appears. A dialog box appears labeled Properties of "chalktalkweb." Change the focus to the Directories tab by clicking on the Directories tab at the top of the window.

3. Check Include Regular Content in WEB-INF and Subdirectories. This should enable the Include WEB-INF Subdirectories list box. Click the Add button to the right of that list box. A dialog box appears requesting a Directory Name or Pattern. Enter **tlds** into the dialog box and click OK. Figure 18.2 shows the Properties for the chalktalkweb dialog box as it now appears.

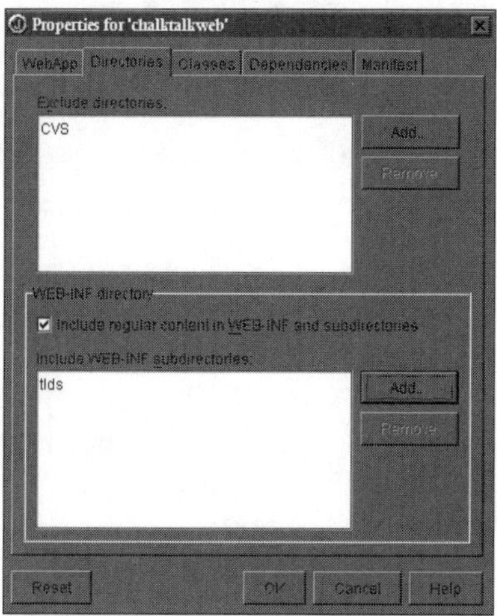

FIGURE 18.2 Properties for chalktalkweb dialog box.

4. Click OK to close the Properties for "chalktalkweb" dialog box.

5. Open the chalktalktaglib.tld file in the Content pane and switch to the Source tab at the bottom. The Content and Project panes appear as in Figure 18.3.

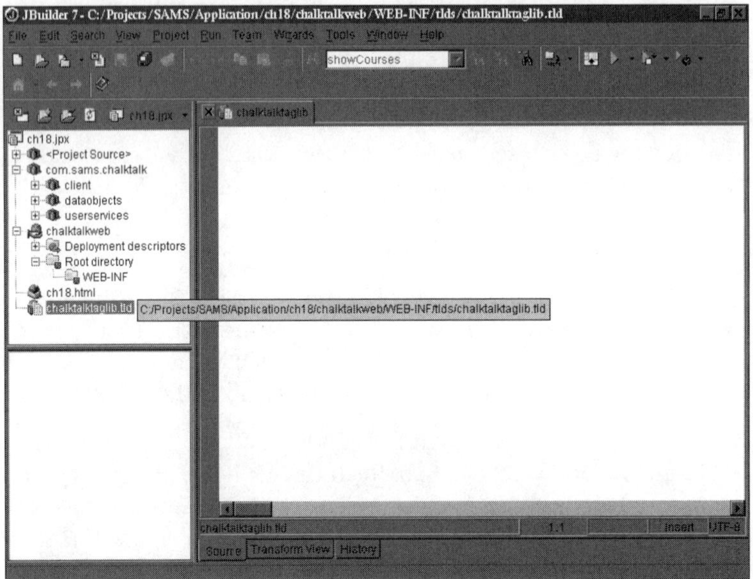

FIGURE 18.3 Content and Project panes.

6. Modify the chalktalktaglib.tld file to match the TLD in Listing 18.20.

LISTING 18.20 chalktalktaglib.tld

```
<?xml version="1.0" encoding="UTF-8"?>
<!DOCTYPE taglib PUBLIC
"-//Sun Microsystems, Inc.//DTD JSP Tag Library 1.2//EN"
"http://java.sun.com/dtd/web-jsptaglibrary_1_2.dtd">
<taglib>
  <tlib-version>1.0</tlib-version>
  <jsp-version>1.2</jsp-version>
  <short-name>chalktalktaglib</short-name>
  <uri>/chalktalktaglib</uri>
  <tag>
     <name>encodeURL</name>
     <tag-class>com.sams.chalktalk.client.taglib.EncodeURLTag</tag-class>
     <body-content>JSP</body-content>
```

LISTING 18.20 Continued

```
    <description>Encodes the URL with the session id if needed</description>
  </tag>
  <tag>
    <name>coursefield</name>
    <tag-class>com.sams.chalktalk.client.taglib.CourseFieldTag</tag-class>
    <body-content>empty</body-content>
    <description>Prints out the current Date Time</description>
    <attribute>
      <name>field</name>
      <required>true</required>
      <rtexprvalue>false</rtexprvalue>
      <type>java.lang.String</type>
      <description>Field to show from the CourseData record</description>
    </attribute>
  </tag>
  <tag>
    <name>courselist</name>
    <tag-class>com.sams.chalktalk.client.taglib.CourseListTag</tag-class>
    <body-content>JSP</body-content>
    <description>Generate List of Courses</description>
  </tag>
  <tag>
    <name>checksecurity</name>
    <tag-class>com.sams.chalktalk.client.taglib.CheckSecurityTag</tag-class>
    <body-content>empty</body-content>
    <description>
        Redirect the client to the Login page if not logged in
    </description>
  </tag>
</taglib>
```

7. Save and close the chalktalktaglib.tld file in the Content pane.

The TLD file has been created. We will now update the web.xml file to reflect the tag library that we created and add the `Login` servlet.

Configuring the WebApp Deployment Descriptor (web.xml) File

In this section we will modify the deployment descriptor for the Web application to intercept every request to the `CourseList` servlet that we created.

1. Open the deployment descriptor file for the Web application. Figure 18.4 shows the WebApp DD Editor.

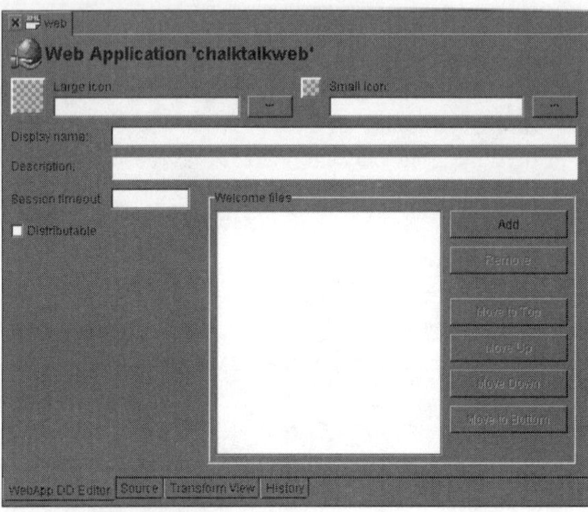

FIGURE 18.4 WebApp DD Editor.

2. Click on the tag library node in the Structure pane to bring up the tag libraries for the chalktalkweb screen in the Content pane. Click the Add button on the right side of the Content pane to add a `<taglib>` mapping element. Enter **/chalktalktaglib** in the TagLib URI column and enter **/WEB-INF/tlds/chalktalktaglib.tld** into the TagLib Location column. Figure 18.5 shows the tag libraries for the "chalktalkweb" screen as it now appears.

3. Right-click on the Structure pane and select the Add Servlet item from the pop-up menu. Enter **Login** as the servlet name in the New Servlet dialog box. This creates a node labeled Login below the Servlets node.

4. Click on the Servlets node in the Structure pane to bring up the Servlet Mappings list in the Content pane as shown in Figure 18.6. Click on the Add button in the Content pane to create a new Servlet mapping. Enter **/login** for the URL pattern and **Login** for the Servlet Name.

5. Set the properties for the filter. Click on the Login Servlet node in the Structure pane to bring up the Servlet properties in the Content pane as shown in Figure 18.7. Enter **`com.sams.chalktalk.client.web.Login`** for the `Servlet` class.

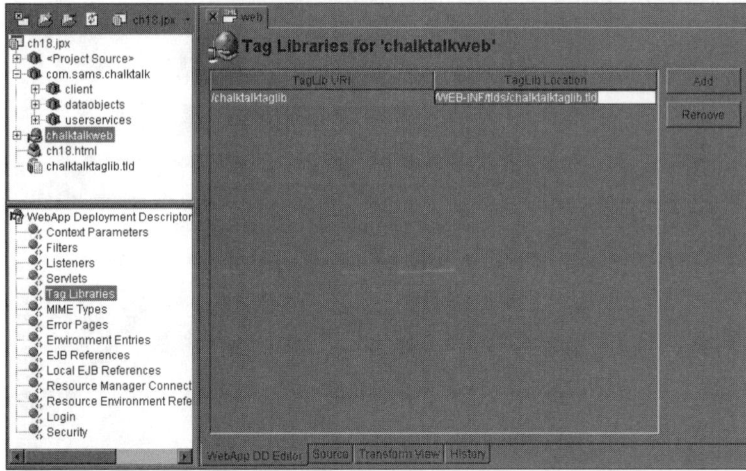

FIGURE 18.5 WebApp DD Editor: Tag Libraries for "chalktalkweb."

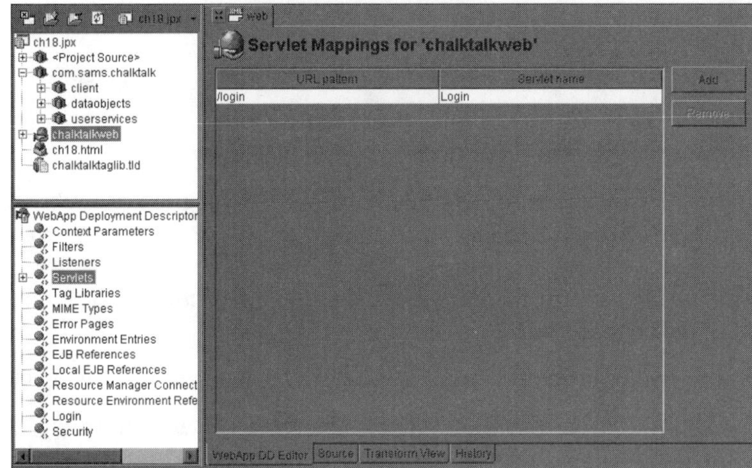

FIGURE 18.6 WebApp DD Editor: Servlet Mappings.

We have completed the configuration of the WebApp deployment descriptor. We will now create the Login JSP.

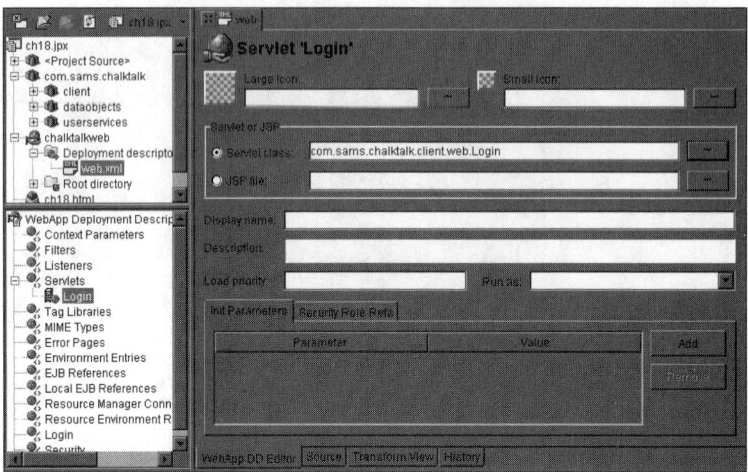

FIGURE 18.7 WebApp DD Editor: Servlet Properties.

Designing the Login JSP

We will design the Login JSP to use the custom tags that we have created:

1. Select File, New to bring up the Object Gallery. On the Web tab, double-click on the Java Server Page icon to bring up the JSP Wizard.
2. On the first screen of the JSP Wizard, make sure that chalktalkweb is specified as the Web App for this JSP. Enter **Login** as the name of the JSP. Uncheck the Generate Submit Form check box. Uncheck the Declare InternetBeans tag library check box. Uncheck the Generate Error Page and the Generate Sample Bean check boxes. Click Next.
3. On the second screen of the JSP Wizard, no changes are needed. Click Next.
4. On the third screen of the JSP Wizard, check the Create a Runtime Configuration check box. Enter **Login – JSP** as the name of the runtime configuration and leave the Base configuration as None. Click Finish.
5. Attempt to run the project from the Run, Run Project menu (shortcut key is F9) to verify that all the settings have been correctly set up and are working. The output is simply that of the Login JSP that we have created, displaying the message "JBuilder Generated JSP."
6. Open the Login JSP in the Content pane and switch to the Source tab at the bottom. The code should look like a plain HTML file.

7. Replace the existing HTML code with the code in Listing 18.21. The new logic will show a login page and use the `encodeURL` custom tag to perform session tracking.

LISTING 18.21 Login.jsp

```
<%@ taglib uri="/chalktalktaglib" prefix="chalk" %>
<html>
<head><title>Course Registration Login</title></head>
<body>
<form action="<chalk:encodeURL>login</chalk:encodeURL>" method="POST">
UserName: <input name="username"><br>
Password: <input type="password" name="password"><br>
<input type="submit" name="Submit" value="Login">
<input type="reset" value="Reset">
</form>
</body>
</html>
```

8. Run the project to verify that the changes are working. Figure 18.8 shows the output of the Login JSP while running the project within JBuilder.

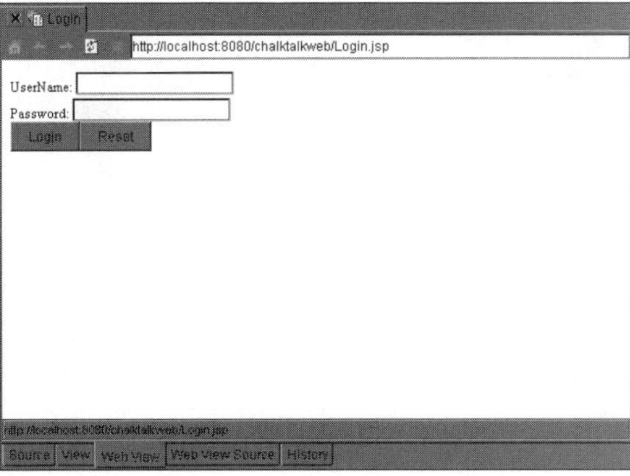

FIGURE 18.8 Output of Login.jsp.

The Web application now provides a Login page. We will now design the new CourseList.jsp page to use the new custom tags.

Designing a View Course List JSP

We will design the View Course List JSP to use the custom tags to generate the course list without any Java code embedded in the JSP.

1. Select File, New to bring up the Object Gallery. On the Web tab, double-click on the Java Server Page icon to bring up the JSP Wizard.
2. On the first screen of the JSP Wizard, make sure that chalktalkweb is specified as the Web App for this JSP. Enter **CourseList** as the name of the JSP. Uncheck the Generate Submit Form check box. Uncheck the Declare InternetBeans Tag Library check box. Uncheck the Generate Error Page and the Generate Sample Bean check boxes. Click Next.
3. On the second screen of the JSP Wizard, no changes are needed. Click Next.
4. On the third screen of the JSP Wizard, check the Create a Runtime Configuration check box. Enter **CourseList – JSP** as the name of the runtime configuration and leave the Base configuration as None. Click Finish.
5. Open the CourseList.jsp file in the Content pane and switch to the Source tab at the bottom.
6. Replace the existing HTML code with the code in Listing 18.22.

LISTING 18.22 CourseList.jsp

```
<%@ taglib uri="/chalktalktaglib" prefix="chalk" %>
<chalk:checksecurity />
<html>
<head>
<title>
CourseList
</title>
</head>
<body>
<A HREF="<chalk:encodeURL>login?Submit=Logout</chalk:encodeURL>">Logout</A>
<A HREF="<chalk:encodeURL>CourseList.jsp</chalk:encodeURL>">View Course List</A>
<HR>

<table border=1>
<tr><td>Id</td><td>Title</td><td>Description</td></tr>
<chalk:courselist>
<tr>
    <td><chalk:coursefield field="Id" /></td>
    <td><chalk:coursefield field="Title" /></td>
    <td><chalk:coursefield field="Description" /></td>
```

LISTING 18.22 Continued

```
</tr>
</chalk:courselist>
</table>

</body>
</html>
```

7. Run the project to verify that the `CourseList` JSP can be executed and is correct. Choose the CourseList - JSP Runtime Configuration from the Choose Runtime Configuration dialog box to view the output of the `CourseList` JSP. The Login page appears first. Click on the Login button to move to the CourseList.jsp page. Figure 18.9 shows the output that should be shown on the screen. The CourseList JSP includes the `checksecurity` tag, which has been designed to redirect the user to display the Login JSP if the user is not currently logged in. If the user is currently logged in, the CourseList JSP will be displayed.

When running this application, it may not always force a login before accessing the CourseList.jsp file. This is due to an attempt to persist session information across various runs of the application. A more extensive explanation of the issue is included in the sidebar "Session Persistence" at the end of the Chapter 16 "In Practice" section.

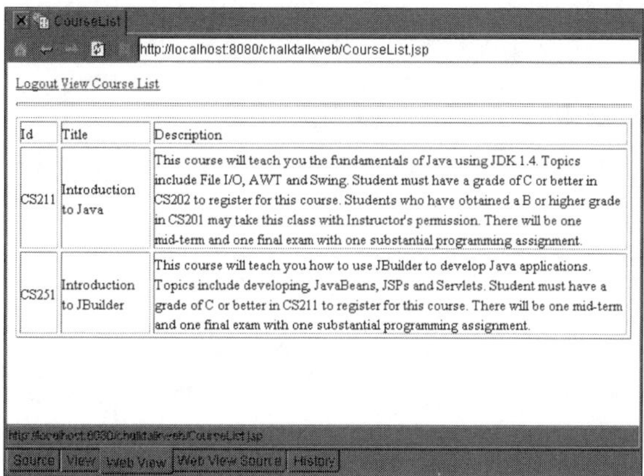

FIGURE 18.9 Output of CourseList.jsp.

The chalktalkweb application now works with the Custom Tag library we created. Neither of the JSPs contain any Java code.

Summary

The Java Server Pages API defines both standard actions and custom actions to support the generation of dynamic Web content using Java. This chapter described the structure of the custom actions called tag libraries and how to develop them using JBuilder. As we discussed, the tag libraries consist of a set of tag handlers that implement the desired functionality to be used by the JSP along with a tag library descriptor (TLD) file. The TLD describes the attributes and the usage of each of the tags included in the library. After the tag library has been created and included in a Web application, a JSP in the Web application may use any of the tag handlers by simply placing the custom tag in the appropriate location and referencing the tag library at the top of the page.

The use of tag libraries may permit the removal of commonly used Java code from a JSP and permit its reuse throughout any number of Web applications. This has the potential to speed up the development of Web applications and reduce errors by reusing previously tested Java code.

Reflections

- What are some potential uses of custom tags and their benefits as compared to the use of JSPs only?
- In the "In Practice" section, we used the `checksecurity` custom tag to verify that the user has logged in and to redirect to the Login JSP if necessary. What are some benefits and drawbacks to security validation with this technique?
- We briefly discussed the validations performed on the JSP during translation into a servlet. The `TagLibraryValidator` and the `TagExtraInfo` classes may be optionally created by the author of the custom tags to assist in verifying correct usage of the custom tags. In what types of applications or environments would it be beneficial for the author to implement these classes with the tag library?

19 InternetBeans Express

IN THIS CHAPTER

- InternetBeans Express in Detail
- Using InternetBeans with Servlets
- Using InternetBeans Express with JSPs
- Design Guidelines

InternetBeans Express was created to solve a problem with developing dynamically Web-based applications. For example, when using a servlet, it joins the presentation (HTML) and business logic (Java) within the same package. Before InternetBeans Express, when you wanted to make a change to the HTML page, you had to go into code, change the HTML, and redeploy. This works for a small number of changes, but you would not want to do this in today's always-need-a-new-Web-layout world. In comes the first version of InternetBeans to merge dynamic content within an HTML page. Then Sun released Java Server Pages (JSPs), and developers rejoiced. You can now define HTML outside the servlet source file. This allows you to deal with dynamic pages as pages rather than code.

InternetBeans Express in Detail

The perfect world is the merging of JSPs for HTML presentation with placeholders or tags to replace with dynamic data. JBuilder's InternetBeans Express provides this functionality to both JSPs and servlets. You can use a static HTML template file (not a JSP file), which is then processed by a `PageProducer` to merge in the dynamic data. If you are partial to using JSPs for templates, you can use a 1.1 tag library extension to accomplish this also. These custom tags relate ultimately to a real component, which includes the functionality to replace the tag with appropriate dynamic data. Many different components are available. Table 19.1 lists the different components provided by InternetBeans Express.

TABLE 19.1 Available Components Within InternetBeans Express

Component	Description
`IxPageProducer`	Not only reads but also parses static HTML files to identify custom tags for ultimate insert of custom data. This component is used within servlets to then merge HTML with dynamic data.
`IxControl`	Determines at runtime which components this control should emulate. This component must be used with `IxPageProducer` if you are using servlet.
`IxTable`	Generates an HTML table based on the results of a result `Set`.
`IxImage`	Adds an HTML image either linked or not linked to the HTML page.
`IxLink`	Represents an HTML hyperlink.
`IxSpan`	Replaces a custom span tag with a property with its dynamic equivalent.
`IxCheckBox`	Creates an HTML check box.
`IxComboBox`	Creates an HTML combo box.
`IxHidden`	Creates an HTML hidden attribute.
`IxImageButton`	Represents an image in HTML in which you can attach a submit form.
`IxListBox`	Represents an HTML list box.
`IxPassword`	Represents a password field, where the echo characters can be hidden or overridden.
`IxPushButton`	Represents an HTML pushbutton.
`IxRadioButton`	Represents an HTML radio button.
`IxSubmitButton`	Represents a form submit button.
`IxTextArea`	Generates a `TextArea` within your HTML document.
`IxTextField`	Generates a `TextField` within your HTML document.

In this chapter we will look at how to use InternetBeans Express. First we look at using InternetBeans with servlets and then with JSPs.

Using InternetBeans with Servlets

Since Java started to move to the Web, servlets have become the foundation of the success for all Web development done in Java. Even with the proliferation of JSPs, they ultimately get compiled into a servlet, giving you an equal, if not slightly less amount of work. So to add dynamic data capability to a Web page, you would have to do a lot of string manipulation to create the desired result. Let's take a look at a simple servlet, shown in Listing 19.1, that just gives the time and date.

LISTING 19.1 Java Servlet to Present the Current Date and Time Within HTML

```
package ibesample;

import javax.servlet.*;
import javax.servlet.http.*;
```

LISTING 19.1 Continued

```
import java.io.*;
import java.util.*;
import java.text.DateFormat;

/**
 * <p>Title: Welcome Servlet</p>
 * <p>Description: This servlet demonstrates dynamic content</p>
 * <p>Copyright: Copyright (c) 2002</p>
 * <p>Company: SAMS Publishing</p>
 * @version 1.0
 */

public class Today extends HttpServlet {
  static final private String CONTENT_TYPE = "text/html";
  //Initialize global variables
  public void init() throws ServletException {
  }
  //Process the HTTP Get request
  public void doGet(HttpServletRequest request,
       HttpServletResponse response) throws ServletException, IOException {
    response.setContentType(CONTENT_TYPE);
    PrintWriter out = response.getWriter();
    Locale locale = new Locale("nl","NL");

    DateFormat df = DateFormat.getDateTimeInstance(DateFormat.FULL,
       DateFormat.FULL,locale);


    out.println("<html>");
    out.println("<head><title>Today</title></head>");
    out.println("<body>");
    out.println("<H1>Welcome</H1>");
    out.println("<p>");
    out.println(df.format(new Date()));
    out.println("</p>");
    out.println("</body></html>");
  }
  //Clean up resources
  public void destroy() {
  }
}
```

In this simple servlet, if someone changes his mind on the presentation, you have to change code. Imagine a complex HTML implementation, which could contain hundreds if not thousands of lines of HTML code. The solution is to design something that allows the presentation to be separate from the business logic/code. Now look at an example using InternetBeans Express. Listing 19.2 takes the preceding servlet, creates an HTML template, and replaces the servlet logic for HTML generation with an `IxPageProducer` component.

LISTING 19.2 Create a Page with Dynamic Data Using an `IxPageProducer`

```
package ibesample;

import java.io.*;
import java.text.*;
import java.util.*;

import javax.servlet.*;
import javax.servlet.http.*;

import com.borland.internetbeans.*;

/**
 * <p>Title: </p>
 * <p>Description: </p>
 * <p>Copyright: Copyright (c) 2002</p>
 * <p>Company: </p>
 * @author unascribed
 * @version 1.0
 */

public class SPhoneList extends HttpServlet {
  static final private String CONTENT_TYPE = "text/html";
  private IxPageProducer page = new IxPageProducer();
  private IxSpan spanTime = new IxSpan();
  //Initialize global variables
  public void init() throws ServletException {
  }
  //Process the HTTP Get request
  public void doGet(HttpServletRequest request,
        HttpServletResponse response) throws ServletException, IOException {
    page.getObjects();
```

LISTING 19.2 Continued

```
    String language = spanTime.getAttribute("language");
    String country = spanTime.getAttribute("country");

    Locale locale = new Locale(language,country);

    DateFormat df = DateFormat.getDateTimeInstance(DateFormat.FULL,
          DateFormat.FULL,locale);

    spanTime.setValue(df.format(new Date()));
    page.servletGet(this, request, response);

  }
  //Clean up resources
  public void destroy() {
  }

  public SPhoneList() {
    try {
      jbInit();
    }
    catch(Exception e) {
      e.printStackTrace();
    }
  }
  private void jbInit() throws Exception {
    spanTime.setColumnName("");
    spanTime.setElementId("time");
    spanTime.setPageProducer(page);
    page.setHtmlFile("C:\\Project\\JBuilder Book\\19 -InternetBeans
Express\\Sample\\IBESample\\template.html");
  }
}
```

Notice that you see no HTML within this servlet. So where does the HTML come from? The template that HTML uses for page production is defined using the `IxPageProducer.setHtmlFile()` method. As you see in Listing 19.2, the HTML template is template.html. Listing 19.3 shows the template with the introduction of the special tag to show the date and time. At runtime, the page is parsed once, and the tag locations are identified. During a request for a given page, the special tags are dynamically replaced with the contents of the tag value. In other words, the parsing of the template is done once regardless of the number of requests for the given page.

LISTING 19.3 Nezzer Chocolate Factory HTML File for Our Phone Book

```
<HTML>
    <BODY>
        <H1>Nezzer Chocolate Factory</H1>
        <H2><span id="time" language="nl" country="NL">as of</span></H2>
        <TABLE BORDER="2">
            <TR>
                <TD>Name</TD>
                <TD>Address</TD>
                <TD>Tel</TD>
                <TD>Fax</TD>
                <TD>Email</TD>
            </TR>
            <TR>
                <TD>Nebby K. Nezzer</TD>
                <TD>911 Somewhere Circle, Babylon</TD>
                <TD>(++612) 12345</TD>
                <TD>(++612) 12345</TD>
                <TD>nezzer@nezzerchocolate.com</TD>
            </TR>
            <TR>
                <TD>Rack</TD>
                <TD>121 Zootle Road, Babylon </TD>
                <TD>(++2721) 531 9090</TD>
                <TD>(++2721) 531 9090</TD>
                <TD>rack@nezzerchocolate.com </TD>
            </TR>
            <TR>
                <TD>Shack</TD>
                <TD>30 Animal Road, Babylon </TD>
                <TD>(++1) 3000 12345</TD>
                <TD>(++1) 3000 12345</TD>
                <TD> shack@nezzerchocolate.com </TD>
            </TR>
            <TR>
                <TD>Benny</TD>
                <TD>1143 Winners Lane, Babylon </TD>
                <TD>(++94) 17 12345</TD>
                <TD>(++94) 17 12345</TD>
                <TD>benny@nezzerchocolate.com </TD>
            </TR>
        </TABLE>
    </BODY>
</HTML>
```

Now replace the table to be dynamically generated from data within a JDBC-compliant database. The process is simple to replace the static HTML table with a dynamic set from the database. Replacing the HTML template as seen in Listing 19.3 will be used as the master for the `IxPageProducer`. A more simplified page will ultimately be used for the dynamic generation of the page, shown in Listing 19.4. This page becomes the template used by `IxPageProducer` to create the desired page with the merging of the dynamic data.

LISTING 19.4 The Template File for Dynamic Generation of the Phone List (template.html)

```
<HTML>
    <BODY>
        <H1>Nezzer Chocolate Factory</H1>
        <H2><span id="time" language="nl" country="NL">as of</span></H2>
        <TABLE id = "PhoneList" BORDER="2">
            <TR>
                <TD>First Name</TD>
                <TD>Last Name</TD>
                <TD>Phone</TD>
            </TR>
        </TABLE>
    </BODY>
</HTML>
```

To accomplish the replacement of the tag with dynamic data, using more than one module is required. The servlet will be used to substitute the template with the dynamic data, as shown in Listing 19.5. The data module will be used to encapsulate all the data access, as shown in Listing 19.6. As you traverse through the code in Listing 19.5, you should notice the two main sections of an InternetBeans Express servlet. The first is the `doGet()` method. This method is responsible for the runtime response to the Web server with the resulting HTML page. It also iterates through the population of all the InternetBeans Express custom tags. The last is the `jbInit()` method. This method initializes all the tags and specifies the template HTML page to the `IxPageProducer` class.

LISTING 19.5 Servlet to Substitute Dynamic Data for the Table

```
package ibesample;

import java.io.*;
import java.text.*;
import java.util.*;
```

LISTING 19.5 Continued

```
import javax.servlet.*;
import javax.servlet.http.*;

import com.borland.internetbeans.*;

public class SPhoneList extends HttpServlet {
  static final private String CONTENT_TYPE = "text/html";
  private IxPageProducer page = new IxPageProducer();
  private IxSpan spanTime = new IxSpan();
  private IxTable PhoneList = new IxTable();
  private dmEmployee dmEmployee1;
  //Initialize global variables
  public void init() throws ServletException {
  }
  //Process the HTTP Get request
  public void doGet(HttpServletRequest request,
     HttpServletResponse response) throws ServletException, IOException {
    page.getObjects();

    String language = spanTime.getAttribute("language");
    String country = spanTime.getAttribute("country");

    Locale locale = new Locale(language,country);

    DateFormat df = DateFormat.getDateTimeInstance(DateFormat.FULL,
       DateFormat.FULL,locale);

    spanTime.setValue(df.format(new Date()));
    page.servletGet(this, request, response);

  }
  //Clean up resources
  public void destroy() {
  }

  public SPhoneList() {
    try {
      jbInit();
    }
    catch(Exception e) {
      e.printStackTrace();
    }
```

LISTING 19.5 Continued

```
  }
  private void jbInit() throws Exception {
    dmEmployee1 = ibesample.dmEmployee.getDataModule();
    spanTime.setColumnName("");
    spanTime.setElementId("time");
    PhoneList.setDataSet(dmEmployee1.getEmployee());
    PhoneList.setElementId("PhoneList");
    PhoneList.setPageProducer(page);
    spanTime.setPageProducer(page);
    page.setHtmlFile("C:\\Project\\JBuilder Book\\19 -InternetBeans
Express\\Sample\\IBESample\\template.html");
  }
}
```

LISTING 19.6 Data Module for Encapsulating Data Communication into One Nodule

```
package ibesample;

import com.borland.dx.dataset.*;
import com.borland.dx.sql.dataset.*;

public class dmEmployee implements DataModule {
  static private dmEmployee myDM;
  private Database database1 = new Database();
  private QueryDataSet employee = new QueryDataSet();
  private Column LAST_NAME = new Column();
  private Column FIRST_NAME = new Column();
  private Column PHONE_EXT = new Column();
  public static dmEmployee getDataModule() {
    if (myDM == null) {
      myDM = new dmEmployee();
    }
    return myDM;
  }

  public dmEmployee() {
    try {
      jbInit();
    }
    catch(Exception e) {
      e.printStackTrace();
    }
```

LISTING 19.6 Continued

```
  }
  private void jbInit() throws Exception {
    PHONE_EXT.setCaption("Phone Extension");
    PHONE_EXT.setColumnName("PHONE_EXT");
    PHONE_EXT.setDataType(com.borland.dx.dataset.Variant.STRING);
    PHONE_EXT.setPrecision(4);
    PHONE_EXT.setTableName("EMPLOYEE");
    PHONE_EXT.setServerColumnName("PHONE_EXT");
    PHONE_EXT.setSqlType(12);
    FIRST_NAME.setCaption("First Name");
    FIRST_NAME.setColumnName("FIRST_NAME");
    FIRST_NAME.setDataType(com.borland.dx.dataset.Variant.STRING);
    FIRST_NAME.setPrecision(15);
    FIRST_NAME.setTableName("EMPLOYEE");
    FIRST_NAME.setServerColumnName("FIRST_NAME");
    FIRST_NAME.setSqlType(12);
    LAST_NAME.setCaption("Last Name");
    LAST_NAME.setColumnName("LAST_NAME");
    LAST_NAME.setDataType(com.borland.dx.dataset.Variant.STRING);
    LAST_NAME.setPrecision(20);
    LAST_NAME.setTableName("EMPLOYEE");
    LAST_NAME.setServerColumnName("LAST_NAME");
    LAST_NAME.setSqlType(12);
    employee.setQuery(new com.borland.dx.sql.dataset.QueryDescriptor(
      database1, "SELECT EMPLOYEE.LAST_NAME,EMPLOYEE.FIRST_NAME," +
      "EMPLOYEE.PHONE_EXT FROM EMPLOYEE ORDER BY EMPLOYEE.LAST_NAME,
      EMPLOYEE. FIRST_NAME",
      null, true, Load.ALL));
   database1.setConnection(new com.borland.dx.sql.dataset.ConnectionDescriptor(
      "jdbc:borland:dslocal:C:\\Development\\JBuilder7\\samples\\" +
      "JDataStore\\datastores\\employee.jds", "Sample", "", false,
      "com.borland.datastore.jdbc.DataStoreDriver"));
    employee.setColumns(new Column[] {LAST_NAME, FIRST_NAME, PHONE_EXT});
  }
  public Database getDatabase1() {
    return database1;
  }
  public QueryDataSet getEmployee() {
    return employee;
  }
}
```

You should start to see that they encapsulate and separate the presentation, logic, and persistence into single focused components. This pattern is simple and effective for producing a high-performance, flexible Web site. The remaining components work similarly; each one looks for a specific tag that will be represented by a custom tag within your HTML template.

Using InternetBeans Express with JSPs

The implementation of InternetBeans Express in JSPs has different requirements and different needs. For example, JSPs naturally implement a separation between the presentation and logic so that the need for an `IxPageProducer` is diminished. The other big difference is that instead of the use of components placed on the JSP, they are implemented with custom tags. This custom tag library is loaded using the following command:

```
<%@ taglib uri="/internetbeans.tld" prefix="ix" %>
```

This tag library is added to your project when you use the wizard to create a JSP. Figure 19.1 shows the JSP Wizard and the option to load the InternetBeans Express. After the wizard has created the JSP, it then makes the new custom tags available with the prefix specified.

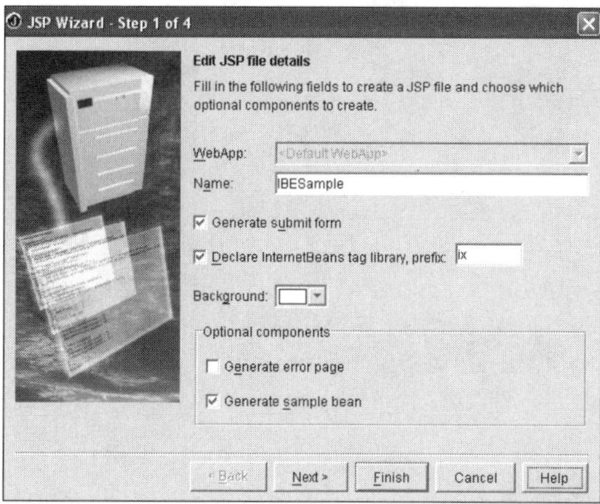

FIGURE 19.1 JSP Wizard—add custom tags for InternetBeans Express to your JSP.

We'll now implement the same solution you created with a servlet. The major items you will notice that will be different will be the removal of an HTML template, and the merging of our template and InternetBeans Express tags within the JSP, as shown in Listing 19.7.

LISTING 19.7 JSP Using the InternetBeans Express Tags

```
<%@ page import="com.borland.internetbeans.*,
➥ com.borland.dx.dataset.*,com.borland.dx.sql.dataset.*" %>
<%@ taglib uri="/internetbeans.tld" prefix="ix" %>
<HTML>
    <BODY>
        <H1>Nezzer Chocolate Factory</H1>
<ix:database id="database1" driver="com.borland.datastore.jdbc.DataStoreDriver"
  url="jdbc:borland:dslocal:C:\\Development\\JBuilder7\\samples\\JDataStore\\" +
  "datastores\\employee.jds"
username="Sample">
<ix:query id="employeeList" statement="SELECT EMPLOYEE.LAST_NAME," +
   "EMPLOYEE.FIRST_NAME,EMPLOYEE.PHONE_EXT " +
   "FROM EMPLOYEE ORDER BY EMPLOYEE.LAST_NAME,EMPLOYEE.FIRST_NAME">
<ix:table dataSet="employeeList">
        <TABLE id = "PhoneList" BORDER="2">
            <TR>
                <TD>First Name</TD>
                <TD>Last Name</TD>
                <TD>Phone</TD>
            </TR>
        </TABLE>
</ix:table>
</ix:query>
</ix:database>
    </BODY>
</HTML>
```

As you look at the solution, you should notice that all the configuration information for each object is embedded within the JSP. This makes the JSP the only required component to re-create the servlet in Listing 19.7. These changes allow you to modify and re-layout the HTML anytime you want using any HTML design tool.

Design Guidelines

Design guidelines for using InternetBeans Express are simple. Whether using servlets or JSPs, the implementation is restricted to only a few patterns. With the separation of the different responsibilities of each component, InternetBeans force the implementation to work the designed way, which is an HTML template having tags that will be substituted with dynamic data.

Use Existing HTML Files

JBuilder and InternetBeans Express are intentionally not HTML designers. When InternetBeans Express adds data-awareness to elements in an existing HTML page, it does not change their size or position. So, when binding InternetBeans Express components to a Web page, the look of the page doesn't change, except that its elements are now data aware. There should only be a couple of small changes to use an existing HTML page:

- `<TABLE>`, `<IMG>`, `<DIV>`, `<SPAN>`, and other HTML tags can be made data aware by binding them to InternetBeans Express components. When you do this, a tag's ID attribute, which is otherwise optional, must be defined.
- Each submit button must have a different name. Servlets allow them to share a name and use the value of the `VALUE` attribute to know which button was selected. In InternetBeans Express, each button is bound by name to its own InternetBeans Express component.

Use Data Modules

An InternetBeans Express application should usually use a data module. If only one data set is being used, define the data set directly in the servlet or JSP. Even then, if several data-enabled pages in the application use the same data, it's simpler and better to define all the Data Express components just once in a data module. When you want to bind InternetBeans Express components in a single servlet or JSP to more than one data set, you must use a data module.

Summary

InternetBeans Express is a powerful group of components that allow the inclusion of data with the static presentation of HTML. These components create a great framework for creating data-aware Web sites with good functionality and flexibility. In addition to those features, it can create these data-aware pages quickly.

Reflections

- When should I use InternetBeans Express?
- How many templates should I create?
- How should I structure my data access?

PART V

JBuilder for Enterprise Applications

IN THIS PART

20

XML

IN THIS CHAPTER

- Structured Graphical Markup Language (SGML)
- HTML
- XML Overview
- Using JBuilder's XML Tools
- Design Guidelines

Extensible Markup Language, or XML, is responsible for a quiet revolution in data formats and is rapidly transforming network landscapes everywhere. These landscapes are quickly becoming a jungle of intertwined technologies and newly sprouted grammars that can strike fear into the hearts of engineers everywhere. Fear not! JBuilder has become a tool the XML adventurer can use to tame and utilize XML effectively. We will look at the following:

- History of XML
- XML specifics
- XML usage in JBuilder

JBuilder provides many facilities besides just a parsing editor. For example, JBuilder generates a set of classes to read and manipulate XML documents. These classes allow for quick and easy integration of XML documents within your enterprise application.

XML inherited a number of features from many similar specifications. It pulled from the structures of SGML and the simplicities of HTML.

Structured Graphical Markup Language (SGML)

SGML became an ISO standard in 1986 and has changed little over the years. It was intended to solve the problems created by procedural markup. Applications such as WordPerfect, Microsoft Word, and others each use their own version of markup to describe how a document looks on the printed page. For example, a document created in Microsoft Word is saved with the file extension .doc. The .doc file extension is more than a simple naming convention—it also identifies the type of markup used to re-create the document on the printed page. This process, of re-creating a printed page, is not only tedious but also unfriendly. If you have attempted to use SGML, you more than likely have had experience with these document types and have experienced the headaches of trying to move documents between applications. The fact is, although you can move data created in one application into another application, the results are not always acceptable.

In the following document saved in Rich Text Format (RTF) from WordPad, as shown in Listing 20.1, you can see that in addition to the data or information, the markup also describes the formatting of the document. For example, the markup contains information about the font used in the document, Arial.

LISTING 20.1 RTF File Created Using Notepad

```
{\rtf1\ansi\ansicpg1252\deff0\deflang1033{\fonttbl{\f0\fswiss\fcharset0 Arial;}}
\viewkind4\uc1\pard\f0\fs20 Jeff Swisher\par
Dunn Solutions Group, Inc\par
5550 West Touhy Ave\par
Skokie, IL 60077\par
}
```

HTML

The Hypertext Markup Language (HTML) revolutionized the way in which you—and in fact most companies—share information. The reason for such a large and fast change is that HTML is not platform-dependent; sharing information now is as trivial as using a word processor to print a document. In addition, HTML is simple. It contains a limited number of tags, and, when you understand those, creating a document in HTML is straightforward. HTML also has a number of tools ranging from the simple to the powerful for creating these HTML pages visually, so remembering the tags is not even an issue.

In addition to being easy for developers to learn, HTML is also easy to deploy to just about any environment. It is typically inexpensive for a company to post documents and other information to the Web. Also, the major browsers that display HTML documents are free.

If HTML is easy to use and widely adopted, why do we need XML? HTML has one overwhelming problem: HTML contains a limited tag set, and that tag set has no relation to the content it surrounds. Take the following HTML example:

```
<h1>Jeff Swisher</h1>
<h2>Dunn Solutions Group</h2>
<h2>5550 West Touhy Ave</h2>
<h2>Skokie, IL 60077</h2>
<p>847-673-0900</p>
```

The tags give no indication as to the type of content they enclose. It would be nearly impossible to extract information from the document based solely on the HTML codes themselves. For example, it would be difficult to extract the phone number of Dunn Solutions Group because the instance is hidden in a tag `<p>`. Even searching through the HTML would make it difficult to attain. Now observe the same document in XML:

```
<Name>Jeff Swisher</Name>
<Company>Dunn Solutions Group</Company>
<Address>5550 West Touhy Ave</Address>
<City>Skokie</City><State>IL</State><Zip>60077</Zip>
<Phone>847-673-0900</Phone>
```

The XML document's tags describe the content they enclose. Thus, it is easy to identify the phone number for Dunn Solutions Group because it is contained within the tag `<Phone>` and easily extracted.

XML IS BORN

If you cross the benefits of SGML in containing data, HTML presentation agnosticism, and a well-defined data structure, a child is born. We will call him XML. Joking aside, XML originally was seen by many—myself included—as nothing more than a glorified text file. Even starting with this view of XML, it does not take long to see many of the benefits XML provides. By disregarding the more complex aspects of SGML, XML is much simpler to learn and implement. The most important feature of SGML that XML retains is its extensibility. You can use XML to create your own markup language just as you could use SGML to create new markups. Unlike HTML, which is limited to a certain number of tags, XML allows you to create your own tags—tags that give a deeper meaning to content. Add to this the fact that developers can define the structure of an XML language, and you will see that XML is a self-describing database. Just like SGML, XML is a metalanguage.

XML Overview

XML is extensible; you can use it to give meaning to information, much more than just structure. After you create an XML document, you can repurpose the document to conform to any output you want—for example, one source of data with multiple views for presentation, as shown in Figure 20.1. Like SGML, XML markup is not tied to one application or even a single use. You can take the XML document and publish it one way to a paper and another to the Web and yet another to a CD.

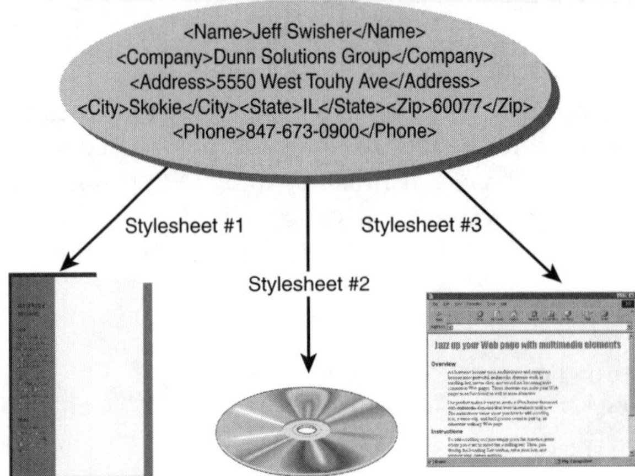

FIGURE 20.1 XML documents can be repurposed into multiple presentations using the same data.

In addition to enabling many different information presentation outputs, XML makes it easier to share information. For example, you might be surprised to know that in 1999 Sears spent more than $150 million in moving information from one location to another. Although the capability to output information to different formats is important, XML's capability to make information exchange easier is its most important and sought-after feature. Because XML is extensible and nonproprietary, it can be used by any company or industry, just as SGML was used in the past. As companies and industries create Document Type Definitions (DTDs), Schema, and other XML-based standards of information exchange, XML's full potential will be realized. For example, the World Wide Web Consortium (W3C) and the Object Management Group (OMG) have sponsored a number of standard implementations of XML.

XML is good for the following:

- Sharing data—With XML, plain text files can be used to share data. Because XML data is stored in plain text format, XML provides a software- and hardware-independent way of sharing data.
- Storing data—XML can also be used to store data in files or in databases. Applications can be written to store and retrieve information from the store, and generic applications can be used to display the data.

- Making your data more useful—Because XML is independent of hardware, software, and applications, you can make your data available to more than only standard HTML browsers.
- Creating new languages—The Wireless Markup Language (WML) used to mark up Internet applications for handheld devices such as mobile phones is written in XML.
- Separating data from HTML—When HTML is used to display data, the data is stored inside your HTML. With XML, data can be stored in separate XML files. This way, you can concentrate on using HTML for data layout and display, and be sure that changes in the underlying data do not require any changes to your HTML.
- Exchanging data—Converting the data to XML can greatly reduce this complexity and create data that can be read by many different types of applications.

Using XML Document Types

The idea of a document type should not be unfamiliar to you. You see document types every day; you just do not look at the window while driving and tell your two-year-old, look at the document type running free. For example, if you see a list of names and phone numbers, you might not know the numbers and names, but you know by the structure that it is a phone book. A document type is defined by each of the contained elements. These document types define how and what the document contains. Two document types are available:

- Document Type Definition (DTD)—The notation that defines an XML document.
- Schema—Defining the structure of data versus documents.

Document Type Definition (DTD)

The purpose of a DTD is to define the legal building blocks of an XML document. I look at the DTD as being a Lego™ set you just purchased. You have 500 different blocks, and they look nothing like the picture on the box. As you slowly assemble the blocks one at a time, they start to have the appearance of the car on the box. That is the same with the DTD; it slowly defines not only each element but also the interrelationships between all the XML data elements. You then will have the full picture of what the XML information is trying to convey.

A validating parser compares an XML document against its DTD. Not all parsers validate XML documents. Many simply check that the XML is well formed—having an open tag and an associated close tag. In fact, Internet Explorer, using the built-in parser, does not validate XML by default, although it is capable of doing so. Look at an example XML document as shown in Listing 20.2, and its associated DTD in Listing 20.3.

LISTING 20.2 Sample XML Defining an E-mail Message

```
<?xml version="1.0"?>
<!DOCTYPE note SYSTEM "note.dtd">
<note>
<to>Jeff</to>
<from>Mike</from>
<heading>Reminder</heading>
<body>Don't forget to get that done!</body>
</note>
```

LISTING 20.3 Sample DTD Validating an E-mail Message

```
<!ELEMENT note (to,from,heading,body)>
<!ELEMENT to (#PCDATA)>
<!ELEMENT from (#PCDATA)>
<!ELEMENT heading (#PCDATA)>
<!ELEMENT body (#PCDATA)>
```

Why do you need to use a DTD? With a DTD, each of your XML files can carry a description of its own format within it. With a DTD, independent developers can agree to use a common DTD for interchanging data, similar to a legal contract between two individuals or companies. Your application can then implement a standard DTD to verify that the data you receive from the outside world is valid. You can also use a DTD to verify your own data, custom information not encompassed by a standard. The main building blocks of both XML and HTML documents are tagged elements, such as `<body>....</body>`. Seen from a DTD point of view, all XML documents (and HTML documents) are made up of the following simple building blocks:

- Elements—The main building blocks of both XML and HTML documents. Examples of HTML elements are `body` and `table`. Examples of XML elements could be `note` and `message`. Elements can contain text or other elements, or they can be empty. Examples of empty HTML elements are `hr`, `br`, and `img`.
- Tags—Used to mark up elements. A starting tag such as `<element_name>` marks up the beginning of an element, and an ending tag such as `</element_name>` marks up the end of an element.

- Attributes—Provide extra information about elements. Attributes are always placed inside the starting tag of an element. Attributes always come in name/value pairs.
- Entities—Variables used to define common text. Most of you will know the HTML entity reference ` `. This no break space entity is used in HTML to insert an extra space in a document. Entities are expanded when a document is parsed by an XML parser.
- PCDATA—PCDATA stands for *parsed character data*. Think of character data as the text found between the start tag and the end tag of an XML element. PCDATA is text that is parsed by a parser. Tags inside the text are treated as markup, and entities are expanded.
- CDATA—CDATA means *character data*. CDATA is text that is not parsed by a parser. Tags inside the text are not treated as markup, and entities are not expanded.

Schema

DTDs are useful if you want to describe the structure of a document. They have been successfully used for this purpose for more than a decade. Unfortunately, DTDs are deficient when it comes to the needs of XML application developers rather than the document/content managers. The fact is that XML is being used, and will continue to be used, to create data-intensive applications. XML is not used to simply mark up a document anymore; it is used to mark up data. Although documents and data are similar, the requirements of data are actually much more demanding in defining the associated structure. For example, Internet businesses such as Dell and Amazon use XML to describe the stuff they sell. This stuff is rarely in the form of a document, if ever. If this gives you the impression that XML servers are performing databaselike functions for these companies, you're correct. In fact, many popular database server vendors are starting to implement many features specifically geared to the needs of the XML application. The purpose of a Schema is to define the legal building blocks of an XML document, just like a DTD. An XML Schema contains the following:

- Elements within a document
- Attributes that can appear within a document
- Which elements are child elements
- Sequence in which the child elements can appear
- Number of child elements
- Required elements

- Data types for elements and attributes
- Default values for elements and attributes

Many organizations still use DTDs, and they are still popular in many situations. DTDs are especially still present in the whole document management/content management space. We think that very soon XML Schemas will replace the use of DTDs in a number of environments, maybe even completely. Here are some reasons:

- Easier to learn than DTD
- Extensible to future additions
- Richer and more useful than DTDs
- Written in XML
- Support data types
- Support namespaces

Let's look at an example. Listing 20.4 creates an order. This order is much more structured than a DTD would handle effectively.

LISTING 20.4 W3C Schema Defining a Music Order

```
<?xml version="1.0"?>
<shipOrder>
  <shipTo>
    <name>Jeff Swisher</name>
    <street>500 North 3300 South</street>
    <address>Skokie, IL 60077</address>
    <country>USA</country>
  </shipTo>
  <items>
    <item>
      <title>Kansas - Two for the Show</title>
      <quantity>1</quantity>
      <price>10.90</price>
    </item>
    <item>
      <title>OC Supertones - Strike Back</title>
      <quantity>1</quantity>
      <price>9.90</price>
    </item>
  </items>
</shipOrder>
```

The order consists of a root element <shipOrder>, with two child elements <shipTo> and <items>. The <items> element contains <item> elements. An <item> element contains <title>, <quantity>, and <price> elements. The XML Schema in Listing 20.5 defines the element <shipOrder> to be of the type order. order is a complex type element consisting of the elements <shipTo> and <items>. The <shipTo> element is of the type shipAddress—a complex type element consisting of the elements <name>, <street>, <address>, and <country>. The <items> element is of the type cdItems—a complex type element consisting of <item> elements. The <item> element is of the type cdItem—a complex type element consisting of <title>, <quantity>, and <price> elements. The <title> element is a normal element of the type string.

LISTING 20.5 Schema Defining the Structure of a Web Order

```
<xsd:schema xmlns:xsd="http://www.w3.org/1999/XMLSchema">

<xsd:element     name="shipOrder" type="order"/>

<xsd:complexType name="order">
  <xsd:element   name="shipTo"    type="shipAddress"/>
  <xsd:element   name="items"     type="cdItems"/>
</xsd:complexType>

<xsd:complexType name="shipAddress">
  <xsd:element   name="name"      type="xsd:string"/>
  <xsd:element   name="street"    type="xsd:string"/>
  <xsd:element   name="address"   type="xsd:string"/>
  <xsd:element   name="country"   type="xsd:string"/>
</xsd:complexType>

<xsd:complexType name="cdItems">
  <xsd:element   name="item"      type="cdItem"/>
</xsd:complexType>

<xsd:complexType name="cdItem">
  <xsd:element   name="title"     type="xsd:string"/>
  <xsd:element   name="quantity"
   type="xsd:positiveInteger"/>
  <xsd:element   name="price"     type="xsd:decimal"/>
</xsd:complexType>

</xsd:schema>
```

Parsers

Before you delve into the grove of the XML Document Object Model (DOM) and Simple API for XML (SAX), you should revisit some of the basic concepts of XML. When an XML document is opened, it is parsed by an XML parser, as shown in Figure 20.2. If an external application written in Java needs to access the XML, it needs a way to interface with this document. This is done through the use of said parser. Two parsers available for this use are SAX and DOM. The XML DOM and SAX offer two ways for an application to interface with XML. XML DOM and SAX are different in the way in which they enable access to XML, as you will see here.

FIGURE 20.2 The parser is an integral part of XML and an application.

The XML DOM or SAX is a middleman that sits between the XML document and an application built to access the XML document. If you chose not use the XML DOM or SAX, you would need to write your application to connect directly to the XML document and parse it. If you have ever attempted to do this, you will appreciate the simplicity of using a parser. By using standardized interpretation of an XML document, such as DOM or SAX, you can load a document, create a document, and access and manipulate the information and structures contained within the XML document.

DOM

The W3C standardized an API for working with XML. It is called the Document Object Model (DOM), and it is available in many different browsers. But the DOM is not only for use in browsers. It can also be used on the server side. You can use the DOM to read, write, and transmit XML in your framework.

The DOM is popular for general XML processing. It has been implemented, for example, for use with just about every major language including languages, such as Python and Perl scripts, and with C++ and Java programming languages, among others. In fact, Microsoft's DOM implementation is a built-in part of the Windows OS itself.

SAX

The Simple API for XML (SAX) is an event-based API for XML. As you saw in DOM, the XML DOM is a tree-based API. It must build a document tree through which applications can navigate. SAX, on the other hand, reports parsing events directly to the application. For example, SAX can be used to report the start of an element back to the application. This technique reduces the stress on the server because it does not require an entire document tree to build. It only reports to the application the information that the application requests.

Different versions of SAX are available, with the current version being SAX2. SAX was developed by members of the XML-DEV mailing list. The purpose of its development was to find a better way to handle large XML documents. As you've already seen in the DOM, the XML DOM needs to create a map on an XML document before you can traverse the document. Because this map must be created in memory, it can result in performance problems on your server, especially if you're working with large XML documents. Let's put it this way: Imagine trying to build an XML DOM tree for all the books sold by Amazon.com. The XML document would be huge, and it would take a lot of server memory to build the DOM. If you were looking for only a small piece of information, using XML DOM would be a waste of time and resources.

Judging from the preceding paragraph, you might think that SAX is always the best choice when you need an XML API. This is not the case. The XML DOM does have advantages over SAX. For one thing, the XML DOM is an approved W3C recommendation. To use an automotive metaphor, the XML DOM is a company-approved dealership. It has a relationship with the parent company for which it sells cars. On the other hand, SAX is an independent dealership. This is not necessarily a bad thing, but it might not always be what you want. The advantages the XML DOM has over SAX include the capability to modify the XML document stored in memory (SAX is not designed to write XML documents) and easier random or multiple access to data.

Using JBuilder's XML Tools

JBuilder provides several features that will enhance and improve your use of XML within your application development. These features are designed with the developer in mind and not the content manager. In other words, it focuses on the implementation and not as much on the XML document. These XML tools include

- Manually creating XML-related documents
- Creating XML-related documents using the JBuilder wizards
- Hierarchical XML viewer
- XML document validation
- XML presentation

XML Document Creation Using JBuilder

Creating an XML file is actually easy within JBuilder. The process of building the XML file is just exercising the editor within JBuilder. The process is simple:

1. Right-click on the project pane and select Add Files/Package.
2. Type in the name of the XML file to create or select an existing one.
3. If this is a new XML document, it prompts you to create the file.

This is not the only method for creating an XML document. You may create an XML document using the wizard. The problem with using the wizard is that you must have a DTD or Schema. The steps for creating an XML document from a DTD are as follows:

1. Choose File, New and select the XML tab. From the XML tab, choose DTD to XML. The DTD to XML Wizard dialog box appears as shown in Figure 20.3.

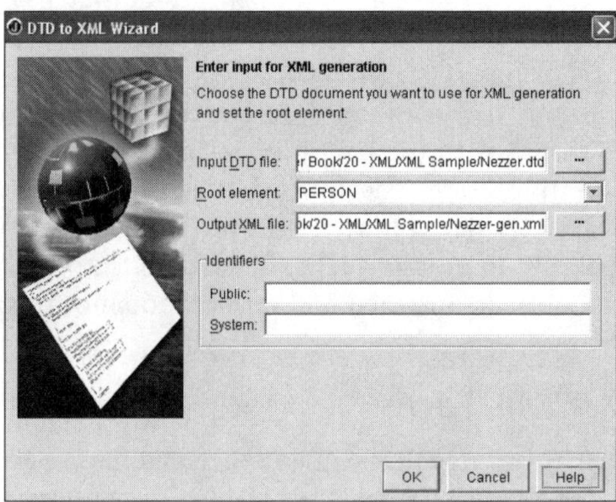

FIGURE 20.3 Generate an XML document from a DTD.

2. Supply the DTD and the target generated XML file.
3. Supply the root of the XML document. The root is the first element within the DTD that you want to generate the DTD.
4. Click Finish. The code created appears in Listing 20.6.

LISTING 20.6 Generation of DTD to XML Wizard

```
<?xml version="1.0" encoding="UTF-8"?>
<PEOPLE>
    <PERSON PERSONID="nmtoken">
        <NAME>pcdata</NAME>
        <ADDRESS>pcdata</ADDRESS>
        <TEL>pcdata</TEL>
        <FAX>pcdata</FAX>
        <EMAIL>pcdata</EMAIL>
    </PERSON>
</PEOPLE>
```

Using the File, New wizards is not the only way to create either a new DTD or XML document. Right-clicking on a DTD or XML document allows you to either generate a DTD or generate an XML document. The same wizards are used regardless of the methods.

Presenting XML Documents

JBuilder provides a number of facilities for viewing or presenting an XML document. These facilities are important to give you a flexible presentation of your XML data. The two major types of XML presentations are as follows:

- eXtensible Stylesheet Language (XSL)
- Cocoon

eXtensible Stylesheet Language (XSL)

XSL can be confusing because it can refer to several different things. When people talk about XSL, they're usually referring to XSL Transformations (XSLTs) and the Path Language (XPath). XSL also includes a formatting language, but the W3C hasn't approved the final recommendation for this part of XSL. The formal recommendation for the XSLT language was approved by the W3C on 26 November 1999.

The origins of XSL are in Cascading Stylesheets (CSSs), where a stylesheet is used to add formatting to an HTML file. The syntax to use a stylesheet in XSLT is similar to the syntax in CSS. However, XSLT stylesheets have a different function than CSSs. CSS allows you to define the colors, backgrounds, and font types for an HTML Web page, whereas XSLT allows you to transform an XML file into an HTML file or another text-based format. If you only need Web page formatting, you might still choose to use CSS because it is less complicated and more widely implemented for general HTML formatting.

Let's now take a look at a complete example using XML and XSLT. One of the best ways to learn a new topic is to see it in practice within an example. Suppose that we want to create a phone directory for our chocolate factory. We will start the information about our employees within an XML file and create a DTD to define its structure. Figure 20.4 demonstrates the ultimate goal for creating the phone directory.

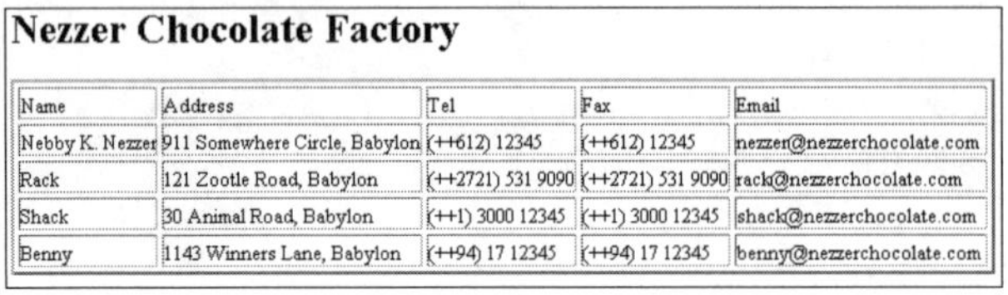

Nezzer Chocolate Factory

Name	Address	Tel	Fax	Email
Nebby K. Nezzer	911 Somewhere Circle, Babylon	(++612) 12345	(++612) 12345	nezzer@nezzerchocolate.com
Rack	121 Zootle Road, Babylon	(++2721) 531 9090	(++2721) 531 9090	rack@nezzerchocolate.com
Shack	30 Animal Road, Babylon	(++1) 3000 12345	(++1) 3000 12345	shack@nezzerchocolate.com
Benny	1143 Winners Lane, Babylon	(++94) 17 12345	(++94) 17 12345	benny@nezzerchocolate.com

FIGURE 20.4 Building a Web page to display the Nezzer Chocolate Factory phone directory.

In the example, it is easiest to start with the HTML page and work backward to produce the XSLT. Having the ultimate end goal makes it easier to create the steps. The following steps were used to create the necessary components of this example:

1. Create the HTML source for the desired result (see Listing 20.7).

LISTING 20.7 HTML Source Page of the Phone Directory

```
<HTML>
    <BODY>
        <H1>Nezzer Chocolate Factory</H1>
        <TABLE BORDER="2">
            <TR>
                <TD>Name</TD>
                <TD>Address</TD>
                <TD>Tel</TD>
                <TD>Fax</TD>
                <TD>Email</TD>
            </TR>
            <TR>
                <TD>Nebby K. Nezzer</TD>
                <TD>911 Somewhere Circle, Babylon</TD>
                <TD>(++612) 12345</TD>
                <TD>(++612) 12345</TD>
                <TD>nezzer@nezzerchocolate.com</TD>
            </TR>
            <TR>
                <TD>Rack</TD>
```

LISTING 20.7 Continued

```
                <TD>121 Zootle Road, Babylon </TD>
                <TD>(++2721) 531 9090</TD>
                <TD>(++2721) 531 9090</TD>
                <TD>rack@nezzerchocolate.com </TD>
            </TR>
            <TR>
                <TD>Shack</TD>
                <TD>30 Animal Road, Babylon </TD>
                <TD>(++1) 3000 12345</TD>
                <TD>(++1) 3000 12345</TD>
                <TD> shack@nezzerchocolate.com </TD>
            </TR>
            <TR>
                <TD>Benny</TD>
                <TD>1143 Winners Lane, Babylon </TD>
                <TD>(++94) 17 12345</TD>
                <TD>(++94) 17 12345</TD>
                <TD>benny@nezzerchocolate.com </TD>
            </TR>
        </TABLE>
    </BODY>
</HTML>
```

2. Design the XML document to contain the desired data. Make sure to create a sample of each type of information you intend to display. Listing 20.8 shows the creation of this document.

LISTING 20.8 Sample XML Document for the Nezzer Chocolate Factory Phone Directory

```
<?xml version="1.0"?>
<!DOCTYPE PEOPLE SYSTEM "nezzer.dtd">
<!-- *********** Nezzer Chocolate Directory *********** -->
<PEOPLE>
  <PERSON PERSONID="p1">
    <NAME>Nebby K. Nezzer</NAME>
    <ADDRESS>911 Somewhere Circle, Babylon</ADDRESS>
    <TEL>(++612) 12345</TEL>
    <FAX>(++612) 12345</FAX>
    <EMAIL>nezzer@nezzerchocolate.com</EMAIL>
  </PERSON>
```

LISTING 20.8 Continued

```
  <PERSON PERSONID="p2">
    <NAME>Rack</NAME>
    <ADDRESS>121 Zootle Road, Babylon </ADDRESS>
    <TEL>(++2721) 531 9090</TEL>
    <FAX>(++2721) 531 9090</FAX>
    <EMAIL>rack@nezzerchocolate.com </EMAIL>
  </PERSON>

  <PERSON PERSONID="p3">
    <NAME>Shack</NAME>
    <ADDRESS>30 Animal Road, Babylon </ADDRESS>
    <TEL>(++1) 3000 12345</TEL>
    <FAX>(++1) 3000 12345</FAX>
    <EMAIL> shack@nezzerchocolate.com </EMAIL>
  </PERSON>

  <PERSON PERSONID="p4">
    <NAME>Benny</NAME>
    <ADDRESS>1143 Winners Lane, Babylon </ADDRESS>
    <TEL>(++94) 17 12345</TEL>
    <FAX>(++94) 17 12345</FAX>
    <EMAIL>benny@nezzerchocolate.com </EMAIL>
  </PERSON>

</PEOPLE>
```

3. Using JBuilder, create a DTD for the given XML document. This is accomplished by adding the XML document to your project. After this is done, right-click on the XML document and select Generate DTD. Listing 20.9 shows the results of creating the required DTD.

LISTING 20.9 DTD for Defining the Phone Directory

```
<?xml version="1.0" encoding="UTF-8" ?>
<!ELEMENT TEL ( #PCDATA ) >
<!ELEMENT PERSON ( NAME, ADDRESS, TEL, FAX, EMAIL ) >
<!ATTLIST PERSON PERSONID NMTOKEN #REQUIRED >
<!ELEMENT EMAIL ( #PCDATA ) >
<!ELEMENT FAX ( #PCDATA ) >
<!ELEMENT PEOPLE ( PERSON+ ) >
<!ELEMENT ADDRESS ( #PCDATA ) >
<!ELEMENT NAME ( #PCDATA ) >
```

4. Create the XSLT using the DTD and XML document starting with the existing HTML page. Slowly replace all the static HTML data elements with the associated XSLT commands. Listing 20.10 is the ultimate end game.

LISTING 20.10 XSLT Stylesheet Will Convert XML to HTML

```
<?xml version="1.0"?>
<xsl:stylesheet xmlns:xsl="http://www.w3.org/1999/XSL/Transform" version="1.0"
xmlns:java="http://xml.apache.org/xslt/java"
exclude-result-prefixes="java">
<xsl:output method="xml" indent="yes"/>
<xsl:output encoding="ISO-8859-1"/>
<xsl:strip-space elements="*"/>

<xsl:template match="/">
<HTML>
<BODY>
<H1>Nezzer Chocolate Factory</H1>
<TABLE BORDER="2">
    <TR>
        <TD>Name</TD>
        <TD>Address</TD>
        <TD>Tel</TD>
        <TD>Fax</TD>
        <TD>Email</TD>
    </TR>
    <xsl:for-each select="PEOPLE/PERSON">
    <TR>
        <TD><xsl:value-of select="NAME"/></TD>
        <TD><xsl:value-of select="ADDRESS"/></TD>
        <TD><xsl:value-of select="TEL"/></TD>
        <TD><xsl:value-of select="FAX"/></TD>
        <TD><xsl:value-of select="EMAIL"/></TD>
    </TR>
    </xsl:for-each>
</TABLE>
</BODY>
</HTML>
</xsl:template>
</xsl:stylesheet>
```

5. Assign the stylesheet to the XML document to be transformed. This is accomplished by entering the properties editor of the XML document and selecting the XML tab, and then attaching the XSLT.

6. Test the transformation by selecting the XML document and clicking on the Transform View tab within the JBuilder Designer.

Using Cocoon in JBuilder

Apache Cocoon is an XML publishing framework that makes using XML and XSLT for server applications much simpler. This was specifically designed for performance and scalability using the SAX parser. Cocoon is designed to offer a flexible environment based on a separation of content, logic, and style. The Cocoon model divides its content into three different categories:

- XML creation—XML is created by the content provider within the framework specified.
- XML processing—The XML files are processed for logical rules.
- XSL presentation—The XML is rendered to a number of different resource outputs (HTML, PDF, WML, XHTML, and so on).

JBuilder offers only the capability to run a Cocoon project within JBuilder. For information on building a Cocoon project visit `www.cocoon.org`.

Manipulating XML Documents Within JBuilder

JBuilder has a number of wizards to aid in the use of SAX, the Simple API for XML. SAX sends events directly to the application through callbacks, allowing processing to take place. The application then implements handlers to deal with each of the different events, similar to event handling in a graphical user interface. For example, Listing 20.11 will be parsed using SAX, and the resulting parsing events are included in Listing 20.12.

LISTING 20.11 The Sample XML Document to Parse

```
<?xml version="1.0"?>
<page>
   <title>Save the World</title>
   <content>Hello, world!</content>
</page>
```

LISTING 20.12 Parsing Events for the Sample XML Document

```
start document
start element: page
start element: title
```

LISTING 20.12 Continued

```
characters: Save the World
end element: title
start element: content
characters: Hello, world!
end element: content
end element: page
end document
```

Using the XML Databinding Wizard, we can automate this process for building an XML parser for our selected document. We will continue to use the XML document shown earlier in Listing 20.7. The following steps create a class to parse this XML document:

1. Open an existing project containing an XML document.
2. Choose File, New under the XML tab. Choose the SAX Handler Wizard.
3. Specify the name of the package and the events you want to override. Override the method `characters` under the `ContentHandler` group.
4. Call your class `MyParser`.
5. After clicking Next, leave the rest of the options with the default setting by clicking the Finish button.
6. Print the elements as they are read from the parser. Add the following code to the parser to demonstrate the parsing process. This code should be added to the overriding method `characters`.

```
String s = new String(ch, start, length);
if (ch[0] == '\n')
 return;
System.out.println(" Value: " + s);
```

BorlandXML

BorlandXML provides a mechanism to generate the associated classes for accessing an XML structure. This allows you to access the XML document as if it was a set of classes. In addition to parsing the document for access, it also gives you a facility to modify and generate an XML document of a given structure defined by a given DTD. This facilitates a number of useful features for the XML developer:

- JavaBean manipulation—Manipulate a Bean to easily construct and access an XML document.

- Marshalling and unmarshalling—Convert an XML document to be accessed through the Beans and converted back to XML.
- Document validation—Validate the XML contained within the JavaBean before marshalling the XML stream.
- PCDATA customization—Customize the PCDATA types to be Java primitives rather than a string.
- Variable names—Modify the names, prefixes, and suffixes for any element within the XML document.

To generate the wrapper BorlandXML classes, execute the following steps:

1. Right-click on a DTD within your project and select Generate Java.
2. Select BorlandXML for the parser. Figure 20.5 demonstrates the wizard's first step.

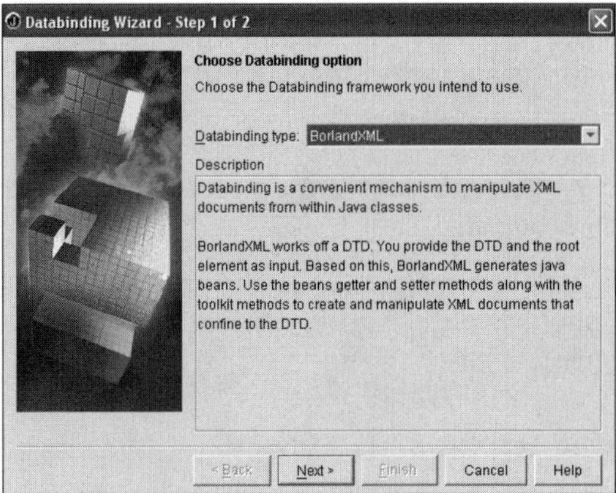

FIGURE 20.5 Step 1 of 2 generating the Java for accessing the XML document.

3. Assign the root element of the DTD. For example, if we continue to use Listing 20.3, the root element is `Person`.
4. Specify the system identifier DTD in the System field. Select the Finish button. Figure 20.6 shows step 2 of the JBuilder Wizard.
5. Use the classes that have been generated. For example, you might want to add code to create a new XML document. Add the following code where you want to create a new XML file based on the designed structure:

```
PERSON p = new PERSON();
try {
```

```
      p.setPERSONID("8821");
      p.setNAMEText("Jeff Swisher");
      p.setADDRESSText("5550 West Touhy Ave");
      p.setEMAILText("JeffS@dunnsolutions.com");

      p.marshal(new java.io.FileWriter("C:\\TEMP\\new.XML"));
    }
    catch (IOException ex) {
      ex.printStackTrace();
    }
```

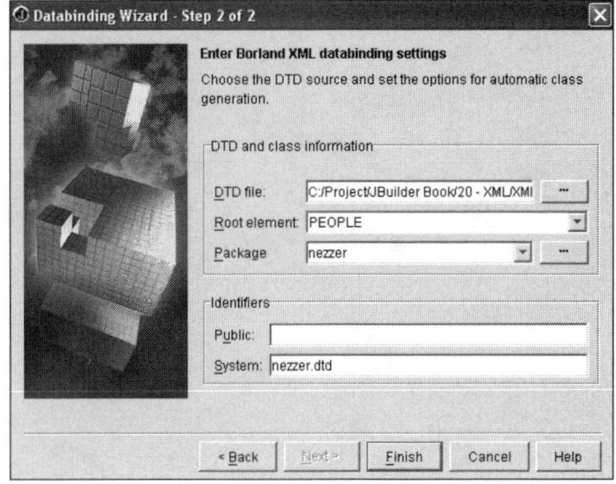

FIGURE 20.6 Step 2 of 2 generating the Java for accessing the XML document.

Using Castor in JBuilder

Castor is similar to BorlandXML in its overall purpose; it wraps the XML parsing in easy-to-use classes. The major difference between Castor and BorlandXML is the inputs to the wizard. Castor uses XMLSchema only. Just like BorlandXML, Castor then takes the Schema and generates a series of classes in which the developer can access and manipulate the XML document contents. Let's look at the same example from Nezzer Chocolate Factory. Listing 20.13 contains the source listing input, XMLSchema, and Listing 20.14 contains the resulting generated Java classes within JBuilder. Listing 20.15 shows PEOPLEDescript.java.

LISTING 20.13 XMLSchema Created for the Phone Directory (nezzer.xsd)

```
<?xml version="1.0" encoding="UTF-8"?>
<xsd:schema xmlns:xsd="http://www.w3.org/2001/XMLSchema"
➥elementFormDefault="qualified">
```

LISTING 20.13 Continued

```
        <xsd:element name="TEL" type="xsd:string"/>
        <xsd:element name="EMAIL" type="xsd:string"/>
        <xsd:element name="FAX" type="xsd:string"/>
        <xsd:element name="ADDRESS" type="xsd:string"/>
        <xsd:element name="NAME" type="xsd:string"/>
        <xsd:complexType name="PERSON">
                <xsd:sequence>
                        <xsd:element ref="TEL"/>
                        <xsd:element ref="EMAIL"/>
                        <xsd:element ref="FAX"/>
                        <xsd:element ref="ADDRESS"/>
                        <xsd:element ref="NAME"/>
                </xsd:sequence>
        </xsd:complexType>
        <xsd:element name="PEOPLE">
                <xsd:complexType>
                        <xsd:sequence>
                                <xsd:element name="PERSON"
➥ type="PersonType" maxOccurs="unbounded"/>
                        </xsd:sequence>
                </xsd:complexType>
        </xsd:element>
</xsd:schema>
```

LISTING 20.14 Our Collection Class for the Group of Employees Called PEOPLE (PEOPLE.Java)

```
/**
 * This class was automatically generated with
 * <a href="http://castor.exolab.org">Castor 0.9.3</a>, using an
 * XML Schema.
 * $Id$
 */

package nezzer;

  //---------------------------------/
 //- Imported classes and packages -/
//---------------------------------/
```

LISTING 20.14 Continued

```
import java.io.Reader;
import java.io.Serializable;
import java.io.Writer;
import java.util.ArrayList;
import java.util.Enumeration;
import org.exolab.castor.xml.*;
import org.exolab.castor.xml.MarshalException;
import org.exolab.castor.xml.ValidationException;
import org.xml.sax.DocumentHandler;

/**
 *
 * @version $Revision$ $Date$
**/
public class PEOPLE implements java.io.Serializable {


      //--------------------------/
     //- Class/Member Variables -/
    //--------------------------/

    private java.util.ArrayList _PERSONList;


      //----------------/
     //- Constructors -/
    //----------------/

    public PEOPLE() {
        super();
        _PERSONList = new ArrayList();
    } //-- nezzer.PEOPLE()


      //-----------/
     //- Methods -/
    //-----------/

    /**
     *
     * @param vPERSON
    **/
```

LISTING 20.14 Continued

```
    public void addPERSON(PERSON vPERSON)
        throws java.lang.IndexOutOfBoundsException
    {
        _PERSONList.add(vPERSON);
    } //-- void addPERSON(PERSON)

    /**
     *
     * @param index
     * @param vPERSON
    **/
    public void addPERSON(int index, PERSON vPERSON)
        throws java.lang.IndexOutOfBoundsException
    {
        _PERSONList.add(index, vPERSON);
    } //-- void addPERSON(int, PERSON)

    /**
    **/
    public void clearPERSON()
    {
        _PERSONList.clear();
    } //-- void clearPERSON()

    /**
    **/
    public java.util.Enumeration enumeratePERSON()
    {
        return new org.exolab.castor.util.IteratorEnumeration(_
➥PERSONList.iterator());
    } //-- java.util.Enumeration enumeratePERSON()

    /**
     *
     * @param index
    **/
    public PERSON getPERSON(int index)
        throws java.lang.IndexOutOfBoundsException
    {
        //-- check bounds for index
        if ((index < 0) || (index > _PERSONList.size())) {
```

LISTING 20.14 Continued

```
            throw new IndexOutOfBoundsException();
        }

        return (PERSON) _PERSONList.get(index);
    } //-- PERSON getPERSON(int)

    /**
    **/
    public PERSON[] getPERSON()
    {
        int size = _PERSONList.size();
        PERSON[] mArray = new PERSON[size];
        for (int index = 0; index < size; index++) {
            mArray[index] = (PERSON) _PERSONList.get(index);
        }
        return mArray;
    } //-- PERSON[] getPERSON()

    /**
    **/
    public int getPERSONCount()
    {
        return _PERSONList.size();
    } //-- int getPERSONCount()

    /**
    **/
    public boolean isValid()
    {
        try {
            validate();
        }
        catch (org.exolab.castor.xml.ValidationException vex) {
            return false;
        }
        return true;
    } //-- boolean isValid()

    /**
     *
     * @param out
```

LISTING 20.14 Continued

```
    **/
    public void marshal(java.io.Writer out)
        throws org.exolab.castor.xml.MarshalException,
➥org.exolab.castor.xml.ValidationException
    {

        Marshaller.marshal(this, out);
    } //-- void marshal(java.io.Writer)

    /**
     *
     * @param handler
    **/
    public void marshal(org.xml.sax.DocumentHandler handler)
        throws org.exolab.castor.xml.MarshalException,
➥org.exolab.castor.xml.ValidationException
    {

        Marshaller.marshal(this, handler);
    } //-- void marshal(org.xml.sax.DocumentHandler)

    /**
     *
     * @param vPERSON
    **/
    public boolean removePERSON(PERSON vPERSON)
    {
        boolean removed = _PERSONList.remove(vPERSON);
        return removed;
    } //-- boolean removePERSON(PERSON)

    /**
     *
     * @param index
     * @param vPERSON
    **/
    public void setPERSON(int index, PERSON vPERSON)
        throws java.lang.IndexOutOfBoundsException
    {
        //-- check bounds for index
        if ((index < 0) || (index > _PERSONList.size())) {
```

LISTING 20.14 Continued

```
            throw new IndexOutOfBoundsException();
        }
        _PERSONList.set(index, vPERSON);
    } //-- void setPERSON(int, PERSON)

    /**
     *
     * @param PERSONArray
    **/
    public void setPERSON(PERSON[] PERSONArray)
    {
        //-- copy array
        _PERSONList.clear();
        for (int i = 0; i < PERSONArray.length; i++) {
            _PERSONList.add(PERSONArray[i]);
        }
    } //-- void setPERSON(PERSON)

    /**
     *
     * @param reader
    **/
    public static nezzer.PEOPLE unmarshal(java.io.Reader reader)
        throws org.exolab.castor.xml.MarshalException,
➥org.exolab.castor.xml.ValidationException
    {
        return (nezzer.PEOPLE)
➥Unmarshaller.unmarshal(nezzer.PEOPLE.class, reader);
    } //-- nezzer.PEOPLE unmarshal(java.io.Reader)

    /**
    **/
    public void validate()
        throws org.exolab.castor.xml.ValidationException
    {
        org.exolab.castor.xml.Validator validator =
➥new org.exolab.castor.xml.Validator();
        validator.validate(this);
    } //-- void validate()

}
```

LISTING 20.15 Descriptor Class Generated by Castor (PEOPLEDescript.java)

```
/*
 * This class was automatically generated with
 * <a href="http://castor.exolab.org">Castor 0.9.3</a>, using an
 * XML Schema.
 * $Id$
 */

package nezzer;

  //---------------------------------/
 //- Imported classes and packages -/
//---------------------------------/

import org.exolab.castor.mapping.AccessMode;
import org.exolab.castor.mapping.ClassDescriptor;
import org.exolab.castor.mapping.FieldDescriptor;
import org.exolab.castor.xml.*;
import org.exolab.castor.xml.FieldValidator;
import org.exolab.castor.xml.TypeValidator;
import org.exolab.castor.xml.XMLFieldDescriptor;
import org.exolab.castor.xml.handlers.*;
import org.exolab.castor.xml.util.XMLFieldDescriptorImpl;
import org.exolab.castor.xml.validators.*;

/**
 *
 * @version $Revision$ $Date$
**/
public class PERSONDescriptor extends
➥org.exolab.castor.xml.util.XMLClassDescriptorImpl {


      //--------------------------/
     //- Class/Member Variables -/
    //--------------------------/

    private java.lang.String nsPrefix;

    private java.lang.String nsURI;

    private java.lang.String xmlName;
```

LISTING 20.15 Continued

```
    private org.exolab.castor.xml.XMLFieldDescriptor identity;


      //----------------/
     //- Constructors -/
    //----------------/

    public PERSONDescriptor() {
        super();
        xmlName = "PERSON";
        XMLFieldDescriptorImpl  desc           = null;
        XMLFieldHandler         handler        = null;
        FieldValidator          fieldValidator = null;

        //-- set grouping compositor
        setCompositorAsSequence();
        //-- initialize attribute descriptors

        //-- initialize element descriptors

        //-- _TEL
        desc = new XMLFieldDescriptorImpl(java.lang.String.class,
➥"_TEL", "TEL", NodeType.Element);
        desc.setImmutable(true);
        handler = (new XMLFieldHandler() {
            public Object getValue( Object object )
                throws IllegalStateException
            {
                PERSON target = (PERSON) object;
                return target.getTEL();
            }
            public void setValue( Object object, Object value)
                throws IllegalStateException, IllegalArgumentException
            {
                try {
                    PERSON target = (PERSON) object;
                    target.setTEL( (java.lang.String) value);
                }
                catch (Exception ex) {
                    throw new IllegalStateException(ex.toString());
                }
            }
```

LISTING 20.15 Continued

```
            public Object newInstance( Object parent ) {
                return null;
            }
        } );
        desc.setHandler(handler);
        desc.setRequired(true);
        desc.setMultivalued(false);
        addFieldDescriptor(desc);

        //-- validation code for: _TEL
        fieldValidator = new FieldValidator();
        fieldValidator.setMinOccurs(1);
        { //-- local scope
            StringValidator sv = new StringValidator();
            sv.setWhiteSpace("preserve");
            fieldValidator.setValidator(sv);
        }
        desc.setValidator(fieldValidator);

        //-- _EMAIL
        desc = new XMLFieldDescriptorImpl(java.lang.String.class,
➥"_EMAIL", "EMAIL", NodeType.Element);
        desc.setImmutable(true);
        handler = (new XMLFieldHandler() {
            public Object getValue( Object object )
                throws IllegalStateException
            {
                PERSON target = (PERSON) object;
                return target.getEMAIL();
            }
            public void setValue( Object object, Object value)
                throws IllegalStateException, IllegalArgumentException
            {
                try {
                    PERSON target = (PERSON) object;
                    target.setEMAIL( (java.lang.String) value);
                }
                catch (Exception ex) {
                    throw new IllegalStateException(ex.toString());
                }
            }
            public Object newInstance( Object parent ) {
```

LISTING 20.15 Continued

```
                return null;
            }
        } );
        desc.setHandler(handler);
        desc.setRequired(true);
        desc.setMultivalued(false);
        addFieldDescriptor(desc);

        //-- validation code for: _EMAIL
        fieldValidator = new FieldValidator();
        fieldValidator.setMinOccurs(1);
        { //-- local scope
            StringValidator sv = new StringValidator();
            sv.setWhiteSpace("preserve");
            fieldValidator.setValidator(sv);
        }
        desc.setValidator(fieldValidator);

        //-- _FAX
        desc = new XMLFieldDescriptorImpl(java.lang.String.class, "_FAX",
➥"FAX", NodeType.Element);
        desc.setImmutable(true);
        handler = (new XMLFieldHandler() {
            public Object getValue( Object object )
                throws IllegalStateException
            {
                PERSON target = (PERSON) object;
                return target.getFAX();
            }
            public void setValue( Object object, Object value)
                throws IllegalStateException, IllegalArgumentException
            {
                try {
                    PERSON target = (PERSON) object;
                    target.setFAX( (java.lang.String) value);
                }
                catch (Exception ex) {
                    throw new IllegalStateException(ex.toString());
                }
            }
            public Object newInstance( Object parent ) {
                return null;
```

LISTING 20.15 Continued

```
            }
        } );
        desc.setHandler(handler);
        desc.setRequired(true);
        desc.setMultivalued(false);
        addFieldDescriptor(desc);

        //-- validation code for: _FAX
        fieldValidator = new FieldValidator();
        fieldValidator.setMinOccurs(1);
        { //-- local scope
            StringValidator sv = new StringValidator();
            sv.setWhiteSpace("preserve");
            fieldValidator.setValidator(sv);
        }
        desc.setValidator(fieldValidator);

        //-- _ADDRESS
        desc = new XMLFieldDescriptorImpl(java.lang.String.class, "_ADDRESS",
➥"ADDRESS", NodeType.Element);
        desc.setImmutable(true);
        handler = (new XMLFieldHandler() {
            public Object getValue( Object object )
                throws IllegalStateException
            {
                PERSON target = (PERSON) object;
                return target.getADDRESS();
            }
            public void setValue( Object object, Object value)
                throws IllegalStateException, IllegalArgumentException
            {
                try {
                    PERSON target = (PERSON) object;
                    target.setADDRESS( (java.lang.String) value);
                }
                catch (Exception ex) {
                    throw new IllegalStateException(ex.toString());
                }
            }
            public Object newInstance( Object parent ) {
                return null;
            }
```

LISTING 20.15 Continued

```
        } );
        desc.setHandler(handler);
        desc.setRequired(true);
        desc.setMultivalued(false);
        addFieldDescriptor(desc);

        //-- validation code for: _ADDRESS
        fieldValidator = new FieldValidator();
        fieldValidator.setMinOccurs(1);
        { //-- local scope
            StringValidator sv = new StringValidator();
            sv.setWhiteSpace("preserve");
            fieldValidator.setValidator(sv);
        }
        desc.setValidator(fieldValidator);

        //-- _NAME
        desc = new XMLFieldDescriptorImpl(java.lang.String.class, "_NAME",
➥"NAME", NodeType.Element);
        desc.setImmutable(true);
        handler = (new XMLFieldHandler() {
            public Object getValue( Object object )
                throws IllegalStateException
            {
                PERSON target = (PERSON) object;
                return target.getNAME();
            }
            public void setValue( Object object, Object value)
                throws IllegalStateException, IllegalArgumentException
            {
                try {
                    PERSON target = (PERSON) object;
                    target.setNAME( (java.lang.String) value);
                }
                catch (Exception ex) {
                    throw new IllegalStateException(ex.toString());
                }
            }
            public Object newInstance( Object parent ) {
                return null;
            }
        } );
```

LISTING 20.15 Continued

```
        desc.setHandler(handler);
        desc.setRequired(true);
        desc.setMultivalued(false);
        addFieldDescriptor(desc);

        //-- validation code for: _NAME
        fieldValidator = new FieldValidator();
        fieldValidator.setMinOccurs(1);
        { //-- local scope
            StringValidator sv = new StringValidator();
            sv.setWhiteSpace("preserve");
            fieldValidator.setValidator(sv);
        }
        desc.setValidator(fieldValidator);

    } //-- nezzer.PERSONDescriptor()


      //-----------/
     //- Methods -/
    //-----------/

    /**
    **/
    public org.exolab.castor.mapping.AccessMode getAccessMode()
    {
        return null;
    } //-- org.exolab.castor.mapping.AccessMode getAccessMode()

    /**
    **/
    public org.exolab.castor.mapping.ClassDescriptor getExtends()
    {
        return null;
    } //-- org.exolab.castor.mapping.ClassDescriptor getExtends()

    /**
    **/
    public org.exolab.castor.mapping.FieldDescriptor getIdentity()
    {
        return identity;
```

LISTING 20.15 Continued

```
    } //-- org.exolab.castor.mapping.FieldDescriptor getIdentity()

    /**
    **/
    public java.lang.Class getJavaClass()
    {
        return nezzer.PERSON.class;
    } //-- java.lang.Class getJavaClass()

    /**
    **/
    public java.lang.String getNameSpacePrefix()
    {
        return nsPrefix;
    } //-- java.lang.String getNameSpacePrefix()

    /**
    **/
    public java.lang.String getNameSpaceURI()
    {
        return nsURI;
    } //-- java.lang.String getNameSpaceURI()

    /**
    **/
    public org.exolab.castor.xml.TypeValidator getValidator()
    {
        return this;
    } //-- org.exolab.castor.xml.TypeValidator getValidator()

    /**
    **/
    public java.lang.String getXMLName()
    {
        return xmlName;
    } //-- java.lang.String getXMLName()

}
```

Other files are generated in addition to the one in Listing 20.15, but the rules are simple. For each complex type defined within a Schema, two classes are generated.

One of the classes provides public access data through the use of accessors and mutators to the parsed document; this is called a *descriptor class*. The second class is used to define the elements contained within the complex type and is given the name of the complex type. In addition the second class is also responsible for XML data validation, and marshalling and unmarshalling of the XML source document.

You may want to start using the newly created classes to access an existing XML document. This process is done by using the classes generated by the XML wrapper interface. For example, Listing 20.16 demonstrates the use of an XML document via the generated interface.

LISTING 20.16 Using the XML Wrapper to Access an XML Document

```
try {
  String fileName = "c:\\temp\\Nezzer.XML";
  System.out.println("== unmarshalling \"" + fileName + "\" ==");
  //Unmarshal XML file.
  PEOPLE p = PEOPLE.unmarshal(new FileReader(fileName));
  System.out.println("Total Number of Persons read = " + p.getPERSONCount());
}
catch (Exception ex) {
  ex.printStackTrace();
}
```

Interfacing with XML

To interface an XML document with JBuilder, you can use the XML document parser or you can use XML components. This set of components is sometimes referred to as *template-based components*. The following are some of the capabilities of the XML components within JBuilder:

- Retrieve data from a database and convert to either an XML or HTML object.
- Retrieve data from a database and map the results to a different structure XML document.

Each XML component has it own customizer, so you will notice that they might look a little different. But the principle is the same for converting either to or from XML.

The following example is the implementation using `XTable`. This example reads data from the employee table and converts the result to XML. The following steps are required to produce a working example:

1. Create a new project and a new application.
2. On your main frame, add an `XTable` component to your frame. This component is located under the tab labeled XML. Notice that you will only see the component under the component tree in the lower left of the UI Designer.
3. Start the customizer as shown in Figure 20.7, by right-clicking on the component within the component tree.

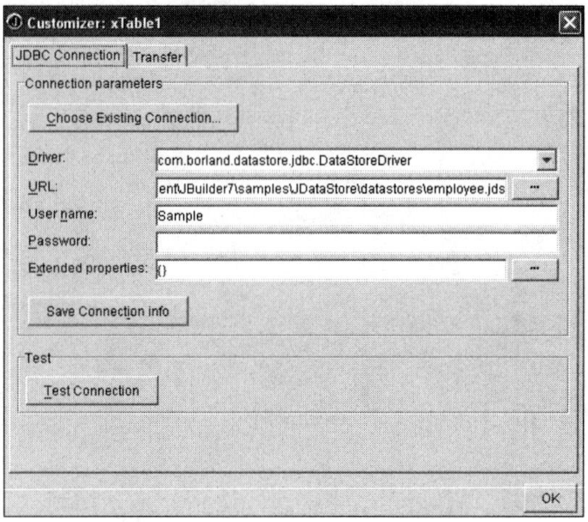

FIGURE 20.7 The `XTable` customizer—supply database connection.

4. Specify the connection string and driver. If you do not have one that you want to use, use the settings as shown in Figure 20.8:

   Name: xTblEmployee

   Driver: `com.borland.datastore.jdbc.DataStoreDriver`

   URL: `jdbc:borland:dslocal:C:\Development\JBuilder7\ samples\JDataStore\ datastores\employee.jds` (The path changes based on the installation directory of JBuilder.)

   User Name: Sample

5. Supply the transfer information to create the XML document. The following information should be filled in:

   Output Filename: beans_employee.xml

   Column: As Elements

   Output: XML

Element Names: Document: XMLEmployees

Row: XMLEmployee

Table Name: Employee

Keys: `EMP_NO<NL>`

Default: `{EMP_NO=2}`

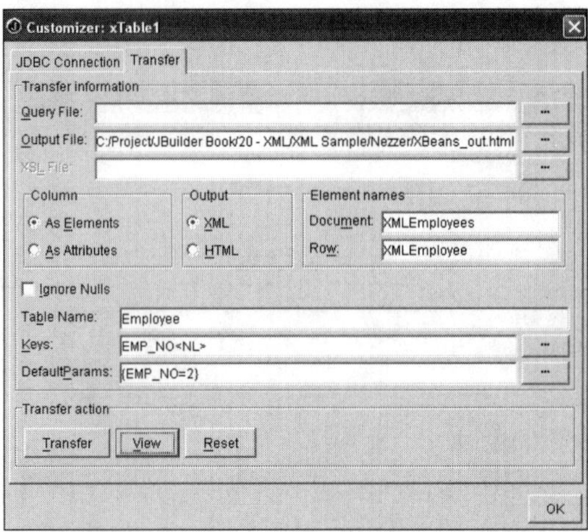

FIGURE 20.8 The `XTable` customizer—supply transfer information.

6. Use the component with the XML document for employee number 2. A number of different methods can be used to gather the information from the document, but the easiest way is to use the method `getOutputAsDom()`. This method returns a DOM parser handle loaded with the document from the `XTable` component. One such method allows us to convert the resulting query to an XML document. Implement the following code on a button event:

```
try {
  xTblEmployee.writeOutputToFile();
}
catch (XException ex) {
  ex.printStackTrace();
}
```

Design Guidelines

XML suffers from an all too common problem with new technologies—"buzzword-itis." Like the Java and multitiered—or was it "n-tiered"—architectures before that,

XML has visibility at the executive level—the nontechnical executive level. This visibility leads to corporate edicts and wondering why the entire system has not been converted to XML. However, like Java and other architectures, XML isn't an answer in and of itself; it's simply a tool you can use to help build your technical solution. We recommend the following six general design guidelines for the judicious use of XML in the data architecture of your systems.

If You Don't Need It, Don't Use It

One thing many architects do not initially see when using XML is that it is just a way to represent information—not take over the world. There really is nothing magical about an XML document: It just shows how various pieces of information relate to one another. When you receive from another source an XML document that includes extraneous information (such as surrogate keys), do not use that information! You can use an XSLT stylesheet to filter out the information you want to keep, drop the information you do not want, and transform it to fit the way you want. If you filter the data to only the data required, it makes your system much more efficient.

For example, if you receive information about seven million customers in one huge XML document, but the information would be more useful to you in separate documents, break it up into multiple XML documents. After all, if you received a fixed-width file from a legacy system, you would not keep it that way; you would transform it to something more useful. Do not be afraid to do the same to your XML documents. Dissect, reorganize, or otherwise modify XML documents to suit your needs as a developer.

Don't Attempt to Find Me

XML does a stellar job of describing and containing data but does not do as well at finding data. Because XML documents are just flat text documents, searching components such as `XPath` requires you to parse the entire document, locate the piece in which you are interested, and return the results. If you are trying to work with a specific XML document, with about seven million customers, searching would be inefficient if not impossible. If you break up the document into smaller documents—say, one per customer—the problem still occurs. To find the particular customer for whom you are looking, parse each document until you find the appropriate one. The only reliable XML search methods are either relation data source searches, which return the results, or native XML indexing tools. A number of XML indexing tools are available in today's market. When you have data-oriented documents (as opposed to text-oriented information, such as a book manuscript) a relational database is well suited for this task, and it provides other benefits as well.

Don't Count on Me

Just like in searching, using XML for summarization is also inefficient. The utility `XPath` contains only the bare minimum of aggregation functionality, and even this is not easily usable if the information you want to summarize is found in more than one document. As in searching, we recommend indexing the information, thus reducing the amount of information to be parsed to discover required pieces needed for aggregation. Alternatively, you could generate an additional document that contains summary information as detailed XML documents that were the basis of the aggregation. However, that would not allow creating your own ad hoc summarization, in addition to creating a complicated XMLSchema. For the best flexibility for summarization tasks, a relational database is really the only good choice; most off-the-shelf XML indexers do not expose the indexes themselves for direct programmatic manipulation.

Presenting with XML

One real power of XML lies in its capability, via XSLT, to present its contents in various forms. This is important if your system needs to support various means of data consumption using a presentation tier, such as HTML within a desktop Web browser, a portable device using WML, or a standard contract agreed on by your industry. Although a relational database can drive presentation, it is not as good at the job. Each possible presentation requires significant coding time.

XML and Legacy Systems

A significant component of any enterprise architecture is the integration of objects and component-based systems with legacy applications. Generally, legacy applications, whether packaged or custom developed, do not contain standard data formats. Furthermore, the information they supply often does not contain standard interfaces or published interfaces at all. In short, these applications are not easily accessible. These special challenges were introduced by integrating two different worlds of technology: the new world of Java/EJB and CORBA objects, and the world of legacy applications still running a majority of mission-critical enterprise applications.

This then reveals how enterprise integration and application servers, message brokers, messaging, and XML can be used to successfully integrate legacy applications into your new enterprise environment. Although various techniques and tradeoffs can be successfully used to deal with the complex issues presented by legacy integration, they normally include XML as the standardized transport layer.

To use XML in this manner is a four-step process that can be time consuming to implement. The following list gives you a road map to integration between components and legacy information using XML:

- Design the interface abstraction—The first step is to review your inventory of legacy transactions and determine which ones you want to integrate with your business-to-business e-commerce processing. Discover the data model and functional model inherent in each. For example, a transaction may involve the addition, modification, and deletion of an object such as a customer record. Then design an interface that reflects a higher level abstraction than the legacy systems typically implement. For example, a suitable business abstraction may be "Modify an existing customer," whereas each of those business-level operations is implemented as a sequence of screen interactions. To create an IT infrastructure that can rapidly respond to changes in the business, you will want to expose an interface that implements the higher level business transaction and not force each developer to painfully execute that sequence of individual screen interactions.
- Expose the legacy transaction—A special challenge with CICS is that the vast majority of applications that were designed to work with the 3270 terminal cannot be called from another MVS program or even other CICS applications. That is, 3270 applications present no callable API—they work only with a terminal. Over the years, IBM has provided a number of approaches to solving this problem. These range from tools that help separate presentation from business logic when you first develop the program to special ways to intercept and replace the 3270 processing with a call, such as FEPI, ECI, EXCI, and most recently, the CICS 3270 bridge.
- Package the higher level business interface—The next step is to define a higher level business abstraction and then map that higher level interface to the sequence of individual CICS screen interactions, which are now exposed with a callable interface. We'll refer to this high level, business abstraction as an *e-business transaction.*
- Implement the logic—After the e-business transaction is defined, the next decision is where to implement the logic that packages the set of transactions together. One approach is to implement the business abstraction packaging logic on a mid-tier component, such as an EJB. The drawback to this approach is that the execution of one e-business transaction would require a number of round-trip communications between the mid-tier component and CICS on the mainframe, resulting in slow performance.

XML Standard Implementations

There are many prewritten and agreed-on implementations covering a range of different vertical industries. There normally is no reason to redevelop the wheel over and over again; the same situation applies to standard implementations. If they exist, use them. Table 20.1 lists many of these standard implementations.

TABLE 20.1 Community Vocabulary Standards for Different Vertical Markets

Vertical XML Standard	Description
ChemML	Chemical Markup Language
ASDML	Astronomical Dataset Markup Language
MathML	Mathematical Markup Language
LegalXML	Legal Markup Language
EML	Electoral Markup Language
NewsML	News/Print Markup Language
BIOML	BioTech Markup Language
OFX	Open Financial eXchange
MISMO	Mortgage Industry Standards Maintenance Organization
CPExc	Customer Personal Exchange Format
aecXML	Architecture, Engineering Construction XML
RecipeML	Yes, even recipes have a standard.

In Practice

It is important to understand that you can implement XML in a number of different ways within JBuilder. In this section, we are going to mark up the information about our course catalog in XML. The information will then be presented using a number of different methods.

As we look at this problem, we will divide the solution into a number of different parts. These parts will then be divided into small and deliberate steps. The following are the steps for which we are going to divide our application:

1. Create a sample XML file containing enough appropriate samples to generate a DTD.
2. Generate a DTD and modify it to support features not identified by the sample.
3. Create the HTML page to display the sample.
4. Convert the HTML file to XSLT.

Creating a Sample XML

It is easiest to create a sample XML file first, before creating the required DTD or Schema. We will create two XML files: one containing the course listing information and one containing the course detail.

1. Create a new project.
2. Add a file to your project to contain the course listing. Either create the file outside JBuilder or specify a name and JBuilder then creates a blank XML file.

Call the file CourseListing.XML. The following XML document represents our course listing information:

```
<?xml version="1.0" encoding="UTF-8"?>
<Courses>
  <Course id="1">
    <Category>Java</Category>
    <Name>Introduction to Java</Name>
    <Duration>3 Days</Duration>
  </Course>
  <Course id="2">
    <Category>Java</Category>
    <Name>Introduction to JBuilder</Name>
    <Duration>5 Days</Duration>
  </Course>
  <Course id="3">
    <Category>Design</Category>
    <Name>In Search of Excellent Requirements</Name>
    <Duration>5 Days</Duration>
  </Course>
</Courses>
```

3. Create an XML file called CourseDetail.XML. The following code contains the detail XML document for course information:

```
<?xml version="1.0" encoding="UTF-8"?>
<Course Id="1">
  <Category>Java</Category>
  <Name>Introduction to JBuilder</Name>
  <Duration>5 Days</Duration>
  <Description>JBuilder 7.0 Application Development is a five-day course
➥designed to ensure that Java developers using JBuilder 7 have an
➥understanding of, and can successfully use the features of,
➥JBuilder 7 in developing data-aware applications. Concepts are
➥taught through instructor led exercises and individual lab
➥exercises, that build on each other to create a data-aware
➥application. JBuilder concepts covered include IDE, projects,
➥debugger, data model, dataModules, data-aware components, and
➥the use of many wizards to simplify and decrease development time.
➥Java concepts covered include language basics, objected oriented
➥programming, event handling ,exception handling, and introduction
➥to JavaBeans, EJBs, Servlets, and CORBA. This course helps prepare
➥students for the Borland Product Certified JBuilder 7 exam.</Description>
</Course>
```

Creating a DTD

It is easier to create a DTD from a sample XML document instead of creating the DTD by hand. It is usually easier for a developer to visualize sample data rather than a nebulous DTD. The following steps are required to create the DTD:

1. Right-click on each XML document and choose Generate DTD. Leave the default name for the DTD.
2. Add to the CourseListing.XML the following line directly after `<?xml...?>`.

   ```
   <!DOCTYPE Courses SYSTEM "CourseListing.dtd">
   ```

3. Add to the CourseDetail.XML the following line directly after `<?xml...?>`.

   ```
   <!DOCTYPE Course SYSTEM "CourseDetail.dtd">
   ```

4. Validate both XML documents using the right-click menu for validation.

NOTE

If your XML document no longer validates, verify the case of your `!DOCTYPE` line. Mismatched case is a common reason for this.

Creating a Simple Presentation

We will make a simple user interface to display the course listing and the course detail. These views will be developed using HTML completely. Although this form will be simple, you can make a complex one if you want. The following steps are required to create the HTML page within JBuilder. Listing 20.17 contains the sample HTML for our presentation of our course listing.

1. Right-click on your project node and select Add Files/Package.
2. Type in the name of the HTML file in the filename box—in this case, **`Nezzer.html`**.
3. If the file is new, JBuilder asks `Do you wish to create it?`
4. The new HTML file is created and added to your project.

LISTING 20.17 Sample Course Listing

```
<HTML>
    <BODY>
        <H1>Public Course Listing</H1>
```

LISTING 20.17 Continued

```
        <TABLE BORDER="2">
            <TR>
                <TD>Category</TD>
                <TD>Title</TD>
                <TD>Duration</TD>
            </TR>
            <TR>
                <TD>Java</TD>
                <TD>Introduction to Java</TD>
                <TD>3 Days</TD>
            </TR>
            <TR>
                <TD>Java</TD>
                <TD>Introduction to JBuilder</TD>
                <TD>5 Days</TD>
            </TR>
            <TR>
                <TD>Design</TD>
                <TD>In Search of Excellent Requirements</TD>
                <TD>5 Days</TD>
            </TR>
        </TABLE>
    </BODY>
</HTML>
```

Converting HTML to XSLT

As stated earlier, it is simpler to create the HTML page, and then slowly convert the HTML page to XSLT. The process is actually simple if you attempt to convert only a small chunk of HTML at a time. The following steps are required to accomplish this task:

1. Save the HTML file to a new name that ends in `.xsl`. In this case, we named the HTML file `CourseListing.html`, so the XSL file would be `CourseListing.xsl`.

2. Add the XSLT header information to the newly converted HTML file. The following lines of code accomplish this:

   ```
   <?xml version="1.0"?>
   <xsl:stylesheet xmlns:xsl="http://www.w3.org/1999/XSL/Transform"
   ➥version="1.0"
   xmlns:java="http://xml.apache.org/xslt/java"
   ```

```
exclude-result-prefixes="java">
<xsl:output method="html" indent="yes"/>
<xsl:output encoding="ISO-8859-1"/>
<xsl:strip-space elements="*"/>
```

3. Add the template end information by adding the following information to the end of the XSL page:

```
</xsl:template>
</xsl:stylesheet>
```

4. Add the element you want to start parsing. This indicates where in the XML hierarchy the parsing will begin. This is like setting the directory you are starting in. The code to do this is simple—just one line:

```
<xsl:template match="/">
```

5. Add the looping construct to go around the detail portion of the table. In this example, it is around the `<TR>`, and `</TR>` indicators for each row of data. Then remove all the rows of detail information, leaving one. This shows you whether you are really traversing through the XML data. After you have done this, your XSL should look as shown in Listing 20.18.

LISTING 20.18 Start Building Your Looping Construct Within the XSLT for Transformation

```
<?xml version="1.0"?>
<xsl:stylesheet xmlns:xsl="http://www.w3.org/1999/XSL/Transform" version="1.0"
xmlns:java="http://xml.apache.org/xslt/java"
exclude-result-prefixes="java">
<xsl:output method="html" indent="yes"/>
<xsl:output encoding="ISO-8859-1"/>
<xsl:strip-space elements="*"/>

<xsl:template match="/">
<HTML>
<BODY>
<H1>Public Course Listing</H1>
<TABLE BORDER="2">
        <TR>
                <TD>Category</TD>
                <TD>Title</TD>
                <TD>Duration</TD>
        </TR>
```

LISTING 20.18 Continued

```
        <xsl:for-each select="Courses/Course">
        <TR>
                <TD>Java</TD>
                <TD>Introduction to Java</TD>
                <TD>3 Days</TD>
        </TR>
        </xsl:for-each>
</TABLE>
</BODY>
</HTML>
</xsl:template>
</xsl:stylesheet>
```

6. Change the data in the row to be replaced with the XML element values. This is accomplished by using the `<xsl:value-of select="Category"/>`. You will then repeat that for each of the elements.

The final result should be an XSL document that transfers the XML document to be presented within an HTML browser. The XSL shown in Listing 20.19 is the completed XSL to accomplish this task.

LISTING 20.19 Final Completion of the XSLT Template

```
<?xml version="1.0"?>
<xsl:stylesheet xmlns:xsl="http://www.w3.org/1999/XSL/Transform" version="1.0"
xmlns:java="http://xml.apache.org/xslt/java"
exclude-result-prefixes="java">
<xsl:output method="html" indent="yes"/>
<xsl:output encoding="ISO-8859-1"/>
<xsl:strip-space elements="*"/>

<xsl:template match="/">
<HTML>
<BODY>
<H1>Public Course Listing</H1>
<TABLE BORDER="2">
        <TR>
                <TD>Category</TD>
                <TD>Title</TD>
                <TD>Duration</TD>
        </TR>
```

LISTING 20.19 Continued

```
        <xsl:for-each select="Courses/Course">
        <TR>
                <TD><xsl:value-of select="Category"/></TD>
                <TD><xsl:value-of select="Name"/></TD>
                <TD><xsl:value-of select="Duration"/></TD>
        </TR>
        </xsl:for-each>
</TABLE>
</BODY>
</HTML>
</xsl:template>
</xsl:stylesheet>
```

You should now have enough information to follow the same steps to create an XSL file for the transformation of course detail information.

Summary

In this chapter we looked at the history of XML and at many key ideas associated with using XML. XML has many roots in other technologies that have been proven in many different implementations. XML should then be just as proven; in fact, many important applications use XML successfully today.

XML has become one of the most important new technologies since HTML. It is used in many applications and is available in many different implementations in just about every language and platform.

Reflections

- Is XML an important service that I must use within my application to meet the desired requirements?
- Has someone already developed an XML document structure that will meet my needs?
- Will XML continue to be a prevalent exchange language or will something better come along?
- How will the use of XML affect my performance requirements?

21

An Architectural Overview of Enterprise JavaBeans

IN THIS CHAPTER

- Ancient History or Not So Ancient
- Client/Server Saves the Day
- Application Servers
- Enterprise JavaBeans and Component-based Middleware
- Enterprise JavaBeans Goals
- How EJB Systems Work
- The Enterprise JavaBeans Component
- The Enterprise JavaBeans Container
- Remote Interface
- The Home Interface
- Where Do I Get an EJB Object Class?
- Enterprise JavaBeans Types
- How Does It All Work?

Enterprise JavaBeans (EJB) have generated a lot of press since their introduction March 1998. In fact, today I doubt that you can enter any major organization or open a trade magazine without seeing some representation of Enterprise JavaBeans. This chapter takes a high-level look at what exactly Enterprise JavaBeans are. We will explore how EJB differs from the original JavaBeans component model and discuss why EJB has generated such an enormous amount of interest.

With the introduction of the Enterprise JavaBean framework in JBuilder 5, it is important to not just understand what wizards do, but how they really work. To find out what they are doing inside, we must first look at the architectural framework.

In this chapter, we will not be looking at code; the chapter will be an architectural overview. EJB covers a lot of territory, so it is important first to understand the basic concepts. These concepts are required to make the code we will look at in subsequent chapters meaningful. This architecture is not complex, but it is rather wide, so we will explore the major features.

One important aspect of understanding an architecture such as EJB is understanding the historical perspective that contributed to its features. We will first look at the history of the most related architectures starting with client/server systems. Although many architectures contributed small portions to EJB, we will concentrate only on those with the greatest impact. We will then look at the different components that make up not just EJB but also the entire J2EE architecture of which EJB is just a small portion. We will also talk about the different types of EJB components and their usage. Finally, we will look at the usage of EJBs and their effectiveness in that environment.

Ancient History or Not So Ancient

In the beginning, there was a mainframe computer. And it was good as far as we were aware at the time. At this time, computers would barely fit in your garage, let alone in your car. These computers consisted primarily of big, expensive machines used by large organizations to support and facilitate their daily business operations.

Then came the minicomputers, mini only in the sense that they were smaller than the others. You might be able fit one in the back of a pickup truck now. In addition to the size limitation, the practice of timesharing this power increased the accessibility of computing power, but information and processing were still centralized on a few individual machines.

Then the first personal computers arrived in the 1980s and quickly changed the corporate culture. You just needed to part with $15,000 for a floppy and 64K of memory. My new calculator, which has Borland on it, has more power. These personal computers soon cluttered the corporate landscape with thousands of tiny islands of information. Each person had his own Lotus 1-2-3 spreadsheets or Ashton Tate dBase databases, all the while churning out reports of variable quality and quickly becoming inconsistent with each other.

Client/Server Saves the Day

The client/server architecture was the first mainstream architecture to address the needs of both centralized data control and widespread data accessibility. This need came about from the unresponsiveness and politicalizing of many IS departments. When using the client/server systems, data or information is maintained in a relatively centralized manner or is dispersed or replicated among distributed database servers. This facilitates control and consistency of data while still providing access to the data users need.

Client/server systems, which still exist in every major and most minor organizations, are now commonly built with various numbers of tiers. These tiers took the traditional portions of the mainframe system, which ran on one computer, and divided them to run over a number of systems. Mainframe-based processing has been referred to as *monolithic* or *single-tier architecture*. Single-tier applications were common in every environment because they are relatively easy to manage and maintain a high degree of data consistency. Unfortunately, a better solution to the monolithic systems was needed because their limited scalability and lack of redundancy were disadvantages to businesses. The old saying was "If the one computer is down, the whole business is down."

In come the first client/server systems to rescue the weary IS personnel. These were constructed with a two-tier design. The first tier was responsible for running the user interface, which ran on the client. The second tier was the persistence tier—in other words, where the data lived. (I cannot think of a single client in which a client/server system is not still in operation.) One common implementation of this type of two-tier architecture performs most, if not all, of the business logic on the client. The data is then updated to a shared data source by sending streams of Structured Query Language (SQL) to a database server. This implementation gave organizations a flexible solution. With such a system, an organization could modify the business rules to reflect new business conditions and access the same data structure, as demonstrated in Figure 21.1.

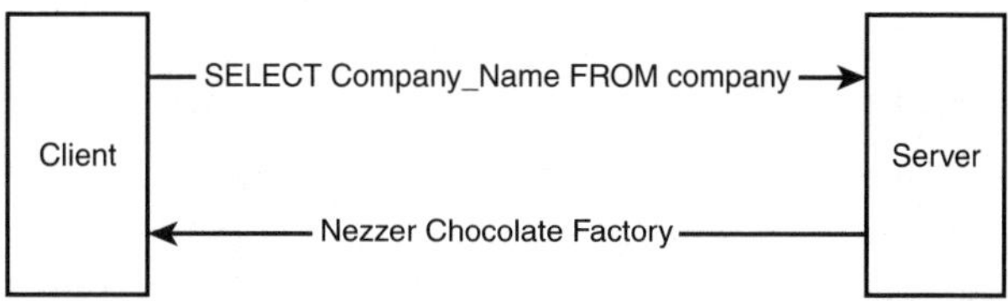

FIGURE 21.1 Sample implementation of the client/server two-tiered architecture.

One major liability within this model is the integration of business logic and the presentation of the data together. This raised a problem that every time business logic needed to change, the client needed to change along with it. Many solutions were proposed and even implemented to address this need—for example, the implementation of business logic within the persistence tier, stored procedures. The problem with this solution is that every database vendor implemented its own "standard" dialect. In addition to the coupling of the business logic and presentation tier, it was discovered that this architecture did not scale well for large-scale enterprise applications. As many different solutions continued to be investigated and implemented, in moved a new concept, the application server.

Application Servers

The application server was not entirely a new concept—just an old one rehashed from other, not so popular, architectures. An application server environment is typically implemented using three different tiers: presentation, business logic, and persistence (see Figure 21.2). These tiers have specific responsibilities, and seldom do the lines of these responsibilities blur.

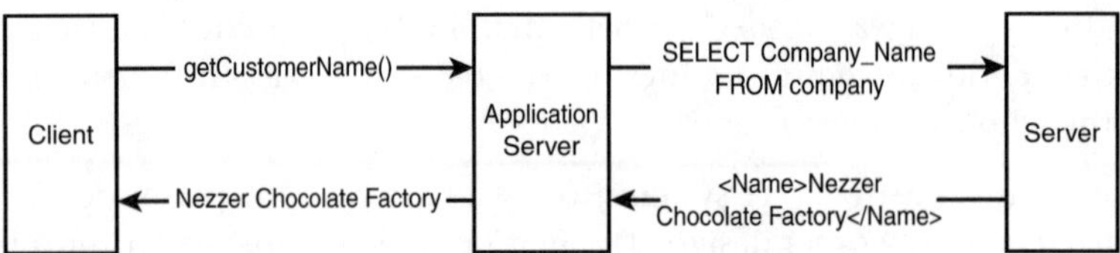

FIGURE 21.2 Sample implementation of an application server based on three-tiered architecture.

In this environment, the client usually executes business methods on the application server and uses the server mostly for persistence and enforcing data integrity. With this scenario, the client and application server typically use a protocol to facilitate the communication between the high-level business method and the underlying physical transactions (tables and rows). In addition to providing an encapsulation and abstraction layer for business logic, these tiers typically implement load balancing and fault tolerance. For example, with fault tolerance, when a client makes a call to the middle tier and the middle tier fails, the transaction is automatically rolled over to the backup middle tier.

These types of application servers are typically referred to as *middleware*. Middleware products provide communication protocols, consolidation of requests, request traffic management (fault tolerance and load balancing), and transaction support. Multitier architectures provided the much-needed flexibility and interoperability lacking in the two-tiered model. Many different middleware categories of products exist, such as the following:

- Remote procedural (RMI, Tuxedo, and DCE)
- Message-oriented middleware (MQseries and JMS)
- Object broker (CORBA and DCOM)
- Component-based middleware (EJB and .NET)

For example, object-oriented languages and techniques became so prevalent that the existing middleware products based on remote procedures became passé. Common Object Request Broker Architecture (CORBA) allowed for objects to be located somewhere on a distributed network and to be reachable. This level of encapsulation became a huge contributor to the component-based middleware products, of which EJB is one. These CORBA servers were interoperable across many languages and platforms, which made it appealing to organizations large and small.

Enterprise JavaBeans and Component-based Middleware

Now that we have spent some time looking into the past and you have an understanding of what application servers are, we'll take a look at Enterprise JavaBeans and see what features they offer. The rudimentary purpose behind Enterprise JavaBeans is to provide a framework for which components may be designed and then "plugged" into a server. This server then extends the components' capabilities by offering services for which it will supply "plumbing" and other necessary amenities. Enterprise JavaBeans are sometimes seen as similar to the original JavaBeans component specification, but in reality they only share some properties, methods, and the same surname: JavaBean. In fact, EJB technology is governed or directed by the specifications for a JavaBeans component.

A component-based middleware approach adopted by the J2EE platform has several benefits:

- It reduces the overall complexity of development with a simplified architecture. The business logic of the application runs within an Enterprise JavaBean container. The supplied vendor containers implement all the necessary plumbing and management.
- It is highly scalable. As the demands of an enterprise system increase, the logic can be easily loaded onto other middle tiers.
- Application integration looks to integrate with existing information systems. This is provided as an API to SQL databases and other enterprise data sources in addition to supporting CORBA servers and custom integration using enterprise connectors.
- Container services provide security implementation of varying types of security models. J2EE technologies are designed with security in mind.
- Many different development tools, servers, and components can be interchanged or integrated. The developers can choose from the solutions that are best for their needs and requirements, without becoming dependent on a given vendor.

Enterprise JavaBeans Goals

As stated in the goals of EJB specification 1.2, the following goals are indicated for Enterprise JavaBeans and their associated specification:

- Makes it easy for developers to create applications, freeing them from low-level system details of managing transactions, threads, load balancing, and so on. Application developers can concentrate on business logic and leave the plumbing details of managing the data processing to the framework, the plumber.
- Defines the major structures of the EJB framework, and then specifically defines the contracts between them. The responsibilities of the client, the server, and the individual components are all clearly spelled out.
- Aims to be the standard way for client/server applications to be built in the Java language. Just as the original JavaBeans (or Delphi components, or whatever) from different vendors can be combined to produce a custom client, EJB server components from different vendors can be combined to produce a custom server.
- Is compatible with and uses other Java APIs, can interoperate with non-Java apps, and is compatible with CORBA.

How EJB Systems Work

To understand how the entire system operates using an EJB architecture, more accurately/commonly called a J2EE architecture, it is important to understand all the components included in this architecture (see Figure 21.3).

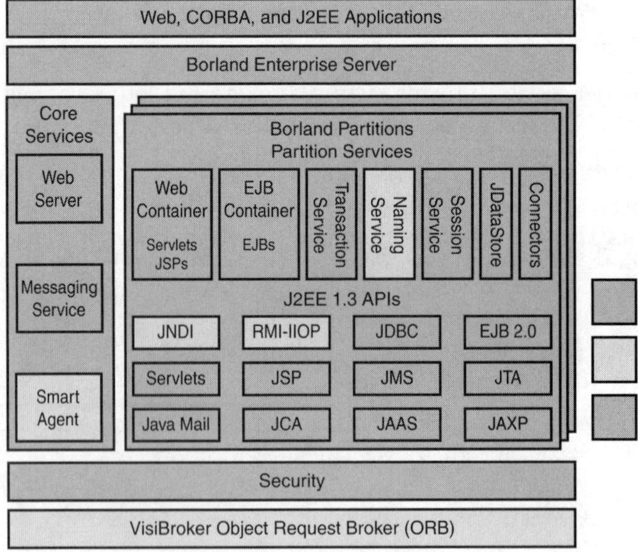

FIGURE 21.3 J2EE architectural blueprint using Borland's Enterprise Server.

This J2EE architecture is made up of a number of services to allow the developer to focus on the business rather than the plumbing and architecture. Table 21.1 describes these components and their usage.

TABLE 21.1 Components That Make Up Borland's Enterprise Server

Component	Description
Web Server	Borland's Enterprise service includes a version of Apache.
Messaging Service	The SonicMQ Message Broker is provided as a core service of the Borland Enterprise Server—AppServer edition.
Smart Agent	The Smart Agent is part of the Visibroker CORBA infrastructure and provides a distributed directory service of CORBA object implementations.
Web Container	Facility to run JSPs and servlets. Borland Enterprise Server uses Tomcat.
EJB Container	A container to manage and host EJB components.
Transaction Service	A service to manage transactions either within the container or external to the container.
Session Service	Java Session Service (JSS) contains session information either stored in JDatastore or a valid JDBC data source.
Naming Service	A directory of components and their location and capabilities.
JNDI	Java Naming Directory Interface—This is the specification for the location of an object within a directory.
RMI-IIOP	Remote Method Invocation over Internet Interoperability Protocol—In other words, the capability to encapsulate RMI within an IIOP packet.
JDBC	Java DataBase Connectivity—Interface to connect to a relation or nonrelational data store.
EJB	Enterprise JavaBeans—Specifications for creating components and managing remote and local Java components.
JMS	Java Messaging Service—The message services provided to either accomplish asynchronous or synchronous message handling.
JavaMail	API allowing for the interface to SNMP mail systems.
JCA	Java Connectivity Architecture—Interface to create connectors to desperate systems.

The Enterprise JavaBeans Component

An Enterprise JavaBean is a component with a well-defined interface. This interface is defined by the EJB specifications. Enterprise JavaBeans are contained, executed, and managed within an EJB container. Any server that can host an EJB container and provide it with the necessary services can be an EJB server. This EJB component is either an implementation of an interface or extends an EJB class. This component is simply a Java class, written by an EJB developer, which implements the desired business logic and persistence.

The Enterprise JavaBeans Container

The EJB container is the home for all EJB components. An EJB component can "live" only inside an EJB container. The container then provides services to components to give functionality. These container services include transactional management, resource management, versioning, scalability, mobility, persistence, and security. These services are used by any of the components contained in the container. Because you do not have to write your own services, you can concentrate on implementing the business logic. For example, you might decide that the current transaction should be rolled back. Simply tell the container, and the transaction will be canceled, including the notification of the other participating components.

Remote Interface

When the client program is ready to execute a remote method from the EJB object, the object communicates to the remote implementation through the remote interface. This remote interface represents all the business methods defined within the EJB component. The remote interface is actually a delegate for the EJB component.

The EJB object and the EJB component are actually separate classes, but they implement the same interface. The client then sees the EJB object and EJB component as the same object. Although both the object and the component implement the same interface, they have completely different responsibilities. The EJB component runs on the server in an EJB container and implements all the business logic. The EJB objects runs within the client and remotely executes the call within the EJB component. For example, imagine a VCR as your EJB component. The object is analogous to the remote control. The buttons on the remote control and the buttons on the VCR accomplish the same result. The VCR does the operation, not the remote.

Similarly, a call to the `addCompany()` method on an EJB object packages up the call. The packaged-up call will then be received by the EJB component—in this case, the `addCompany()` method on the EJB component. In reality, the call goes through the EJB container. In addition, the Enterprise JavaBean also has a home interface, which we will discuss in the following section. This interface helps you to find your remote interface.

The Home Interface

A client locates an application server and requests a specific Enterprise JavaBean to be created. As the object is created, the client can request the Bean to do processing with data on its behalf. This Bean is contained and managed within the EJB container. The server responds with the creation of a server-side object, the EJB component's instance. The application server then returns a proxy object, which is the EJB object. The interface of this object is the same interface as the EJB component's implementation to allow for operations on the client's behalf. From this point forward, the client uses the EJB object as if it was a local object, not aware that the object is actually a remote object on another computer. After the remote object, also known as a *proxy object,* is available, all remaining operations involving the life cycle of the server-side Beans are the responsibility of the EJB container.

Where Do I Get an EJB Object Class?

The actual creation of an EJB object is generated by a code-generation tool that comes with the specific vendor's EJB container. This tool comes packaged either with your IDE (JBuilder), or your application server (Borland Enterprise Server). To the client, an EJB object looks just like the implementation interface. The EJB object is just a stand-in for the actual EJB component, running within the EJB container (see Figure 21.4). This is the core concept to features such as network ubiquity of the EJB application server.

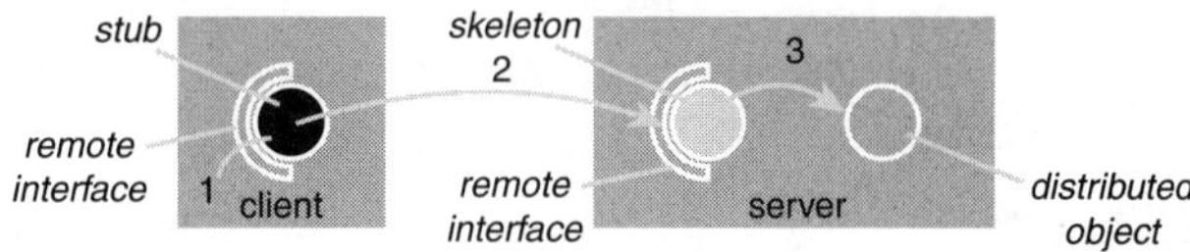

FIGURE 21.4 EJB object interaction with a J2EE client.

Let's look in detail at Figure 21.4, investigating the interactions between the components. The numbers of the following list match the numbers in the diagram:

1. The client communicates to the remote interface of the Bean. This is an interface generated by the tools accompanying the application server. In other words, it provides all the plumbing for the Enterprise JavaBean framework.

2. The call is then marshalled/serialized and encapsulated to send over the wire to a duplicate of the remote interface within the container. This interface provides the fixture at the other end of our plumbing.

3. The call is then passed on to the implementation to execute the business logic.

Enterprise JavaBeans Types

To meet the diverse requirements needed for implementing an enterprise application, the Enterprise JavaBean specification designed different Beans. Each Bean is designed to accomplish a set of application and business requirements. The specification describes three basic types of Enterprise JavaBeans to accomplish the varying tasks:

- Session Beans
- Entity Beans
- Message-Driven Beans

Session Bean

Session Beans are large-grained objects that implement high-level services. Such services include order entry, portfolio management, and service provision. When combined with Entity Beans, a Session Bean would typically perform processing in conjunction with many Entity Beans. For example, an Order Entry Session Bean would invoke behaviors of Customer, Order, and Product Entity Beans. Without Entity Beans, a Session Bean would itself implement all the business and data access logic that would otherwise reside in the Entity Beans. Note that a Session Bean does not have the option of using container-managed persistence. It must implement its own persistence management.

In its deployment descriptor, a Session Bean indicates whether it is *stateful* or *stateless*. A stateful Session Bean can change state after method invocations. Therefore, it must remain running after each method invocation, and a client must connect with the same instance for each method call within the same session. A stateless Session Bean always has the same state. Therefore, it may be destroyed after each method invocation, and a client can connect to a new instance every time. For example, a Flight Reservation Session Bean would be stateful because making a reservation requires executing a set of dependent tasks. However, a Flight Finder Session Bean would be stateless because finding a flight does not change the state of any variables.

As with Entity Beans, a Session Bean developer or a development tool must create both home and remote interfaces. As mentioned previously, the Session Bean's container implements the home interface to control its life cycle and the remote interface to broker communication between the client and the Session Bean instance. Clients use the home and remote interfaces as stubs so that they can create Session Beans and invoke their methods.

Entity Bean

Entity Beans are relatively fine-grained objects with a persistent representation. This representation may be in a flat file, a database, or a packaged application. Entity Beans are optional in version 1.0 of the EJB specification. They will be required in the 2.0 specification. The most typical way for developers to construct Entity Beans is to assemble a group of logically related records from back-end databases and add appropriate behaviors. For example, to build a Customer Entity Bean, a developer would identify records from all the tables in all the databases that contain customer information and declare corresponding object variables. He would then implement object methods related to customer management such as `newCustomer()`, `getOrders()`, and `fileComplaint()`.

Each Entity Bean has a unique identity that persists across client sessions as well as an object state that resides in one or more data sources. So that clients can locate an Entity Bean with a particular identity, developers must provide an EJB class with a primary key and at least one find method in the home interface that returns a reference to the EJB based on a primary key lookup. So that an Entity Bean's persistence state can be stored in and retrieved from its parent databases, it must either implement its own data access code or delegate this function to its container. If it implements its own data access code, it specifies Bean-managed persistence in its deployment descriptor. If it delegates data access to its container, it specifies container-managed persistence.

An Entity Bean developer or a development tool must create both home and remote interfaces. As mentioned previously, the Entity Bean's container implements the home interface to control its life cycle and the remote interface to broker communication between the client and the Entity Bean instance. Clients use the home and remote interface as stubs so that they can find Entity Beans and invoke their methods.

Message-Driven Bean

Message-Driven Beans (MDBs) are a new type of Bean added in the EJB 2.0 specification. They were added because there was no way in EJB 1.1 to handle asynchronous invocation. The primary reason for this is that an EJB could never be invoked from other object through anything other than its remote interface. Therefore, a Bean could never set itself up as a listener for asynchronous invocation.

This limitation is overcome by MDBs. An MDB is a Bean without a remote interface; the container sets itself up as a listener for asynchronous invocation of the MDB and handles the invocation of the concrete Bean. Otherwise, MDBs follow all the usual rules for EJBs.

MDBs are primarily focused on JMS. An MDB is either a topic or a queue subscriber. A topic Bean is the model for implementing multiple subscribers and multiple publishers or any combination. A queue is designed to implement point-to-point communication between one or more publishers and only one subscriber. One nice feature of MDBs is that one gets multithreaded subscribers (even for topics) without having to deal with the subtle difficulties of writing multithreaded code for JMS message consumers.

How Does It All Work?

Every EJB component class contains an interface called a *home interface*, which defines all the methods for creating, initializing, destroying, and optionally finding EJB instances within the application server container. The home interface is the contract between the EJB component class and the container. The container then defines the construction, destruction, and lookup of all EJB instances.

The EJB home interface extends the interface defined within the Sun specifications. The `javax.ejb.EJBHome` defines base-level functionality for a home interface. Every method in the interface must be RMI-compatible—in other words, they must be usable by the `java.rmi` package. The EJB home interface also defines all the `create()` methods (see Figure 21.5). There must be a minimum of one and an additional one for each signature required. The return for each `create()` method must be the remote interface for the EJB. This remote interface consists of all the business methods provided by the EJB component.

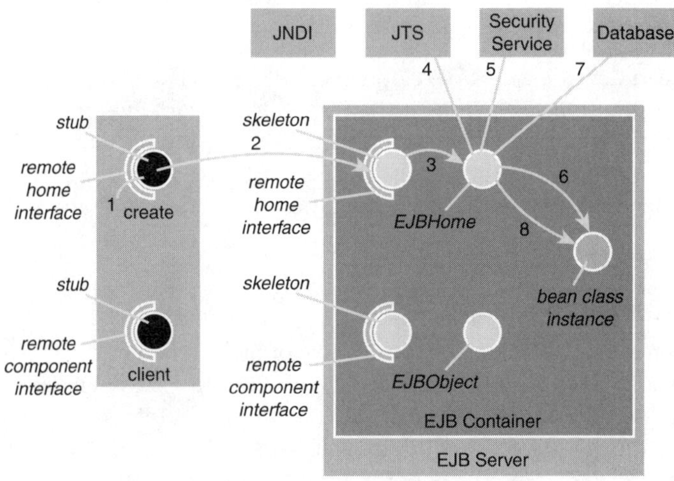

FIGURE 21.5 Client and server intercommunication between the different tiers.

If the client application desires to create a server-side Bean, it uses the JNDI to locate the component's home interface for the desired Bean. JNDI is an extension of the Java core server that allows a client to look up, in a directory, any desired component. After the client has found the home interface for the desired EJB component it wants to create, it calls one of the `create()` methods. The `create()` method then calls the EJB container on the server, which in turn creates the EJB component and returns the object's remote interface.

After the client obtains a reference to the component's home interface, it calls the `create()` method on that home interface to instantiate the EJB component. The home interface then returns an EJB object to the client. The client then calls the EJB object's methods, which are then serialized and sent to the container. The container then defers the execution to the implementation on the instantiated EJB component.

Summary

EJB application servers are sophisticated pieces of software and offer a number of services to greatly increase the productivity of the development process. These servers offer more than just plumbing; they offer services for transactions, security, and many other useful services. Although many components make up a J2EE application, all these components interrelate and communicate the same way. The fundamental goals of a server component architecture are to

- Create a server whose methods are extensible at runtime.
- Deploy an accounting package, drop it into a running server, and use the client software that came with the package to access the server functionality, all without even shutting down the server, much less recompiling it.

The answer that Enterprise JavaBeans provide is to create the client in terms of remote interfaces. The remote interfaces are implemented on the client as remote method invocations of one sort or another, and the same interface is implemented on the server side as domain functionality. The EJB server uses JNDI to publish the availability of these services. The client uses JNDI to locate a new class's home interface by name, and then uses the home interface to create objects with the remote interface that provides the service. This late-binding between available interfaces on a server and the interface names makes an EJB server runtime extensible.

Reflections

- Which Beans should I use and when should I use them?
- Should I use container-specific variations or remain loyal to the EJB specification?
- With all the choices for Beans, how do I prevent analysis paralysis? In other words, how do I solve the problem without getting stuck in design?
- Which container vendor should I choose?

22

Developing Session Beans

IN THIS CHAPTER

- Session Bean in Detail
- Writing a Client
- Writing a Session Bean
- Design Guidelines

Session Beans are large-grained objects that implement high-level services such as shopping carts, order management systems, and content management systems. Sessions Beans are normally never used alone but are combined with Entity Beans. The Session Bean typically performs processing in conjunction with many Entity Beans. For example, an Order Entry Session Bean would invoke behaviors of Customer, Order, and Product Entity Beans. Without Entity Beans, a Session Bean would itself implement all the business and data access logic that would otherwise reside in the Entity Beans.

NOTE

A Session Bean does not have the option of using container-managed persistence; in other words, you must either use an Entity Bean or connect to the data store yourself.

As we discuss Session Beans, we will look at the following information:

- Session Bean detail
- Developing a Session Bean manually
- Using the JBuilder wizards for developing Session Beans

As in other chapters, we will also look at design guidelines using Session Beans, in addition to looking at a real example in the section "In Practice."

Session Bean in Detail

When using Session Beans, you might need different types of Beans to accomplish the desired outcome. Sometimes you will need to share Beans with multiple users, and other times you will want a dedicated Bean for each session. As we examine the different capabilities and requirements for implementing the solution, we need different Session Beans to accomplish this.

Stateful Session Beans

Stateful Session Beans are components dedicated to a single client and maintain the state for that client only. For example, consider a shopping cart Session Bean for a Web site. The shopping cart must maintain an individual list for each user. As the shopper in an online store selects items he wants to purchase, the items need to be added to the user's individual shopping cart. This is accomplished by storing the selected items in a list within the shopping cart, which is a member within a Session Bean object.

The following rules were defined by Sun for the implementation of Stateful Session Beans:

- The Bean class instance is dedicated to one client.
- Each method call from the same client is serviced by the same instance.
- Inactive Bean class instances can be *passivated* (swapped to a secondary storage device).

Stateless Session Beans

Stateless Session Beans do just the opposite of a stateful Bean; each session shares a Bean, so no state is maintained. Therefore, they can be pooled for use by many clients. For example, consider a Session Bean that returns a list that contains customer information—the `getCustomers()` business method. The client would invoke `getCustomers()`, passing it a criteria for the list. The `getCustomers()` method would then pass back to the client a list of customers.

The following rules were defined within the Enterprise Java Beans (EJB) specification for stateless Session Beans:

- Bean class instances can be swapped freely between EJB objects controlled by the container.
- Subsequent client calls can be serviced by different instances.
- Idle Bean class instances are stored in the pool.
- Bean instances are not destroyed until the container is shut down.

Session Bean Life Cycle

To improve your overall understanding of Session Beans, we will look at the life cycle of these Beans. We will also look at the life cycle of the Bean both from the client's point of view and then the view from the Bean itself. If you are developing a client, it is important for you to understand the life cycle of the Bean; likewise, if you are developing a Bean, it is important to understand how the container will manage it.

The life cycle of a Session Bean is controlled by the client's communication to that Bean. The Bean typically represents some nonpersistent component that the client will access. Figure 22.1 shows the different stages of the life cycle of a Session Bean from the client's perspective.

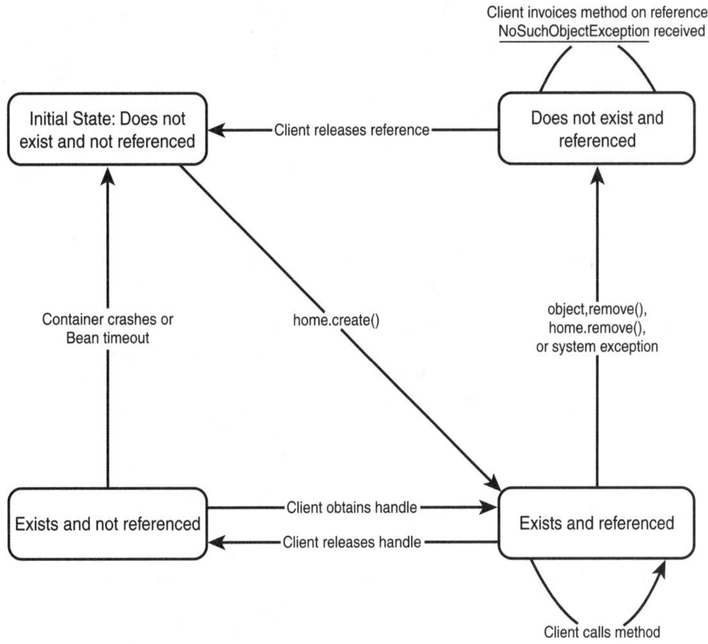

FIGURE 22.1 Client's perspective of the states of a Session Bean.

The starting/initial state of the Bean is located in the top-left state—`Does not exist and not referenced`. The client creates a Bean instance by calling the method `create()` of the home object interface. At this stage, the container creates the Bean. After that point, the client can call any method available on the Session Bean. The client may then remove the Bean when it is completed by using the `remove()` method on the remote object or the `remove()` method of the home interface.

NOTE

After the client informs the Bean of its desire to remove it, the client should mark the reference to `null`. This moves the client view of the Bean from `Exists and not referenced` to `Does not exist and not referenced`.

Now let's look at the state from the Bean's perspective rather than the client's perspective. The state diagram of the stateless Session Bean is actually simple. It contains only two states: exists or does not exist (see Figure 22.2). Either the Bean has not been created or it is located in a pool available for usage.

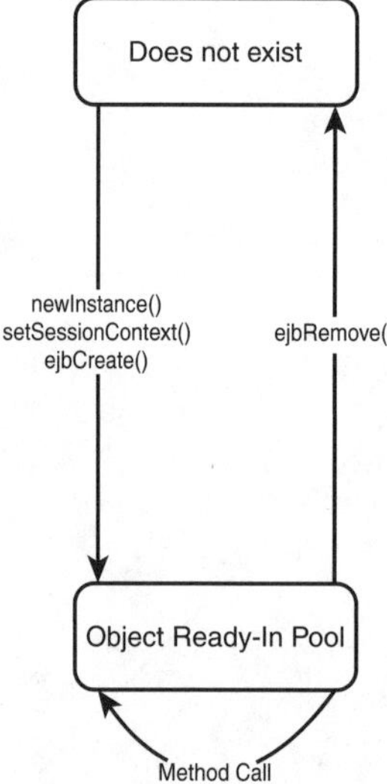

FIGURE 22.2 Stateless Session Beans state transaction diagram.

When the Bean is created, it enters a pool of available stateless Beans. The client then executes a method on a specific Bean, using a Bean removed from the Bean pool. After the method has completed, it is then returned to the pool of available Beans for another client request.

Writing a Client

The best way to learn how to use EJBs is to look at some examples. The process for a client to connect to a Bean is rather simple. For a client to work with an EJB, the client must perform the following:

- Get a reference to a JNDI server.
- Get a reference to the desired Bean's home object.

- Get a reference to a remote object by calling the `create()` method or a finder method.
- Invoke the desired business method.

Now we'll create a client that communicates to a weather Session Bean. This Bean simply connects to a Bean and returns to the client the current temperature. The following steps are required to create a client to connect to the weather Bean:

1. Create a client application:

```
package sessionbean;

class WeatherClient {
  public static void main(String[] args) {
  }
}
```

2. Obtain a reference to JNDI. This is required to find the home interface of the desired object.

```
//get naming context
Context ctx = new InitialContext();
```

3. Look up the desired object within the naming service:

```
//look up jndi name
Object ref = ctx.lookup("WeatherStation");
```

4. Cast the object to the proper interface. Notice that we do not use typical Java casting but the `narrow()` method to accomplish this.

```
//cast to Home interface
weatherStationHome = (WeatherStationHome) PortableRemoteObject.narrow(ref,
WeatherStationHome.class);
```

5. Ask the container to supply you an object of this type:

```
WeatherStation station = stationHome.create();
```

6. Call the desired method. In this case, ask the Bean for the current temperature within a given ZIP Code:

```
station.currentTemp("46304");
```

7. Make sure that you remember to catch the exceptions. JBuilder guides you and indicates which exceptions must be caught (see Listing 22.1).

LISTING 22.1 Complete Source for Testing Our Session Bean

```
package sessionbean;

import java.rmi.*;

import javax.ejb.*;
import javax.naming.*;

class WeatherClient {
  public static void main(String[] args) {
    try {
      InitialContext ctx = new InitialContext();
      Object objRef = ctx.lookup("WeatherStation");
      WeatherStationHome stationHome  =
(WeatherStationHome)javax.rmi.PortableRemoteObject.narrow(objRef,
➥WeatherStationHome.class);
      WeatherStation station = stationHome.create();
      System.out.println("Current Temperature is:");
      System.out.println(station.currentTemp("46304"));
    }
    catch (RemoteException ex) {
      System.err.println("Remote Exceptoion:" + ex);
    }catch (CreateException ex) {
      System.err.println("Create Exceptoion:" + ex);
    }catch (NamingException ex) {
      System.err.println("Naming Exceptoion:" + ex);
    }catch (ClassCastException ex) {
      System.err.println("Cast Exceptoion:" + ex);
    }
  }
}
```

Creating the client requires only a few lines of code that you might not be familiar with. The beauty of an EJB client is that most of the required functionality is implemented within the stubs and skeletons. These generated pieces of code hide the complexity required to implement the plumbing portion of EJBs.

As we look at the client, it is important to understand what happens when I call the methods to communicate with the Bean. If we look at this implementation of a weather station in two different ways, it will help you understand the underlying details. First we will look at a component diagram of what happens with the implementation at runtime (see Figure 22.3). Second we will look at the implementation using a sequence diagram (see Figure 22.4).

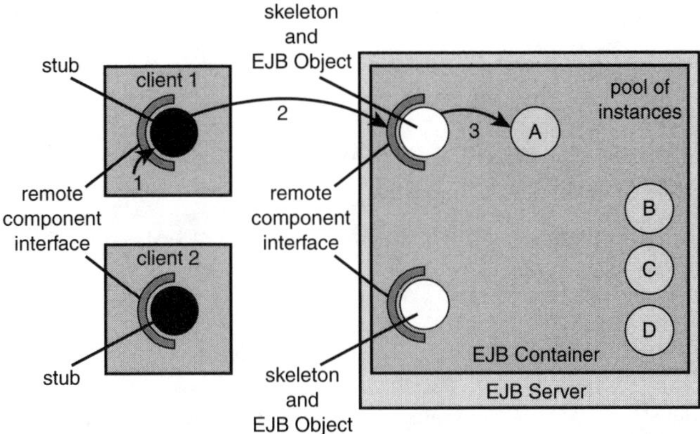

FIGURE 22.3 Component diagram for client-to-EJB component communication.

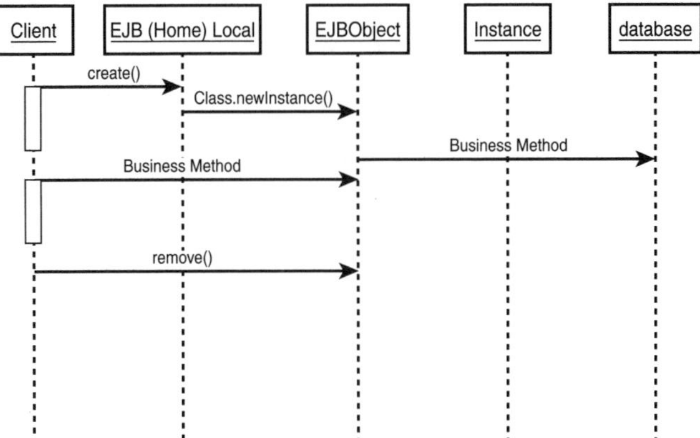

FIGURE 22.4 Sequence diagram from client to component.

Let's walk through the sequence diagram in Figure 22.4, which shows a simple scenario of using a stateless Session Bean.

1. Before calling a Bean's business methods, a remote client needs to create a new Bean instance or remove one from the pool managed by the container using the remote home interface.
2. In response, the container creates a new EJB object, and a reference of the remote component interface is then passed back to the client for use.
3. The client can then make invocations using the business methods defined in the Bean's remote interface.
4. After receiving a request by the EJB object, the container allocates a Bean class instance to service the request.
5. This might involve creating a new instance, if no instances are available in the pool. The client's call is forwarded to the instance.
6. After all necessary invocations are made by the client, the client should remove the Bean.

NOTE

When no more invocations are required to be executed on a given Bean class instance, the Bean instance should be removed by the client. The Bean class instances are not destroyed, however. Instead, the EJB object element is destroyed, and the reference to the remote component interface is invalidated.

Although our weather station was a stateless Session Bean, you will notice that the client does not need to change to use a stateful Bean. All that changes is how you may use the Bean. For example, instead of passing in the ZIP Code, we will use a mutator and then call the method (see Listing 22.2).

LISTING 22.2 Using a Stateful Session Bean in a Client

```
package sessionbean;

import java.rmi.*;

import javax.ejb.*;
import javax.naming.*;

class WeatherClient {
  public static void main(String[] args) {
    try {
      InitialContext ctx = new InitialContext();
      Object objRef = ctx.lookup("WeatherStation");
```

LISTING 22.2 Continued

```
      WeatherStationHome stationHome  =
(WeatherStationHome)javax.rmi.PortableRemoteObject.narrow(objRef,
➥WeatherStationHome.class);
      WeatherStation station = stationHome.create();
      station.setZipcode("46304");
      System.out.println("Current Temperature is:");
      System.out.println(station.currentTemp());
    }
    catch (RemoteException ex) {
      System.err.println("Remote Exceptoion:" + ex);
    }catch (CreateException ex) {
      System.err.println("Create Exceptoion:" + ex);
    }catch (NamingException ex) {
      System.err.println("Naming Exceptoion:" + ex);
    }catch (ClassCastException ex) {
      System.err.println("Cast Exceptoion:" + ex);
    }
  }
}
```

Writing a Session Bean

Now it is time, for the Bean. As stated earlier, we have two types of Session Beans: stateful and stateless. These Beans actually are similar to each other in development and code. However, what changes are the deployment descriptor and the design of the object. As we build these Session Beans, you will notice that JBuilder offers many facilities to aid in this process. For example, a Bean designer allows you to develop your Beans graphically instead of with code. The following productivity features have been integrated within the JBuilder environment to allow for quick development and deployment of your EJB application:

- EJB Designer—This designer allows you to graphically build the interrelationship between your JavaBeans. This designer is not as beneficial for Session Beans as it is for Entity Beans.
- Various wizards—JBuilder wizards aid the user in the development, management, and deployment of EJB projects. For example, the EJB module takes care of the archiving in addition to the containership of the EJB components placed within it.

- Test clients—It is not uncommon for the developer of the EJB components to not be the developer who creates the user interface. Because of this reality, these components need to be unit tested before moving on through the development process. The Test Client Wizard generates a test client to exercise your EJB components and defined methods.
- Support for many vendors—JBuilder supports not only Borland Enterprise Server but many other vendors as well. Other implemented vendor support includes IBM's WebSphere, BEA WebLogics, and Sun's IPlanet as well as facilities to add support for others within the environment using the customer application server option.

We are now ready to create a Session Bean. The process entails many steps at the onset; however, many of the steps are short, focused tasks. The following process is required to accomplish the task; we will go into more detail later in this chapter.

The following preparation tasks are not directly related to creating a Session Bean, but nonetheless are required to build any EJB project within JBuilder's IDE:

1. Configure the enterprise server target.
2. Create a project.
3. Create an EJB module.

The following production tasks are directly related to building your Session Bean, either stateless or stateful:

1. Create a 1.x or 2.0 Session Bean.
2. Implement Business Logic.
3. Compile and archive the Beans.
4. Create/modify the deployment descriptors.
5. Create a test client for unit testing of your component.
6. Test your Enterprise JavaBean.
7. Implement your client.

Preparing the Landscape

When you are ready to start your EJB project, you first must prepare JBuilder to integrate and understand your vendor's EJB server and associated capabilities. If you do not configure JBuilder's IDE, you will not be able to use any of JBuilder's productivity features for enterprise development. In fact, JBuilder's components under the Enterprise tab within the Object Gallery will all be disabled. Now it's time to prepare JBuilder to allow us to build an EJB Session Bean.

Configuring JBuilder

JBuilder supports a wide variety of different application servers. To have JBuilder properly communicate to these environments, you must configure JBuilder to recognize them. When an application server environment is selected, JBuilder then configures the features, code generators and wizards, command-line utilities, class paths, and deployment and runtime options for the vendor's specific implementation requirements. The JBuilder Enterprise and Studio product ships with Borland Enterprise Server—Application Server Edition, which is an EJB application server, in addition to supporting VisiBroker (CORBA Orb), WebServices, and HTTP using Apache. We will use this application server for building our application; however, the same principles apply regardless of the application server brand or versions selected. To access JBuilder's configuration of application servers, we must enter the Editor by choosing Tools, Configure Servers from the menu (see Figure 22.5) and enable the application servers you want to use within JBuilder. This is not a one-time setup for each developer's login, but you can change these parameters by reentering the editor anytime.

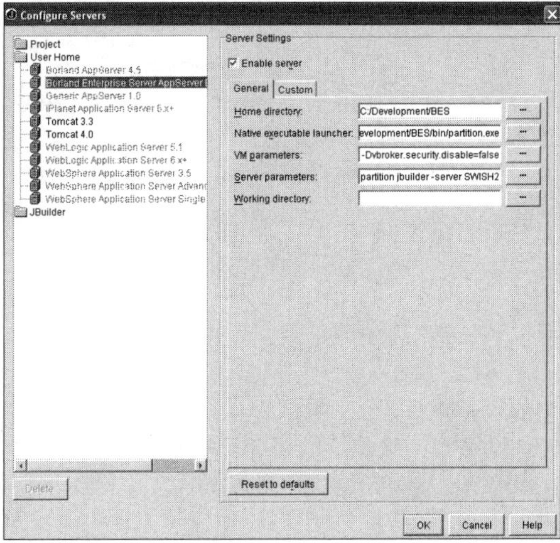

FIGURE 22.5 Application server setup within the JBuilder environment.

To enable the desired application server, select it in the list on the left and click the Enable server check box for that application server configuration. You now have full access to the features available within the given application server. For example, if you choose an application server that does not support EJB 2.0 Entity Beans, it will not allow you to build 2.0 Entity Beans within your application.

Starting the Project

To create a project, simply choose File, New Project from the menu. This creates an empty JBuilder project for you. The specialized task you must do next is select which EJB application will be used for this project; many times, you may have more than one vendor or version of application server available. You must add the libraries for your application server to your project using the Project Properties Editor by choosing Project, Project Properties from the menu. After you are in the dialog box, select the Required Libraries tab under the Paths tab and add the appropriate libraries, as shown in Figure 22.6.

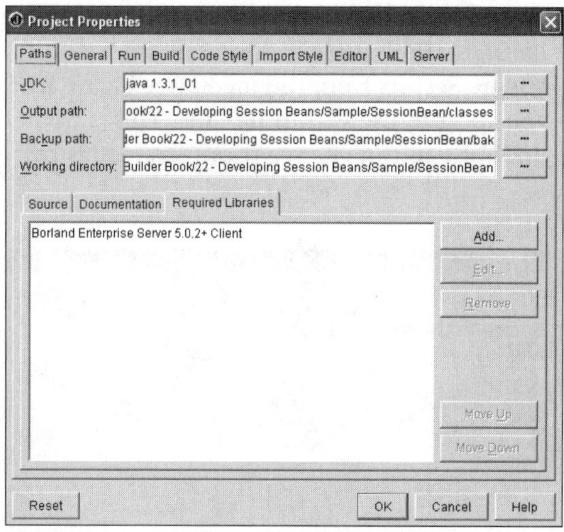

FIGURE 22.6 Project Properties Editor for our EJB project.

Creating an EJB Module

Every enterprise Bean you create must belong to a JBuilder EJB module, unless you want to hand code all your Beans. In other words, the EJB module is the facilitator for the graphical design of your EJBs. An EJB module is just a way for JBuilder to logically group all your Beans, in addition to producing the deployment descriptors and JAR files for deployment. When creating an EJB module, you will be confronted with two formats: XML or binary. *XML format* is simply an XML document stored in a text file, describing the context of your module. A *binary* is essentially a ZIP archive containing information about the deployment.

The easiest method to create an EJB module is using JBuilder's EJB Module Wizard. This wizard takes you through the properties that need to be set to create your module (see Figure 22.7).

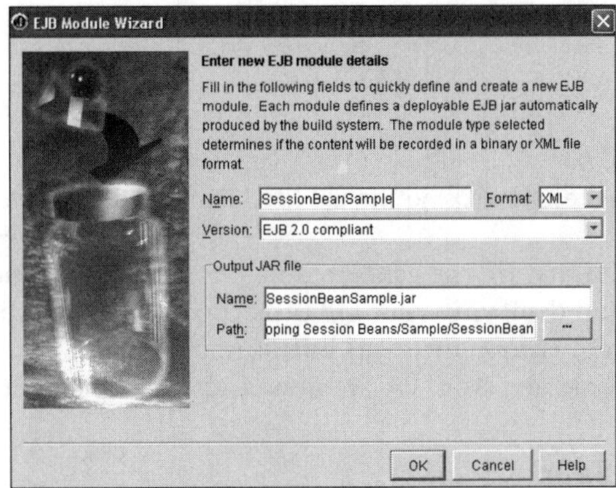

FIGURE 22.7 Using the EJB Module Wizard builds a container for all EJB components.

The properties listed in Table 22.1 are required to be assigned to create your EJB module.

TABLE 22.1 Properties to Set when Building an EJB Module

Property	Description	Example
`Name`	The logical name of your EJB module, this name will typically be the same as your JAR file but does not necessarily have to be.	`SessionBeanSample`
`Format`	Identifies the format for which the Session Bean is contained, either XML or binary. XML is easier to modify and the most commonly used.	XML
`Version`	Informs JBuilder of the restriction of the capabilities of JBuilder wizards and the Jbuilder environment regarding either EJB 1.x compliance or 2.0.	EJB 2.0 compliant
`Output JAR Name`	Specifies the JAR filename when you build your EJB components.	`SessionBeanSample` *<Same as Module Name>*
`Path`	Specifies the path to store the EJB JAR file.	C:\Project\Sample\SessionBean

After these properties are supplied, JBuilder then generates some new nodes within your project for building, managing, and customizing your EJB (see Figure 22.8).

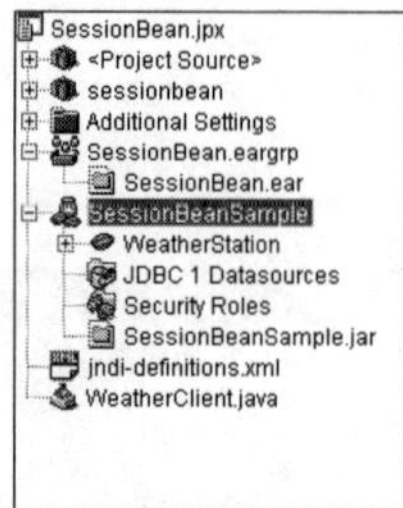

FIGURE 22.8 The results of using the EJB Module Wizard to create an EJB module.

The files and nodes that will be generated help to accomplish many important activities in building and deploying your EJB project. For example, the JAR that will be used for deployment is contained within this node, in addition to the JDBC data sources used to persist the data. We are now ready to implement our business logic.

Creating the Bean

When creating a Session Bean within the JBuilder environment, tools are available to ease the pain. One of these tools includes the EJB Designer. For example, the capability to create the interface graphically helps visualize what the interface will look like. The processes for building the Bean, using the EJB design or hand coding, are broken into three distinct steps:

1. Create the interface that surfaces the business implementation logic.
2. Implement the business methods within the structure of the code generated.
3. Prepare the Bean for deployment to the desired environment.

Creating the Interface

The interfaces to your Beans are the most often rushed steps in building effective EJBs. The problem of rushing the design is that it can manifest new design flaws and propagate old ones. This is due to the contractual agreement between the services your Bean agrees to provide and the manner in which the client agrees to use them. Just as a reminder, the client does not necessarily have to be only a "client" application running on the desktop but anyone who wants to use the given service. In our example, the weather station might be available to just a client application, or it might be used by an air conditioner to optimize its usage for the current outdoor temperature.

Using the JBuilder EJB Designer, we are going to create a Session Bean that uses the interface we implemented in our earlier client application. To build this Session Bean, we are simply going to traverse through a set of steps within the JBuilder's IDE:

1. Double-click on the EJB module you want to use as the container for your new Session Beans.
2. Right-click on the design window or on the node and select New Session Bean.
3. Name and configure your Session Bean (see Figure 22.9). Configure the following properties:

Bean name:	`weatherStation`
Interfaces:	`Remote`
Session type:	`Stateless`

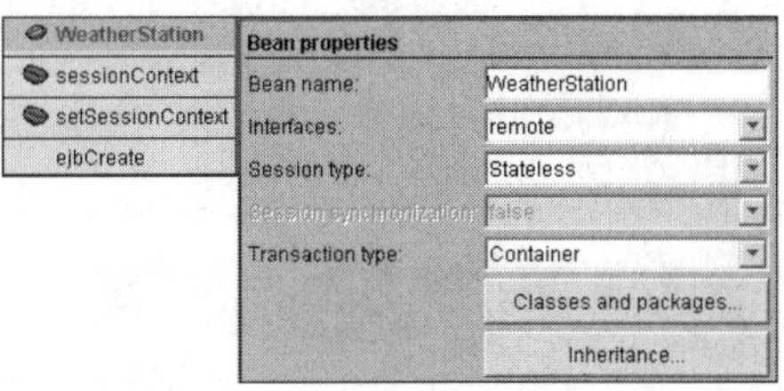

FIGURE 22.9 Configure your Session Bean by changing the properties through the EJB Designer.

4. Right-click on the new Session Bean and add a method. This process is similar to adding a new field (see Figure 22.10). The method we want to add is the following (see Figure 22.11):
   - Method name: `getCurrentTemp`
   - Return type: `Int`
   - Input parameters: `java.lang.String zipcode`
   - Interfaces: `Remote`

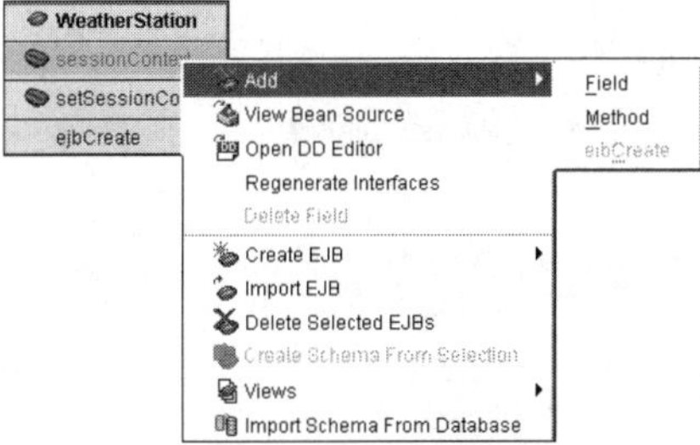

FIGURE 22.10 Using the context menu to add methods or fields to your Session Bean graphically.

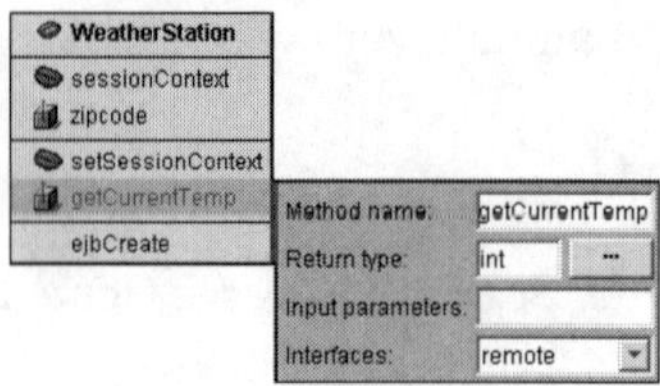

FIGURE 22.11 Configuring your method and assigning the given properties.

5. Assign the desired names to the generated code for the Bean implementation, as shown in Figure 22.12. For example, we want to change the default package of our Session Beans to `com.sams.weatherstation.session`. This is accomplished by selecting the classes and packages buttons on the properties for the entire Bean. If you do not see this button on the properties popup panel of the Bean, reselect the title of the Bean.

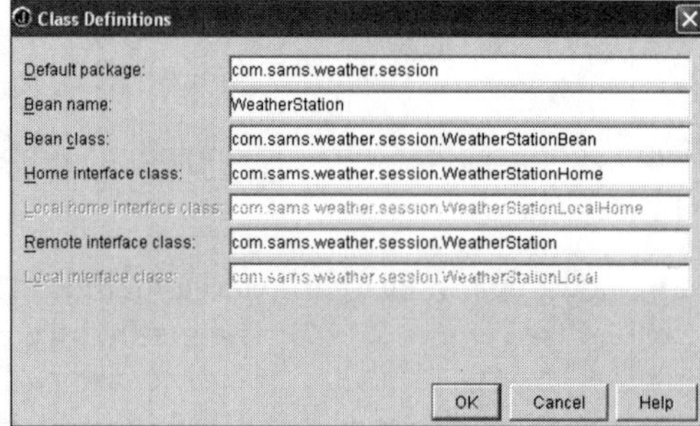

FIGURE 22.12 Assign default packages and change the names of generated source.

We have now completed the generation of our interface for our Session Bean. The process of defining the interface is simple; however, the process of designing a good interface is more difficult. The design guidelines of this chapter will help you design a good interface for your Session Beans. The result of this process creates a number of different Java class files, each one with a varying purpose, as shown in Table 22.2.

TABLE 22.2 The Different Files Created Using the EJB Designer Within JBuilder

File	Description
`WeatherStation.java`	Java interface file that contains the contract our Bean will implement (see Listing 22.3).
`WeatherStationBean.java`	A Java class in which we will implement the desired business logic. Notice that it also implements the interface we agreed on (see Listing 22.4).
`WeatherStationHome.java`	The interface for which we will create, find, and remove instances of our Bean class, managed by the container via this interface (see Listing 22.5).

LISTING 22.3 Java Interface Generated by the EJB Designer for Our Weather Station

```
package com.sams.weather.session;

import java.rmi.*;

import javax.ejb.*;

public interface WeatherStationHome extends javax.ejb.EJBHome {
  public WeatherStation create() throws CreateException, RemoteException;
}
```

LISTING 22.4 Java Class Generated by the EJB Designer for Our Weather Station Implementation

```
package com.sams.weather.session;

import javax.ejb.*;

public class WeatherStationBean implements SessionBean {
  SessionContext sessionContext;
  public void ejbRemove() {
    /**@todo Complete this method*/
  }
  public void ejbActivate() {
    /**@todo Complete this method*/
  }
  public void ejbPassivate() {
    /**@todo Complete this method*/
  }
  public void setSessionContext(SessionContext sessionContext) {
    this.sessionContext = sessionContext;
  }
  public int getCurrentTemp(java.lang.String zipcode) {
    /**@todo Complete this method*/
    return 0;
  }
  public void ejbCreate() throws CreateException {
    /**@todo Complete this method*/
  }
}
```

LISTING 22.5 Java Interface That Defines Our Home Interface to Be Used to Create, Find, or Remove an EJB Object

```
package com.sams.weather.session;

import java.rmi.*;

import javax.ejb.*;

public interface WeatherStationHome extends javax.ejb.EJBHome {
  public WeatherStation create() throws CreateException, RemoteException;
}
```

Implementing the Business Methods

Now it is time for what you have all been waiting for, developing and implementing the business logic. We built the framework to give access to our business logic; now we need to implement the business logic within this framework. After all, the preceding steps just generated an implementation framework for which the `getCurrentTemp` method will be implemented, as shown in Listing 22.6. We have only one real step to implement the business logic—or if you want to get picky, two steps.

LISTING 22.6 Before the Bean Has Implemented `getCurrentTemp()`, We Generated the Necessary Framework

```
package com.sams.weather.session;

import java.util.*;

import javax.ejb.*;

/**
 *
 * <p>Title: Weather Station Session Bean</p>
 * <p>Description: Implementation Class for our weatherStation session bean</p>
 * <p>Copyright: Copyright (c) 2002</p>
 * <p>Company: </p>
 * @author SAMS Publishing
 * @version 1.0
 */
public class WeatherStationBean implements SessionBean {
  SessionContext sessionContext;
  public void ejbRemove() {
```

LISTING 22.6 Continued

```
    /**@todo Complete this method*/
  }
  public void ejbActivate() {
    /**@todo Complete this method*/
  }
  public void ejbPassivate() {
    /**@todo Complete this method*/
  }
  public void setSessionContext(SessionContext sessionContext) {
    this.sessionContext = sessionContext;
  }
  public int getCurrentTemp(java.lang.String zipcode) {
    /**@todo Complete this method*/
  }
  public void ejbCreate() throws CreateException {
    /**@todo Complete this method*/
  }
}
```

The following steps guide you through the process of implementing the business logic within a Session Bean:

1. Find the Bean where the implementation is to be placed. Typically, if you let JBuilder name the file, the name will be `<BeanName>Bean.java`. In our case, the file is WeatherStationBean.java.

2. Find the method where our business logic must be implemented. The easiest way to find it is to look in the Structure pane of this class file under the to-do folder. JBuilder then takes you directly to the code that needs to be implemented. You will probably notice that many other methods also need to be implemented; we will look at those methods later in this chapter. Listing 22.7 shows what our method should look like after implementation.

LISTING 22.7 After the Bean Has Implemented `getCurrentTemp()`

```
package com.sams.weather.session;

import java.util.*;

import javax.ejb.*;
```

LISTING 22.7 Continued

```
/**
 *
 * <p>Title: Weather Station Session Bean</p>
 * <p>Description: Implementation Class for our weatherStation session bean</p>
 * <p>Copyright: Copyright (c) 2002</p>
 * <p>Company: </p>
 * @author SAMS Publishing
 * @version 1.0
 */
public class WeatherStationBean implements SessionBean {
  SessionContext sessionContext;
  public void ejbRemove() {
    /**@todo Complete this method*/
  }
  public void ejbActivate() {
    /**@todo Complete this method*/
  }
  public void ejbPassivate() {
    /**@todo Complete this method*/
  }
  public void setSessionContext(SessionContext sessionContext) {
    this.sessionContext = sessionContext;
  }

  /**
   * Get the current temperature by randomly generating one
   * @param zipcode
   * @return current temp
   */
  public int getCurrentTemp(java.lang.String zipcode) {
    int currentTemp;
    Random rnd = new Random(System.currentTimeMillis());
    currentTemp = rnd.nextInt(110);
    return currentTemp;
  }
  public void ejbCreate() throws CreateException {
    /**@todo Complete this method*/
  }
}
```

Getting Ready to Deploy Your Bean

Each EJB created must have a deployment descriptor, and the Session Bean we created earlier is no different. The deployment descriptor describes the type and configuration of the Session Bean to the container. The container then uses this descriptor to manage the Bean. Listing 22.8 is the deployment descriptor we need to deploy our `WeatherStation` Bean.

LISTING 22.8 Deployment Descriptor for Our Newly Created Bean JAR File

```
<?xml version="1.0" encoding="UTF-8"?>
<!DOCTYPE ejb-jar PUBLIC "-//Sun Microsystems, Inc.//
➥DTD Enterprise JavaBeans 2.0//EN"
"http://java.sun.com/dtd/ejb-jar_2_0.dtd">
<ejb-jar>
    <enterprise-beans>
        <session>
            <display-name>WeatherStation</display-name>
            <ejb-name>WeatherStation</ejb-name>
            <home>com.sams.weather.session.WeatherStationHome</home>
            <remote>com.sams.weather.session.WeatherStation</remote>
            <ejb-class>com.sams.weather.session.WeatherStationBean</ejb-class>
            <session-type>Stateless</session-type>
            <transaction-type>Container</transaction-type>
        </session>
    </enterprise-beans>
    <assembly-descriptor>
        <container-transaction>
            <method>
                <ejb-name>WeatherStation</ejb-name>
                <method-name>*</method-name>
            </method>
            <trans-attribute>Required</trans-attribute>
        </container-transaction>
    </assembly-descriptor>
</ejb-jar>
```

As you will see, the deployment descriptor for our `WeatherStation` Bean contains all the important information about our Bean. The `<home>` and `<remote>` tags inform the container of the interfaces for the `WeatherStation` we will make available to the client. The `<ejb-class>` informs the container of the implementation class of the Bean. The last import tag `<session-type>` informs the container of the type of Session Bean—either stateful or stateless. Although we could enter the deployment descriptor by hand, JBuilder creates one for us; this descriptor was completed using JBuilder. If you want to edit your deployment descriptor, a number of editors are available to aid this process without your having to know or care about the structure within the deployment descriptor Document Type Definition (DTD)—for example, if we want to add a description to a Session Bean that will then be displayed within our container console, see Figure 22.13.

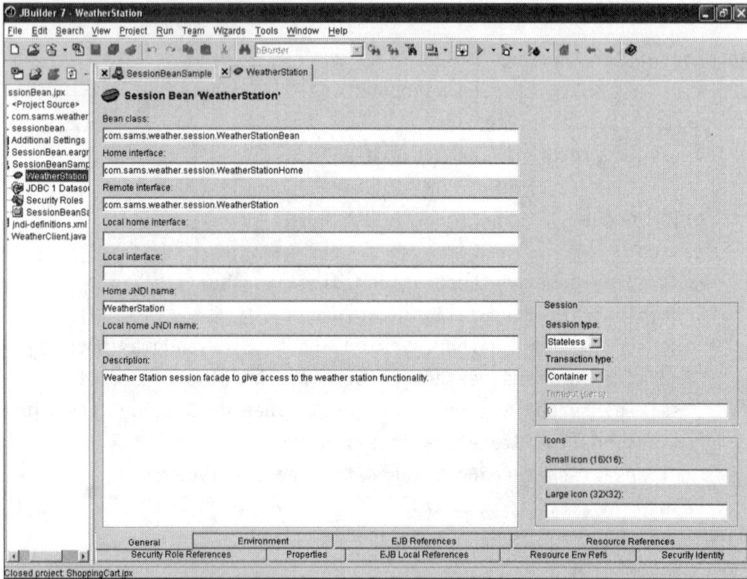

FIGURE 22.13 Assign information to our Session Bean that will be included within our deployment descriptor.

The deployment descriptor for Session Beans is simple in comparison to Entity Beans. In fact, JBuilder normally configures 90% of all Session Bean deployment descriptors within the designer.

Deploy Your Bean

The Session Bean we just created must be deployed on an application server before any client can access the Bean. The process varies slightly depending on the version or brand of your application server. JBuilder attempts to insulate you from most of the differences, but nonetheless you have to know a little bit about your deployment environment. The process for deploying our Bean is accomplished in the following two steps:

1. Create an EAR node.

2. Deploy to an application server.

The topmost archive used for deployment is an Enterprise Archive (EAR) file. The EAR file contains all the JAR and WAR files required for deployment and execution of our enterprise middle-tier services. It also contains an application.xml file describing the manifest of the entire archive for the container to identify the contents. In other words, it allows you to completely package your application into one deliverable, self-contained.

Let's now create an EAR file for our application, containing at this point only our Session Bean:

1. Choose File, New and select the Enterprise tab.

2. Select the EAR node to add to your project.

3. Specify the name of your EAR file and node name. In this case, we want to keep the name similar to our sample project `SessionBean` (see Figure 22.14 through Figure 22.19).

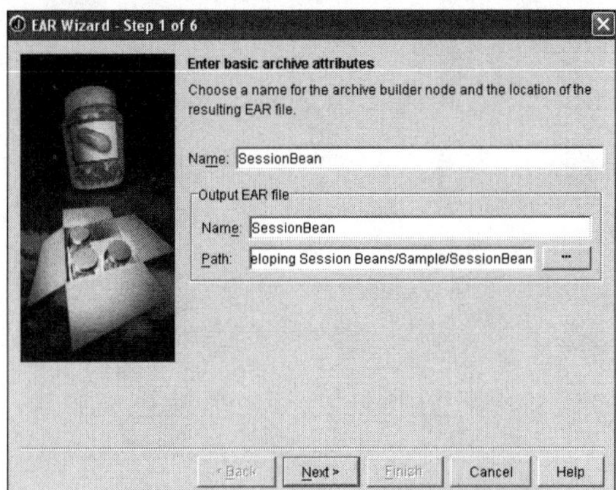

FIGURE 22.14 Step 1 of 6—Creating an EAR file for deployment.

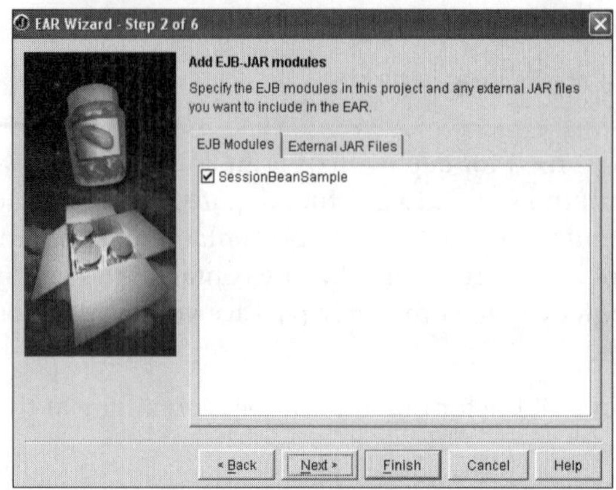

FIGURE 22.15 Step 2 of 6—Specify the EJB modules to be included within the EAR.

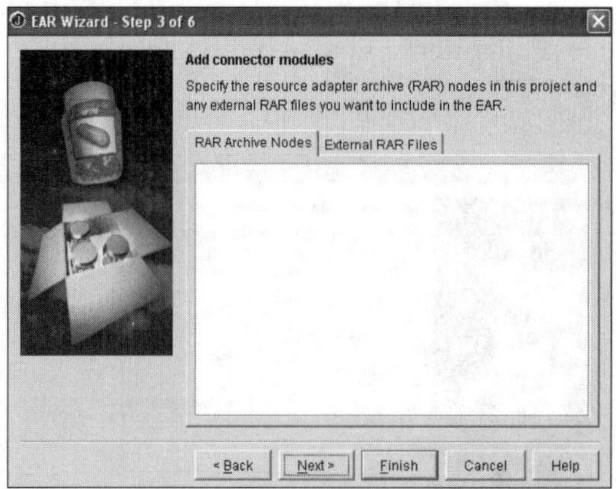

FIGURE 22.16 Step 3 of 6—Add resource adapter archives to the EAR module.

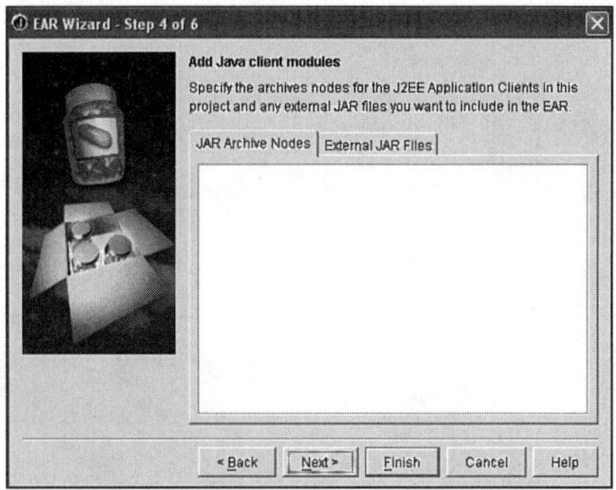

FIGURE 22.17 Step 4 of 6—Add other archive nodes to an EAR.

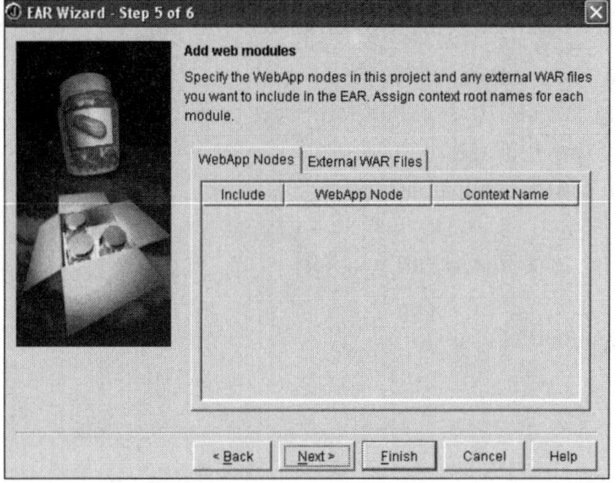

FIGURE 22.18 Step 5 of 6—Add all Web modules to an EAR.

4. Right-click on your new node SessionBean.eargrp and select make. This creates both a SessionBean.ear and, contained within this, an application.xml descriptor (see Listing 22.9).

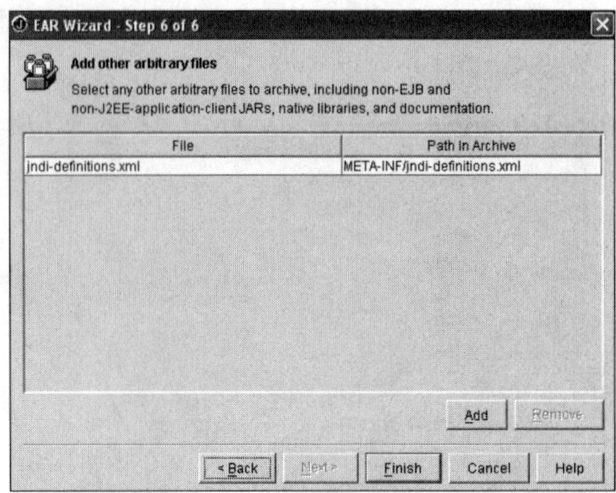

FIGURE 22.19 Step 6 of 6—Add other resources required for an EAR.

LISTING 22.9 After the Bean Has Implemented `getCurrentTemp()`

```
<?xml version="1.0" encoding="UTF-8"?>
<!DOCTYPE application PUBLIC "-//Sun Microsystems, Inc.//
➥DTD J2EE Application 1.3//EN"
➥"http://java.sun.com/dtd/application_1_3.dtd">
<application>
  <display-name>SessionBean</display-name>
  <module>
    <ejb>SessionBeanSample.jar</ejb>
  </module>
</application>
```

5. Right-click the `SessionBean.eargrp` and choose to deploy your bean. Make sure that your application server is running. If it is not, start your application server and deploy your Bean again.

Write a Test Client

We have now deployed our Bean; however, we are not confident that our Bean works properly. We need to test our Bean, but the actual user interface might not be completed yet or even started. In comes the Test Client Wizard to allow us to quickly create a client to exercise our Bean. Typically, you will not want to include these unit testing interfaces in your entire project. To provide a separation between production code and testing code, we place them in a different package. The wizard, shown in Figure 22.20, gives us the facilities to generate this test client without writing any code.

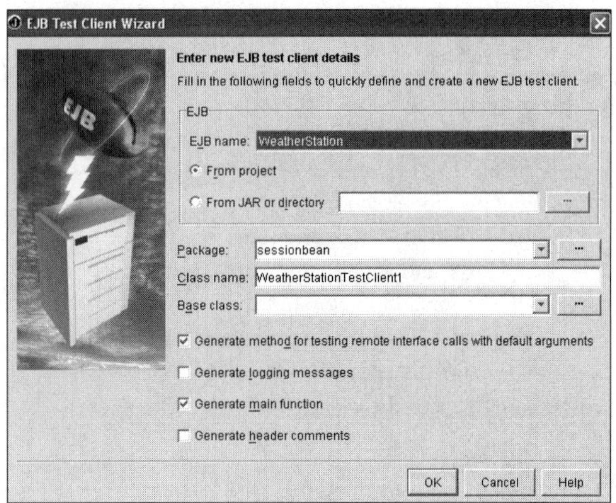

FIGURE 22.20 Create a test client using the EJB Test Client Wizard.

The process for accessing the wizard is accomplished by selecting File, New from the menu and choosing the Enterprise tab. The EJB Test Client Wizard then appears. We'll now take a look at all the different properties we can set for our test client, as shown in Table 22.3.

TABLE 22.3 Properties and Definitions Within the EJB Test Client Wizard

Property	Description	Example
EJB name	Specifies the EJB you want to test. This allows you to select only an EJB within the current project. If you want to select another Bean, specify the JAR file for which it is located.	`WeatherStation`
Package	The package for which the wizard defines the test client. It is important not to mix up testing code with production code.	`com.sams.testclient`
Class name	The name of the generated class for which the testing code will be placed.	`WeatherStationTestClient`
Base class	This is normally not used unless you have a framework for all your test clients to inherit from.	`SamsTestFrame`
Generate method for testing remote interface calls with default arguments	This box adds a `testRemoteCallsWithDefaultArguments()` method, which calls all the remote interface calls with default argument values.	`getCurrentTemp()` takes a string so that the call would look like `getCurrentTemp("")`.

TABLE 22.3 Continued

Property	Description	Example
Generate logging messages	Generates code that displays log messages tracing execution and timing. This option also generates wrappers for all the methods declared in the home and remote interfaces and initialization functions.	N/A
Generate main function	Adds the main function to the client to allow us to run the test client.	N/A
Generate header comments	Generates Default JavaDoc header comments to the client.	N/A

There are multiple ways to test your client application after the test client has been generated. The first and easiest way is to add code to exercise the desired method with the given set of parameters, as shown in Listing 22.10.

LISTING 22.10 `WeatherStationTestClient` Generated by the EJB Test Client Wizard in Addition to the Code Added to Test the Interface

```
package com.sams.testclient;

import com.sams.weather.session.*;
import javax.naming.*;
import javax.rmi.PortableRemoteObject;

/**
 * <p>Title: Session Bean Client</p>
 * <p>Description: </p>
 * <p>Copyright: Copyright (c) 2002</p>
 * <p>Company: </p>
 * @author SAMS Publishing
 * @version 1.0
 */

public class WeatherStationTestClient {
  static final private String ERROR_NULL_REMOTE =
➥"Remote interface reference is null. It must be
➥created by calling one of the Home interface methods first.";
  static final private int MAX_OUTPUT_LINE_LENGTH = 100;
  private boolean logging = true;
```

LISTING 22.10 Continued

```
  private WeatherStationHome weatherStationHome = null;
  private WeatherStation weatherStation = null;

  //Construct the EJB test client
  public WeatherStationTestClient() {
    long startTime = 0;
    if (logging) {
      log("Initializing bean access.");
      startTime = System.currentTimeMillis();
    }

    try {
      //get naming context
      Context ctx = new InitialContext();

      //look up jndi name
      Object ref = ctx.lookup("WeatherStation");

      //cast to Home interface
      weatherStationHome = (WeatherStationHome)
➥PortableRemoteObject.narrow(ref, WeatherStationHome.class);
      if (logging) {
        long endTime = System.currentTimeMillis();
        log("Succeeded initializing bean access.");
        log("Execution time: " + (endTime - startTime) + " ms.");
      }
    }
    catch(Exception e) {
      if (logging) {
        log("Failed initializing bean access.");
      }
      e.printStackTrace();
    }
  }

  //----------------------------------------------------------
  // Methods that use Home interface methods to generate a
➥Remote interface reference
  //----------------------------------------------------------
```

LISTING 22.10 Continued

```
public WeatherStation create() {
  long startTime = 0;
  if (logging) {
    log("Calling create()");
    startTime = System.currentTimeMillis();
  }
  try {
    weatherStation = weatherStationHome.create();
    if (logging) {
      long endTime = System.currentTimeMillis();
      log("Succeeded: create()");
      log("Execution time: " + (endTime - startTime) + " ms.");
    }
  }
  catch(Exception e) {
    if (logging) {
      log("Failed: create()");
    }
    e.printStackTrace();
  }

  if (logging) {
    log("Return value from create(): " + weatherStation + ".");
  }
  return weatherStation;
}

//----------------------------------------------------------------------
// Methods that use Remote interface methods to access data through the bean
//----------------------------------------------------------------------

public int getCurrentTemp(String zipcode) {
  int returnValue = 0;
  if (weatherStation == null) {
    System.out.println("Error in getCurrentTemp(): " + ERROR_NULL_REMOTE);
    return returnValue;
  }
  long startTime = 0;
  if (logging) {
    log("Calling getCurrentTemp(" + zipcode + ")");
    startTime = System.currentTimeMillis();
  }
```

LISTING 22.10 Continued

```
    try {
      returnValue = weatherStation.getCurrentTemp(zipcode);
      if (logging) {
        long endTime = System.currentTimeMillis();
        log("Succeeded: getCurrentTemp(" + zipcode + ")");
        log("Execution time: " + (endTime - startTime) + " ms.");
      }
    }
    catch(Exception e) {
      if (logging) {
        log("Failed: getCurrentTemp(" + zipcode + ")");
      }
      e.printStackTrace();
    }

    if (logging) {
      log("Return value from getCurrentTemp(" + zipcode + "): " +
➥returnValue + ".");
    }
    return returnValue;
  }

  public void testRemoteCallsWithDefaultArguments() {
    if (weatherStation == null) {
      System.out.println("Error in testRemoteCallsWithDefaultArguments(): "
➥+ ERROR_NULL_REMOTE);
      return ;
    }
    getCurrentTemp("");
  }

  //----------------------------------------------------------------------
  // Utility Methods
  //----------------------------------------------------------------------

  private void log(String message) {
    if (message == null) {
      System.out.println("-- null");
      return ;
    }
    if (message.length() > MAX_OUTPUT_LINE_LENGTH) {
```

LISTING 22.10 Continued

```
      System.out.println("-- " + message.substring(0, MAX_OUTPUT_LINE_LENGTH) +
➥" ...");
    }
    else {
      System.out.println("-- " + message);
    }
  }
  //Main method

  public static void main(String[] args) {
    WeatherStationTestClient client = new WeatherStationTestClient();
    // Use the client object to call one of the Home interface wrappers
    // above, to create a Remote interface reference to the bean.
    // If the return value is of the Remote interface type, you can use it
    // to access the remote interface methods. You can also just use the
    // client object to call the Remote interface wrappers.
    /* Added code to test the interface */
    client.create();
    System.out.println(client.getCurrentTemp("46304"));
  }
}
```

Now that we have looked at the test client, let's look at the results of the test client (see Listing 22.11). This result gives you, as a developer, confidence with your deployment, in addition to some simple performance metrics. Make sure that you call all the methods that you want to exercise, and make sure that you test with good and incorrect parameter data. For example, you might want to test a `getCustomer()` method with a customer that is found, not found, and passing in a `null`.

LISTING 22.11 Test Client Results for the `WeatherStation` Bean

```
-- Initializing bean access.
-- Succeeded initializing bean access.
-- Execution time: 3124 ms.
-- Calling create()
-- Succeeded: create()
-- Execution time: 40 ms.
```

LISTING 22.11 Continued

```
-- Return value from create():
➥Stub[repository_id=RMI:com.sams.weather.session.WeatherStation:000000000 ...
-- Calling getCurrentTemp(46304)
-- Succeeded: getCurrentTemp(46304)
-- Execution time: 10 ms.
-- Return value from getCurrentTemp(46304): 16.
```

Many times you might want to add other Beans to your test, or you have a Bean for which the results of one Bean is the input of another. The EJB Test Client Wizard facilitates this by giving you a different interface and capabilities for the same wizard. If you select the wizard by choosing Wizards, EJB, Use EJB Test Client from the menu, you are prompted with a first step that is different from the one in the Object Gallery, (see Figure 22.21). By selecting the EJB test client class already exists check box, you will then add the new Bean within the same test client already generated. The second frame, if you do not make this selection, still looks the same as the first (shown previously in Figure 22.20), or it allows you only to choose a Bean and field to hold the instance (see Figure 22.22).

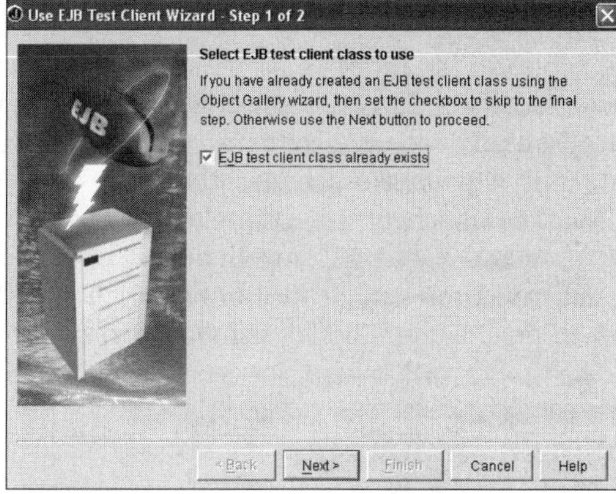

FIGURE 22.21 Use an existing test client with a different Bean.

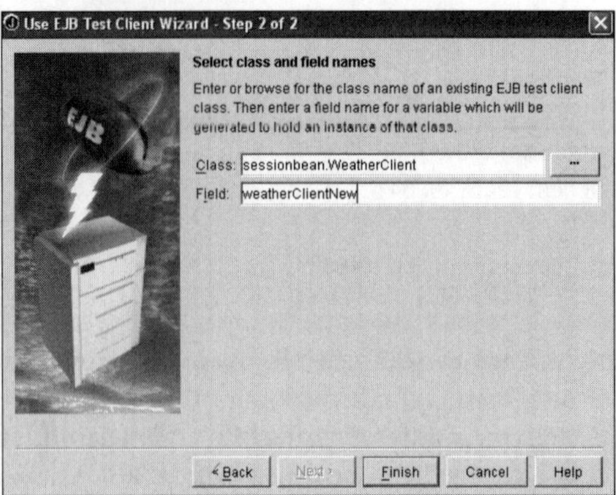

FIGURE 22.22 Specify the class and field to add to your existing test client.

Design Guidelines

As I sat and thought about what to place in "Design Guidelines," I could not decide where to stop. Notice that I did not say "where to begin." Entire books are written on design patterns for J2EE implementation. In fact, I think I own at least five on that single topic, let alone all the other books with that topic included. The problem with so much material on a subject is that it's difficult to know what is important and what is extraneous. I have seen two extreme reactions to these principles. First, design principles are used regardless of whether they fit or not—just for the sheer fact that someone wants to use them. For example, I have seen more than one organization attempt to use Model/View/Controller (MVC) for everything when a simpler pattern would have been sufficient, if not better. This section takes many of these patterns and best practices and boils them down to their root causes and rudimentary solutions.

Wrap Entities with Session Beans

A multitiered, distributed system ultimately requires method invocations to be sent over the wire. These clients do not and should not be exposed to the changes of persistence and transactional management. As a result, the presentation tier becomes vulnerable to changes in the persistence service. Figure 22.23 demonstrates one such solution for us.

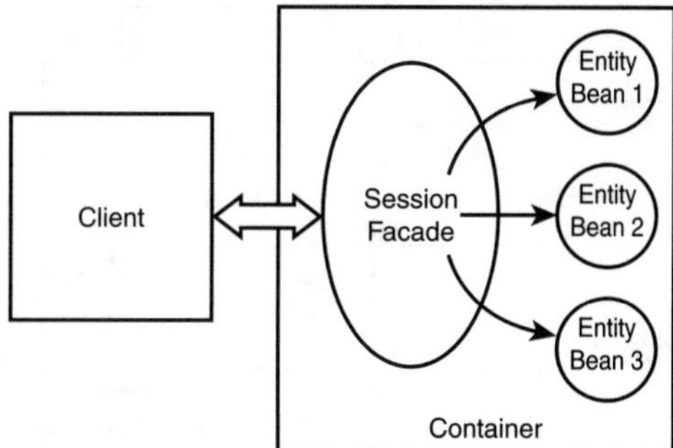

FIGURE 22.23 Wrap entities with a Session Bean.

Inspiration

Although we are talking about Entity Beans before we cover them, it is important to understand that they are defined as coarse-grained persistence objects managed by the container. Each call to a remote object requires a remote invocation, which can be expensive. We need an alternative to this expensive operation especially when a use case or business transaction typically spans multiple Beans.

In addition to the remote cost, the client must also know the transactional context of each Entity Bean rather than the business tier being responsible for its own transaction management. As you will quickly see, you should not access an entity directly but via a Session Bean within the same container.

Inner Workings

A number of different patterns enable this type of operation. We will look at the potential solution and then we will name the pattern for you. Two main patterns are used to accomplish this task. The first and most common for a number of reasons is the session facade pattern. Figure 22.24 contains the sequence diagram for a sample session facade. This is accomplished by implementing a Session Bean to provide a unified access layer for all Entity Beans. The second pattern is the extract class pattern, which is simply moving the business logic to the middle tier. So you might ask what the difference is between the two. A session facade combines multiple disparate types of methods into one Bean, whereas an extract class is singular in purpose.

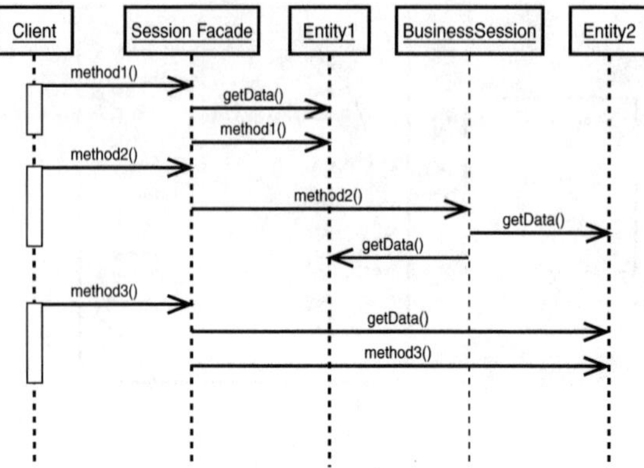

FIGURE 22.24 Sequence diagram of a session facade.

Using Business Delegates

The coupling of the presentation tier to the business tier within a complex environment provides a number of challenges. Some of the challenges are realized by these forces:

- The presentation tier must access business services to function.
- Different clients using different presentation methods must also access the required business services.
- Clients need only use the business rules and not the underlying API within the architecture.

Figure 22.25 demonstrates a client communicating to the delegate not knowing nor caring whether the object is local. As we look into this design guideline, you will notice that this is a fundamental goal of the EJB architecture. "Network Ubiquity" does not know where, does not care.

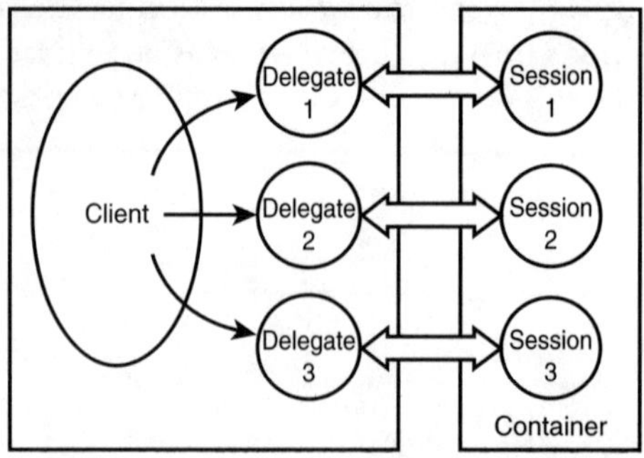

FIGURE 22.25 Using business delegates to surface Session Beans.

Inner Workings

Using a Business Delegate pattern reduces the coupling between the client (presentation tier) and the corresponding business services. This pattern hides all the underlying detail of the specific implementation. It also includes many service requirements such as lookup and details of the EJB architecture. For example, Figure 22.26 shows the sequence of this Business Delegate pattern.

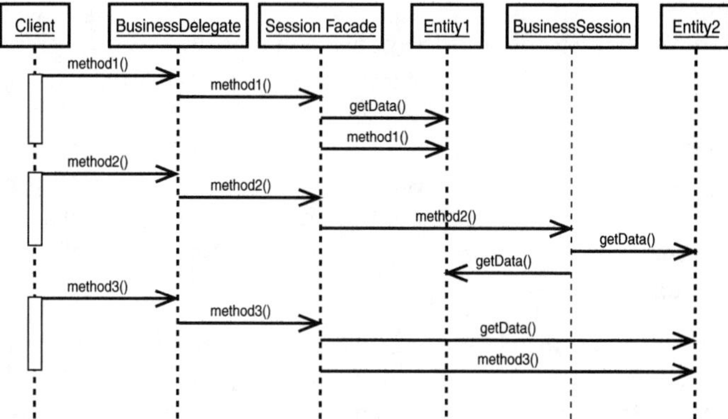

FIGURE 22.26 Business Delegate sequence diagram.

Fold Multiple Session Beans Together

Enterprise Beans encapsulate the business logic and business persistence by exposing them via an interface. Ultimately, the complexity of this interface becomes more important as a system grows. Minimizing the complexity by making the interface as simple as possible is imperative (see Figure 22.27).

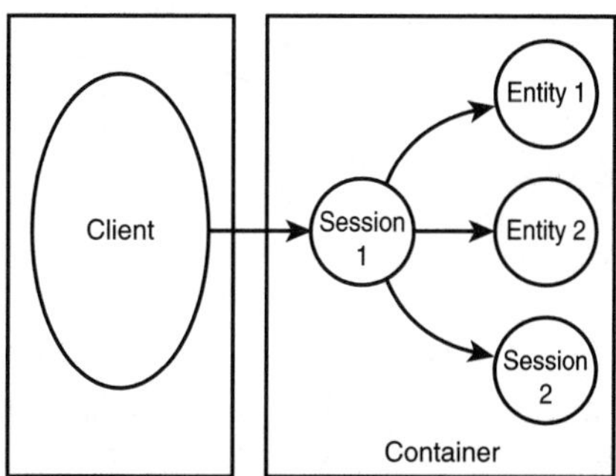

FIGURE 22.27 Merge Session Beans tighter into one consolidated Bean.

Inspiration

When designing an EJB-based solution, it is tempting to do either a one-to-one mapping to Entity Beans or a one-to-one mapping to an individual use case. You are simply using the Session Bean as a proxy to the Entity Beans. Some developers think the purpose of this wrapping is to insulate the user/developer from the Entity Bean's implementation. The motivation is, more importantly, a way to not require the client to manage multiple connections to the EJB container, in addition to the management of these connections by the container. As you saw when testing your Bean with metrics, the single most expensive operation in Session Bean communication is to connect to the home interface; the second is creating the Bean instance.

Inner Workings

You need to implement a Session Bean to supply the required business methods wrapped into one Bean or just a few. Ultimately, a Session Bean will include many different or even sometimes unrelated methods; this is not usually a problem, but it might seem odd at first.

Consolidate a set of all closely related interactions that involve one or more Entity Beans or Session Beans; see the class diagram in Figure 22.28. This ultimately results in a fewer number of Session Beans required for the client to communicate with the middle tier.

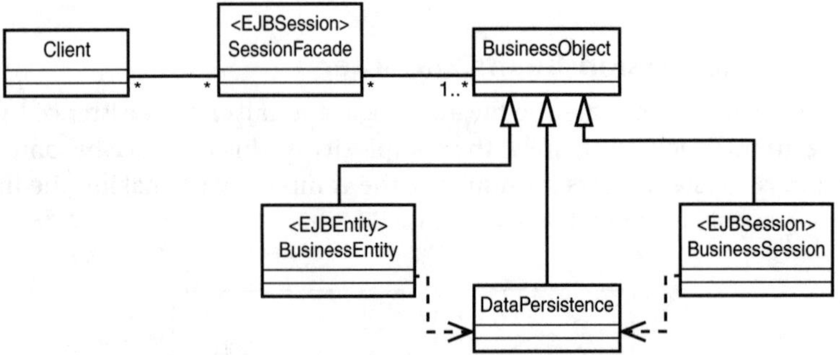

FIGURE 22.28 Session facade class diagram.

Value Objects

Applications must exchange data. If you start with the absolute, you must then focus on the most efficient and simplest method to implement the solution. It is safe to say that you will not be the first to move data from a business service to the presentation tier. Accepting this precept, you can learn from the triumphs and tragedies of others.

Inspiration

Transferring business data between a client and a server is one of the most common operations in EJB applications, and thus it needs to be designed and implemented carefully. A naive, incorrect approach is to implement data transfer between a client and an EJB. For instance, an Entity Bean would need to make multiple invocations, over the wire, using accessor (if data is to be transferred from the EJB to the client) or mutator methods (if data is to be transferred from the client to the EJB) defined in the EJB component interface.

For example, to obtain the topic and times of a meeting, a client could make three calls to the `Meeting` Entity Bean. Such an approach, applied to many objects, results in an inefficient use of network bandwidth; see Figure 22.29 for an example.

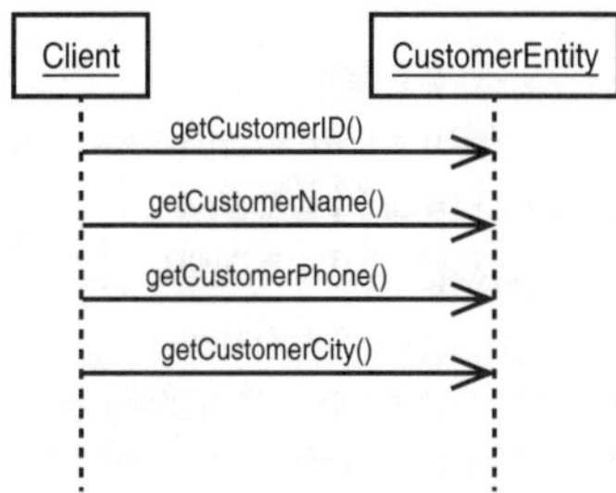

FIGURE 22.29 Sequence diagram for communicating to a customer entity.

Inner Workings

A way to improve efficiency of data transfer between clients and EJB components is to design and use *value objects* as envelopes containing multiple data attributes. A value object is a regular, serializable Java object, capable of storing multiple data attributes to be exchanged between a client and an EJB. Value objects can be used for both reading and update operations; in other words, you can pass it both directions.

If a client wants to read data, it invokes a single method of an EJB (see Figure 22.30). The invoked method of the EJB component creates a value object, populates the object with data, and returns the value object as a result. After receiving the result, the client can access all the data attributes via local invocations of a value object's accessor methods. If a client wants to update data, the client creates a value object, populates the value object with new data attributes, and invokes a method of an EJB component passing the data back. The value object can simply contain multiple data attributes to be updated as a parameter of the invoked method. The EJB component extracts the values from the value objects and performs the update of the database (accessing the database directly, or via interactions with other EJB components, such as Entity Beans).

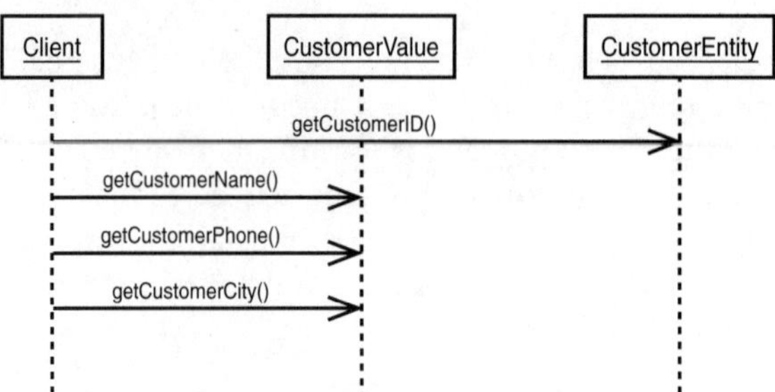

FIGURE 22.30 Sequence diagram for communicating to the value object.

In Practice

It is time to implement the Session Beans for our ChalkTalk system. We will implement a portion of the system giving you a taste of the implementation process. A brief description of the objects to be implemented is as follows:

- `Course`—Represents all the courses offered by the school at one time or another. A `Course` might not be in offering now or might even have been cancelled (for example, "Introduction to JBuilder").
- `CourseInstance`—A particular instance of a `Course` being offered. A `CourseInstance` is a course when it is actually taught in the school. One `Course` might have multiple (or zero) `CourseInstances` at any given time. A `CourseInstance` must have between 3 and 20 `Students` (both limits inclusive).
- `Student`—Any person who registers to take a `CourseInstance`.
- `Instructor`—A person who can teach a `Course`. An `Instructor` is authorized to teach `Courses` for which he is qualified. An `Instructor` might be selected to teach zero or more `CourseInstances`.
- `Room`—Where a `CourseInstance` is scheduled to be held or taught. The `Room` class represents a fixed resource that cannot be created nor destroyed for the purpose of the ChalkTalk application.
- `Calendar`—Represents a set of dates and times on which a particular `CourseInstance` is offered. A `Calendar` class can represent all the possible scheduling scenarios for a `CourseInstance` (recurring or one-off time slots, and so on).

The Business Services package describes the operations that can be performed on the classes that are part of the Data Services package. At this level of analysis, all these operations are in only one class called `BusinessOperations`.

Table 22.4 lists all the operations that can be performed on the different Data Services classes. Each column represents a Data Services class, and each row corresponds to an operation. The letters A, S, and I indicate that the operations will be performed by Administrators, Students, and Instructors. (This information is not needed at this level of abstraction, but will be needed when we design the client tiers.)

TABLE 22.4 The Operations (Methods) of the `BusinessOperations` Class in the Business Services Package

	Course	Student	Instructor	CourseInstance	Room	Calendar
Add	No	Yes (S)	No	Yes (A)	No	No
Remove	No	Yes (S)	No	Yes (A)	No	No
Modify	Yes (A)	Yes (S)	Yes (I)	Yes (A)	No	No

Preparing the Project

1. Create a new project or use the existing "In Practice" exercise from an earlier chapter.
2. Assign project properties to indicate the enterprise server.
3. Create an EJB module: `ChalkTalk`. This will be used to encapsulate all the EJBs within a design unit. This will then allow us to develop our EJBs graphically using the EJB Designer.

Building the Session Interface

1. Create value objects for our session facade.
2. Create a Session Bean: Stateless/`ChalkTalkFacade`.
3. Classes and Packages: `com.sams.chalktalk.beans`.
4. Add all the business methods found in Table 22.5.

TABLE 22.5 The Operations (Methods) of the `BusinessOperations` Class in the Business Services Package

	Add	Remove
Course	`addCourse`	`removeCourse`
Student	`addStudent`	`removeStudent`
Instructor	`addInstructor`	`removeInstructor`
Room	`addRoom`	`removeRoom`
Calendar	`addCalendar`	`removeCalendar`

TABLE 22.5 Continued

	Modify	Find
Course	`modifyCourse`	`findCourse`
Student	`modifyStudent`	`findStudent`
Instructor	`modifyInstructor`	`findInstructor`
Room	`modifyRoom`	`findRoom`
Calendar	`modifyCalendar`	`findCalendar`

Building the Value Objects Interface

1. Select File, New Class to construct our value objects.
2. Specify the following values for these properties:
   - Package: **`com.sams.chalktalk.data`**
   - Class name: **`RoomData`**
   - Bean class: **`java.lang.Object`**
   - Options: Public, Generate Default Constructor
3. Click Finish.
4. Repeat this step for every instance of data you want to pass from client to server. For information about the Value Object pattern, see the "Design Guidelines" section.
5. Define the structure for the class to match the data you want to marshal between the client and the server. Listing 22.12 is one of those structures demonstrating the implementation of our room Entity Bean.

LISTING 22.12 Implementing a Value Object for Our Room Entity Bean

```
package com.sams.chalktalk.data;

public class roomData {

  private String name;
  private int key;
  private int capacity;
  private String location;
  public roomData() {
  }
```

LISTING 22.12 Continued

```
  public roomData(int key, String name, int capacity, String location){
    this.key = key;
    this.name = name;
    this.capacity = capacity;
    this.location = location;
  }
  public void setName(String name) {
    this.name = name;
  }
  public String getName() {
    return name;
  }
  public void setKey(int key) {
    this.key = key;
  }
  public int getKey() {
    return key;
  }
  public void setCapacity(int capacity) {
    this.capacity = capacity;
  }
  public int getCapacity() {
    return capacity;
  }
  public void setLocation(String location) {
    this.location = location;
  }
  public String getLocation() {
    return location;
  }
}
```

6. Repeat this process for each required value object.
7. Save and compile. Remove errors and address warning.

Building the Integration Between Business Services and Value Objects

1. Enter the EJB Designer for the `ChalkTalk` EJB module.
2. Add the appropriate value object to the method signature. For example, the `addRoom` method needs to receive a copy of the room instance you want to add to your data store.
3. Add validation and business rules to the method implementation. For example, a room with a negative capacity is not allowed (see Listing 22.13).

LISTING 22.13 Implementation of a Business to Validate the Room Data Added to Our Persistence Store

```
public void addRoom(com.sams.chalktalk.data.RoomData room) {
  if (room.getCapacity() <= 0){
    throw new EJBException("Capacity <= 0 not allowed");
  }
}
```

4. Save and compile. Remove errors and address warning.

Deploying the Bean

1. Add an EAR node to our project. This is accomplished by selecting File, New.
2. Within the Object Gallery, choose the Enterprise tab. Create an EAR.
3. Specify the following parameters to the wizard:
   - Name: `ChalkTalk`
   - Output archive name: `ChalkTalk`
4. Click Finish.
5. Save and build your project.
6. Right-click on your `ChalkTalk.ear` and deploy it to your EJB container.

Creating a Test Client

It is time to test the client we have created. The easiest way to test our session facade is to build a client dedicated to testing our interface. The following steps build a test client to exercise this facade:

1. Select File, New on the JBuilder menu.
2. Within the Object Gallery under the Enterprise tab, select the EJB Test Client.
3. Specify the following parameters to build our test client:
    - EJB name: `ChalkTalkFacade`
    - Package: `com.sams.chalktalk.data`
    - Class name: `ChalkTalkFacadeTestClient`
    - Generate method for testing remote interface calls with arguments: Checked
    - Generate logging messages: Checked
    - Generate main functions: Checked
    - Generate header comments: Checked
4. Add the following code to the `main` method to test your Session Bean interface:

```
//create a Remote interface
client.create();

//Add a room
client.addRoom(new RoomData(5,"Small Room",5,"2nd Floor"));

//Add with invalid capacity
client.addRoom(new RoomData(3,"Error Room",0,"3rd Floor"));
```

5. Save, compile, and run your test application.

Summary

As we looked at Session Beans, you learned that they are a powerful portion of the entire Enterprise Java Bean (EJB) suite. As we looked at the development of both stateless and stateful Session Beans, you saw that each has a different purpose or goal. The development and deployment of both stateless and stateful Session Beans do not differ that much. The following aspects are important in developing Session Beans:

- You must develop two interfaces, an implementation class, and the deployment descriptor to create a Session Bean. Stateless Session Beans and stateful Session Beans are identical except for the Bean type in the deployment descriptor.

- Create a JAR file that contains the interfaces, class, and deployment descriptor for a given EJB module. It then can be deployed to a J2EE container for management and delivery or combined with other archives into an EAR.
- When developing a Session Bean client, you must create, locate, and utilize the Session Bean's business operations.

Reflections

- How many Session Beans are required?
- Why should I use stateless or stateful Session Beans?
- Why do I need a value object?

23

Developing Entity Beans

IN THIS CHAPTER

- A Closer Look at Entity Beans
- Developing a CMP Bean
- Developing a BMP Bean
- Advanced Container-Managed Persistence
- Transactions
- Container Security
- Design Guidelines

Entities have a singular purpose: to represent an entity of data from a given data source. This typically represents a record within a database. The beauty of this component is the capability to manipulate the data stored within a data store through a standard interface instead of having to send manipulation calls directly to the data source in any manner. This technique of wrapping manipulation to a data source is not new; you might know it as *object to relational mapping*.

This object mapping requires that an entity bean be responsible for inserting, updating, selecting, and removing data within the data source. This process of managing the communication between the component and the data source is called *persistence*. In other words, persistence is this process of writing the information to an external data source. As you discovered in Chapter 21, "An Architectural Overview of Enterprise JavaBeans," we defined two types of entity beans. Using the first entity type, the container manages all the persistence itself. This entity type is called *container managed persistence (CMP)*. The other type informs the container that you, the developer, are required to manage all the manipulation to your given data source. This type is called *bean managed persistence (BMP)*.

The most current version of entity beans is defined within the EJB 2.0 specification. The EJB 2.0 specification does not abandon support for 1.1 beans. There are a number of significant changes between 1.1 and 2.0, such that you cannot develop one bean that will work with both specifications.

As we work to understand Enterprise JavaBeans, and more specifically in this section entity beans, we will look at examples and even put them into practice. We will explore the following topics:

- Developing CMP and BMP beans
- Deploying entity beans
- Using entity beans

A Closer Look at Entity Beans

As we look at an entity, you will see that it is an object-oriented representation of the data contained within a data source. This important feature allows you as a developer to easily represent data in a relational data source as an object within Java. Ultimately, Java requires data to be represented within an object footprint, and this makes the process simple.

It is important for you to understand that entity beans are a single representation of data, whereas a session bean can have multiple instances of the bean representing data. This implies an important difference between entity beans and session beans: The life span of a session bean is dependent on the life span of the client, whereas the life span of an entity bean is a relationship to data.

Bean Life Cycle

Unlike session beans, an entity bean survives beyond the client session using it. Even though the client creates an instance of an entity bean, the entity bean remains available until the container and only the container decides to remove it.

If we investigate the sequence diagram, shown in Figure 23.1, we can see that, as in the session bean, the entity's sequence diagram has a similar-looking state transition diagram (refer to Figure 22.2).

When the client invokes the `create()` method on the home interface, the bean is then created and placed within the pool of available beans. This pool contains all currently instantiated entity beans of this type. In the sequence diagram, you will see that the transition from `Does not exist` to `pooled` varies between BMP and CMP.

At some point, the container may decide to "garbage" collect pooled beans. The container calls `unsetEntityContext()` to deallocate the current associated entity of data. The EJB specification does not define the frequency or trigger for this action to execute, only that the bean must have the capability to accomplish this. In other words, different vendors trigger the garbage collector at different times. For example, Borland's Enterprise Server executes it on the length of inactivity of the bean.

If the client then invokes one of the finder methods, the bean finds the instance of the data in the data source, copies the primary key into the instance's member variables, and finally returns the bean to the pool. In many instances, this does not cause the entire instance to be loaded into the entity bean. This happens when the `ejbLoad()` method is called to synchronize the data with the data source.

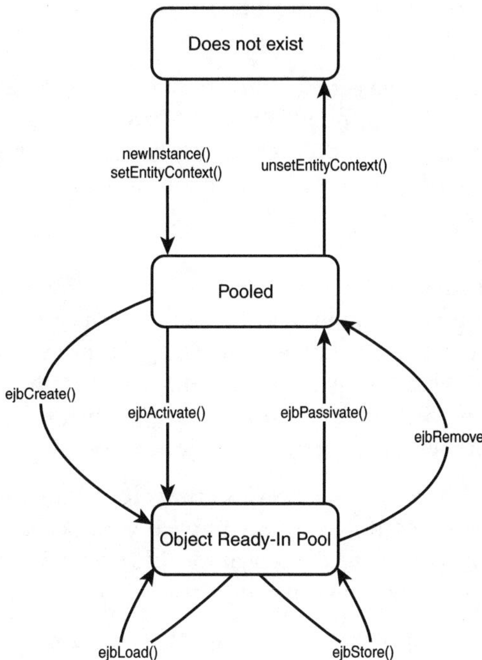

FIGURE 23.1 Client's perspective of the state of an entity bean.

What Are CMP and BMP Anyway?

The main goal for having two different types of entity beans is to give developers the ultimate flexibility for implementing entity beans as they see fit, but clients of the bean do not have to be aware or concerned with the implementation.

This is accomplished by giving you container managed persistence and bean managed persistence. First, container managed persistence addresses one of the main goals of Enterprise JavaBeans, which is to split work between the component developer and the container. The goals for container managed persistence are basic and important:

- Free up the developer to work on business logic rather than persistence. This is accomplished by allowing the container to manage all the persistence and loading of data. For example, if you are developing an order entry system, you can communicate only to a data source using SQL, thus the communication is well defined and fairly repetitive except for the data context.

- Persistence services can be developed by persistence specialists. In other words, this means that persistence is most likely going to run faster, with more transactional safety, and scale better. Using the EJB 2.0 specification has expanded greatly the performance and capabilities of the container managed persistence bean.
- CMP beans are portable across EJB containers and data sources. EJB containers that support the EJB 2.0 specification facilitate the movement of an entity bean from one container to another rather seamlessly. In fact, some containers even attempt to work in specific database vendor features for performance and scalability but still allowing portability.

Finally, bean managed persistence is an alternative to using container managed persistence. Just as the name implies, it allows the bean to persist the instance in which the bean developer must implement. The goals of bean managed persistence are slightly more nebulous. For example, anything you cannot accomplish in a container managed persistence bean, you can accomplish in a bean managed persistence component. Some of these include the following:

- You might have specific JDBC features that are required for your DBMS vendor. For example, you might need to accomplish your persistence with stored procedures or bulk inserts. Note: Some vendors have added stored procedure communication to container managed persistence.
- You might have proprietary object-to-relational mapping provided by another tool. For example, TopLink is a popular object mapping tool that generates the code for bean managed persistence.
- You might need to encapsulate communicating to a nonrelational data store. For example, you might want to communicate to a mainframe or mini using a proprietary data store for a given application.

It is unlikely that you cannot accomplish all of an application's persistence requirements using container managed persistence. The EJB 2.0 specifications include many new features for CMP beans that make BMP almost obsolete in most occasions.

EJB 2.0 Versus EJB 1.1

There were two large problems with the EJB 1.1 specification as it related to entity beans. The EJB 2.0 specifications focused on these two problems:

- It was difficult to build coarse-grained entity beans.
- Finder methods lacked portability.

The Enterprise JavaBean 2.0 specifications have provided a number of new features to fill some of the gaps found in the EJB 1.1 specification. Table 23.1 presents some of the problems found after many applications were written using the EJB 1.1 specification and how the 2.0 specification resolves them.

TABLE 23.1 EJB 1.1 Specification Versus EJB 2.0 Specifications

EJB 1.1 Problem	EJB 2.0 Solution
No good pattern to represent dependent objects within an entity bean	The introduction of local interfaces, which allow for modeling of dependent objects as another bean but still allow for good performance.
Load-on-demand and dirty checking of data	EJB 2.0 CMP has abstract methods available for the implementation of load-on-demand and dirty checking.
No portable way to ensure the contents of a collection within a container's persistence strategy	The EJB container maintains collection classes that simplify the object-to-relational mapping.
Data-aliasing contention created when two or more entities reference the same dependent object	Dependent objects are managed as entity objects by the container. The container then manages the state of the entity component. This ultimately allows for synchronization within the transaction with multiple entities being represented as multiple aliases.
No portable implementation of finder methods	A portable query language was implemented based on a subset of SQL.

With these new features, most of which have been added to container managed persistence, entity beans have become extremely powerful and efficient. A developer can simply model most if not all of the persistence requirements within JBuilder allowing you to work on your business methods rather than plumbing.

Primary Keys

As we have looked at entity beans to this point, the key consideration is that relational data is represented in the object world. Therefore, just as the relational world represents a unique instance of data with a primary key, you must do the same in the object world. This special class is called the *primary key*. Its sole purpose is to uniquely identify an instance of an entity bean. In other words, the primary key class contains all the information required to find an entity within the persistent data store. To accomplish this successfully, a number of rules must be followed:

- The primary key instances must be any legal type in RMI/IIOP. In other words, it must be serializable.
- It must provide a `hashcode()` and `equals()` method.

- It must uniquely identify a single instance of the data stored within the persistent data store. For example, the primary key of the table is probably a good primary key for the entity.
- In container managed persistence, the class must have a constructor that takes no arguments. Because the container is responsible for creating instances, it must have the capability to create a primary key class.

The Interface

The beauty of entity beans is that, whenever you develop a CMP or BMP, the interface is the same to the client. This allows for the user of the bean to be isolated from the overall implementation of the bean. This is where session beans and entity beans differ greatly; a session bean has a method for each business method required. For CMP beans, you let the container provide the implementation of the interface, whereas with BMP beans you, as the developer, implement the interface. We'll now take a look at the interface provided for Enterprise JavaBeans (see Listing 23.1).

LISTING 23.1 `EntityBean` Interface for Implementation by the Entity Bean

```
// JBuilder API Decompiler stub source generated from class file
// Jul 5, 2002
// -- implementation of methods is not available

package javax.ejb;

// Imports
import java.rmi.RemoteException;

public abstract interface EntityBean extends EnterpriseBean {

  // Methods
  void ejbActivate() throws EJBException, RemoteException;
  void ejbLoad() throws EJBException, RemoteException;
  void ejbPassivate() throws EJBException, RemoteException;
  void ejbRemove() throws RemoveException, EJBException, RemoteException;
  void ejbStore() throws EJBException, RemoteException;
  void setEntityContext(EntityContext entityContext)
➥throws EJBException, RemoteException;
  void unsetEntityContext() throws EJBException, RemoteException;
}
```

In addition to implementation of the preceding interface, the bean developer is required to also implement an `ejbCreate()` and an `ejbPostCreate()` that correspond with each `create()` method signature within the home interface.

As you look at this interface, you will see that it supports the four basic operations required of any persistent data store; they are known as CRUD. The four basic operations you might want to perform on data are

- Create (C)
- Read (R)
- Update (U)
- Delete (D)

Each of the four operations of a persistent data store is represented by a corresponding entity interface callback method. Create relates to `ejbCreate()` and `ejbPostCreate()`. Reading is implemented using `ejbLoad()`. Update is implemented using the `ejbStore()`, and finally delete is implemented using `ejbRemove()`. These callbacks are then managed by the container based entirely on the life cycle of the entity bean.

In addition to the CRUD requirements, you also have a few other methods to implement. If you compare the `ejbActivate()` and `ejbPassivate()` methods to that defined within a session bean, you will notice they are similar. By default, an entity bean saves its instance data to a secondary data store so that the requirements of activation and passivation are not as important. More importantly, it uses `ejbActivate()` as a notification mechanism when the entity bean's instance has been associated with a primary key class. `ejbPassivate()` is then called to notify the entity that the primary key is being disassociated with the primary key class and is available to another instance.

Finally, the last two methods are `setEntityContext()` and `unsetEntityContext()`. The `setEntityContext()` method allows a bean to access the bean's context. This is important when using entity beans because you use the context to associate the primary key to an instance. The `unsetEntityContext()` allows you to remove the allocation of resources.

Developing a CMP Bean

It is now time to look at the process of building an entity bean. We will develop a simple CMP bean, but spend most of our time investigating and perfecting the process.

The process has some similarities to creating session beans. The following is the process we are going to use to investigate and build an entity bean:

- Implement the home interface.
- Define the appropriate finder methods.
- Implement the component interface.
- Define the bean implementation class.
- Build the deployment descriptor.
- Deploy the bean.
- Test the bean.

Defining the Home Interface

The home interface for an entity bean is similar to the home interface of a session bean. To review, its purpose is to create an instance, find existing instances, or remove an instance; the same rules apply to an entity bean (see Listing 23.2).

LISTING 23.2 Home Interface for Our `Employee` Entity Bean

```
import javax.ejb.*;
import java.util.*;

public interface EmployeeHome extends javax.ejb.EJBLocalHome {
  public Employee create(Short empNo) throws CreateException;
  public Employee findByPrimaryKey(Short empNo) throws FinderException;
}
```

The `create()` method is used to create an instance of a class based on this primary key. For our employee table, the `empNo` is the primary key, thus we will also use `empNo` as the primary key of our entity bean. The second method type is called a finder method. With entity beans, to create an instance we use the `create()` method, but finding an existing instance is just as important if not more important. With that requirement, we need finder methods to provide the capability to locate a specific instance or collection of instances of data.

The `findByPrimaryKey()` is a method that has an argument representing the primary key; in our case, it is `empNo`. This searches for an employee with the given primary key either returning a remote interface to the instance or through an exception.

NOTE

The `findByPrimaryKey()` method is required by all entity beans; any other finders are optional.

Finder methods do not just return a single instance, but they can also return a collection of instances. These types of finder methods are typically used when the primary key or an alternative unique key is not used. For example, we might want to be able to find employees who have a certain salary range, as shown in Listing 23.3. This finder method should return a collection of employees rather than a single instance.

LISTING 23.3 Home Interface for Our `Employee` Entity Bean with the Addition of New Finder Methods

```
import javax.ejb.*;
import java.util.*;
import java.math.*;

public interface EmployeeHome extends javax.ejb.EJBLocalHome {
  public Employee create(Short empNo) throws CreateException;
  public Collection findSalaryRange(BigDecimal low, BigDecimal high)
➥throws FinderException;
  public Employee findByPrimaryKey(Short empNo) throws FinderException;
}
```

Notice that the `findSalaryRange()` does not return a single instance like the `findByPrimaryKey()` but a `java.lang.Collection`. This collection contains instances of the primary key, not the entire instance; the container then translates for you this instance into the remote interface. This method might return a huge collection of records, so it is important to make sure that you design the beans appropriately.

Defining the Component Interface

Our `Employee` interface defines all the methods required for us to access and mutate the data within the bean. For example, `setFirstName()` and `getFirstName()` methods are required to get access to the instance variables (see Listing 23.4).

LISTING 23.4 Component Interface for the `Employee` Bean

```
import javax.ejb.*;
import java.util.*;
import java.sql.*;
import java.math.*;
```

LISTING 23.4 Continued

```
public interface Employee extends javax.ejb.EJBLocalObject {
  public Short getEmpNo();
  public void setFirstName(String firstName);
  public String getFirstName();
  public void setLastName(String lastName);
  public String getLastName();
  public void setPhoneExt(String phoneExt);
  public String getPhoneExt();
  public void setHireDate(Timestamp hireDate);
  public Timestamp getHireDate();
  public void setDeptNo(String deptNo);
  public String getDeptNo();
  public void setJobCode(String jobCode);
  public String getJobCode();
  public void setJobGrade(Short jobGrade);
  public Short getJobGrade();
  public void setJobCountry(String jobCountry);
  public String getJobCountry();
  public void setSalary(BigDecimal salary);
  public BigDecimal getSalary();
  public void setFullName(String fullName);
  public String getFullName();
}
```

Implementing the Bean

One misconception about CMP beans is that you do not have to have a bean implementation class. This class supplies the necessary implementations required for the container to manage the persistence, as shown in Listing 23.5.

LISTING 23.5 EmployeeBean Implementation Class

```
import javax.ejb.*;

abstract public class EmployeeBean implements EntityBean {
  EntityContext entityContext;
  public java.lang.Short ejbCreate(java.lang.Short empNo)
➥throws CreateException {
    setEmpNo(empNo);
    return null;
  }
```

LISTING 23.5 Continued

```
public void ejbPostCreate(java.lang.Short empNo) throws CreateException {
  /**@todo Complete this method*/
}
public void ejbRemove() throws RemoveException {
  /**@todo Complete this method*/
}
public abstract void setEmpNo(java.lang.Short empNo);
public abstract void setFirstName(java.lang.String firstName);
public abstract void setLastName(java.lang.String lastName);
public abstract void setPhoneExt(java.lang.String phoneExt);
public abstract void setHireDate(java.sql.Timestamp hireDate);
public abstract void setDeptNo(java.lang.String deptNo);
public abstract void setJobCode(java.lang.String jobCode);
public abstract void setJobGrade(java.lang.Short jobGrade);
public abstract void setJobCountry(java.lang.String jobCountry);
public abstract void setSalary(java.math.BigDecimal salary);
public abstract void setFullName(java.lang.String fullName);
public abstract java.lang.Short getEmpNo();
public abstract java.lang.String getFirstName();
public abstract java.lang.String getLastName();
public abstract java.lang.String getPhoneExt();
public abstract java.sql.Timestamp getHireDate();
public abstract java.lang.String getDeptNo();
public abstract java.lang.String getJobCode();
public abstract java.lang.Short getJobGrade();
public abstract java.lang.String getJobCountry();
public abstract java.math.BigDecimal getSalary();
public abstract java.lang.String getFullName();
public void ejbLoad() {
  /**@todo Complete this method*/
}
public void ejbStore() {
  /**@todo Complete this method*/
}
public void ejbActivate() {
  /**@todo Complete this method*/
}
public void ejbPassivate() {
  /**@todo Complete this method*/
}
public void unsetEntityContext() {
  this.entityContext = null;
```

LISTING 23.5 Continued

```
    }
    public void setEntityContext(EntityContext entityContext) {
      this.entityContext = entityContext;
    }
}
```

The client first calls the `create()` method of the entity bean's home interface. Remember that this is the client of the bean, not necessarily an end-user client. This then translates through the container to the implementation bean. These methods are called by the container for the persistence to take place properly. Let's take a look in detail at how the bean actually works. The best method to view the operation is to use a sequence diagram.

First, let's look at the creation of a new instance of an entity bean, as shown in Figure 23.2. The `create()` method tags arguments, which is typically a signature containing the primary key of an instance. After that, the container takes complete control going forward.

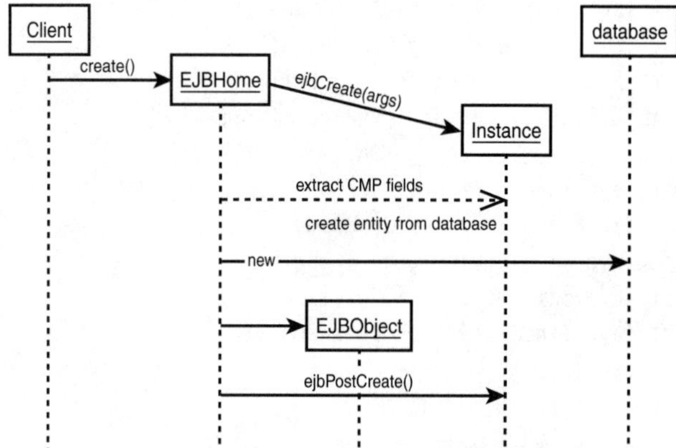

FIGURE 23.2 Sequence diagram for a client creating an entity bean.

Second, we might need to remove a bean. The `remove()` method is called by the client, allowing for the instance to be removed from the data source (see Figure 23.3). Again, the only call the client needs to make is `remove()`; the container then manages the rest of the interaction to remove the instance.

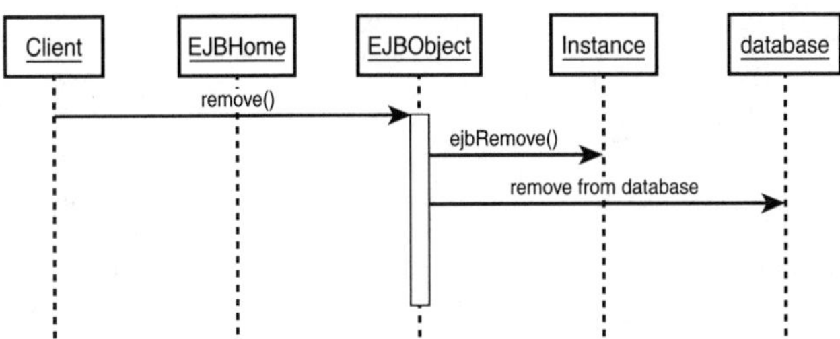

FIGURE 23.3 Sequence diagram for a client removing an entity bean.

Finally, let's look at a finder method, shown in Figure 23.4. When the client makes a call to one of the finder methods on the home interface, the home interface uses the data source to return the matching elements either singularly using the remote interface or by a list using a `java.lang.Collection`.

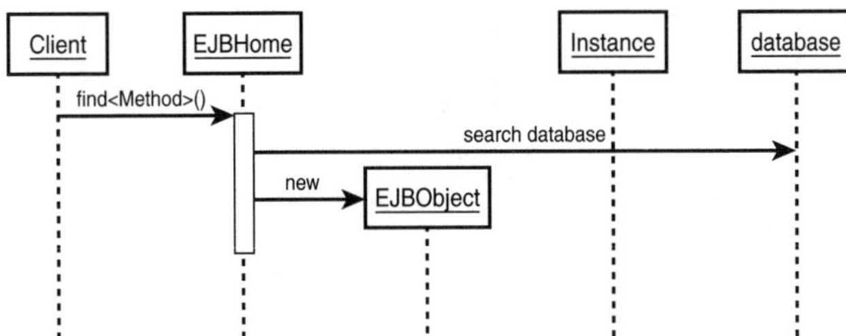

FIGURE 23.4 Sequence diagram for a client using one of the finder methods.

Deployment Descriptor

The role of the deployment descriptor is to ultimately provide information about each EJB that is to be bundled and deployed within a particular JAR file. Its intent is to inform the consumer, in this case the container, what the JAR file contains and how it is to be implemented. If you are developing your bean, it is typically your responsibility to create the deployment descriptor. The deployment descriptor keeps the following information:

- Defines the types, or names, of the classes for the home/local home and remote/local interfaces and the bean class.
- JNDI names, which define the name of the interface advertised to the naming service.
- Fields to enable container managed persistence.
- Transactional policies for the bean's transactional behavior.

- Security attributes for the enterprise beans.
- Deployment-specific information; these include special information for the deployed container brand.

To alleviate the confusion between vendor-specific deployment descriptors and general deployment descriptors, they are divided into two different descriptors. The first of which is the deployment descriptor, which contains the configuration information for our `Employee` CMP bean (see Listing 23.6).

LISTING 23.6 Deployment Descriptor Containing Our `Employee` CMP Bean (ejb-JAR.xml)

```
<?xml version="1.0" encoding="UTF-8"?>
<!DOCTYPE ejb-JAR PUBLIC "-//Sun Microsystems, Inc.//DTD
➥Enterprise JavaBeans 2.0//EN" "http://java.sun.com/dtd/ejb-JAR_2_0.dtd">
<ejb-JAR>
    <enterprise-beans>
        <entity>
            <display-name>Employee</display-name>
            <ejb-name>Employee</ejb-name>
            <local-home>com.sams.samples.entity.EmployeeHome</local-home>
            <local>com.sams.samples.entity.Employee</local>
            <ejb-class>com.sams.samples.entity.EmployeeBean</ejb-class>
            <persistence-type>Container</persistence-type>
            <prim-key-class>java.lang.Short</prim-key-class>
            <reentrant>False</reentrant>
            <cmp-version>2.x</cmp-version>
            <abstract-schema-name>Employee</abstract-schema-name>
            <cmp-field>
                <field-name>empNo</field-name>
            </cmp-field>
            <cmp-field>
                <field-name>firstName</field-name>
            </cmp-field>
            <cmp-field>
                <field-name>lastName</field-name>
            </cmp-field>
            <cmp-field>
                <field-name>phoneExt</field-name>
            </cmp-field>
            <cmp-field>
                <field-name>hireDate</field-name>
            </cmp-field>
```

LISTING 23.6 Continued

```
            <cmp-field>
                <field-name>deptNo</field-name>
            </cmp-field>
            <cmp-field>
                <field-name>jobCode</field-name>
            </cmp-field>
            <cmp-field>
                <field-name>jobGrade</field-name>
            </cmp-field>
            <cmp-field>
                <field-name>jobCountry</field-name>
            </cmp-field>
            <cmp-field>
                <field-name>salary</field-name>
            </cmp-field>
            <cmp-field>
                <field-name>fullName</field-name>
            </cmp-field>
            <primkey-field>empNo</primkey-field>
            <query>
                <query-method>
                    <method-name>findBySalaryRange</method-name>
                    <method-params>
                        <method-param>java.math.BigDecimal</method-param>
                        <method-param>java.math.BigDecimal</method-param>
                    </method-params>
                </query-method>
                <ejb-ql>select OBJECT(e) from employee e where
➥e.salary between (low,high)</ejb-ql>
            </query>
        </entity>
    </enterprise-beans>
    <assembly-descriptor>
        <container-transaction>
            <method>
                <ejb-name>Employee</ejb-name>
                <method-name>*</method-name>
            </method>
            <trans-attribute>Required</trans-attribute>
        </container-transaction>
    </assembly-descriptor>
</ejb-JAR>
```

As you look at this descriptor, you will notice that all the information regarding our bean is contained within the deployment descriptor. This descriptor will be deployed in the JAR with the bean. Now let's look at the deployment descriptor specific to an enterprise application server container—specifically, in this case, Borland's Enterprise Server, shown in Listing 23.7.

LISTING 23.7 Application-Specific Deployment Descriptor for Borland's Enterprise Server (ejb-borland.xml)

```
<?xml version="1.0" encoding="UTF-8"?>
<!DOCTYPE ejb-JAR PUBLIC "-//Borland Software Corporation//DTD
➥Enterprise JavaBeans 2.0//EN"
"http://www.borland.com/devsupport/appserver/dtds/ejb-JAR_2_0-borland.dtd">
<ejb-JAR>
    <enterprise-beans>
        <entity>
            <ejb-name>Employee</ejb-name>
            <bean-local-home-name>Employee</bean-local-home-name>
            <cmp2-info>
                <cmp-field>
                    <field-name>empNo</field-name>
                    <column-name>EMP_NO</column-name>
                </cmp-field>
                <cmp-field>
                    <field-name>firstName</field-name>
                    <column-name>FIRST_NAME</column-name>
                </cmp-field>
                <cmp-field>
                    <field-name>lastName</field-name>
                    <column-name>LAST_NAME</column-name>
                </cmp-field>
                <cmp-field>
                    <field-name>phoneExt</field-name>
                    <column-name>PHONE_EXT</column-name>
                </cmp-field>
                <cmp-field>
                    <field-name>hireDate</field-name>
                    <column-name>HIRE_DATE</column-name>
                </cmp-field>
                <cmp-field>
                    <field-name>deptNo</field-name>
                    <column-name>DEPT_NO</column-name>
                </cmp-field>
```

LISTING 23.7 Continued

```
                <cmp-field>
                    <field-name>jobCode</field-name>
                    <column-name>JOB_CODE</column-name>
                </cmp-field>
                <cmp-field>
                    <field-name>jobGrade</field-name>
                    <column-name>JOB_GRADE</column-name>
                </cmp-field>
                <cmp-field>
                    <field-name>jobCountry</field-name>
                    <column-name>JOB_COUNTRY</column-name>
                </cmp-field>
                <cmp-field>
                    <field-name>salary</field-name>
                    <column-name>SALARY</column-name>
                </cmp-field>
                <cmp-field>
                    <field-name>fullName</field-name>
                    <column-name>FULL_NAME</column-name>
                </cmp-field>
                <table-name>EMPLOYEE</table-name>
            </cmp2-info>
            <property>
                <prop-name>ejb-designer-id</prop-name>
                <prop-type>String</prop-type>
                <prop-value>Employee</prop-value>
            </property>
        </entity>
    </enterprise-beans>
    <table-properties>
        <table-name>EMPLOYEE</table-name>
        <column-properties>
            <column-name>EMP_NO</column-name>
        </column-properties>
        <column-properties>
            <column-name>FIRST_NAME</column-name>
        </column-properties>
        <column-properties>
            <column-name>LAST_NAME</column-name>
        </column-properties>
        <column-properties>
```

LISTING 23.7 Continued

```
            <column-name>PHONE_EXT</column-name>
        </column-properties>
        <column-properties>
            <column-name>HIRE_DATE</column-name>
        </column-properties>
        <column-properties>
            <column-name>DEPT_NO</column-name>
        </column-properties>
        <column-properties>
            <column-name>JOB_CODE</column-name>
        </column-properties>
        <column-properties>
            <column-name>JOB_GRADE</column-name>
        </column-properties>
        <column-properties>
            <column-name>JOB_COUNTRY</column-name>
        </column-properties>
        <column-properties>
            <column-name>SALARY</column-name>
        </column-properties>
        <column-properties>
            <column-name>FULL_NAME</column-name>
        </column-properties>
        <property>
            <prop-name>datasource</prop-name>
            <prop-type>String</prop-type>
            <prop-value>serial://datasources/DataSource</prop-value>
        </property>
    </table-properties>
    <assembly-descriptor />
</ejb-JAR>
```

Deploying Your Entity Bean

Deploying the bean is exactly the same as deploying the bean with a session bean. The entity bean we just created must be deployed on an application server before any client can access the bean. The process varies slightly depending on the version or brand of your application server. JBuilder insulates you from most of the differences, but nonetheless you have to know a little bit about your deployment environment. The process for deploying our bean is accomplished in two steps:

1. Create an EAR node.
2. Deploy it to the application server.

The topmost archive used for deployment is an Enterprise Archive File (EAR). The EAR file contains all the JAR and WAR files required for deployment and execution of our enterprise application. It also contains an application.xml file describing the manifest to the entire archive. In other words, it allows you to completely package your application into one deliverable, self-contained entity.

Let's now create an EAR file for our application, containing at this point only our session bean:

1. Choose File, New from the menu and select the Enterprise tab.
2. Select the EAR node to add to the project.
3. Specify the name of the EAR file and node name. In this case, keep the name similar to the sample project SampleBeans.
4. Right-click on the new node `SampleBean.EARgrp` and select Make. This creates a SampleBean.EAR, and contained within this is an application.xml descriptor.
5. Right-click on the `SampleBean.EARgrp` and choose Deploy Your Bean. Note: Make sure that your application server is running; if it is not, start your application server and deploy the bean again.

Using Your Entity Bean

It is easiest to test any bean using the remote interface. If you want to test your local interface, you must communicate to that local interface with another object that encapsulates that call with a remote interface. For example, we will test our local interface using a session bean. But first let's test our entity bean's remote interface. The test client in this case only tests the finder method, as shown in Listing 23.8.

LISTING 23.8 Test Client for Verifying the Operation of Our `Employee` Entity Bean (EmployeeTestClient.java)

```
package testclient;

import javax.naming.*;
import javax.rmi.*;

import com.sams.samples.entity.*;

/**
```

LISTING 23.8 Continued

```
 * <p>Title: Empoyee Entity Test Client</p>
 * <p>Description: </p>
 * <p>Copyright: Copyright (c) 2002</p>
 * <p>Company: SAMS Publishing</p>
 * @author SAMS Publishing
 * @version 1.0
 */

public class EmployeeTestClient {
  private EmployeeRemoteHome employeeRemoteHome = null;

  //Construct the EJB test client
  public EmployeeTestClient() {
    try {
      //get naming context
      Context ctx = new InitialContext();

      //look up jndi name
      Object ref = ctx.lookup("EmployeeRemote");

      //cast to Home interface
      employeeRemoteHome = (EmployeeRemoteHome) PortableRemoteObject.narrow(ref,
➥EmployeeRemoteHome.class);

      Short empNo = new Short("5");

      EmployeeRemote employee = employeeRemoteHome.findByPrimaryKey(empNo);

      System.out.println(employee.getFirstName());
      System.out.println(employee.getLastName());
    }
    catch(Exception e) {
      e.printStackTrace();
    }
  }


  //-----------------------------------------------------------------------
  // Utility Methods
  //-----------------------------------------------------------------------
```

LISTING 23.8 Continued

```
  public EmployeeRemoteHome getHome() {
    return employeeRemoteHome;
  }
  //Main method

  public static void main(String[] args) {
    EmployeeTestClient client = new EmployeeTestClient();
    // Use the getHome() method of the client object to call Home interface
    // methods that will return a Remote interface reference. Then
    // use that Remote interface reference to access the EJB.
  }
}
```

The other option for our entity bean, or for that matter even a session bean, is a local interface. This local interface is available only to another bean running inside the same JVM. Listing 23.9 is the session bean developed to test the bean, and Listing 23.10 is the client used to exercise the session bean.

NOTE

The purpose of the local interface is simple—*performance*. This performance gain is accomplished primarily in passing data. With a remote interface, the data is passed by value. In other words, the data is copied and serialized to another object on the client. The local interface passes by reference, giving a huge performance increase.

LISTING 23.9 Session Façade to Access the `Employee` Entity Bean (EmployeeFacadeBean.java)

```
package com.sams.samples.ejb;

import javax.ejb.*;
import javax.naming.*;
import javax.rmi.*;


public class EmployeeFacadeBean implements SessionBean {
  SessionContext sessionContext;
  public void ejbCreate() throws CreateException {
    /**@todo Complete this method*/
  }
  public void ejbRemove() {
```

LISTING 23.9 Continued

```
    /**@todo Complete this method*/
  }
  public void ejbActivate() {
    /**@todo Complete this method*/
  }
  public void ejbPassivate() {
    /**@todo Complete this method*/
  }
  public void setSessionContext(SessionContext sessionContext) {
    this.sessionContext = sessionContext;
  }
  public java.lang.String getEmployeeFirstName(java.lang.Short empNo) {
    try {
      //get naming context
      Context ctx = new InitialContext();

      //look up jndi name
      Object ref = ctx.lookup("java:comp/env/ejb/employee");

      //cast to Home interface
      EmployeeHome employeeHome = (EmployeeHome) PortableRemoteObject.narrow(ref,
➥EmployeeHome.class);

      Employee employee = employeeHome.findByPrimaryKey(empNo);

      return employee.getLastName();
    }
    catch(Exception e) {
      e.printStackTrace();
    }
    return null;
  }
}
```

LISTING 23.10 Client Testing the Session Façade, Which in Turn Accesses the `Employee` Entity Bean (EmployeeFacadeTestClient.java)

```
package testclient;

import com.sams.samples.ejb.*;
import javax.naming.*;
```

LISTING 23.10 Continued

```
import javax.rmi.PortableRemoteObject;

/**
 * <p>Title: Session Facade Test Client</p>
 * <p>Description: Testing the entity beans local interface via the session</p>
 * <p>Copyright: Copyright (c) 2002</p>
 * <p>Company: SAMS Publishing</p>
 * @author unascribed
 * @version 1.0
 */

public class EmployeeFacadeTestClient {
  static final private String ERROR_NULL_REMOTE = "Remote interface reference
➥is null. It must be created by calling one of the Home interface
➥methods first.";
  static final private int MAX_OUTPUT_LINE_LENGTH = 100;
  private boolean logging = true;
  private EmployeeFacadeHome employeeFacadeHome = null;
  private EmployeeFacade employeeFacade = null;

  //Construct the EJB test client
  public EmployeeFacadeTestClient() {
    long startTime = 0;
    if (logging) {
      log("Initializing bean access.");
      startTime = System.currentTimeMillis();
    }

    try {
      //get naming context
      Context ctx = new InitialContext();

      //look up jndi name
      Object ref = ctx.lookup("EmployeeFacade");

      //cast to Home interface
      employeeFacadeHome = (EmployeeFacadeHome) PortableRemoteObject.narrow(ref,
➥EmployeeFacadeHome.class);
      if (logging) {
        long endTime = System.currentTimeMillis();
        log("Succeeded initializing bean access.");
        log("Execution time: " + (endTime - startTime) + " ms.");
```

LISTING 23.10 Continued

```
      }

      java.lang.Short empNo = new java.lang.Short("5");
      EmployeeFacade employeeFacade = this.create();
      System.out.println(employeeFacade.getEmployeeFirstName(empNo));
    }
    catch(Exception e) {
      if (logging) {
        log("Failed initializing bean access.");
      }
      e.printStackTrace();
    }
  }

  //-----------------------------------------------------------------------
  // Methods that use Home interface methods to generate a Remote interface
  // reference
  //-----------------------------------------------------------------------

  public EmployeeFacade create() {
    long startTime = 0;
    if (logging) {
      log("Calling create()");
      startTime = System.currentTimeMillis();
    }
    try {
      employeeFacade = employeeFacadeHome.create();
      if (logging) {
        long endTime = System.currentTimeMillis();
        log("Succeeded: create()");
        log("Execution time: " + (endTime - startTime) + " ms.");
      }
    }
    catch(Exception e) {
      if (logging) {
        log("Failed: create()");
      }
      e.printStackTrace();
    }

    if (logging) {
      log("Return value from create(): " + employeeFacade + ".");
```

LISTING 23.10 Continued

```
    }
    return employeeFacade;
  }

  //-------------------------------------------------------------------------
  // Methods that use Remote interface methods to access data through the bean
  //-------------------------------------------------------------------------

  public String getEmployeeFirstName(Short empNo) {
    String returnValue = "";
    if (employeeFacade == null) {
      System.out.println("Error in getEmployeeFirstName(): " +
➥ERROR_NULL_REMOTE);
      return returnValue;
    }
    long startTime = 0;
    if (logging) {
      log("Calling getEmployeeFirstName(" + empNo + ")");
      startTime = System.currentTimeMillis();
    }

    try {
      returnValue = employeeFacade.getEmployeeFirstName(empNo);
      if (logging) {
        long endTime = System.currentTimeMillis();
        log("Succeeded: getEmployeeFirstName(" + empNo + ")");
        log("Execution time: " + (endTime - startTime) + " ms.");
      }
    }
    catch(Exception e) {
      if (logging) {
        log("Failed: getEmployeeFirstName(" + empNo + ")");
      }
      e.printStackTrace();
    }

    if (logging) {
      log("Return value from getEmployeeFirstName(" + empNo + "): " +
➥returnValue + ".");
    }
    return returnValue;
  }
```

LISTING 23.10 Continued

```
  public void testRemoteCallsWithDefaultArguments() {
    if (employeeFacade == null) {
      System.out.println("Error in testRemoteCallsWithDefaultArguments(): " +
➥ERROR_NULL_REMOTE);
      return ;
    }
    getEmployeeFirstName(null);
  }

  //-----------------------------------------------------------------
  // Utility Methods
  //-----------------------------------------------------------------

  private void log(String message) {
    if (message == null) {
      System.out.println("-- null");
      return ;
    }
    if (message.length() > MAX_OUTPUT_LINE_LENGTH) {
      System.out.println("-- " + message.substring(0, MAX_OUTPUT_LINE_LENGTH) +
➥" ...");
    }
    else {
      System.out.println("-- " + message);
    }
  }
  //Main method

  public static void main(String[] args) {
    EmployeeFacadeTestClient client = new EmployeeFacadeTestClient();
    // Use the client object to call one of the Home interface wrappers
    // above, to create a Remote interface reference to the bean.
    // If the return value is of the Remote interface type, you can use it
    // to access the remote interface methods. You can also just use the
    // client object to call the Remote interface wrappers.
  }
}
```

Building Entity Beans with JBuilder

You may look at the amount of code you need to accomplish a simple task, but JBuilder offers a number of time-saving features to make this process efficient. These features offer a number of capabilities regardless of the EJB vendor you are using. The following are some of those features:

- EJB Designer to build session and entity beans graphically
- Component packaging for deployment
- Deployment Descriptor Editors
- Wizards to automatically produce container managed persistence
- Test client generators

Many of these features were discussed in Chapter 22, "Developing Session Beans." We will concentrate on the ones that specialize in entity beans. We will build the same example we built earlier to access our `Employee` entity and wrap the access with a session façade.

1. Create a project by choosing File, New Project from the menu. Call the project **`EntityBeanSample`**. After you create the project, make sure that the enterprise server is selected using the Project Properties Editor. If you set it as the default for all projects, it will not need to be set.
2. Create a new EJB module called **`EntityBean`**. Make sure the version property is set to **EJB 2.0 compliant**.
3. Double-click on the new EJB module node. This loads the EJB Designer.
4. Right-click on the data sources in the button on the left pane of the IDE and select Import Schema from Database. This process loads all the information from an existing data structure, as shown in Figure 23.5.
5. Fill in the connection information to your data source. In this case, use the employee `jDatastore` database that ships with JBuilder. This process loads the entire schema from the specified database. This is accomplished by clicking on the Choose Existing Connection button.
6. Right-click on the table Employee and create a CMP 2.0 Entity Bean. This creates an entity bean configured to manage the persistence of the entity to the Employee table.
7. Now place both a local and remote interface on the new entity bean. This is accomplished by selecting the bean in the Designer, and then changing the interface's property to local/remote.

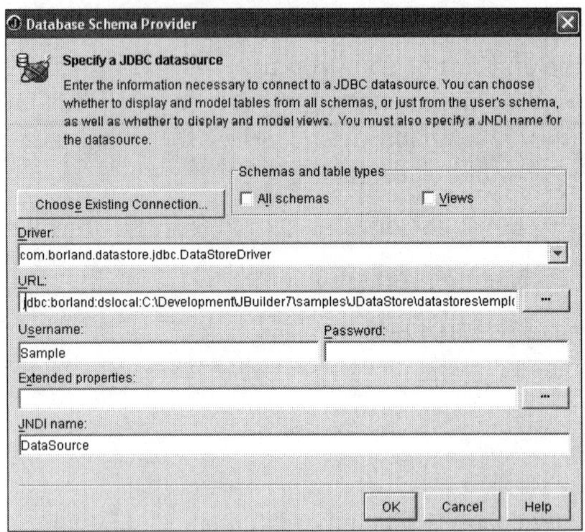

FIGURE 23.5 Import data source definition from external database.

Let's look at what was generated by JBuilder and make sure that you understand the purpose of each generated file (see Table 23.2).

TABLE 23.2 Files Generated when Creating a CMP Entity Bean

Filename	Scope	Description
Employee.java	Local	Interface for providing the accessors and mutators to the attributes
EmployeeHome.java	Local	Home interface for creating, finding, and removing an entity
EmployeeBean.java	Local/remote	Implementation class for CMP beans
EmployeeRemote.java	Remote	Interface for providing the accessors and mutators to the attributes for remote usage
EmployeeRemoteHome.java	Remote	Home interface for creating, finding, and removing an entity for remote usage

8. Compile your application to create a JAR for your EJB entity beans.
9. Add to the project a test client generated for our new `Employee` entity bean, or write your own client as seen in Listing 23.11.

LISTING 23.11 Test Client to Verify Your Entity Bean Operations

```
public EmployeeTestClient() {
  long startTime = 0;
  if (logging) {
```

LISTING 23.11 Continued

```
      log("Initializing bean access.");
      startTime = System.currentTimeMillis();
    }

    try {
      //get naming context
      Context ctx = new InitialContext();

      //look up jndi name
      Object ref = ctx.lookup("EmployeeRemote");

      //cast to Home interface
      employeeRemoteHome = (EmployeeRemoteHome) PortableRemoteObject.narrow(ref,
➥EmployeeRemoteHome.class);
      if (logging) {
        long endTime = System.currentTimeMillis();
        log("Succeeded initializing bean access.");
        log("Execution time: " + (endTime - startTime) + " ms.");
      }

      /* Test your component Interface */
      this.findByPrimaryKey(new java.lang.Short("5"));
      this.getEmpNo();

    }
    catch(Exception e) {
      if (logging) {
        log("Failed initializing bean access.");
      }
      e.printStackTrace();
    }
  }
```

10. Choose Tools, Borland Enterprise Server Management Agent from the menu.
11. Right-click and run either your JAR file or your EAR. This launches a version of the enterprise server inside JBuilder.
12. Run your test application and verify the exercising of the entity bean (see Listing 23.12).

LISTING 23.12 Results of the Test Client Exercising Your Beans Methods

```
-- Initializing bean access.
-- Succeeded initializing bean access.
-- Execution time: 2944 ms.
-- Calling findByPrimaryKey(5)
-- Succeeded: findByPrimaryKey(5)
-- Execution time: 1452 ms.
-- Return value from findByPrimaryKey(5):
➥Stub[repository_id=RMI:entitybeansample.EmployeeRemote:000000 ...
-- Calling getEmpNo()
-- Succeeded: getEmpNo()
-- Execution time: 40 ms.
-- Return value from getEmpNo(): 5.
```

Developing a BMP Bean

In the preceding section, we developed a CMP bean in which the container handled all the persistence. We will now look at the process for building a BMP bean and contrast the process from the CMP bean. For a BMP bean, we must produce the appropriate persistence code for our bean instead of the container accomplishing that task for us.

Most of the changes from EJB 1.1 to EJB 2.0 specifications focused on container managed persistence. There were a few changes to bean managed persistence. The changes are basically two different items:

- The introduction of local interfaces for use within these beans allows for fine-grained objects to be used without a detriment to performance.
- The home interface can contain more than just accessors, mutators, and finder methods; it can contain business methods. These business methods can contain implementations that reference a group of entities versus a single entity.

Bean managed persistence requires you to implement a specific interface. Ultimately, this interface maps to relational SQL, (see Table 23.3).

TABLE 23.3 SQLStatements Relate to Different Relational SQL

Method	SQL Statement
ejbCreate	INSERT
ejbFindByPrimaryKey	SELECT
ejbFindByLastName	SELECT
ejbFindInRange	SELECT

TABLE 23.3 Continued

Method	SQL Statement
ejbLoad	SELECT
ejbRemove	DELETE
ejbStore	UPDATE

Rather than start over with a new example, we will use the `Employee` bean we constructed using a CMP bean. Ultimately, this gives us the ability to compare the new BMP bean to the previously created CMP bean.

Defining the Home Interface

The home interface should look exactly the same as the CMP bean's home interface. This allows the user of the bean to not know whether the bean is CMP or BMP, nor should she be concerned (see Listing 23.13).

LISTING 23.13 Home Interface for Our BMP Bean

```
package entitybeansample;

import javax.ejb.*;
import java.util.*;

public interface EmployeeBMPHome extends javax.ejb.EJBLocalHome {
  public EmployeeBMP create(Short empNo) throws CreateException;
  public EmployeeBMP findByPrimaryKey(Short empNo) throws FinderException;
}
```

Defining the Remote Interface

The remote interface should look identical also. This interface provides us access to all the fine-grained attributes required (see Listing 23.14).

LISTING 23.14 Remote Interface for Our `Employee` BMP Entity Bean

```
package entitybeansample;

import javax.ejb.*;
import java.util.*;
import java.rmi.*;
import java.sql.*;
import java.math.*;
```

LISTING 23.14 Continued

```
public interface EmployeeBMPRemote extends javax.ejb.EJBObject {
  public Short getEmpNo() throws RemoteException;
  public void setFirstName(String firstName) throws RemoteException;
  public String getFirstName() throws RemoteException;
  public void setLastName(String lastName) throws RemoteException;
  public String getLastName() throws RemoteException;
  public void setPhoneExt(String phoneExt) throws RemoteException;
  public String getPhoneExt() throws RemoteException;
  public void setHireDate(Timestamp hireDate) throws RemoteException;
  public Timestamp getHireDate() throws RemoteException;
  public void setDeptNo(String deptNo) throws RemoteException;
  public String getDeptNo() throws RemoteException;
  public void setJobCode(String jobCode) throws RemoteException;
  public String getJobCode() throws RemoteException;
  public void setJobGrade(Short jobGrade) throws RemoteException;
  public Short getJobGrade() throws RemoteException;
  public void setJobCountry(String jobCountry) throws RemoteException;
  public String getJobCountry() throws RemoteException;
  public void setSalary(BigDecimal salary) throws RemoteException;
  public BigDecimal getSalary() throws RemoteException;
  public void setFullName(String fullName) throws RemoteException;
  public String getFullName() throws RemoteException;
}
```

Implementing the Bean

This section contains the complete implementation of our persistence logic. As we implement this interface, we have to be sensitive to the exceptions we need to use. Table 23.4 summarizes the exceptions of the `javax.ejb` package. All these exceptions are application exceptions, except for the `NoSuchEntityException` and the `EJBException`, which are system exceptions.

TABLE 23.4 Exception Summary for Use with Bean-Managed Persistence

Method Name	Exception It Throws	Reason for Throwing
`ejbCreate`	`CreateException`	An input parameter is invalid.
`ejbFindByPrimaryKey` (and other finder methods that return a single object)	`ObjectNotFoundException` (subclass of `FinderException`)	The database row for the requested entity bean cannot be found.

TABLE 23.4 Continued

Method Name	Exception It Throws	Reason for Throwing
`ejbRemove`	`RemoveException`	The entity bean's row cannot be deleted from the database.
`ejbLoad`	`NoSuchEntityException`	The database row to be loaded cannot be found.
`ejbStore`	`NoSuchEntityException`	The database row to be updated cannot be found.
(all methods)	`EJBException`	A system problem has been encountered.

The CMP bean was basically empty, but in a BMP bean, we need to implement the services required. As we continue with our employee example, we need to implement the bean interface generated by the EJB Designer wizards (see Listing 23.15).

LISTING 23.15 `Employee` BMP Implementation Bean (EmployeeBMPBean.java)

```
package entitybeansample;

import java.sql.*;

import javax.ejb.*;
import javax.naming.*;
import javax.sql.*;

public class EmployeeBMPBean implements EntityBean {
  EntityContext entityContext;
  java.lang.Short empNo;
  java.lang.String firstName;
  java.lang.String lastName;
  java.lang.String phoneExt;
  java.sql.Timestamp hireDate;
  java.lang.String deptNo;
  java.lang.String jobCode;
  java.lang.Short jobGrade;
  java.lang.String jobCountry;
  java.math.BigDecimal salary;
  java.lang.String fullName;
  public java.lang.Short ejbCreate(java.lang.Short empNo)
➥throws CreateException {
    setEmpNo(empNo);

    Connection con = null;
```

LISTING 23.15 Continued

```
    try {
      InitialContext initial = new InitialContext();
      DataSource ds = (DataSource)initial.lookup(
➥"java:comp/env/jdbc/EmployeeData");
      con = ds.getConnection();
      PreparedStatement ps = con.prepareStatement(
➥"INSERT INTO employee (empno)" +
          "values (?)");
      ps.setShort(1,empNo.shortValue());
      ps.executeUpdate();
      return empNo;
    }
    catch (SQLException ex) {
      ex.printStackTrace();
    }catch (NamingException ex) {
      ex.printStackTrace();
      throw new CreateException();
    }finally {
      if (con!=null){
        try {
          con.close();
        }
        catch (SQLException ex) {
          ex.printStackTrace();
        }
      }
    }
    return null;
  }
  public void ejbPostCreate(java.lang.Short empNo) throws CreateException {
    /**@todo Complete this method*/
  }
  public void ejbRemove() throws RemoveException {
    Connection con = null;
    try {
      InitialContext initial = new InitialContext();
      DataSource ds = (DataSource)initial.lookup(
➥"java:comp/env/jdbc/EmployeeData");
      con = ds.getConnection();
      PreparedStatement ps = con.prepareStatement("DELETE " +
          "FROM EMPLOYEE WHERE empno = ?");
```

LISTING 23.15 Continued

```
      ps.setShort(1,getEmpNo().shortValue());
      ps.executeUpdate();
    }
    catch (SQLException ex) {
      ex.printStackTrace();
    }catch (NamingException ex) {
      ex.printStackTrace();
      throw new RemoveException();
    }finally {
      if (con!=null){
        try {
          con.close();
        }
        catch (SQLException ex) {
          ex.printStackTrace();
        }
      }
    }
  }
//Getters and Setters for all members
  public void setEmpNo(java.lang.Short empNo) {
    this.empNo = empNo;
  }
  public void setFirstName(java.lang.String firstName) {
    this.firstName = firstName;
  }
  public void setLastName(java.lang.String lastName) {
    this.lastName = lastName;
  }
  public void setPhoneExt(java.lang.String phoneExt) {
    this.phoneExt = phoneExt;
  }
  public void setHireDate(java.sql.Timestamp hireDate) {
    this.hireDate = hireDate;
  }
  public void setDeptNo(java.lang.String deptNo) {
    this.deptNo = deptNo;
  }
  public void setJobCode(java.lang.String jobCode) {
    this.jobCode = jobCode;
  }
```

LISTING 23.15 Continued

```
public void setJobGrade(java.lang.Short jobGrade) {
  this.jobGrade = jobGrade;
}
public void setJobCountry(java.lang.String jobCountry) {
  this.jobCountry = jobCountry;
}
public void setSalary(java.math.BigDecimal salary) {
  this.salary = salary;
}
public void setFullName(java.lang.String fullName) {
  this.fullName = fullName;
}
public java.lang.Short getEmpNo() {
  return empNo;
}
public java.lang.String getFirstName() {
  return firstName;
}
public java.lang.String getLastName() {
  return lastName;
}
public java.lang.String getPhoneExt() {
  return phoneExt;
}
public java.sql.Timestamp getHireDate() {
  return hireDate;
}
public java.lang.String getDeptNo() {
  return deptNo;
}
public java.lang.String getJobCode() {
  return jobCode;
}
public java.lang.Short getJobGrade() {
  return jobGrade;
}
public java.lang.String getJobCountry() {
  return jobCountry;
}
public java.math.BigDecimal getSalary() {
  return salary;
}
```

LISTING 23.15 Continued

```
  public java.lang.String getFullName() {
    return fullName;
  }
//Find an individual instance and return the primary key
  public java.lang.Short ejbFindByPrimaryKey(java.lang.Short empNo)
➥ throws FinderException {
    Connection con = null;
    try {
      InitialContext initial = new InitialContext();
      DataSource ds = (DataSource)initial.lookup(
➥"java:comp/env/jdbc/EmployeeData");
      con = ds.getConnection();
      PreparedStatement ps = con.prepareStatement("SELECT id FROM EMPLOYEE" +
          "WHERE empno = ?");
      ps.setShort(1,empNo.shortValue());
      ResultSet rs = ps.executeQuery();

      if (!rs.next()){
        throw new ObjectNotFoundException();
      }
      return empNo;
    }
    catch (SQLException ex) {
      ex.printStackTrace();
    }catch (NamingException ex) {
      ex.printStackTrace();
      throw new EJBException(ex);
    } finally {
      if (con!=null){
        try {
          con.close();
        }
        catch (SQLException ex) {
          ex.printStackTrace();
        }
      }
    }
    return null;
  }
//Load a single instance from the datasource
  public void ejbLoad() {
    Connection con = null;
```

LISTING 23.15 Continued

```
    try {
      InitialContext initial = new InitialContext();
      DataSource ds = (DataSource)initial.lookup(
➥"java:comp/env/jdbc/EmployeeData");
      con = ds.getConnection();
      PreparedStatement ps = con.prepareStatement(
➥"SELECT EmpNo,DeptNo,FirstName," +
          "FullName,HireDate,JobCode,JobCountry,JobGrade,LastName,
➥PhoneExt,Salary " +
          "FROM EMPLOYEE WHERE empno = ?");
      ps.setShort(1,getEmpNo().shortValue());
      ResultSet rs = ps.executeQuery();
      if (!rs.next()){
        throw new EJBException("Object not found!");
      }

      setDeptNo(rs.getString(2));
      setFirstName(rs.getString(3));
      setFullName(rs.getString(4));
      setHireDate(rs.getTimestamp(5));
      setJobCode(rs.getString(6));
      setJobCountry(rs.getString(7));
      setJobGrade(new java.lang.Short(rs.getShort(8)));
      setLastName(rs.getString(9));
      setPhoneExt(rs.getString(10));
      setSalary(rs.getBigDecimal(11));

    }
    catch (SQLException ex) {
      ex.printStackTrace();
    }catch (NamingException ex) {
      ex.printStackTrace();
      throw new EJBException(ex);
    } finally {
      if (con!=null){
        try {
          con.close();
        }
        catch (SQLException ex) {
          ex.printStackTrace();
        }
      }
```

LISTING 23.15 Continued

```
    }
  }
//Pasivate data to the datasource
  public void ejbStore() {
    Connection con = null;

    try {
      InitialContext initial = new InitialContext();
      DataSource ds = (DataSource)initial.lookup(
➥"java:comp/env/jdbc/EmployeeData");
      con = ds.getConnection();
      PreparedStatement ps = con.prepareStatement("Update employee " +
          "set DeptNo = ?, FirstName = ?, FullName = ?, HireDate = ?," +
          "JobCode = ?, JobCountry = ?, JobGrade = ?, LastName = ?," +
          "PhoneExt = ?, Salary = ? where empno = ?");
      ps.setString(1,getDeptNo());
      ps.setString(2,getFirstName());
      ps.setString(3,getFirstName());
      ps.setString(4,getFullName());
      ps.setTimestamp(5,getHireDate());
      ps.setString(6,getJobCode());
      ps.setString(7,getJobCountry());
      ps.setShort(8,getJobGrade().shortValue());
      ps.setString(9,getLastName());
      ps.setString(10,getPhoneExt());
      ps.setBigDecimal(11,getSalary());

      ps.setShort(12,empNo.shortValue());
      ps.executeUpdate();
    }
    catch (SQLException ex) {
      ex.printStackTrace();
    }catch (NamingException ex) {
      ex.printStackTrace();
      throw new EJBException();
    }finally {
      if (con!=null){
        try {
          con.close();
        }
        catch (SQLException ex) {
          ex.printStackTrace();
```

LISTING 23.15 Continued

```
          }
        }
      }
    }
    public void ejbActivate() {
    }
    public void ejbPassivate() {
    }
    public void unsetEntityContext() {
      this.entityContext = null;
    }
    public void setEntityContext(EntityContext entityContext) {
      this.entityContext = entityContext;
    }
}
```

Deployment Descriptor

The deployment descriptor differs only slightly from the container managed persistence bean created earlier. For example, the `<persistence-type>` changed from `Container` to `Bean` (see Listing 23.16).

LISTING 23.16 Deployment Descriptor for Our Entity Beans

```
<?xml version="1.0" encoding="UTF-8"?>
<!DOCTYPE ejb-JAR PUBLIC "-//Sun Microsystems, Inc.//
➥DTD Enterprise JavaBeans 2.0//EN"
"http://java.sun.com/dtd/ejb-JAR_2_0.dtd">
<ejb-JAR>
    <enterprise-beans>
        <entity>
            <display-name>Employee1</display-name>
            <ejb-name>EmployeeBMP</ejb-name>
            <home>entitybeansample.EmployeeBMPRemoteHome</home>
            <remote>entitybeansample.EmployeeBMPRemote</remote>
            <local-home>entitybeansample.EmployeeBMPHome</local-home>
            <local>entitybeansample.EmployeeBMP</local>
            <ejb-class>entitybeansample.EmployeeBMPBean</ejb-class>
            <persistence-type>Bean</persistence-type>
            <prim-key-class>java.lang.Short</prim-key-class>
            <reentrant>False</reentrant>
```

LISTING 23.16 Continued

```
            <abstract-schema-name>Employee1</abstract-schema-name>
        </entity>
    </enterprise-beans>
    <assembly-descriptor>
        <container-transaction>
            <method>
                <ejb-name>EmployeeBMP</ejb-name>
                <method-name>*</method-name>
            </method>
            <trans-attribute>Required</trans-attribute>
        </container-transaction>
    </assembly-descriptor>
</ejb-JAR>
```

Deploying Your Entity Bean

Deploying your bean is no different from deploying a container managed persistent bean. Just like a CMP bean, the home interface is used to create, find, and remove instances of the entity.

Using Your Entity Bean

The beauty of using bean managed persistence or container managed persistence is that it gives the bean developer the flexibility to choose the implementation that best meets the persistence requirements. In fact, the client of the bean does not need to be concerned with the method of persistence, only that the persistence is accomplished. For example, using the same client used to test our container managed persistent bean, we can now test our bean managed persistent bean. The only change we need to make to the client is to change from using the `Employee` entity bean to the `EmployeeBMP` (see Listing 23.17).

LISTING 23.17 Test Client to Exercise Our New Entity Bean (EmployeeTestClient.java)

```
package entitybeansample;

import java.math.*;
import java.sql.*;

import javax.naming.*;
import javax.rmi.*;

/**
```

LISTING 23.17 Continued

```
 * <p>Title: </p>
 * <p>Description: </p>
 * <p>Copyright: Copyright (c) 2002</p>
 * <p>Company: </p>
 * @author unascribed
 * @version 1.0
 */

public class EmployeeTestClient {
  static final private String ERROR_NULL_REMOTE =
➥"Remote interface reference is null. It must be created by
➥calling one of the Home interface methods first.";
  static final private int MAX_OUTPUT_LINE_LENGTH = 100;
  private boolean logging = true;
  private EmployeeBMPRemoteHome employeeBMPRemoteHome = null;
  private EmployeeBMPRemote employeeBMPRemote = null;

  //Construct the EJB test client
  public EmployeeTestClient() {
    long startTime = 0;
    if (logging) {
      log("Initializing bean access.");
      startTime = System.currentTimeMillis();
    }

    try {
      //get naming context
      Context ctx = new InitialContext();

      //look up jndi name
      Object ref = ctx.lookup("EmployeeBMPRemote");

      //cast to Home interface
      employeeBMPRemoteHome = (EmployeeBMPRemoteHome)
➥PortableRemoteObject.narrow(ref, EmployeeBMPRemoteHome.class);
      if (logging) {
        long endTime = System.currentTimeMillis();
        log("Succeeded initializing bean access.");
        log("Execution time: " + (endTime - startTime) + " ms.");
      }
```

LISTING 23.17 Continued

```
      /* Test your component Interface */
      this.findByPrimaryKey(new java.lang.Short("5"));
      this.getEmpNo();

    }
    catch(Exception e) {
      if (logging) {
        log("Failed initializing bean access.");
      }
      e.printStackTrace();
    }
  }

  //----------------------------------------------------------------------
  // Methods that use Home interface methods to generate a Remote
  // interface reference
  //----------------------------------------------------------------------

  public EmployeeBMPRemote create(Short empNo) {
    long startTime = 0;
    if (logging) {
      log("Calling create(" + empNo + ")");
      startTime = System.currentTimeMillis();
    }
    try {
      employeeBMPRemote = employeeBMPRemoteHome.create(empNo);
      if (logging) {
        long endTime = System.currentTimeMillis();
        log("Succeeded: create(" + empNo + ")");
        log("Execution time: " + (endTime - startTime) + " ms.");
      }
    }
    catch(Exception e) {
      if (logging) {
        log("Failed: create(" + empNo + ")");
      }
      e.printStackTrace();
    }

    if (logging) {
      log("Return value from create(" + empNo + "): " +
➥employeeBMPRemote + ".");
```

LISTING 23.17 Continued

```
    }
    return employeeBMPRemote;
  }

  public EmployeeBMPRemote findByPrimaryKey(Short empNo) {
    long startTime = 0;
    if (logging) {
      log("Calling findByPrimaryKey(" + empNo + ")");
      startTime = System.currentTimeMillis();
    }
    try {
      employeeBMPRemote = employeeBMPRemoteHome.findByPrimaryKey(empNo);
      if (logging) {
        long endTime = System.currentTimeMillis();
        log("Succeeded: findByPrimaryKey(" + empNo + ")");
        log("Execution time: " + (endTime - startTime) + " ms.");
      }
    }
    catch(Exception e) {
      if (logging) {
        log("Failed: findByPrimaryKey(" + empNo + ")");
      }
      e.printStackTrace();
    }

    if (logging) {
      log("Return value from findByPrimaryKey(" + empNo + "): " +
➥employeeBMPRemote + ".");
    }
    return employeeBMPRemote;
  }

  //----------------------------------------------------------------------
  // Methods that use Remote interface methods to access data through the bean
  //----------------------------------------------------------------------

  public Short getEmpNo() {
    Short returnValue = null;
    if (employeeBMPRemote == null) {
      System.out.println("Error in getEmpNo(): " + ERROR_NULL_REMOTE);
      return returnValue;
    }
```

LISTING 23.17 Continued

```
    long startTime = 0;
    if (logging) {
      log("Calling getEmpNo()");
      startTime = System.currentTimeMillis();
    }

    try {
      returnValue = employeeBMPRemote.getEmpNo();
      if (logging) {
        long endTime = System.currentTimeMillis();
        log("Succeeded: getEmpNo()");
        log("Execution time: " + (endTime - startTime) + " ms.");
      }
    }
    catch(Exception e) {
      if (logging) {
        log("Failed: getEmpNo()");
      }
      e.printStackTrace();
    }

    if (logging) {
      log("Return value from getEmpNo(): " + returnValue + ".");
    }
    return returnValue;
  }

  //----------------------------------------------------------------------
  // Utility Methods
  //----------------------------------------------------------------------

  private void log(String message) {
    if (message == null) {
      System.out.println("-- null");
      return ;
    }
    if (message.length() > MAX_OUTPUT_LINE_LENGTH) {
      System.out.println("-- " + message.substring(0, MAX_OUTPUT_LINE_LENGTH) +
➥" ...");
    }
    else {
      System.out.println("-- " + message);
```

LISTING 23.17 Continued

```
    }
  }
  //Main method

  public static void main(String[] args) {
    EmployeeTestClient client = new EmployeeTestClient();
    // Use the client object to call one of the Home interface wrappers
    // above, to create a Remote interface reference to the bean.
    // If the return value is of the Remote interface type, you can use it
    // to access the remote interface methods. You can also just use the
    // client object to call the Remote interface wrappers.
  }
}
```

The test client that is generated can then be tweaked or modified to test the implementation. Test clients are not normally designed to fully test a client or live beyond the life of an appropriate client. Typically, when you want long-term test fixtures, you will use JBuilder's Test Case Wizards. See Chapter 5, "Unit Testing," for more information.

Advanced Container-Managed Persistence

Using the EJB 1.1 specifications, container managed persistence beans were not very powerful. In most cases, bean developers went quickly beyond the capabilities of CMP and had to convert to use bean managed persistence. Many developers shied away from using entity beans altogether. The EJB 2.0 quickly addressed many of these issues. This now allows the bean developer to implement most persistence requirements using container managed persistence. The four features that facilitate this are the following:

- EJB query language
- Finder methods
- Relationship mapping of multiple entity beans
- Business methods implemented within the home interface

The Enterprise JavaBeans Query Language

The Enterprise JavaBeans Query Language (EJB QL) specification defines a query language to be used within finder methods of an entity bean with container managed persistence. Rather than develop a completely new query language, the specification is based on a subset of SQL92. The EJB QL gives you the features to allow navigation over the relationships defined in an entity bean's abstract schema.

Your EJB QL queries will be contained within your deployment descriptor of the entity bean. The container will then translate these queries into the target language of the underlying data store. For example, EJB QL will be translated to true SQL for `JDatastore`. Using this translation allows entity beans using container managed persistence to be portable. In other words, the code is not tied to a specific type of data store or application server vendor.

EJB Query Restrictions

EJB QL has a few restrictions:

- Commenting is not supported within EJB QL.
- Date and time values are always represented in milliseconds and contained within a Java `long`.
- Container managed persistence does not support inheritance. In other words, you cannot compare two entity beans of different types with each other.

Query Syntax

An EJB QL query has three components associated with it: `SELECT`, `FROM`, and `WHERE`. The `SELECT` and `FROM` clauses are the only required portions of EJB QL; the `WHERE` clause is optional. For example, `SELECT OBJECT(e) FROM Employee e` selects all the instances contained within the `Employee` entity.

The `SELECT` component defines the values or objects that will be returned by the created query. The return values can either be a local interface or a remote interface contained within an entity. The `FROM` component defines the scope of the query. It may declare one or more entities. Finally, the `WHERE` component contains a conditional expression that restricts the values retrieved by the query. As mentioned earlier, this portion of the query is optional; it is normally required to meet most entity finder requirements.

Examples Described

```
SELECT OBJECT(e) FROM Employee e
```

This method returns all the instances of employee contained within the entity. In this case, we refer to the `Employee` entity with an alias `e` to make the definition of the query shorter.

```
SELECT DISTINCT OBJECT(e) FROM Employee e WHERE e.empNo = ?1
```

The query returns an employee instance specified by an `empNo`. This query is typically used to find an instance by either a primary key or alternate key. The `DISTINCT` keyword can be used to remove duplicates from the query but this should not happen if you are using a primary key.

```
SELECT DISTINCT OBJECT(e) FROM Employee e, IN (e.salaryHistory)
➥as s WHERE s.Country = ?1
```

This query navigates to related beans using the defined relationship. The `e` variable relates to the `Employee` entity bean, and the `s` variable represents the related bean instances `SalaryHistory`. The `IN` keyword specifies that `SalaryHistory` is a collection of beans related to the `Employee` entity. The query then navigates the relationship to identify all the salary histories within a specific country.

```
SELECT DISTINCT OBJECT(e) FROM Employee e WHERE e.salary BETWEEN ?1 AND ?2
```

The employees whose salaries fall within a given range are returned. The `BETWEEN` keyword returns all salaries within the given range. This expression is useful when using range finder methods.

Expressions and Functions

Just like SQL92 specifications of which EJB QL specifications is a subset, EJB QL describes the functionality of the expressions and functions. The specification does not include a full list of functions like that of SQL92 but simply a subset that should fit most requirements (see Table 23.5).

TABLE 23.5 Expressions and Functions Contained Within EJB QL

Type	Description
Standard comparisons	Just like SQL, you have the operations =, >, >=, <, <=, and <>.
Arithmetic	+, -, *, /
Logical	NOT, AND, OR
Between	The `BETWEEN` expression determines whether a value falls within a range.
In	The `IN` expression determines whether a value is contained within a given set.
Like	The `LIKE` expression evaluates whether a string matches a pattern. For a single character wildcard, use _. To use a wildcard that represents zero or more characters, use %.
Null	The `NULL` comparison expression evaluates whether an attribute or set is null. This is not used to evaluate a null collection; we use the `EMPTY` expression to evaluate collections.

EJB QL also includes several functions, both arithmetic and string, listed in Table 23.6. Most EJB vendors, including Borland's Application Server, allow you to define and implement your own custom functions.

TABLE 23.6 Functional Expressions

Function Syntax	Description
`CONCAT(String, String)`	Concatenate two strings together and return into a third.
`SUBSTRING(String, start, length)`	Return a substring based on the start and length passed in.
`LOCATE(String, String [, start])`	Locate a string within another and return its location.
`LENGTH(String)`	Return the length of a string.
`ABS(number)`	Return the absolute version of the number.
`SQRT(double)`	Return the square root of a number.

Finder Methods

The ability to find an entity is a key requirement of all entity beans. The implementation of finder methods, within EJB specification 1.1, required us to quickly move to bean managed persistence rather than use the simpler container managed persistence beans. Using EJB QL in conjunction with finder methods within a container managed persistent bean, you can meet most requirements for finding an individual or collection of entities.

We'll continue to look at our `Employee` entity and add a more complex finder other than `findByPrimaryKey()`. The requirement we need to implement is the capability to find employees based on a salary range. The following steps are required to build this finder method implementation:

1. Right-click on the `Employee` entity and choose Add, Finder. The results of which display the finder editor.
2. Add the finder properties required to accomplish the given task.
3. Set the following properties (see Figure 23.6):

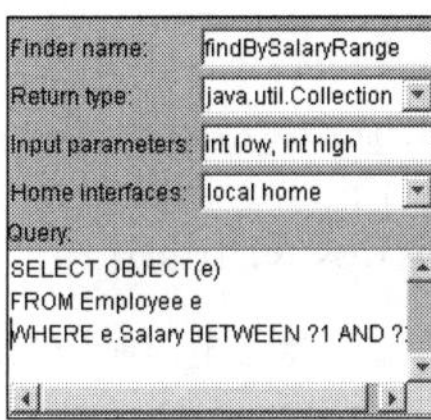

FIGURE 23.6 Finder editor within the EJB Designer.

- Method name: **`findBySalaryRange`**
- Return type: **`java.util.Collection`**
- Input parameters: **int low, int high**
- Home interface: **local home**
- Query: **`SELECT OBJECT(e) FROM Employee e WHERE e.Salary BETWEEN ?1 AND ?2`**

4. Save and compile your project.

The deployment descriptor now contains the information for this finder method (see Listing 23.18). When the bean is deployed to the container, it translates the information contained within the deployment descriptor EJB QL to standard SQL for `JDatastore`.

LISTING 23.18 Portion of the Deployment Descriptor for Defining a Finder Method with EJB QL

```
<query>
  <query-method>
    <method-name>findBySalaryRange</method-name>
    <method-params>
       <method-param>int</method-param>
       <method-param>int</method-param>
     </method-params>
  </query-method>
  <ejb-ql>SELECT OBJECT(e) FROM Employee e WHERE e.Salary
➥BETWEEN ?1 AND ?2</ejb-ql>
</query>
```

Relationship Mapping

As stated earlier the introduction of relationships in EJB 2.0 specifications makes a huge difference. These relationship mappings allow for not only providing the mechanics for managing relationships, but also the capability to model and implement complex business relationships with unidirectional and bidirectional traversal.

Each entity bean typically is not isolated in itself; it relates to other entities within our system. For example, the `Employee` entity we have been working with relates to many other entities within our system such as the salary history. To demonstrate relationships, we will start with one-to-many and move to more complex relationships, such as many-to-many.

One-to-Many Relationships

We can use a simple example for a one-to-many relationship. Using the sample database provided with JBuilder, each employee has a lengthy salary history that we want to make available through the instance (see Figure 23.7).

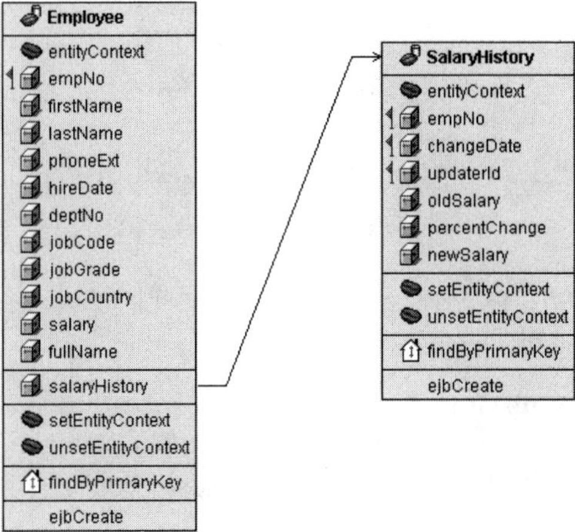

FIGURE 23.7 Model of employee to salary history.

The process for creating this one-to-many relationship within JBuilder is accomplished by using the EJB Designer. The relationship ultimately is exposed via a local interface defined on the `Employee` entity bean. Ultimately, you would access this local interface by way of a session façade bean, but to make the example simple, we will use the remote interface with a test client.

1. Expand the `EmployeeData` source and verify that the `SALARY_HISTORY` table is contained within the source's definition.

2. Right-click on the `SALARY_HISTORY` table and select Create Entity Bean. The bean then appears in the EJB Designer. Make sure that the version property is set to EJB 2.0 compliant.

3. Creating an EJB relationship is accomplished by right-clicking on the parent entity. In this class, right-click on our `Employee` entity and select Add, Relationship. An arrow used to graphically represent our relationship appears within the EJB Designer.

4. Drag the end of the relationship arrow onto the `SalaryHistory` entity.

5. Select the newly created method that contains the relationship. The name assigned by JBuilder's EJB Designer is `salaryHistory`.

6. The Relationship Property editor appears to allow you to change the behavior of the relationship (see Figure 23.8).

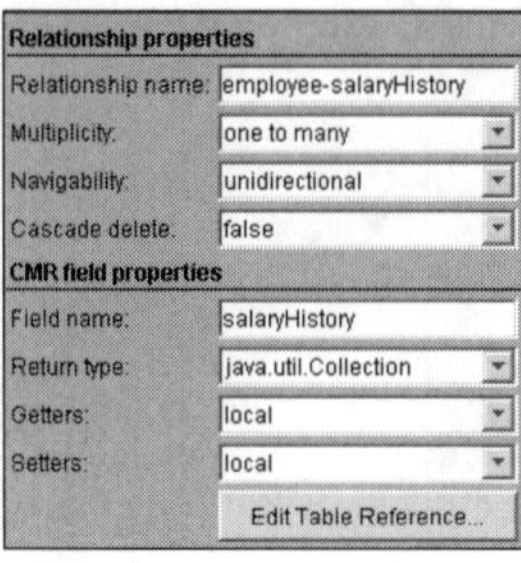

FIGURE 23.8 Relationship Property editor for the `Employee` to `SalaryHistory` relationship.

7. For the relationship properties, Multiplicity should be set to one-to-many, and Navigability should be set to unidirectional. The Navigability is set to unidirectional because it does not make sense to access `Employee` entity information through the `SalaryHistory` entity.

8. Click on the Edit Table Reference button to open the Table Reference editor (see Figure 23.9). We will use this editor to provide the link/keys between the two entities.

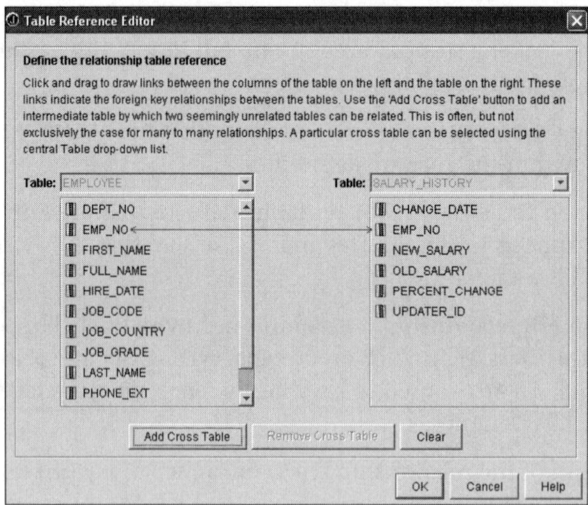

FIGURE 23.9 Table Reference editor for the `Employee` to `SalaryHistory` relationship.

9. Adding a relationship is important because it indicates all the important keys that define the relationship between parent and child entities. Double-click on the `empNo` in the `Employee` entity and drag it onto the `empNo` of the `SalaryHistory` entity. Click OK.

10. You should have a new attribute that contains the relationship between the `Employee` and the employee's salary history. Using the property editor, shown in Figure 23.8, make sure that the return type of the `salaryHistory` method within the `Employee` entity is `java.util.Collection`.

Many-to-Many Relationships

A many-to-many relationship appears frequently in relationship database designs. It is usually implemented through the use of a resolution table because most relational database servers do not support this many-to-many relationship directly, although object modeling supports this relationship well. Although we can create this same resolution entity within our container, why not implement a many-to-many relationship that more accurately represents our actual instances?

For example, our employee system contains a many-to-many relationship implemented through a resolution table (see Figure 23.10).

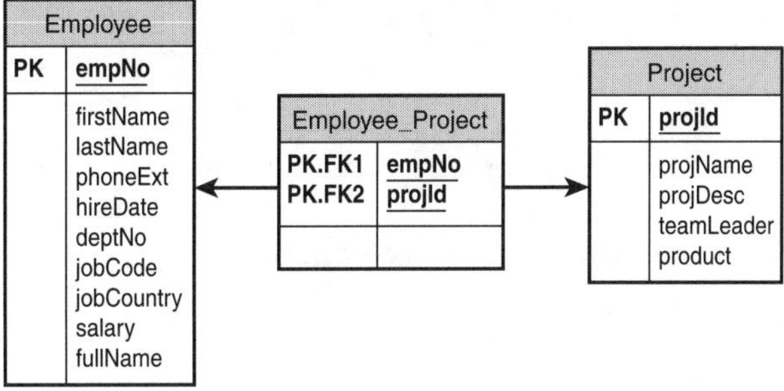

FIGURE 23.10 Employee relational data model.

Let's now create a many-to-many relationship using the existing `employeeData` source. The relationship will be exposed via local interfaces of the `Employee` and `Project` entity beans. To access these interfaces, we will use the local interfaces of the beans created. The following tasks help us create the required relationships and deployment descriptor for these entity beans:

1. Right-click on the `PROJECT` table within the defined data module within the EJB Designer and select Create CMP 2.0 Entity Bean.

2. Create the many-to-many relationship between the `Employee` and `Project` entity beans using the EJB Designer. This is accomplished by right-clicking on

the `Employee` bean and selecting Add, Relationship; then drop the other end of the relationship on the `Project` entity.

3. Select the newly created relationship entity called `Project`, and the relationship editor is created (see Figure 23.11):

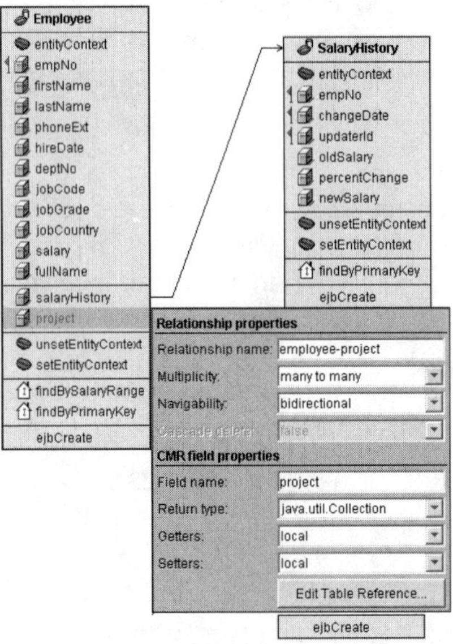

FIGURE 23.11 Relationship editor for a many-to-many relationship.

- Relationship name: employee-project
- Multiplicity: many to many
- Navigability: bidirectional
- Field name: project
- Return type: `java.util.Collection`
- Getters/setters: local

4. Click on Edit Table Reference; this launches the Table Reference editor.
5. Click on Add Cross Table (see Figure 23.12). After you make the appropriate selections, the Add Cross Table button becomes available.

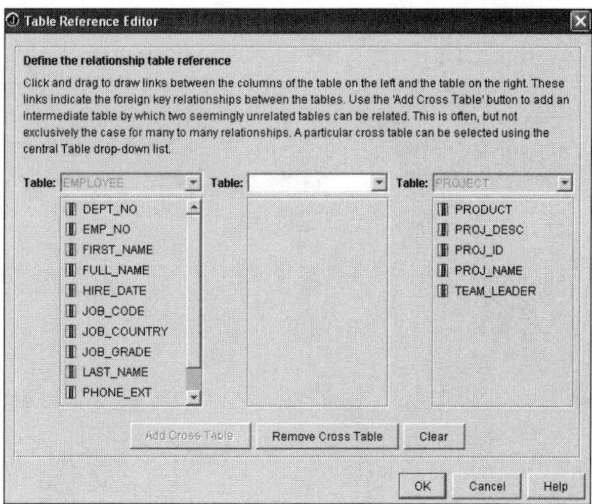

FIGURE 23.12 Table Reference editor to establish a many-to-many relationship.

6. Select the `EMPLOYEE_PROJECT` table as the cross table (see Figure 23.13).

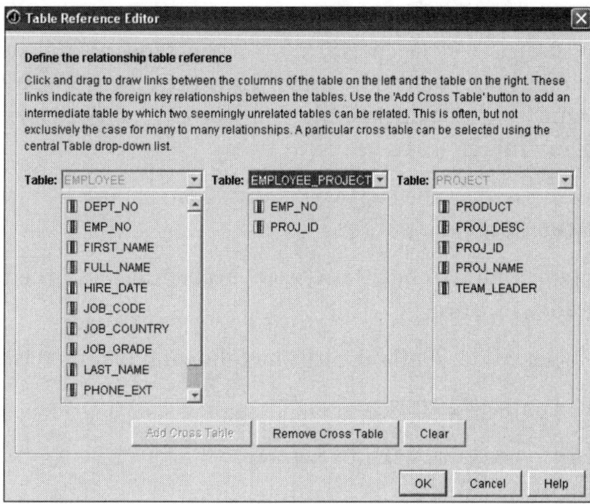

FIGURE 23.13 Table Reference editor to establish a many-to-many relationship using a cross table.

7. Drag `EMPLOYEE EMP_NO` to the `EMPLOYEE_PROJECT EMP_NO` and drag `EMPLOYEE_PROJECT PROJ_ID` to `PROJECT PROJ_ID` (see Figure 23.14).
8. Click OK and compile and save your project.

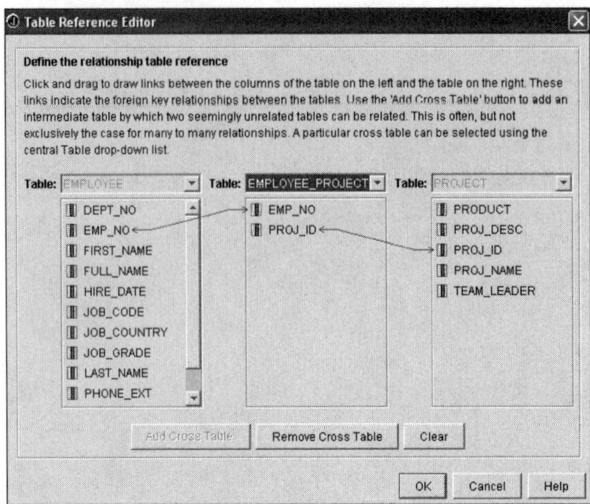

FIGURE 23.14 Build the relationship between the resolution table and the Employee and Project tables with the connected keys.

Home Business Methods

One of the new changes for the specification is the addition and support for collection methods and business methods contained within the home interface. For example, we might want to calculate the total current salary of all employees. The process for building this is simple:

1. Add a new method to the `Employee` entity bean calling it **`calculateTotalSalary`**.
2. Enter the return type to be a **`java.math.BigDecimal`** and the target interface should be **local home**.
3. Create another finder method with the following parameters:
    - Finder name: **`findAll`**
    - Return type: **`java.util.Collection`**
    - Parameter: leave empty
    - Method interface: **local home**
    - Query: **`SELECT OBJECT(e) FROM Employee AS e`**

4. Create a select method with the following properties:
   - Select name: **selectAll**
   - Return type: **java.util.Collection**
   - Parameter: leave empty
   - Result type mapping: **local**
   - Query: **SELECT OBJECT(e) FROM Employee AS e**
5. Most of the code for the Employee entity has been generated by the EJB Wizard. The piece we need to add is the implementation of CalculateTotalSalary.
6. Locate the EmployeeBean class and double-click to view the source.
7. Locate the ejbHomeCalculateTotalSalary() method in the class.
8. Implement the method as follows:

```
public java.math.BigDecimal    ejbHomeCalculateTotalSalary() {
  float res = 0;

  try {
    java.util.Iterator iter = ejbSelectAll().iterator();
    while(iter.hasNext()){
      Employee emp = (Employee)iter.next();
      res = res + emp.getSalary().floatValue();
    }
  }
  catch (FinderException ex) {
    throw new javax.ejb.EJBException(ex);
  }

  return new java.math.BigDecimal(new Float(res).toString());
}
```

Transactions

Transactions play an important role in most application development projects. This is not different when developing an EJB-based solution. Transactions can be complex features to implement, but EJB-based systems require that the vendors implement transaction processing within the container. This does not mean, however, that you do not have to be concerned about transactions.

Simply put, a transaction is a grouping of work that represents a single unit or task. This single unit may contain something as simple as one step or many complex steps to be treated as one. Many times, people ask "Why do I need transactions?" Transactions help to alleviate the complexity of coordinating data or resource access across many clients.

Whenever you use transactions, you need to understand the four main characters: Atomicity, Consistency, Isolation, and Durability, commonly referred to as ACID. These four properties and the basic requirements fulfilled through the use of transactions are shown in Table 23.7.

TABLE 23.7 Properties of a Successful Transaction

Property	Description
Atomicity	All or none of a transaction's effects are kept.
Consistency	Transactions preserve data integrity and consistency.
Isolation	Intermediate results of a transaction are not visible outside that transaction.
Durability	Committed effects survive system failures.

Transaction Attributes

With declarative demarcation you specify to the container which methods are going to be included within transactional processing. Each method is given a transactional context that it uses to participate within the given transaction. Enterprise JavaBeans define seven different types of transaction attributes, each having a slightly different implementation, as shown in Table 23.8.

TABLE 23.8 Transaction Attributes Available for EJB Transactional Implementation

Transactional Attribute	Description
Required	Guarantees that the work performed by the method is within a global transaction context. If the caller already has a transaction context, the container uses the same context. If the caller has not been assigned a transaction context, the container begins a new transaction automatically. The attribute makes it easy to implement multiple beans and coordinate the work of all the beans using the same global transaction for all the beans within the same transaction.
RequiresNew	The container invokes the enterprise bean method with a new transaction it has started with. The container ends this transaction when the invocation completes. The transaction is ended either by a rollback or commit request.
Mandatory	This allows bean methods to declare that they must be invoked by clients within transactions. Typically, such bean methods are not intended to be used on their own but are expected to be one part of a larger transaction.

TABLE 23.8 Continued

Transactional Attribute	Description
Supports	The beans participate in interactions without causing new transactions to be started, yet using them if they are present. Only application logic that can function correctly both within a transaction and without one should be allowed to use this mode.
NotSupported	Allows bean methods with implementations that can't or shouldn't be invoked with a transaction. This might happen, for instance, if a bean does not want the client's transaction to propagate to resources that it may contact during its processing.
Never	This allows a bean method to declare that it must never be invoked by clients running transactions. Typically, this is because the bean's method performs some activity that can provide ACID properties. This attribute has been deprecated in EJB 2.0 specifications.
Bean-managed	This is also known as *programmatic transactional control*. In other words, the transactions are implemented within the source of the bean.

Transaction Usage

Transaction usage within the container is specified within the deployment descriptor. JBuilder's EJB Designer provides an easy-to-use interface that gives access to the transactional attributes. This interface makes it simple to define a transactional context that will ultimately be contained within the deployment descriptor. For example, let's look at our `Employee` entity bean again. The following process is used to define the transactional context for the entity bean:

1. Select a bean to define a transaction attribute.
2. Underneath the `Employee` entity you will see a child node entitled Container Transaction.
3. Double-click on the Container Transaction; this loads the Container Transaction editor, shown in Figure 23.15.
4. Using the drop-down combo boxes, select the interface—either Home, Remote, LocalHome, or Local. After you select an interface, you are then allowed to either select all the methods (*) or specify a method.
5. Finally, select the appropriate transactional attribute.

The results of this process are placed in the deployment descriptor, as shown in Listing 23.19.

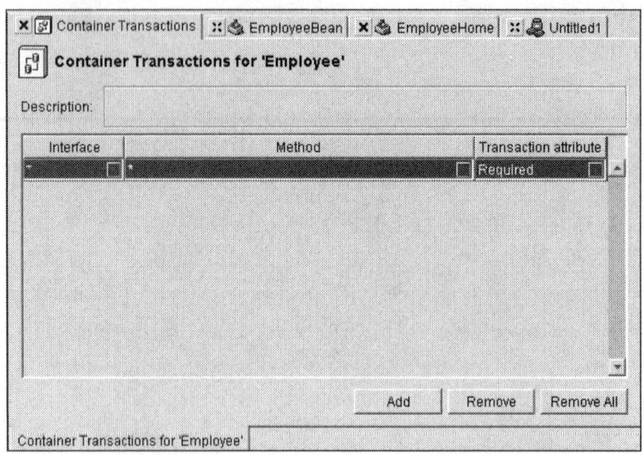

FIGURE 23.15 Define a transaction attribute using the Container Transaction editor.

LISTING 23.19 Portion of the Deployment Descriptor Containing the Transaction Attributes

```
<container-transaction>
    <method>
        <description />
        <ejb-name>Employee</ejb-name>
        <method-intf>LocalHome</method-intf>
        <method-name>create</method-name>
        <method-params>
            <method-param>java.lang.Short</method-param>
        </method-params>
    </method>
    <trans-attribute>Required</trans-attribute>
</container-transaction>
<container-transaction>
    <method>
        <description />
        <ejb-name>Employee</ejb-name>
        <method-intf>LocalHome</method-intf>
        <method-name>findAll</method-name>
        <method-params />
    </method>
    <trans-attribute>Supports</trans-attribute>
</container-transaction>
```

Container Security

Security is an important issue in the development and deployment of all enterprise-based applications. This security is implemented using the container's support for security specified within the EJB specification. The EJB framework is designed to have security built within the container allowing the implementation of security to be effortless.

The EJB security model is designed for the enterprise-based applications and should not be used if EJBs are not being used. The process of implementing this security within EJBs is defined based on the security requirements needed within your implementation. Implementing this typically requires the following:

- Defining users and groups
- Associating application resources to users or groups
- Providing efficient and different methods of maintaining security
- Implementing logic to validate security at runtime
- Implementing tools to mange users, groups, and privileges

Authentication

Authentication is the process of verifying that a client is who they claim to be. Authentication is the basis from which the remaining portions of the security model are constructed—the foundation. Many different authentication mechanisms are available in most EJB containers. For example, Borland's Enterprise Server contains authentication with JDBC, LDAP, JDatastore, or the implementation of a custom security class.

Authorization

Authorization is the process of giving rights to the underlying implementation. For example, you might require a certain set of rights to call a given method. Authentication can be implemented via the container, or you can programmatically implement the security within the bean home interface. To help visualize the implementation of the authorization mechanisms, take a look at the security sequence diagram shown in Figure 23.16.

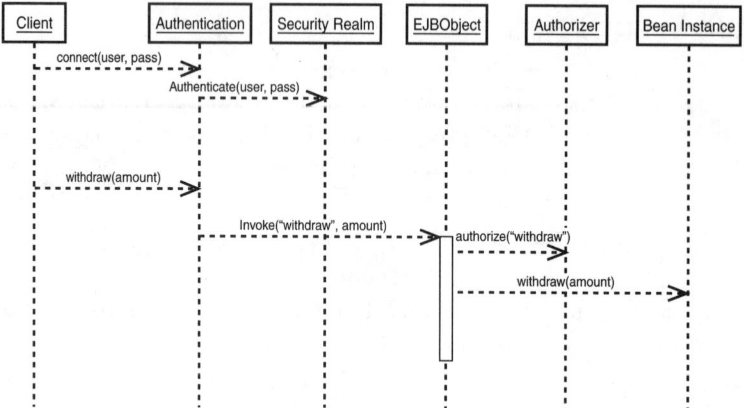

FIGURE 23.16 Sequence diagram for illustrating server-based authentication.

Secure Communication

Secure communication is probably the simplest to implement but the most complex if you look at what is hidden from you in the details. JBuilder does not offer any special features to either manage or implement secure communication; this is simply a feature of the container. For example, Borland Enterprise Server can communicate either between the clients or between other J2EE servers using SSL configured through the use of the container's console.

JBuilder's Support

JBuilder's support is actually simple. It is divided into two sections. The first is the capability to define the roles that will be available to the security editor in order (see Figure 23.17).

The second is the capability to assign security to any interface or method based on the role of the end-user (see Figure 23.18).

Design Guidelines

Using entity beans is a practice that many users of application servers do not want to venture into. Part of this is due to the lack of understanding; the other part is due to the lack of capabilities in earlier versions of the EJB specification. As we look at entity beans, keep in mind two important considerations when designing the architecture:

- Using local interfaces versus remote interfaces
- Container managed persistence versus bean managed persistence

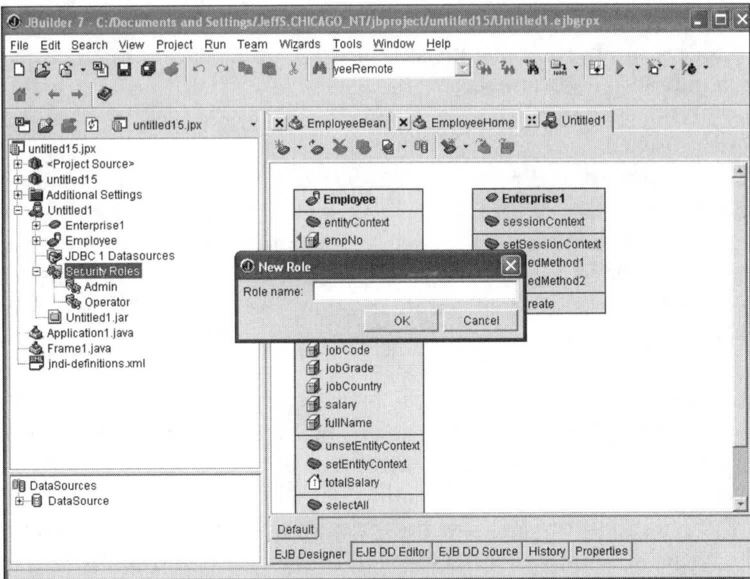

FIGURE 23.17 Building new roles for the security domain.

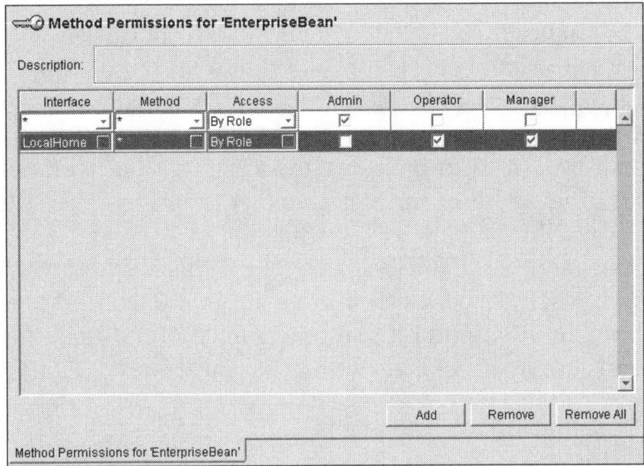

FIGURE 23.18 Assigning roles to either an interface, method, or both.

Use the Local Interface

When accessing data remotely, the result of the data has to be moved from one location to another, thus, data has to be serialized. This process of serialization is expensive. In other words, the latency of serializing data, sending it over the wire, and rematerializing the data on the client can be time consuming. With the introduction of EJB 2.0 specification, the capability to call and communicate to an entity bean with a local interface was defined.

Inspiration

The inspiration of local interfaces is specifically to address the performance issues related to serializing data. With the use of session façades or the use of value objects, the need for network ubiquity and serializing data has become less important. Without the need for serialized data, an alternative was needed. This alternative is to pass data by reference rather than value. In other words, instead of copying/ serializing the data, a reference to the data is passed.

Inner Workings

The inner workings of this change in the design are rather simple. If the entity bean runs within the same process, you can access the entity bean using its local interface and pass all data by reference rather than value. There is a drawback to using this method of communication: You lose the concept of network ubiquity. In other words, the client needs to know the location of the bean you want to use, but you gain what was lost in higher performance throughput.

Use CMP Before BMP

When I first started to use J2EE servers, the idea of letting the container manage all the persistence for me seemed unsettling. So I found myself developing persistence code. The process was neither desirable nor ultimately a good, efficient process for developing large-scale applications. I was developing huge portions of code that did nothing other than save, read, and remove instances of data. They were virtually identical except for the details of the SQL statements and member attributes.

Inspiration

With the changes in the EJB specification from 1.1 to 2.0, container managed persistence became all the more important and powerful. Without these necessary changes to the specifications, many developers found that most uses of CMP were limited to simple persistence.

Inner Workings

Container managed persistence supports most of the persistence requirements that any enterprise application needs. Using the container for accomplishing these tasks is not only quicker to develop, but the performance is usually better. If those two reasons are not enough, container managed persistence is by far the most portable of the components within the J2EE architecture.

In Practice

The ChalkTalk application needs the capability to read and save data to the database structure. We have read and written data to the database using JDBC; now it is time to accomplish the same task using entity beans. The process of building the beans is rather simple; most of our work will be executed in the session facade.

Building the Persistence Layer

The creation of the persistence layer using JBuilder depends on the appropriate data structure being completed. In Chapter 15, "Database Connectivity," we created the necessary data store for our application. We will now create the entity beans to manage this persistence. The following steps are used to build the necessary entity beans:

1. Import a schema from our data source in the EJB module containing our session beans. This is accomplished by right-clicking on the data source node when we are in the EJB Designer and selecting Import Schema from Datasource.
2. Set the following database parameters:
    - Driver: **`com.borland.datastore.jdbc.DataStoreDriver`**
    - URL: **`jdbc:borland:dslocal:C:\JBDG\db\ChalkTalk.jds`**
    - Username: leave blank
    - Password: leave blank
3. Right-click on each table and create a CMP 2.0 entity bean for each table. For example, right click on the table Room and create a CMP 2.0 bean.
4. Define relationships.

Configuring an Entity Bean

Typically each entity bean that has been created requires more finder methods than just a `findByPrimaryKey`. Our `Room` entity bean is a perfect example.

1. Right-click on our `Room` entity bean. Add a finder method.
2. Configure the following properties for the finder method:
    - Name: **`findAll`**
    - Return type: **`java.util.Collection`**
    - Input parameters: leave empty

  - Home interfaces: **Local Home**
  - Query: **SELECT OBJECT(o) FROM RoomSchema AS o**

3. Compile and save.

Creating an EJB Connection Factory

This factory supplies caching to both local and remote interfaces. Although this connection factory differentiates between local and remote interfaces, you have the capability to make this interface ubiquitous. The following steps build your EJB connection factory:

1. Create a new class within your project, calling it **EJBConnectionFactory**.
2. Move the newly created class to the package **com.sams.chalktalk.beans**.
3. Add the following code to implement the connection to both local and remote beans in addition to placing them into a cache when the connection has been established:

```
package com.sams.chalktalk.beans;

import javax.naming.*;
import java.util.*;
import javax.ejb.*;

class EJBHomeFactory {

  private static EJBHomeFactory instance = null;
  private Context initialContext;
  private Map ejbHomes;

  private EJBHomeFactory() throws NamingException {
    initialContext = new InitialContext();
    ejbHomes = Collections.synchronizedMap(new HashMap());
  }

  public static EJBHomeFactory getInstance() throws NamingException {
    if(instance == null) {
      instance = new EJBHomeFactory();
    }
    return instance;
  }
```

```
    public EJBLocalHome lookupByLocalEJBReference(String ejbReferenceComponent)
      throws NamingException {

      java.lang.Object home = ejbHomes.get(ejbReferenceComponent);
      if(home == null) {
        home = initialContext.lookup("java:comp/env/ejb/" +
                                     ejbReferenceComponent);
        ejbHomes.put(ejbReferenceComponent, home);
      }
      return (EJBLocalHome) home;
    }

    public EJBHome lookupByRemoteEJBReference(String ejbReferenceComponent,
        Class homeClass)
      throws NamingException {

      java.lang.Object home = ejbHomes.get(ejbReferenceComponent);
      if(home == null) {
        java.lang.Object obj =
          initialContext.lookup("java:comp/env/ejb/" + ejbReferenceComponent);
        home = javax.rmi.PortableRemoteObject.narrow(obj, homeClass);
        ejbHomes.put(ejbReferenceComponent, home);
      }
      return (EJBHome) home;
    }
  }
```

4. Compile and save your project.

Creating a Manager Bean

A manager bean surfaces the business logic and ultimately interfaces to the persistence utilizing the entity beans. These manager beans will then be attached to the session facade to consolidate the middle-tier access. The following steps are required to create one of the manager beans:

1. Create a new class, naming the class **RoomManager** and placing the new class in the package **com.sams.chalktalk.beans**.
2. The following code surfaces the required business logic. The requirements of the manager class are used to implement all the appropriate business logic, such as checking to make sure that a room has a capacity.

```
package com.sams.chalktalk.beans;

import javax.naming.*;
import javax.ejb.*;
import java.util.*;

class RoomManager {
  //Add a home factory for caching the home interfaces
  private EJBHomeFactory homeFactory;
  private static RoomManager instance = null;

  //Use the RoomValueFactory to create
  private RoomValueFactory roomValueFactory;

  private RoomManager() throws NamingException {
    homeFactory = EJBHomeFactory.getInstance();
  }

  public static RoomManager getInstance() throws NamingException {
    if(instance == null) {
      instance = new RoomManager();
    }
    return instance;
  }

  public String createRoom(RoomValue roomValue)
      throws FinderException, NamingException {

    try {
      RoomHome roomHome =
          (RoomHome) homeFactory.lookupByLocalEJBReference("Room");
      Room room = roomHome.create(roomValue.getLocation(),roomValue.
getCapacity()
➥,roomValue.getName(),roomValue.getKey());
      return room.getName();
    }
    catch(Exception e) {
      throw new EJBException(e);
    }
  }
```

```
  public void updateRoom(RoomValue roomValue)
      throws FinderException, NamingException {

    try {
      Room room = roomValueFactory.findRoom(roomValue.getKey());
      room.setCapacity(roomValue.getCapacity());
    }
    catch(Exception e) {
      throw new EJBException(e);
    }
  }

  public void removeRoom(Short key)
      throws FinderException, NamingException {

    try {
      Room room = roomValueFactory.findRoom(key);
      room.remove();
    }
    catch(Exception e) {
      throw new EJBException(e);
    }
  }

  public void removeAllRooms()
      throws FinderException, NamingException {

    try {
      Collection rooms = roomValueFactory.findAllRooms();
      Iterator iterator = rooms.iterator();
      Room room = null;
      while(iterator.hasNext()) {
        room = (Room) iterator.next();
        room.remove();
      }
    }
    catch(Exception e) {
      throw new EJBException(e);
    }
  }
}
```

Attaching the Session Facade

Our session facade wraps multiple manager beans together into one session bean. In other words, we will access all functionality for our ChalkTalk system utilizing this one session bean. The following steps are required to attach the facade to our manager bean:

1. Define a private member for each type of bean manager you want to use. For example, the following code defines one for our `RoomManager`:

   ```
   private RoomManager roomManager;
   ```

2. Create an instance of our manager bean within `ejbCreate()`. The following demonstrates the implementation using our `RoomManager`:

   ```
   public void ejbCreate() throws CreateException {
     try {
       roomManager = RoomManager.getInstance();
     }
     catch (NamingException ex) {
       //pass exception to the container
       throw new EJBException(ex);
     }
   ```

3. Attach the manager bean call to be called from the corresponding session bean method. If the client calls the `createRoom` method of the session bean, it then needs to pass the information to the manager class. The following code demonstrates such an implementation:

   ```
   public void createRoom(RoomValue room) {
     try {
       roomManager.createRoom(room);
     }
     catch (Exception ex) {
        throw new EJBException(ex);
     }
   }
   ```

4. Compile and save your project.

Testing the Implementation

It is time to test the client we created. The easiest way to test the session facade is to build a client dedicated to testing the interface. The following steps build a test client to exercise this facade:

1. Select File, New from the JBuilder menu.
2. Within the Object Gallery, under the Enterprise tab, select the EJB Test Client.
3. Specify the following parameters to build our test client:
   - EJB name: **ChalkTalkFacade**
   - Package: **com.sams.chalktalk.client**
   - Class name: **ChalkTalkFacadeTestClient**
   - Generate Method for Testing Remote Interface Calls with Arguments: Checked
   - Generate Logging Messages: Checked
   - Generate Main Functions: Checked
   - Generate Header Comments: Checked
4. Add the following code to the `main` method to test your session bean interface:

```
//create a Remote interface
client.create();

//Add a room
client.addRoom(new RoomData(5,"Small Room",5,"2nd Floor"));

//Add with invalid capacity
client.addRoom(new RoomData(3,"Error Room",0,"3rd Floor"));
```

5. Save, compile, and run your test application.

Summary

Using entity beans is a question for design, experience, need, and implemented technology. Entity beans are designed to handle all the persistence requirements for most enterprise applications. Entity beans, like session beans, are designed to be distributed objects with the following characteristics:

- Entity beans provide persistence.
- Entity beans are transactional.
- Entity beans are multiuser.

- Entity beans are long-lived.
- Entity beans survive the life of the container.

The introduction of more advanced container managed persistence and the other important features added to the EJB specification has made building and ultimately managing an application much more efficient.

Reflections

- Should I use container managed or bean managed persistence?
- Should I design for use with local or remote interfaces?
- Should entity beans be used to encapsulate nontraditional data access?

24 Message-Driven Beans

IN THIS CHAPTER

- Point-to-Point Versus Publish/Subscribe
- Writing a Message-Driven Bean
- Testing the Message-Driven Bean
- Building a Message-Driven Bean with JBuilder
- Design Guidelines

Message-driven beans, introduced in the EJB 2.0 specification, reduced the complexity of building a message-based application. The beans simply implement an `onMessage()` that implements the appropriate response to the message received. The container then handles all the required plumbing to implement and wrap Java Message Server (JMS). In other words, message-driven beans simply wrap up JMS functionality into a simple bean component. A message may be initiated from a client application, Web page, or another bean, and the message may also be consumed by anyone of these.

A message-driven bean (MDB) is essentially a message consumer that implements some business logic. The MDB registers itself to a JMS queue or topic of its choosing. The MDB must then implement the MessageListener interface and finally awaits the arrival of a message (see Figure 24.1).

A message-driven bean works similarly to stateless session beans: A single instance is shared by multiple clients of the bean (refer to Figure 24.1). The process of this communication is simple. A publisher produces a message and sends it to the message bean. If the message is synchronous or asynchronous, it simply determines whether the client will then be blocked. The message-driven bean then handles all the required integration to the subscribers.

The design model for message-driven beans implementation has three basic rules that define its interaction:

1. A message producer creates a message and sends it to a specified topic.
2. A message consumer subscribes with a topic to receive messages.
3. The message is delivered from the topic to the request subscribers.

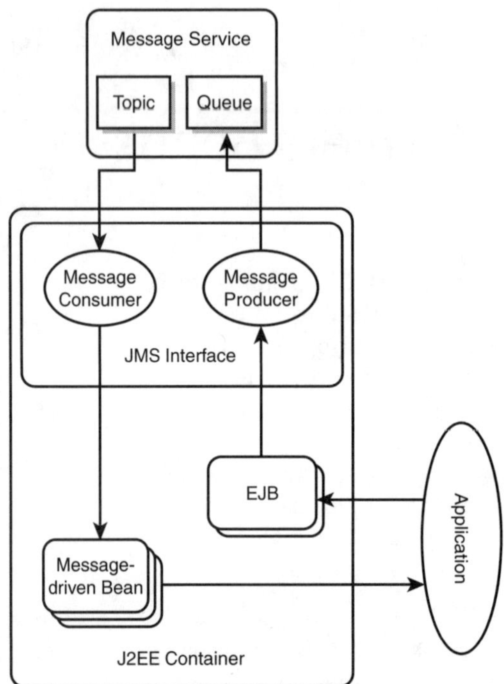

FIGURE 24.1 Message-driven component view model.

As we look at creating a message-driven bean, you will see the facilities that JBuilder offers. The EJB Designer makes it simple to create the bean; however, you will still have to implement the business logic.

Point-to-Point Versus Publish/Subscribe

The point-to-point communication model is always used when a message is consumed only by a single consumer. For example, a system may inform a client of a processed order. This order can be received and processed by only one client. This model is referenced as a message queue (see Figure 24.2).

In this model, a message producer sends a message to a given queue. Each queue is supplied with a unique name in the container's naming service. The message then is consumed by the queue. Finally the queue delivers the message to a single registered client.

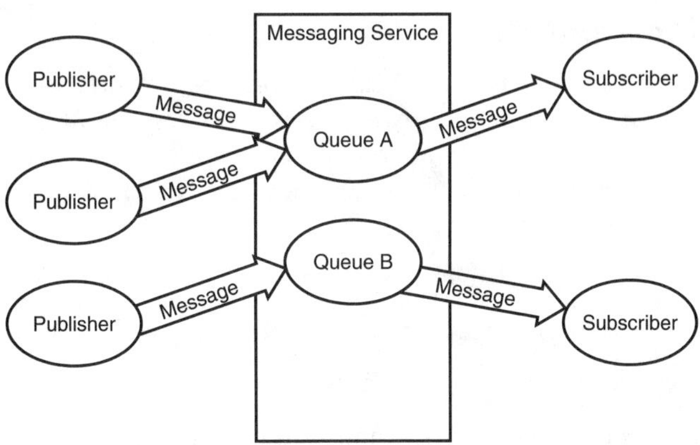

FIGURE 24.2 Message queue model.

NOTE

One limitation of message-driven beans compared to standard JMS listeners is that a given message bean deployment can be associated with only one queue or topic. If your application requires a single JMS consumer to service messages from multiple queues or topics, you must use a standard JMS consumer, or deploy multiple message-driven bean classes.

The publish/subscribe model is typically used for general broadcasts. For example, an inventory management system periodically transmits the current inventory levels to many clients. In this model, the message server defines a topic, for each of which a subject is created for handling messages. A message is then produced by a consumer and is sent to a given topic. The topic consumes the message and then delivers the message to all the parties who have registered for the given message (see Figure 24.3).

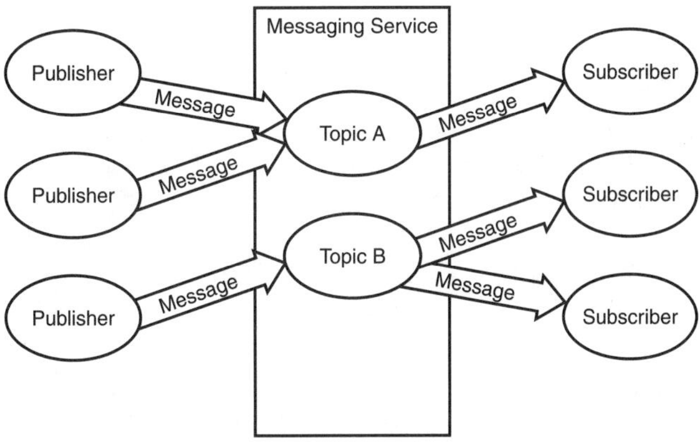

FIGURE 24.3 Topic publish/subscribe model.

Writing a Message-Driven Bean

The task of writing a message-driven bean is simplified, in comparison to a JMS implementation, in that you only create a bean class. This message-driven bean does not have either a remote/local home or remote/local interface, but it is communicated to by a publisher via a message. The following tasks are required to build a message-driven bean:

1. Create a class that implements the `javax.ejb.MessageDrivenBean` interface.
2. Implement the `javax.jms.MessageListener` interface.
3. Create a public constructor that contains no arguments.
4. Implement the `ejbCreate()` method taking no arguments. This method should be declared as public. Its return type must be void, and it must declare any application exceptions.

Implementing the Interfaces

The `javax.ejb.MessageDrivenBean` interface contains only two methods that must be implemented, as shown in Listing 24.1.

LISTING 24.1 Interface for Message-Driven Beans

```
package javax.ejb;

public abstract interface MessageDrivenBean extends EnterpriseBean {

  // Methods
  void ejbRemove() throws EJBException;
  void setMessageDrivenContext(MessageDrivenContext messageDrivenContext)
➥throws EJBException;
}
```

The implementation of this interface is required for the message-driven bean to be managed by the container. The listener interface only implements the method to process the incoming messages, as shown in Listing 24.2.

LISTING 24.2 Interface for Message-Driven Beans Listener

```
package javax.jms;

public abstract interface MessageListener {
```

LISTING 24.2 Continued

```
  // Methods
  void onMessage(Message message);
}
```

Implementing the Required Methods

The container calls the message-driven bean's `ejbCreate()` and `ejbRemove()` methods when creating or removing an instance of the bean class. As with other EJB types, the `ejbCreate()` method in the bean class should prepare any resources required for the bean's operation. The `ejbRemove()` method should release those resources so that they are freed before the container removes the instance.

Message-driven beans should also perform some form of regular clean-up routine outside the `ejbRemove()` method. The beans cannot rely on `ejbRemove()` being called under all circumstances (for example, if the EJB throws a runtime exception).

Processing the Message

The message-driven bean's `onMessage()` method performs all the business logic for the EJB. WebLogic Server calls `onMessage()` when the EJB's associated JMS queue or topic receives a message, passing the full JMS message object as an argument. It is the message-driven EJB's responsibility to parse the message and perform the necessary business logic in `onMessage()`.

Make sure that the business logic accounts for asynchronous message processing. For example, it cannot be assumed that the EJB receives messages in the order they were sent by the client. Instance pooling within the container means that messages are not received or processed sequentially, although individual `onMessage()` calls to a given message-driven bean instance are serialized, as shown in Listing 24.3.

LISTING 24.3 Message-Driven Bean Source with Implementation (EmployeeMDBBean.java)

```
package messagebean;

import java.text.*;
import java.util.*;

import javax.ejb.*;
import javax.jms.*;
import javax.naming.*;
```

LISTING 24.3 Continued

```
/**
 * The MessageBean class is a message-driven bean.  It implements
 * the javax.ejb.MessageDrivenBean and javax.jms.MessageListener
 * interfaces. It defines a constructor and the methods
 * setMessageDrivenContext, ejbCreate, onMessage, and
 * ejbRemove.
 */
public class EmployeeMDBBean implements MessageDrivenBean,
    MessageListener {

  private transient MessageDrivenContext mdc = null;
  private Context context;
  public EmployeeMDBBean() {  }

  public void setMessageDrivenContext(MessageDrivenContext mdc)
  {
    this.mdc = mdc;
  }

  public void ejbCreate() { }

  public void onMessage(Message inMessage) {
    try {
      if (inMessage instanceof MapMessage){
        MapMessage map = (MapMessage)inMessage;

        System.out.println("Fire Notice");
        System.out.println("Name:" + map.getString("name"));

        sendNote(map.getString("Email"));
      } else {
        System.out.println("Wrong message type");
      }
    }
    catch (Exception ex) {
      ex.printStackTrace();
    }
  }

  private void sendNote(String recipient){
    try {
```

LISTING 24.3 Continued

```
      Context initial = new InitialContext();
      javax.mail.Session session = (javax.mail.Session)
         initial.lookup("java:comp/env/MailSession");

      javax.mail.Message msg = new  javax.mail.internet.MimeMessage(session);

      msg.setFrom();

      msg.setRecipients(javax.mail.Message.RecipientType.TO,
                        javax.mail.internet.InternetAddress.parse
➥ (recipient,false));
      msg.setSubject("Just letting you know!");
      DateFormat dateFormater = DateFormat.getDateTimeInstance(
          DateFormat.LONG, DateFormat.SHORT);

      Date timeStamp = new Date();

      String messageText = "You need to pack up today is your last day!!!!" +
                           '\n' + "Your kind boss";

      msg.setText(messageText);

      msg.setSentDate(timeStamp);

      javax.mail.Transport.send(msg);
    }
    catch (Exception ex) {
      throw new EJBException(ex.getMessage());
    }
  }

  public void ejbRemove() {
    System.out.println("EmployeeMDBBean.ejbRemove() called.");
  }
}
```

Deployment Descriptor

Just like session and entity beans, a deployment descriptor describes the interaction between the bean and the container. The descriptor describes not only the container relationships for the bean, but also the resources required, as shown in Listing 24.4.

LISTING 24.4 Deployment Descriptor for the Message-Driven Bean

```
<?xml version="1.0" encoding="UTF-8"?>
<!DOCTYPE ejb-jar PUBLIC "-//Sun Microsystems, Inc.
➥//DTD Enterprise JavaBeans 2.0//EN" "http://java.sun.com/dtd/ejb-jar_2_0.dtd">
<ejb-jar>
    <enterprise-beans>
        <message-driven>
            <display-name>EmployeeMDB</display-name>
            <ejb-name>EmployeeMDB</ejb-name>
            <ejb-class>messagebean.EmployeeMDBBean</ejb-class>
            <transaction-type>Bean</transaction-type>
            <acknowledge-mode>Auto-acknowledge</acknowledge-mode>
            <message-driven-destination>
                <destination-type>javax.jms.Queue</destination-type>
            </message-driven-destination>
            <resource-ref>
                <description />
                <res-ref-name>MailSession</res-ref-name>
                <res-type>javax.mail.Session</res-type>
                <res-auth>Container</res-auth>
            </resource-ref>
            <resource-env-ref>
                <description />
                <resource-env-ref-name>FireQueue</resource-env-ref-name>
                <resource-env-ref-type>javax.jms.Queue</resource-env-ref-type>
            </resource-env-ref>
        </message-driven>
    </enterprise-beans>
    <assembly-descriptor>
        <container-transaction>
            <method>
                <ejb-name>EmployeeMDB</ejb-name>
                <method-name>*</method-name>
            </method>
            <trans-attribute>Required</trans-attribute>
        </container-transaction>
    </assembly-descriptor>
</ejb-jar>
```

Testing the Message-Driven Bean

Testing a message-driven bean is similar to testing a session or entity bean. You must develop a client; a client needs to produce a message to the queue. In this case, our program will be a console-based application (see Listing 24.5).

LISTING 24.5 Client Test Application (MessageClient.java)

```
package messagebean;

import javax.jms.*;
import javax.naming.*;

/**
 * <p>Title: </p>
 * <p>Description: </p>
 * <p>Copyright: Copyright (c) 2002</p>
 * <p>Company: </p>
 * @author unascribed
 * @version 1.0
 */

public class MessageClient {
  public static void main(String[] args) {
    Context cntx = null;
    QueueConnectionFactory qcf = null;
    QueueConnection qcon = null;
    QueueSession qses = null;
    Queue q = null;
    QueueSender qs = null;
    MapMessage message = null;

    final int MSG_CNT;

    if ((args.length < 1)) {
      System.out.println("Usage: MessageClient QueueName");
    }

    try {
      cntx = new InitialContext();

      qcf = (QueueConnectionFactory)cntx.lookup(
➥"java:comp/env/QueueConnectionFactory");
```

LISTING 24.5 Continued

```
      q = (Queue)cntx.lookup(args[0]);

      qcon = qcf.createQueueConnection();
      qses = qcon.createQueueSession(false,Session.AUTO_ACKNOWLEDGE);

      qs = qses.createSender(q);

      message = qses.createMapMessage();
      message.setString("name","Bob the Builder");
      message.setString("email","bob@builder.com");

      qs.send(message);
    }
    catch (NamingException ex) {
      ex.printStackTrace();
    }catch (JMSException ex) {
      ex.printStackTrace();
    }
  }
}
```

Building a Message-Driven Bean with JBuilder

Building a message-driven bean with JBuilder is accomplished by using the EJB Designer. The EJB Designer offers facilities to create the bean and build the deployment descriptor. The process is as follows:

- Create a message-driven bean within an EJB container.
- Build the deployment descriptor for the message-driven bean.
- Debug the bean execution in process.

The following steps are required to build a generic message-driven bean:

1. Right-click in the EJB Designer and create a new message-driven bean.
2. Configure your bean's parameters and name (see Figure 24.4).
3. Edit the deployment descriptor for the message-driven bean (see Figure 24.5). In addition, look at Table 24.1 for a description of all the properties within the editor.

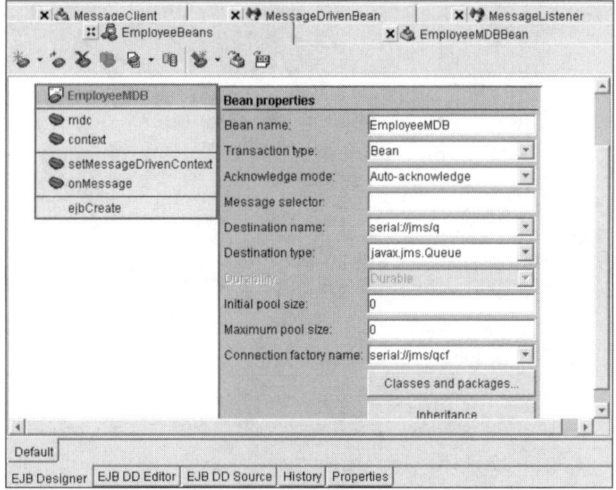

FIGURE 24.4 Message-driven bean designer.

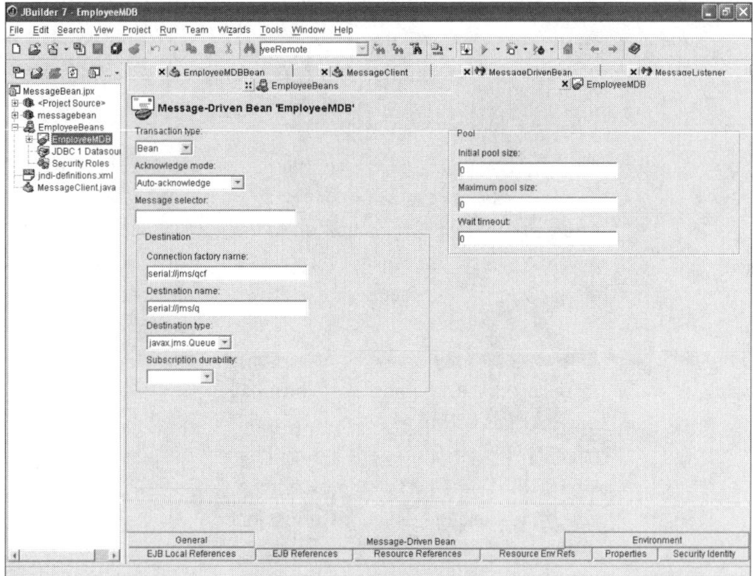

FIGURE 24.5 Message-driven bean deployment descriptor editor.

TABLE 24.1 Table of Properties and Descriptions Within a Message Bean Deployment Descriptor

Property	Description	Example
Bean Name	The name provided for your message-driven bean.	`EmployeeMDB`
Transaction Type	This property specifies the bean's transaction management type. You need to decide whether the bean or the container will manage the transaction handling.	Bean
Acknowledge Mode	The property is valid only if the transaction type value is Bean. Auto-acknowledge mode defines that all messages are acknowledged, and a check is performed to verify that duplicate messages are not acted on. The `Dups-ok-acknowledge` means that all messages are acknowledged and still include all the duplicate messages.	Auto-acknowledge
Message Selector	This property informs the server which messages will be delivered to a given consumer. The selector itself is defined using a string containing SQL QL.	Price between 100.0 and 200.0
Connection Factory Name	The connection factory creates the consumer proxies for the `Queue` or `Topic`. Choose the factor that matches either a `Queue`, `QueueConnectionFactory` and for a topic `Topic`, `TopicConnectionFactory`.	`Serial:/jms/qcf`. This is the JNDI name for a `QueueConnectionFactory` in SonicMQ, which is Borland's Application Server's JMS implementation.
Destination Name	Each topic or queue created has a unique name in the JNDI namespace. This property specifies to which JNDI registered queue or topic the message-driven bean listens. This is the JMS destination from which the message-driven bean instance consumes messages.	`orderConfirm`
Destination Type	This destination type needs to match the associated factory. The choices are either `javax.jms.Queue` or `javax.jms.Topic`. If topic is chosen, durability becomes enabled.	`Javax.jms.Queue`

TABLE 24.1 Continued

Property	Description	Example
Subscription Durability	Durability is when a subscriber will not lose an incoming message even when it is not active. In other words, if the subscriber is not active, the message is stored and maintained until the subscriber reconnects to the topic.	`NonDurable`
Initial Pool Size	The number of message-driven bean instances the container should create as default for the pool.	`0`
Maximum Pool Size	The maximum number of message-driven beans that should be in the pool at any given time. A value of 0 indicates that the maximum pool size is unlimited.	`0`

4. Implement the `onMessage()` method to contain the business process to consume the message.

5. Create a client application to produce a message.

Design Guidelines

It is hard to say "How did we ever live without message-driven beans?" The fact of the matter is that message-driven beans fill a niche for processing asynchronous messages without the need to create complex components using JMS. Because of this, the important design guidelines to apply are as follows:

- When do I use message-driven beans?
- Why should I use message-driven beans instead of JMS?

When to Use Message-Driven Beans

Session beans and entity beans allow you to send JMS messages and to receive them synchronously, but not asynchronously. To avoid tying up server resources, you may prefer not to use blocking synchronous receiving in a server-side component. To receive messages asynchronously, use a message-driven bean.

Using Message-Driven Beans Instead of JMS

The message-driven bean portion of the EJB specification is one of the most exciting and powerful additions to enterprise computing in recent years. It allows messages received via a JMS implementation to be handled by a simple and powerful component model. However, message-driven EJBs have the potential to become the de facto component model for handling any kind of message, not just messages delivered by a JMS.

JMS messages are designed to be interoperable across JMS implementations. This means that a JMS message may have a proprietary implementation under the covers, but the contents can be transparently converted to another proprietary JMS implementation without affecting the message consumer in any way. Because this conversion can be done from one JMS implementation to another prior to message delivery to the client, any arbitrary message format can be converted to a JMS message and delivered to a message-driven bean.

In other words, a message-driven bean can process messages sent by e-mail, HTTP, FTP, or any other protocol, provided that the application server has the facility to convert these protocols into a JMS message. This opens the door to a standard, simple, portable component model that can process any message delivered by any protocol. If the messages are defined in an open, extensible language such as XML, unprecedented interoperability can be achieved in loosely coupled systems in a model that everyone understands. A simple use case for this protocol-independent message processing capability illustrates the power of this technology.

In Practice

This section continues with the use of our ChalkTalk application. We will develop the portions of the system required to process registrations to a course. Figure 24.6 demonstrates the implementation of our `ConfirmationProcessor`.

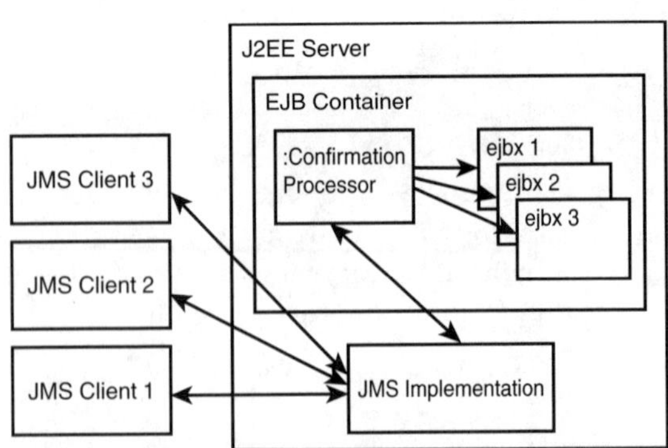

FIGURE 24.6 The `ChalkTalk` components illustrated using a message-driven bean.

Scenario: You want to process course confirmation messages from several different sources such as salespersons, individuals, or corporations.

Solution: Provide an asynchronous method using message-driven beans to process the registration and confirmation (see Figure 24.7).

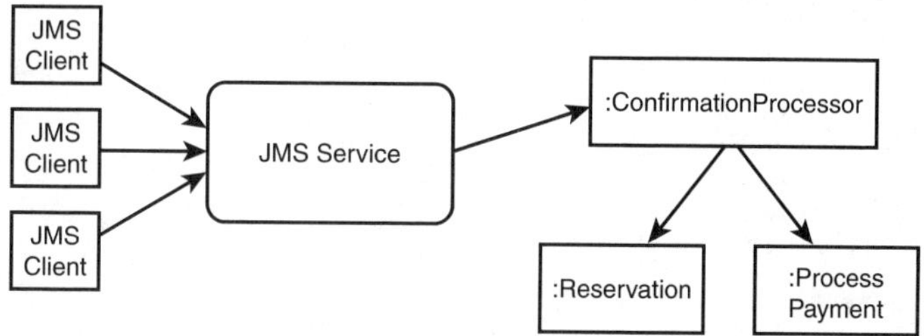

FIGURE 24.7 The design for an automated process for responding to reservations and corresponding confirmations using message-driven beans.

Building the Message-Driven Bean

The message-driven bean we are going to use will process a registration, verify payment, and produce a confirmation. The process for building this bean is similar to the process used to build a message-driven bean earlier. The following is the process required to build such a bean:

1. Open the "In Practice" solution from Chapter 23, "Entity Beans."
2. Right-click in the EJB Designer and create a new message-driven bean.
3. Configure your bean's properties:

Property	Value
Bean name	`ConfirmationProcessor`
Transaction type	`Bean`
Acknowledge mode	`Auto-acknowledge`
Message selector	<empty>
Destination name	<empty>
Destination type	`javax.jms.Queue`
Initial pool size	`0`
Connection factory name	<empty>

4. Change the package name by clicking on the Classes and Packages button to **`com.sams.chalktalk.beans`**.

Implementing the Message Processing

Business logic for the EJB is triggered by the `onMessage()` method of the MDB. The `onMessage()` is called by the container when the JMS `Queue` or `Topic` receives a message. The `onMessage()` does not return any result and has one argument. The full JMS message object is passed as an argument. The following steps implement our `onMessage()` processing:

1. Find the `onMessage()` method located within the `ConfirmationProcessor` bean.
2. Implement the following code to process our message:

```
public void onMessage(Message msg) {
  try {
    MapMessage confMsg = (MapMessage) msg;

    int studentPK = confMsg.getInt("StudentID");
    int coursePK = confMsg.getInt("CourseID");
    int schedulePK = confMsg.getInt("ScheduleID");

    double price = confMsg.getDouble("Price");
    String creditCardNum = confMsg.getString("CreditCard");
    Date creditCardExp = new Date(confMsg.getLong("CreditCardExp"));

    String creditCardType = confMsg.getString("CreditCardType");

    LocalRegisterHome resHome = (LocalRegisterHome)
       jndiContext.lookup("java:comp/env/ejb/LocalRegisterHome");
    resHome.register(studentPK,coursePK,schedulePK);

    Integer confNum = new
        Integer(resHome.processPayment(creditCardNum,creditCardExp,
        creditCardExp,studentPK));

    //deliver confirmation
    Queue queue = (Queue) confMsg.getJMSReplyTo();
    QueueConnectionFactory fact = (QueueConnectionFactory)
        jndiContext.lookup("java:comp/env/jms/QueueFactory");
    QueueConnection connect = fact.createQueueConnection();
    QueueSession session = connect.createQueueSession(flase,0);

    QueueSession sender = session.createSender(queue);
    ObjectMessage message = session.createObjectMessage();
```

```
      message.setObject(confNum);

      sender.send(message);

      connect.close();

    }
    catch (JMSException ex) {
      ex.printStackTrace();
    }

  }
```

3. Add this member variable to the message-driven bean:

```
Context jndiContext;
```

4. Locate the `ejbRemove()` method and add the following code:

```
public void ejbRemove() {
  jndiContext.close();
  messageDrivenContext = null;
}
```

5. Compile and save your beans.

6. Deploy your newly created beans to your application server container.

Creating the JMS Client

The `SimpleMessageClient` sends messages to the queue that the `ConfirmationProcessor` listens to. The client starts out by locating the connection factory and queue. The following steps are required to create this client:

1. Create a JMS client application. The following framework is required to implement a runnable class:

```
package com.sams.chalktalk.client;

public class Untitled1 {
  public static void main(String[] args) {
  }
}
```

2. Implement the connection to JMS. The following code implements the connection to JMS and the message to register for a class:

```
package com.sams.chalktalk.client;

import javax.naming.*;
import javax.jms.*;

public class SimpleMessageClient {
  public static void main(String[] args) {
    Context cntx = null;
    QueueConnectionFactory qcf = null;
    QueueConnection qcon = null;
    QueueSession qses = null;
    Queue q = null;
    QueueSender qs = null;
    MapMessage message = null;


    if ((args.length < 1)) {
      System.out.println("Usage: MessageClient QueueName");
    }

    try {

      //Establish Connection
      cntx = new InitialContext();

      qcf = (QueueConnectionFactory)cntx.lookup(
          "java:comp/env/QueueConnectionFactory");

      q = (Queue)cntx.lookup(args[0]);

      qcon = qcf.createQueueConnection();
      qses = qcon.createQueueSession(false,Session.AUTO_ACKNOWLEDGE);

      qs = qses.createSender(q);

      //Create Message
      message = qses.createMapMessage();

      message.setInt("StudentID",100);
      message.setInt("CourseID",30);
```

```
      message.setInt("ScheduleID",15);

      message.setDouble("Price",1700);
      message.setString("CreditCard","1234-1234-1234-1234");
      message.setLong("CreditCardExp",System.currentTimeMillis());

      message.setString("CreditCardType","Visa");

      //Send Message
      qs.send(message);
    }
    catch (NamingException ex) {
      ex.printStackTrace();
    }catch (JMSException ex) {
      ex.printStackTrace();
    }
  }
}
```

3. Save, compile, and run your client application.

Summary

A message-driven bean is a special kind of EJB that acts as a message consumer in the container's JMS messaging system. As with standard JMS message consumers, message-driven beans receive messages from a JMS `Queue` or `Topic` and perform business logic based on the message contents.

EJB deployers create listeners to a `Queue` or `Topic` at deployment time, and the container automatically creates and removes message-driven bean instances as needed to process incoming messages.

Because message-driven beans are implemented as EJBs, they benefit from several key services not available to standard JMS consumers. Most importantly, message-driven bean instances are wholly managed by the EJB container. Using a single message-driven bean class, the container creates multiple EJB instances as necessary to process large volumes of messages concurrently. This stands in contrast to a standard JMS messaging system, where the developer must create a `MessageListener` class that uses a serverwide session pool. The container also provides other standard EJB services to message-driven beans, such as security services and automatic transaction management.

Finally, message-driven beans benefit from the write-once, deploy-anywhere quality of EJBs. Whereas a JMS `MessageListener` is tied to specific session pools, `Queues`, or `Topics`, message-driven beans can be developed independently of available server resources. A message-driven bean's `Queues` and `Topics` are assigned only at deployment time, utilizing resources available on the particular container's instance.

Reflections

- When would I use JMS versus message-driven beans?
- Should I use a `Queue` or a `Topic`?
- Do I need message durability?

25 CORBA

IN THIS CHAPTER

The Common Object Request Broker Architecture (CORBA) is a specification that describes how objects communicate with other objects over a network. The specification provides for vendor and implementation language independence. The Object Management Group (OMG) created and maintains the CORBA specification. OMG has more than 800 members including companies such as 3M, IBM, Citigroup, HP, Sun Microsystems, Fujitsu, Oracle, Bank of America, Chevron, Ford, and Boeing.

The CORBA specification is implemented by many vendors including Borland. Borland's product, Visibroker, is part of the Borland Enterprise Server package and will be used throughout this chapter.

This chapter introduces you to JBuilder's support of CORBA. The following topics will be covered:

- CORBA defined
- Interface Definition Language (IDL)
- Basics of CORBA
- Setting up JBuilder and CORBA
- Building a CORBA server
- Building a CORBA client

CORBA Defined

CORBA defines a specification that allows objects, known as *servants*, to communicate with objects written in different languages running on different platforms. CORBA defines an open standard interface for object communications, language mappings, security, transaction management, naming, and many other services.

Figure 25.1 shows an example of a program on one machine communicating with an object running on another machine. Some obvious problems that come up in this scenario are

- How does a program find an object?
- How does the program communicate with the object?
- How does the program convert parameters to the correct format for the object?
- How does the program handle errors if the object is not running?

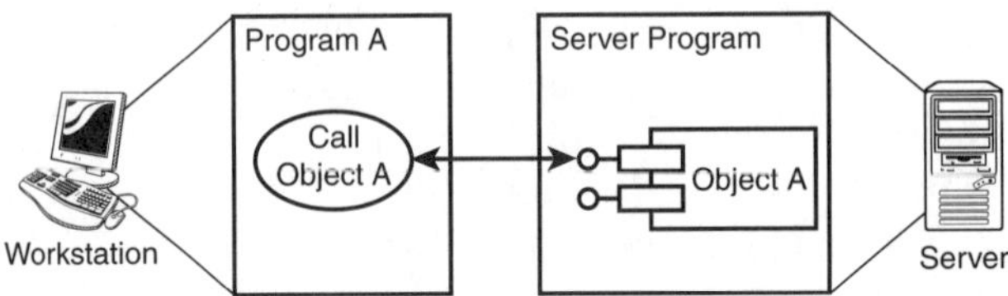

FIGURE 25.1 Sample architecture of object communication.

CORBA answers the question of object interaction by specifying the interfaces to which each part of the system must comply.

How does a program find an object? A program finds an object by locating a CORBA naming service and asking the naming service to provide the location of an object. This enables an application to run regardless of where the object is located.

How does the program communicate with the object? CORBA specifies that an Object Request Broker (ORB) manage the communication between objects. Objects communicate using the Internet Inter-ORB Protocol (IIOP).

How does the program convert parameters to the correct format for the object? CORBA specifies the data type mappings of many languages. CORBA's ORB then marshals the data types from one format to another. This allows a string in one language to be converted to a string in another language. Language mappings exist for COBOL, C, C++, Java, Delphi, and many others.

How does the program handle errors if the object is not running? CORBA specifies the error format for system- and application-level errors. The raising of errors is handled by the ORB libraries. For example, C++ has its own method and standard of raising errors, whereas Java has another method and standard. CORBA bridges these languages by allowing a C++ error to be raised and passed into a Java application.

Other object interoperability models arrived on the scene after CORBA. Microsoft introduced COM, DCOM, and COM+ as object-to-object communication protocols. SUN introduced Remote Method Invocation (RMI) and Enterprise JavaBeans (EJB).

Each of these communication methods is proprietary and has adapters to communicate with CORBA objects. EJB has moved toward full CORBA interoperability by including a CORBA requirement in its specifications.

Despite the flavors of object interoperability models, CORBA remains the only open standard with true vendor and language independence. Figure 25.2 specifies a typical CORBA system and the various components.

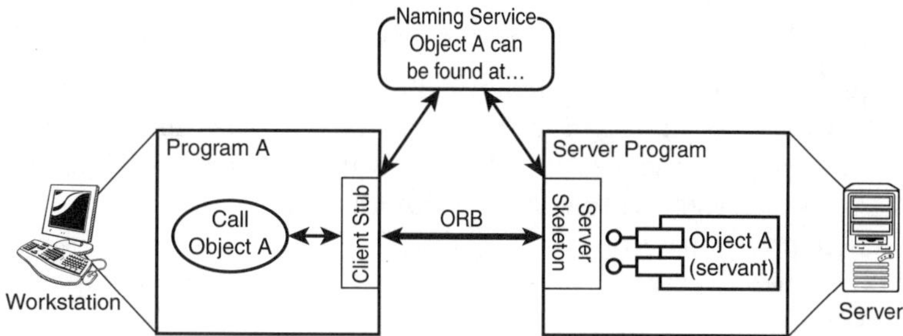

FIGURE 25.2 CORBA view of object communication.

Figure 25.2 identifies an ORB, a client stub, a server skeleton, and a naming service. Each of these components plays an important role in object interoperability.

ORB and IIOP

ORB is a set of communication libraries that enable objects to transparently communicate in a distributed environment. The ORB handles the object communication in process, out of process, and across the network.

The client application making the request does not know the location of the object and in most cases simply makes a standard local method invocation. The ORB libraries take what appears to be a standard local method invocation, marshal the data, locate the object, and invoke the method.

The ORB running on one machine can be different from the ORB running on another machine. These ORBs must have a standard on-the-wire communication protocol so that object references and method invocations can be executed. The on-the-wire protocol is the IIOP.

The OMG group defined a standard communication protocol named the General Inter-ORB Protocol (GIOP). The Internet and growing use of TCP/IP prompted a specialized version of GIOP for the Internet, named IIOP. For an object to communicate across the network with another object, the ORB vendor must support IIOP.

Client Stubs and Server Skeletons

CORBA defines an Interface Definition Language (IDL) that fully describes the public interface of your objects. Using the IDL, client stub and server skeleton code are generated to handle the low-level communication with the ORB libraries, the controlling of network connections, and the marshalling and unmarshalling of data.

Each CORBA vendor provides a utility that takes IDL and generates the client stubs and server skeletons. CORBA vendors differ in the way the code is generated and typically provide their own optimizations.

For example, Visibroker optimizes communication by determining the servant's location. If the servant is running in the same process, local method invocation is used, resulting in huge performance gains. If the servant is running on the same machine in a different process, the interprocess communication method is used, resulting in moderately improved performance. Finally, if Visibroker determines that the object is located on a different server, IIOP is used to communicate with the object resulting in a standard CORBA call.

The client stubs are libraries used by the client application to create client-side proxy objects. The client-side proxy objects transparently invoke methods on the server object. A server object is known as a servant.

The server skeleton provides the servant a framework that provides the CORBA functionality. The server skeleton activates the object, listens for incoming network connections, and handles incoming invocations.

Because much of the CORBA code is automatically generated, your job is to focus on the business implementation of the application or servant.

Object Adapter

An *object adapter (OA)* is the component that manages the servant's interaction with the ORB. The OA generates the object reference and activates the servant. The OA is responsible for managing the method invocations.

In early versions of CORBA, the OA was named the basic object adapter (BOA). Due to the under specifications of the BOA, many vendors implemented the specification differently. The various BOA implementations made the movement of a servant from one vendor to another difficult.

The next release of the specification cleared up the under specification of the BOA and renamed it the portable object adapter (POA). The POA provides control over the creation, lifetime, persistence, and naming of a servant. A single ORB can have multiple POAs created, and each POA can have different policies and servants.

IOR and Naming Service

Finally, a servant is good only if you can locate it. Every servant knows where it is located and how it is listening for connections. Every servant can produce this information as an Interoperability Object Reference (IOR).

The IOR is a standard reference that contains all the information needed to contact and communicate with a servant. The IOR can be written out as a string and is referred to as a *stringified IOR*. The client stubs provide methods to take a stringified object reference and convert it back to an object reference.

Because a CORBA object can create an IOR, the IOR still has to find its way to the client application. One way to accomplish this is to write an IOR to a file and share the file with the client application. Because the IOR can change for an object every time it is run, this is not a very good method. CORBA defined a more elegant solution with its naming service.

The naming service is a hierarchical naming graph that gives a client application the capability to find and bind to a servant. The naming service defined by the CORBA specification can be difficult to use, and many vendors have created much easier naming service implementations.

For example, Visibroker includes support for a naming service called OSAgent. OSAgent support is provided by the stub and skeleton libraries generated by Visibroker. OSAgent runs on a machine and provides a flat naming space. The servants automatically locate and register with the OSAgent using a UDP broadcast. The client applications issue a bind method call that finds the OSAgent on the network and asks for a servant. The OSAgent returns the object reference to the client application.

NOTE

An IOR contains information regarding the IP and port address where a server is running. If you move that server to a new machine or port, a new IOR file would be needed to locate the server.

A naming service allows the dynamic registration of an IOR making up-to-date IOR files unnecessary. The only problem is locating the naming service! After you figure out how to boot strap the naming service, everything gets much easier. OSAgent uses UDP broadcast. Other naming services provide alternate methods.

The following high-level events take place between a Visibroker client application, a Visibroker servant, and the OSAgent naming service:

1. Start the OSAgent service.
2. Start the servant.

3. Servant broadcasts the local subnet to find the OSAgent.
4. The first OSAgent to respond is chosen as the OSAgent for that servant.
5. The servant registers its server name with the OSAgent.
6. Servant sits in a loop waiting for activation by the portable object adapter.
7. Client application begins and broadcasts the local subnet to find the OSAgent.
8. The first OSAgent to respond is chosen as the OSAgent for the client application.
9. The client application invokes a method on the servant.
10. The client application asks the OSAgent for the object reference to the servant.
11. The OSAgent returns the object reference directly or through a chain of OSAgent to OSAgent calls.
12. The client application binds to the object reference and invokes the method.
13. The portable object adapter activates the servant and invokes the method. The results are returned to the client application.
14. The client application can continue to use this object without further need of the OSAgent.

Much of the magic in the communication between a client application and a servant is hidden in the client stubs and server skeletons. The separation of this plumbing code and the business logic makes programming with CORBA a snap!

Interface Definition Language (IDL)

IDL provides the public interface contract made between the servant and the applications accessing the servant. IDL is essential to creating a CORBA object that can be accessed from any language on any platform. The actual IDL file is a text file that JBuilder recognizes based on its .IDL file extension.

IDL models the public interface using a defined set of data types and structures. There are no programming statements or variable definitions in IDL. After the public interface has been created in IDL, an IDL compiler takes the IDL and generates client stubs and server skeletons in your language of choice. The word *compiler* in IDL compiler is misleading. The IDL compiler generates files that take the IDL file and generate the client stubs and server skeleton code. No real "compiling" is done in IDL, just file creation. IDL mimics the syntax of C++ by using curly braces, escape identifiers, and comments.

The vendor of your IDL compiler generates the core client stubs and server skeletons using its implementation of the CORBA specification. This means that the implementation of one vendor's client stubs is not identical to the client stubs generated by another vendor. The client stubs will have the same class names and public interfaces, but the implementation will vary by vendor.

Visibroker's IDL compiler is `idl2java` and can be found in the Borland Enterprise Server directory in the bin subdirectory. The IDL compiler for other CORBA servers can be set up in JBuilder. The "Setting Up JBuilder and CORBA" section that appears later in this chapter explains how to set up other CORBA servers.

IDL provides a number of keywords that are used to construct the definition of a public interface. IDL is a case-sensitive language where all the keywords are in lowercase. The module and interface keywords represent the grouping of objects and the objects themselves.

The IDL keyword `interface` represents a CORBA object. A group of IDL interfaces can be placed in an IDL module. The IDL keyword `module` acts as a container or namespace for the IDL interfaces. Listing 25.1 is an example IDL file.

LISTING 25.1 Sample IDL file (course.idl)

```
module ChalkTalk {

typedef sequence<string> CourseName;

  interface CourseData {
    string getCourseList(inout CourseName names);
  };
};
```

When the IDL file in Listing 25.1 is compiled, it results in the generation of many Java files. These files are explained in the following section "Basics of CORBA."

The `module` statement specifies the name of a Java package that contains the interfaces defined in IDL. Within the scope of the module statement, interfaces and data types can be defined.

In Listing 25.1, the module name generates a Java package named `ChalkTalk`. All the interfaces and data types defined within the module will be placed in the `ChalkTalk` package.

The `ChalkTalk` package contains a new data type named `CourseNames` that consists of a sequence of strings. A *sequence* is a one-dimensional array that may or may not be bounded. A sequence is mapped to a Java array with the same name. The `ChalkTalk` package also contains an interface named `CourseData` and a method called `getCourseList`.

The interface statement in IDL maps to a Java class name. The interface statement contains the data types and method signatures defined within that interface's scope.

In Listing 25.1, the interface `CourseData` maps to a Java class named `CourseData`. The Java class `CourseData` contains a method called `getCourseList` that returns a string and passes the data type `CourseName` as input and output.

Every method definition must contain a return type, method name, parameter direction, parameter data type, and parameter name. The format of an IDL method signature is defined as

```
<return type> methodName( direction datatype name, direction datatype name, ...)
```

The *`return type`* is a valid data type, which includes user-defined data types. Methods are implemented as blocking, and therefore a method call waits until the object returns. IDL does make provisions for nonblocking method calls through the use of the `oneway` modifier.

The direction represents the flow of the parameters. In Java, parameters are passed by value. Therefore, to change the reference of a parameter, support files are generated by the IDL compiler. Table 25.1 identifies the direction values.

TABLE 25.1 Direction Values

Direction	Definition
`in`	The data is being passed from the client to the server.
`out`	The data is being passed from the server to the client.
`inout`	The data is being passed from the client to the server and from the server to the client.

The valid data types include user-defined data types and basic data types. The basic data types are mapped to the Java data types. Table 25.2 shows the mapping of IDL data types to Java data types.

TABLE 25.2 Basic Data Types and Java Mapping

IDL Data Type	Java Data Type	Definition
`boolean`	`boolean`	Standard `boolean` values of true and false.
`char`	`char`	In IDL, `char` is an 8-bit value, and in Java a `char` is a 16-bit value. Java supports Unicode natively, which is a 16-bit character set. If a Java `char` exceeds the 8-bit value, a CORBA data conversion exception is thrown.
`wchar`	`char`	IDL appended the specification to include Unicode and a 16-bit character data type. An IDL `wchar` maps directly to a Java `char`.

TABLE 25.2 Continued

IDL Data Type	Java Data Type	Definition
octet	byte	An octet is an 8-bit value mapped to a Java byte.
string	java.lang.String	In IDL, a string is a sequence of 8-bit character values that may be bounded. In Java, the java.lang.String represents a 16-bit sequence of characters. Similar to char, if a Java string exceeds the acceptable range of the IDL string, a CORBA exception will be thrown.
wstring	java.lang.String	IDL appended the specification to include Unicode and therefore wide strings. A wide string is directly mapped to a Java string. An IDL wide string can be bounded in length. If a Java string exceeds the IDL bounded string length, a CORBA exception will be thrown.
short	short	An IDL short is a signed 16-bit value. In Java, a short is a signed 16-bit value.
unsigned short	short	An IDL unsigned short is an unsigned 16-bit value. All IDL numeric values can be signed or unsigned. In Java, all numeric values are signed. A developer must exercise caution when dealing with unsigned values.
long	int	An IDL long represents a 32-bit value. In Java, an int represents a 32-bit integer. All IDL numeric values can be signed or unsigned. In Java, all numeric values are signed. A developer must exercise caution when dealing with unsigned values.
long long	long	An IDL long long is a 64-bit value. In Java, a long is a 64-bit value. All IDL numeric values can be signed or unsigned. In Java, all numeric values are signed. A developer must exercise caution when dealing with unsigned values.
float	float	An IDL float is identical to a Java float.
double	double	An IDL double is identical to a Java double.

IDL provides constructs for handling enumerations, structures, unions, arrays, and user type definitions. Many resources provide more complete information on IDL. For example, CORBA and IDL are part of the OMG standards and can be found at www.omg.org.

Basics of CORBA

After the interface definition file has been created for a CORBA object, the IDL compiler generates the client stubs and server skeletons.

A single IDL interface results in at least seven Java class files being created. These files are never edited and can be regenerated anytime the IDL is modified. The files make up the client stub, server skeleton, helper methods, operations, holder classes, tie class, and interface definitions. The classes are stored in the hierarchy defined by the module statement in the IDL file.

For example, Listing 25.1 identifies the module `ChalkTalk`, a sequence of strings named `CourseName`, and the interface `CourseData`. Table 25.3 lists the files that will be generated from the IDL file in Listing 25.1.

TABLE 25.3 Generated Files for Listing 25.1

Filename	Description
CourseDataStub.java	Client stub code that manages the communications with the servant.
CourseData.java	Declares the `CourseData` interface.
CourseDataHelper.java	The *xxx*Helper.java class provides helper utilities to bind the object, narrow references, read object, and write object routines.
CourseDataHolder.java	Java supports pass-by value method calls. The *xxx*Holder.java class provides methods for implementing pass-by reference calls in Java.
CourseDataOperations.java	Defines the method signatures based on the IDL file.
CourseDataPOA.java	Server skeleton code that manages the creation and invocation made on the servant.
CourseDataPOATie.java	Server skeleton code that implements the Tie mechanism. The Tie concept is outside the scope of this chapter.
CourseNameHelper.java	Because the IDL defines `CourseName` as a sequence of strings, the `Helper` methods provide serialization of the sequence.
CourseNameHolder.java	Because the IDL defines `CourseName` as a sequence of strings, the `Holder` method makes it possible to pass the array by reference.

Because an IDL file can have multiple interfaces defined, it generates multiple Java class files. The generated files are not modified and are simply referenced when the servant and client applications are created.

After the IDL files have been generated, the server class extends from the portable object adapter (POA) class file. The server class implements the public method call and any constructors that are required.

For example, take the IDL in Listing 25.1. The IDL file creates a `CourseData` interface with the `getCourseList` method. When the IDL is compiled, the files listed in Table 25.3 are generated. The actual implementation of the `getCourseList` method is written in a class that extends from the `CourseDataPOA` class. The typical convention for this class name would be `CourseDataImpl`.

The client application creates the client stub and invokes methods. The method invocations are translated into the appropriate CORBA calls. The typical client application must initialize the ORB libraries, locate the servant, cast the servant to the correct interface definition, and then invoke the method calls.

For example, a client application wants to call the `getCourseList` method on the `CourseData` servant. The client application creates the client stub using the `CourseData` interface. The `CourseDataHelper` class is used to bind the `CourseData` interface to the servant. The `bind` method uses a naming server to locate the servant and bind the interface to the servant. After the interface is bound to a servant, the method `getCourseList` is invoked like a typical method.

The latter sections of this chapter about building a CORBA client and building a CORBA server demonstrate how JBuilder simplifies the building of CORBA client and server applications.

Setting Up JBuilder and CORBA

To enable CORBA support in JBuilder, you must first choose a CORBA ORB product. JBuilder provides out-of-the-box support for Visibroker and Orbix CORBA products. JBuilder Enterprise Edition includes Visibroker as part of the Enterprise Server AppServer Edition.

To set up and enable CORBA support in JBuilder, go to the Tools menu and select the Enterprise Setup menu choice. Figure 25.3 shows the Enterprise Setup dialog box with the CORBA tab selected.

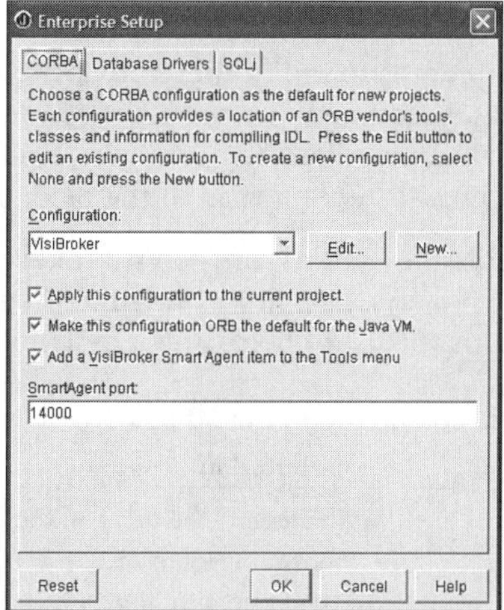

FIGURE 25.3 Enterprise Setup dialog box.

The Enterprise Setup dialog box allows you to choose the ORB vendor using the Configuration field. The dialog box also presents the options in Table 25.4.

TABLE 25.4 CORBA Configuration Options

Option	Description
Apply this configuration to the current project	The current project settings will be modified with the selected configuration.
Make this configuration ORB the default for the Java VM	Modifies the orb.properties file and sets the default ORB class for the Java VM. If you get an error after selecting this option, you may not have rights to change the orb.properties file. Please consult your security administrator.
Add a Visibroker Smart Agent item to the Tools menu	If the selected configuration is Visibroker, you can add the Smart Agent product to the Tools menu. This option is disabled for non-Visibroker products.
SmartAgent port	Sets the port of the local Smart Agent. If the port is changed, the Smart Agent must be stopped and restarted.

NOTE

If you are working on a network with other users of JBuilder, you might want to change the Smart Agent port. By using a different port number, you reduce the risk of activating an object running on another machine. For example, if you are one of several developers working on the same object, make sure that you are activating your copy of the object and not a copy running on another machine.

If you cannot find your ORB vendor in the dialog box, you must create it using the New button. If the ORB vendor is found in the drop-down list but it is installed in a different location, you may need to edit its configuration settings. Figure 25.4 shows the Edit Configuration dialog box. The New Configuration dialog box is identical to the Edit Configuration dialog box except that all the fields are editable and blank.

In Figure 25.4, the only editable options for the Visibroker configuration are Path for ORB tools and Library for projects. In a new configuration example, all the fields are editable. Table 25.5 contains the list of fields and a description of their function.

TABLE 25.5 Fields on Edit Configuration Dialog Box

Field	Description
Name for this configuration	Represents the name in the Configuration drop-down box shown in Figure 25.3.
Path for ORB tools	The location of the ORB vendor's tools. In particular, this is needed for the IDL compiler and the Smart Agent tools.

TABLE 25.5 Continued

Field	Description
Library for projects	These are the necessary library files for the ORB to run. The library is chosen from the list of libraries.
IDL compiler command	The command needed to execute the IDL compiler.
Command option for output directory	The IDL compiler option required to redirect the generated server skeleton and client stub files to a new location.

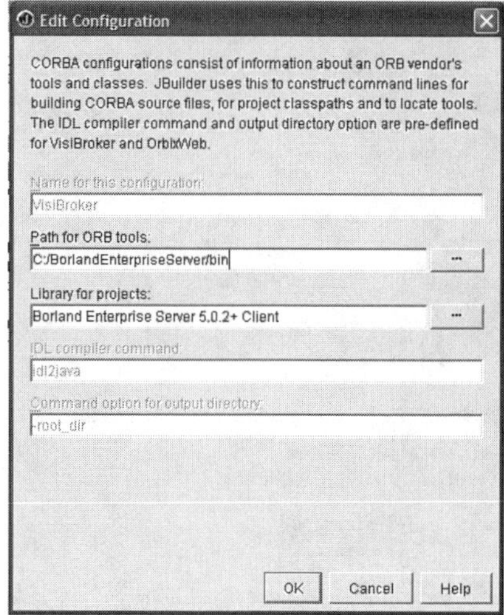

FIGURE 25.4 Edit Configuration of a CORBA vendor.

After the CORBA vendor has been selected and set up, the Object Gallery should contain a CORBA tab, and the items should be enabled. Figure 25.5 shows the CORBA tab from the Object Gallery. The Object Gallery can be displayed by selecting File, New from the menu.

The CORBA tab provides different CORBA items used to create a CORBA application. Table 25.6 explains the different CORBA items.

TABLE 25.6 CORBA Items in the Object Gallery

CORBA Item	Description
Sample IDL	Creates an IDL file based on a template file. It is a quick way to get started with writing your own IDL file.
CORBA Client Interface	Takes an existing IDL file and generates a basic CORBA client application.
CORBA Server Interface	Takes an existing IDL file and generates the implementation skeleton for a basic CORBA server class based on a selected interface.

TABLE 25.6 Continued

CORBA Item	Description
HTML CORBA Client	Takes an existing IDL file and generates a basic CORBA HTML client application using Java Server Pages (JSP).
CORBA Server Application	Takes an existing IDL file and generates a default server application for all the interfaces. Logging and CORBA object monitoring code is written in the server application.

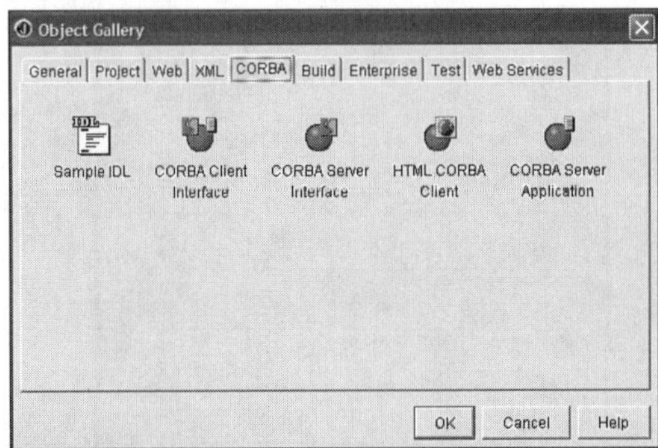

FIGURE 25.5 CORBA tab in the Object Gallery.

Building a CORBA Server

When building a server application, time and energy must be spent on designing the public interface or API. The public interface is the contract between the server application and all applications using the server. If the public interface is changed, all applications using that interface will now be broken. Therefore, care must be taken in designing a suitable interface.

NOTE

It is common practice to maintain compatibility with original interfaces while providing new functionality through extensions of the original interface.

For example, new functionality and values are available for an interface named `getCreditScore`. Instead of modifying the original interface, a new interface is created named `getCreditScoreEx`. This allows existing applications to function while new applications can take advantage of the extended capabilities.

The steps in creating a CORBA server are

1. Define the interface in an IDL file.
2. Compile the interface into server skeleton files.
3. Implement a server using a CORBA wizard.
4. Start the naming service.
5. Start the CORBA server.
6. Validate that the CORBA server is running.

Defining the Interface in IDL

Imagine that you are writing a credit scoring system that takes your name and returns a credit score. The credit score could be retrieved from a database, an elaborate set of calculations, or in our example, from a random number generator.

The sample IDL for this interface is shown in Listing 25.2.

LISTING 25.2 Credit Rating/Scoring Interface (SearchDatabase.IDL)

```
module dbCorba {

  interface CreditRating {
    short getCreditScore(in string name, out long creditscore);
  };
};
```

Listing 25.2 creates a global namespace named `dbCorba` with an interface named `CreditRating`. There is one method for the interface `CreditRating` named `getCreditScore`. The method parameters are an input variable of type `string` that contains a person's name and an output variable of type `long` named `creditscore` that returns the person's score. The method's success is returned as a short integer.

Compiling the Interface into Server Skeleton Files

JBuilder is aware of files with a .IDL extension and automatically calls the `idl2java` compiler. The `idl2java` compiler generates the client stub and server skeleton files from the IDL file.

Prior to making the IDL file, the project properties should be checked to verify that the IDL compiler has been set up. Figure 25.6 displays the Project Properties dialog box that appears when you choose Project, Project Properties from the menu.

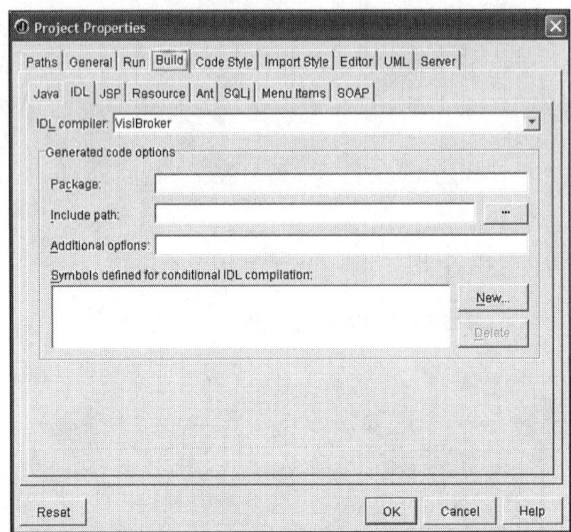

FIGURE 25.6 Project Properties Build tab and IDL sub-tab.

Figure 25.6 displays the Build tab and the IDL sub-tab. The IDL sub-tab allows you to set the IDL compiler and additional options. The IDL compiler drop-down box displays the different CORBA servers that JBuilder has been set up to recognize. The Visibroker IDL compiler has been chosen.

Under the Generated code options section, there are four additional fields:

- The Package field allows you to specify a package name to prefix the generated files.
- The Include path specifies the location where the IDL compiler looks to find included IDL files.
- The Additional options can be used to set additional command-line arguments for the IDL compiler.
- Finally, the Symbols defined for conditional IDL compilation option is used to set values for conditional compilation.

Additional IDL settings can be made by selecting the IDL file, right-clicking to bring up the pop-up menu, and selecting the Properties menu choice. The IDL properties dialog box in Figure 25.7 appears when the IDL compiler in Project Properties is set to Visibroker.

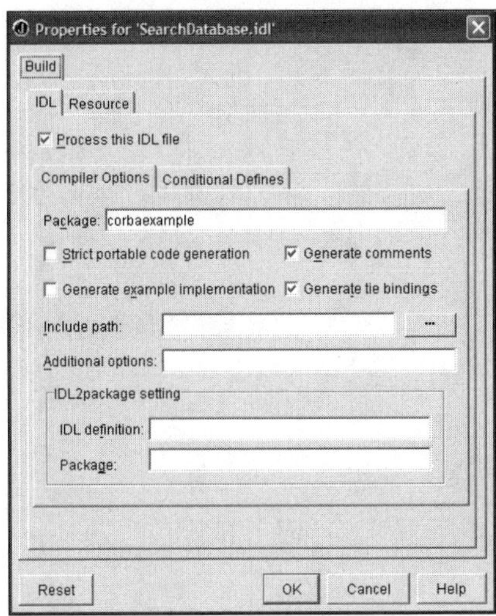

FIGURE 25.7 Visibroker IDL properties.

The IDL properties box allows you to set additional IDL compilation options. These options are listed in Table 25.7.

TABLE 25.7 Visibroker IDL Properties Tab on an IDL File

Option	Description
Process this IDL file	By checking this option, the IDL file will be compiled. If this option is not checked, the IDL file will not be recompiled.
Package	This field specifies the prefix to the IDL file's module statement.
Strict portable code generation	Forces all the code generation to be compliant with the CORBA specifications. Visibroker-specific enhancements are removed from the code.
Generate example implementation	An example class is generated.
Generate comments	Comments are generated in the code.
Generate tie bindings	Generates the TIE set of classes.
Include path	Contains the path location of IDL files included in the project's IDL file.
Additional options	Allows the user to enter additional command-line options.
IDL definition	Allows scope name substitution in the generated code.
Package	The Java package for the IDL definition settings.
Conditional Defines	Allows you to set conditional defines for the IDL preprocessor.

Figure 25.8 is displayed when the IDL compiler is set to Orbix.

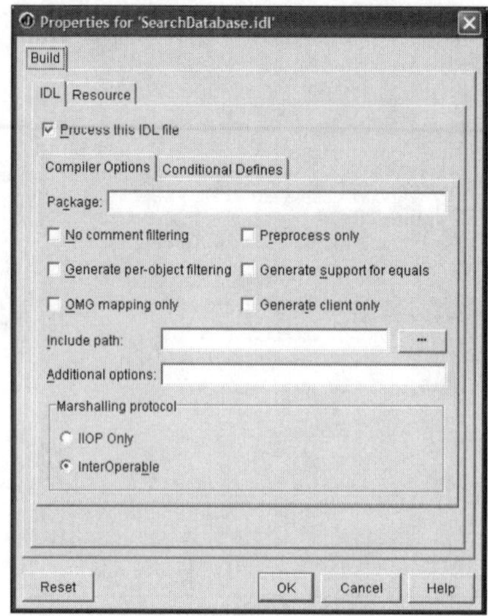

FIGURE 25.8 Orbix IDL properties.

Table 25.8 explains the different Orbix options available.

TABLE 25.8 Orbix IDL Properties

Option	Description
Process this IDL file	By checking this option, the IDL file will be compiled. If this option is not checked, the IDL file will not be recompiled.
Package	This field specifies the prefix to the IDL file's module statement.
No comment filtering	Determines whether comments should be included in the generated code. Selected means comment will be generated.
Generate per-object filtering	Determines whether per-object filtering code will be generated. Selected means that code will be generated.
OMG mapping only	Select this option to remove all vendor-specific code. Generate code compliant with the CORBA specifications.
Preprocess only	Only run the IDL preprocessor.
Generate support for equals	Adds the `equals()` method in the generated code.
Generate client only	Generates the client stubs only. The server skeleton code is not generated.
Include path	Contains the path location of IDL files included in the project's IDL file.
Additional options	Allows the user to enter additional command-line options.
Marshalling protocol: IIOP only	Only generate objects with IIOP communication protocol.
Marshalling protocol: InterOperable	Generate objects with IIOP communication protocol and with OrbixWeb-specific protocol.
Conditional defines	Allows you to set conditional defines for the IDL preprocessor.

After the IDL settings have been made, the IDL file needs to be compiled. To compile the IDL file, right-click on the IDL file in the Project pane. From the pop-up menu, select the *make* menu choice. The IDL file compiles and generates the client sub and server skeleton files. These files can be displayed by expanding the IDL file in the Project pane.

Implementing a Server Using a CORBA Wizard

JBuilder provides a wizard to generate a CORBA server application. Select File, New from the JBuilder menu to bring up the Object Gallery. On the Object Gallery, select CORBA Server Application located on the CORBA tab. After you click OK, the CORBA Server Application Wizard begins with Figure 25.9.

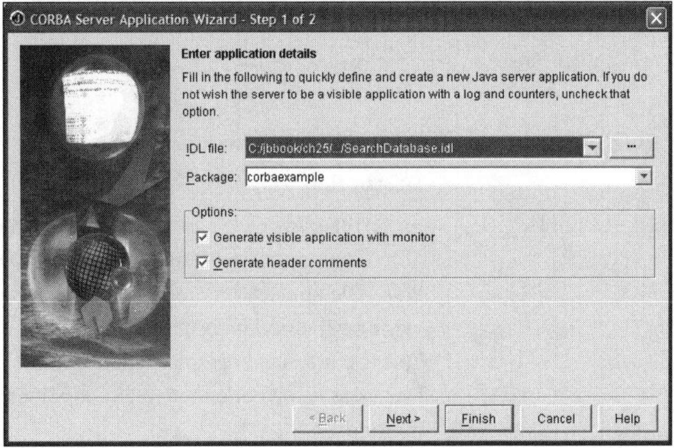

FIGURE 25.9 CORBA Server Application Wizard—Step 1 of 2.

The JBuilder Wizard allows you to select the IDL file and package location for the generated server application. The JBuilder options provide a unique logging and monitoring system. The logging and monitoring system records all method invocations and object creations for the generated CORBA server. This option can be disabled. Finally, the server application code can include header comments.

The final step in the wizard allows you to create a new runtime configuration. Figure 25.10 displays the last step in the CORBA server application creation.

After Finish is selected, the wizard generates the files listed in Table 25.9.

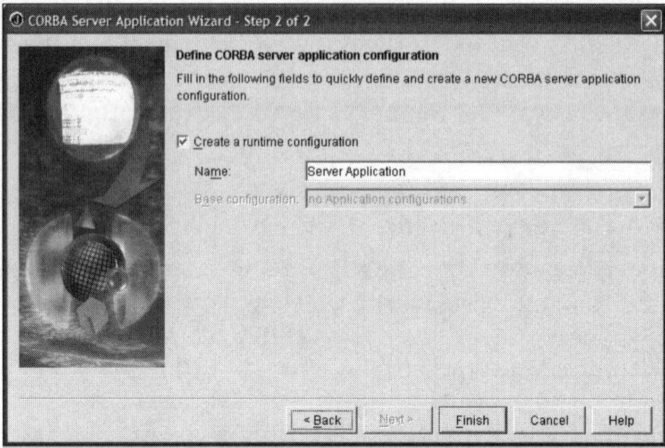

FIGURE 25.10 CORBA Server Application Wizard—Step 2 of 2.

TABLE 25.9 CORBA Server Application Wizard Generated Files

Filename	Description
dbCorbaAppGenFileList.html	An HTML page with a listing of all the generated files.
dbCorbaServerApp.java	The main server application file that creates the servant and POA. The application registers the servant with the POA and waits for method invocations.
CreditRatingImpl.java	This is the actual implementation of the `CreditRating` interface. This is the code that will be modified to implement our methods.
ServerFrame.java, ServerMonitor.java, ServerMonitorPage.java, ServerResources.java	These files make up the monitoring and logging functionality for the server application.

The wizard has generated everything needed to make the CORBA server application work. The `CreditRatingImpl.java` is the only class that will be modified so that the method `getCreditScore` is implemented according to our rules.

The `getCreditScore` method in the CreditRatingImpl.java file will be modified to Listing 25.3. The modified lines are in bold.

LISTING 25.3 `getCreditScore` Method in CreditRatingImpl.java

```
public short getCreditScore(String name,
➥org.omg.CORBA.IntHolder creditscore)  {
   Random rnd = new Random();
   ServerMonitor.log("(" + _name + ") CreditRatingImpl.java getCreditScore()");
```

LISTING 25.3 Continued

```
    creditscore.value = rnd.nextInt();
    return (short)0;
  }
```

The CORBA Server Application Wizard generates everything including the method signature and sample code. To complete the server, you have to write the specific implementation for your methods.

Starting the Naming Service

If you are using Visibroker, select the Visibroker Smart Agent from the Tools main menu. The Visibroker Smart Agent runs like a typical Java application in the JBuilder environment.

The naming service must be started prior to starting the server application. If a naming service is not present, the server application appears to run although it could never register itself with a naming service.

Starting the CORBA Server

To start the CORBA server, make sure that the naming service is running. After the naming service is running, select Run, Run Project from the menu. Figure 25.11 displays the Server Monitor form created when the server is running.

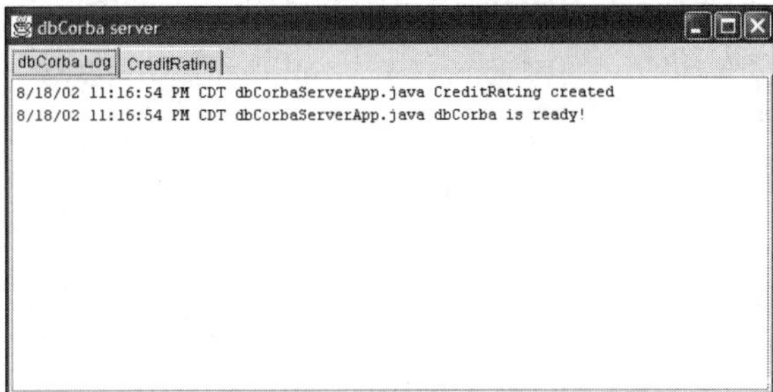

FIGURE 25.11 Server Monitor and Log dialog box.

Validating That the CORBA Server Is Running

In Visibroker, you can confirm that the CORBA server is up and running. Visibroker provides an `osfind` command that locates the Visibroker Smart Agent and discovers the server objects that have registered with it.

Figure 25.12 shows the command screen with the `osfind` command being executed. Notice that the server registered its name as the interface name with a _poa suffix.

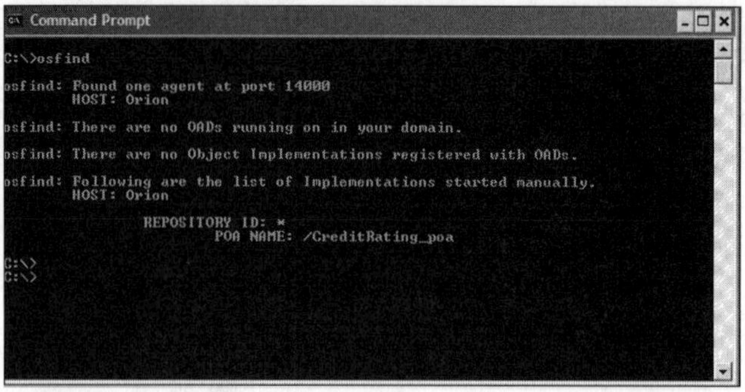

```
C:\>osfind

osfind: Found one agent at port 14000
        HOST: Orion

osfind: There are no OADs running on in your domain.

osfind: There are no Object Implementations registered with OADs.

osfind: Following are the list of Implementations started manually.
        HOST: Orion

                REPOSITORY ID: *
                        POA NAME: /CreditRating_poa

C:\>
C:\>
```

FIGURE 25.12 `osfind` command locates the `CreditRating_poa` server.

If you are connected to a network, the `osfind` program attempts to locate all Visibroker Smart Agents on the subnet. If other Visibroker Smart Agents are running across the network on the same port, `osfind` returns the registered server objects.

JBuilder also comes with the Visibroker console application. The Visibroker console application shows the different Smart Agents and the CORBA objects they are running. The Visibroker console application is in the Visibroker bin subdirectory.

Building a CORBA Client

Building a CORBA client is just as easy as building a CORBA server. JBuilder provides wizards that generate client application code. The typical steps in creating a CORBA client application are

1. Initialize the CORBA ORB.
2. Create an instance of the CORBA client stub.
3. Locate the CORBA server.
4. Bind the CORBA server to the client stub.
5. Call methods on the CORBA client stub.

The steps in calling a method on a CORBA server always involve creating a client stub, locating the CORBA server, and binding to the CORBA server. This code is necessary for every CORBA server that is needed.

JBuilder simplifies CORBA client code by providing a wizard that creates a wrapper class around the client stub files. The wrapper provides the ORB initialization, locating the server, and binding to the server. Using the JBuilder wizards, the modified steps in creating a CORBA client application are

1. Generate a CORBA client class wrapper.
2. Create an instance of the CORBA client class wrapper.
3. Call methods on the CORBA client class wrapper.

The class wrapper can be created two different ways. The first method creates the CORBA client interface using the Object Gallery. The second method is the Use CORBA Interface menu option under the Wizards menu. The second method takes the process a step further by creating an instance variable and adding the imports to your client application.

Generating a CORBA Client Class Wrapper

A CORBA client class wrapper encapsulates the client stubs from the IDL and adds the ORB initialization and the binding of the class to the server object.

To generate the client class wrapper, select File, New from the menu. The Object Gallery is displayed. Select the CORBA Client Interface from the CORBA tab on the Object Gallery. The CORBA Client Interface selection starts the wizard shown in Figure 25.13.

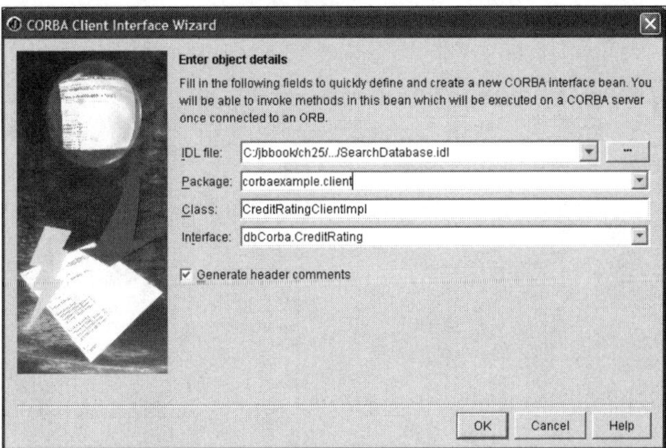

FIGURE 25.13 CORBA Client Interface Wizard.

Figure 25.13 contains the fields listed in Table 25.10.

TABLE 25.10 CORBA Client Interface Fields

Field	Description
IDL file	The location of the IDL file that contains the interface to be wrapped
Package	The name of the package the client wrapper class belongs to
Class	The name of the class that will be generated from the IDL file and the selected interface
Interface	The name of the interface in the IDL file that is to be generated into a class
Generate header comments	Adds the project information settings to the generated class file

The code in Listing 25.4 is generated to encapsulate the interface described in Listing 25.2.

LISTING 25.4 Generated Code: CreditRatingClientImpl.java

```
package corbaexample.client;

import java.awt.*;
import org.omg.CORBA.*;

public class CreditRatingClientImpl {
  private boolean bInitialized = false;
  private dbCorba.CreditRating _creditRating;
  private com.borland.cx.OrbConnect orbConnect1;
  private String _name = "CreditRating";

  public CreditRatingClientImpl() {
    try  {
      jbInit();
    }
    catch (Exception ex) {
      ex.printStackTrace();
    }
  }

  private void jbInit() throws Exception {
  }

  public boolean init() {
    if (!bInitialized) {
      try {
```

LISTING 25.4 Continued

```
        org.omg.CORBA.ORB orb = null;
        if (orbConnect1 != null) {
          orb = orbConnect1.initOrb();
        }
        if (orb == null) {
          orb = org.omg.CORBA.ORB.init((String[])null,
                                       System.getProperties());
        }
        _creditRating = dbCorba.CreditRatingHelper.bind(orb,
                         "/" + _name + "_poa", _name.getBytes());
        bInitialized = true;
      }
      catch (Exception ex) {
        ex.printStackTrace();
      }
    }
    return bInitialized;
  }

  public dbCorba.CreditRating getCorbaInterface() {
    return _creditRating;
  }

  public void setCorbaInterface(dbCorba.CreditRating intf) {
    _creditRating = intf;
  }

  public com.borland.cx.OrbConnect getORBConnect() {
    return orbConnect1;
  }

  public void setORBConnect(com.borland.cx.OrbConnect orbConnect) {
    this.orbConnect1 = orbConnect;
  }

  public short getCreditScore(String name,
               org.omg.CORBA.IntHolder creditscore)  {
    init();
    return _creditRating.getCreditScore(name, creditscore);
  }
}
```

The generated code implements the CORBA interface Bean and creates all the defined methods from the IDL file. Each method calls the `init()` method prior to returning the method call from the client stub. The `init()` method initializes the ORB, locates the server object, and binds a client stub instance to the server.

Creating an Instance of the CORBA Client Class Wrapper

To use the CORBA client class wrapper, you can manually add the imports and instance variable to your client application, or you can select Wizards, Use CORBA Interface from the JBuilder main menu.

The first step is to select the client application file that needs access to the CORBA server. After that is loaded, select Wizards, Use CORBA Interface from the menu. The dialog box shown in Figure 25.14 appears.

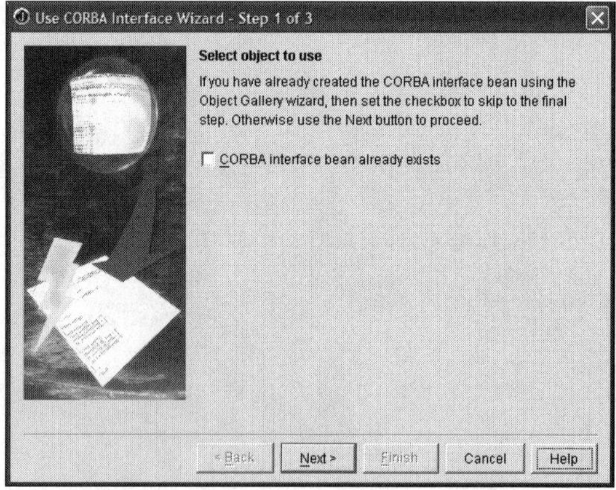

FIGURE 25.14 Use CORBA Interface Wizard—Step 1 of 3.

The Use CORBA Interface Wizard asks you whether the CORBA interface Bean already exists. If the CORBA interface Bean does not exist, the second step in the wizard is identical to Figure 25.13 except that it says Step 2 of 3 in the window title bar.

If the bean is already created, check the option, and the wizard jumps to the final step, shown in Figure 25.15. The final step asks for the class that is the CORBA interface Bean and the field name of the instance variable to create.

NOTE

If you checked the option, the wizard jumps to the final step, and the dialog displays Step 2 of 2. The strange thing about this is that the previous dialog box displayed Step 1 of 3.

Because Step 2 of 3 is skipped with the option checked, JBuilder changes the number of steps from 3 to 2.

If the option is not checked, Figure 25.13 is displayed, and the words Step 2 of 3 are added to the window title bar.

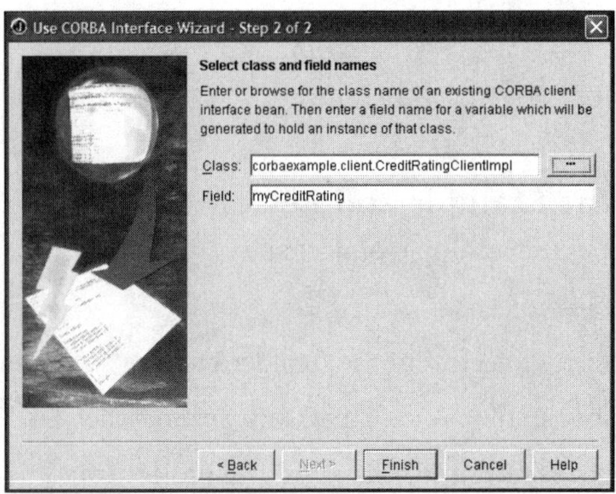

FIGURE 25.15 Use CORBA Interface Wizard—Step 2 of 2.

After you complete the Use CORBA Interface Wizard, the instance variable you defined is added to the class. In addition, the imports are updated to include the CORBA interface Bean's package.

Call Methods on the CORBA Client Class Wrapper

To begin using your CORBA client class wrapper, take the instance variable that was created and use it like any other object. For example, Listing 25.5 shows sample code that calls the `getCreditScore` method of the server object.

LISTING 25.5 Sample Usage of Generated Class Wrapper

```
org.omg.CORBA.IntHolder iData = new org.omg.CORBA.IntHolder();
myCreditRating.getCreditScore("Michael Landy", iData);
```

The first line of code creates the parameters needed to invoke the method. The next line uses the instance variable created with the Use CORBA Interface Wizard and executes the `getCreditScore` method.

In Practice

The "In Practice" lab creates a CORBA server that returns a list of course information. Taking the example application from Chapter 15, "Database Connectivity," the method browseCourses in the CommonOperations.java file calls a CORBA server. The lab covers the following tasks:

1. Create the IDL file.
2. Implement the server code.
3. Implement the client code.
4. Execute the new code.

Step 1: Open the Example and Review the Class

In this step, you open the example project and review the source code file.

To open the example project

1. Select File, Open Project from the JBuilder menu.
2. Locate the jbbook/ch25/swing/ChalkTalk.jpx and click OK.
3. The project opens in the Project pane. The project contains many files. Open the file CommonOperations.java located in the userservices folder.
4. Double-click on the CommonOperations.java. The Content pane displays the file.

Step 2: Locate the Method browseCourses

Search the file and locate the method browseCourses. Listing 25.6 shows the current code for browseCourses.

LISTING 25.6 browseCourses Method

```
public java.util.Collection browseCourses(CourseFilter courseFilter) {
  Vector v = new Vector();

  v.add(
    new CourseData(
      "Introduction to Java",
      "CS211",
      "This course will teach you the fundamentals of Java using JDK 1.4.
➥ Topics include File I/O, AWT and Swing. Student must have a grade
```

LISTING 25.6 Continued

```
➥of C or better in CS202 to register for this course. Students who
➥have obtained a B or higher grade in CS201 may take this class with
➥Instructor's permission. There will be one mid-term and one final
➥exam with one substantial programming assignment.")
      );
    v.add(
      new CourseData(
        "Introduction to JBuilder",
        "CS251",
        "This course will teach you how to use JBuilder to develop Java
➥applications. Topics include developing, JavaBeans, JSPs and
➥Servlets. Student must have a grade of C or better in CS211 to
➥register for this course. There will be one mid-term and one
➥final exam with one substantial programming assignment.")
      );

    return Collections.unmodifiableCollection(v);
  }
```

Notice that this method creates a vector, statically adds data to the vector, and then returns a collection to the calling method.

Step 3: Create the IDL File

1. Add an IDL file to your application by choosing File, New from the main menu. From the Object Gallery, select the Sample IDL on the CORBA tab shown in Figure 25.16. Click OK when ready.

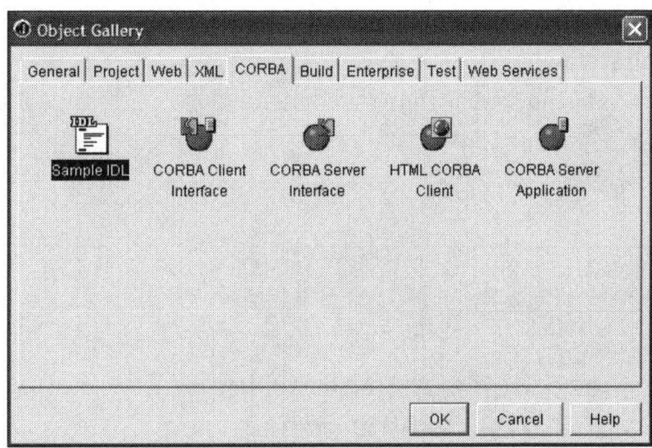

FIGURE 25.16 Sample IDL on the CORBA tab.

2. The Sample IDL Wizard asks for the package and IDL filename. Fill in the fields based on Figure 25.17.

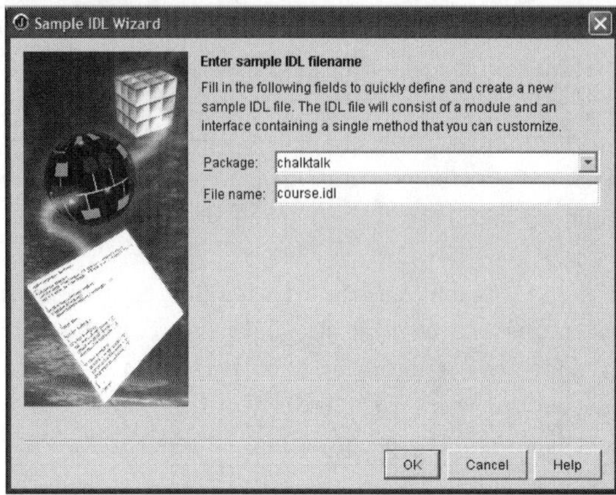

FIGURE 25.17 Sample IDL Wizard.

The Package field should be set to `chalktalk`.

The File name field should be set to course.idl.

3. The course.idl file should be in the Content pane with an example IDL template. Erase the contents of the file and add the code shown in Listing 25.7.

LISTING 25.7 Course.idl File Contents

```
module course {

typedef sequence<string> StringData;

  interface CourseDataCorba {
  string getCourseList(inout StringData names, inout StringData coursenumber,
➥ inout StringData description);
  };
};
```

4. Save the file.
5. Compile the course.idl file by right-clicking on the filename in the Project pane and selecting make from the pop-up menu.

6. The following files will be created under the course.idl file:

   CourseDataCorbaStub.java

   CourseDataCorbaPOA.java

   CourseDataCorba.java

   CourseDataCorbaPOATie.java

   CourseDataCorbaHelper.java

   StringDataHelper.java

   CourseDataCorbaHolder.java

   StringDataHolder.java

   CourseDataCorbaOperations.java

Step 4: Implement the Server Code

Now that the interface has been defined, the server application has to be created. To create the server application, use the CORBA Server Application Wizard:

1. Choose File, New. From the Object Gallery select the CORBA Server Application. Click OK. (Refer to Figure 25.16 for a view of the Object Gallery dialog box.)
2. The CORBA Server Application Wizard in Figure 25.18 is displayed. Set the IDL file to course.idl and the package to `chalktalk`. Finally, check the Generate visible application with monitor and the Generate header comments options. Click Next.

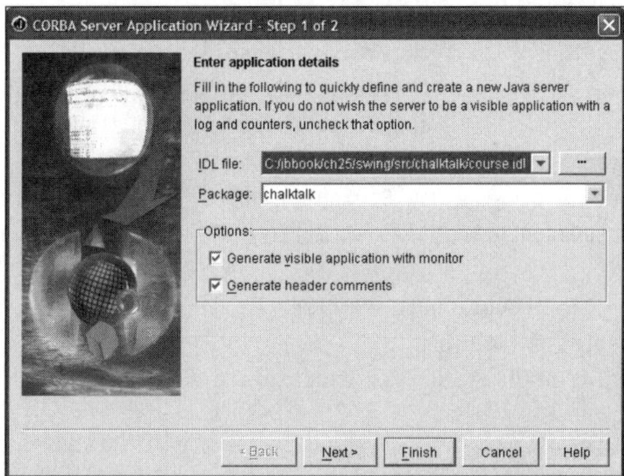

FIGURE 25.18 CORBA Server Application Wizard—Step 1 of 2.

3. The next step in the wizard is to create a runtime configuration. Check the Create a runtime configuration box. Set the name to **`Server Application`** as shown in Figure 25.19.

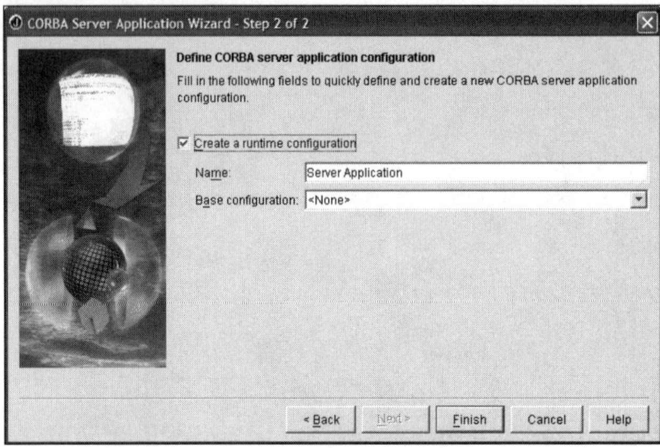

FIGURE 25.19 CORBA Server Application Wizard—Step 2 of 2.

4. Expand the chalktalk.course.server tree in the Project pane.
5. Select the `CourseDataCorbaImpl.java` class. Double-click on the class to load it in the Content pane. This class will hold our server implementation.
6. Locate the method `getCourseList`. Modify the method so that it appears the same as Listing 25.8.

LISTING 25.8 Updated `getCourseList` Method

```
public String getCourseList(chalktalk.course.StringDataHolder names,
                            chalktalk.course.StringDataHolder coursenumber,
                            chalktalk.course.StringDataHolder description)  {
  String sCourse[] = new String[2];
  String sCourseNumber[] = new String[2];
  String sCourseDescription[] = new String[2];

  sCourse[0] = "Introduction to JBuilder";
  sCourseNumber[0] = "CS251";
  sCourseDescription[0] = "Course description is coming from a CORBA Server";

  sCourse[1] = "Introduction to Java";
  sCourseNumber[1] = "CS211";
```

LISTING 25.8 Continued

```
    sCourseDescription[1] = "Intro to Java - Course description
➥ from a CORBA Server";

    names.value = sCourse;
    coursenumber.value = sCourseNumber;
    description.value = sCourseDescription;

    ServerMonitor.log("(" + _name + ") CourseDataCorbaImpl.java
➥ getCourseList()");
    return "";
  }
```

Listing 25.8 creates string arrays and populates them with data. The data could have come from any source. The string arrays are set to the `StringDataHolder` class using the `value` property.

7. Save the file.
8. Choose Tools, Visibroker Smart Agent from the menu. This starts the naming service.
9. Right-click on the courseServerApp.java file and select Run using the Server Application configuration. If you have correctly typed the information, you will see the dialog box shown in Figure 25.20.

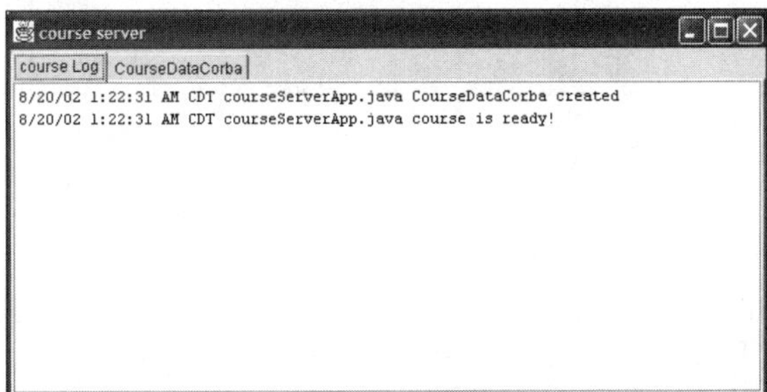

FIGURE 25.20 Course Server is running.

Step 5: Implement the Client Code

In step 2, you reviewed the `browseCourses` method in the `CommonOperations.java` class. The code in this method will be replaced with code to call the new CORBA server.

1. Open the CommonOperations.java file in the Content pane.
2. Select Wizards, Use CORBA Interface from the menu.
3. The Use CORBA Interface Wizard—Step 1 of 3 dialog box is displayed. Make sure that the CORBA interface bean already exists check box is not checked. Click Next.
4. The next dialog box shows Step 2 of 3. Set the field settings to those shown in Figure 25.21.

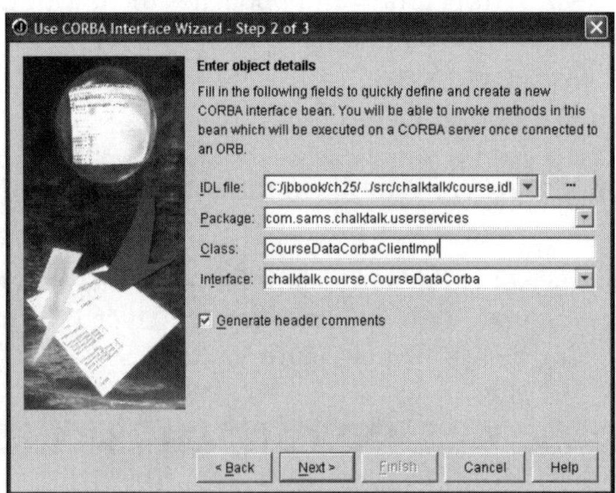

FIGURE 25.21 Use CORBA Interface Wizard—Step 2 of 3.

5. Click Next.
6. The final dialog box for the Use CORBA Interface Wizard appears. The Field value should be set to `myCourseDataCorba` as shown in Figure 25.22.
7. Click Finish.
8. Add the following line to the `import` section of the `CommonOperations.java` class:

```
import chalktalk.course.StringDataHolder;
```

9. Rewrite the `browseCourses` method as shown in Listing 25.9.

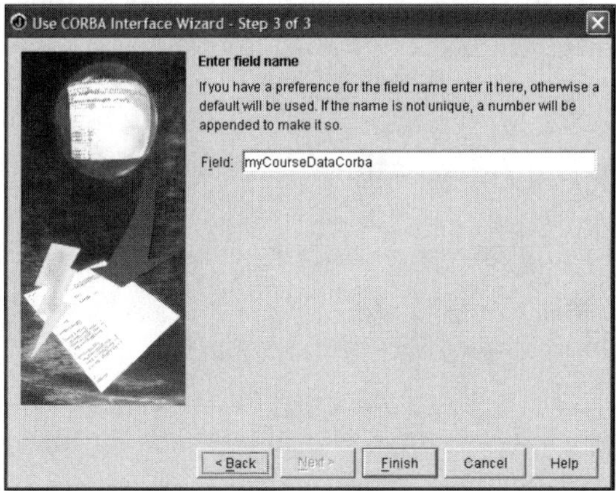

FIGURE 25.22 Use CORBA Interface Wizard—Step 3 of 3.

LISTING 25.9 Updated browseCourses Method

```
public java.util.Collection browseCourses(CourseFilter courseFilter) {
   Vector v = new Vector();
   int x;
   StringDataHolder coursenames = new StringDataHolder();
   StringDataHolder coursenumbers = new StringDataHolder();
   StringDataHolder coursedescriptions = new StringDataHolder();

   // Needed so as not to pass a null pointer (Not CORBA accepted)
   coursenames.value = new String[0];
   coursenumbers.value = new String[0];
   coursedescriptions.value = new String[0];

   myCourseDataCorba.getCourseList(coursenames,coursenumbers,
                                   coursedescriptions);
   for(x=0;x<coursenames.value.length;x++)
   {
     v.add(
       new CourseData(
         coursenames.value[x],
         coursenumbers.value[x],
         coursedescriptions.value[x])
       );
   }

  return Collections.unmodifiableCollection(v);
}
```

The `browseCourses` method has been modified to call the CORBA client wrapper to locate the server object. The data is retrieved from the server object and read into the collections array.

Step 6: Execute the Application

To run the ChalkTalk application, the Visibroker Smart Agent must be running, the course server must be running, and finally the ChalkTalk application must be running.

1. Start the Visibroker Smart Agent. Choose Tools, Visibroker Smart Agent from the menu.
2. Right-click the courseServerApp.java and select Run with the Use Server Application configuration.
3. Choose Run, Run Project from the menu. A Choose Runtime Configuration dialog box is displayed. Select the ChalkTalkClient configuration.
4. From the client application, browse classes. The class description will be coming from the CORBA server.

Summary

This chapter shows how JBuilder's features have been updated to support Visibroker and other CORBA-compliant ORBs. JBuilder makes it easier to take an Interface Definition file and generate code that can be used as a server or a client.

Reflections

- What benefits does CORBA offer?
- How does CORBA benefit n-tier design?
- What situations would make you more likely to choose one distributed technology over another?

26

Debugging Your Enterprise Application

IN THIS CHAPTER

- Remote Debugging Explained
- Setting Up the Debugging Environment
- Debugging a Remote Application
- Cross-Process Breakpoints
- Configuration Settings for Application Servers

As applications become more complex and are distributed across the corporate enterprise, debugging your code becomes more difficult. In Chapter 6, "Debugging," you learned how to debug code running on your local machine. This chapter explores how to debug your code running across the network.

In today's environment, the standard architecture for constructing an application is the n-tier model. The code written to support an n-tier model will use CORBA, Enterprise JavaBeans, or Remote Method Invocation. The code may take advantage of one of these application servers running on a separate machine. Learning how to debug an application running across the network is a necessary skill.

In Java 2, Sun introduced the Java Platform Debugger Architecture (JPDA). JPDA provides the infrastructure needed for debuggers to communicate across the network.

JBuilder implements a JPDA-compliant debugger allowing you to attach and debug an application running on another machine. This chapter explores the remote debugging features of JBuilder. The following topics are covered:

- Remote debugging explained
- Setting up the debugging environment
- Debugging a remote application
- Cross-process breakpoints
- Configuration settings for application servers

Remote Debugging Explained

Remote debugging allows you to debug an application running on another machine. The capability to debug an application across the network is increasingly important with the proliferation of application servers. Remote debugging does not necessarily have to be across the network. The applications could be running on the same machine but in a completely different Java Virtual Machine (JVM). For this chapter, remote debugging will be illustrated as occurring on two separate machines.

An application server typically provides a context and set of services for building distributed applications. For example, application servers provide services to manage database transactions, database resource pooling, and user security rights.

Installing and configuring an application server on every developer's machine would not help because your application runs within the context of the application server. Therefore, to debug your code, you would log operations and review them after the application executed.

Figure 26.1 shows how your application would run inside an application server. Notice how the application code takes advantage of the application server's database pooling and security context.

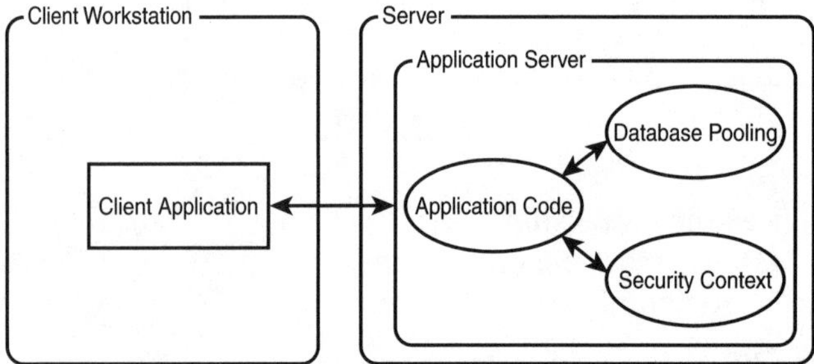

FIGURE 26.1 Application running in application servers.

The need to debug code running in an application server is not the only need for remote debugging. You may need to debug code running on a different platform that uses resources available only on that machine.

In Java 2, Sun addressed the need for remote debugging and introduced the JPDA. The intent of the JPDA is to allow Java debugging tools to be written without regard to platform specifics such as hardware, operating system, and virtual machine implementation.

The JPDA consists of a protocol, two interfaces, and changes to the Java virtual machines. The protocol describes the format of debugging information on the wire.

The Java virtual machine must implement the Java Virtual Machine Debug Interface (JVMDI).

The JDK versions on different machines do not need to match as long as they both implement the JPDA. This allows the application code to be debugged across the network, on different platforms, using different versions of Java.

JBuilder built a JPDA-compliant debugger that meets the specifications on debugging without regard to platform specifics. As discussed in Chapter 6, JBuilder has a powerful debugger where you can set breakpoints, watch variables, and modify values.

Setting Up the Debugging Environment

To support remote debugging, the virtual machine (VM) needs to be passed command-line options to turn on the debugging option for that VM. One VM acts as the server and listens for a debug connection. Another VM acts as a client and connects to the server VM.

To negotiate a debugging connection, the client VM needs to know about the server VM. The command-line options for the VM set up the connection properties. Table 26.1 displays a list of the common command-line options.

TABLE 26.1 Virtual Machine Debug Options

Option	Description
`-classic`	Some VMs may not support this option. This option selects the classic VM as opposed to a Just In Time VM.
`-Xdebug`	Enables debugging in the VM.
`-Xnoagent`	Disables the original debug agent contained in `sun.tools.debug`. The JPDA has its own debug agent.
`-Djava.compiler=NONE`	Disables the JIT compiler. Debugging requires that the JIT compiler be disabled.
`-Xrunjdwp:<sub-options>`	Loads the JPDA implementation. The suboptions control how the debugger works. Table 26.2 explains the suboptions.

NOTE

The VM should have the Just In Time (JIT) compiler disabled. In most cases, this is required for the application to be debugged properly. JDK 1.4.1 now supports full-speed debugging and other new enhancements.

The main part of the debugging setup is contained in the suboptions for the JPDA option `-Xrunjdwp`. The suboptions are name-value pairs separated by commas. Table 26.2 contains the suboptions for the JPDA setup.

```
-Xrunjdwp:name1=value1,name2=value2,...
```

TABLE 26.2 JPDA Suboptions

Option	Description
`transport`	Required. Transport type used in connecting to the debugger application. Possible values are `dt_socket` and `dt_shmem`. `dt_socket` uses TCP/IP to connect to the debugger and is the most versatile. `dt_shmem` uses shared memory, and the reference implementation is currently available on Windows.
`server`	Not required. Default = `n`. If `server` is set to `y`, the application is set to be the server application. This means that the application listens for the debugger to connect. If the `address` option is specified, the debugger connects at that address location; otherwise, the server application prints to the standard out listening address.
`address`	Required if `server` = `n`. If the `server` option is `n`, the `address` option specifies the debugger connection address. If the `server` option is `y`, the address option specifies the server listening address. When the transport is `dt_socket`, the address refers to the host and port number that the application server is listening on. Failure to specify an address causes the application to randomly pick and print out a listening port number. To prevent continuous adjustments to the port number on the client configuration settings, specifying a port address is recommended.
`suspend`	Not required. Default = `y`. If the `suspend` option is `y`, the application will be suspended immediately when it is started. If the `suspend` option is `n`, the application will run until it encounters a breakpoint.

Using the debugging options, you can set up your server environment to run your application in a debug VM. After your server is running in debug mode, only one debugger can be attached to it at any one time.

Debugging a Remote Application

Before you can easily debug remote applications, you must set up your client-side debugging environment. Assuming that you have JBuilder running on the client machine and a JPDA-compliant JDK running on a server, the following processes are necessary:

- Launch the remote application using debug settings.
- Copy the remote application files to the client.

- Set up a runtime configuration for the remote server.
- Set breakpoints in the code.

Launch the Remote Application Using the Debug Setting

If your server is running a JPDA-compliant JDK, the following command line shows a command for starting your server application so that it can be remotely debugged:

```
java -Xdebug -Xnoagent -Djava.compiler=NONE -Xrunjdwp:transport=dt_socket,
➥server=y,address=5000,suspend=n -classpath <CLASSPATH> <MyClass>
```

If your server is running in JBuilder, add the following options to the VM parameters in the runtime configuration settings:

```
-classic -Xdebug -Xnoagent -Djava.compiler=NONE -Xrunjdwp:transport=dt_socket,
```

The sample command-line and parameter settings start the Java VM in debug mode. The application `MyClass` is identified as the server application, and the debugger listens on port 5000. The server application runs without waiting for a debugger connection.

If your server application runs within the context of an application server, you may need to change the application server's configuration files. Some of the more common application servers are shown in the section "Configuration Settings for Application Servers" later in this chapter.

After the remote application is running in debug mode on the server, no other configuration options are needed. The remainder of the configuration options is set on the client.

Copy the Remote Application Files to the Client

To correctly debug the remote application, the remote application's .java and .class files need to be identical on the server and on the client. If the .class files do not match on either side, strange and unpredictable behavior will occur during the debugging process.

It does not matter whether you compile the application code on the server or on the client as long as the files are identical on both machines. The debugger uses the local copy of the remote application files to set breakpoints and debug the remote application.

Set Up a Runtime Configuration for the Remote Application

To set breakpoints on the remote application, a runtime configuration needs to be set up on the client machine. Using the remote application files, create a runtime configuration entry in JBuilder. JBuilder uses this configuration entry to create an attachment to the remote application.

To create the runtime configuration for the server, choose Run, Configuration from the menu. The Project Properties configuration dialog box shown in Figure 26.2 is displayed.

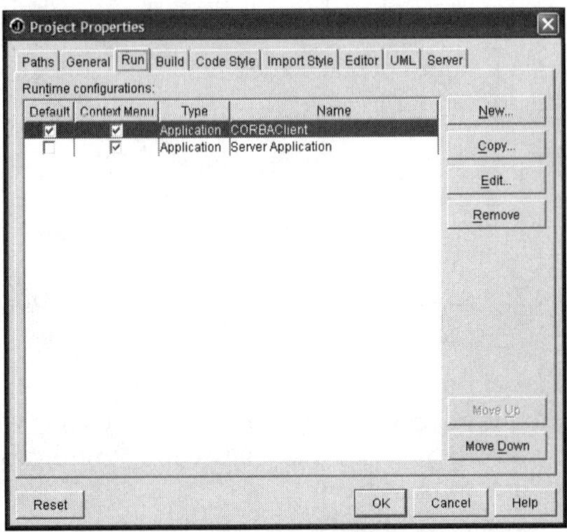

FIGURE 26.2 Runtime configuration settings.

The New, Copy, and Edit buttons on the Run tab of the Project Properties dialog box are used to maintain runtime configurations. Figure 26.3 shows the Runtime Properties dialog box.

Figure 26.3 shows the Application subtab on the Run tab. The Main Class field should identify the main class in your remote application. After that has been set, the debug options need to be configured for the remote application. Figure 26.4 displays the Debug tab.

Figure 26.4 identifies the available remote debug options. Table 26.3 describes the remote debugging options.

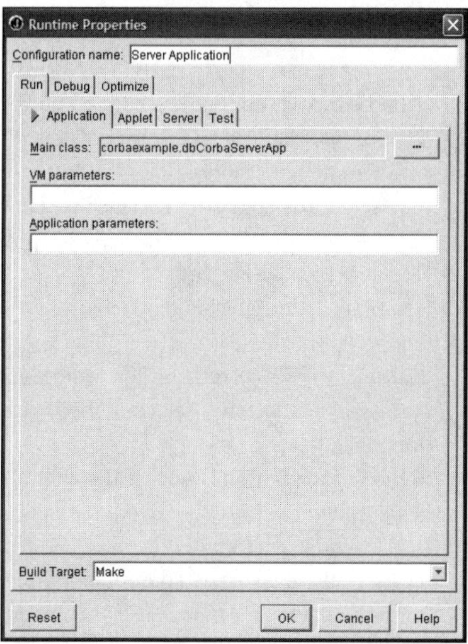

FIGURE 26.3 Runtime Properties dialog box—Run tab.

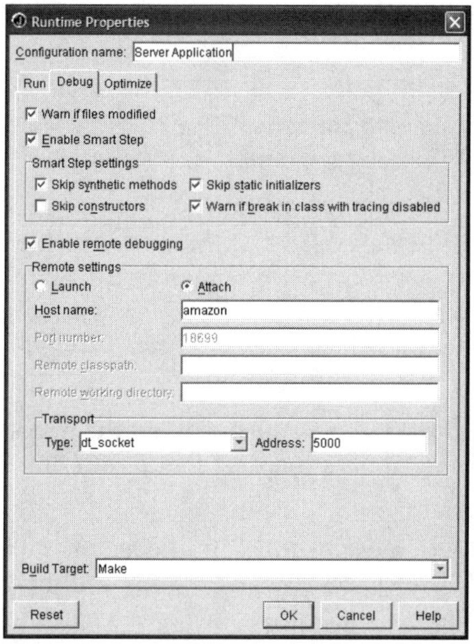

FIGURE 26.4 Runtime Properties Dialog box—Debug tab.

TABLE 26.3 Remote Debugging Options

Option	Description
Enable remote debugging	When checked, the runtime configuration does not actually run the application, but instead implements the JPDA functionality to connect to a remote application.
Launch	If selected, the application is launched on the remote machine. This requires the use of the DebugServer application located in the JBuilder/remote directory.
Attach	If selected, the application attaches to an already running remote application.
Host name	Name of the server running the remote application.
Port number	If the Launch button is selected, the port address of the Debug Server is entered here.
Remote classpath	If the Launch button is selected, the remote classpath is entered here.
Remote working directory	If the Launch button is selected, the remote working directory for the application is entered here.
Transport Type	Provides the `dt_socket` and optionally the `dt_shmem` options. In most cases, the `dt_socket` is the preferred and only method for remote debugging.
Address	When the remote application is started under the debug VM, it either sets a listening port or randomly chooses one. The Address field holds the port number that the debugger will connect to for the remote application.

JBuilder can communicate with the remote application by either attaching to the remote application or launching the remote application.

To attach to the remote application, you must select the Attach radio button, type in the host name, and type in the address. The address is either decided on when you launched the remote application, or it is randomly chosen by the remote application. In either case, the Address field must contain the address determined in the remote application. After these fields are set, JBuilder attempts to attach to the remote application.

JBuilder can also launch the remote application on the remote machine. To accomplish this, the DebugServer application that comes with JBuilder must be installed on the remote machine.

The DebugServer application can be found in the remote subdirectory in the main JBuilder directory. DebugServer consists of a .jar file and shell scripts for Unix and DOS/Windows. The DebugServer.jar file needs to be copied to the remote machine. If the remote machine is a Unix machine, copy over the DebugServer script file. If the remote machine is a DOS- or Windows-based machine, copy over the DebugServer.bat file.

The DebugServer script has the following syntax:

```
DebugServer <debugserver.jar_dir> <jdk_home_dir> <-port portnumber>
➥<-timeout milliseconds>
```

The parameters for the DebugServer script are listed in Table 26.4.

TABLE 26.4 DebugServer Script Parameters

Parameter	Description
`debugserver.jar_dir`	The directory on the remote machine where the DebugServer.jar file is located.
`jdk_home_dir`	The directory on the remote machine where the JDK home directory is located.
`-port portnumber (optional)`	The port number the DebugServer listens on for launch commands from the debugger. This port number corresponds to the Port Number option in Table 26.3. Default: 18699
`-timeout milliseconds (optional)`	The number of milliseconds the DebugServer waits while trying to connect the remote computer to the client computer. Default: 60,000

After the DebugServer is set up and running, the launch functionality in the runtime configuration settings start your remote application.

Whether you choose to launch or attach to your remote application, the debugging process is identical. JBuilder runs the server runtime configuration, and a connection to the remote application is made.

Set Breakpoints in the Code

Open the remote application code and place a line breakpoint. Refer to Chapter 6 for information about setting breakpoints. After the breakpoint has been set, debug the remote application using the runtime configuration. The remote application code stops processing when the breakpoint has been reached.

If the remote application was started with the `suspend` option set to `y`, the remote application will wait for the debug connection before starting. In this situation, when JBuilder starts to debug the remote application on the client machine, the debug window immediately pauses. By clicking the resume debugging button, the remote application starts running on the server.

The client-side application can be run or debugged in JBuilder. In either case, if the client application is running and encounters the line that has been marked with a breakpoint, the JBuilder debugger halts the execution at the breakpoint. The JBuilder debugger can be used to modify and evaluate the variables and step through the code.

Cross-Process Breakpoints

Cross-process breakpoints cause the debugger to stop when you step into a class in a separate process. You can specify whether to stop on any method call or a specific method call. Using a cross-process breakpoint allows you to step into a server process from a client process instead of having to set breakpoints in both the client and server processes.

To set a cross-process breakpoint, open a source code file on your server project. Choose Run, Add Breakpoint, Add Cross Process Breakpoint from the menu. Figure 26.5 shows the Add Cross-Process Breakpoint dialog box.

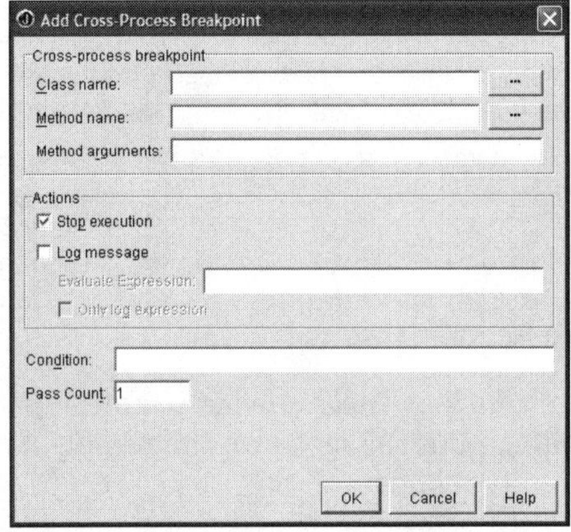

FIGURE 26.5 Add Cross-Process Breakpoint dialog box.

The Add Cross-Process Breakpoint dialog box requires only that the Class name field be completed. If Class name is the only field filled in, the breakpoint stops execution when any method in the class is executed.

If the method name is selected, a dialog box of the available methods in the selected class is displayed. Figure 26.6 displays a list of methods available.

When a method is selected, the method's arguments are automatically filled in the Method arguments field in the Add Cross-Process Breakpoint dialog box. The arguments are used to identify the correct function signature because overloaded methods are possible in Java.

The remaining fields in the Add Cross-Process Breakpoint dialog box are identical to the breakpoint fields identified in the section "More Debugging Options" in Chapter 6. In summary, the fields allow you to stop execution and/or log expressions to a file. The breakpoint can be activated based on a condition or a number of execution passes.

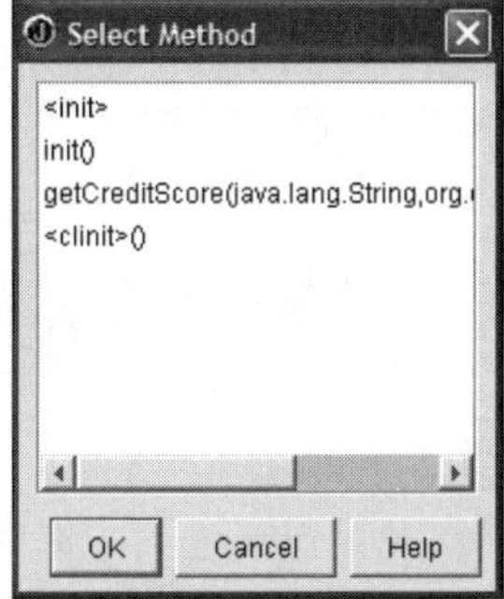

FIGURE 26.6 Select Method dialog box.

NOTE

When you are remotely debugging an application, you can set a breakpoint on a line of code in the server application code. The breakpoint behaves the same as using a cross-process breakpoint.

Configuration Settings for Application Servers

Application servers are primarily used to provide a framework of services to your application. Your application can take advantage of an application server's database caching, database pooling, resource management, transaction management, and security management services.

Application servers manage the life of your application by controlling the VM. Because the application server controls the VM of your application, you must modify the application server's process of starting the VM. The application server needs to be told to start the VM in debug mode.

If you can begin the application server in debug mode, the most important parameter is the listening address of the application server. The listening address is needed so that the debugger can remotely attach to the running server.

There are many different application servers, and their configurations differ dramatically. Here are a few of the popular application servers and how to set them up for remote debugging.

Inprise Application Server 5.x

If you are using Inprise Application Server, the EJB containers/partitions can be set to support JPDA. Figure 26.7 shows the configuration properties for the standard EJB partition. You can get to the configuration properties by right-clicking on the partition name and selecting the configuration menu option.

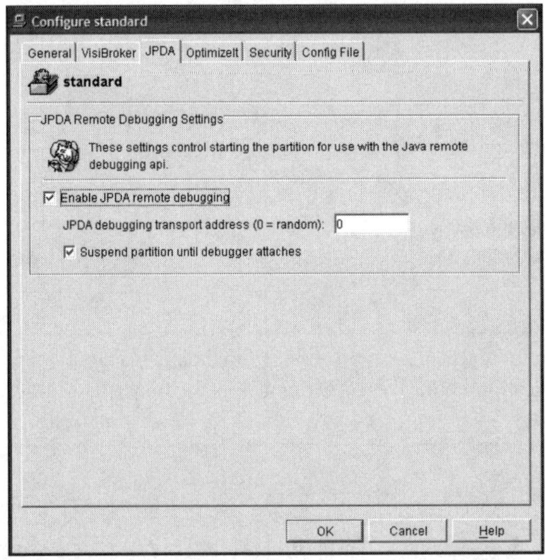

FIGURE 26.7 Configure Standard dialog box.

The JPDA tab in the configuration dialog box allows you to enable JPDA support. The JPDA debugging address can be set to a particular number. The number entered into this field must match the number in the address field in Figure 26.4. The final option for JPDA support is whether to suspend the application when started.

Weblogic Server 7.0

To enable remote debugging, the Weblogic Server must be started with the debugging options. Weblogic Server starts its application server by executing command scripts. The command scripts need to be modified to turn on remote debugging.

To be safe, the following instructions make copies of the modified command scripts:

1. For your application, find the startWeblogic.cmd file. This can usually be found in the c:\bea\user_projects\mydomain directory. Copy this file and rename it startRemoteWeblogic.cmd.
2. Open the startRemoteWeblogic.cmd file and find the line

   ```
   call "c:\bea\weblogic700\server\bin\startWLS.cmd"
   ```

3. The line should be modified to the following:

   ```
   call "c:\bea\weblogic700\server\bin\startRemoteWLS.cmd"
   ```

4. Save the file.
5. Go to the c:\bea\weblogic700\server\bin directory and find the file startWLS.cmd. Copy and rename the file to startRemoteWLS.cmd.
6. Open the file startRemoteWLS.cmd.
7. Make the following changes to the startRemoteWLS.cmd file. Listing 26.1 shows the code modifications necessary to enable remote debugging. The address for the debugging port has been set to 6000.

LISTING 26.1 startRemoteWLS.cmd

```
set CLASSPATH=%JAVA_HOME%\lib\tools.jar;C:\Borland\JBuilder7\lib\jaxrpc.jar;
➥C:\Borland\JBuilder7\lib\jds.jar;C:\Borland\JBuilder7\lib\j
➥dsremote.jar;C:\Borland\JBuilder7\lib\jdsserver.jar;
➥%WL_HOME%\server\lib\weblogic_sp.jar;
➥%WL_HOME%\server\lib\weblogic.jar;%CLASSPATH%

@rem Start Server
@echo off
if "%ADMIN_URL%" == "" goto runAdmin
@echo on
"%JAVA_HOME%\bin\java" -classic %MEM_ARGS% -Xdebug -Xnoagent
➥-Djava.compiler=NONE -Xrunjdwp:transport=dt_socket,server=y,
➥address=6000,suspend=n %JAVA_OPTIONS% -classpath"%CLASSPATH%"
➥-Dweblogic.Name=%SERVER_NAME% -Dbea.home="C:\bea"
➥-Dweblogic.management.username=%WLS_USER%
➥-Dweblogic.management.password=%WLS_PW%
➥-Dweblogic.management.server=%ADMIN_URL%
➥-Dweblogic.ProductionModeEnabled=%STARTMODE%
➥-Djava.security.policy="%WL_HOME%\server\lib\weblogic.policy"
```

LISTING 26.1 Continued

```
➥-Daxis.enableListQuery=true weblogic.Server
goto finish

:runAdmin
@echo on
"%JAVA_HOME%\bin\java" -classic %MEM_ARGS% -Xdebug -Xnoagent
➥-Djava.compiler=NONE -Xrunjdwp:transport=dt_socket,server=y,
➥address=6000,suspend=n %JAVA_OPTIONS% -classpath"%CLASSPATH%"
➥-Dweblogic.Name=%SERVER_NAME% -Dbea.home="C:\bea"
➥-Dweblogic.management.username=%WLS_USER%
➥-Dweblogic.management.password=%WLS_PW%
➥-Dweblogic.ProductionModeEnabled=%STARTMODE%
➥-Djava.security.policy="%WL_HOME%\server\lib\weblogic.policy"
➥-Daxis.enableListQuery=true weblogic.Server

:finish
```

In step 7, you modify the command used to start the `weblogic.Server` application. The command has been modified to turn on debugging.

When the server is started, remote debugging is enabled at port address 6000. Modify the runtime configuration shown in Figure 26.4 for your server application in JBuilder to match the same address.

Websphere Server 4

Websphere has native support for the JPDA. The problem is identifying the address number used for the debugger.

1. To begin, load the Websphere console.
2. Locate the application servers in the tree view. After the application server is selected, a configuration panel appears on the right side of the console.
3. Select the JVM Setting tab.
4. Click on the Advance Settings button. You may need to scroll the screen to see the button.
5. In the dialog box, select the Enable distributed debugger check box.
6. Shut down the server and the console.
7. Start up the server. When the server starts, it displays the status information onscreen. One of the last lines in the server startup reads `"Debug support is`

`available on port:`". The number that appears at the end of this line must match the Address field in Figure 26.4.

Remember to modify your project properties in Figure 26.4. After this has been done, you will be able to attach to the EJB server and debug your code.

iPlanet Server

iPlanet has a Web-based administration program in which you can set the JVM options.

Under the JVM options settings, set the following values:

```
-Xdebug,-Xnoagent,-Xrunjdwp:transport=dt_socket,server=y,suspend=n,address=5000
```

The JVM options are set in the jvm12.conf file.

NOTE

The Web administration program in iPlanet has a bug. When the preceding options are entered, iPlanet forces a hard carriage return in the middle of the options. The incorrectly formatted options are then read in by iPlanet causing the debug JVM not to be set correctly.

To correct this, open the jvm12.conf file and manually add the options to the jvm.option settings.

If you use the Web administration program to adjust these settings later, your changes will be lost, and you will have to remodify the jvm12.conf file.

Other Servers

If you have a different application server than the ones mentioned previously, search that application server's documentation for remote debugging or JPDA support. In addition, Borland's developer site provides helpful hints and tricks on other application servers.

In Practice

To run this "In Practice" section, you need the following:

- A client machine running JBuilder and the Borland Enterprise Server 5.0x.
- A server machine running JDK 1.3.1 or better and the Borland Enterprise Server.
- The machines must be accessible to each other on the network via TCP/IP.

The "In Practice" exercise is broken down into the following steps:

1. Set up the server application on the server machine.
2. Set up the server application on the client machine.
3. Debug the server application on the client machine.

The exercise uses the CORBA application developed in Chapter 25, "CORBA." A copy of the solved CORBA application is placed in the Chapter 26 directory.

Set Up the Server Application on the Server Machine

In this step, you copy the server application files from the client machine to the server machine. The exercise assumes that the files will be installed on drive C on the server machine.

1. Locate the jbbook\ch26\swing\classes\chalktalk directory on the client machine and copy the chalktalk subdirectory over to the server machine. Remember the location on the server.
2. On the server machine, make sure that the location of the chalktalk subdirectory is included in the CLASSPATH environment variable. For example, if you copied the chalktalk directory to c:\jbbook\ch26, type in the following command:

   ```
   set CLASSPATH=C:\jbbook\ch26\.;%CLASSPATH%
   ```

3. After the path has been set, type in the following command to start the server in debug mode with a debug address of 5000:

   ```
   java -classpath %CLASSPATH% -Xdebug -Xnoagent -Djava.compiler=NONE
   ➥-Xrunjdwp:transport=dt_socket,server=y,address=5000,
   ➥suspend=n chalktalk.courseServerApp
   ```

4. If you have correctly installed the server application onto the server machine, you should see the dialog box in Figure 26.8.

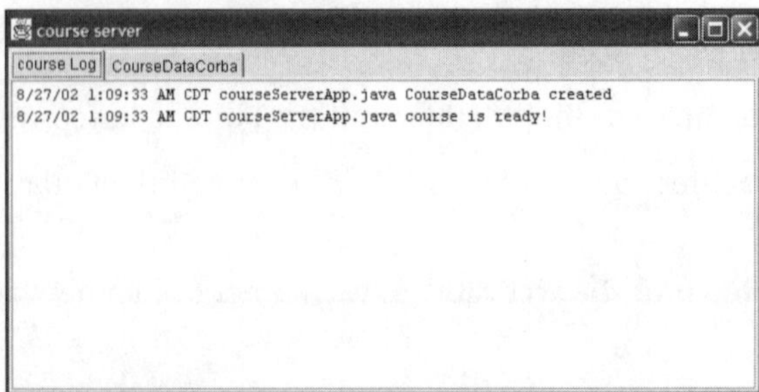

FIGURE 26.8 Course Server Application dialog box.

Set Up the Server Application on the Client Machine

In this step, you open the JBuilder application on the client machine.

To open the example project

1. Select File, Open Project from the JBuilder menu.
2. Locate jbbook\ch26\swing\ChalkTalk.jpx and click OK.
3. Select Run, Configurations from the JBuilder menu. Figure 26.9 displays the Run tab in the Project Properties dialog box.

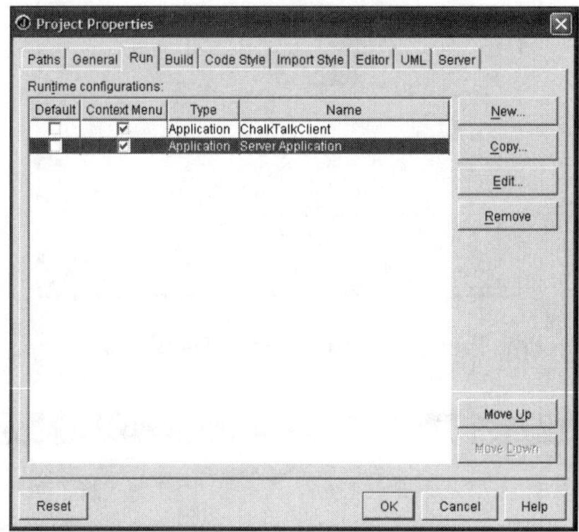

FIGURE 26.9 Project Properties dialog box—Run tab.

4. Select the Server Application configuration and click the Edit button. Figure 26.10 displays the Runtime Properties dialog box with the Debug tab selected.
5. Check the Enable remote debugging box.
6. Select the Attach button.
7. Type the name of the server machine into the Host name field. In Figure 26.10, the example server machine name is AMAZON.
8. Type **5000** into the Address field.
9. Click OK.
10. Click OK in the Project Properties dialog box.
11. Right-click on the courseAppServer file in the Project pane. Select Debug, Use Server Application from the pop-up menu. If the correct settings were made, Figure 26.11 displays.

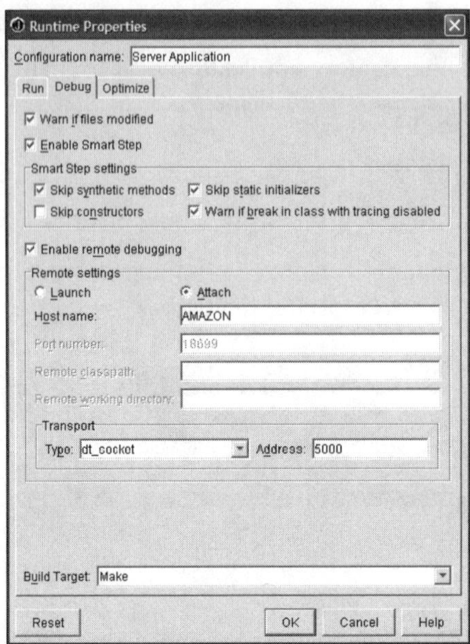

FIGURE 26.10 Runtime Properties dialog box—Debug tab.

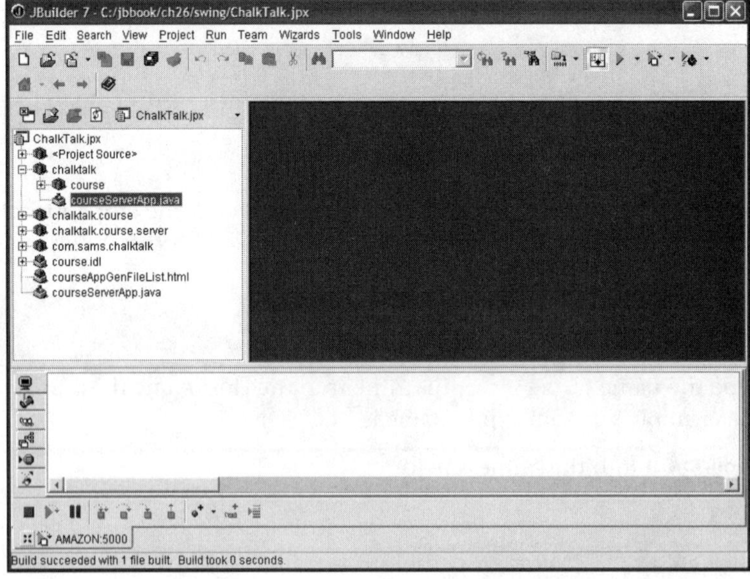

FIGURE 26.11 Server application running on AMAZON, address 5000.

At this point, the server application on the client machine has successfully attached to the server application running on the server machine.

Debug the Server Application on the Client Machine

The client application will be executed against the server application. We will set a breakpoint in the server application code to stop execution when a certain line is reached. We will modify a variable and make sure that the server returns the modified data:

1. Locate the CourseDataCorbaImpl.java file in the Project pane under the chalktalk.course.server tree node.
2. Double-click on the CourseDataCorbaImpl.java file so that the contents appear in the Content pane.
3. Go to line 61, which reads as follows:

   ```
   sCourseNumber[0] = "CS251";
   ```

4. Set a breakpoint on this line by pressing the F5 key while on the line, or right-clicking on the line and selecting Toggle Breakpoint from the pop-up menu.
5. Locate the ChalkTalkClient.java file in the Project pane under the com.sams.chalktalk.client.swing tree node.
6. Right-click on the ChalkTalkClient.java file and select Run, Use ChalkTalkClient from the pop-up menu.
7. The application will run. Select File, Browse Courses from the main menu. JBuilder notifies you that the server application has stopped at the breakpoint. Figure 26.12 shows the stopped server application.
8. Right-click on the Content pane and select Evaluate/Modify from the pop-up menu.
9. Type the following line into the Expression field on the Evaluate/Modify dialog box:

   ```
   sCourse[0] = "Introduction to Remote Debugging"
   ```

10. Click the Evaluate button. If you successfully changed the value, the dialog box will look like Figure 26.13.

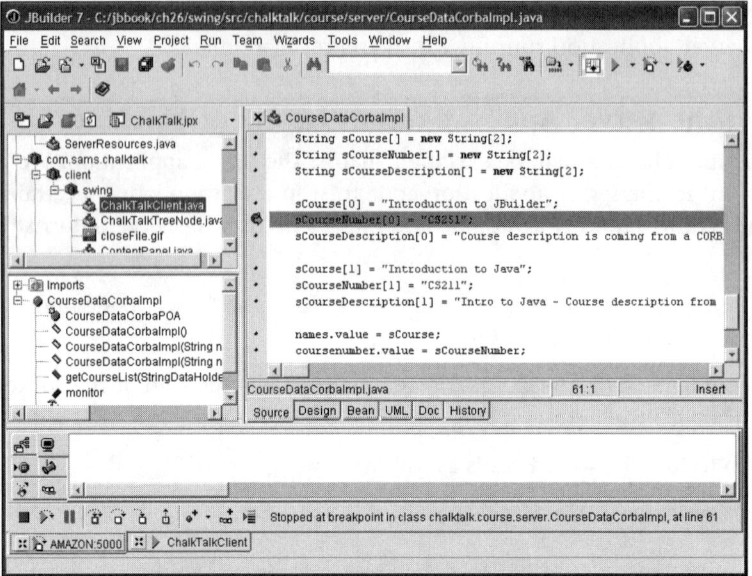

FIGURE 26.12 Server application stopped at breakpoint.

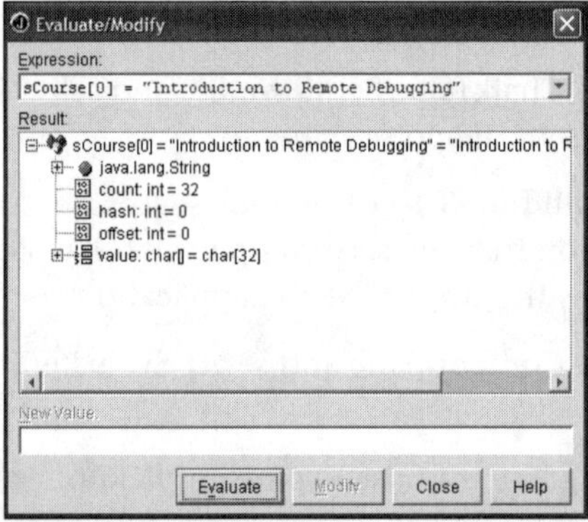

FIGURE 26.13 Evaluate/Modify dialog box.

11. Click the Close button on the Evaluate/Modify dialog box.
12. Click the Resume Debugging Session button on the command bar.
13. Look at the client application and verify that the data has been changed. Figure 26.14 shows the client application with the modified data.

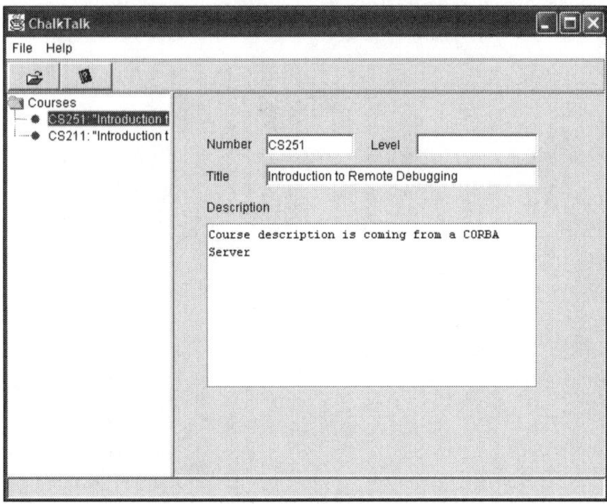

FIGURE 26.14 Client application with modified data.

This section started our server application on a server machine. We attached to the server application on the client machine by setting the remote debugging options. Finally, we set a breakpoint in the server application that was triggered by the client application.

Summary

In today's enterprise application server environment, the skill to remotely debug an application is required. Take advantage of the remote debugging capabilities of JBuilder to solve remote application problems.

This chapter covered the steps necessary to enable remote debugging, set up remote debugging, and configure some of today's application servers.

Reflections

- What situation do you find yourself in today where remote debugging would help you?
- When users tell you the program does not work on their machine, do you believe them? Now you can check out what is happening!

27

Development and Deployment for WebLogic and WebSphere

IN THIS CHAPTER

- Using WebLogic with JBuilder
- Using IBM WebSphere with JBuilder

JBuilder's support for multiple application servers makes this the most versatile IDE on the market. The support includes not only the writing of code but deploying, debugging, and wizards also. As we look at the difference between WebLogic and WebSphere, you will notice JBuilder's capability to mask the differences from application server to application server. The following processes are important to examine for each application server:

- Installing the application server
- Developing a JSP and/or servlet
- Creating EJBs
- Deploying your application
- Remote debugging your application

Using WebLogic with JBuilder

BEA WebLogic Application Server is a full-featured, standards-based application server providing the foundation on which an enterprise can build its applications. For all the crucial tasks of application development and deployment—from integrating enterprise systems and databases to delivering services and collaborating over the Internet—the starting place is BEA WebLogic Server. With its comprehensive set of features, compliance with open standards, multitiered architecture, and support for component-based development, WebLogic Application Server is the choice of Internet-savvy businesses to develop and deploy best-of-breed applications. As we look at the integration between WebLogic and JBuilder, we will look at the following key elements for using the best-of-breed IDE:

- Installing WebLogic
- Configuring JBuilder for WebLogic
- Developing servlets and JSPs
- Developing EJBs
- Deploying your application components
- Debugging

Installing WebLogic Application Server

To create and install WebLogic Application Server, you typically follow the installation directions provided by BEA. The process for creating a server varies from platform to platform, but this chapter shows specifically how to configure and set up a single server within the Windows environment. To develop and debug your WebLogic application, it is most advantageous to install the server locally with your installation of JBuilder. The following steps are required to set up a WebLogic Application Server—single server.

1. Install the WebLogic Application Server into the C:\BEA directory. Use the supplied setup either downloaded from the BEA Web site or using the BEA distribution CD.
2. Create and configure a server using the Configuration Wizard. This wizard is accessed by clicking on Start, All Programs, BEA WebLogic Platform 7.0, Configuration Wizard.
3. Supply the following properties to the Configuration Wizard:

Property	Value
Domain name	**dev**
Server type	**Single Server**
Domain location	**C:\bea\user_projects**

NOTE

From this point forward, the domain location will actually be the domain location plus the name of the domain. For example, in this instance the directory location is actually c:\bea\user_projects\dev.

Configuring JBuilder with WebLogic

JBuilder supports a wide variety of different application servers, WebLogic being one of them. To have JBuilder properly communicate with these environments, you must configure JBuilder to recognize them. When an application server environment is selected, JBuilder then configures the features, code generators and wizards, command-line utilities, classpaths, and deployment and runtime options for the vendor's specific implementation requirements. To access JBuilder's configuration of application servers, you must enter the editor by choosing Tools, Configure Servers from the menu (see Figure 27.1) and enable the application servers you want to use within JBuilder. This is not a one-time setup for each developer's login, but you can change these parameters by reentering the editor anytime.

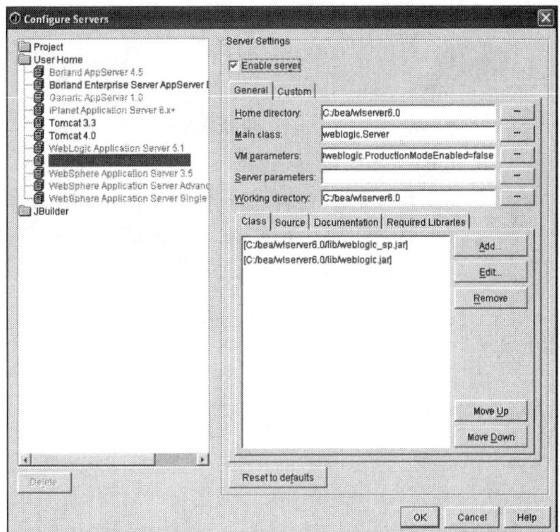

FIGURE 27.1 Application server setup within the JBuilder environment for WebLogic integration.

To enable the desired application server, select it in the list on the left and click the Enable server check box for that application server configuration. You now have full access to the features available within the given application server. For example, if you choose an application server that does not support EJB 2.0 Entity Beans, it will not allow you to build 2.0 Entity Beans within your application.

WebLogic 7.0 is not specifically supported within the JBuilder environment but can easily be configured to work. The following steps set up WebLogic 7.0 within the JBuilder environment:

1. Click Tools, Configure Servers.
2. Select WebLogic Application Server 6.x+.
3. Click the Enable server check box.
4. Enter the following properties for the WebLogic Application Server:

Property	Value
Home directory	**c:\bea\weblogic\server**
Main class	`weblogic.Server`

VM parameters	`-ms64m -mx64m`
	`-Djava.library.path=/bea/wlserver6.0/bin`
	`-Dbea.home=/bea`
	`-Dweblogic.Domain=mydomain`
	`-Dweblogic.Name=myserver`
	`-Djava.security.policy==/bea/wlserver6.0/lib/weblogic.policy`
	`-Dweblogic.management.discover=false`
	`-Dweblogic.ProductionModeEnabled=false`

Working directory	**c:\bea\user_projects\dev**

Using Servlets and JSPs with WebLogic

When using JBuilder, the IDE isolates the differences between the application server containers within its wizards. For example, the process for creating JSPs and servlets is exactly the same as that of BES, with one exception. This exception is to specify which container will supply the necessary services for implementation. The following steps are necessary to create a BEA JSP and servlet project:

1. Select File, New, Project tab from the Object Gallery.
2. Choose Project.
3. In the Project Wizard - Step 1 of 3, specify the project name and other important properties.

4. Select Finish.
5. Choose Project, Project Properties.
6. Select the Server tab (see Figure 27.2).

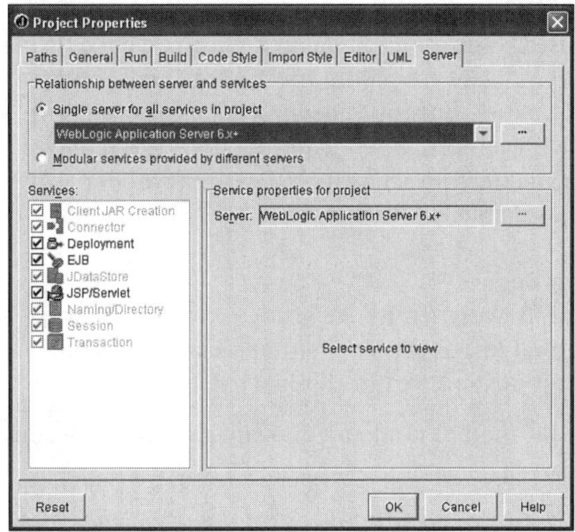

FIGURE 27.2 Project Properties window for the newly created project.

NOTE

JBuilder not only allows for development and deployment to multiple application servers, but also allows for a mixing of service providers across the same project.

7. Select the WebLogic Application Server 6.x+ in the combo box.
8. Compile and save your project.

All other processes for creating JSPs and servlets are exactly the same.

The following process is used to create a Web application using WebLogic Application Server:

1. Create a Web application. Select File, New, Web tab in the Object Gallery.
2. Select a Web application. Make sure to choose the check box Generate WAR.
3. Click File, New, Web tab in the Object Gallery.
4. Select the JavaServer page.

5. Compile and save the project.
6. Right-click on the JSP and select Web Run using <name>.jsp.

Working with EJBs

Creating an EJB-based solution implemented within WebLogic is similar to creating a JSP. The preparatory tasks of specifying the application server are exactly the same. The only difference happens if the version of WebLogic supports varying forms of EJB specification. For example, when using versions of WebLogic prior to version 6.5, you will have a limited feature set available within JBuilder. CMP 2.0 is one such feature that is not available.

Creating a Session Bean

Using the JBuilder EJB Designer, we are going to create a Session Bean that uses the interface implemented in our earlier client application. To build this Session Bean, we will perform a set of steps within JBuilder's IDE:

1. Double-click on the EJB module you want to use as the container for your new Session Bean.
2. Right-click on the design window or on the node and select New Session Bean.
3. Name and configure your Session Bean (see Figure 27.3). Configure the following properties:

   Bean name: **weatherStation**

   Interfaces: **Remote**

   Session type: **Stateless**

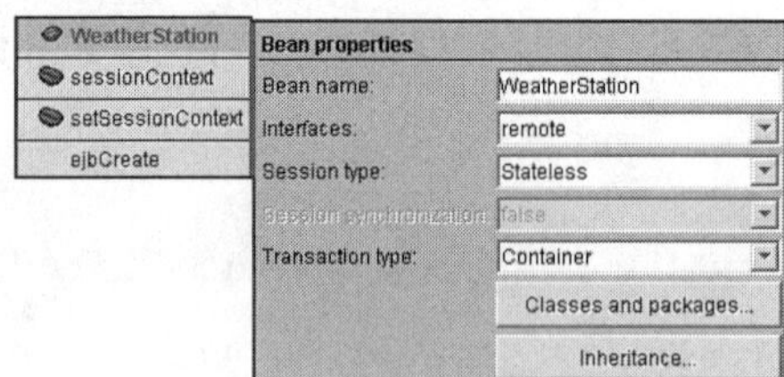

FIGURE 27.3 Configure your Session Bean by changing the properties through the EJB Designer.

4. Right-click on the new Session Bean and add a method. This process is similar to adding a new field (see Figure 27.4). The method you want to add is the following (see Figure 27.5):

   Method name: **`getCurrentTemp`**

   Return type: **`int`**

   Input parameters: **`java.lang.String zipcode`**

   Interfaces: **Remote**

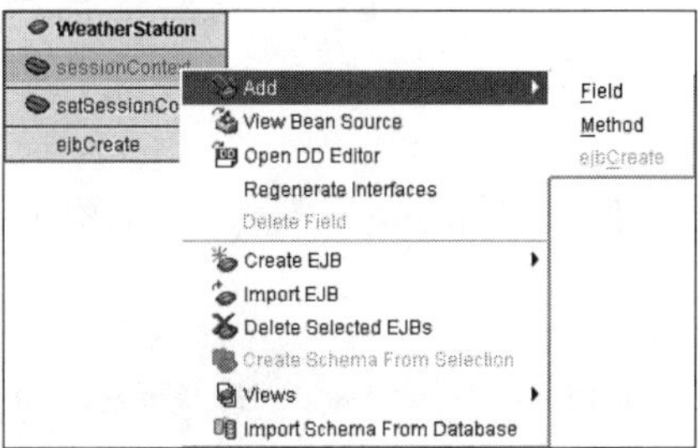

FIGURE 27.4 Using the context menu to add methods or fields to your Session Bean graphically.

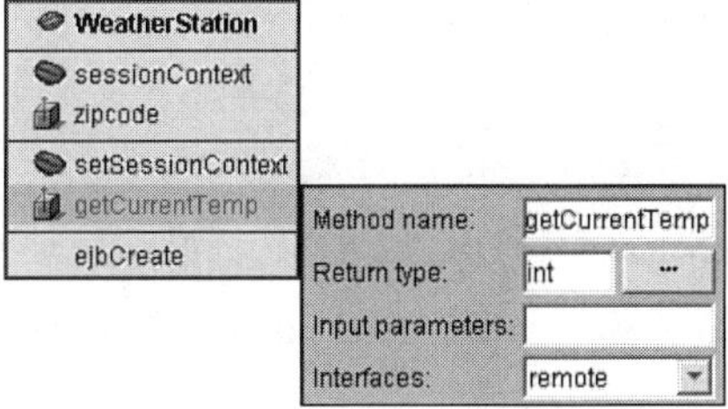

FIGURE 27.5 Configuring your method and assigning the given properties.

5. Assign the desired names to the generated code for the Bean implementation, as shown in Figure 27.6. For example, change the default package of the Session Beans to `com.sams.weatherstation.session`. This is accomplished by selecting the classes and packages button on the properties for the entire Bean. If you do not see this button on the properties pop-up panel of the Bean, reselect the title of the Bean.

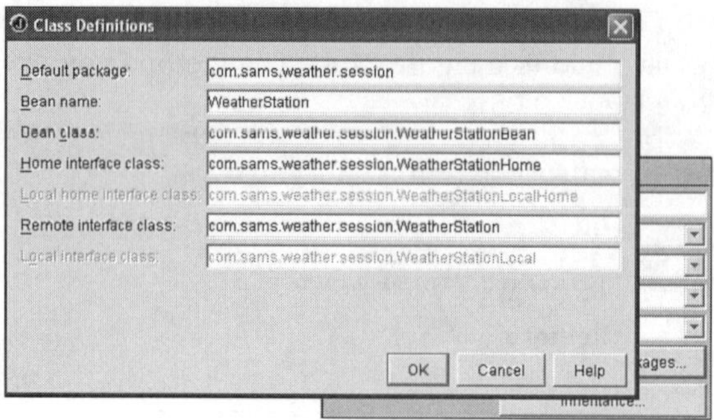

FIGURE 27.6 Change the default package for a Session Bean.

6. Compile and save your project.

Creating an Entity Bean

Just like Session Beans, the Entity Bean usage does not change dramatically more than the BES development and deployment. The following steps create an Entity Bean using the WebLogic environment:

1. Import a schema from the data source in the EJB module containing your Session Beans. This is accomplished by right-clicking on the data source node when you are in the EJB Designer and selecting Import Schema from Datasource.
2. Set the following database parameters:
   - Driver: **`com.borland.datastore.jdbc.DataStoreDriver`**
   - URL: **`jdbc:borland:dslocal:C:\JBDG\db\ChalkTalk.jds`**
   - Username: leave blank
   - Password: leave blank
3. Right-click on each table and create a CMP 2.0 Entity Bean for each table. For example, right-click on the table room and create a CMP 2.0 Bean.
4. Define relationships.
5. Compile and save your project.

Deploying Your Application

JBuilder insulates you from the details of the implementation that are WebLogic specific. For example, the deployment descriptor has some WebLogic-specific information contained within many of its components (see Listing 27.1).

LISTING 27.1 WebLogic Deployment Descriptor for a Sample Project (weblogic-ejb-jar.xml Located within the Deployment JAR)

```
<?xml version="1.0" encoding="UTF-8"?>
<!DOCTYPE weblogic-ejb-jar PUBLIC '-//BEA Systems, Inc.
➥//DTD WebLogic 7.0.0 EJB//EN'
➥'http://www.bea.com/servers/wls700/dtd/weblogic-ejb-jar.dtd'>
<weblogic-ejb-jar>
    <weblogic-enterprise-bean>
        <ejb-name>Cart</ejb-name>
        <reference-descriptor>
            <ejb-local-reference-description>
                <ejb-ref-name>ejb/Orderitem</ejb-ref-name>
                <jndi-name>Orderitem</jndi-name>
            </ejb-local-reference-description>
            <ejb-local-reference-description>
                <ejb-ref-name>ejb/ShoppingCart</ejb-ref-name>
                <jndi-name>ShoppingCart</jndi-name>
            </ejb-local-reference-description>
            <ejb-local-reference-description>
                <ejb-ref-name>ejb/ServerDataModule</ejb-ref-name>
                <jndi-name>ServerDataModule</jndi-name>
            </ejb-local-reference-description>
            <ejb-local-reference-description>
                <ejb-ref-name>ejb/User</ejb-ref-name>
                <jndi-name>User</jndi-name>
            </ejb-local-reference-description>
        </reference-descriptor>
        <jndi-name>Cart</jndi-name>
...
    </weblogic-enterprise-bean>
    <weblogic-enterprise-bean>
        <ejb-name>Sequence</ejb-name>
        <entity-descriptor>
            <persistence>
                <persistence-use>
                    <type-identifier>WebLogic_CMP_RDBMS</type-identifier>
                    <type-version>6.0</type-version>
                    <type-storage>META-INF/weblogic-cmp-rdbms-jar.xml
➥</type-storage>
                </persistence-use>
            </persistence>
        </entity-descriptor>
```

LISTING 27.1 Continued

```
        <local-jndi-name>Sequence</local-jndi-name>
    </weblogic-enterprise-bean>
</weblogic-ejb-jar>
```

This file contains all the WebLogic-specific configurations required for the deployment of your application.

Remote Debugging

JBuilder contains the facilities to remotely debug an application running within another JVM process. To remotely debug this application deployed on the application server, specifically WebLogic Server, you must start your server in debug mode. The following process is required to create the hooks necessary for remote debugging within WebLogic:

1. Copy startWebLogic.cmd to startRemoteWeblogic.cmd. This file is located in your user project directory plus your WebLogic domain name—for example, c:\bea\user_projects\dev.
2. Make the following change to your newly copied startRemoteWeblogic.cmd file:

```
@rem Call WebLogic Server
call "c:\bea\weblogic700\server\bin\startRemoteWLS.cmd"
```

3. Copy from c:\bea\weblogic700\server\bin the file startWLS.cmd to startRemoteWLS.cmd.
4. Make the following changes to startRemoteWLS.cmd:

Modification 1—Change the classpath.

```
set CLASSPATH=%JAVA_HOME%\lib\tools.jar;
➥c:\borland\jbuilder7\lib\jaxrpc.jar;
➥c:\borland\jbuilder7\lib\jds.jar;
➥c:\borland\jbuilder7\lib\jdsremote.jar;
➥c:\borland\jbuilder7\lib\jdsserver.jar;
➥%WL_HOME%\server\lib\weblogic_sp.jar;
➥%WL_HOME%\server\lib\weblogic.jar;%CLASSPATH%
```

Modification 2—Change command switches for starting WebLogic Server.

```
@rem Start Server
@echo off
if "%ADMIN_URL%" == "" goto runAdmin
@echo on
"%JAVA_HOME%\bin\java" -classic %MEM_ARGS% -Xdebug -Xnoagent
➥-Djava.compiler=NONE
➥-Xrunjdwp:transport=dt_socket,server=y,address=5555,suspend=n
➥%JAVA_OPTIONS%
➥-classpath "%CLASSPATH%" -Dweblogic.Name=%SERVER_NAME%
➥-Dbea.home="C:\bea" -Dweblogic.management.username=%WLS_USER%
➥-Dweblogic.management.password=%WLS_PW%
➥-Dweblogic.management.server=%ADMIN_URL%
➥-Dweblogic.ProductionModeEnabled=%STARTMODE%
-Djava.security.policy="%WL_HOME%\server\lib\weblogic.policy"
➥-Daxis.enableListQuery=true
weblogic.Server
goto finish

:runAdmin
@echo on
"%JAVA_HOME%\bin\java" -classic %MEM_ARGS% -Xdebug -Xnoagent
➥-Djava.compiler=NONE
➥-Xrunjdwp:transport=dt_socket,server=y,address=5555,suspend=n
➥%JAVA_OPTIONS%
➥-classpath "%CLASSPATH%" -Dweblogic.Name=%SERVER_NAME%
➥-Dbea.home="C:\bea" -Dweblogic.management.username=%WLS_USER%
➥-Dweblogic.management.password=%WLS_PW%
➥-Dweblogic.ProductionModeEnabled=%STARTMODE%
-Djava.security.policy="%WL_HOME%\server\lib\weblogic.policy"
➥-Daxis.enableListQuery=true
weblogic.Server

:finish
```

5. Start the WebLogic Application Server by executing c:\bea\user_projects\dev\startRemoteWebLogic.
6. Create a new run configuration. Select Run, Configuration.
7. Click the New button to create a new configuration.
8. Click the Debug tab to edit the runtime properties (see Figure 27.7).

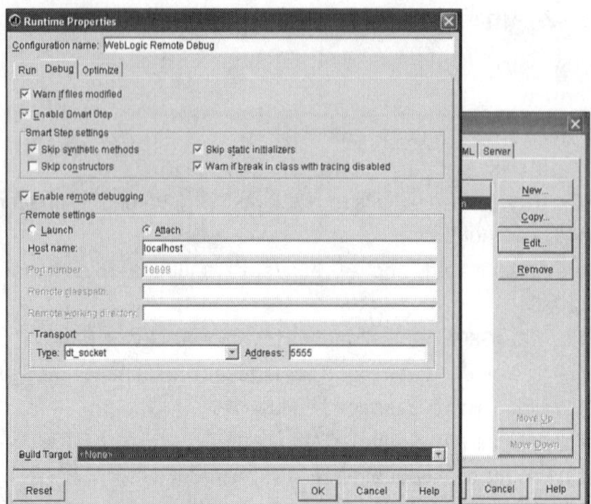

FIGURE 27.7 Debug runtime configuration for remotely debugging a WebLogic deployment.

9. Assign a configuration name to the newly created configuration. Check the Enable Remote Debugging check box.
10. Click the Attach within the Remote Settings panel.
11. Enter the address as **5555** and change the Build Target to <NONE>.
12. Assign breakpoints to the remote code.
13. Select Run, Debug Project. Select the Remote Debug configuration created earlier. This starts your application in debug mode.
14. Debug your application.

Using IBM WebSphere with JBuilder

The IBM WebSphere software platform for e-business is a comprehensive set of award-winning, integrated e-business solutions. It's a software platform based on industry standards—making it flexible and pluggable, which can allow you to adapt on-the-fly as markets shift and business goals change. Building on this robust platform, you can integrate diverse IT environments to maximize current investments, deliver core business applications to the Web, grow these applications to meet changing needs and increasing demand, and create a differentiated e-business that sets your business apart from the competition. As we look at the integration between JBuilder, we will look at the following key elements for using the best-of-breed IDE:

- Installing WebSphere
- Configuring JBuilder for WebSphere
- Developing servlets and JSPs
- Developing EJBs
- Deploying your application components
- Debugging

Installing WebSphere

IBMWebSphere is delivered in three different versions: Standard, Advanced, and Enterprise. When developing with JBuilder for the WebSphere platform, working with the Advanced Single Server Edition installed locally on your development workstation is advantageous.

NOTE

For consistency throughout this chapter, we suggest you install IBM WebSphere within c:\WebSphere.

Configuring JBuilder with WebSphere

JBuilder supports a wide variety of different application servers, WebSphere being one of them. To have JBuilder properly communicate with these environments, you must configure JBuilder to recognize them. When an application server environment is selected, JBuilder then configures the features, code generators and wizards, command-line utilities, class paths, and deployment and runtime options for the vendor's specific implementation requirements. We will use this application server for building our application; however, the same principles apply regardless of the application server brand or versions selected. To access JBuilder's configuration of application servers, enter the editor by choosing Tools, Configure Servers from the menu (see Figure 27.8) and enable the application servers you want to use within JBuilder. This is not a one-time setup for each developer's login, but you can change these parameters by reentering the editor anytime.

To enable the desired application server, select it in the list on the left and click the Enable server check box for that application server configuration. You now have full access to the features available within the given application server. For example, if you choose an application server that does not support EJB 2.0 Entity Beans, it will not allow you to build 2.0 Entity Beans within your application.

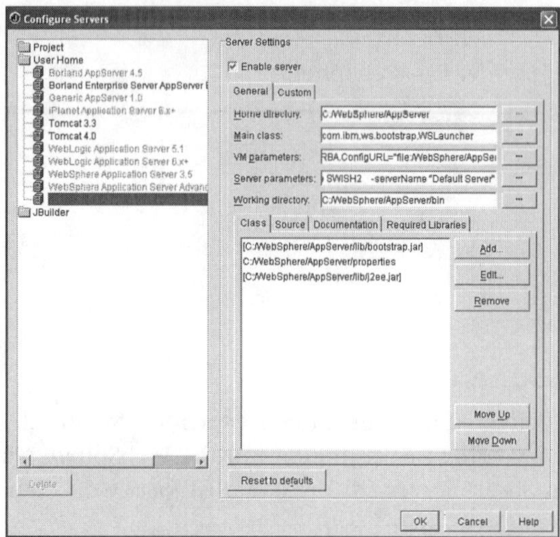

FIGURE 27.8 Application server setup within the JBuilder environment for WebSphere integration.

WebSphere 4.0 is not specifically supported within the JBuilder environment but can easily be configured to work. The following steps set up WebSphere 4.0 within the JBuilder environment:

1. Click Tools, Configure Servers.
2. Select WebSphere Application Single Server 4.0.
3. Click the Enable Server check box.
4. Enter the following properties for the WebSphere Application Server:

Property	Value
Home directory	**c:/WebSphere/AppServer**
Main class	`com.ibm.ws.bootstrap.WSLauncher`
VM parameters	**`-Xms17m -Xmx128m -Xminf0.15 -Xmaxf0.25 -Djava.library.path="/WebSphere/AppServer/bin;/WebSphere/AppServer/java/bin;/WebSphere/AppServer/java/jre/bin;/DB2/bin;/DB2/lib" -Dws.output.encoding=console -Djavax.rmi.CORBA.UtilClass=com.ibm.CORBA.iiop.Util -Dcom.ibm.CORBA.iiop.noLocalCopies=true -Dws.ext.dirs="/WebSphere/AppServer/java/lib;/WebSphere/AppServer/classes;/WebSphere/AppServer/lib;/WebSphere/AppServer/lib/ext;/WebSphere/AppServer/web/help"`**

Property	Value
Server parameters	`com.ibm.ejs.sm.server.AdminServer -bootFile /WebSphere/AppServer/bin/admin.config -nodeRestart`
Working directory	**c:/WebSphere/AppServer/bin**

Using Servlets and JSPs with WebSphere

When using JBuilder, the IDE isolates the differences between the application server containers within its wizards. For example, the process for creating JSPs and servlets is exactly the same as that of BES, with one exception. This exception is to specify which container will supply the necessary services for implementation. The following steps are necessary to create a BEA JSP and servlet project:

1. Select File, New, Project tab from the Object Gallery.
2. Choose Project.
3. In the Project Wizard—Step 1 of 3, specify the project name and other important properties.
4. Select Finish.
5. Choose Project, Project Properties.
6. Select the Server tab.

NOTE

JBuilder not only allows for development and deployment to multiple application servers, but also allows for a mixing of service providers across the same project.

7. Select the WebSphere Application Advanced Single Server 4.0 in the combo box.
8. Compile and save your project.

All other processes for creating JSPs and servlets are exactly the same.

The following process is used to create a Web application using WebSphere Application Server:

1. Create a Web application by selecting File, New, Web tab in the Object Gallery.
2. Select a Web application. Make sure to choose the check box Generate WAR.
3. Click File, New, Web tab in the Object Gallery.

4. Select the JavaServer page.
5. Compile and save the project.
6. Right-click on the JSP and select Web Run using <name>.jsp.

Developing EJBs with WebSphere

Each Enterprise Bean you create must belong to a JBuilder EJB module. The restriction with developing the EJB module for IBM WebSphere is that you will not be able to use EJB 2.0. An EJB module is a logical grouping of one or more Beans that will be deployed in a single JAR file, using IBM WebSphere only using EJB 1.x Beans.

Developing Session Beans

To create an EJB 1.x module and build some Session Beans within the module, follow these steps:

1. Create an EJB module within a project. The restriction placed on your project by IBM WebSphere requires the EJB module to be version 1.x (see Figure 27.9).

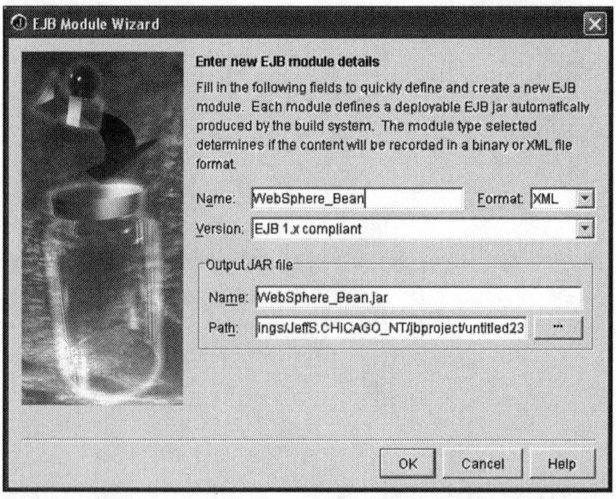

FIGURE 27.9 Building an EJB module with JBuilder for IBM WebSphere.

2. To create a Session Bean, select File, New. Select the Enterprise tab and choose Enterprise JavaBean 1.x (see Figure 27.10).
3. Click Next, which assigns the existing EJB module (see Figure 27.11).

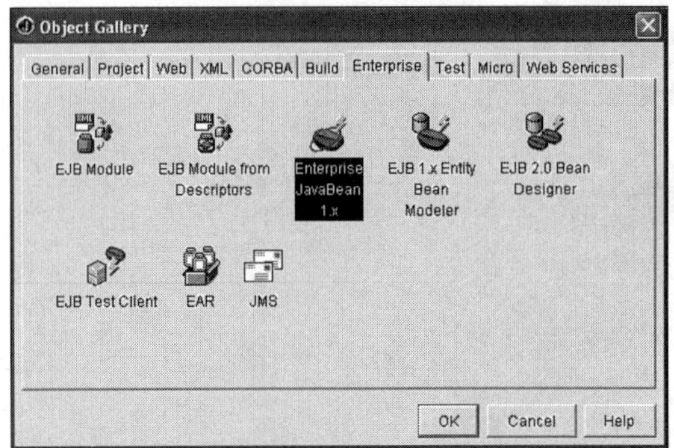

FIGURE 27.10 Select the Enterprise JavaBean 1.x from the Object Gallery.

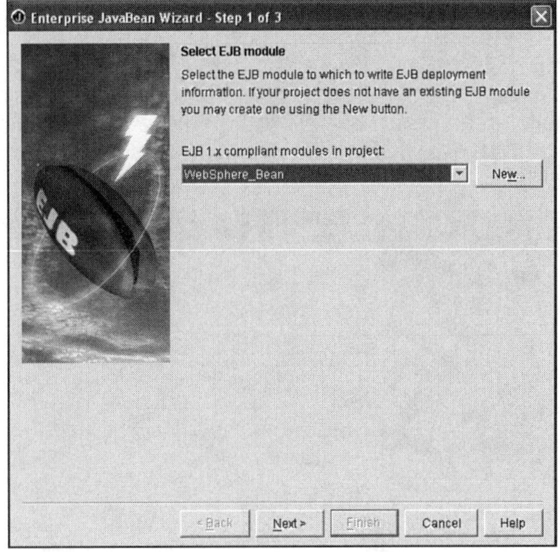

FIGURE 27.11 Building a Session Bean with Enterprise JavaBean 1.x; Select EJB Module (Step 1 of 3).

4. Assign the properties shown in Figure 27.12 to your Session Bean and click Next.
5. View the package names and JNDI settings for your Session Bean and click Finish (see Figure 27.13).

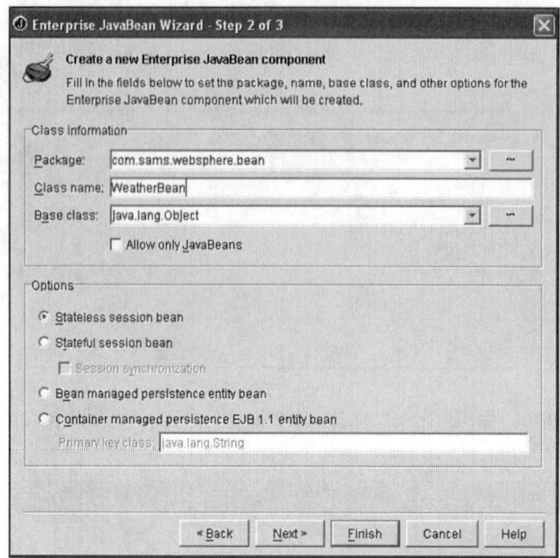

FIGURE 27.12 Building a Session Bean with Enterprise JavaBean 1.x; Create a New EJB Component (Step 2 of 3).

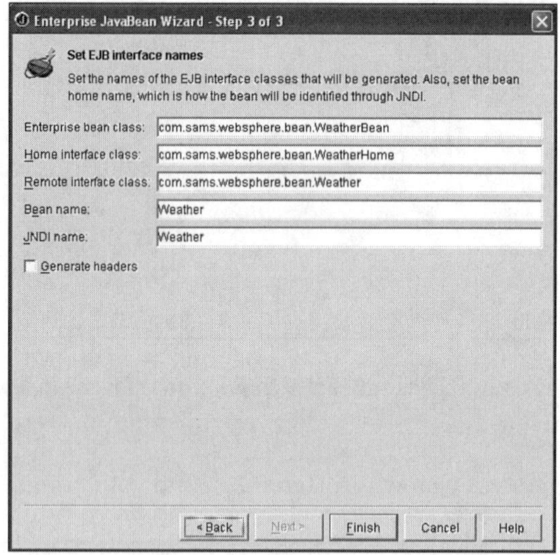

FIGURE 27.13 Building a Session Bean with Enterprise JavaBean 1.x; assign JNDI names and other properties (Step 3 of 3).

6. Add your business logic using the source created by the wizard.

Developing Entity Beans with WebSphere

Using BEA WebLogic or Borland Enterprise Server, you used the EJB 2.0 Designer for implementing Entity Beans. As noted earlier, IBM WebSphere supports only EJB 1.x, thus we must use the 1.x Entity Bean Modeler. The following process builds Entity Beans using IBM WebSphere:

1. Select File, New and select the Enterprise tab within the Object Gallery.
2. Select the EJB 1.x Entity Bean Modeler.
3. Leave the default EJB module. The name should be `WebSphere_Bean` (see Figure 27.14). Click Next.

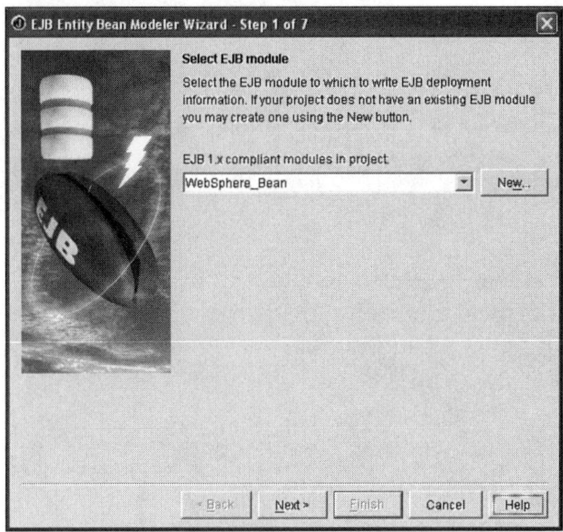

FIGURE 27.14 EJB 1.x Entity Bean Modeler (Step 1 of 7); Select EJB Module.

4. Supply the connection information to the data source (see Figure 27.15). The following parameters use the JDataStore employee database:

Property	Value
Drive	**com.borland.datastore.jdbc.DataStoreDriver**
URL	**`jdbc:borland:dslocal:C:\Development\JBuilder7\samples\JDataStore\datastores\employee.jds`**
Username	**Sample**
JNDI name	**`EmployeeDataSource`**

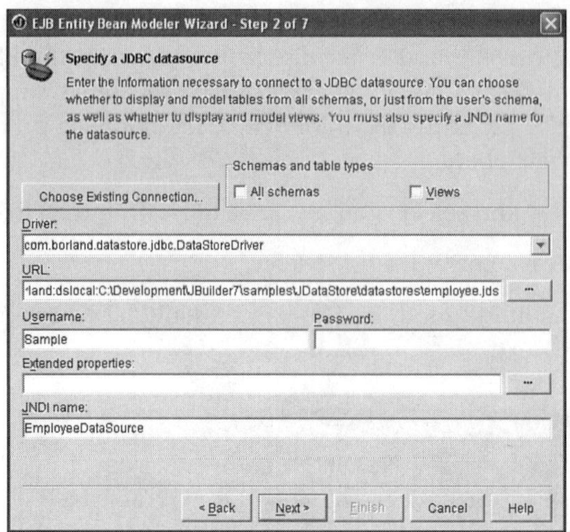

FIGURE 27.15 EJB 1.x Entity Bean Modeler (Step 2 of 7); supply JDBC connection properties.

5. This step allows you to select the tables from the database. The left panel shows the list of available tables for the database you selected in the previous window; the right panel shows the selected tables. The only table we will provide as an Entity Bean is Employee (see Figure 27.16).

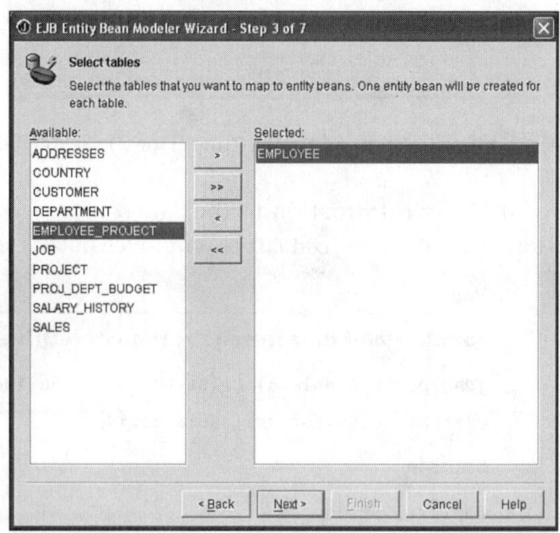

FIGURE 27.16 EJB 1.x Entity Bean Modeler (Step 3 of 7); select tables to make an Entity Bean.

6. Assign the columns to make available within the Entity Bean (see Figure 27.17). Make all the columns available to the Entity Bean.

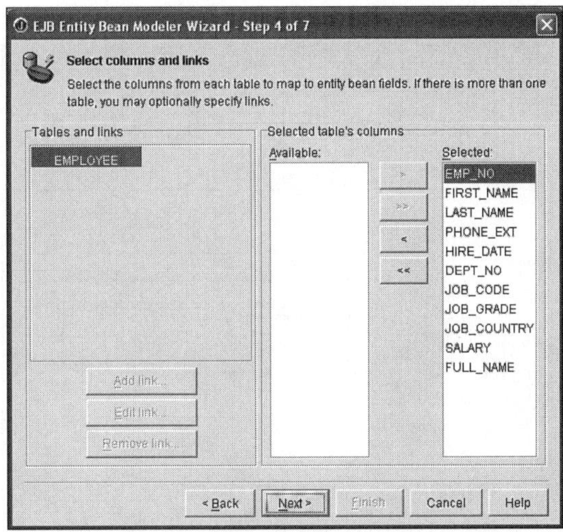

FIGURE 27.17 EJB 1.x Entity Bean Modeler (Step 4 of 7); assign available columns to the Entity Bean.

7. Specify the names and types of each property within the Entity Beans (see Figure 27.18). Leave the settings with the default values.

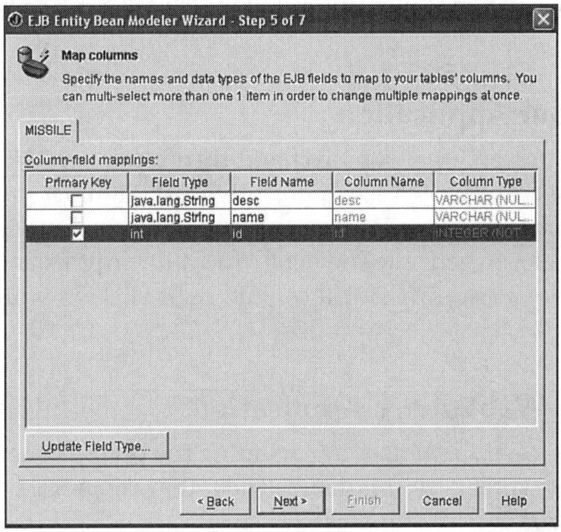

FIGURE 27.18 EJB 1.x Entity Bean Modeler (Step 5 of 7); supply the column types and names.

8. Change the default package name to **`com.sams.websphere`** (see Figure 27.19). Although we are going to leave the remaining properties as the defaults, you can also change the names of any of the interfaces or change the JNDI names.

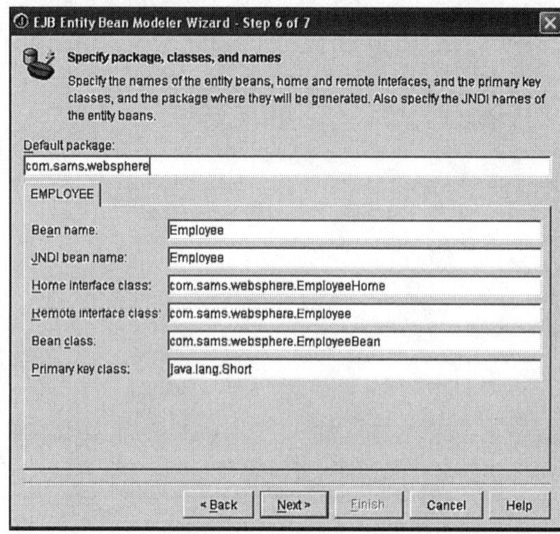

FIGURE 27.19 EJB 1.x Entity Bean Modeler (Step 6 of 7); supply the interface and package names.

9. Assign the properties for the Entity Bean. These properties control the Bean's behavior when deployed. Leave all the properties with the defaults, except check Generate findAll() method in the home interface (see Figure 27.20).

Deploying Your Application

To run the Session Bean, open a project and then create an EAR file, deploy the EAR file, and restart WebSphere. To accomplish this task, JBuilder provides a number of tasks important in the process. At the time of project make, JBuilder runs the WebSphere compiler to generate the deployment descriptors and container-generated files. For the deployment of your JAR or EAR, right-click on your archive and select Deploy.

Debugging a WebSphere Application

WebLogic can be started remotely by providing the options `-debugEnable-jdwpPort <Port #>` to the `startServer` command. The following process enables you to debug your application:

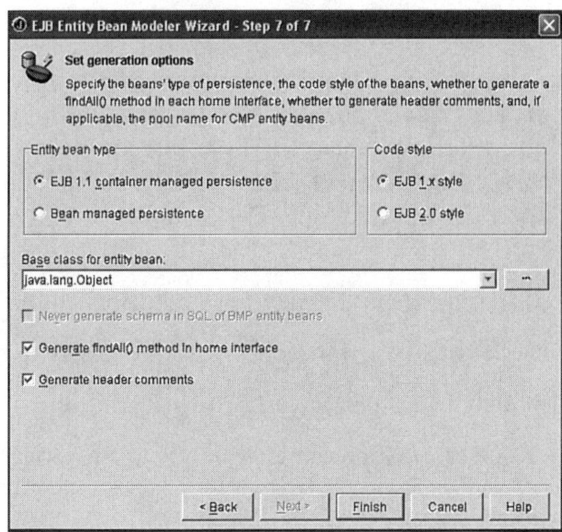

FIGURE 27.20 EJB 1.x Entity Bean Modeler (Step 7 of 7); change the generation options for the deployed Bean.

1. Start an MS-DOS window.
2. Type **C:\WebSphere\AppServer\bin\startServer –debugEnable –jdwpPort 5555**. This starts your server in debug mode.
3. Click Run, Configurations and select the Run tab.
4. Click New and select the Debug tab.
5. Enter the configuration name as **Remote Debug WebSphere**. Check Enable Remote Debugging.
6. Click Attach in the Remote Settings panel. Enter the address of the debug port—for example, port **5555**.

NOTE

The address specified here must be the same as the port number specified in the server as debug options. JBuilder opens a socket connection to the WebSphere server and attaches using the port number 5555.

7. Set your breakpoints and debug your application.

Summary

The J2EE is an architecture for a Java development platform for distributed enterprise applications. It was designed by Sun Microsystems, with input from the development community, including Borland, IBM, and BEA. Many different implementations of the J2EE platform exist, such as the Borland Enterprise Server, IBM WebSphere, and BEA WebLogics, and offer the developer the capability of building applications with these benefits:

- Scalability so that business transactions are processed quickly
- Reliability so that business transactions are processed accurately
- Security to protect users' privacy and the integrity of the enterprise's data
- Availability to meet the increasing demands of the global business environment
- Portability to ensure that dependence on a specific vendor is minimized

JBuilder is a Java integrated development environment that, when coupled with a supported application server from companies such as Borland, BEA, IBM, and Sun-Netscape, greatly simplifies and speeds the development of J2EE applications.

Reflections

- How much do I need to know about the differences between EJB vendors?
- Should I install WebLogic locally and remotely?
- How much should my design change from application server to application server?
- Should I write generically for any implementation?

28

Web Services

IN THIS CHAPTER

- Simple Object Access Protocol (SOAP)
- WSDL Component of Web Services
- UDDI Component of Web Services
- JBuilder Web Services Toolkit

Web services is the latest buzzword. Combine the promise of complete application interoperability, open standards, platform independence, universal vendor support, and the muscle of XML, and you've got an idea why so many industry vendors and users are excited about Web services.

CORBA addressed interoperability and vendor neutrality to some extent, but it failed to gain complete vendor support the way that Web services have (at least in momentum).

The following are the key technologies in Web services:

- SOAP (Simple Object Access Protocol)—SOAP provides the means by which to exchange messages between systems. The SOAP specification defines message content (including data types, headers, and the body), encoding rules of custom data types, transport protocol bindings (such as HTTP), and examples of common patterns used today, such as Remote Procedure Calls (RPCs).
- WSDL (Web Services Description Language)—The WSDL provides a means to completely describe Web services at a particular location. It contains the details necessary to programmatically use a Web service. It's constructed in such a way (XML) that tools can automate much of the process of consuming Web services.
- UDDI (Universal Description, Discovery, and Integration)—UDDI provides the capability to describe Web services, such that systems and users may discover them in a standard fashion. UDDI registries publish system contact information (responsible parties) and WSDL documents used to access the services.

- XML (Extensible Markup Language)—The key word is *extensible*. The authors of the SOAP specification used XML as the means to describe the content of the messages.

Simple Object Access Protocol (SOAP)

SOAP is a protocol specification used to access services across distributed networks. SOAP was created to address the need to use HTTP as a transport mechanism for messaging. SOAP standardizes using HTTP as a transport protocol to invoke XML messages and remote calls in a portable and open fashion. HTTP is an important protocol because it's firewall friendly, and most networks let HTTP traffic through their firewalls. Most other solutions require proprietary solutions, or "tunneling" through HTTP. SOAP was designed to be transport independent, so it's possible to use SMTP or other protocols to send messages.

It's important to note that SOAP is being shaped by the W3C standards body, not by a single vendor, to evolve into a useful specification. In fact, representatives from competing technologies (Sun and Microsoft, for example) are part of the expert groups for SOAP and XML.

Implementations of SOAP are available for major platforms by Microsoft and open source groups such as Apache. Numerous projects are in development and production exchanging SOAP calls with different vendor implementations of SOAP.

Apache SOAP is the first generation SOAP implementation for Java. Based on the SOAP 1.1 specification, Apache SOAP is a Java solution initially based on IBM's SOAP4J implementation.

Apache Axis is the second generation SOAP implementation for Java. Based on the SOAP 1.1 specification, Apache Axis provides a rich set of tools for generating Java classes based on WSDL documents.

SOAP Envelope

The first major component of SOAP is the envelope. The SOAP envelope is an XML document that represents a complete message to a SOAP service. In this chapter, we will develop a SOAP stock symbol lookup service to illustrate many of the topics. A SOAP envelope contains an optional header and a body. Listing 28.1 shows a simple SOAP message sent over HTTP as a POST message. Note that the `SOAP-ENV` is the first element in the XML document, and the `SOAP-ENV:Body` element is contained within the `SOAP-ENV` element.

LISTING 28.1 SOAP Request (SOAPRequest.txt)

```
POST /axis/services/StockQuoteServicePort HTTP/1.0
Content-Length: 510
Host: 127.0.0.1
Content-Type: text/xml; charset=utf-8
SOAPAction: ""

<?xml version="1.0" encoding="UTF-8"?>
<SOAP-ENV:Envelope SOAP-ENV:encodingStyle=
➥http://schemas.xmlsoap.org/soap/encoding/
➥ xmlns:SOAP-ENV="http://schemas.xmlsoap.org/soap/envelope/"
xmlns:xsd="http://www.w3.org/2001/XMLSchema"
➥xmlns:xsi="http://www.w3.org/2001/XMLSchema-instance" xmlns:SOAP-
ENC="http://schemas.xmlsoap.org/soap/encoding/">
 <SOAP-ENV:Body>
  <ns1:getQuote xmlns:ns1="http://webservicetest">
   <symbol xsi:type="xsd:string">BORL</symbol>
  </ns1:getQuote>
 </SOAP-ENV:Body>
</SOAP-ENV:Envelope>
```

The corresponding response to the preceding request message is shown in Listing 28.2.

LISTING 28.2 SOAP Response (SOAPResponse.txt)

```
HTTP/1.1 200 OK
Content-Type: text/xml; charset=utf-8
Content-Length: 487
Date: Sat, 20 Jul 2002 01:38:46 GMT
Server: Apache Tomcat/4.0.3 (HTTP/1.1 Connector)

<?xml version="1.0" encoding="UTF-8"?>
<SOAP-ENV:Envelope xmlns:SOAP-ENV="http://schemas.xmlsoap.org/soap/envelope/"
xmlns:xsd="http://www.w3.org/2001/XMLSchema"
➥xmlns:xsi="http://www.w3.org/2001/XMLSchema-instance">
 <SOAP-ENV:Body>
  <ns1:getQuoteResponse SOAP-ENV:encodingStyle=
➥"http://schemas.xmlsoap.org/soap/encoding/" xmlns:ns1="http://webservicetest">
   <getQuoteResult xsi:type="xsd:double">10.3</getQuoteResult>
  </ns1:getQuoteResponse>
 </SOAP-ENV:Body>
</SOAP-ENV:Envelope>
```

Encoding

Encoding is the second major component of SOAP. Encoding is fundamentally the rules that describe how application-defined types and built-in types can be encoded within the body of the envelope and decoded by the receiver. This is in contrast to sending custom data types in XML and parsing them by using a SAX or DOM parser. Encoding makes it possible, for example, to return a JavaBean as output from a message and have it translated by the SOAP client (on any platform) with no knowledge of Java or its data types. The following line of code is from the previous request SOAP envelope and shows the encoding of the single string parameter in the message:

```
<symbol xsi:type="xsd:string">BORL</symbol>
```

The preceding SOAP message consists of the following elements:

- `symbol`—The name of the argument.
- `xsi:type`—Refers to the xsi namespace defined earlier in the message. This one in particular refers to XML data types.
- `xsd:string`—Refers to the string data type as defined in the XML data types.
- `BORL`—The literal text passed as the argument. Note that it's a string.

This example points back to the *S* part of SOAP, *Simple*. When debugging traditional distributed applications, it's a luxury to be able to inspect the message coming across the wire. With this being the case, it's possible to determine the exact cause of a problem when different vendor solutions are sending the exact same message, but the format could be slightly different.

The preceding section shows an elementary example of passing a simple string argument and returning a simple double type. The following example shows how to return a user-defined Java class as a complex type. The following element is a piece of a SOAP response and contains the results from a message call. The returned object is a complex type. The information has been serialized automatically by the SOAP implementation.

```
<ns1:getQuoteResponse SOAP-ENV:encodingStyle=
➥"http://schemas.xmlsoap.org/soap/encoding/"
➥xmlns:ns1="http://webservicetest">
   <getQuoteResult href="#id0"/>
  </ns1:getQuote3Response>
  <multiRef id="id0" SOAP-ENC:root="0" xsi:type="ns2:StockInfo" xmlns:SOAP-
ENC="http://schemas.xmlsoap.org/soap/encoding/"
➥xmlns:ns2="http://webservicetest">
```

```
  <description xsi:type="xsd:string">BORLAND SOFTWARE CORP</description>
  <symbol xsi:type="xsd:string">BORL</symbol>
  <price xsi:type="xsd:double">10.3</price>
</multiRef>
```

Points of interest:

- `xmlns:SOAP-ENC=http://schemas.xmlsoap.org/soap/encoding/`—The namespace for SOAP encoding
- `xsi:type="ns2:StockInfo"`—Defines the namespace for our custom data type
- `description`, `symbol`, and `price`—The properties of the custom data type

To give you an idea of what the Java code looks like, the method definition for the original Java code looks like the following:

```
public StockInfo getQuote(String symbol);
```

Encoding in Apache SOAP or Axis for the most part is automated. This process is accomplished with serializers, much the same way that Beans are serialized in Java. Note that the end product of object serialization in SOAP messages must be a valid XML element and will look nothing like the traditional objects serialized because they must be deserialized/serialized in a standard way by non-Java implementations as well.

Data Types

The SOAP specification provides several data types. All the following data types must be implemented in a SOAP implementation in order to be compliant:

- Simple—`int`, `float`, `negativeInteger`, and many more that map to most data types in Java. The exhaustive list of simple types can be found at `http://www.w3.org/TR/xmlschema-2/#built-in-primitive-datatypes`. An example mapping of a simple type is `xsi:type="xsd:string"`.
- Compound—Contain components of different types. `StockInfo` in the preceding code is an example of a compound type. Compound types are often referred to as complex types.
- Arrays—Contain a list of elements. The items in the array can be of any type at any point within the array. The following shows an array of double values being returned:

  ```
  <getHighLowResult xsi:type="SOAP-ENC:Array"
  ➥SOAP-ENC:arrayType="xsd:double[2]" xmlns:SOAP-
  ```

```
ENC="http://schemas.xmlsoap.org/soap/encoding/">
    <item xsi:type="xsd:double">10.3</item>
    <item xsi:type="xsd:double">9.98</item>
   </getHighLowResult>
```

Note that the `xsd:double[2]` denotes the type of the elements in the array along with the size of the array. The actual data are in the item elements and are 10.3 and 9.98, respectively.

- Enumerations—Used when a distinct set of names or types is required. An example would be (apple, orange, pear). The definition for an enumeration looks similar to a compound type in that there is a named type followed by the possible values.

SOAP Faults

A SOAP fault is similar to a Java exception. A *fault* is a standard SOAP concept to indicate that an exception occurred and that different behavior may be required. A SOAP fault may indicate that the SOAP container was unable to process the request and may indicate a malformed URL. In other words, the host indicated could be correct, but the service requested may be incorrect. Listing 28.3 is an example of how a SOAP fault appears in a response to a malformed request. The `SOAP-ENV:fault` appears inside the `SOAP-ENV:Body` element.

LISTING 28.3 SOAP Fault (SOAPFault.txt)

```
<SOAP-ENV:Fault>
   <faultcode xmlns:ns1="http://xml.apache.org/axis/">
➥ns1:Server.NoService</faultcode>
   <faultstring>The AXIS engine could not find a target service to invoke!
➥  targetService is StockQuoteService999Port</faultstring>
   <detail>
    <ns2:stackTrace xmlns:ns2="http://xml.apache.org/axis/">The AXIS engine
➥could not find a target service to invoke!  targetService is
➥StockQuoteService999Port&#xd;
    at org.apache.axis.server.AxisServer.invoke(AxisServer.java:282)&#xd;
    at org.apache.axis.transport.http.AxisServlet.doPost
➥ (AxisServlet.java:547)&#xd;
    at javax.servlet.http.HttpServlet.service(HttpServlet.java:760)&#xd;
    at javax.servlet.http.HttpServlet.service(HttpServlet.java:853)&#xd;
    at org.apache.catalina.core.ApplicationFilterChain.internalDoFilter
➥ (ApplicationFilterChain.java:247)&#xd;
    at org.apache.catalina.core.ApplicationFilterChain.doFilter
➥ (ApplicationFilterChain.java:193)&#xd;
```

LISTING 28.3 Continued

```
    at org.apache.catalina.core.StandardWrapperValve.invoke
➥ (StandardWrapperValve.java:243)&#xd;
    at org.apache.catalina.core.StandardPipeline.invokeNext
➥ (StandardPipeline.java:566)&#xd;
    at org.apache.catalina.core.StandardPipeline.invoke
➥ (StandardPipeline.java:472)&#xd;
    at org.apache.catalina.core.ContainerBase.invoke
➥ (ContainerBase.java:943)&#xd;
    at org.apache.catalina.core.StandardContextValve.invoke
➥ (StandardContextValve.java:190)&#xd;
    at org.apache.catalina.core.StandardPipeline.invokeNext
➥ (StandardPipeline.java:566)&#xd;
    at org.apache.catalina.core.StandardPipeline.invoke
➥ (StandardPipeline.java:472)&#xd;
    at org.apache.catalina.core.ContainerBase.invoke
➥ (ContainerBase.java:943)&#xd;
    at org.apache.catalina.core.StandardContext.invoke
➥ (StandardContext.java:2343)&#xd;
    at org.apache.catalina.core.StandardHostValve.invoke
➥ (StandardHostValve.java:180)&#xd;
    at org.apache.catalina.core.StandardPipeline.invokeNext
➥ (StandardPipeline.java:566)&#xd;
    at org.apache.catalina.valves.ErrorDispatcherValve.invoke
➥ (ErrorDispatcherValve.java:170)&#xd;
    at org.apache.catalina.core.StandardPipeline.invokeNext
➥ (StandardPipeline.java:564)&#xd;
    at org.apache.catalina.valves.ErrorReportValve.invoke
➥ (ErrorReportValve.java:170)&#xd;
    at org.apache.catalina.core.StandardPipeline.invokeNext
➥ (StandardPipeline.java:564)&#xd;
    at org.apache.catalina.core.StandardPipeline.invoke
➥ (StandardPipeline.java:472)&#xd;
    at org.apache.catalina.core.ContainerBase.invoke
➥ (ContainerBase.java:943)&#xd;
    at org.apache.catalina.core.StandardEngineValve.invoke
➥ (StandardEngineValve.java:174)&#xd;
    at org.apache.catalina.core.StandardPipeline.invokeNext
➥ (StandardPipeline.java:566)&#xd;
    at org.apache.catalina.core.StandardPipeline.invoke
➥ (StandardPipeline.java:472)&#xd;
    at org.apache.catalina.core.ContainerBase.invoke
➥ (ContainerBase.java:943)&#xd;
```

LISTING 28.3 Continued

```
    at org.apache.catalina.connector.http.HttpProcessor.process
➥ (HttpProcessor.java:1012)&#xd;
    at org.apache.catalina.connector.http.HttpProcessor.run
➥ (HttpProcessor.java:1107)&#xd;
    at java.lang.Thread.run(Thread.java:484)&#xd;
</ns2:stackTrace>
   </detail>
  </SOAP-ENV:Fault>
```

Note the full stack trace as part of the additional fault string. The main fault text is in the `faultstring` element. SOAP faults usually are accessible as an enumeration of items for convenient processing.

SOAP RPC

The last SOAP component we'll discuss at this point is the concept of Remote Procedure Calls (RPCs) in SOAP. SOAP messages are, by definition, one-way messages. However, the authors of the SOAP specification discuss the information necessary to fulfill an RPC. The basics are a method name, parameters, and the URI of the service in question. SOAP RPC is implemented easily using HTTP as the transport because HTTP is by nature a request and response protocol.

WSDL Component of Web Services

This section discusses the Web Services Definition Language (WSDL) component of Web services. The sections of a WSDL document will be explained, along with some samples of describing a simple Web service. A WSDL document is an XML document that adheres to the schema defined within the document. In other words, a WSDL document is an XML file with a schema that it uses for validation. A WSDL document is the roadmap for potential clients (called *consumers*) to follow to access the Web service.

The tool that you are working with typically generates WSDL documents. Rarely will you need to generate the document manually. It is necessary to know the composition of a WSDL document because you will be relying on them when consuming or producing Web services. At least a fundamental understanding of WSDL is necessary for situations when your code is using a WSDL document to consume a Web service. Also, especially in the early days of Web services, sometimes it's necessary to modify portions of the WSDL document because of an error generated by the tool.

Listing 28.4 shows an example of a WSDL document, using SOAP 1.1 bindings.

LISTING 28.4 WSDL Document Sample (sample.wsdl)

```
<?xml version="1.0" encoding="UTF-8"?>
<wsdl:definitions targetNamespace="http://webservicetest"
➥xmlns="http://schemas.xmlsoap.org/wsdl/" xmlns:SOAP-ENC=
➥"http://schemas.xmlsoap.org/soap/encoding/"
➥xmlns:impl="http://webservicetest-impl" xmlns:intf=
➥"http://webservicetest" xmlns:wsdl="http://schemas.xmlsoap.org/wsdl/"
xmlns:wsdlsoap="http://schemas.xmlsoap.org/wsdl/soap/"
➥xmlns:xsd="http://www.w3.org/2001/XMLSchema">
    <types>
        <schema targetNamespace="http://webservicetest"
➥xmlns="http://www.w3.org/2001/XMLSchema">
            <complexType name="StockInfo">
                <sequence>
                    <element name="symbol" nillable="true" type="xsd:string"/>
                    <element name="description" nillable="true"
➥type="xsd:string"/>
                    <element name="price" type="xsd:double"/>
                </sequence>
            </complexType>
            <element name="StockInfo" nillable="true" type="intf:StockInfo"/>
        </schema>
    </types>
    <wsdl:message name="getQuote3Response">
        <wsdl:part name="return" type="intf:StockInfo"/>
    </wsdl:message>
    <wsdl:message name="getQuote3Request">
        <wsdl:part name="symbol" type="SOAP-ENC:string"/>
        <wsdl:part name="test" type="xsd:int"/>
    </wsdl:message>
    <wsdl:portType name="StockQuoteServicePortType">
        <wsdl:operation name="getQuote3" parameterOrder="symbol test">
            <wsdl:input message="intf:getQuote3Request"/>
            <wsdl:output message="intf:getQuote3Response"/>
        </wsdl:operation>
    </wsdl:portType>
    <wsdl:binding name="StockQuoteServicePortSoapBinding"
➥type="intf:StockQuoteServicePortType">
        <wsdlsoap:binding style="rpc"
➥transport="http://schemas.xmlsoap.org/soap/http"/>
        <wsdl:operation name="getQuote3">
            <wsdlsoap:operation soapAction=""/>
            <wsdl:input>
```

LISTING 28.4 Continued

```
                <wsdlsoap:body
➥encodingStyle="http://schemas.xmlsoap.org/soap/encoding/"
➥namespace="http://webservicetest" use="encoded"/>
            </wsdl:input>
            <wsdl:output>
                <wsdlsoap:body
➥encodingStyle="http://schemas.xmlsoap.org/soap/encoding/"
➥namespace="http://webservicetest" use="encoded"/>
            </wsdl:output>
        </wsdl:operation>
    </wsdl:binding>
    <wsdl:service name="StockQuoteService">
        <wsdl:port binding="intf:StockQuoteServicePortSoapBinding"
➥name="StockQuoteServicePort">
            <wsdlsoap:address
➥location="http://localhost:8080/axis/services/StockQuoteServicePort"/>
        </wsdl:port>
    </wsdl:service>
</wsdl:definitions>
```

The following list describes the major components of a WSDL document:

- Types—This section defines any complex data types used in the message elements. The standard data types are not defined in this section.
- Message—Multiple messages are in the document. Each message represents one distinct communication with the service. To achieve an RPC, two message elements make up the operation (described next in port type).
- Port type—Consists of operations (that is, methods), each consisting of input and output message elements. This is simply the list of input arguments and any output arguments (responses). Another thing you might notice when using SOAP is that a method defined returning "void" still contains an output message element. This is because SOAP messages sent over HTTP are modeled as an RPC, and a response is required.
- Binding—Defines the encoding and protocol for a port type. Notice that the type for the binding relates to the port type.
- Port—Commonly referred to as an endpoint, a port defines an address. See the location attribute of the address element.
- Service—A service defines a set of ports together to expose it as a single service.

At first glance, a WSDL document is complex. The complexity is really in the linking of the different elements that comprise a single service. Generally it's useful to examine a single service method and to highlight the distinct pieces and how the pieces all fit together.

UDDI Component of Web Services

This section focuses on the Universal Description, Discovery, and Integration (UDDI) component of Web services. UDDI is a repository of business information, designed to be the central point between business partners and their customers. UDDI allows programmatic and human queries against metadata stored by businesses. This metadata can be queried by various criteria, including business type or industry, region within a particular country, and so forth. In other words, UDDI helps businesses find other businesses that provide online transaction capabilities. The UDDI registry also contains technical information necessary to conduct transactions with those businesses. Technical information such as a WSDL document that describes the business services provided is available and thus is a roadmap to the particular service that a business offers.

An example of a typical business instance is integrated package tracking for a Web site. An online business might want to provide online and integrated package tracking through its various shipping vendors (FedEx, UPS, and so on). That online business would look up the specific shipping vendors in the UDDI registry, gather the particular technical details for its IT staff, and build an integrated package tracking mechanism within its Web site. Of course, this is an oversimplification, but this is a typical business scenario that will repeat itself. This is a standard way to perform application integration using Web services that can bridge platforms, languages, and all the other Web services benefits.

WSDL documents can usually be obtained from UDDI servers and thus serve as a complete repository for discovering and consuming Web services.

JBuilder Web Services Toolkit

Borland developed the Web services toolkit for JBuilder 7 Enterprise to provide the productivity enhancements expected by JBuilder developers. The Web Services Toolkit packages the Apache Axis distribution along with several wizards that make JBuilder the most productive environment for building Web services.

With the Web Services Toolkit, it's possible to perform the following actions inside JBuilder:

- Import a WSDL document to build a test client for a Web service that you've found through the UDDI registry.
- Build a SOAP server to act as the base for your Web services.

- Expose a simple Java class as a Web service.
- Expose an EJB Session Bean as a Web service.
- Debug a Web service and a Web service client concurrently.

Apache Axis

The Apache Axis distribution contains a great deal of functionality that the JBuilder Web Services Toolkit uses. The following list summarizes these features:

- WSDL generation from a Java class—This is the WSDL2Java tool that can be run from the command line with the Axis distribution.
- Java class generation—Builds a set of proxy client classes for a WSDL document. This is the WSDL2Java tool also run from the command line.
- Web service deployment descriptor (WSDD) generation—When a new class is exposed as a Web service, deployment settings for Axis are generated.
- EJB provider for exposing stateless EJBs as Web services—This provides the necessary glue for instantiating an EJB exposed as a Web service.
- TCP Monitor—This monitors requests and responses from within JBuilder. To use this, the client must direct calls to a port that the TCP Monitor is listening on. The TCP Monitor then redirects these calls to the Web service. This tool is useful for snooping requests sent (debugging) and for understanding SOAP requests in general.

Examples Primer

To build a SOAP service, follow these steps:

1. Code and test your business logic class.
2. Expose the class as a Web service.
3. Generate a SOAP server in JBuilder to contain the Web services.
4. Run the Web application using the Tomcat Web container. This deploys the Web service for testing.
5. Modify the test case generated by step 3 to test the Web service.
6. Run the test client to test functionality.

To test an external Web service, perform the following steps:

1. Obtain the WSDL document through the Web Services Explorer or through other means.
2. Add the WSDL document to your project.
3. Import the WSDL document to generate Java classes.
4. Modify the test case to include parameters that will provide a meaningful test.
5. Run the test client to test functionality.

In Practice

This section provides working examples for building a Web service and importing an external Web service. It also shows you how to use the TCP Monitor and Web Services Explorer tools.

Building a Web Service

The sample Web service will be the often-used example of providing stock quotes based on a stock ticker symbol. This example is trivial but illustrates some key concepts you will initially encounter when developing Web services.

Example steps:

1. Create a new, blank project for this example. Call this project **`ch28-stockquote`**. This project contains the Stock Quote service.
2. Inspect the server properties of this project by selecting Project, Project Properties. The Server tab is the last tab. In the top group box, make sure that the first radio box (Single server for all services in project) is selected and choose Tomcat 4.0 from the list. If this is not an available option, go to the Tools, Configure Servers menu and enable this server. By default, Tomcat 4.0 is installed with JBuilder.
3. Select File, New Class to bring up the Class Wizard.. Enter **`ch28`** as the package name and **`StockQuote`** as the class name. Make sure that the base class contains **`java.lang.Object`**. Choose the Public option and uncheck the remaining four options.
4. Create a new method called `getPrice()`. The signature of the method should look like this:

   ```
   public double getPrice(String symbol)
   ```

Listing 28.5 shows the completed `StockQuote` class.

LISTING 28.5 Simple Stock Quote (StockQuote.java)

```
package ch28;

public class StockQuote {
    public StockQuote() {
    }

    public double getPrice(String symbol) {
        return 43.5;
    }

    // simple test
    public static void main(String[] args) {
        StockQuote stockQuote1 = new StockQuote();
        System.out.println( stockQuote1.getPrice("BORL"));
    }
}
```

The preceding example is similar to a Hello World example in that it really does nothing more than test the fundamentals of a new technology. In fact, this example will never really obtain real-time stock quotes but will be a simulation of a real-world Web service.

After you run the simple class to verify that it's working, we can move on to exposing it as a Web service.

Exposing the Java Class As a Web Service

This step creates the files necessary to expose the `StockQuote` class as a Web service. In this step, we will select the methods that we want to expose, set the default namespace mappings, and select the options for importing the WSDL document we will create.

To expose the `StockQuote` class as a Web service, one of the following methods can be used:

- Right-click on the class in the Project pane and choose Export Class as a Web Service.
- Choose File, New (or the New icon in the toolbar). Select the Export Class as a Web Service item in the Web Services tab in the Object Gallery.

Either step brings up the Export Class as a Web Service Wizard shown in Figure 28.1. Make sure that the `ch28.StockQuote` class is displayed in the Interface or class text area. For this simple example, leave the other options at their default settings. The name of the service should be `StockQuoteService`. The Generate client stub check box should be selected. Click the Next button to proceed to step 2.

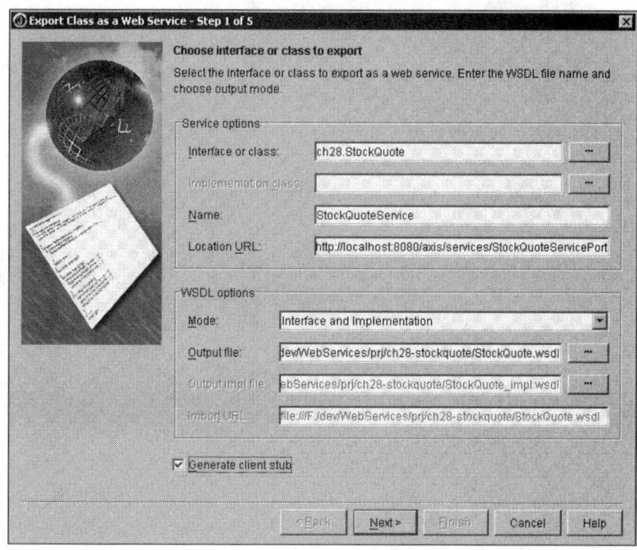

FIGURE 28.1 Export Class as a Web Service.

Step 2 displays the methods that we want to expose as Web services (see Figure 28.2). The default is to expose all methods, but you might want to examine the functionality of this step. You can change the Selection mode to Allow selected methods and choose only the new method, `getPrice()`. Click Next to proceed to step 3.

Step 3 displays the namespace mapping to be used for packages (see Figure 28.3). If your project contains package names, these package names will be mapped into the namespace. For example, if your package name is `stockserver`, the namespace will be `http://stockserver`. This information appears later in the generated WSDL document. For our example, the `DefaultNamespace` will be used. Click Next to proceed to step 4.

Step 4 is used to set the options for WSDL document importing (see Figure 28.4). The WSDL file will be generated as part of this wizard, but this step serves as the setup for the files generated to access this Web service. By default, the package will be set to the package name of the Web service (or `DefaultNamespace` if there is no package name) with `_generated` appended. For now, select only the Generate JUnit test case check box. Click Next to proceed to step 5.

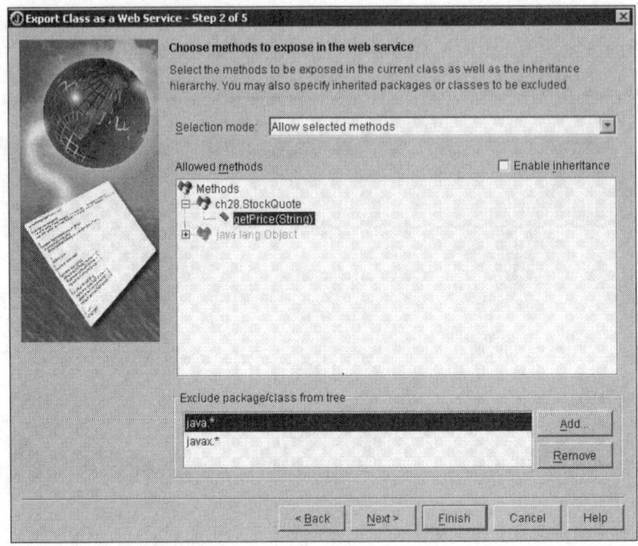

FIGURE 28.2 Select the methods to expose.

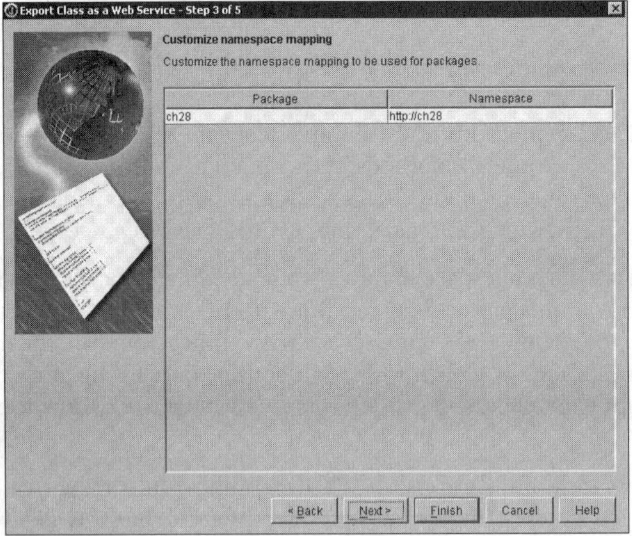

FIGURE 28.3 Customize namespace mapping.

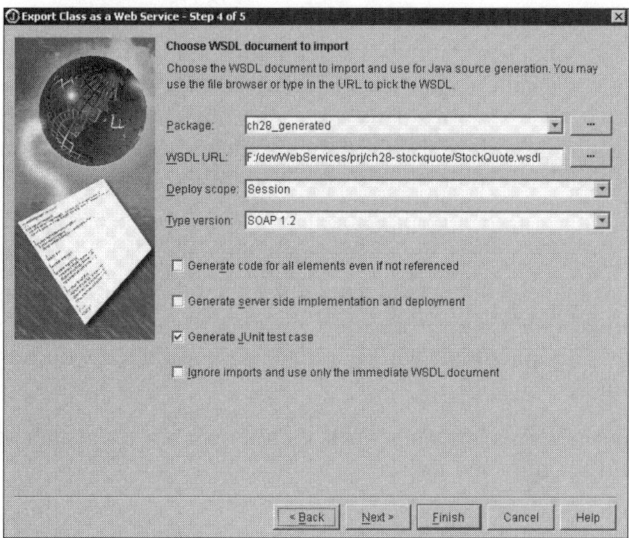

FIGURE 28.4 Import WSDL document.

NOTE

It's generally a good idea to keep generated code in a package separate from your business logic code because you can blow away a package that contains generated classes without worrying about impacting your code.

Step 5 is the final step of this wizard. This step is used to customize the namespaces to package names. Note the default mappings from the package names to the namespaces and click the Finish button to complete this wizard.

At the completion of this wizard, you will see the new WSDL document and the `DefaultNamespace_generated` package in the project pane along with the generated class files. At this point, save all the generated files and make the project to verify that no errors are present.

The following is a summary of each generated file:

- `StockQuoteService`—Extends the RPC service (`javax.xml.rpc.Service`) interface.
- `StockQuoteServiceLocator`—Implements the `StockQuoteService` interface. Returns the port address and a `StockQuoteServicePortType` instance.

- `StockQuoteServicePortSoapBindingStub`—Encapsulates all the SOAP calls to the Web service. There should be one public method per Web service method (because it implements the remote interface `StockQuoteServicePortType`). The other methods are private. This class will not be used directly by the code you write, but it's important to know the details because you may have to compose a similar stub class to be more flexible. An example of a more flexible case would be when you want to provide a WSDL document at production time and don't want to have to hard-code the port details into a class.
- `StockQuoteServicePortType`—This is the remote interface for the Web service. You will see a method in this interface for each method you choose to expose. This class is synonymous with a remote class you'd use when using EJBs or Java RMI.
- `StockQuoteServiceTestCase`—This is the JUnit test case that serves as a simple test client for this Web service.

Creating a New SOAP Server

It's now necessary to create a SOAP server, which is necessary to provide the infrastructure to service client requests. The previous step of exposing the class simply generated the WSDL document and the stub classes to access the Web service. This process creates a Web application, which you can then use to deploy your Web services under. This step is necessary to test your Web service under the typical conditions that Web services are deployed and to verify that your Web service methods can be accessed.

To create a new SOAP server, invoke the Object Gallery by selecting File, New or by selecting the New icon from the toolbar. Select the Web Services tab. The SOAP Server option will be the first item in the list. Figure 28.5 shows the create SOAP Server option in the Object Gallery.

This wizard is a two-step process. The first step builds a Web application (see Figure 28.6). The screen prompts for a name and a directory. The name is the name of the Web application. The directory is the document root for your Web application. Typically, these two fields should be the same. For our example, we'll follow the typical procedure of using "axis" for our name and directory. Go ahead and select the Generate WAR check box; this specifies that the WAR should be generated each time the project is built. You can turn off this option later because it slows down the build process slightly. Click OK to proceed to the SOAP Server Wizard.

Step 1 of the SOAP Server Wizard prompts for a Web application to use (WebApp) and a Web Services Toolkit to base the SOAP server on (see Figure 28.7). The defaults should be the Web application created in the previous step (axis), and the Toolkit should be "Apache Axis," respectively. If these options are not selected by default, select them and then click Next to continue to step 2.

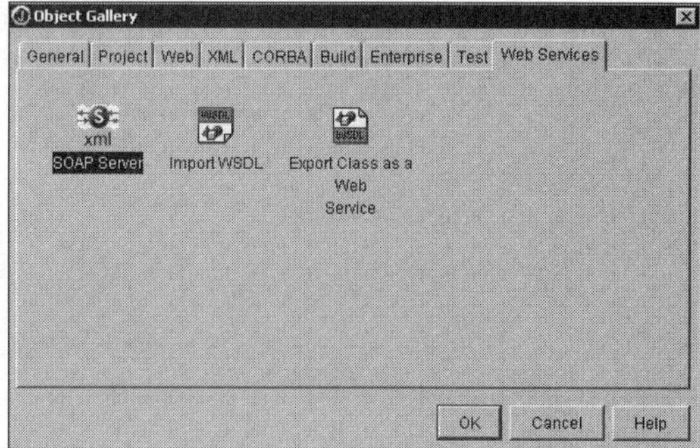

FIGURE 28.5 Create SOAP Server.

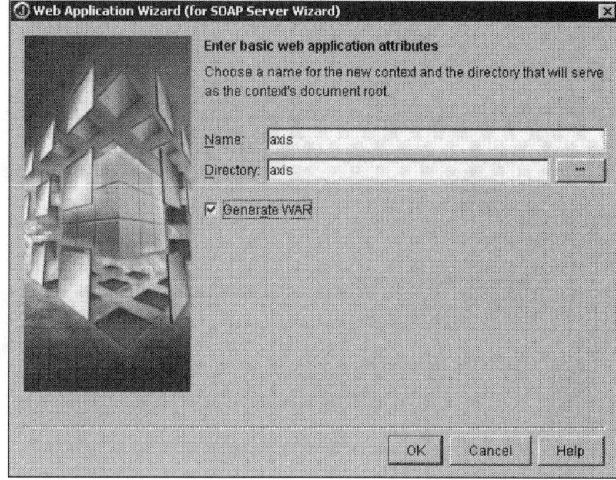

FIGURE 28.6 Web Application Wizard.

NOTE

The Copy admin/console to webapp check box copies the necessary files to the Web application's document root to administer this Web application after it's deployed.

Step 2 creates a runtime configuration in which to launch the Web application containing the Web services (see Figure 28.8). This allows you to run or debug the Web application inside JBuilder. This option is unnecessary if a runtime configuration already exists to run the application as a Web application. Click the Finish button to complete this wizard. You should now see a runtime configuration called Web Services Server under the Run menu.

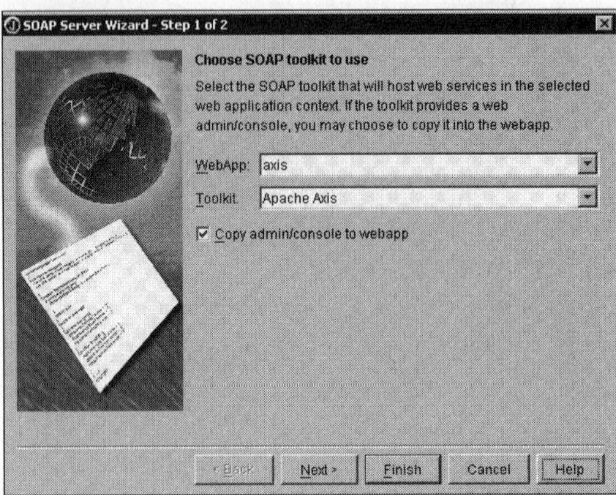

FIGURE 28.7 Choose a SOAP Toolkit.

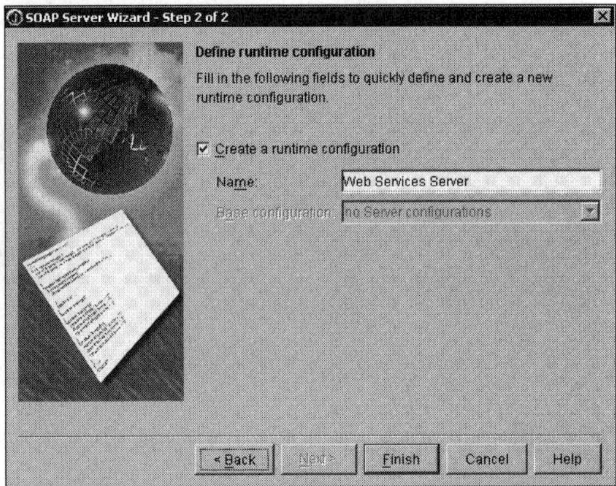

FIGURE 28.8 Create a runtime configuration.

Notice a Web application icon in the Project pane. If you expand this node and look under the SOAP: Apache Axis toolkit subnode, you will see the deployment descriptor for this Web service (wsdd extension). You can double-click on this item to view the contents. Notice the `className` parameter and the value. The value is the original class exposed as a Web service. The Apache Axis container uses this information to determine which classes are exposed and which methods can be invoked. Close this file before continuing to the next step.

Testing the New Web Service

At this point, we're ready to test the new Web service. Select the run configuration from the menu option under the Run menu or the configuration under the run icon. If you're unsure of which item to use, go to the configurations (under the project properties, Run tab) and look at which configuration has the Server type. Upon invoking the proper run configuration, you'll see a new tab open in the message pane area of the AppBrowser (see Figure 28.9). The Tomcat 4.0.3 information appears first, followed by a lot of WebappLoader messages, which mean that the Web service application, axis, is being deployed automatically.

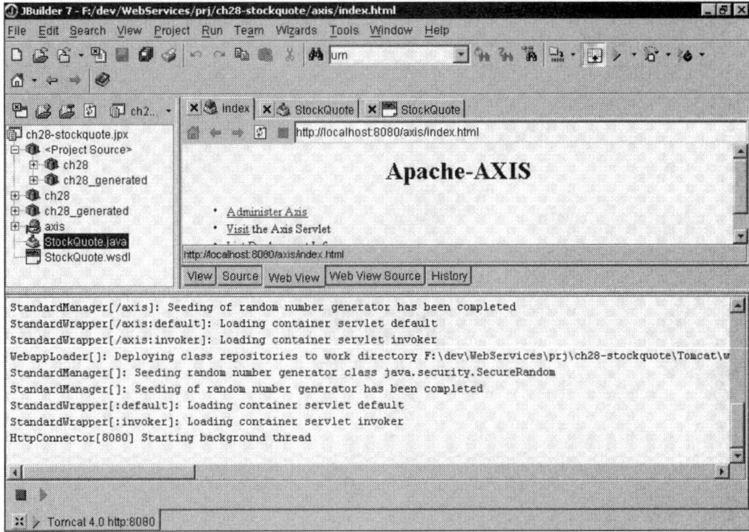

FIGURE 28.9 Output of running Web application.

Now that the Web service is running, find the `StockQuoteServiceTestCase` class in the Project pane. Run the test case by selecting the Run Test `StockQuoteServiceTestCase` using defaults item from the Run menu. Note that you must have the test case class open for this menu option to appear. This starts up the JUnit testing environment, and you will see the success indicators next to the test method. Figure 28.10 shows the expected results.

That's it. A basic Web service has been created and tested. You'll probably want to look at the `StockQuoteServiceTestCase` test class to really get a feel for how the generated classes interact. The best way to do this, of course, is to debug the test class, the Web service, or both.

At this point, stop the Web server by selecting the Tomcat 4.0 message tab and clicking the Reset icon just above the tab.

Debugging the New Web Service

To debug the Web service, start the Web application in Debug mode, as you normally would any other servlet or JSP Web application. Because the JBuilder Web Services Wizard created a runtime configuration, simply start up the application using the Run/Debug Project menu option. This starts the JVM that Tomcat runs inside in Debug mode. Now, set a breakpoint inside the `StockQuote` class's `getPrice` method. Now, start the JUnit test case, `StockQuoteServiceTestCase`, as in the previous example. JBuilder stops at the breakpoint line and allows you to inspect the environment. This is a somewhat trivial example of debugging, but this is a productive manner in which to develop new Web services, especially if you're unfamiliar with the new class libraries (Axis).

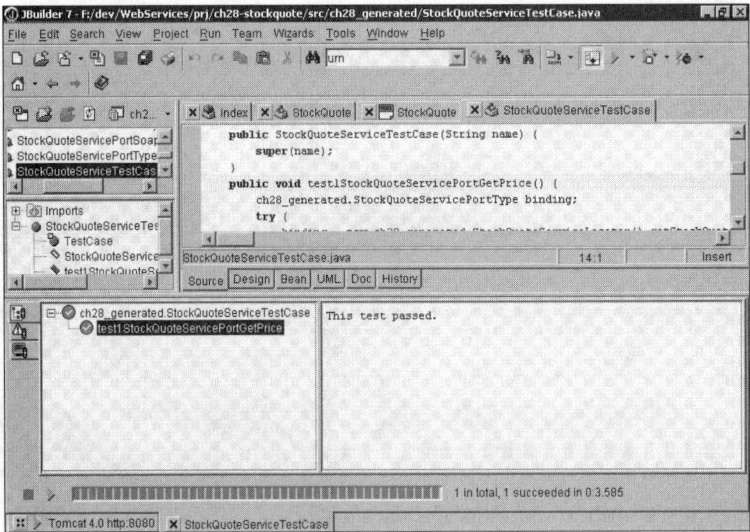

FIGURE 28.10 Output of the `StockQuoteServiceTestCase`.

Debugging the Test Case

To debug the test case, set a breakpoint in the `StockQuoteServiceTestCase` class. Try initially setting the breakpoint on the line that instantiates the binding object:

```
binding = new ch28_generated.StockQuoteServiceLocator().
➥getStockQuoteServicePort();
```

Select the Debug Test StockQuoteServiceTestCase.java using the default menu item from the Run menu. JBuilder starts up the JUnit testing environment and stops at the breakpoint you set before debugging this test case. Try stepping into (the shortcut is F7) the `getStockQuoteServicePort()` method to see how the generated classes operate. The `StockQuoteServiceLocator` class will be important in the next section on viewing the SOAP envelopes in JBuilder.

Utilizing the TCP Monitor Tool

As described earlier, Apache Axis is delivered with several useful tools. One of these tools is the TCP Monitor. The TCP Monitor tool allows you to view the SOAP envelopes exchanged between your Web services and any test clients. The TCP Monitor listens on a specific port for SOAP packets, displays them, and sends the request to an alternate port. The alternate port is typically the Web container running the Web service. There are several different ways to accomplish viewing the SOAP requests. The simplest way is to perform the following steps:

1. Stop any JBuilder running processes (Web applications, debug sessions, client running sessions).
2. Stop any external Tomcat sessions. (You'll be amazed how many times you may forget to do this.)
3. Open the TCP Monitor tool (found on the Tools menu, directly above Configure Tools).
4. Stop the TCP Monitor tool. By default, this tool is waiting for a connection on the default port (8082). Click on the Stop button to stop TCP Monitor.
5. Change the port that the TCP Monitor tool is listening on. Change the entry in the Listen Port to 8080. Change the port entry to 8082. Click on the Start button.
6. Start the Web application. You should notice Tomcat startup on a port other than 8080. It should, by default, start on 8082. You can tell which port it's listening on by looking at the tab at the bottom of the environment. Look for something such as Tomcat 4.0 http:8082.
7. Run the test case as performed earlier. The test case should run successfully as before. Now, switch to the TCPMonitor running application (see Figure 28.11). You should see an entry in the application for the request that was sent.

NOTE

Tomcat looks for an unused port when starting up. To view this information, go to the Web Services run configuration (Run/Configurations menu option) and select the configuration you're using to run the server. Click the Edit button to view the configuration. The Server tab should be selected for this configuration by default. Select the JSP/Servlet entry on the Services category (lower left-hand side of the dialog) list box. The Search for unused port check box should be checked. The default port number that Tomcat uses is in the Port number box to the left.

You'll notice some other interesting features of the TCP Monitor:

- You can resend a particular request. You could potentially perform a debug session, attempt to find a problem, and then resend the previous problematic request.
- You can change the layout to be horizontal (side-by-side) rather than vertical.
- You can save request-response information to a file. This saves a text file representing the currently selected item.

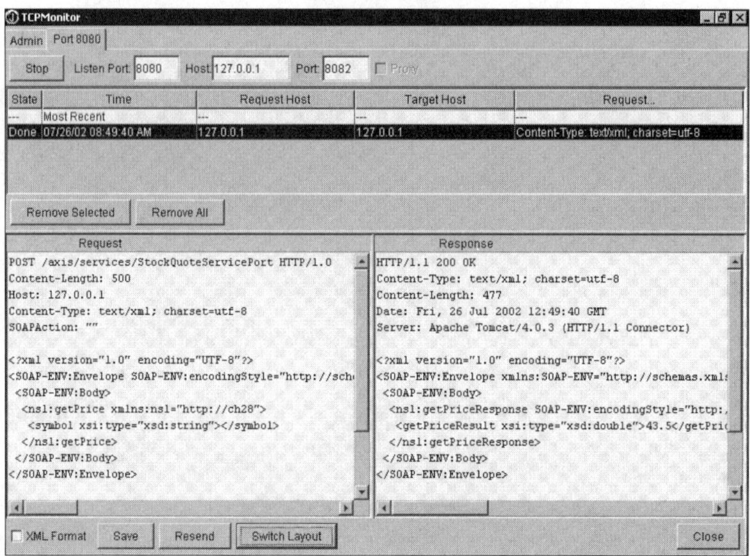

FIGURE 28.11 TCPMontitor tool.

Enhancing the Simple Web Service

Beyond a simple Web service, complex data types are the next logical step for the sample Web service. For the example, we'll create a `StockInfo` class that can return more information than just the current stock price. This complex type returns the stock's description and the price. For this example, we'll just create a new Bean, `StockInfo`. Create a Java class as you normally would and place it into the `ch28` package as the `StockQuote` class. Listing 28.6 shows the new class, which holds the complete stock information.

LISTING 28.6 Stock Quote Information (StockInfo.java)

```
package ch28;
public class StockInfo {
    private String symbol;
    private String description;
    private double price;

    public StockInfo() {
    }
    public String getDescription() {
        return description;
    }
    public void setDescription(String description) {
        this.description = description;
    }
    public void setPrice(double price) {
        this.price = price;
    }
    public double getPrice() {
        return price;
    }
    public String getSymbol() {
        return symbol;
    }
    public void setSymbol(String symbol) {
        this.symbol = symbol;
    }
}
```

After you've created the JavaBean to contain the stock information, add the `getInfo()` method specified in Listing 28.7.

LISTING 28.7 Enhanced Stock Quote (StockQuote.java)

```
package ch28;

public class StockQuote {

    public double getPrice(String symbol) {
        System.out.println("getPrice("+symbol+")");
        return 43.9;
    }
```

LISTING 28.7 Continued

```
    public StockInfo getInfo(String symbol) {
        System.out.println("getInfo("+symbol+")");

        StockInfo stockInfo = new StockInfo();
        stockInfo.setSymbol(symbol);
        stockInfo.setPrice(43.9);
        stockInfo.setDescription("Sample stock");
        return stockInfo;
    }

    // simple test
    public static void main(String[] args) {
        StockQuote stockQuote1 = new StockQuote();
        System.out.println( stockQuote1.getPrice("BORL"));

        StockInfo stockInfo = stockQuote1.getInfo("BORL");
        System.out.println("returned from getInfo(): description="+
➥stockInfo.getDescription());
    }
}
```

Because our Web services can be easily generated, you can safely export the `StockQuote` class as a Web service once again using the same settings as before. Note that you'll lose any code you may have changed in the JUnit test case class (StockQuoteServiceTestCase.java). The new class contains only the code necessary to test the methods specified for export. (By default, all methods will be exposed.)

NOTE

You may have noticed that the `StockInfo` class is not marked as serializable as is traditional in EJB development. This is because Bean serialization is not used with Web services. Utility classes included with Apache Axis provide the serialization. Remember that the information is not serialized in the Java serialization, but it is serialized to XML in a format that can be deserialized by other platforms and software.

If you're curious, open the deploy.wsdd (under the webapp node, under the `<SOAP: Apache Axis toolkit>` item) file. You'll notice a `typeMapping` element after exporting the class as a Web service. The Serializer attribute specifies the class to use for serialization, and the Deserializer provides the deserialization part of this object. In other words, these classes know how to translate Java classes to and from XML. This is similar to traditional JavaBean serialization. Of course it causes no harm to add this interface to your Bean class. The WSDL2Java tool actually includes this in the class it generates.

You can inspect the results of the serialization/deserialization process by using the TCP Monitor.

After exporting the `StockQuote` class as a Web service, you'll notice a new class in the `ch28_generated` package: `StockInfo.java`. This class was generated by the Apache Axis WSDL2Java tool. Remember that complex types are defined in the WSDL by the service provider. It just so happens that we're the provider and the consumer of this Web service. This may seem a bit confusing—just imagine that you're using a Web service from another company. You'll want to use the generated classes to separate the dependencies from your code. Also, the provider might not be a Java service at all. It could very well be a .NET service providing this complex type. Listing 28.8 shows the portion of the StockQuote.wsdl file that was used to generate `ch28_generated.StockInfo.java`.

LISTING 28.8 StockQuote Service Types (StockQuote.wsdl)

```
<types>
  <schema targetNamespace="http://ch28"
➥xmlns="http://www.w3.org/2001/XMLSchema">
    <complexType name="StockInfo">
     <sequence>
      <element name="symbol" nillable="true" type="xsd:string"/>
      <element name="description" nillable="true" type="xsd:string"/>
      <element name="price" type="xsd:double"/>
     </sequence>
    </complexType>
    <element name="StockInfo" nillable="true" type="intf:StockInfo"/>
  </schema>
 </types>
```

This concludes the example walk-through for building a sample Web service. The next example builds on the information in this example and shows how to consume an external Web service. You'll notice many of the same concepts as well as some of the same wizard screens.

Consuming a Web Service

This example walks through the process of consuming a Web service. In other words, you will use a Web service created by a third party and published on a public UDDI site. To begin this example, create a new project in JBuilder called `ch28-explorer`.

After the project is created, open the Web Services Explorer, which is located on the Tools menu directly above the TCP Monitor. Double-click on the UDDI sites to expand the list of known UDDI sites. Expand the XMethods node and select the Business List element. Figure 28.12 shows the Web Services Explorer tool.

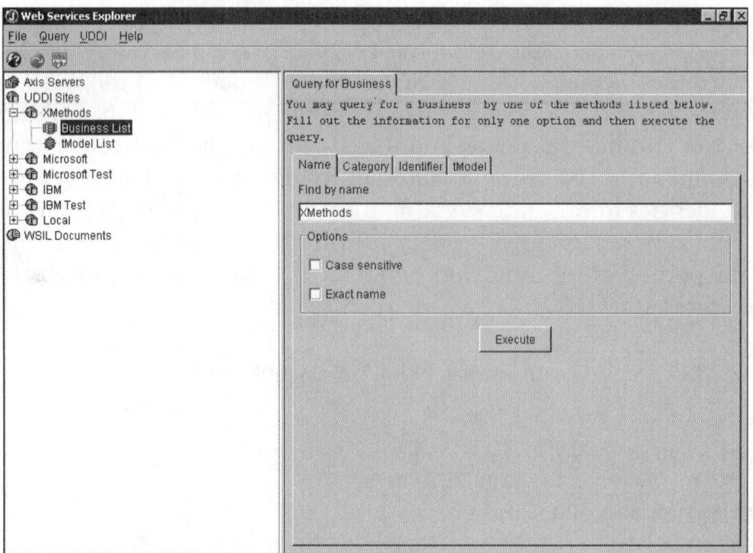

FIGURE 28.12 Web Services Explorer.

Enter **`XMethods`** into the Find by name text box and click on the Execute button. This returns the services offered on the XMethods server. Several interesting services are available on this server. We'll be importing and using the Barnes and Noble Price Quote service. Find this service under the XMethods node and expand this node until you see the Barnes and Noble Price Quote node. Figure 28.13 shows how the Web Services Explorer should look.

Select this node and click on the Import WSDL toolbar icon, or select the File, Import WSDL menu option. This launches a familiar dialog box to import the service's WSDL document into the new project. For simplicity's sake, leave the default options checked (Generate server side implementation and deployment and Generate JUnit test case), and click the Finish button. This generates the classes necessary to access the Web service. Figure 28.14 shows the Import WSDL Wizard with the default options checked.

This Web service makes it possible to look up the price of a book at the Barnes and Noble online bookstore based on the book's ISBN. To test this service, find the generated class `BNQuoteServiceTestCase.java` and find the line in the `test1BNQuotePortGetPrice()` method that has the `binding.getPrice(new java.lang.String())` code in it. Replace the instantiation of a blank string with an actual ISBN, such as `0743211375`, the latest Stephen King book, *From a Buick 8*. Immediately following this line, you'll probably want to see the return value, so add

```
System.out.println("price="+value);
```

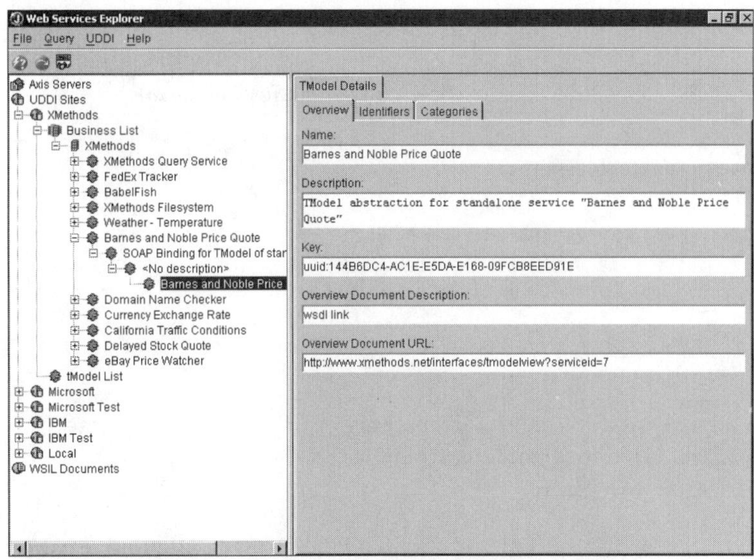

FIGURE 28.13 Web Services Explorer TModel view.

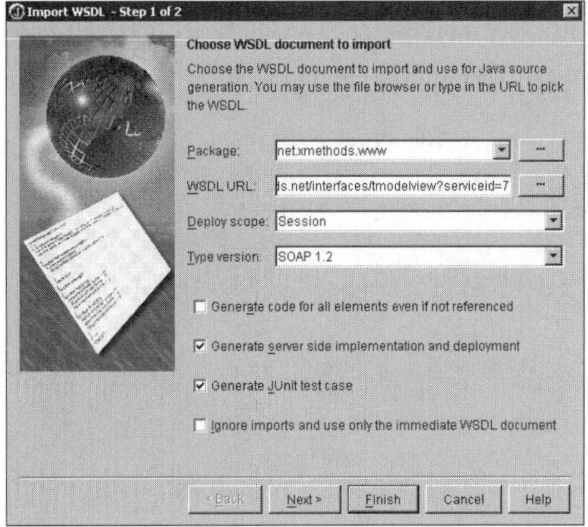

FIGURE 28.14 Import WSDL document.

Listing 28.9 shows the completed JUnit test class.

LISTING 28.9 ISBN Price Lookup (BNQuoteServiceTestCase.java)

```
/**
 * BNQuoteServiceTestCase.java
 *
 * This file was auto-generated from WSDL
 * by the Apache Axis Wsdl2java emitter.
 */

package net.xmethods.www;

public class BNQuoteServiceTestCase extends junit.framework.TestCase {
    public BNQuoteServiceTestCase(String name) {
        super(name);
    }

    public void test1BNQuotePortGetPrice() {
        net.xmethods.www.BNQuotePortType binding;
        try {
            binding = new net.xmethods.www.BNQuoteServiceLocator().
➥getBNQuotePort();
        }
        catch (javax.xml.rpc.ServiceException jre) {
            throw new junit.framework.AssertionFailedError(
➥"JAX-RPC ServiceException caught: " + jre);
        }
        assertTrue("binding is null", binding != null);

        try {
            float value = -3;
            value = binding.getPrice("0743211375");
        System.out.println("price="+value);
        }
        catch (java.rmi.RemoteException re) {
            throw new junit.framework.AssertionFailedError(
➥"Remote Exception caught: " + re);
        }
    }

}
```

Now, compile the classes and run the test case. The test case should finish successfully. Also, you should see the standard output from the test case in the Test Output window. Figure 28.15 shows the output from the completed test case.

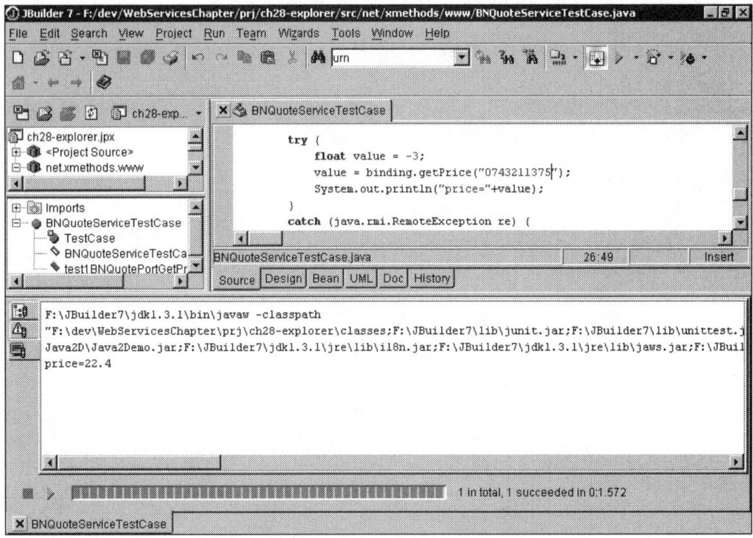

FIGURE 28.15 Output from running `BNQuoteServiceTestCase`.

The really interesting part about this example is that you can see how simple it would be to extend this service to include multiple booksellers to allow you to build a portal site that could find the best price for a particular title.

You can see how Web services allow you to build powerful applications and how the JBuilder Web Services Toolkit leverages Apache Axis and Web service's standards to allow rapid development of Web services.

Summary

Web services provide a powerful new way for applications to communicate in a standard and flexible manner. JBuilder provides the tools necessary to become acclimated with Web services and provides the productivity tools necessary in an enterprise development environment.

29 Using JBuilder with J2ME

IN THIS CHAPTER

- Introducing the Micro Edition
- JBuilder's MobileSet Environment
- Design Guidelines

At the JavaOne Conference in June 1999, Sun Microsystems announced a new edition of the Java 2 platform: the Java 2 Micro Edition (J2ME). The purpose of the Micro Edition is to enable Java applications to run on small computing devices. This announcement revolutionized the handheld and personal phone industry and caused a frenzy among hardware producers and wireless network hosts to evaluate and create solutions that work with the J2ME specification. In this chapter, we discuss what J2ME is and what it is not. We look closely at one of its key pieces, a new virtual machine optimized for small devices. We also look at how other related pieces of Java technology—things such as EmbeddedJava and PersonalJava—fit into the J2ME puzzle.

Introducing the Micro Edition

Sun Microsystems' Web site describes J2ME this way:

"Java 2 Platform, Micro Edition, is a highly optimized Java runtime environment targeting a wide range of consumer products, including pagers, cellular phones, screenphones, digital set-top boxes, and car navigation systems."

As we look as Sun's description of the J2ME environment, one key phrase should not be overlooked: "highly optimized Java runtime environment." We must emphasize that J2ME does not define a new kind of Java but instead adapts Java for consumer products that incorporate or are based on some kind of small computing device. A Java application written for the Micro Edition will also work with the Standard Edition and even the Enterprise Edition, assuming that the Application Programming Interfaces (APIs) it uses are available in each edition. In other words, there are similarities between all three versions of Java.

There are constraints, but the architecture of Java never changes. Writing Java code that runs unchanged in all three editions is possible and in many cases desirable. In other words, will the application work correctly on a specific set or family of devices? To accomplish this, the Micro Edition has a number of the key features that will answer this question.

JBuilder implements the Micro Edition with an add-in OpenTool, called the JBuilder MobileSet.

A New Virtual Machine

The Java 2 Standard Edition (J2SE) platform currently supports two different virtual machine configurations: the so-called classic virtual machine and the newer HotSpot/Just-in-Time (JIT) virtual machine. Swapping out the classic virtual machine configuration and replacing it with a HotSpot/JIT virtual machine gives J2SE programs an immediate and measurable performance boost without making any other changes to the runtime environment. The J2ME virtual machine needed to be redesigned from the ground up to run within these constrained environments and implement the lessons learned from developing the JIT JVM. That is exactly what J2ME does with the KVM, which is short for Kuaui VM (an early name). The J2ME is a completely new implementation of a Java virtual machine, an implementation optimized for use on small devices.

New and Changed Classes

One of the keys to getting Java to run on a small device is to reduce significantly the overall size of the runtime classes. The Micro Edition accomplishes this task by removing unnecessary classes to form a new set of core classes for micro applications. In addition to removing classes, a similar pruning occurs within the classes themselves removing unnecessary or duplicate methods. What is left is a true subset of the J2SE runtime classes designed to fit within a small footprint. Specific implementations of the Micro Edition are also free to "ROMize" the core classes. In other words, any classes provided as part of the basic runtime environment can be stored by using the virtual machine's internal format instead of the normal class-file format, such as a chip. J2ME also augments the runtime environment by defining new classes suitable for smaller devices. Some of these classes replace similar classes in J2SE, whereas others provide new functionality not found in the other editions.

Configurations and Profiles

Realizing that the one-size-fits-all principle implemented within the Standard Edition does not work on small devices, the Micro Edition uses configurations and profiles to customize the Java runtime environment. A configuration defines the basic J2ME runtime environment as a virtual machine and a set of core classes that run on a family of devices that have similar capabilities. Two configurations are currently defined:

- Connected Limited Device Configuration (CLDC) is used specifically with the KVM for 16-bit or 32-bit devices with limited amounts of memory. This is the configuration (and the virtual machine) used for developing small J2ME applications. Its size limitations make CLDC more interesting and challenging (from a development point of view) than CDC. CLDC is also the configuration that we will use for developing our drawing tool application.
- Connected Device Configuration (CDC) is used with the C virtual machine (CVM) and is used for 32-bit architectures requiring more than 2MB of memory. An example of such a device is a Net TV box.

Each configuration provides a minimal set of features that all devices in the configuration must support. The CDC uses the classic virtual machine, whereas the CLDC uses the KVM (as shown in Figure 29.1).

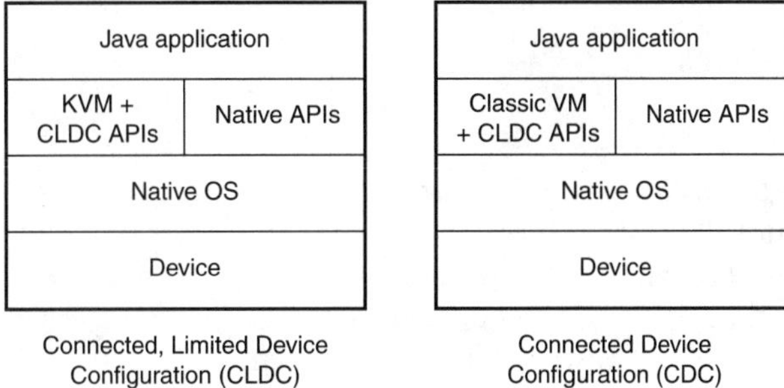

FIGURE 29.1 The two different J2ME configurations.

The profile defines the type of devices supported by your application. Specifically, it adds domain-specific classes to the J2ME configuration to define certain uses for devices. Profiles are built on top of configurations. Two profiles have been defined for J2ME and are built on CLDC: KJava and Mobile Information Device Profile (MIDP). These profiles are geared toward smaller devices. A profile adds domain-specific classes to a particular J2ME configuration. Unlike configurations, which are device oriented, profiles are more application oriented. They provide classes geared toward specific kinds of applications (or more accurately, specific uses of devices). Examples are user interface classes, persistence mechanisms, messaging infrastructures, and so on. Figure 29.2 shows how profiles and configurations work together to provide a complete Java runtime environment.

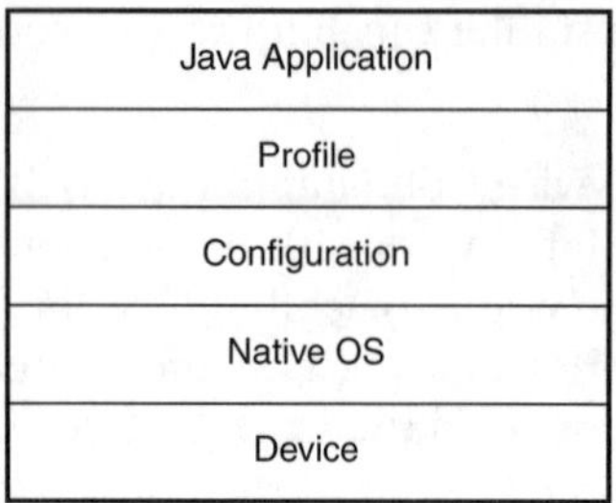

FIGURE 29.2 J2ME profiles and configurations.

A profile not only defines important and necessary functionalities but also limits your application's portability to the other editions of Java or even to other profiles. Such restrictions are not unexpected or unreasonable, however, because the need to run a single application on all possible platforms is rare. Although no Java developer really wants another set of APIs to learn (it is hard enough keeping track of all the new classes added to the Standard Edition), profiles keep the developer using a familiar language and familiar development tools. This is a key feature of all three editions of Java.

KVM

Many perceive the KVM to be the heart of the Micro Edition. Strictly speaking, of course, this is not the case. The KVM is one of two virtual machines provided by Sun Microsystems for use with J2ME. Although most implementations of J2ME use or port the Sun virtual machines, vendors are also free to implement their own virtual machines as long as they adhere to the J2ME specifications and pass Sun's compatibility tests. If the KVM is not the heart of J2ME, however, it is certainly an important part of it. As mentioned, when Sun first announced J2ME at the JavaOne Conference, an early version of the KVM was made available to attendees (preloaded on a Palm V that they could buy as a show special). The KVM soon found its way onto the Internet, causing considerable excitement in both the Palm and Java development communities.

Make Room for MIDP

As mentioned earlier in this section, KJava is a proprietary Sun API. It was not intended as a full-featured profile, but rather as a demonstration of how a profile could work with CLDC. According to the CLDC Release Notes included with the CLDC download:

> The GUI classes provided in package `com.sun.kjava` are not part of the Connected Limited Device Configuration (CLDC). Official GUI classes for Java 2 Platform, Micro Edition, will be defined separately through the Java Community Process and included in J2ME profiles.

In spite of this fact, the KJava profile has been widely used by early adopters. At the 2001 JavaOne Developer Conference, Sun announced early access availability of MIDP for Palm OS (initial releases of the MID Profile focused mostly on wireless phones). The specification of MIDP for CLDC was defined by the Java Community Process (JCP) and is, therefore, vendor independent.

JBuilder's MobileSet Environment

JBuilder MobileSet is an OpenTool that you add to an existing JBuilder installation. The environment of the MobileSet works similarly to any other project within JBuilder. With the addition of tabs and wizards to support the creation and management of J2ME applications, JBuilder provides the tools necessary to be effective. JBuilder provides the following features to aid in the creation of a MobileSet application:

- MIDlet wizards
- MIDP Displayable Wizard
- New components to create MobileSet applications

We will look at each of these features using samples and practical applications as opposed to just theoretical examples.

Creating an MIDP Application

The steps for creating a MIDlet (an MIDP is a MID Profile application) project are not much different from creating a normal J2SE project, with one exception: the runtime environment. To start a new project, use JBuilder's Project Wizard to generate the basic framework of files, directories, paths, and preferences automatically. Follow these steps to create an MIDP application:

1. Create a new project by selecting File, New Project.
2. Provide the name and directory structure for the new project (see Figure 29.3). When you are finished setting up these properties, choose Next.

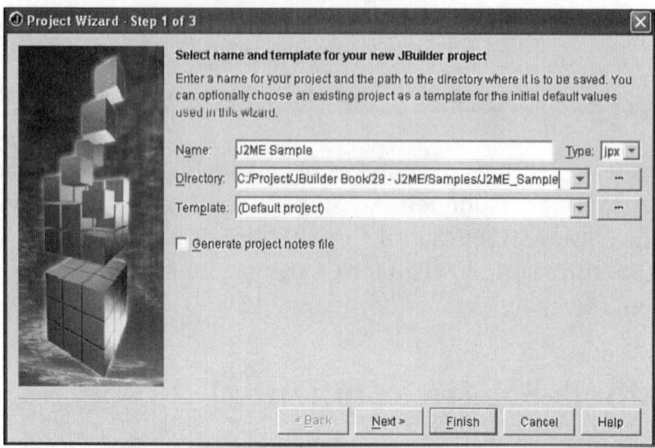

FIGURE 29.3 JBuilder Project Wizard—Step 1 of 3.

3. Provide information about the project runtime. In this case, you only need to change one item, the JDK (see Figure 29.4). After you change all the appropriate parameters for your project, as shown in Figure 29.5, choose Next.

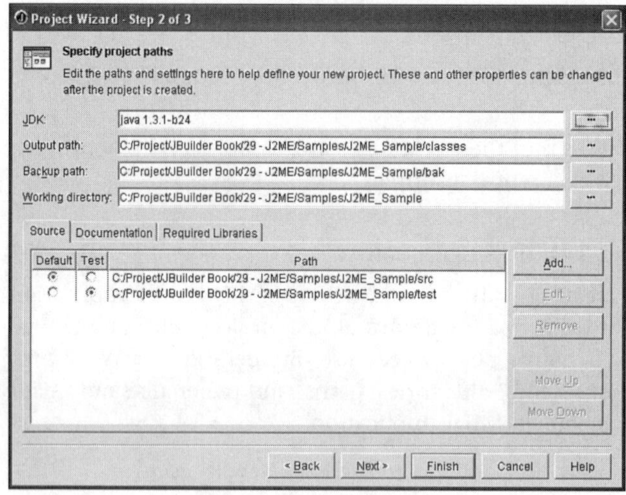

FIGURE 29.4 JBuilder Project Wizard—Step 2 of 3.

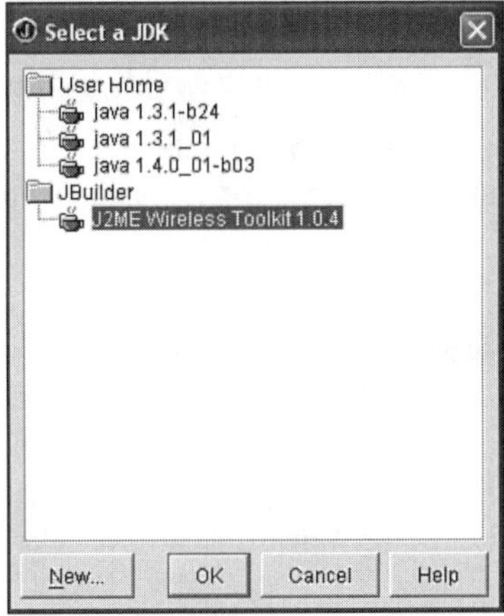

FIGURE 29.5 Select the J2ME Wireless Toolkit.

4. Provide project Javadoc comments and project encoding information (see Figure 29.6).

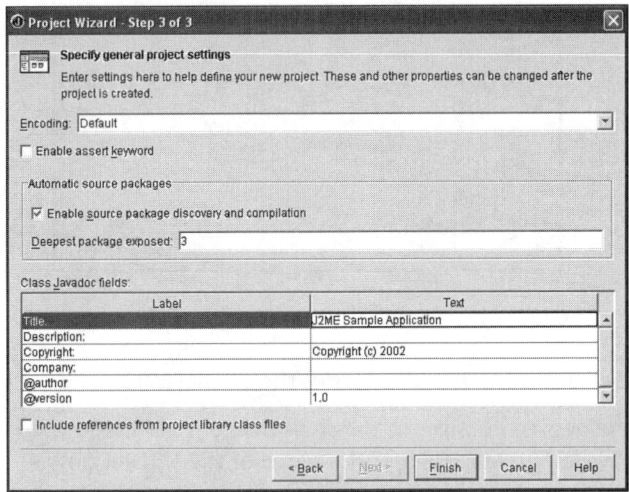

FIGURE 29.6 JBuilder Project Wizard—Step 3 of 3.

5. Save your newly created project.

Designing and Creating an MIDP

The MIDlet Wizard consists of two files that it adds to the currently open project:

- A skeleton MIDlet class that extends `javax.microedition.midlet.MIDlet`. This class implements the methods `startApp()`, `pauseApp()`, and `destroyApp()`, which are analogous to `start()`, `stop()`, and `destroy()` in J2SE.
- A default Displayable class that can extend `javax.microedition.lcdui.Canvas`, `javax.microedition.lcdui.Form`, `javax.microedition.lcdui.List`, or `javax.microedition.lcdui.TextBox`. You can customize the `Displayable` class visually in the MIDP designer.

Creating a MIDlet using the MIDlet Wizard is simple. The following steps guide you through this process:

1. Choose File, New, and select the Micro tab in the Object Gallery (see Figure 29.7).

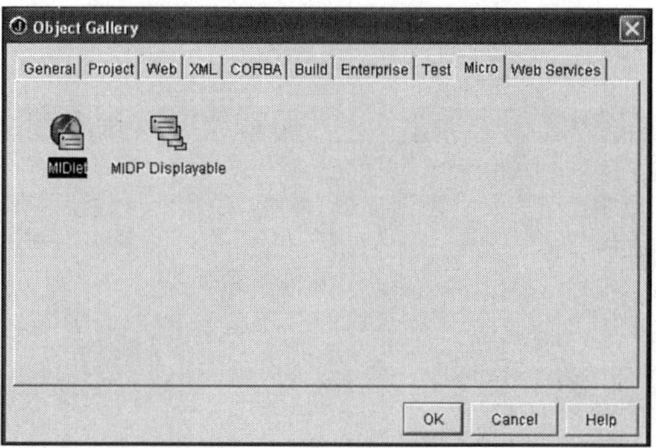

FIGURE 29.7 The Object Gallery's Micro tab.

2. Double-click the MIDlet icon to run the MIDlet Wizard.
3. Make the desired changes to the steps of the wizard, and then click Next (see Figure 29.8). This step defines the name of the MIDlet only.
4. Define the information for a Displayable class (see Figure 29.9):

   CLASS: `DSPLYMAIN`

   TITLE: DISPLAYABLE MAIN

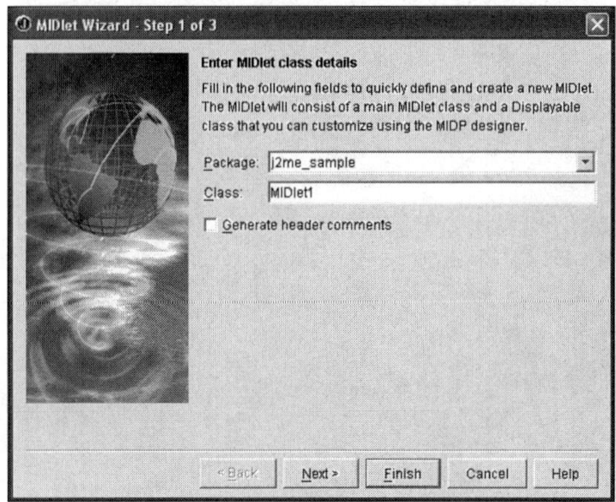

FIGURE 29.8 MIDlet Wizard—Step 1 of 3.

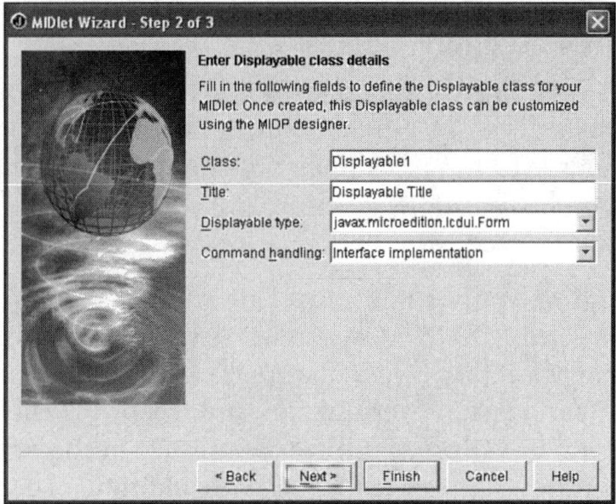

FIGURE 29.9 MIDlet Wizard—Step 2 of 3.

5. Define the runtime configuration (see Figure 29.10). Typically this is left as the default setting.

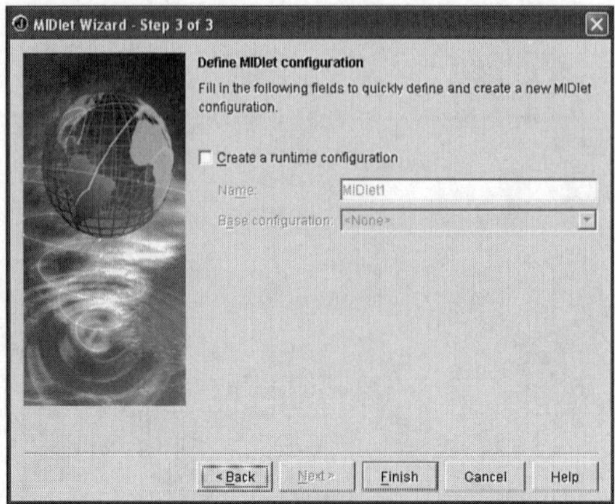

FIGURE 29.10 MIDlet Wizard—Step 3 of 3.

Creating an MIDP Screen

The J2ME MIDP UI components were created specifically for limited configuration devices because the standard AWT components were unsuitable in a number of ways. The AWT components used too much memory and did not fit with the requirements of user interaction on handheld devices. Also, MIDP devices do not use a pointing mechanism, which AWT requires.

For a device to be MIDP compliant, it must base its implementation on the J2ME MIDP specification. The MIDP UI APIs were written at a high level to be more abstract and provide portability across platforms. At the same time, however, MIDP user interface APIs limit control over the look and feel of the UI. Each manufacturer of a device can extend the MIDP API to take advantage of specific features on its device. But, the more you supplement MIDP with additional UI classes, the less cross-platform it becomes. Creating the `Displayable` class is simplified by using the built-in designer. The following steps demonstrate the use of the designer:

1. Select the Design tab of your `Displayable` class. A `Displayable` class is similar to a frame or panel in your typical AWT or Swing project.
2. Choose the MIDP tab and place a ticker component on your form:

   Name: **Ticker1**

   Text: **Isn't This Great!!!!!**
3. Select the frame and change the property ticker to point to the newly created ticker.

4. Compile and run.
5. Select the Launch button for executing the newly created application (see Figure 29.11).

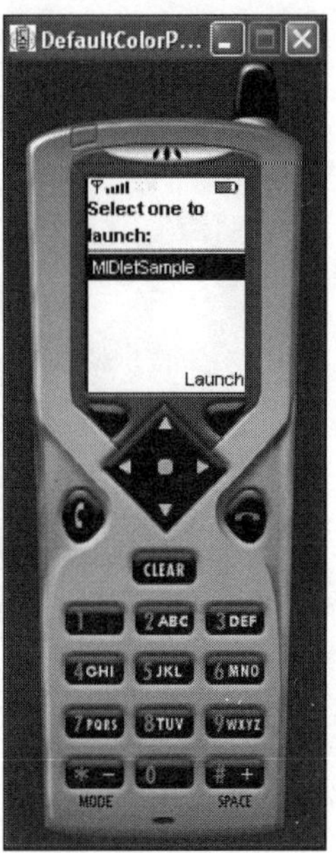

FIGURE 29.11 Phone J2ME application launcher.

6. Notice the ticker scrolling your message (see Figure 29.12).

Component Overviews

Because of the small display screens on handheld devices, and limited memory and processing power, MIDP uses a special class called `Displayable` to display a UI on the device rather than the typical windowing system. This limitation/requirement not only removes the typical components from being utilized but also introduces a new list of components.

Table 29.1 describes each of the `Displayable` components capable of being placed on a screen. This palette is available on the MIDP Screens tab.

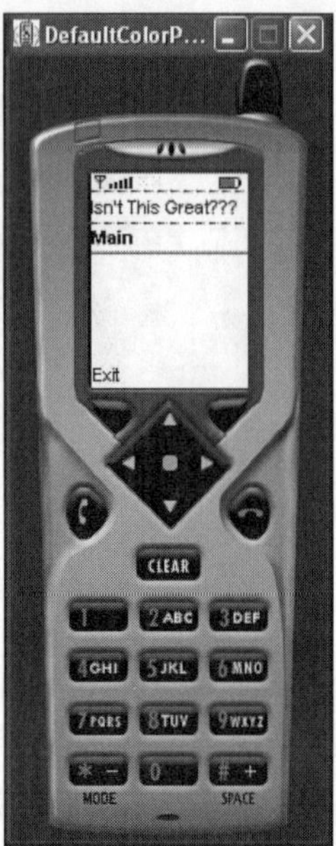

FIGURE 29.12 Phone J2ME application running.

TABLE 29.1 MIDP Screens Available Within JBuilder MobileSet

MIDP Screens	Description
`Alert`	Displays text and an image via the user interface and waits for a specified length of time before closing, or until the user responds. It is primarily used to report error messages and other exceptional conditions.
`Form`	The only MIDP component that can contain other components. In other words, it is the foundation for the building of the screen and supplies user interaction. The form may also scroll by using the device's default scroll mechanism.
`List`	Displays one of three different types of lists: `IMPLICIT`, which can be used as a menu; `EXCLUSIVE`, a single-choice list; and `MULTIPLE`, which allows more than one selection.
`TextBox`	A screen in which the user can enter and edit text. Just like other text components, it takes String values and also lets you set its maximum size (or capacity). If the text cannot be displayed within the current screen width, it allows the user to scroll the text.

Table 29.2 lists the MIDP UI components delivered on the palette in JBuilder. The icon used by the MIDP designer to represent it in the component tree and on the palette is located in front of each component name.

TABLE 29.2 MIDP Components Available Within JBuilder MobileSet

Component	Description
`ChoiceGroup`	A list of one or more String choices displayed on the user interface. Each String can have an optional image associated with each choice.
`DateField`	An editable date and time field. You can choose to display just the date or the time or a combination of both.
`Gauge`	A gauge representing a range of values.
`ImageItem`	A container for displaying an image in the PNG format.
`StringItem`	A noneditable text field that can also have an associated label.
`TextField`	An editable text field. This `TextField` can also contain a label. Multiple `TextField` components can be added to a `Form` for user input.
`Ticker`	A String that scrolls across the screen based on the direction and speed of the device.

Design Guidelines

Developing applications for small devices requires you to keep certain strategies in mind during the design phase. It is best to strategically design an application for a small device before you begin coding. Too many times, you will attempt to go beyond the device's capabilities or design. Correcting the code because you failed to consider all the gotchas before developing the application can be a painful process. Here are some design strategies to consider:

- Keep it simple. Remove unnecessary features, possibly making those features a separate, secondary application.
- Smaller is better. This consideration should be a no brainer for all developers. Smaller applications use less memory on the device and require shorter installation times. Consider packaging your Java applications as compressed Java Archive (JAR) files.
- Minimize runtime memory usage. To minimize the amount of memory used at runtime, use scalar types in place of object types. In addition, do not depend on the garbage collector to do all your cleaning. Manage the memory efficiently yourself by setting object references to `null` when you are finished with them. This removes the reference to the component. Another way to reduce runtime memory is to use lazy instantiation, only allocating objects on an as-needed basis. Other ways of reducing overall and peak memory use on small devices are to release resources quickly, reuse objects, and avoid exceptions.

The same rule of thumb applies for mobile device development as mentioned for small device development: Design and then code. Let's examine some design recommendations to consider when developing applications for mobile devices:

- Let the server do most of the work. Move the computationally intensive tasks to the server, and let the server run them for you. Let the mobile device handle the interface and minimal amounts of computations, and let the server do the intensive work. Of course, the mobile device for which you are developing plays a factor in how easy and how often the device can connect to a server.
- Choose the language carefully. J2ME still is in its infancy and may not be the best option. Other object-oriented languages, such as C++, could be a better choice, depending on your needs.

Here are some ways to code with the aim of achieving the best performance:

- Use local variables. It is quicker to access local variables than to access class members.
- Avoid string concatenation. String concatenation decreases performance and can increase the application's peak memory usage.
- Use threads and avoid synchronization. Any operation that takes more than 1/10 of a second to run requires a separate thread. Avoiding synchronization can increase performance as well.
- Separate the model using the model-view-controller (MVC). MVC separates the logic from the code that controls the presentation.

In Practice

This "In Practice" section creates a user interface to access course information. To make it simple, we are not going to hook this frontend to any backend. An overview of the MIDlet we are going to create appears in Figure 29.13.

The ChalkTalk MIDlet contains five classes:

- `ChalkTalk.java`—The MIDlet main class that handles saving and loading any user options
- `MainMenu.java`—A `Displayable` class that displays the menu onscreen
- `ListClasses.java`—A `Displayable` class that contains the basic functionality for displaying a list of available classes

- `DetailClasses.java`—Provides the functionality to show the class detail
- `FindClasses.java`—Provides a class name and returns a list of matching classes

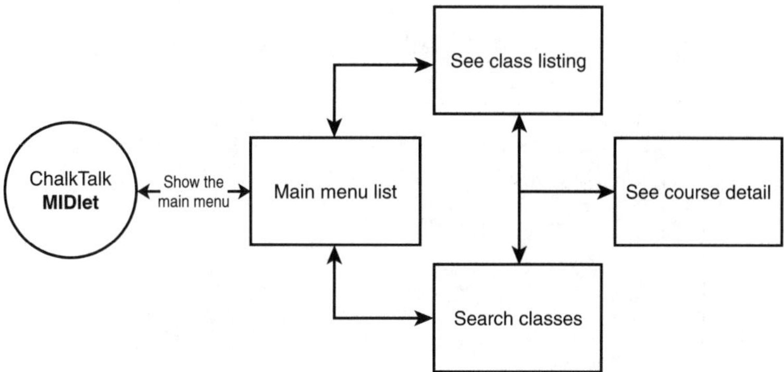

FIGURE 29.13 MIDlet overview for the ChalkTalk J2ME client.

Creating a Project for the MIDlet

We will limit this process to the important steps required:

1. Choose File, New Project to open the Project Wizard (see Figure 29.14).

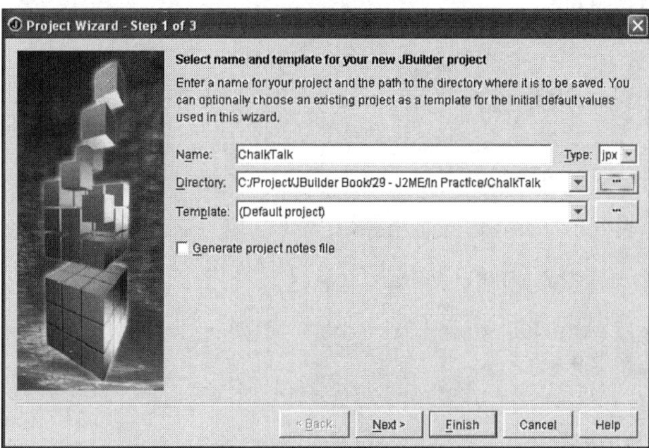

FIGURE 29.14 Project Wizard—Step 1 of 3 for the ChalkTalk project.

2. Supply a name for the ChalkTalk application.

   Name: **ChalkTalk**

3. Leave the rest of the fields at the default setting and click Next.

4. Click the ellipsis beside the JDK field and select the MIDP/CLDC JDK you want to use for this MIDlet (see Figure 29.15).

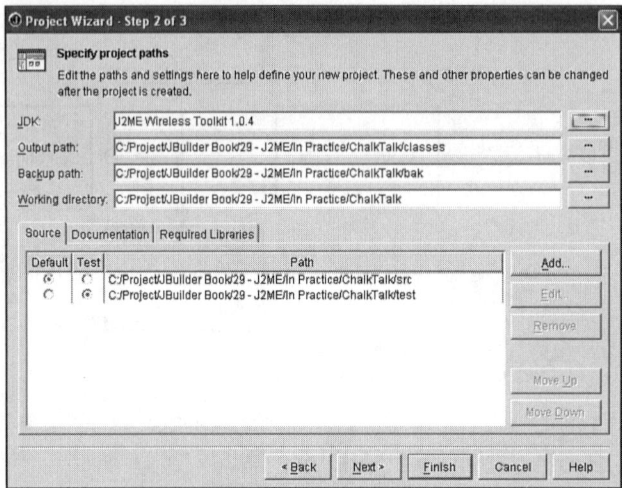

FIGURE 29.15 Project Wizard—Step 2 of 3 for the ChalkTalk project.

5. Leave the default settings on the last step and click Finish.

Creating the MIDlet Files

Now that you have a project, you can use the MIDlet Wizard to generate the skeleton MIDlet files for the project:

1. Choose File, New and click the Micro tab in the Object Gallery.

2. Double-click the MIDlet Wizard icon.

3. Replace the default name of the main MIDlet class (MIDlet1) with **`ChalkTalk`** (see Figure 29.16).

4. Click Next.

5. Replace the `Displayable` class name with MainMenu and the title with ChalkTalk menu.

6. Click the down arrow beside the `Displayable` type field and choose `javax.microedition.lcdui.list`.

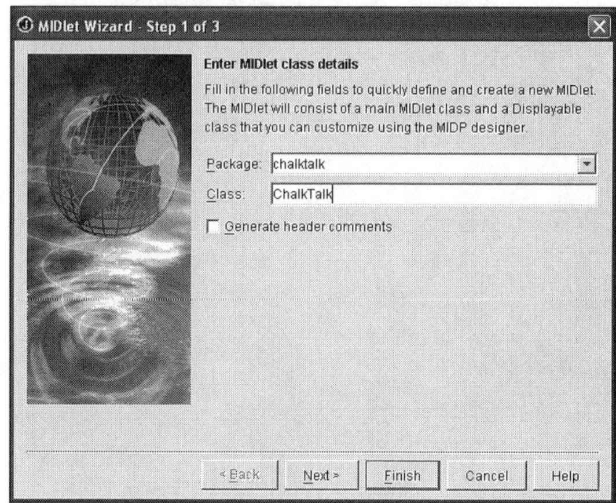

FIGURE 29.16 MIDlet Wizard—Step 1 of 3 for the ChalkTalk project.

7. Leave the default command Handling field as interface implementation (see Figure 29.17).

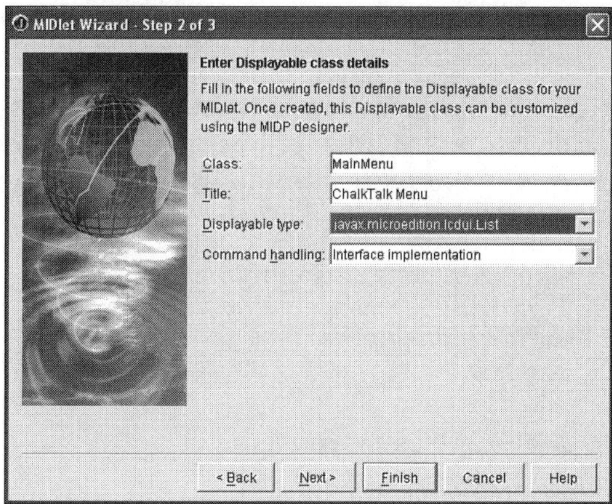

FIGURE 29.17 MIDlet Wizard—Step 2 of 3 for the ChalkTalk project.

8. Check Create a Runtime Configuration in step 3; then click Finish (see Figure 29.18).

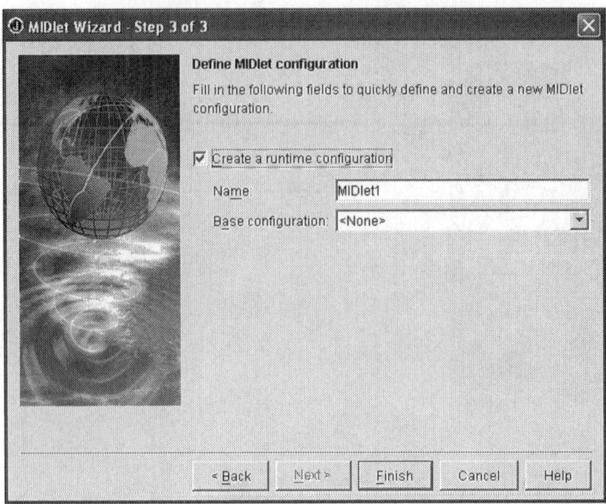

FIGURE 29.18 MIDlet Wizard—Step 3 of 3 for the ChalkTalk project.

Creating the `mainmenu`

The process of creating a main menu to supply navigation to our application is accomplished by using the `ListDisplay` component. The following steps create the required menu:

1. Place the cursor after the open bracket at the end of the first line of the constructor (`public class mainmenu extends list implements commandlistener {`) and press Enter a couple of times to open up some blank lines.

2. Insert the following class constants in this space:

```
// These are our menu choices that will be in our List.
  private static final String[] MENU_CHOICES = new String[2];
  static {
    MENU_CHOICES[0] = "Class Listing";
    MENU_CHOICES[1] = "Find A Class";
  };
```

3. Next, you need to create the following instance variable for the `classlistdisplay` screen that will be created later in the exercise. Place the cursor on the next line after the class constants you just created and enter the following instance variable:

```
   // ClassList screen.
  private ClassListDisplay classListDisplay = new ClassListDisplay(this);
```

4. Replace the `super()` method called in the `mainmenu` constructor contents to add the menu choices:

```
super("ChalkTalk Menu",  // List title.
      List.IMPLICIT,     // List type.
      MENU_CHOICES,      // Our defined array of menu choices.
      null);             // Images.  (we're not including any images).
```

5. Replace the method `commandAction` in class `mainmenu` with the following code:

```
public void commandAction(Command command, Displayable displayable) {
  // First, get the type of command that was just received.
  int commandType = command.getCommandType();

  // Now perform an action based on the type of command received.
  if (commandType == Command.EXIT) {
    // We just received the EXIT command (user just pressed EXIT),
    // so quit the MIDlet.
    ChalkTalk.quitApp();
  }
  else {
    // User must have selected one of the menu items.  Find out what is
    // selected and display the appropriate screen.
    String selectedItem = getString(getSelectedIndex());
    if (selectedItem.equals(MENU_CHOICES[0])) {
      // Show the ClassList screen.
      Display.getDisplay(ChalkTalk.instance).
➥setCurrent(ClassListDisplay);
    }
  }
}
```

6. Finally, add a method for cleaning up the variables when quitting the MIDlet. The following method sets the variable references to `null`:

```
void destroy() {
  ClassListDisplay.destroy();
  ClassListDisplay = null;
}
```

Creating the `ClassList`

1. Choose File, New and click the Micro tab in the Object Gallery.
2. Double-click the MIDP Displayable Wizard icon.
3. Replace the default name of the main MIDlet class (`displayable2`) with class name as `CourseListDisplay` and a title of Course Listing (see Figure 29.19).

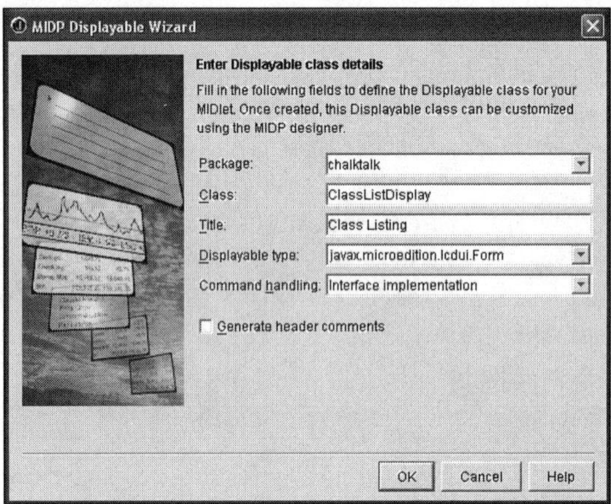

FIGURE 29.19 MIDP Displayable Wizard to build the Course List form.

4. Click the Finish button.
5. Add a private variable to the created class to keep a copy of the calling menu.
6. Modify the constructor to save a copy of the calling menu:

```
public ClassListDisplay(MainMenu mainMenu) {
// Save the MainMenu instance so that we can access it later when we
// want to switch back to the MainMenu screen.
this.mainMenu = mainMenu;

// Initialize the canvas.
try {
  jbInit();
}
catch(Exception e) {
  e.printStackTrace();
}
```

7. Add a `destroy` method to provide cleanup code to our class:

```
  void destroy() {
}
```

Summary

This chapter covered topics such as the K Virtual Machine (KVM) and the KJava profile used in conjunction with the Connected Limited Device Configuration (CLDC) API. We also discussed the Mobile Information Device Profile (MIDP), which also uses CLDC. We also briefly discussed the Connected Device Configuration (CDC), which is used for larger applications.

Although still in its infancy, Java for mobile devices already has changed the way people conduct business and personal communications. As J2ME evolves and mobile devices become more sophisticated, so will the applications that support business and personal mobile communications.

Reflections

- Which JVM should I use for my device?
- Do I need the functionality of a JVM or should I simply use WAP and WML?
- How do you effectively test a mobile application?

30

Team Development with JBuilder

IN THIS CHAPTER

- Why Is Team Development Important?
- Design Guideline: Team Structure and Responsibility
- Using JBuilder with Version Control Systems

Software engineering is a team sport. Rarely will you find yourself working alone on all but the most trivial programming projects. All practical software methodologies encourage or require practices such as code reviews and testing, which require a team rather than an individual. Extreme Programming even advocates the habit of pair programming, where two programmers simultaneously assist each other in developing code.

With this in mind, we will look at the JBuilder features that facilitate team development, specifically those features that allow multiple programmers to write code in a controlled manner.

Why Is Team Development Important?

Is it possible to be a lone ranger in the field of software development? Isn't writing code akin to other forms of creative writing (poetry or an op-ed piece) that must intrinsically be a lonesome activity? In practice (as well as in the opinion of these authors), the answer is not exactly. Authoring code (like any other engineering discipline) gains stability and maturity when it is pursued as a team effort, where the instruments of peer review and critique help balance the negative effects of personal bias and accustomed (but irksome) habits.

An example is due. For the longest time, one of the authors of this book was in the habit of using a Java class to contain all the constants (`public static final` variables). These constants would then be used wherever they were needed using constructs like the following:

```
// somewhere in the middle of a method in class "User"
int length = Constants.DEFAULT_LENGTH;
```

The problem with this was the repetitive wart-like presence of `Constants.` in front of every usage of any constant. Also, if there was any variable called `DEFAULT_LENGTH` in class `User`, the compiler would not flag it, and there would be needless confusion (because `DEFAULT_LENGTH` and `Constants.DEFAULT_LENGTH` were different!). The simple solution to these two problems was suggested by one of the colleagues of the author, who advocated using an interface with the `public static final` constants rather than a class. Then, the user class could simply implement the interface like this:

```
public class User extends SomeClass implements SomeInterface, Constants
```

And reference to the variables could be straightforward:

```
int length = DEFAULT_LENGTH
```

Furthermore, the compiler would now catch erroneous re-declarations of variables such as `DEFAULT_LENGTH` in the same scope.

The point is that a second (or a third) pair of eyes looking at the same code likely will come up with a different, possibly more elegant way to solve known problems. It never hurts to write software as part of a team.

Design Guideline: Team Structure and Responsibility

A well-known organizational design pattern, known as XXX's Law, says that "when software is written by a team of programmers, the structure of the software and the structure of the team are isomorphic." In other words, teams produce software architecturally analogous to the internal team structure.

This may seem like a radical idea. (If horses had gods, they would look like horses!) However, there is empirical evidence that XXX's Law is plausible. We do not need to prove it mathematically. If team structure has a bearing on the software produced by the team, we should be careful in constituting our teams.

Here are some suggestions on how to allocate responsibilities to team members. It is by no means an attempt to indoctrinate a particular software process, only a set of useful hints.

- Try to assign cohesive software entities (a class, or at least a substantial business method) to individual team members. This increases cohesion within that class (or method).

- Try to reduce communication between team members to minimize the coupling between the classes designed by different team members.
- The team members must be able to clearly describe the responsibilities of the class(es) they are developing, and the behavior they expect from other classes. Using modeling techniques such as CRC cards may help team members to play out the roles of their classes.
- Watch out when teams contain many organizational layers. More than three organizational layers should be a concern for a small project; more than five layers is almost guaranteed to be a problem. The problems with communication make deeply hierarchical teams unmanageable. And the software will most likely show this lack of focus.

Again, the preceding points are not meant to be hard-and-fast rules, but merely strong suggestions on how to form productive teams for successful projects.

Using JBuilder with Version Control Systems

In this section, we'll see how JBuilder jives with different commercially available version control systems (VCS). We'll start by looking at CVS (which is bundled with the professional edition of JBuilder) and then examine Microsoft's Visual SourceSafe and Rational's ClearCase. We'll also mention some useful rules for using version control systems collaboratively in a team environment.

Before we delve into these specifics, it is helpful to define some simple yet key terms that are significant in any version control system. We will use the standard terms used by CVS, and note the slight variations in the other version control systems at the appropriate junctures.

- *Repository*—The shared directory where the version-controlled files are placed. The repository belongs to the project and the team (not to any individual developer) and hence is a precious, central resource. It is highly advisable to house the repository on a networked computer whose hard drive is periodically backed up. In other words, if you damage a repository that has not been backed up, you lose all the changes and historical versions of your code. Enough said!
- *Workspace*—One developer's personal directory where the latest versions of the files she is working on are kept. As such, there is (at least) one workspace per developer, usually on her own computer's hard drive. It is not necessary to back up the workspace (in fact, a key reason for using a version control system is to avoid having to back up dozens of hard drives). If you damage the workspace of one developer, you lose all the changes that developer made since the last time she checked in her files.

- *Check out*—The act of obtaining a file from the version control system for the purpose of making possible changes to it. A version control system may support one of two kinds of checkouts: *locking* checkout and *unlocking* checkout. A locking checkout prevents two users (programmers) from simultaneously checking out the same file. An unlocking checkout places no such restrictions. Thus, version control systems may be classified as *pessimistic* (disallowing multiple checkouts) or *optimistic* (allowing such checkouts).
- *Commit or Check in*—Placing a file back in the version control system. For pessimistic VCSs, the file must already be checked out.
- *Merge*—In optimistic VCSs, the merge command allows the user to compare the differences between the repository and workspace versions of a file. Each change is flagged using some kind of visual icon. The user can then accept or reject each change, thereby merging her workspace version with the version in the repository.

Version Control Etiquette

Just like playing a sport, you must first learn the rules and regulations before using any software tool effectively. The following is a set of rules for using any version control system with the most benefits:

1. One developer must first create the project in the repository. Initially, the project will be minimal. It may contain only the project files (.jpr or .jpx), a read me file and some initial source code or resource files.
2. All other developers should then check out the project from the repository.
3. Every developer should first update (by running a merge or update command) his or her local workspace file with the repository version immediately before making changes to that file. This ensures that any last-minute changes already committed to the repository will be reflected in her workspace. Pessimistic VCSs enforce this requirement: A file must be checked out (for writing) before the VCS allows any changes.
4. Every developer should periodically merge her code with the code in the repository. This not only allows the other team members to benefit from the latest code but also ensures that any unforeseen event on the developer's machine (a hard-drive crash) causes minimal overall damage (because code is in the repository). Having said this…
5. Every developer should ensure that only code that works (at minimum, compiles and passes unit tests) is placed in the repository. Few things are as frustrating as getting the latest and greatest code base from the repository, only

to find that something that worked yesterday is broken now because someone placed new but unfinished (or untested) code in the repository.

Observing these rules makes using a version control a pure joy for the whole team!

JBuilder and CVS

To use any version control system, you must first select it using the Team, Select Project VCS menu option. This brings up the Select Project VCS dialog box shown in Figure 30.1.

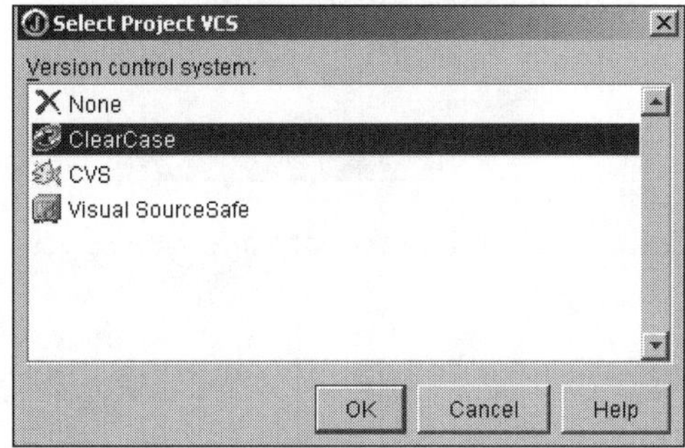

FIGURE 30.1 The Select Project VCS dialog box lets you select the version control system you want to use.

The version control system you choose on this dialog box enables appropriate options in the context-sensitive menus on the Navigation pane and in the Team menu.

After you select a specific version control system, you can proceed with the specific steps of creating a project in the VCS, checking out the project from VCS, and updating files in the VCS. Next, we'll look at these steps specifically for the CVS version control system.

Creating a Project in CVS

Immediately after you select CVS from the Select Project VCS dialog box, the Team menu looks as shown in Figure 30.2.

As you can see, most menu options are disabled at this time. The first thing you must do is create a repository and place the project in it.

Figure 30.3 displays the Create a Local CVS Repository dialog box. Enter the repository directory and click OK.

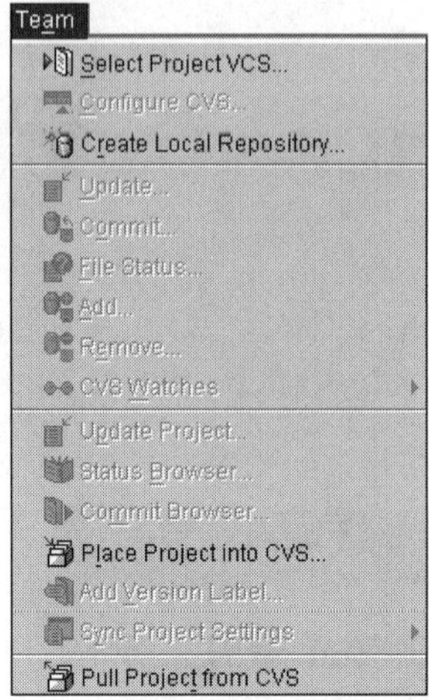

FIGURE 30.2 The Team menu as it looks right after you select CVS as the version control system.

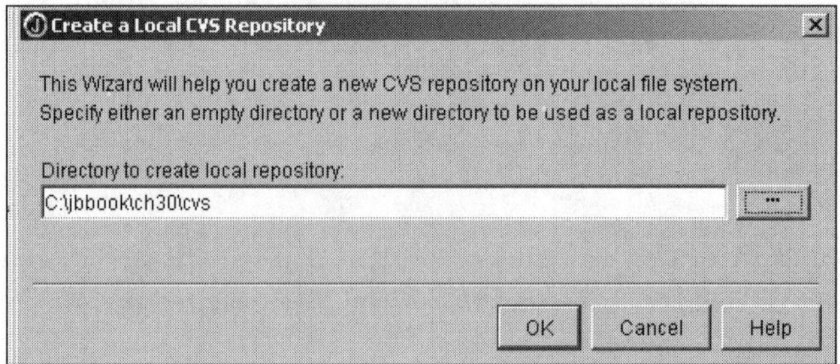

FIGURE 30.3 Create a local CVS repository.

NOTE

In Figure 30.3, the repository is created on the local hard drive. In team development, the repository would be set on a shared network drive.

If the repository was successfully created, the dialog box in Figure 30.4 will be displayed.

After a repository is created, the project must be stored in the repository. Choose Team, Place Project in CVS from the menu to begin the process of putting your project into the CVS repository.

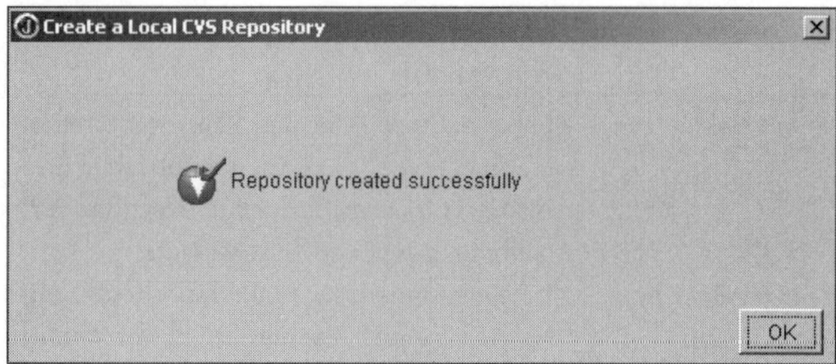

FIGURE 30.4 Repository successfully created.

Figure 30.5 shows the Place Project into CVS Wizard. The CVS properties need to be set up for a project so that it can find the repository.

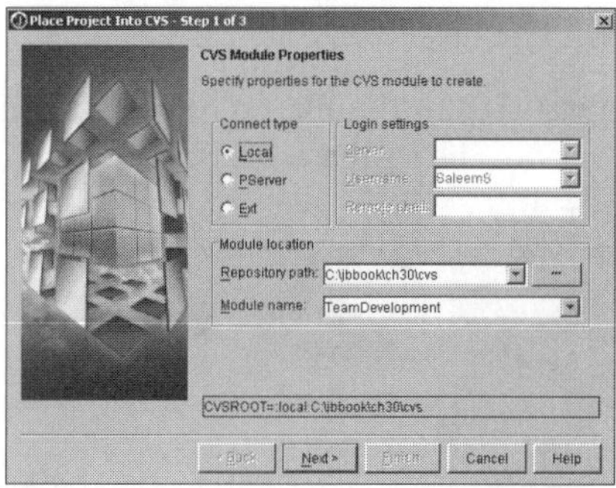

FIGURE 30.5 Place Project into CVS—Step 1 of 3.

Table 30.1 lists the project configuration settings needed to hook the project into CVS.

TABLE 30.1 Place Project into CVS—Step 1 of 3

Setting	Description
Connect Type—Local	Specifies that the repository resides on a local or network drive.
Connect Type—PServer	Specifies that the repository resides on a server.
Connect Type—Ext	Specifies that the repository resides on a secure server.
Login settings—Server	If connect type is local, no server name is required. If connect type is PServer or Ext, the server name refers to the machine name hosting the CVS server.
Login settings—Username	If connect type is local, no username is required. If connect type is PServer or Ext, the username is required to log in to the CVS server.

TABLE 30.1 Continued

Setting	Description
Login settings—Remote shell	If connect type is local or PServer, no remote shell is required. If connect type is Ext, the Remote shell is required. Typically this refers to a secure shell of executing CVS commands—for example, the ssh on Unix variants.
Module location—Repository Path	If connect type is local, the repository path is required. If connect type is PServer or Ext, the repository path is not required.
Module location—Module name	The module name under which the repository stores the project files.

At the bottom of Figure 30.5, the environment variable `CVSROOT` is set to the repository location. The environment variable is required if you want to run CVS commands outside the JBuilder environment.

Figure 30.6 displays the next step in the Place Project into CVS Wizard. Step 2 of 3 asks for a module description to be stored with the project.

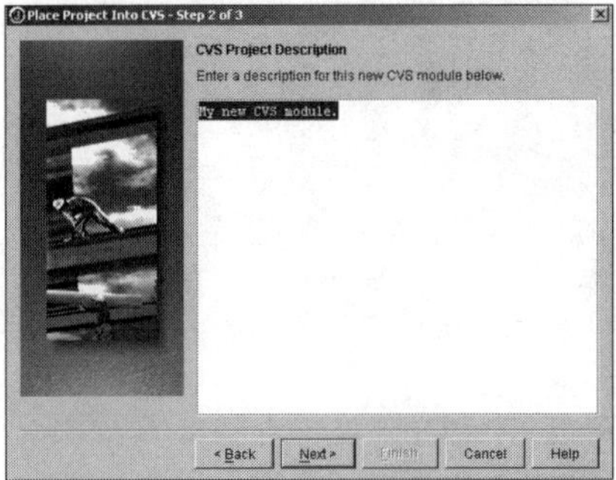

FIGURE 30.6 Place Project into CVS—Step 2 of 3.

The comment field is free-form and can be used for a description of the module.

TIP

We recommend that your team discuss how to use comments effectively. We suggest that you have a standard module comment and a standard check-in comment. Without agreeing to standard documentation on version control, the comment fields are meaningless, and it becomes difficult to understand the history of the code.

The final dialog box you have to fill in during the Place Project into CVS Wizard is the selection of what files should be included in the repository. Figure 30.7 displays the final step.

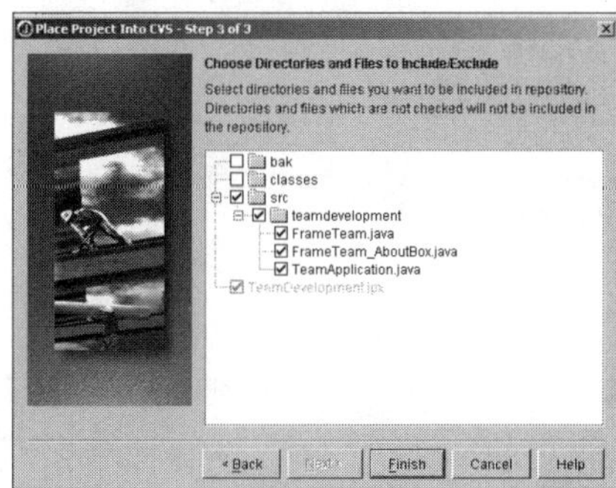

FIGURE 30.7 Place Project into CVS—Step 3 of 3.

Most of the time, you want to select only the source code files and not compiled code. CVS handles files of any data type; however, the handling and CVS's capability to merge code depends on the file type. For example, CVS can handle binary file types but cannot merge two different binary files into one.

After the files are selected, clicking Finish begins the file versioning process. Figure 30.8 displays the progress of CVS as it locates the repository, checks for an existing module name, and uploads the files into the repository.

CVS supports a command-line interface for checking files in and out of the repository. These commands can be found in the online CVS and JBuilder documentation.

Checking a Project Out of the Repository

When a new user comes on board, the first thing she must do is get the latest version of all the project files from the version control system. In other words, she must pull the project from CVS.

The Team menu contains a Pull Project from CVS menu item that brings forth the Pull Project from CVS Wizard, shown in Figure 30.9.

The first screen of the wizard requires the target directory into which the project files will be pulled. As Figure 30.9 shows, this directory can be different for each individual user and almost always resides on the user's local drive.

The second screen, shown in Figure 30.10, provides details on how to connect to the server.

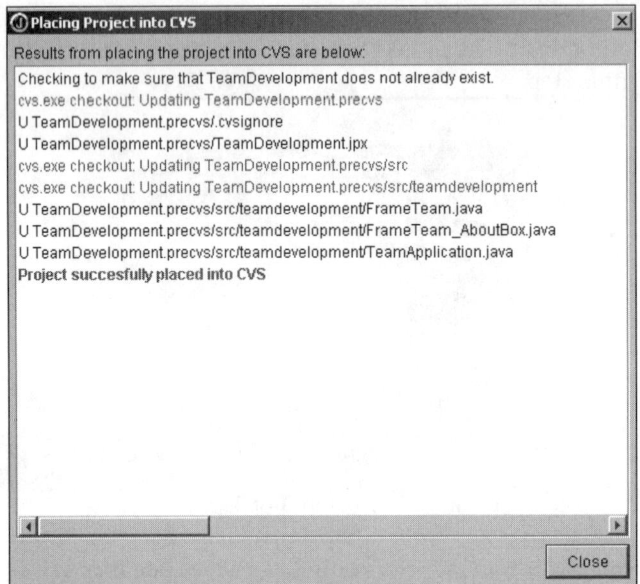

FIGURE 30.8 Files successfully placed into CVS.

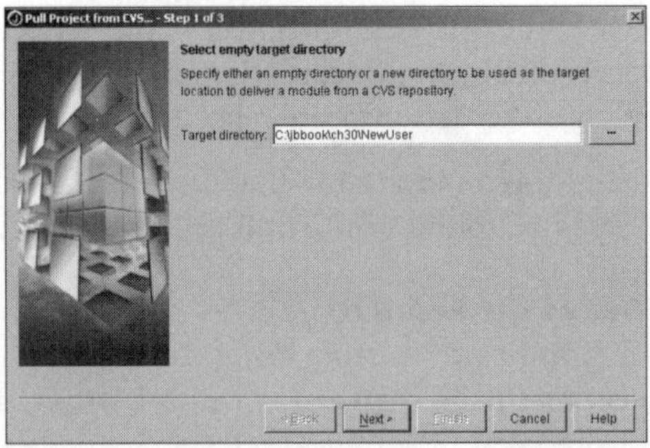

FIGURE 30.9 Pulling a project from CVS.

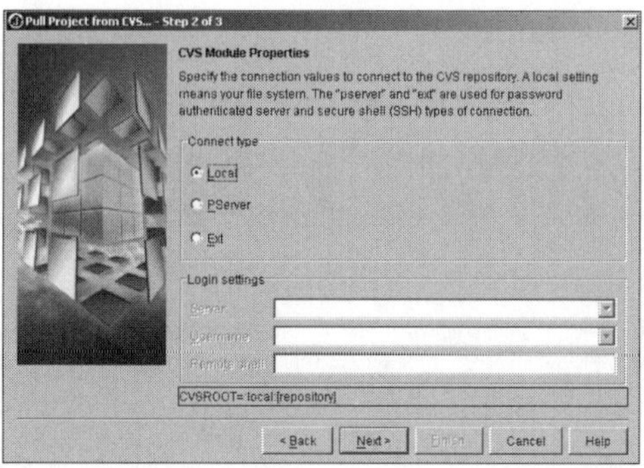

FIGURE 30.10 Specifying connection properties on the Pull Project from CVS Wizard.

NOTE

In Figure 30.10, as in Figure 30.3, the repository exists on the local hard drive. In team development, the repository would be set on a shared network drive. In such cases, the machine name and username would be specified in the appropriate places in Figure 30.10.

The next step is to specify the repository path on the server and the name of the module in the repository. This is shown in Figure 30.11.

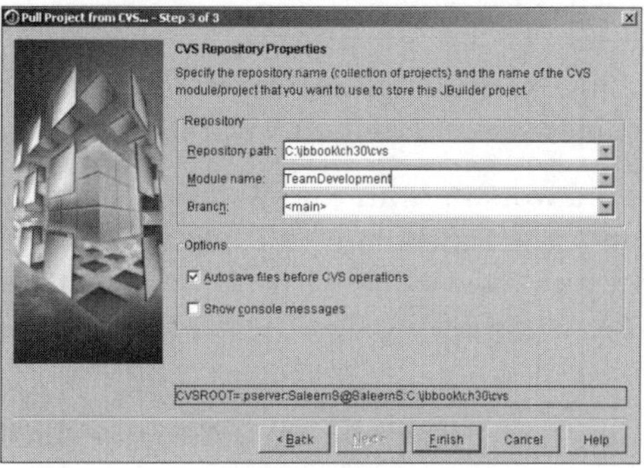

FIGURE 30.11 Specifying the repository path and module name on the Pull Project from CVS Wizard.

You can see that the repository path and the module name are the same as those entered when the project was placed into CVS. The developer (project leader) who initially places the project in CVS would provide these values to the rest of the development team.

After the project is pulled from CVS, the results are displayed, as shown in Figure 30.12.

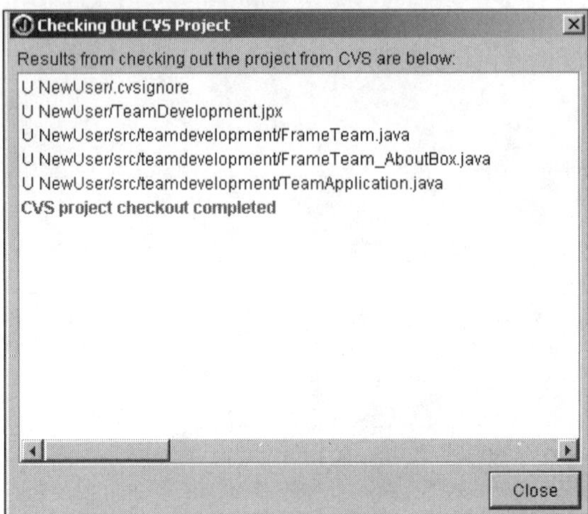

FIGURE 30.12 Results of pulling a project from CVS.

The results dialog box shows the details for all the files pulled from the repository and problems (if any).

Updating the Repository

CVS uses optimistic change control. This demands that you have a discipline to update all your project files from the repository prior to making changes.

To make sure that you are working with the latest files, choose the Team, Status Browser menu command. The Status Browser compares your local files against the repository files and lets you know whether there are any differences. Figure 30.13 displays the Commit Browser showing that the file FrameTeam.java has differences between the repository version and my workspace version.

With the FrameTeam.java file selected, the Status Browser allows you to review your workspace version of the file, the repository version of the file, or the differences between your version and the repository version of the file. The Workspace Diff tab displays the line that was added with a plus symbol, and the line that was removed with a minus symbol.

If you want to overwrite your changes with the repository version of the file, select the Team, Update Project menu item.

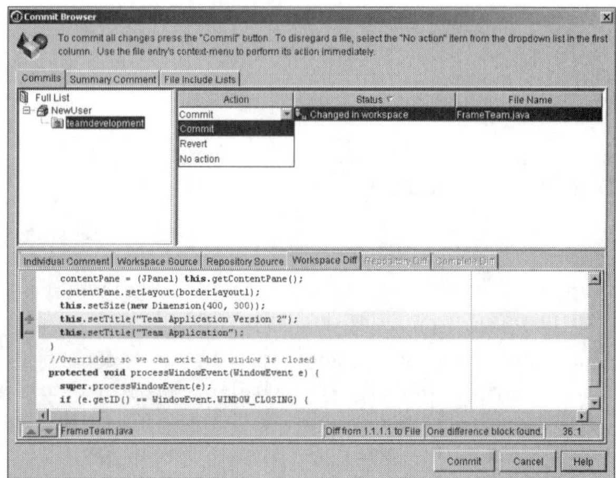

FIGURE 30.13 Commit Browser.

For each file with one or more differences, you have three choices:

- Commit your changes to the repository.
- Revert to the version in the repository, overwriting any changes in your local copy of the file.
- Do nothing.

These three choices are embodied by the Commit, Revert, and No Action choices in the Action drop-down combo box, shown previously in Figure 30.13.

Of course, the choice you make depends on the individual circumstances.

When you are about to start making changes to any file, you should always select Revert. This is because any discrepancies between your local and repository copies of the file are because your local file is stale, and hence should be updated.

After you modify a file for a while, and then attempt to update the repository, you would obviously see the discrepancies created by your modifications. In this case, you should choose Commit to put your changes in the repository.

However, what if you see other changes in addition to the ones you made—changes you do not recognize. What should you do then?

If you dutifully reconciled your file before you started making changes, clearly these unidentified discrepancies are the result of another developer modifying the file while you were making your changes. The two of you were blissfully unaware of each other's actions. Unfortunately, this blissful state lasts only until the second developer (you, in this case) has to update the repository!

The solution to this is described in the following sidebar.

RECONCILING DISPARATE CHANGES IN CVS

Let's clearly define the problem first. You pull a file from the repository, make some changes to it, and attempt to update it in the repository only to find that in addition to your changes, the Commit Browser shows other, strange changes. These changes must have been made (and updated) in the repository by another developer while you were making your changes.

Also, to make the problem solvable, let's assume that the two sets of changes are noninterfering—that is, they deal with different sections of the file, and no change overlaps another change. (If two developers modify the same line of code two different ways, they have to agree whose change wins.) Figure 30.14 shows this scenario.

When concurrent changes are made to a file, they would show up as strange lines of code in the Commit Browser. For example, let's assume that you added the `this.setBackground (Color.cyan);` line as shown in Figure 30.15.

The other changed line, `this.setTitle("Team Application Version 2");` is the line that's unfamiliar to you. It was added by another developer while you were changing your copy of the file.

You cannot select Update or Commit for individual changes to a file; it's all or nothing.

To merge these two sets of files, we'll use a simple recipe: Save your changes, update the file from the repository, reconcile through the local backups to put back your changes, and commit the file to the repository.

You must make sure that you have turned on backups. The Editor tab of the Tools, Editor Options dialog box shows the number of backups JBuilder creates, as shown in Figure 30.16.

Now make sure that you have saved your file (with your changes). Then, back in the Commit Browser, select Update from the action drop-down combo box and then click the Commit button, as shown previously in Figure 30.15. Now view the file in JBuilder's Editor pane.

What! Did you think we tricked you into losing your changes? Not at all! Switch to the History tab at the bottom of the Content pane, and then the Diff tab within the History tab (see Figure 30.17).

You will see a From and a To list. Select the latest saved version (~9~ in Figure 30.17) in the From list and the Buffer in the To list. This shows you the differences before and after you Updated the file from CVS.

Notice that the Diff view looks similar to the CVS Commit Browser. However, there is one significant difference: You can accept and reject individual blocks of change. As Figure 30.17 shows, we want to undo the deletion of the one line of code we added and retain the other block of code. This is done by clicking on the small Redo button and then selecting the Undo above changes menu.

If you switch back to the Source tab, you'll see that you have reverted to your new line of code as well as keeping the modified line from CVS—the best of both worlds. All you need to do now is save the file and commit it in CVS.

That is, unless someone else changed something in CVS in the meantime!

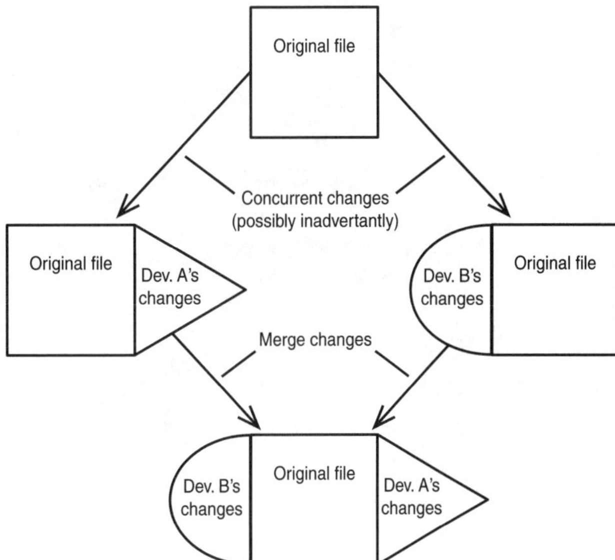

FIGURE 30.14 Two distinct sets of changes made concurrently to a file.

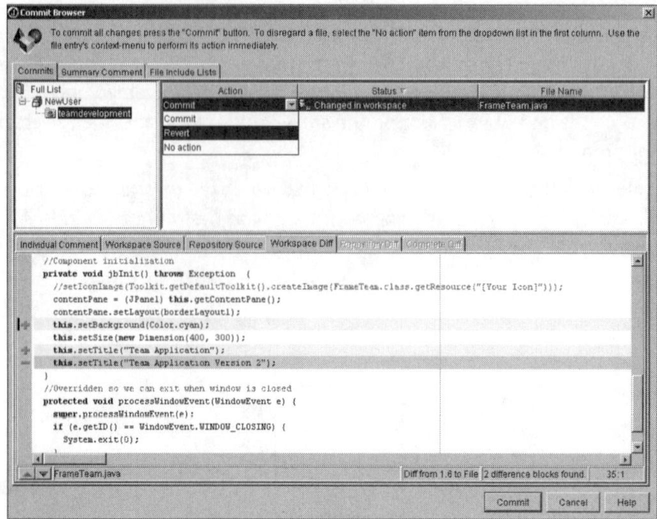

FIGURE 30.15 Multiple blocks of changes in the Commit Browser.

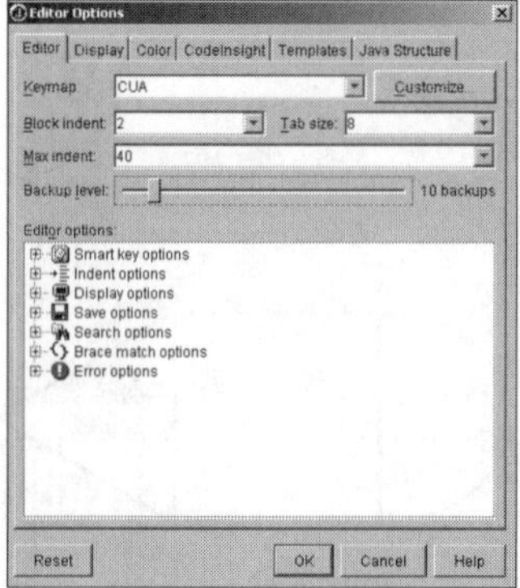

FIGURE 30.16 The Editor Options dialog box lets you specify, among other things, if and how many backups JBuilder should create.

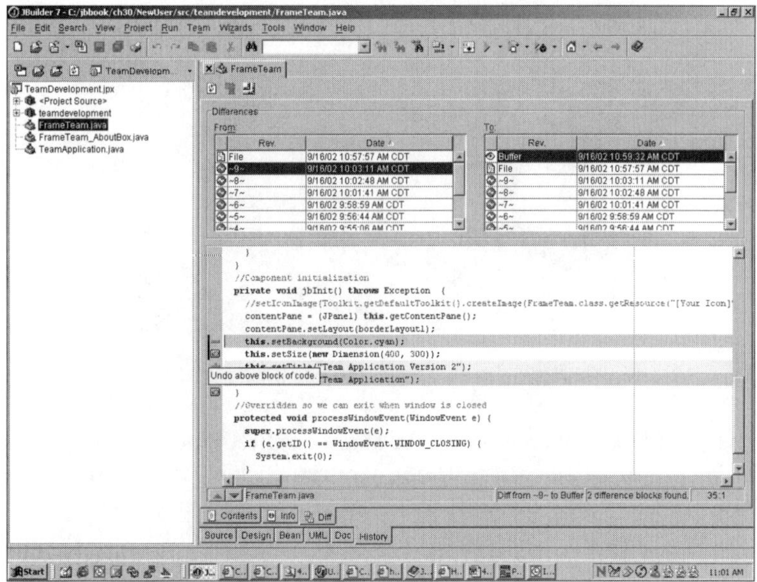

FIGURE 30.17 The Diff tab within the History tab lets you compare (and revert to) earlier versions of your files.

JBuilder and Microsoft Visual SourceSafe

To use Microsoft Visual SourceSafe (VSS), you must first have VSS installed on your computer. Then you can select Visual SourceSafe from the Select Project VCS dialog box, shown earlier in Figure 30.1.

After selecting VSS, you can proceed with the version control operations as before.

Creating a Project in VSS

After you select VSS from the Select Project VCS dialog box, the menu options in the Team menu change to reflect VSS-specific choices.

The first thing to do is place the current project in VSS by choosing the Team, Place Project into VSS menu option. This launches the Place Project into Visual SourceSafe Wizard, shown in Figure 30.18.

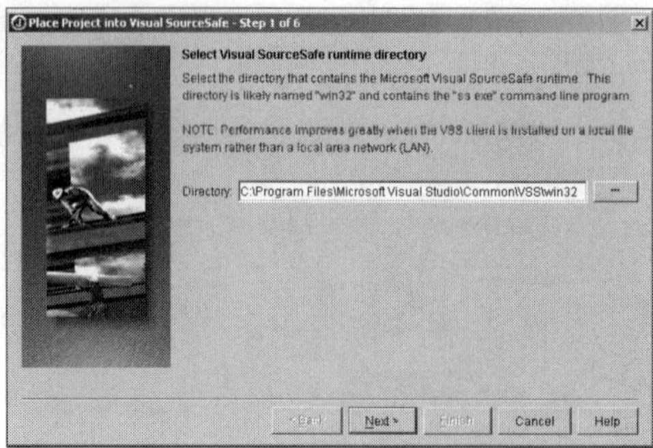

FIGURE 30.18 The first page of the Place Project into Visual SourceSafe Wizard.

If you installed Visual SourceSafe in the standard directories, the default value in the Directory field should be correct. If not, you can click on the ellipsis button to navigate to the directory that contains the ss.exe file.

The second page of the wizard prompts you for the directory where the VSS database is located. This can be any directory, as long as it contains a file named srcsafe.ini. This file contains some environment variables used by VSS. If the selected directory does not have a srcsafe.ini file, a "Directory is not valid" message will be displayed at the bottom of the wizard.

TIP

To start a brand-new VSS database, you can copy the starter srcsafe.ini file that comes with Visual Source Safe. This file is located at C:\Program Files\Microsoft Visual Studio\Common\VSS for the default installation.

On the third page, you have to enter the username and password information required to authenticate yourself to Visual SourceSafe.

On the fourth page, shown in Figure 30.19, you can select which directories and files to put in VSS. The project files are always selected. In addition, the source directory (and all its files) is selected by default. You can specify other project files to be saved, although the default values are usually sufficient.

On the fifth page, you can select whether you want to check out any files immediately (see Figure 30.20).

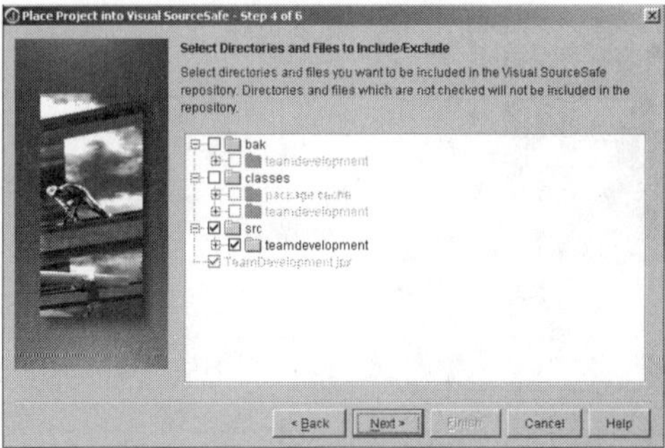

FIGURE 30.19 The fourth page of the Place Project into Visual SourceSafe Wizard lets you select which files to put in the repository.

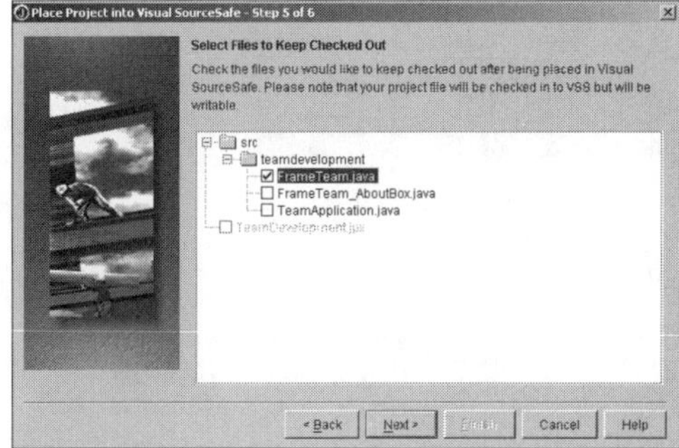

FIGURE 30.20 The fifth page of the Place Project into Visual SourceSafe Wizard.

On the last page of the wizard, shown in Figure 30.21, you select a project name that will be created in the VSS database. You can choose to put the project under the root (indicated by the $ sign in the Location drop-down), or you can put it inside some existing project in the database.

At the conclusion of this step, a VSS repository for the project is created. The message box, shown in Figure 30.22, indicates the files placed in VSS.

At this point, other developers can check files in and out of the repository for modifications.

Checking a Project Out of the Repository

The first thing that a new member of the development team should do is to pull the project from VSS. This is done via the Team, Pull Project from VSS menu option, which brings up the Pull Project from Visual SourceSafe Wizard shown in Figure 30.23.

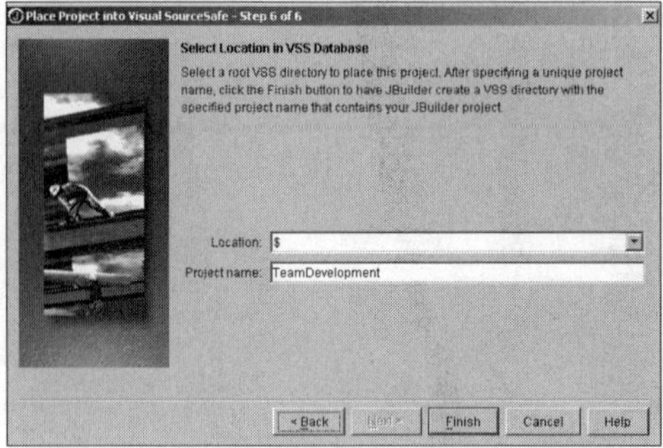

FIGURE 30.21 The last page of the Place Project into Visual SourceSafe Wizard lets you specify the project name and location.

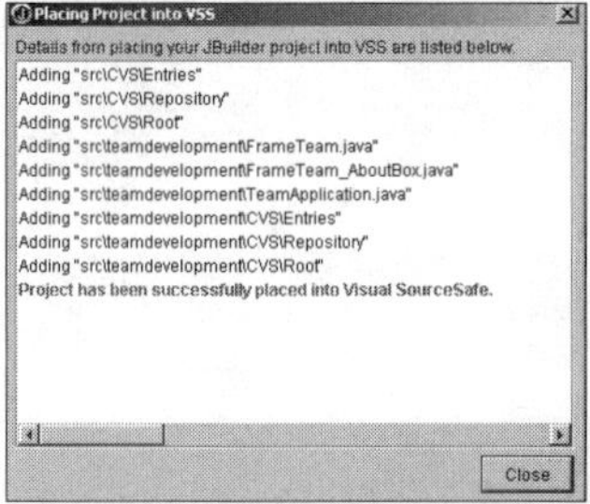

FIGURE 30.22 The Placing Project into VSS dialog box provides information and error messages (if any).

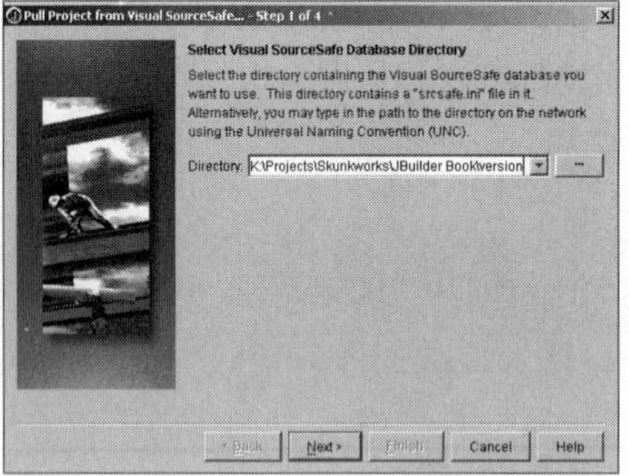

FIGURE 30.23 The first page of the Pull Project from Visual SourceSafe Wizard requires you to specify the VSS repository directory.

On the second page, you enter a valid username and password for VSS. On the third page, shown in Figure 30.24, you specify the project within the VSS repository that you want to check out.

FIGURE 30.24 The third page of the Pull Project from Visual SourceSafe Wizard lets you select a specific project from the repository.

The last page of the wizard, shown in Figure 30.25, lets you specify the target directory where the project files will be pulled.

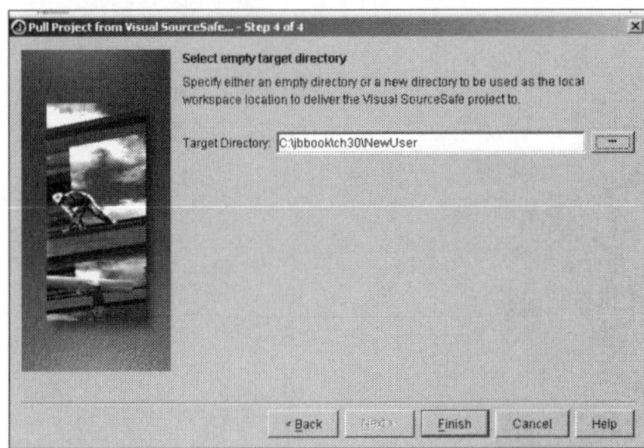

FIGURE 30.25 The last page of the Pull Project from Visual SourceSafe Wizard lets you specify the target directory.

If everything goes well, you see an information dialog box indicating the success of the operation, as shown in Figure 30.26.

At this point, the project files have been pulled (copied) into the target directory.

Updating the Repository

Visual SourceSafe uses pessimistic locking. This means that before you can modify a file, you must check it out. The Team, Check Out menu option is used to accomplish this. Alternatively, the context-sensitive menu shown in Figure 30.27 can also be used to achieve the same result.

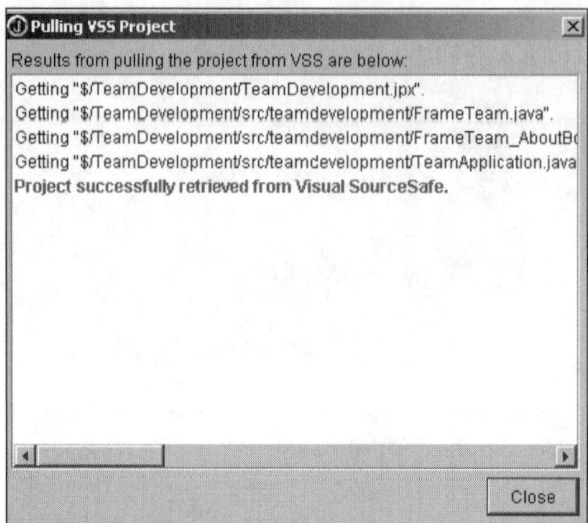

FIGURE 30.26 The Pulling VSS Project dialog box informs you of the results of the pull operation.

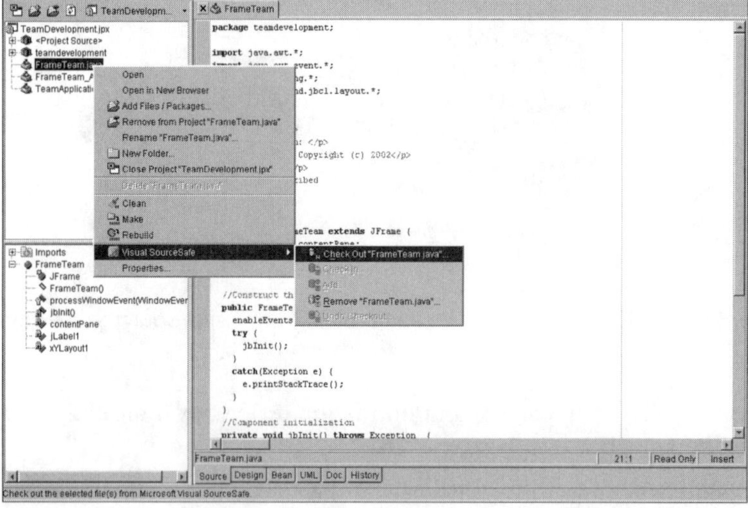

FIGURE 30.27 The context-sensitive menu is another way to check out files from VSS.

An informational Check Out File dialog box appears before the file is checked out. After you click OK on this dialog box, the file is checked out of VSS and becomes writable (the Read-Only flag shown in Figure 30.27 disappears).

At this point, you can start making changes to this file. Furthermore, no other developer can check out this file from VSS. Thus, when you are ready to check the modified file into VSS, you are guaranteed that there will be no strange modifications in the repository version. This guarantee is provided by the nature of a pessimistic VCS like Visual SourceSafe.

To check a file back in, use the Check In menu option, either from the Team menu or from the context-sensitive Navigation pane menu.

Summary

The use of a version control system is a key aspect of developing software in a team. JBuilder provides out-of-the-box support for commercially available VCSs, as well as bundling the simple but effective CVS version control system with the Enterprise edition. This built-in support for team development is the difference between a single-developer code IDE and an enterprisewide software development tool.

Reflections

- Why should I use version control?
- What are the benefits of using version control?
- If I am a single developer, why does version controlling help?

31

Struts and JBuilder

IN THIS CHAPTER

Struts, from the Jakarta Project, is a development framework for Java servlet applications based on the Model-View-Controller (MVC) design paradigm. An MVC system untangles and separates the business logic, server-side processing, and display logic into distinct components. This separation allows each component to be easily reused and interchanged with other components. Struts is comprised of a controller servlet, beans and other Java classes, configuration files, and tag libraries. This means that when you use the Struts framework you will have the following available

- A controller for your application (the Struts servlet acts as a common controller for the whole application)
- A collection of JavaBeans and other helper classes that you use in the Model part of your application
- A collection of tag libraries used in your Java Server Pages

To glue these components together, Struts uses a set of configuration files (see Figure 31.1). Together this gives you the skeleton that you can use to strut your application, thus the name. Struts has been designed to give you modularity and loose couplings in your application. If you're building a simple, small application, you might find it complicated to have to create and handle so many files. You might even be tempted to put all your code in a single JSP. Don't be tempted; the extra effort of using a modular framework will soon be rewarded.

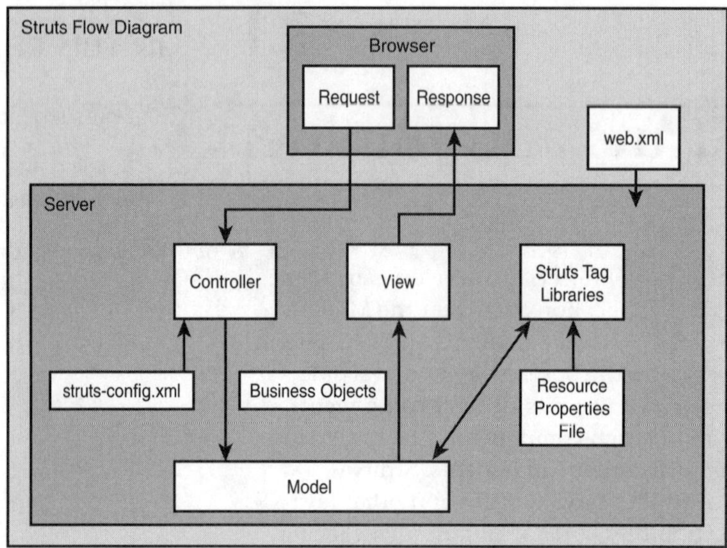

FIGURE 31.1 Struts application framework.

In addition to looking at the Struts framework, we will also look at JBuilder's support for the framework. The following topics will be covered in this chapter:

- Struts tag library
- Building a Struts application
- Deploying a Struts application

Struts Tag Libraries

The Struts tag libraries are Strut components to allow the easy integration of the Struts framework within the application's logic. These tag libraries hide most of the work of using Struts behind simple-to-use tag statements. The Struts distribution includes four tag libraries for the JSP framework:

- Bean tag library
- HTML tag library
- Logic tag library
- Template tag library

Bean Tag Library

The Struts bean tag library encapsulates most features needed to display static and dynamic Web pages. This includes creating beans to store and display data, write internationalized messages, and embed scriptlets for JSPs.

Some tags included in the Struts bean tag library are

- `define`—Define a new attribute and make it available at a specified scope such as request, page, session, or application.
- `include`—Include pages and snippets from other files in the source of the current file.
- `message`—Use this tag to internationalize by requesting messages from the Resources file and replacing the current tag with a properly internationalized message, in any language, following the standard internationalization for the Java programming language.
- `write`—Write data from beans exposed at any level—that is, write the attributes of objects.

HTML Tag Library

The Struts HTML tag library encapsulates tags for all the standard HTML controls typically used in HTML code and JSPs. This makes it easy to create and maintain forms, buttons, and other HTML controls as well as store and retrieve data.

The HTML tag library supplies two important features *linking* and *internationalization*. These HTML tags are used to create links between pages in two formats: hyperlink or anchor. Ultimately, the HTML tags also provide easy-to-use mechanisms to gather locales from the HTTP request, and then use the `message` tag in the bean tag library to format text in the appropriate language.

Because the functions of the HTML tag library are not as simple as those of the other libraries, we can expect to find some challenges in using some of the tags. Here are some representative HTML tags shown with potential benefits and issues:

- Struts logic tag library
- Struts template tag library

Logic Tag Library

The Struts logic tag library is responsible for all basic first and second order logic functions used to describe the flow and function of JSPs and the controls they provide, contingent on the state of the form beans and input forms. Most binary logic tags are included.

Template Tag Library

The template tag library is useful in creating dynamic templates based on the JSP framework for pages that share a common format. These tags provide capabilities similar to style sheets or the standard include directive in JSP technology, but they are dynamic rather than static.

There are three template tags:

- `Get`—Retrieve content from a request scope bean.
- `Insert`—Insert the retrieved content into the specified template.
- `Put`—Create a request scope bean that specifies the content to be used by the `get` tag. Content can be printed directly or included from a JSP or HTML file.

Building a Struts Application with JBuilder

Our Struts example consists of the following files. These files will be created as we go through the process of creating this example.

- submit.jsp
- SubmitAction.java
- SubmitForm.java
- struts-config.xml

Starting a New Struts Project

Using JBuilder to create a Struts application is simple. The following steps guide you through the process of creating a simple struts project framework:

1. Select File, New Project. This starts the Project Wizard (see Figure 31.2). Supply the name of your project to be **sampleProject**. The remaining properties in the Project Wizard can be filled in with any properties.
2. Create a Web application using the Web Application Wizard. This wizard is started by selecting File, New; then within the Object Gallery, select the Web tab.
3. Select the Web Application icon. This starts the Web Application Wizard (see Figure 31.3).

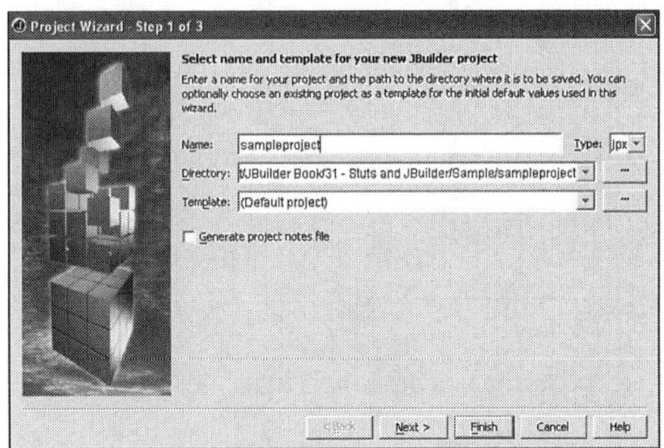

FIGURE 31.2 Creating a new project with the Project Wizard.

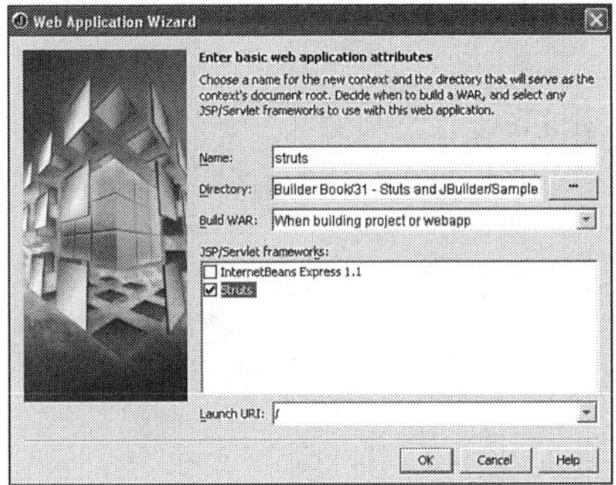

FIGURE 31.3 Creating a Web application using the Web Application Wizard.

4. Supply the following properties to the Web Application Wizard:

Property	Value
Name	**Struts**
Directory	**C:\Sample**
JSP/Servlet framework	check **struts**
Launch URL	/

The web.xml File

The JSP container checks the web.xml configuration file and determines what Strut action servlets exist. The JSP container then maps all appropriate file requests to go to the correct action servlet. The file contains three sections:

- Definition of the Struts servlet named ActionServlet
- URL mapping for the calls to this servlet
- Definitions of the Struts tag libraries

Although we will not change this file for our sample, you need to be aware of the components of the file (see Listing 31.1)

LISTING 31.1 Struts Configuration File—web.xml

```
<?xml version="1.0" encoding="UTF-8"?>
<!DOCTYPE web-app PUBLIC
   "-//Sun Microsystems, Inc.//DTD Web Application 2.3//EN"
   "http://java.sun.com/dtd/web-app_2_3.dtd">
<web-app>
  <servlet>
    <servlet-name>action</servlet-name>
    <servlet-class>org.apache.struts.action.ActionServlet</servlet-class>
    <init-param>
      <param-name>config</param-name>
      <param-value>/WEB-INF/struts-config.xml</param-value>
    </init-param>
    <init-param>
      <param-name>debug</param-name>
      <param-value>2</param-value>
    </init-param>
    <load-on-startup>2</load-on-startup>
  </servlet>
  <servlet-mapping>
    <servlet-name>action</servlet-name>
    <url-pattern>*.do</url-pattern>
  </servlet-mapping>
  <taglib>
    <taglib-uri>/WEB-INF/struts-bean.tld</taglib-uri>
    <taglib-location>/WEB-INF/struts-bean.tld</taglib-location>
  </taglib>
  <taglib>
    <taglib-uri>/WEB-INF/struts-html.tld</taglib-uri>
    <taglib-location>/WEB-INF/struts-html.tld</taglib-location>
  </taglib>
  <taglib>
    <taglib-uri>/WEB-INF/struts-logic.tld</taglib-uri>
```

LISTING 31.1 Continued

```
    <taglib-location>/WEB-INF/struts-logic.tld</taglib-location>
  </taglib>
  <taglib>
    <taglib-uri>/WEB-INF/struts-template.tld</taglib-uri>
    <taglib-location>/WEB-INF/struts-template.tld</taglib-location>
  </taglib>
</web-app>
```

JBuilder provides a number of editors to facilitate easy maintenance and creation of the web.xml file. Table 31.1 shows a subset of the 15 editors for modifying the web.xml file.

TABLE 31.1 Subset of Editors for the web.xml File

Editor	Purpose	Figure
Web Application	Edit the main deployment descriptor for a Web application.	See Figure 31.4.
Servlet Mapping	Create mappings from a URL pattern to an action class.	See Figure 31.5.
Tag Library	Define the available tag libraries used for this configuration of struts.	See Figure 31.6.
Servlet	Specify the available action servlet class parent.	See Figure 31.7.

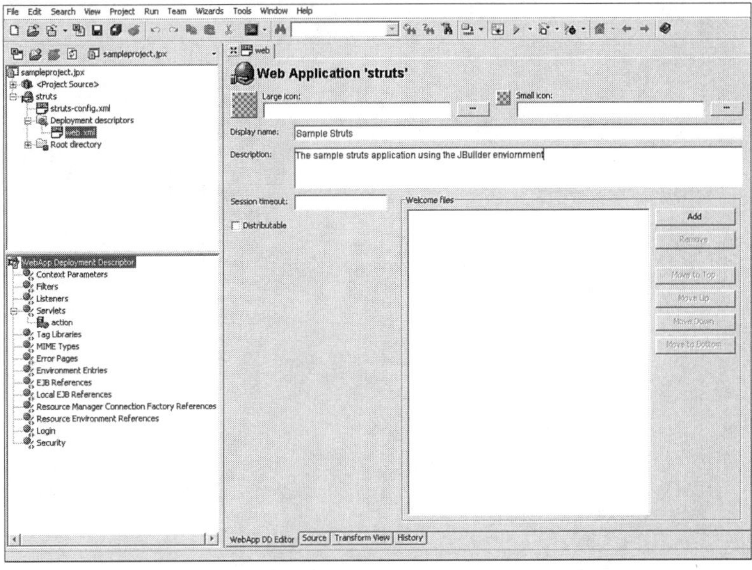

FIGURE 31.4 Web Application Editor Main section.

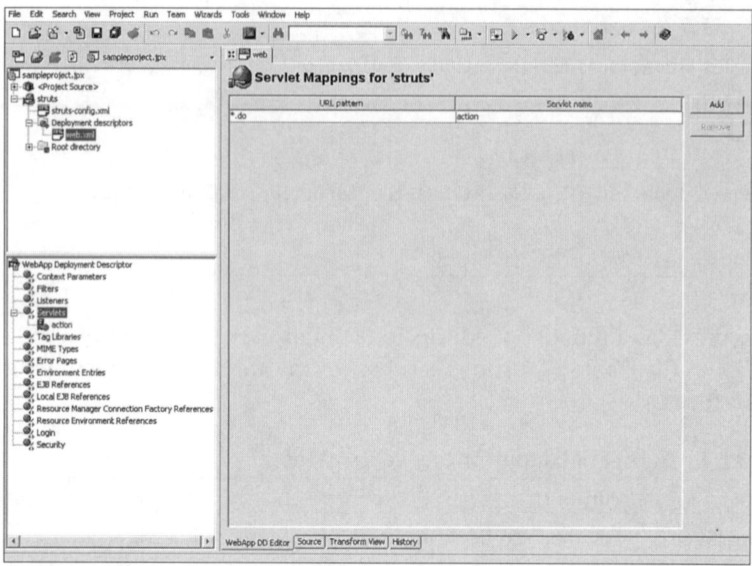

FIGURE 31.5 Servlet Mapping Editor.

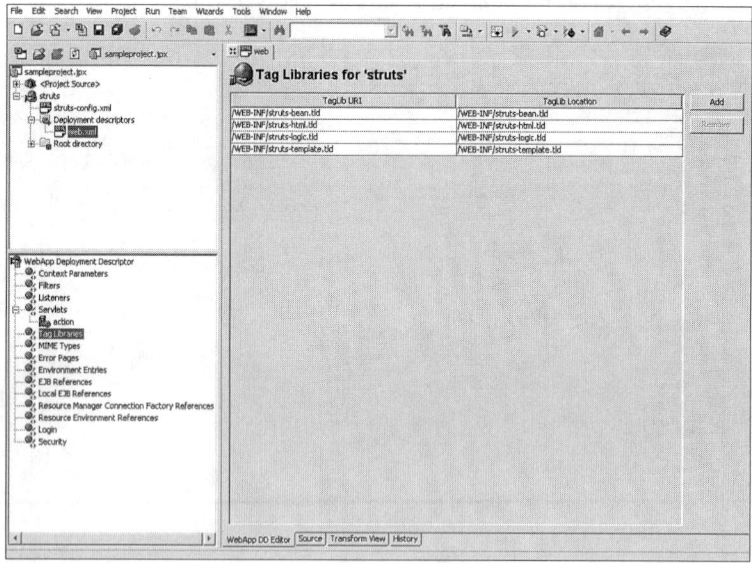

FIGURE 31.6 Tag Library Editor.

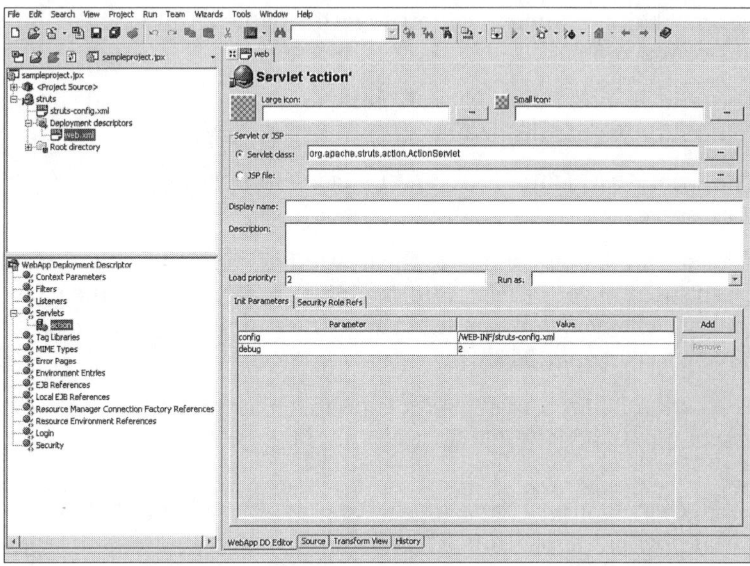

FIGURE 31.7 Servlet Editor.

The struts-config.xml File

To help make life more modular, Struts has a configuration file to store mappings of actions. The advantage of this system is the prevention of hard coding the module to be called within a component. This means that it is easy to swap around different actions by merely changing a single initialization file. The controller checks the struts-config.xml file to determine which modules to call upon an action request. This makes the struts-config.xml file the central heart of Struts. Struts reads only the `struts-config.xml` upon startup. When you use Struts then, part of this interaction is as follows:

- The Struts servlet automatically transfers the data from your form into a JavaBean that you should supply. This bean is called the `ActionForm` bean because your bean must extend the Struts `ActionForm` class. Think of this bean as a buffer between the browser and your database. The `ActionForm` bean may also be used to initialize form controls and to validate the data entered by the user.

- The Struts servlet calls a class that you specify, and it is referred to as the `Action` class. This class may use the data in the `ActionForm` bean. The `Action` class is where your application coding starts. When your class finishes, it returns control to the Struts servlet.

JBuilder provides four different editors to facilitate the creation and maintenance of the struts-config.xml:

- The Struts-config Data Sources Editor allows the creation and editing of data sources for your Struts framework.
- The Form Beans Editor is utilized to define form beans made available to the framework.
- The Forward Editor configures the forward declarations within the file. These can be used in your JSPs, for links to other pages, by using the name. Thus, if the path changes, you can just change the struts-config.xml file without having to edit your JSPs.
- The Action Editor is used to edit two different types of forms: JSPs that don't accept input and JSPs that do accept input.

We need to create a struts-config.xml file to provide the framework required for our simple implementation of Struts. The following process guides us through the creation of the XML file.

1. Create a form bean by selecting the Form Beans editor. Click the Add Button and enter the name of the form bean—**`submitForm`**.
2. Click the Edit button on the newly created form called `submitForm`. The form bean launches to edit the `submitForm` properties (see Figure 31.8). Specify the `Implementation` class property to contain the class `com.sams.sample.submitForm`.
3. Add a new action mapping using the Add button within the Action Mappings Editor. The /path name for our action mapping should be **`/submit`**.
4. Select the newly created action mapping and click the Edit button. The Action Mapping Editor then launches (see Figure 31.9). Instead of editing the config-struts.xml file using the editor, we will make this change using the source XML file.
5. Select the Source tab of the struts-config.xml file. Edit the file until the content matches Listing 31.2.

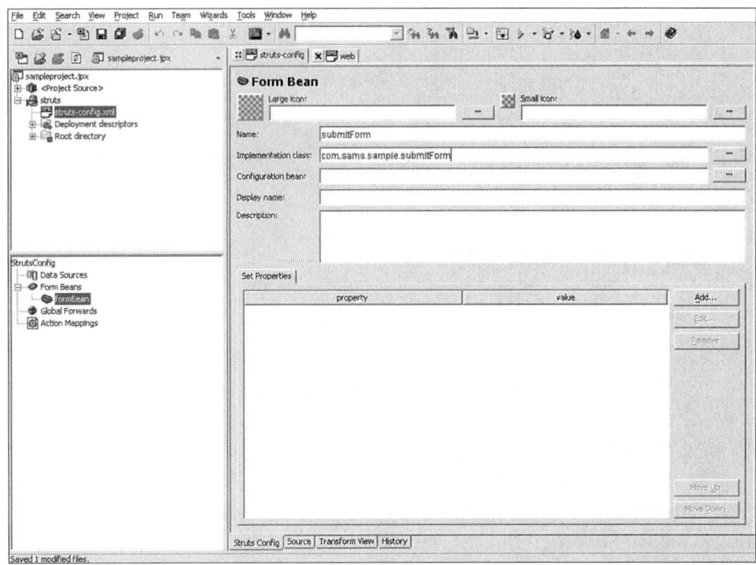

FIGURE 31.8 Form Bean Editor.

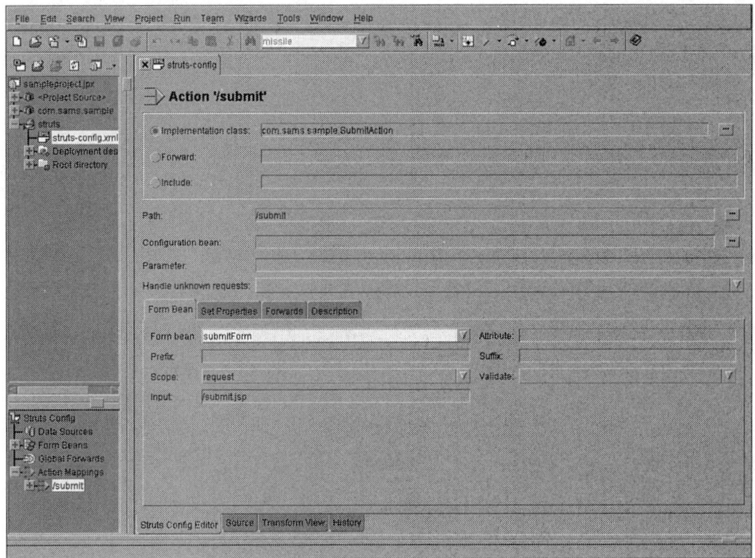

FIGURE 31.9 Action Mapping Editor.

LISTING 31.2 struts-config.xml File for a Simple Application

```
<?xml version="1.0" encoding="ISO8859_1"?>
<!DOCTYPE struts-config PUBLIC
   "-//Apache Software Foundation//DTD Struts Configuration 1.0//EN"
   "http://jakarta.apache.org/struts/dtds/struts-config_1_0.dtd">
<struts-config>
    <form-beans>
        <form-bean name="submitForm"
                   type="com.sams.sample.submitForm" />
    </form-beans>
    <action   path="/submit"
              type="coms.sams.sample.SubmitAction"
              name="submitForm"
              input="/submit.jsp"
              scope="request">
    <forward name="success" path="/submit.jsp"/>
    <forward name="failure" path="/submit.jsp"/>
    </action>

</struts-config>
```

6. Save your application.

Building the Java Server Page

For the `ActionForm` bean to work, you must use Struts's own tags for creating the HTML form and the controls defined within it. As we go into detail about these tags, you'll see that they're clearly modeled after the real HTML tags. Figure 31.10 demonstrates the user interface we are going to create using the Struts framework.

1. Create a JSP by selecting File, New from the menu. This launches the Object Gallery. Select the Web tab and click on Java Server Page (see Figure 31.11).
2. Configure the following properties for your newly created JSP:

Property	Value
Name	**`submitForm`**
Tag Libraries	Check `struts-bean` and `struts-html`.
Generate	Uncheck all the Generate options.

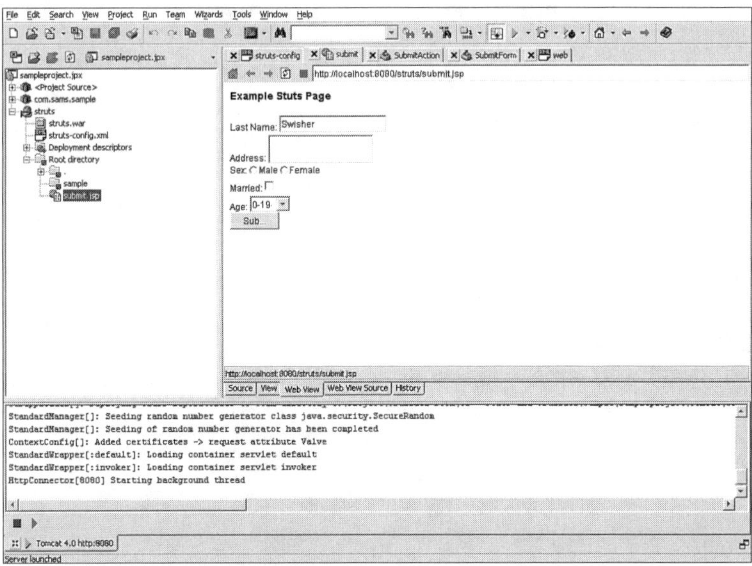

FIGURE 31.10 Simple user interface (submit.jsp).

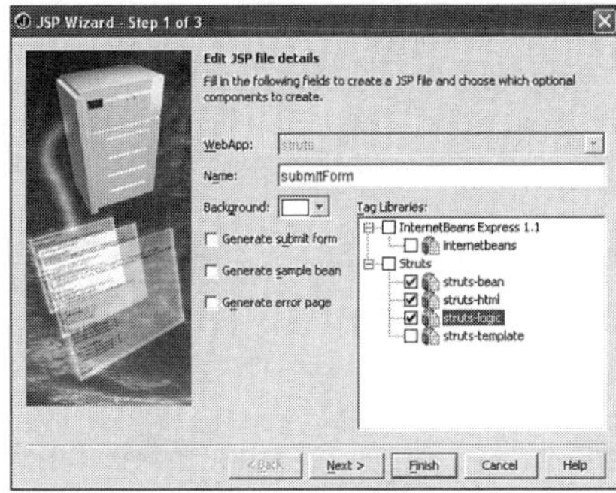

FIGURE 31.11 Create a Java Server Page using the Struts framework.

3. Click Finish.

4. Create your JSP. Listing 31.3 demonstrates the implementation of the user interface shown in Figure 31.10.

LISTING 31.3 Submit.jsp Using the Struts Framework

```
<%@ taglib uri="/WEB-INF/struts-logic.tld" prefix="logic" %>
<%@ taglib uri="/WEB-INF/struts-html.tld" prefix="html" %>
```

LISTING 31.3 Continued

```
<%@ taglib uri="/WEB-INF/struts-bean.tld" prefix="bean" %>
<html>
<head><title>Stuts Framework Sample</title></head>
<body>

<h3>Example Stuts Page</h3>

<html:errors/>

<html:form action="submit.do">
Last Name: <html:text property="lastName"/><br>
Address:   <html:textarea property="address"/><br>
Sex:       <html:radio property="sex" value="M"/>Male
           <html:radio property="sex" value="F"/>Female<br>
Married:   <html:checkbox property="married"/><br>
Age:       <html:select property="age">
             <html:option value="a">0-19</html:option>
             <html:option value="b">20-49</html:option>
             <html:option value="c">50-</html:option>
           </html:select><br>
           <html:submit/>
</html:form>

</body>
</html>
```

Coding the `ActionForm` Class

The Struts framework generally assumes that you have defined an `ActionForm` bean. The `ActionForm` class is a Java class extending the `ActionForm` class for each input form required in your application. `ActionForm` beans are sometimes just called *form beans*. As you code your `ActionForm` beans, keep the following principles in mind:

- It is used to identify the role these particular beans play in the overall architecture.
- The class also offers a standard validation mechanism. If you override a stub method and provide error messages in the standard application resource, Struts automatically validates the input from the form calling your method.
- Define properties with associated `get`*`Xxx`*`()` and `set`*`Xxx`*`()` methods for every field on the form. This can be accomplished quickly using JBuilder's JavaBean Editor.

- This class must extend the Struts `ActionForm` and must have setters and getters for all the form controls in the JSP. Optionally, it may have a validation method.

As we go through the process of creating our `ActionForm` class, it will be a simple implementation. The process would still be similar if we needed to implement something more complex.

1. Select File, New class.
2. Assign the following values to these properties:

Property	Value
Package	**`com.sams.sample`**
Name	**`SubmitForm`**
Base Class Name	**`org.apache.struts.action.ActionForm`**
Options:Public	Check Public

3. Using the JavaBeans Express, we can create properties, accessors, and mutators rather easily. This is started by selecting the Bean tab. Specify the properties shown in Figure 31.12.

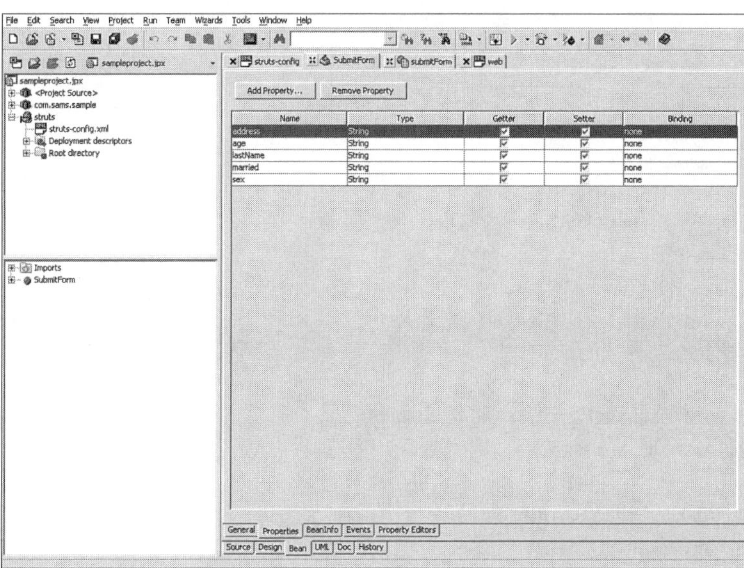

FIGURE 31.12 Create the SubmitForm.java using the JavaBeans Express.

4. Compare the source created using JavaBeans Express to Listing 31.4.

LISTING 31.4 The Newly Created SubmitForm.java

```
package com.sams.sample;

import org.apache.struts.action.ActionForm;

public class SubmitForm extends ActionForm {
  private String lastName = "Swisher"; //Setting a Default Value
  private String address = null;
  private String sex = null;
  private String married = null;
  private String age = null;
  public String getAddress() {
    return address;
  }
  public String getAge() {
    return age;
  }
  public String getLastName() {
    return lastName;
  }
  public String getMarried() {
    return married;
  }
  public String getSex() {
    return sex;
  }
  public void setSex(String sex) {
    this.sex = sex;
  }
  public void setMarried(String married) {
    this.married = married;
  }
  public void setLastName(String lastName) {
    this.lastName = lastName;
  }
  public void setAge(String age) {
    this.age = age;
  }
  public void setAddress(String address) {
    this.address = address;
  }
}
```

5. Compile and save your application.

Coding the `Action` Class

The `Action` class is the heart of the application implementation. This is where your implementation must decide how the application will be partitioned. Most often the `Action` class should be kept as "thin" as possible, placing business logic in other beans or even EJBs, CORBA on other servers. The rules for the implementation of our `Action` class are similar to the rules for implementation for the `ActionForm` class:

- The `Action` class being created must extend the `Action` class.
- The `Action` class must contain a perform method for an `ActionForm` class.

The process for creating and coding our `Action` class is also similar to creating an `ActionForm` class. As we do so in the following steps, remember that typically a more complex implementation is not only desired but required:

1. Select File, New class.
2. Assign the following values to these properties:

Property	Value
Package	**`com.sams.sample`**
Name	**`SubmitAction`**
Base Class Name	**`org.apache.struts.action.Action`**
Options:Public	Check Public

3. Implement the class using the code found in Listing 31.5.

LISTING 31.5 The Newly Created SubmitAction.java

```
package com.sams.sample;

import org.apache.struts.action.*;
import javax.servlet.http.*;


public final class SubmitAction extends Action {

  public ActionForward perform(ActionMapping mapping,
      ActionForm form,
      HttpServletRequest request,
      HttpServletResponse response) {
```

LISTING 31.5 Continued

```
    SubmitForm f = (SubmitForm) form; // get the form bean

    String lastName = f.getLastName();
    request.setAttribute("lastName", lastName.toUpperCase());

    // Forward control to the success page - looked up in
    // the struts-config.xml
    return (mapping.findForward("success"));
  }
}
```

4. Compile and save your application.

Design Guidelines

As I sat and thought about what to place in "Design Guidelines," I could not decide where to stop. (Notice that I did not say where to begin.) Entire books are written on design patterns for J2EE implementation of which Struts is an implementation to facilitate usage of the specification. A number of important principles need to be addressed if you want to have a successful implementation of Struts.

Using Validation

The `validate()` method is called by the controller servlet after the bean properties have been populated, but before the corresponding action class's `perform()` method is invoked. The `validate()` method has the following options:

```
public ActionErrors validate(ActionMapping actionMapping,
                             HttpServletRequest httpServletRequest)
  {
    return null;
  }
```

The `validate()` method is then called by the controller servlet after the bean properties have been populated from the form. It is important to note that the `validate()` method is called before the `perform()` method. The `validate()` method has a number of decision paths that it must perform:

- After performing the appropriate validations and no errors are found—This is indicated by either returning a null or a zero-length `ActionError` class instance.
- When performing the validations and an error is found—The `validate()` method must return an instance of the `ActionError` class.

The following process can be used to validate our sample application:

1. Create a file called ApplicationResources.properties and save the file in your com.sams.sample directory.

2. Place the following text within the file:

```
error.address.required=<li>address is required
```

3. Add validation code to the SubmitForm.java. This is accomplished by overriding the `validate()` method.

```
public ActionErrors validate(ActionMapping actionMapping,
                             HttpServletRequest httpServletRequest)
{
  ActionErrors errors = new ActionErrors();
  if ((address == null) || (address.length() < 1))
    errors.add("address", new ActionError("error.address.required"));
  return errors;
}
```

4. Add an initialization property to your `ActionServlet`. This is placed within your web.xml (see Figure 31.13).

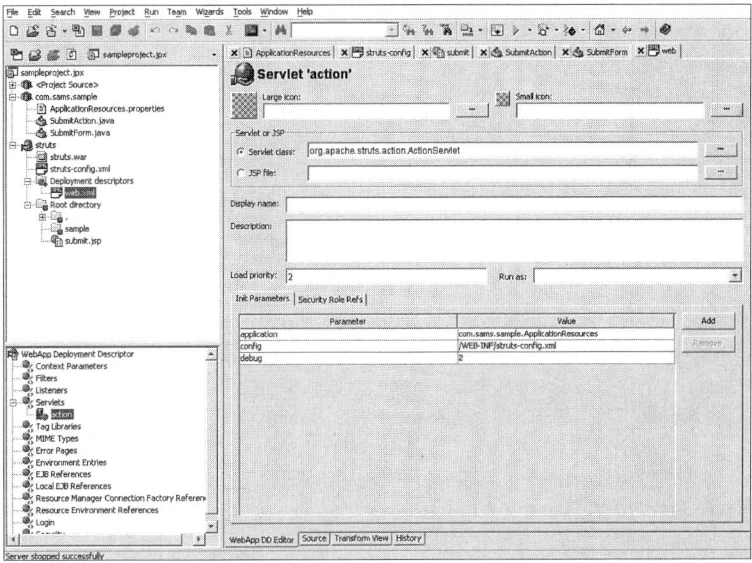

FIGURE 31.13 Editing the web.xml file—adding an initialization property.

5. Compile and run your application. Verify that your validation code is executed.
6. Notice the null before and after the error. To remove that, define an error header and error footer. Add the following text to your ApplicationResources.properties file:

```
errors.header=<h3><font color="red">Error: <UL>
errors.footer=</ul></font><hr>
```

7. Compile and restart your application.

Use a Forwarding Action for Static Pages

When using static pages, use the generic forwarding `Action` as a handler. In other words, if your needs change, you can just update the `struts-config.xml`, and you can hide the true page's location (see Listing 31.6).

LISTING 31.6 Generic Action Forward Class

```
/**
* Generic dispatcher to ActionForwards.
* @author Ted Husted
* @version $Revision: 1.1 $ $Date: 2001/08/01 $
*/
public final class DispatchForward extends Action {

// ---------------------------------------------------------- Public Methods

/**
* Forward request to "cancel", {forward}, or "error" mapping, where {forward}
* is an action path given in the parameter mapping or in the request as
* "forward=actionPath".
*
* @param mapping The ActionMapping used to select this instance
* @param actionForm The optional ActionForm bean for this request (if any)
* @param request The HTTP request we are processing
* @param response The HTTP response we are creating
*
* @exception IOException if an input/output error occurs
* @exception ServletException if a servlet exception occurs
*/
public ActionForward perform(ActionMapping mapping,
ActionForm form,
```

LISTING 31.6 Continued

```
HttpServletRequest request,
HttpServletResponse response)
throws IOException, ServletException {

// -- isCancelled?
if (isCancelled(request)) {
form.reset(mapping,request);
return (mapping.findForward("cancel"));
}

// -- Locals
ActionForward thisForward = null;
String wantForward = null;

// -- Check internal parameter for forward
wantForward = mapping.getParameter();

// -- If not found, check request for forward
if (wantForward==null)
wantForward = request.getParameter("forward");

// -- If found, consult mappings
if (wantForward!=null)
thisForward = mapping.findForward(wantForward);

// -- If anything not found, dispatch error
if (thisForward==null) {
thisForward = mapping.findForward("error");
ActionErrors errors = new ActionErrors();
errors.add(ActionErrors.GLOBAL_ERROR,
new ActionError("action.missing.parameter"));
saveErrors(request, errors);
}

return thisForward;

} // end perform

} // end Action
```

Organize `ActionMappings` into a Structure

JSP developers often refer to query strings as the universal command line. This rings especially true of `ActionMappings`, which usually leads to some type of dynamic operation. Because `ActionMappings` can be named in any convenient manner, name them after the command structure. A set of mappings for a file management system might read file/Save, file/Open, and file/Exit, regardless of how the source tree or JSP tree is organized.

Submit Once, Validate Twice

The standard way of implementing validation is at least two levels. First is the simple domain-type checking—for example, it should contain only numerals. Second is business-logic validation—for example, a customer number should be greater than 1000, or the username and password should match.

Simple domain-type validation is easy to implement and doesn't require access to the business logic, so we have a standard method that you can override if you want to do that as part of your `ActionForm`. Business-logic validation gets to be application specific and is usually handled in the `Action` perform method. Because you are already overriding perform for other operations, there doesn't seem to be much value in providing yet another method to override here for validation.

Follow a Good Development Life Cycle

The following is one simple approach to develop an effective Struts application:

- Develop the screen requirements in terms of their structure. We will not describe the look/colors, but identify what data entities must be collected or displayed. In addition to entities, it is also important to identify workflow. Develop helper classes to meet screen requirements. This often means also defining value object beans to hold the data required by the screens and passed through the helpers.
- Develop the workflow requirements. Document the workflow or movement of a user through the application. This can often result in an extended flowchart or storyboard.
- Define a system of `ActionMappings` to meet the workflow requirements. This can result in a command hierarchy that would ultimately represent the navigation section of your application.
- Create stub JSPs to demonstrate workflows using the `ActionMappings`. It is useful to create stub pages that demonstrate the navigation and workflow.

- Develop `Actions` to be called by the `ActionMappings`, which in turn call the appropriate helpers and forward to requisite JSPs.
- Update stub JSPs to use production properties.

In Practice

Many times, when working with a project, the need to create new pages or logic from scratch is not the norm. In other words, we are going to refactor our existing solution to use Struts. JBuilder includes a number of features to expedite the conversion of standard JSPs to the use of Struts. The following tasks convert our ChalkTalk JSPs created in Chapter 17, "Java Server Pages," to use Struts.

1. Open the "In Practice" exercise from Chapter 17.
2. Right-click on the Login.jsp and select Convert to Struts; Figure 31.14 is step 1 of 3.

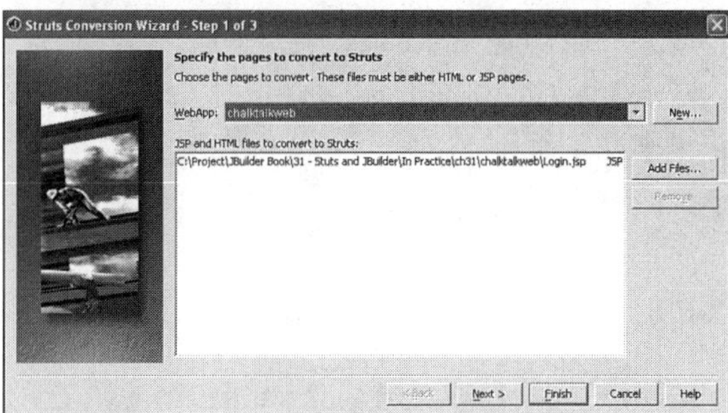

FIGURE 31.14 Convert to Struts Wizard—Supply JSP Information—Step 1 of 3.

3. Step 2 of 3 identifies the tags to be replaced (see Figure 31.15).
4. Select the following, as shown in Figure 31.16:

   Include `<html:base/>` tag

   Remove 'value' attributes in text input tags

   Include only required Struts tag imports

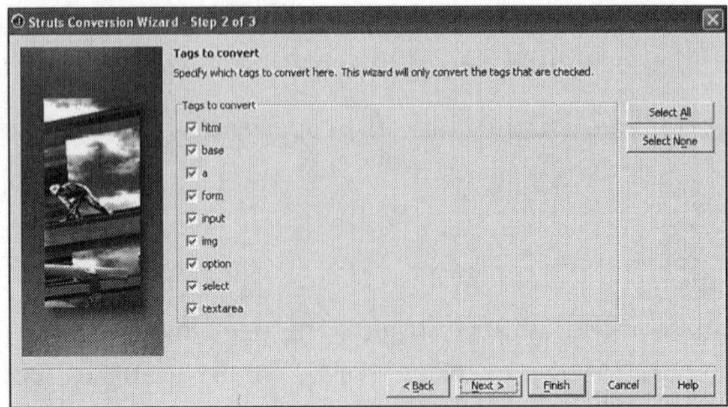

FIGURE 31.15 Convert to Struts Wizard—Supply Tag Replacement Criteria—Step 2 of 3.

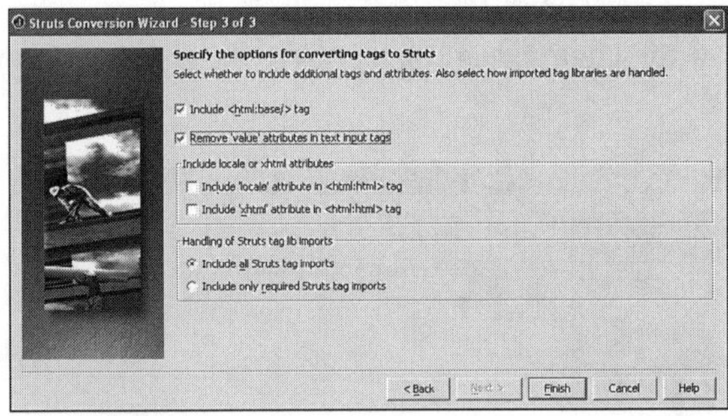

FIGURE 31.16 Convert to Struts Wizard—Replacement Options—Step 3 of 3.

5. Verify your resulting JSP. It should look similar to Listing 31.7.

LISTING 31.7 login.jsp After Being Converted to Use Struts

```
<%@ taglib uri="/WEB-INF/struts-logic.tld" prefix="logic" %>
<%@ taglib uri="/WEB-INF/struts-template.tld" prefix="template" %>
<%@ taglib uri="/WEB-INF/struts-bean.tld" prefix="bean" %>
<%@ taglib uri="/WEB-INF/struts-html.tld" prefix="html" %>
<html:html>
<head><title>Course Registration Login</title><html:base/>
<html:base/>
</head>
<body>
<html:form action=""><%= response.encodeURL("login")%>" method="POST">
UserName: <html:text property="username"/><br>
Password: <html:password property="password"/><br>
```

LISTING 31.7 Continued

```
<html:submit value="Login" property="Submit"/>
<html:reset value="Reset"/>
</html:form>
</body>
</html:html>
```

6. Refresh your project, and you will notice the appearance of a struts-config.xml file within the WebApp node.
7. Create an `ActionForm` Class; select File, New. When the Object Gallery appears, select the Web tab, and then select ActionForm Wizard (see Figure 31.17).

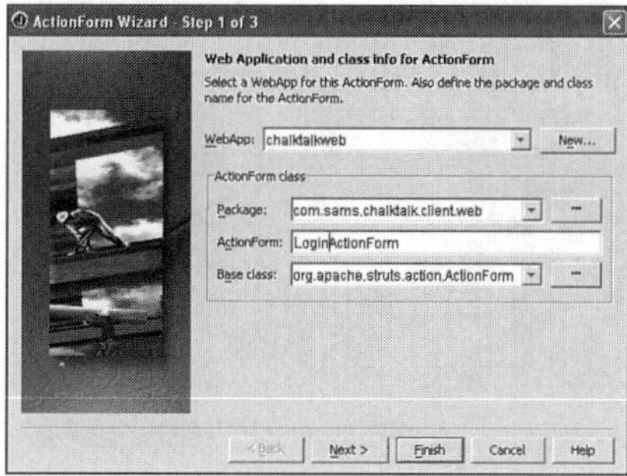

FIGURE 31.17 ActionForm Wizard—Identify ActionForm Requirements—Step 1 of 3.

8. Specify the following property values within the ActionForm Wizard:

Property	Value
Package	`com.sams.chalktalk.client.web`
ActionForm	`LoginActionForm`

9. Define the properties required for the `ActionForm` (see Figure 31.18). Build these properties by selecting the Add from JSP, and selecting the login.jsp.
10. Add the `ActionForm` to the struts-config.xml file (see Figure 31.19).
11. Create an `Action` class; select File, New. From the Web tab, select the Action Wizard (see Figure 31.20).

Property	Value
Package	`com.sams.chalktalk.client.web`
Action	`LoginAction`

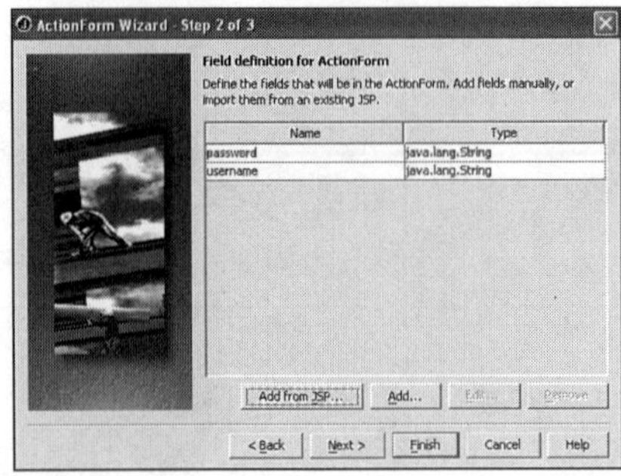

FIGURE 31.18 ActionForm Wizard—Retrieve Properties from a JSP—Step 2 of 3.

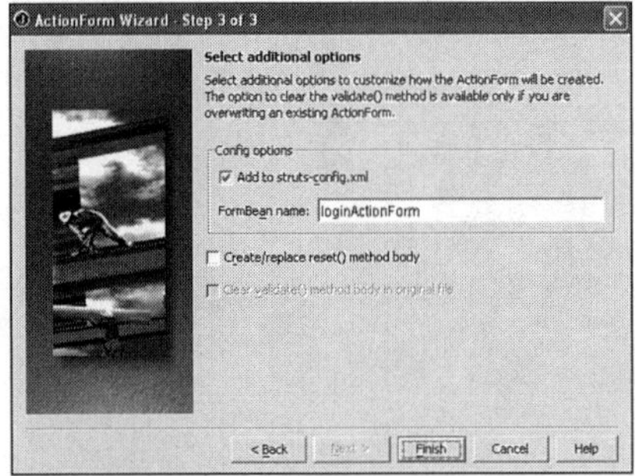

FIGURE 31.19 ActionForm Wizard—Add to the struts-config.xml file—Step 3 of 3.

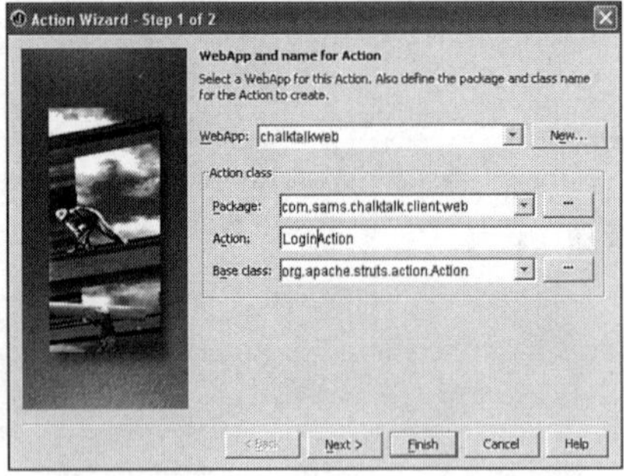

FIGURE 31.20 Action Wizard—Create a Struts Action Class—Step 1 of 2.

12. Assign the properties to the struts-config.xml (see Figure 31.21).

Property	Value
FormBean name	`loginActionForm`
Scope	Session
Input JSP	`/Login.jsp`

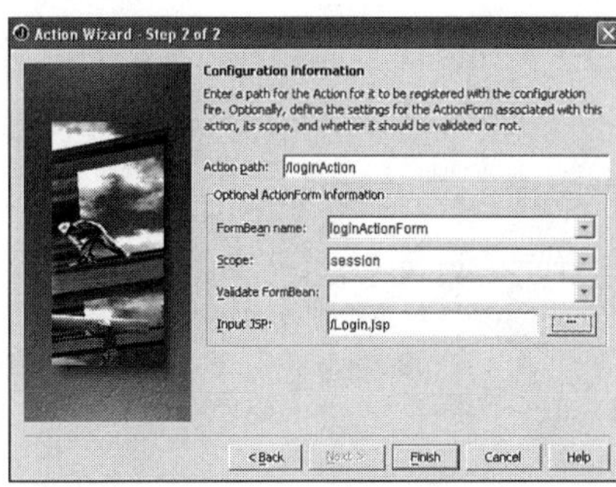

FIGURE 31.21 Action Wizard—Specify struts-config.xml Information—Step 2 of 2.

13. Change the following line:

```
<html:form action=""><%= response.encodeURL("login")%>" method="POST">
```

to

```
<html:form action="/loginAction" method="POST">
```

14. Using the Action Mappings Editor, add two action forwards. This is accessed by selecting the struts-config.xml file. After the Struts Config Editor is activated, the Structure pane is then populated with the parsed struts-config.xml file. Expand the Action Mappings node to see the available action mappings.
15. Select the `/loginAction` node.
16. Add two forwards. The first calls `success` and forwards to /CourseListing.jsp. The second calls `failure`, and it forwards back to the /login.jsp.
17. Code the LoginAction.java class; Listing 31.8 demonstrates a sample implementation.

LISTING 31.8 LoginAction.java Sample Implementation

```
package com.sams.chalktalk.client.web;

import org.apache.struts.action.*;
import javax.servlet.http.*;
import com.sams.chalktalk.userservices.*;

public class LoginAction
    extends Action {

  private CommonOperations commonOps;

  public ActionForward perform(ActionMapping actionMapping,
                               ActionForm actionForm,
                               HttpServletRequest httpServletRequest,
      HttpServletResponse httpServletResponse) {
    //Setup Session Variable
    HttpSession sess = httpServletRequest.getSession();

    commonOps = (CommonOperations) sess.getAttribute("oOperation");
    if (commonOps == null) {
      commonOps = new CommonOperations();
      sess.setAttribute("oOperation", commonOps);
    }
    //Login Business Operations
    commonOps.login();

    //Login sucessfull
    sess.setAttribute("LoggedIn", new Boolean(true));

    return (actionMapping.findForward("success"));
  }
}
```

18. Compile, save, and execute.

Summary

Although it takes time to learn Struts, it will pay off in the end for Web applications of varying sizes. A good understanding of Struts as a whole in conjunction with a solid foundation in J2EE technology (more specifically, EJB components) makes any team using these technologies become immediately productive. As the Struts framework continues to mature, you will see it become a full-fledged framework for all applications.

Reflections

- Should I use Struts or hand-coded JSPs?
- How should I validate the end-user input?
- How much should be implemented in the `Action` class and how much in a middle-tier?

Index

Symbols

A

B

D

E

G

H

I

J

K

L

M

N

O

P

Q

R

S

T

U

V

W

X-Y-Z

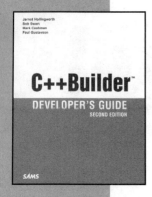

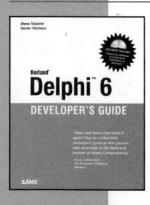

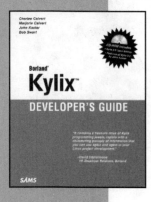